The Chancellor as Courtier

Chancellor Bernhard von Bülow in military uniform, *c* 1905

The Chancellor
as Courtier

Bernhard von Bülow and the
Governance of Germany
1900–1909

KATHARINE ANNE LERMAN

Lecturer in Modern European History
St David's University College, Lampeter

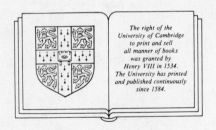

The right of the
University of Cambridge
to print and sell
all manner of books
was granted by
Henry VIII in 1534.
The University has printed
and published continuously
since 1584.

CAMBRIDGE UNIVERSITY PRESS

Cambridge
New York   Port Chester
Melbourne   Sydney

Published by the Press Syndicate of the University of Cambridge
The Pitt Building, Trumpington Street, Cambridge CB2 1RP
40 West 20th Street, New York, NY 10111, USA
10 Stamford Road, Oakleigh, Melbourne 3166, Australia

First published 1990

Printed in Great Britain at Redwood Press Ltd, Melksham, Wiltshire

British Library cataloguing in publication data

Lerman, Katharine Anne
The Chancellor as courtier: Bernhard von Bülow and
the governance of Germany, 1900–1909.
1. Germany, 1871–1918
I. Title
943.08'3

Library of Congress cataloguing in publication data

Lerman, Katharine Anne.
The Chancellor as courtier: Bernhard von Bülow and the governance
of Germany, 1900–1909/Katharine Anne Lerman.
p.   cm.
Bibliography.
Includes index.
ISBN 0 521 38 155 X
1. Bülow, Bernhard, Fürst von, 1849–1929. 2. Statesmen–Germany–
Biography. 3. Germany – Politics and government–1888–1918.
I. Title
DD231. B8L47 1990
943.08 092–dc20   89–34312 CIP
[B]

ISBN 0 521 38155   X

Contents

Illustrations

Thanks are due to Ullstein Bilderdienst for the following illustrations:
frontispiece, 3, 4, 5, 6, 8 and 10.

Abbreviations

BA	Bundesarchiv
BA–MA	Bundesarchiv–Militärarchiv
BP	Bülow Papers
FCO	Foreign and Commonwealth Office
GLA	Generallandesarchiv
HHSA	Haus- Hof- und Staatsarchiv
HSA	Hauptstaatsarchiv
HSA–KA	Hauptstaatsarchiv–Kriegsarchiv
KE	Kleine Erwerbungen (Minor Acquisitions)
Landtag	*Stenographische Berichte über die Verhandlungen des Preussischen Hauses der Abgeordneten*
MA	Militärarchiv
PA	Politisches Archiv
PRO	Public Records Office
Reichstag	*Stenographische Berichte über die Verhandlungen des Reichstags*
SA	Stadtarchiv
ZSA	Zentrales Staatsarchiv

To my parents
Denise and Peter Coppock

Preface

This book is concerned with the political position and effectiveness of Imperial Germany's fourth Reich Chancellor, Bernhard von Bülow. It has long been recognised that the years of Bülow's Chancellorship are of crucial importance in the history of Germany before the First World War. Bülow held the highest responsible political office in the *Kaiserreich* at a time when Germany was experiencing rapid social and economic change and seeking to assert a new and dynamic role for herself in world affairs. He became Chancellor after the protracted constitutional struggles of the 1890s and, for the first time since Bismarck's dismissal in 1890, it was believed that Germany had found a man with the necessary stature and intelligence to occupy this prestigious and onerous position. His appointment marked the beginning of a new period of optimism and confidence in the German leadership. It was hoped that, notwithstanding the extreme volatility and immaturity of Kaiser Wilhelm II and the advance of mass politics, a new degree of stability and consistency in German decision-making could be achieved, which would demonstrate the viability and durability of the Bismarckian political system in the absence of its creator.

The wide discrepancy between the high expectations which Bülow's Chancellorship aroused and the reality of his role within the German government system is a central theme of this book. For Bülow's Chancellorship never fulfilled its political promise. Bülow was the man who, as Foreign Secretary in 1897, had promised Germany 'a place in the sun'. Yet between 1900 and 1909 Germany's international position deteriorated dramatically with the formation of the Anglo–French and Triple ententes, the crises over Morocco and Bosnia–Herzegovina and the intensification of the Anglo–German naval armaments race, all of which are now familiar landmarks on the road to 1914. With respect to imperial domestic politics, too, Bülow left a legacy of bitterness and disillusionment, political polarisation and financial debt, which in a real sense narrowed the options open to the German leadership in the few remaining years of peace. Bülow had more skill and imagination than most of his contemporaries in the German ruling élite but, as this study will reveal, although he became Chancellor at a critical juncture in the political evolution of the *Kaiserreich*, he had no great vision or far-sighted plans for tackling Germany's problems, and despite some short-term successes his Chancellorship was ultimately devoid of creative or reformist initiatives. Personally vain and egocentric, he increasingly subordinated political considerations to the task of securing his personal position and reputation, cultivating a public image of his Chancellorship which diverged sharply from the reality of his role. Having chosen to base his position on a close relationship with the monarch, Wilhelm II, Bülow ultimately reduced the role of the Chancellor to that of a courtier who was content with the appearance rather than the substance of power. He resigned in 1909, an embittered and lonely figure with little trace of the vigour and self-confidence he had exuded during his early political career.

The book is based on official and private papers in fourteen archives in the German Federal Republic, German Democratic Republic, Austria and England. A full list of sources is provided with the bibliography, and my main debts will be clear from the notes. The private papers of Bülow, Otto Hammann, Oswald von Richthofen and Friedrich Wilhelm von Loebell were particularly valuable for the insights they gave into the personal preoccupations of the Chancellor. The files of the Reich Chancellery and Foreign Office, the minutes of the Prussian Ministry of State, the files of the Kaiser's Civil Cabinet and the Kaiser's correspondence in the Royal Household archives provided the indispensable government framework for an assessment of Bülow's activities. A very useful parliamentary dimension to Bülow's Chancellorship was supplied by the private papers of the Reichstag deputy, Karl Bachem. The intelligent and colourful reports of the Bavarian, Württemberg, Baden and Austrian ambassadors in Berlin together constituted a revealing commentary on the functioning of the government machine at the centre.

The book could not have been completed without the invaluable assistance of the archivists and staff at the following archives: the Bundesarchiv in Koblenz, the Bendesarchiv–Militärarchiv in Freiburg, the Politisches Archiv in Bonn, the Generallandesarchiv in Karlsruhe, the Hauptstaatsarchiv and Militärarchiv in Stuttgart, the Hauptstaatsarchiv and Kriegsarchiv in Munich, the Stadtarchiv in Cologne, the Haus- Hof- und Staatsarchiv in Vienna, the Zentrales Staatsarchiv in Potsdam and Merseburg, and the Public Records Office and Foreign and Commonwealth Office in London. I should like to record my thanks to them all, and also to Herr Wolfgang von Loebell for permission to read the private papers of his father and to Dr Bernd Sösemann, who permitted me to look at the private papers of Theodor Wolff.

My thanks are also extended to the Economic and Social Research Council for providing me with a three-year research grant and generous financial assistance during the year I spent in foreign archives; and to the Research

Committee of St David's University College, Lampeter, which funded a further trip to Germany after the completion of my D.Phil. thesis. I am also indebted to all those friends and acquaintances in Germany and Austria, in particular Alfred and Ursula Loose and Christa and Detlev Siebeck, whose hospitality ensured that the months of research would be particularly memorable and enjoyable.

Professors James Joll, Wolfgang J. Mommsen, Geoffrey Best and Geoff Eley read the original thesis, and I am very grateful to them for their valuable comments and general encouragement. In a wider sense I am also indebted to all my colleagues working in the field of German history whose ideas and insights I have assimilated during discussions at conferences and elsewhere. The participants at two conferences on the role of Kaiser Wilhelm II, in Corfu in 1979 and Munich in 1987, deserve special mention in this respect. Thomas Kohut, whom I met in Corfu, not only read the final draft of this book but also had an uncanny knack of choosing to cross the Atlantic just when my spirits were flagging.

Finally, I should like to express my gratitude to two people: the supervisor of my thesis at the University of Sussex, Professor John Röhl, who awakened my interest in Wilhelmine Germany when I was an undergraduate, guided me gently through the complexities of the Wilhelmine political system, supported this project warmly and enthusiastically from its inception and has lost neither his patience nor his interest in the publication of this book despite the delays and procrastinations which the arrival of two children have inevitably produced; and my husband, Tony, without whose constant support and encouragement this book would never have been written. I hope that what follows does justice to their efforts.

Introduction

> Bernhard von Bülow is clean-shaven and pasty, with a shifty look and an almost perpetual smile. Intellectually plausible rather than penetrating. He has no ideas in reserve with which to meet all contingencies, but appropriates other people's ideas and skillfully retails them without acknowledging the source. In this way he often flatters the originator of the idea.[1]

This unfavourable judgement of the man who was to become the longest-serving Reich Chancellor of Imperial Germany under Kaiser Wilhelm II was recorded in his diary by the influential Counsellor in the German Foreign Office, Friedrich von Holstein, in 1884. Holstein was certainly not alone in observing the young diplomat's ingratiating approach and aggressive insincerity, both of which were to be mercilessly exploited in his pursuit of high office and indispensable aids to his political survival as Chancellor. For while Bülow's political skill and intellectual capacity were frequently acknowledged by contemporaries, their assessment of his character was invariably critical, questioning his loyalty and integrity. A smooth conversationalist, the fourth Chancellor was nicknamed 'the eel', so adept was he at slithering out of uncomfortable situations and slipping through the fingers of his political opponents.[2]

Bülow's oleaginous qualities help to explain his relative neglect by recent historical scholarship. Certainly a general lack of sympathy for his character, as well as the absence of a strong tradition of political biography in Germany,[3] have discouraged serious scrutiny of his political career and effectiveness. The methodological bias in favour of social history in recent years has also rendered unfashionable the traditional preoccupation of historians with high politics, governments and statesmen, and this is particularly marked in the case of Imperial Germany. Despite what is now an abundance of literature on the *Kaiserreich*,[4] the new and refreshing multiplicity of views and approaches,[5] and the ever-expanding boundaries of the political realm as new studies analyse the political parties, pressure groups, key industries and localities,[6] one specialist has recently admitted 'just how ignorant we still remain about the detailed political history of the *Kaiserreich*'.[7] The Bülow period from 1900 to 1909 represents a sizeable slice of German history before the First World War, years which are generally seen as 'the high Wilhelmine era' and the most stable period of Wilhelm II's rule.[8] Yet there is no serious study of Bülow's Chancellorship which can lay any claim to being comprehensive in scope. Ironically, the length and importance of the Bülow period seem to have encouraged historians to analyse specific aspects of his Chancellorship – the early years of his foreign policy, the naval programme or the reorganisation of the tariff laws – rather than to seek an overview or to consider his political role in general.[9]

This neglect of the fourth Chancellor is particularly evident at a time when traditional assumptions about the political evolution of the *Kaiserreich* are being challenged and qualified and when it is no exaggeration to say that a 'Bülow problem' has emerged in German historical scholarship. As a more differentiated picture of the *Kaiserreich* has begun to be drawn,[10] so it has become increasingly evident that generalisations about the political system cannot apply to the entire period between 1890 and 1914 and that the power relationships within Wilhelmine Germany changed over time. Bülow's Chancellorship is of central importance to any discussion about the 'parliamentarisation' or democratisation of Germany before 1914 and its potential for change.[11] Its importance is also undeniable with respect to the debate about the government's strategy before 1914 and the economic and social foundations of imperial domestic politics.[12] In addition, it has now become central to the issue of the Kaiser's power before 1914. For the thesis that the monarch practised 'personal rule' from 1897 above all hinges on Bülow's role as Chancellor and the extent to which he initiated and controlled German policy.

It is now over sixty years since Johannes Haller published *Die Aera Bülow*, a damning indictment of the fourth Chancellor for cowardice, indecision, poor leadership and deception,[13] and until fairly recently there existed a virtual consensus, based mainly on memoir sources and older works without access to primary evidence, that Bülow was an ambitious, egotistical and vain schemer, whose principal aim was to preserve his own position.[14] Bülow himself, who during twenty years in retirement did his utmost to cultivate the image of the experienced elder statesman who would have averted the First World War if he had still been Chancellor in 1914, contributed to this negative assessment of his personality by becoming, as was said at the time, 'the only man to commit suicide after his death'.[15] The posthumous publication of his memoirs,[16] four volumes of 'futile erudition'[17] and lies, provoked a storm of public protest and did irreparable damage to his already sullied reputation.[18] The impression was confirmed that Bülow 'was not even intelligent enough to recognise his own actions for what they were'.[19]

In the early literature Bülow was variously blamed for the mistakes in German foreign policy before 1914, for not restraining Kaiser Wilhelm II, for his desultory treatment of domestic issues and his failure to exploit the alleged opportunities for reform such as those presented by the so-called 'Bülow Bloc' parliamentary coalition between 1907 and 1909.[20] Implicit or explicit in these works was the idea that Imperial Germany stood at a crossroads during Bülow's Chancellorship and that the Chancellor had to bear much of the moral and political blame for the path it eventually took. Yet the picture these assessments painted of the Chancellor's responsibility for German policy and decision-making during his nine-year Chancellorship was altogether more ambiguous. While some were categorical in their conviction that Bülow was responsible for 'all the reasons and all the resentments that made war inevitable',[21] Haller, for example, represented Bülow in certain respects as a helpless wedge between Kaiser Wilhelm II on the one hand and the *éminence grise* in the German Foreign Office, Friedrich von Holstein, on the other. Bülow, too, in his memoirs pursued a zig-zag course between attempting to justify or excuse 'his' policies and indicating that political mistakes were not his fault.[22]

This lack of clarity about Bülow's role as Chancellor was compounded by studies which appeared on the Bülow years in the 1950s and 1960s. Here again, in so far as they touched on Bülow's position and even though they made use of archival sources, the picture they presented was confused and contradictory. Karl-Erich Born argued that for most of his Chancellorship, Bülow was prepared to take second place in domestic policy behind the State Secretary of Interior, Arthur von Posadowsky-Wehner. Bülow, he claimed, concentrated his interest on foreign policy.[23] A doctoral thesis on administrative reform in Germany between 1907 and 1918 also concluded that Bülow's 'profound unconcern for domestic affairs' was partly responsible for the administrative anarchy which the author maintained characterised the German system during these years.[24] Such conclusions about Bülow's lack of real involvement in German domestic policy would perhaps have seemed more acceptable if, as these works implied, he had indeed concentrated on foreign policy. But here a similar confusion arose. Bernhard Dehmelt, who studied Bülow's Moroccan policy between 1902 and 1905, vainly searched the Foreign Office files for evidence of 'mature consideration' on Bülow's part and blamed Bülow above all for the contradictions in German foreign policy. 'He used his office as a mediator and compromiser rather than as a leader. He permitted both Kaiser and Foreign Office a remarkable degree of independence.'[25] And Norman Rich, in his exemplary biography of Friedrich von Holstein, presented an essentially similar view of Bülow's role in German foreign policy. Bülow, he argued, claimed the credit for foreign policy successes and made Holstein the scapegoat for his failures. He was too maleable in the face of pressure – from the Kaiser, public opinion, the colonial and naval enthusiasts – and, at decisive junctures such as the Moroccan crisis of 1905–6, he never had 'a policy of his own' and failed to impose unity on the policies of others.[26] Bülow's position in the government thus appeared elusive, with historians who had looked at German domestic policy claiming that he concentrated on foreign policy and historians of German foreign policy also finding scant indication of his leadership. The evidence seemed to point towards a kind of shadow Chancellor, weak, indecisive and unable to fulfil the role assigned to him – a picture completely at variance with contemporary opinion for, as Sebastian Haffner has said, 'one should not overlook [the fact] that Bülow was an extremely popular Chancellor', and the first since Bismarck who was seen to have the necessary stature and esteem worthy of the role.[27]

This issue of Bülow's position within the government system was given new significance by the work of John Röhl, whose book *Germany Without Bismarck* and later publication of the Eulenburg Papers asked new questions about the nature of decision-making in Wilhelmine Germany.[28] In his book, published in 1967, Röhl focused his attention on the ten years between Bismarck's dismissal in 1890 and the appointment of Bülow as Chancellor in 1900, and he presented what is still the classic account of the constitutional struggles during these years. Röhl argued that the chief beneficiary of the political crises in the 1890s was the Kaiser, who practised a 'personal rule' between 1897 and 1900: he determined the broad outlines of government policy, and the Chancellor's importance correspondingly declined. With Bülow's promotion to the Chancellorship in 1900, the aim of the Kaiser and his principal 'irresponsible' adviser, Philipp Eulenburg, was achieved. Bülow was to be Kaiser Wilhelm II's Bismarck, a Chancellor 'who would stay for twenty years or more'.[29] However, he was not to be an obstacle to Wilhelm's 'personal rule', but rather an instrument of it. Bülow was to be the monarch's 'executive tool' and ensure that the members of the Wilhelmine government and bureaucracy were the pliant servants of the Crown.

As with Erich Eyck and Norman Rich before him,[30] it is Röhl's wish to place Kaiser Wilhelm II at the centre of any discussion of the nature of Wilhelmine government and society, and he has tirelessly uncovered new material and organised academic conferences with the aim of exploring the monarch's role.[31] Röhl is generally seen to have succeeded in presenting the Kaiser as 'an important subject of scholarly consideration',[32] but it is the issue of the Kaiser's power which has aroused the most controversy. The immense powers granted to the Kaiser by the Bismarckian constitution have long been recognised, but the full significance of his imperial prerogatives and function is still being clarified and assessed. Since the publication of *Germany Without Bismarck* Röhl has considerably refined his thesis about 'personal rule' (which was the phrase used by contemporaries), and he insists that he has never argued that the Kaiser's powers exceeded those of Bismarck. Recognising that no one ever rules alone and that even the power of so-called 'absolute' rulers was relative,[33] he has suggested that 'personal rule' was an institution-alised system of government in which 'pliant tools of the imperial will' had been appointed to all the key offices. Under 'personal rule – in the good sense' (Bülow), the less the Kaiser felt obliged to intervene, Röhl argues, the better the system was working; and he has also suggested the concept of 'negative personal rule' as an explanation of the way in which the monarch acted as a barrier or block to certain initiatives and options. Even if 'personal rule' *were* merely a legal fiction, Röhl has argued that it had fatal institutional consequences, for example in the multiplication of positions which carried the right of direct access to the Kaiser (*Immediatstellen*). Röhl's application of Norbert Elias's concept of *Königsmechanismus* (kingship mechanism) to the Wilhelmine political system has proved particularly useful in demonstrating the pervasive political and social effects of the Kaiser's powers of patronage. The rivalry of individuals and groups for the monarch's favour was not confined to a highly elaborate Court apparatus in Germany before 1914. Rather, it was a permanent, institutionalised feature of political life within the higher echelons of the Berlin executive and (as this study will further demonstrate) an important determinant of political and social behaviour.[34]

The nature of the Kaiser's personality and the extent of his political influence have recently attracted growing public and professional interest. The German press, radio and television debates on the role of Kaiser Wilhelm II, occasioned by the centenary anniversary of his accession to the throne in 1888, have once again placed the issue of 'who ruled in Berlin' in the decades between Bismarck's dismissal and the outbreak of the First World War in the forefront of historical debate. Moreover, new research into the Kaiser's personality and psychology, as well as the publication of the Eulenburg Papers and Isabel Hull's work on the structure of the Kaiser's entourage, have rekindled scholarly discussion about the historical significance of Wilhelm in the Wilhelmine era.[35] In a review article on the publication of the Eulenburg Papers, Geoff Eley recognised the 'methodological prejudice' which had led some historians of Wilhelmine Germany to reject out of hand Röhl's thesis on 'personal rule' and his allegedly 'personalistic approach'; and he asserted the importance of Röhl's work 'as one of the very few attempts to study the formation of Imperial policy in general'.[36] Nevertheless, Eley too, while recognising the value of Röhl's concept of 'negative personal rule', ultimately took issue with his claims and urged him 'to abandon the chimera of personal rule'. Eley accepted that the Kaiser's position and personality had effects which limited the governing possibilities for successive Chancellors and their colleagues, but he denied that these had more than 'a limited constructive or systematic importance'. In the final analysis Eley insisted upon a much more complex structure of state power than the concept of 'personal rule' seemed to suggest, although Röhl had never denied that the high-political process must be located within the broader field of political, social, economic and cultural relations.

The problem with words such as 'rule' and 'authority' is that they do not appear to allow scope for pressures from below or for constraints on those who occupy high positions and that they thus suggest a straightforward pyramidal organisation of power which few if any would embrace.[37] Yet as Isabel Hull has argued, the standards by which some historians have tried to measure the existence and extent of the Kaiser's 'personal rule' also ultimately ignore the complexity of governance in general and Wilhelmine decision-making in particular. By insisting that the Kaiser only ruled personally if he had a coherent political programme which he consistently carried out despite opposition, these historians make it impossible to say that any individual ever practised 'personal rule'.[38] The case for 'personal rule' is not that Wilhelm II made all the important day-to-day political decisions. Rather, it rests on evidence of a personalised system of rule in which the monarch had a controlling and corrupting influence over personnel appointments. Under Kaiser Wilhelm II the combined effects of his military and political privileges, his unlimited resources of patronage and his manifest personality defects conspired to produce a government machine which lacked coherence, rationality and efficiency. As Röhl has argued, 'personal rule' is perfectly compatible with Hans-Ulrich Wehler's theory that from 1890 the German decision-making processes degenerated into 'polycratic chaos'.[39] The desire for a 'flesh and blood Kaiser' (Bülow), invested with the ultimate power of command, precluded the possibility that a genuinely collective leadership might emerge after Bismarck's dismissal and ensured that there could be no effective coordination of policy.

The discussion of the Kaiser's 'personal rule' has brought into stark relief the problem of the Kaiser's relations with his 'responsible' political advisers and the extent to which they were willing or able to pursue independent policies. Crucially this problem hinges on the role of the Chancellor for, as Wehler has recently confirmed, the man who headed the German government was dependent on the monarch's confidence until October 1918, and this 'late feudal personalistic loyalty relationship' helped to wreck the chances of a parliamentarisation of German political life under the *Kaiserreich*.[40] Bülow's position is central to any discussion of the role of the Chancellor, not least because he was the only Chancellor selected by Wilhelm II with any degree of forethought and because the implications of Röhl's work on the 1890s for the Bülow period have remained untested, even though they posed all kinds of questions about Bülow's role.[41] While the evidence was conclusive that Bülow was brought into the government with the intention that he should be the Kaiser's 'executive tool', only a detailed examination of the Bülow years can establish whether he was content to fulfil this role and whether the imperial government during his Chancellorship 'was so closely attuned to its Kaiser, that he rarely felt the need to intervene'.[42] Did Bülow take steps to limit the Kaiser's power or to manipulate him and, if so, how successful was he in these manoeuvres? And how far was he able to carry out Wilhelm II's wishes even if he had wanted to, given the existence of the Reichstag which, despite its limitations, had inflicted humiliating defeats on the government and opposed imperial projects in the past?

Moreover, while Röhl's thesis was not incompatible with some of the earlier assessments of Bülow's personality and position, a clarification of the Chancellor's role between 1900 and 1909 was becoming doubly necessary with the appearance of new work seeking to revise Bülow's reputation and present the Chancellor rather than the monarch as the man at the helm. Two important works in the 1970s attempted to counter the interpretation that Bülow was a Chancellor without a foreign policy. Barbara Vogel argued that he did have a consistent programme in foreign policy which came to grief in 1906;[43] and Peter Winzen in his study of the period 1897–1901/2 rejected the idea that Wilhelm II or Holstein determined German foreign policy and insisted that Bülow controlled this area from his appointment as foreign Secretary in 1897. A major weakness of Winzen's work was that his study was confined to the 'early phase' of Bülow's foreign policy, and only fleeting attention was paid to the years after 1901. But this did not prevent him from seeking a major revision of Bülow's role, not only with respect to his involvement in foreign policy but also with respect to domestic policy.

One hardly does justice to the fourth Chancellor when one sees in him – as has happened until now – only an opportunist politician, without principles or ideas, who was simply and solely intent on 'ingratiating himself with the monarch and preserving his position' (Thimme). On the contrary, Bülow possessed a long term programme embracing all aspects of domestic and foreign policy which he was to cling to for nearly a decade.[44]

With respect to domestic policy, too, a reassessment of Bülow's role has been urged. The idea that Bülow's Chancellorship offered Imperial Germany her last opportunity for peaceful reform is not a new one, and in particular the years of the Bülow Bloc, the parliamentary coalition of the liberal and Conservative parties between 1907 and 1909, have been seen as a crucial turning-point, when 'the only serious attempt to reactivate the stagnant domestic life of the *Kaiserreich*' ended in failure.[45] But whereas Theodor Eschenburg, from the vantage-point of the Weimar Republic, blamed the Chancellor for his failure to exploit this alleged opportunity to create a more stable basis for parliamentary government in Germany,[46] Terence Cole, in two recent articles on the later period of Bülow's Chancellorship, has emphatically and explicitly argued that Bülow was 'far more weighty and courageous a statesman than his historical reputation would allow'.[47] According to Cole, Bülow was 'a reforming Chancellor' who soon abandoned his role as defender of the monarchy and, in 1905–6, consciously launched a major campaign to 'reform the constitutional structure of the German Empire'. The Bülow Bloc was just one of 'an intimidating array of weapons in his battle with the Kaiser', and it provided him with 'a powerful base from which he could beat off attacks on him from any quarter'. Bülow was a statesman whose 'objectives must command respect' and whose resignation in 1909 ended any chance that Germany might have resolved her inner conflicts peacefully. 'The politics of realism and responsibility had been overwhelmed by the politics of posture and greed.'

Cole provided very little concrete evidence to substantiate his thesis. Nevertheless the fact that he could present such a dissenting view of Bülow's position and intentions – and that his interpretation aroused so little comment[48] – is indicative of the paucity of documented research into the political history of Bülow's Chancellorship. Bülow's personality, political aims and role within the German government system thus all need clarification, since only a critical evaluation of his Chancellorship can resolve these conflicting interpretations.

This book aims to explore Bülow's position as Chancellor on the basis of archival evidence. It is not a political biography of Bülow and makes no claim to assess his role and achievements in the context of his life; nor is it a political history of Bülow's Chancellorship, and the discussion of political issues has been kept to a minimum. As an analysis of the governance of Germany during his Chancellorship, it cannot pretend either to present a full picture of the Wilhelmine political system and the decision-making process, but seeks to examine them from the point of view of the Reich Chancellor. While the Reich Chancellor occupied the highest political office in the government hierarchy and was subjected to pressures 'from above' and 'from below', it is important to remember that this was not the only hierarchy with political influence in Wilhelmine Germany. Indeed, the political status of the Chancellor cannot be understood unless it is appreciated that his political views were frequently an irrelevance in military circles and that his social inferiority weighed heavily against him at Court. In focusing on what happened to the Chancellorship during Bülow's incumbency, other crucial institutions – the political parties, pressure groups, bureaucracy, Army and Kaiser's entourage – have necessarily been pushed into the background and are touched on only in so far as they affected Bülow's personal position and competence. But all of these have generally been better researched in recent years than the central Reich executive.

Nevertheless, for all its omissions and shortcomings, the book was written on the assumption that these would be more than outweighed by the advantages of obtaining an 'overview' of Bülow's Chancellorship. While the importance of the period has never been in dispute, Bülow's Chancellorship frequently receives very cursory treatment by historians.[49] The present state of research into the structures of the *Kaiserreich* also indicates that a more differentiated approach to Wilhelmine high politics, one which can encompass changes over time and the heterogeneity of the 'ruling élite', is highly desirable. And Bülow's political position has become central to the discussion about how Germany was ruled before 1914. Finally, of course, Bülow himself deserves to be rescued from the murky historical depths into which he has sunk. While this book may give substance to some of the myths which have developed about him, it should also help to resolve some of the contradictions which have emerged in previous portraits of this elusive Chancellor and illuminate why he has been variously seen as the arch-villain, the smooth manipulator, the conscious tool of the Kaiser, the impotent Chancellor, the mediator or compromiser, and the man with admirable or mistaken objectives. For all these reasons a study of this kind seems particularly opportune. Bülow was highly sensitive about his future place in history, and it is only right that a man who occupied the most important political office in Germany for nine critical years before the outbreak of the First World War should be given serious attention.

1

The political rise of Bernhard von Bülow, 1849–1900

The early political career of Bernhard von Bülow, 1849–1897

Bernhard von Bülow was the youngest man to assume the Chancellorship of the German Empire and was under fifty years old when he was appointed State Secretary of the Foreign Office in 1897. Behind him he had twenty-four years of accumulated experience in the German Diplomatic Service and the reputation of being one of its most talented and ambitious members. There was nothing inexorable about Bülow's rise to prominence, and his early political career was not without its temporary disappointments and disillusionment. Nevertheless Bülow's career in the Diplomatic Service suffered no real setbacks and, although his promotion was not always as rapid as he himself would have wished, he encountered few obstacles in his progress to his ultimate aim.

Bernhard Martin Heinrich Carl von Bülow was born at Flottbeck in Holstein on 3 May 1849 and was the eldest son of Bernhard Ernst von Bülow, the Danish Minister at the Federal Diet in Frankfurt and later State Secretary of the German Foreign Office (1873–9). At a natural advantage from birth, Bülow related with pride in his memoirs how he first consciously met Bismarck, then Prussian Minister at Frankfurt, when he was seven or eight years old.[1] He had a classical education, attending a Frankfurt Gymnasium and the Royal Pädagogium at Halle before studying at the universities of Lausanne, Leipzig and Berlin. His school leaving certificate in 1867 attests to his 'enthusiastic industry', his 'friendly disposition' and his 'praiseworthy behaviour in every respect' and indicates his relatively weak academic performance in maths and science subjects.[2] Bülow interrupted his education on the outbreak of the Franco-Prussian War in 1870 and enlisted in the Royal Hussar Regiment at Bonn. Promoted to a commission during the campaign, Bülow was attracted by the military profession and would have happily settled for a military career had not his father insisted that he take the law examination, which he passed in March 1872.[3] After eighteen months practising law at Metz, Bülow entered the Foreign Office as an attaché in November 1873.

Bülow's early political experience was fairly wide. During his first five years in the Service he spent some months at the German missions in Rome,

1 Bernhard von Bülow, attaché in rome, at a fancy dress ball in 1875

St Petersburg, Vienna and Athens; he passed the diplomatic examination with honours in November 1875 and he was employed in the Secretariat of the Congress of Berlin in 1878. In late 1878 he was appointed Second Secretary at the Paris embassy under the ambassador, Prince Chlodwig zu Hohenlohe-Schillingsfürst. Bülow was promoted to First Secretary in 1883 and transferred to St Petersburg in the same capacity one year later. In April 1888 he was appointed German Minister to Bucharest, where he was to remain until December 1893, when he was appointed ambassador to Rome, his final diplomatic post before becoming State Secretary and Prussian Minister in 1897. Bülow thus had first-hand experience of several of Europe's most important capitals. The one glaring omission in his political education was London, where it appears that Bülow spent only four days, visiting Herbert Bismarck in 1884, before taking over the conduct of German foreign policy in 1897.[4]

With remarkable swiftness, Bülow succeeded in establishing a reputation as a diplomat. As early as October 1881 Bismarck was able to express to Hohenlohe Berlin's satisfaction with Bülow's political reports[5] and by 1886 Alfred von Kiderlen-Wächter, Bülow's successor at the Paris embassy, could write to Holstein that 'A comparison with Bülow will naturally always be to my disadvantage' since 'Bülow is . . . known everywhere as an uncommonly capable diplomat.'[6] Bülow clearly devoted much time to his work. He demonstrated skill and initiative, wrote long and colourful political reports and assiduously cultivated social connections. Competent, with a good memory, and a proven negotiator, Bülow was considered for the State Secretaryship of the Foreign Office in 1890 on Bismarck's dismissal.[7]

Both birth and merit contributed to Bülow's political rise but, notwithstanding his manifest diplomatic talents, his success must also be attributed to his ability to manipulate and a propensity to intrigue. He demonstrated great skill in manoeuvering within a system in which personal relationships were a formative influence on politics, and the ambitious young diplomat remorselessly exploited friendships and connections to gain influence, promote his career and achieve a position of power.

In the early 1880s he relied heavily for support and political advancement on Holstein, who 'was especially fond of fostering talented younger members of the diplomatic service'.[8] Holstein was impressed by Bülow's skill and ingenuity in Paris,[9] and his advice, political hints and general goodwill did much to establish Bülow's reputation as a rising young diplomat.[10] Bülow clearly trusted Holstein at this stage of his career, a trust that was to be undermined by the fluctuations in their relationship in later years,[11] but he was also aware of Holstein's susceptibility to praise and flattery. Bülow was always careful to thank Holstein most humbly for his support and to emphasise his endeavour to win Holstein's approval.[12] From December 1881

Bülow began to hint to Holstein that his influence as Second Secretary in Paris was considerably limited, and in January 1883 he openly expressed his hope for promotion.[13] Appointed First Secretary later that year, Bülow wrote gratefully to Holstein, 'Let me tell you once more how earnestly I will endeavour to prove myself worthy of your confidence, to which I am above all indebted for the fulfilment of my hopes.'[14]

Bülow's relationship with Holstein deteriorated in the later 1880s when Holstein began to find Bülow's methods rather transparent and to suspect his motives.[15] During this period Bülow cultivated a close political relationship with Herbert Bismarck, the son of the Reich Chancellor, whom he had known since childhood.[16] Herbert Bismarck soon developed a high opinion of the young Secretary and during a visit to Paris in 1883, he wrote to his father that everyone he met sang Bülow's praises.[17] By June 1884 Herbert's estimation of Bülow's political capacity was, in Bülow's own words, 'such as almost to make me blush'.[18] It was after Bülow's transfer to St Petersburg in July 1884 that the relationship between Bülow and Herbert Bismarck assumed marked political significance. Herbert Bismarck clearly found Bülow a very useful diplomatic instrument in St Petersburg[19] and, with his relationship with Holstein at an all time low, Bülow did his utmost to cultivate his political friendship with Herbert, relying on him almost exclusively for information and support. The relationship between Bülow and Herbert Bismarck must be set within the wider context of Bülow's deep admiration for Herbert's father, and Bülow later claimed that his own father's relationship with the first Chancellor had always served as the model for his feelings towards Herbert.[20] Nevertheless, Bülow without doubt saw in his private correspondence with the Reich Chancellor's son an excellent means of furthering his career despite his consciousness of the dangers of staking his ambitions on one man.[21] Herbert passed on Bülow's interesting political reports to the Kaiser's young grandson, Prince Wilhelm, with whom he had developed a close friendship.[22] When Herbert Bismarck became State Secretary of the Foreign Office in April 1886 Bülow considered the possibility of becoming his Under State Secretary (though he denied this ambition to others).[23] And in April 1887, in a very sycophantic letter in which he again denied any personal ambition, Bülow openly expressed to Herbert his desire to leave St Petersburg and be promoted to a European Legation (*Gesandtschaft*).

At all events it was my only endeavour – in the past as in the present and for all the future – to win your satisfaction and to show you thereby how I am devoted to you with all my heart, to you personally and to your cause, which indeed for me coincides with everything I have loved, revered and believed in since my earliest childhood.[24]

Bülow, however, had to wait another year before he was appointed Minister to Bucharest.

Bülow was not the only young aspirant in the German Diplomatic Service, and was doubtless not unique in his desire to find out from as many sources as possible what was being said of him in Berlin and how he might improve his chances of promotion. Nevertheless he did seem prepared to go to further lengths to obtain such information than the majority of his contemporaries. To Karl Lindenau, an official in the German Foreign Office whose friendship Bülow also assiduously cultivated in the 1880s, Bülow was prepared to write five letters before getting a single reply.[25] Bülow was obviously concerned that this further private link with the Foreign Office should remain a secret, and he always promised Lindenau that he destroyed his letters, but he also did not hide from him how valuable he found them. 'Your letters are useful to me to a *high* degree', Bülow told Lindenau in October 1883.

Nothing is more interesting for me than to hear what the Reich Chancellor remarks on my reports *in margine* or has expressed orally. Also Holstein's remarks, whether laudatory or cautionary, are very important for me as direction.[26]

Bülow continued his correspondence with Lindenau throughout the 1890s even though it is likely that the two men had not met for years and Lindenau is not mentioned in Bülow's memoirs.

Bülow repeatedly proved more conscientious and more energetic in writing letters than his correspondents. Philipp Eulenburg, who had met Bülow in 1881 as Third Secretary at the Paris embassy when Bülow was Second, repeatedly apologised for the long delays before he replied to Bülow's letters but admired the persistence of his friend, which he saw as a sign of his loyalty and devotion.[27] Moreover, in his private correspondence with his chosen friends Bülow did what he could to create an atmosphere of confidentiality and deep affection, and to each he gave the impression that he regarded their relationship as something special. 'I think it has something to do with my nature that I find it difficult to come out from a certain polite reserve and cannot easily express my inner feelings', he told Herbert Bismarck in 1883. 'But I have always felt a far greater sympathy for you than I perhaps showed . . .'[28] 'You know how I am fond of you with all my heart', he wrote to Eulenburg in 1886. 'To be with you, dearest friend, is such a joy for me.'[29] 'There are few people whom I like as much as you', Bülow told Lindenau in 1887.[30]

Bülow's methods and approach did not, however, meet with unqualified success in the 1880s, and it could be argued that he might have done better under the Bismarckian regime to omit the flattery and rely exclusively on his diplomatic talents. By the mid 1880s Bülow had alienated Holstein. In his diary Holstein recorded that Bülow was a liar and 'aggressively insincere'; he adopted the 'smooth approach' in handling people and could not 'look anyone straight in the eye'; he was a place-seeker and a schemer who set men against each other with his 'insinuating smile'.[31] In part Holstein's change of heart about Bülow may be attributed to Holstein's own suspicious nature and the growing political divergence between the two men over Bismarck's Russian policy,[32] but Herbert Bismarck was also not impressed by Bülow's technique. He was disgusted by Bülow's letter in April 1887 asking for promotion, which he recognised was larded with flattery and protestations of goodwill in order to achieve a European Legation.[33] Herbert continued to be friends with Bülow and found him 'stimulating and entertaining', but 'terribly time-consuming'.[34] His father seems to have become more convinced of Bülow's unreliability.[35]

Bülow's methods could thus repel as well as attract, and by the mid 1880s he was already gaining a reputation as someone whose behaviour could be explained by his ambition.[36] Moreover Bülow was at times disappointed by how little effect his methods had,[37] and there is no doubt that he felt his promotion was painfully slow. He had to drop hints to Holstein for over a year before he was made First Secretary at Paris. Despite his assertion in his memoirs that it was not easy to leave St Petersburg after four interesting and happy years,[38] Bülow had been anxious to leave for months, complaining to Lindenau and Philipp Eulenburg as well as Herbert Bismarck about the effects of the Russian climate on his health and his general dissatisfaction with the post.[39] In 1887 he wrote to Lindenau,

It is frankly silly how all the Ministers [*Gesandten*] imagine that I want their positions when in reality I am advancing more slowly rather than more quickly than the average. I only wish that all the diplomats thought as little of their dear persons and as much of the cause [*die Sache*] as I do.[40]

He was initially enthusiastic about Bucharest,[41] but after two years he was sick and tired of Romanian politics and anxious to get an embassy.[42] But Bülow had to languish in the relatively insignificant Romanian capital for five years and be frustrated in his hopes to get promoted to the ambassadorships at Paris and St Petersburg[43] before Philipp Eulenburg came to his rescue by facilitating his appointment to Rome.[44]

Bülow's political aspirations were not masked by his frequent denials of personal ambition,[45] but there is one episode in Bülow's early political career which is perhaps not easily reconciled with the emerging picture of the ambitious young diplomat. Bülow's long liaison with Countess Marie von Dönhoff and their eventual marriage in January 1886 when Bülow was thirty-six years old can be seen in some respects as politically motivated, but ultimately defies explanation except as a love match.

In his memoirs Bülow claimed he met Marie von Dönhoff in Florence in 1875,[46] though in a letter to Holstein in 1884 he claimed he met and fell in love with her in Vienna in 1876.[47] The Italian-born princess, Marie Beccadelli di Bologna, had married the German diplomat Count Karl von Dönhoff in 1867, and there is no doubt that Bülow was responsible for the protracted negotiations which led to their divorce in 1883.[48] It is possible that Bülow saw certain political advantages in marrying Marie, who was nine months his senior. Marie von Dönhoff was an intimate friend of the Crown Princess, and Bülow might have hoped to ingratiate himself with the future Kaiser. Holstein interpreted Bülow's passion in this way and noted that they would be 'a dangerous couple: she, the Crown Princess's favourite, he, the world's worst intriguer'.[49] Moreover, in the 1870s the young Prince Wilhelm also seems to have become infatuated with his mother's frequent companion. Wilhelm wrote several letters to his new 'dear and beloved friend'[50] and, although Marie cannot be accused of trying to exploit the friendship (she proved a very unreliable correspondent[51]), her relationship with the later Kaiser Wilhelm II remained affectionate and even survived the bitterness of Bülow's resignation in 1909.[52]

Nevertheless, for all the potential and real advantages of the match for Bülow there were at least as many obstacles and disadvantages in the 1880s. The idea of Bülow's marrying a Catholic divorcee with two children, the former wife of another member of the Diplomatic Service and the close friend of the Crown Princess, was bound to be repugnant to the Bismarcks and meet with official disapproval. Bülow anticipated this opposition, which partly explains why he took Holstein into his confidence about the affair in 1884, but he was either secretly confident that the opposition of the Bismarcks could be overcome without great damage to his career and friendship with them (a confidence that was ultimately justified) or he was prepared to run the risk of permanently alienating the Bismarck family. 'If I were to give up this – intellectually and emotionally – exceptionally gifted woman, who is life itself to me, who has afforded me so many proofs of love and loyalty and wholly entrusted herself to me, I would not know another happy moment and would be a broken man', Bülow told Holstein, and he was adamant that if his request to marry the Countess was not granted he would resign from the Service.[53]

In his letter to Holstein Bülow expressed his resolve to marry Marie in December 1884, and at this stage it is clear that the couple were planning that she would convert from Catholicism to Protestantism. Bülow claimed he was not able to afford a papal annulment and he was unwilling to promise that 'even any possible daughters' be brought up as Catholics. It may have been pressure from Marie's Catholic relatives which caused the marriage eventually to be delayed until a papal annulment was granted in late 1885.[54]

But it is more likely that the Bismarcks and members of Bülow's own family, who also disapproved of the prospective marriage, put pressure on Bülow and insisted that the Countess's first marriage be annulled by the Papacy, either to placate Catholic circles or, more probably, to delay and ultimately prevent the marriage.[55] Bülow finally married Marie in a Catholic ceremony on 9 January 1886 and it was his friend, Philipp Eulenburg, who played a major role in overcoming the hostility of the Bismarcks to the match and thus in enabling Bülow ro remain in the Diplomatic Service.[56] Herbert Bismarck had earlier expressed his revulsion at 'the idea of seeing our friend saddled with this shrivelled-up lemon-skin, which he himself has squeezed utterly dry, in so far as others have left anything',[57] but the majority of reports attest to the many charms and talents of Bülow's wife.[58] Bülow himself was ecstatic and convinced, as he was to maintain throughout his life, that the years of waiting had been worth while.[59]

If Bülow had hoped that his marriage would help his career under the future Kaiser he was to be sadly disappointed. The brief rule of Kaiser Friedrich, the accession of Wilhelm II and the subsequent dismissal of Bismarck in 1890 could not have been anticipated, and in a letter to Herbert Bismarck in April 1890 Bülow was pessimistic about his chances of getting on well under the New Course. He did not know the new Chancellor, General Leo von Caprivi, or the new State Secretary of the Foreign Office, Adolf Marschall von Bieberstein, who was a novice in foreign affairs.[60] Moreover Bülow was well aware of Holstein's enmity, though he could not explain it.[61] The future of Germany and Bülow's own prospects seemed uncertain but, as Germany plunged into a prolonged constitutional crisis, Bülow was to find that he did not need the support of a weakened 'responsible government'.[62] In his friendship with Philipp Eulenburg Bülow had the best guarantee of a successful career under the New Course.

Without doubt Bülow's friendship with Philipp Eulenburg in the 1880s was sincere, beginning at a time when neither could have foreseen the other's usefulness.[63] Nevertheless in 1887 Eulenburg had told Bülow about his developing intimacy with Prince Wilhelm,[64] and by 1890 at the latest Bülow had come to appreciate the value of the connection.[65] Bülow's protestations of affection and friendship reached new heights in his correspondence with Eulenburg in the 1890s.[66] Attuning himself to Eulenburg's sensitive nature, Bülow gave free rein to a poetic, but nevertheless calculated emotion.[67] When Eulenburg wrote to Bülow in 1893 addressing him with the familiar *Du*, Bülow's response was ecstatic.[68]

Bülow's manoeuvres during the critical years of the 1890s were as skilful as any during his later Chancellorship. He had already persuaded many of his friends both of his eminent qualifications for the State Secretaryship and of his lack of interest in the post.[69] Now he succeeded in convincing Eulenburg that he would be the ideal Chancellor of Germany under Kaiser Wilhelm II, and he sufficiently inspired the royal favourite to ensure that he would work consistently throughout the 1890s to achieve that goal.[70] Eulenburg was prepared to intrigue against the Kaiser and the Chancellor to secure Bülow's appointment as ambassador to Rome in December 1893;[71] and, with customary finesse, Eulenburg not only proved able to persuade Wilhelm II of the desirability of Bülow's appointment as Chancellor but also impressed on him the need for restraint until Bülow could be eased into the highest responsible position with the minimum expenditure of his political capital.[72] Bülow reinforced Eulenburg's efforts by cultivating his own relationship with Wilhelm II[73] and by managing to regain Holstein's confidence so that he would be prepared to continue working in the Foreign Office after 1897.[74]

Bülow's appointment to the State Secretaryship of the Foreign Office in 1897 can be seen as the first stage in the execution of plans discussed by Bülow and Eulenburg as early as 1893.[75] Nevertheless, in the spring of 1897, when it became clear that the Kaiser could no longer tolerate Marschall as State Secretary and that he had set his heart on Bülow's immediate appointment,[76] both Eulenburg and Bülow were worried that the time was inopportune for Bülow to go to Berlin. If the Chancellor, Hohenlohe, had resigned as well as Marschall, a potentially serious crisis could have arisen and Bülow risked being associated with a reactionary regime.[77] In the event, the reshuffle of June 1897 was very smooth and Hohenlohe stayed on as Chancellor. But this did not prevent Bülow from securing a written assurance that he would be given a European embassy again, and first and foremost Rome, if he had to resign as State Secretary.[78]

Bülow had frequently maintained to others (including his wife) that he did not want the State Secretaryship.[79] However, his appointment in 1897 was a major step towards the attainment of an ambition that he had long harboured though rarely expressed. Moreover, the State Secretaryship had only become less attractive to Bülow after he realised that he could play for higher stakes. The Württemberg ambassador in Berlin, Varnbüler, reported in July 1897 that he had been surprised to find the new State Secretary in elegiac mood, lamenting that the beautiful days in the Palazzo Caffarelli in Rome were over. Bülow, he went on, was not at all sentimental by nature, and at the beginning of his diplomatic career all his thoughts and endeavours had been directed towards the attainment of the reputation and position he had now acquired.[80] Bülow had now equalled the achievement of his father and could look forward to the most coveted prize. He owed this success to the persuasive influence of Philipp Eulenburg, who greeted the appointment of his protégé with relief, convinced of the identity of their political views and that they shared a similar conception of Bülow's future role as Chancellor.

The early political ideas of Bernhard von Bülow, 1849–1897

In 1897, when Bülow was appointed to the State Secretaryship, he was widely regarded as one of the most talented and capable members of the German Diplomatic Service. Doubts were sometimes expressed about his character and personal qualities, but there is little evidence to suggest that anyone questioned his intelligence or qualifications for the post. Even Philipp Eulenburg had proved willing to work for Bülow's appointment as much because he was impressed by Bülow's trenchant political comments and because he became sincerely convinced that Bülow's appointment would correspond to the national interest, as because his friend seduced him with ingratiating flattery and calculated protestations of affection.[81] Bülow's formative political experience and early political conceptions without doubt influenced his later political activity. As Henry Kissinger, the former American Secretary of State has indicated, high office teaches decision-making but not necessarily substance, and 'the convictions that leaders have formed before reaching high office are the intellectual capital they will consume as long as they continue in office'.[82] But a discussion of the development of Bülow's political views and ideas is doubly significant and pertinent to a study of his later Chancellorship because Bülow was the only Reich Chancellor of the German Empire who *knew* that he might well assume the highest Reich office several years before he was appointed. Bülow had ample opportunity and leisure to reflect on his future role as Chancellor and to create the intellectual capital on which he would later be called to draw.

The importance of intellectual influences is always difficult to gauge, but as a young diplomat Bülow read avidly and extensively, and in his early correspondence with friends there are frequent references to the works of history, philosophy and literature which he had particularly enjoyed and recommended. Especially during his years in Bucharest Bülow had plenty of time to spend reading and studying, and the diplomat Anton von Monts later claimed that it was during this period that Bülow collected the numerous quotations and historical anecdotes with which he impressed his audiences in later years.[83] It would doubtless be misleading to attribute undue significance to any one particular work which Bülow cited in his early years, especially when his literary comments were frequently neither expansive nor probing.[84] He had a particular passion for classical literature, especially Homer, but the frequent historical parallels he drew in his political reports reflected a broad knowledge of history and he also familiarised himself with the great works of German literature and philosophy.[85] In his memoirs Bülow claims he was attracted to Marie von Dönhoff when he discovered that she knew Goethe and Schiller, Hölderlin and Kleist, Schopenhauer (his favourite philosopher) and even Immanuel Kant 'almost better than I did myself.[86]

When abroad Bülow immersed himself in the country's history and culture, but there is no doubt that he considered German culture to be superior. Goncharov's *Oblomov*, in which the Russian hero is plagued by existential indecision while his German friend reaps all the material rewards of life, was described by Bülow as 'the finest available portrayal of the Russian character'.[87] The Romanians' misfortune was to mimic the 'pseudo-civilisation' of Paris instead of drinking their fill of German culture.[88] Bülow's strong sense of German nationalism and the pre-eminence of German culture may have derived to some extent from his reading of Treitschke. Bülow later claimed in his memoirs that Treitschke's *German History* and Bismarck's speeches constituted the foundations of his political thought and feelings.[89] Treitschke was undoubtedly a formative intellectual influence on Bülow,[90] and when he died in 1896, Bülow wrote to Monts how much he had loved and respected the historian.[91] However, Bülow never knew Treitschke personally, and his influence on the fourth Chancellor has probably been exaggerated.[92] Bülow's knowledge and image of Bismarck as a statesman operating in the realm of practical politics were at least as important as intellectual influences for the development of his ideas.

All his life Bülow lived under the shadow of the awesome achievements of Germany's first Chancellor. Bülow was only twenty-one years old when he enlisted in the Prussian Army in order to fight in the Franco-Prussian War, and the wars of unification were without doubt the most formative experience in his adolescence. For Bülow, Bismarck was 'the greatest German statesman',[93] who 'with a mighty effort retrieved in the space of years what had been mismanaged and neglected for centuries',[94] and Bülow's memoir account of Bismarck's diplomacy in the 1860s is strewn with references to his genius, his vision and his complete mastery of the art of statecraft.[95] Bülow was always to profess great love and admiration for the Chancellor whom he associated with his own father.[96] But in the 1880s there was almost a religious or mystical quality in Bülow's adulation. To hear Bismarck talk was 'like a Shakespearian drama come alive', he wrote after visiting Varzin in 1884; 'you believe you are hearing history itself speaking'.[97]

Throughout his life Bülow claimed that politically he was a staunch Bismarckian,[98] but this needs considerable qualification. Especially after 1890 Bülow was critical of aspects of Bismarck's domestic policy (in particular, the *Kulturkampf* against the Catholics),[99] and, despite the conviction of his friends in 1897 that he would follow in Bismarck's tradition in foreign policy,[100] the evidence suggests that certainly in the 1870s and 1880s Bülow did not always understand the reasons behind Bismarckian diplomacy.[101] For all his skill and ingenuity as a young diplomat Bülow's approach to international relations was frequently simplistic and confused. He admitted that he saw foreign powers merely as pawns in a chess game, to be pushed about in Germany's interest;[102] in his political reports he could indulge in sweeping generalisations about foreign peoples[103] and 'eccentric conjectures' of the kind sharply criticised by Bismarck himself in 1887;[104] and even given the changing diplomatic circumstances between 1873 and 1897 Bülow's tergiversations with respect to his political opinions and suggested strategies reflect a remarkable fickleness and inconsistency, unlikely to contribute to the ascendancy of Germany within a stable Europe which, as a professed Bismarckian, he presumably wanted.[105] In March 1890 Bülow confessed to Eulenburg that he disagreed with a central element of Bismarck's diplomacy, his policy towards Russia.[106] All this indicates that Herbert Bismarck was suffering from a fundamental misconception, not least fostered by Bülow's pandering to the Bismarcks' views,[107] when he told Bülow in 1885 that he was 'really the only one of all our diplomats who lets himself be penetrated by the political ideas of my father'.[108]

It would thus be misleading to suggest that Bülow absorbed all the political conceptions of Otto von Bismarck or even that he was greatly impressed by the details of Bismarck's policy. What Bülow meant when he maintained he was a Bismarckian was that he appreciated Bismarck's brand of *Realpolitik* and that he wholeheartedly endorsed Bismarck's political loyalties and achievements. As Bülow was told by his father:

Genius cannot be copied . . . Nothing would be more foolish than to want to imitate Bismarck. But what one can learn from him is the vision for the realities in politics, the contempt for theory which has always been so precious to us Germans. Bismarck will also hear nothing of the scientific methods which are frequently advocated in Germany. For him politics is not a science but an art. Learn from our great Bismarck above all and for your entire life conscientiousness in matters great and small, caution, deliberation, passionate, unerring patriotism, unshakeable devotion to Prussia, to *Deutschtum*, to the monarchy, to the Army, to everything which has made us great and which alone can keep us great.[109]

The confirmation of Prussian values, tempered by Reich necessities, and his lifelong rejection of morality and 'dogmatic beliefs' in politics were above all else what Bülow learnt from Bismarck.[110]

Bismarck's Chancellorship taught Bülow other lessons. In later years Bülow attached great importance to the continuity and stability of the Bismarckian era which he saw as one of the main reasons for the success of the 'old course'.[111] More significantly, he came to appreciate Bismarck's invaluable role as a national symbol and the personification of the national idea. In foreign capitals he was able to experience at first hand the impact of the Chancellor's personality and stature, and he recognised that Bismarck was Germany's most prestigious asset, the embodiment of national solidarity at home and German power abroad. Russia would continue to have great respect for Germany 'so long as we have your great father and the Army', he told Herbert Bismarck in 1885;[112] Russia's fear of Germany had been significantly increased by 'the colossal speech of the Reich Chancellor', he wrote in 1888.[113] Watching the domestic troubles in Germany following the death of Kaiser Wilhelm I Bülow recognised not only the dangers of political instability within Germany but also the vital role played by Bismarck in promoting German prestige abroad. 'You at the centre', he told Herbert Bismarck, 'can scarcely imagine how greatly the unqualified machinations against the Reich Chancellor and the *Staatsraison* he embodies undermine [*erschüttern*] here on the periphery respect and confidence in Germany, that is, the foundations of our power position and of world peace.'[114] A clearer exposition of how closely Bülow associated the appearance of power with its substance could scarcely be found.

Bülow opposed Bismarck's abrupt dismissal in 1890. Recognising that the Chancellor's years were numbered, he believed that it would have been in the best interests of the country and Kaiser to have Bismarck's powers dismantled gradually. 'To unburden the Reich Chancellor gradually, to accustom the nation gradually to the fact that sooner or later, whether we want it or not, we will have to get on without this phenomenal figure [*phänomenale Erscheinung*] is a vital question for us', he wrote to Eulenburg shortly before Bismarck's departure was confirmed.[115] But once Bismarck's dismissal was a fact, Bülow displayed a strong sense of realism. The main task now, he wrote on several occasions, was to prove 'that the Reich can also be ruled without him'.[116] In the 1890s Bülow further distanced Bismarck's personality from his achievement and significance as a national symbol. He became more critical of Bismarck's policies as Chancellor;[117] and he condemned Bismarck's hostile attitude to the New Course, which he considered detrimental to Germany's interests.[118] Individuals were transitory phenomena, he repeated to Eulenburg; the national idea was more important than the lives of mortals.[119] While Bülow insisted that he would remain 'loyal to the Bismarck of former times and to the spirit of his great period',[120] by 1897 he could write in a personal memorandum that he hoped Bismarck would die soon because he only made the task of governing more difficult.[121]

Of course Bismarck's dismissal came at a time when Bülow was already emancipating himself from the influence of the Bismarck family and had already recognised the usefulness of his friendship with Philipp Eulenburg; and to Philipp Eulenburg at least Bülow was already arguing that many of the real and symbolic functions fulfilled by Bismarck could just as easily be assumed by the new Kaiser, Wilhelm II. As early as 1887 Bülow had expressed optimism about the future reign of the young Prince,[122] and this confidence was to be repeated frequently in his correspondence with Eulenburg in future years. To Eulenburg Bülow praised Wilhelm's personal qualities and individuality,[123] and even before Bismarck's dismissal Bülow welcomed the new Kaiser's desire to be more personally active in politics since he alone was in the position eventually to take the place of the Chancellor.[124] 'We cannot be grateful enough', he wrote to Eulenburg in August 1890,

that we have such a master, who always reminds me of the heroic Salier and Hohenstaufen Kaisers of our Middle Ages. He is – as I wrote to you, *ni fallor*, a year ago – made of the wood from which our Lord God loves to carve the great, the very great rulers.[125]

'The stuff is obviously there', he continued later that year. But for the first time Bülow qualified his praise. 'If he finds loyal and clever servants he will also one day take a great place in world history.'[126]

This was the theme that Bülow was to develop persistently and to good effect in his correspondence with Eulenburg in subsequent years. The Kaiser himself was not to blame for his declining prestige and the problems of the 1890s. His ideas and plans were all correct and often had the mark of genius; it was the executors of his policies who were at fault.[127] Despite all the indications to the contrary, Bülow continued to minimise Wilhelm II's personal defects and emphasise his 'splendid qualities'.[128] In this way Bülow convinced Eulenburg of his devotion to Wilhelm II and of his supreme qualifications for the Chancellorship.[129]

Once Bülow had persuaded Eulenburg of his eligibility for the Chancellorship, he elaborated on his conception of the role. He insisted that his overriding aim was to facilitate the Kaiser's personal rule.

I would be a different kind of Chancellor from my predecessors. Bismarck was a power in his own right, a Pepin, a Richelieu. Caprivi and Hohenlohe regarded or regard themselves as the representatives of the 'Government' and to a certain extent of the Parliament against His Majesty. I would regard myself as the executive tool of His Majesty, so to speak his political Chief of Staff. With me, personal rule – in the good sense – would really begin.[130]

Bülow held out to Eulenburg the prospect that his Chancellorship would obviate the need for extreme solutions to Germany's problems. The Kaiser would not be forced to embark on a reactionary, *coup d'état* policy against the German Reichstag. By recourse to new, more subtle methods of social and political control, Bülow would ensure that such a confrontation was averted but that the Kaiser's will would still prevail.

Bülow had a remedy for all the problems of the 1890s, and his optimism sustained Eulenburg at times when the royal favourite was despondent about the chances of ever finding a satisfactory solution. The main task, Bülow insisted, was to preserve the Kaiser's authority, independence and power, and to strengthen the bonds which existed between the imperial Crown and the nation.[131] Dislike of a strong and, to a certain extent, autocratic Kaiser was not as widespread as some people imagined.[132] Contact between the Kaiser and the nation had been loosened, but this could soon be corrected.[133] By steadiness and consistency the Crown would make an impression in Germany, and gradually the Kaiser and nation would grow together.[134]

Bülow had no doubt that the monarchy was not an antiquated system of rule and that it would be able to overcome the problems Germany faced at the end of the nineteenth century.[135] Foremost among these problems, in Bülow's opinion, was the evil of particularism. Prussia's future was not inseparably linked with that of the Reich, he told Eulenburg, and any weakening of the Reich idea would be a step on the road to disaster.[136] Particularist sentiment could be countered by broadening the basis of monarchical support to include moderate liberals and clericals[137] and by enhancing nationalist feeling through fostering an atmosphere of external crisis.[138] With skill and patience they would have to win over the South Germans, who had been particularist, 'Great German', ultramontane and even in favour of the Napoleonic Confederation of the Rhine but who had never supported the Hohenzollern.[139] Germany's entire internal and external future, Bülow wrote, ultimately depended on the progressive strengthening of the ties between the South German states and the Reich, on the nurturing of the national idea.[140]

Similarly German Catholics would have to be harnessed to support the monarchy. Divisive policies such as the *Kulturkampf* were to be avoided, now only because Bismarckian methods could only be employed by Bismarck himself,[141] but also because they weakened the Reich idea. 'Rather', Bülow argued, 'we must do everything compatible with the well-being of the whole [*des Ganzen*] in order to merge the Centre – basically still the old Germany which fought in the Thirty Years War under the imperial Habsburg flag – gradually with the new Reich of the Hohenzollern. Otherwise our unity and future will stand only on one leg.'[142] National Liberals and the more moderate left-wing liberals would also have a place in imperial domestic politics, Bülow told Eulenburg: 'on the one hand we need this to maintain the Reich's unity, on the other to create a broad front in our fight against the social revolution'.[143] Even the masses, with their socialist tendencies, were to submit to the monarchy in the end, according to Bülow's formula. Reforms would improve their material standard of living while violent opposition would be mercilessly suppressed. 'The horses may kick and bite as much as they like', Bülow wrote complacently, 'but in the end they will come before a carriage and be steered by a coachman with reins and whip.'[144]

While it is impossible not to notice the lack of sincerity and the calculated ambition in many of Bülow's letters to Eulenburg in the 1890s, it is still clear that Bülow's correspondence with Eulenburg remains the most important source for the development of his political conceptions during this period. To no one but Eulenburg did Bülow insist quite so unreservedly that he was confident in Wilhelm II's strength and genius;[145] to no one but Eulenburg did he develop quite so persistently the theme that the 'mediocrities' surrounding the Kaiser had to be replaced.[146] But many of the ideas expressed by Bülow to Eulenburg were repeated in his correspondence with other friends such as Lindenau, Monts and even Holstein. The emphasis on developing the Germans' sense of nationality; on tailoring foreign and domestic policy so as to encourage national solidarity; on broadening the basis of imperial domestic politics; on the need for moderation, calm, consistency, continuity – all this can be found elsewhere.[147] In his notebooks Bülow copied down quotations which supported these ideas: 'The solidarity of the citizens is the elementary basis of the state idea'; 'the ultimate aim of politics is to induce the individual to subordinate his egoism consciously to the aims recognised as useful for all'; and he was impressed by a remark in Goethe's *Elective Affinities* that the states ruled by a politically educated class, such as Rome, Venice and England, lasted longest. 'This is still lacking in Prussia, we are too dependent on individual personalities [*zu sehr auf einzelnen Persönlichkeiten gestellt*]. Therefore, in order to create such a class, we must aspire to fuse the Junker class and the "intelligentsia", Army–Civil Service and bourgeoisie, Conservatives and National Liberals.'[148]

Bülow's political conceptions in the 1890s, and especially his preoccupation with national solidarity, reflected to a great extent what he considered to be the fundamental weaknesses of the New Course. German policy was no longer being conducted with the same unanimity or assurance, the prestige of the monarchy and the government was declining, and the country's domestic instability was having an adverse effect on German foreign policy. Bülow lamented the dissatisfaction in Germany and the prevalent mood of pessimism, which he found exaggerated and unpatriotic. They were simply living through a transitional period which always had its unpleasant and inconvenient sides, he told Eulenburg, but when it was doubly necessary for everyone to hold his head high and do his duty without ill-humour for the great cause.[149]

The central issue in looking at Bülow's political conceptions before 1897 is his attitude to the Kaiser, and it seems appropriate to question how serious Bülow was in his professed intention to implement 'personal rule – in the good sense' if this meant that as Chancellor he would merely be the Kaiser's 'executive tool'. The insincerity of many of Bülow's declarations of devotion to Wilhelm II in his correspondence with Eulenburg has already been noted, and as one historian has pointed out, 'Bülow repeated these sentiments in letter after letter, long after they should have seemed a cruel mockery.'[150] Bülow was certainly too sensible not to see Wilhelm's shortcomings, however susceptible he may have been to his charms. Moreover many of Bülow's recommendations to Eulenburg about how German policy should be conducted after Bismarck's dismissal can be interpreted as indirect criticism of Wilhelm personally. Bülow's emphasis on consistency, caution and the avoidance of sudden or extreme measures was scarcely compatible with the behaviour of the monarch, who was all too impetuous in his conduct of affairs. Finally, even before 1897 a discrepancy is discernible between Bülow's apparent conception of his future role as Chancellor and Wilhelm II's conception of Bülow's role, as developed in response to Eulenburg's influence. While Bülow saw himself as the 'alternative solution' to Germany's problems – the other alternative being a *coup d'état* – Wilhelm already saw Bülow as 'his Bismarck', who would help him 'clean up this rubbish heap of parliamentarism and the party system at home'.[151] Thus the Kaiser was under the misapprehension that Bülow would be the Prussian Chancellor who, if necessary, would be prepared to undertake a *Staatsstreich*, while this was the very course Bülow sought to avoid. For all these reasons it is necessary to examine more closely Bülow's conception of his future Chancellorship and how he viewed his future relationship with Kaiser Wilhelm II.

Without doubt the monarchy occupied a central position in Bülow's political conceptions for it embodied 'an eternal principle' and was 'the symbol and crown of Germany unity'.[152] Although after the collapse of the monarchy in 1918 Bülow was to imply that the dismissal of Bismarck should have been followed by a slow evolution towards a more parliamentary system of government,[153] there was no hint of this kind of sentiment in the 1890s. Bülow dismissed parliamentarism as unsuited to the German national character,[154] and suggested that if Kaiser Friedrich had lived long enough to inaugurate parliamentary rule in Prussia, 'Prussia would today be a kind of Belgium or Baden, if it still existed at all.'[155] Instead, Bülow emphasised his fanatical love for the Prussian state, the Prussian Army and above all the Prussian monarchy. Bülow maintained at different times that both the Army and the monarchy were the true representatives of the German people.[156]

Bülow was thus a royalist by conviction, and he also claimed that he was emotionally bound to the monarchy.[157] Nevertheless, much of what he wrote about the monarchy indicated that his ideal conformed more to the personality and style of Wilhelm I than that of Wilhelm II. For Bülow, the monarch had an elevated and symbolic status which it was imperative not to damage in the public eye.[158] He conceived of a monarch whose ultimate power was unquestioned but who nevertheless distanced himself to a not inconsiderable extent from the hurly-burly of political life. In his letters to Eulenburg, he praised the Kaiser when he acted with restraint[159] and also implied that once the Kaiser had demonstrated the principle of his absolute authority, he could allow his Ministers to be conciliatory about the specific details of policy.[160]

While Bülow conceived of a Kaiser who remained lofty and benevolent, it was the Chancellor who would exercise the monarch's political functions and 'interpret' his plans. The Chancellor would be the Kaiser's direct representative in government[161] and stand in the forefront of German politics. In Prussia he would be above the other Ministers, the *de facto* Prime Minister and not simple *primus inter pares*, who controlled the Prussian Ministry in the name of the King.[162] Clearly in this scheme of things there was room too for the Chancellor to assume a symbolic role. The Chancellor could come to embody the nation's political unity and, especially in the case of a Chancellor who came to believe that one of his major tasks was to restore to the Chancellorship the prestige, seriousness and authority it had lacked for a decade,[163] might well run the risk of eclipsing the monarch.

The cornerstone of such a system would be the relationship between Kaiser and Chancellor, and Bülow attributed many of the difficulties of Bismarck and his successors to the unsatisfactory nature of their relations with Wilhelm II.[164] To some extent Bülow seems to have preserved an extraordinary optimism about the personality of Wilhelm II, doubtless facilitated by the infrequency of their meetings before 1897, and he may well have believed that the Kaiser's strong will and lively temperament would always bow to the dictates of *raison d'état*.[165] However, even before 1897 Bülow openly indicated to Eulenburg that he would not take every word of his high-spirited master too seriously[166] and in private he was already critical of the monarch. Wilhelm, he wrote in April 1897, was seen by many as 'mentally eccentric'; in any case his imagination got the better of his knowledge and strength of judgement. The Kaiser provoked public opinion but was nevertheless afraid of it. He appeared insufficiently serious, too concerned with externals and trivialities. He was too 'dangerous', not knowing the value of moderation, and he did not recognise the limits of his knowledge and ability. Philipp Eulenburg's influence on the monarch was considered harmful because he flattered Wilhelm too much. People saw in the Ministers the only defence against 'eccentricities from above'. 'If His Majesty would only keep quiet for a few months', Bülow wrote, 'everything could be put to rights.'[167]

Wilhelm's unpredictability in the spring of 1897 clearly made Bülow very preoccupied with the dangers of Germany's domestic situation. Further personal, pencilled notes reveal that Bülow had heard from his brother, Alfred, that the South German princes were prepared to take up a common position in the event of 'eccentric' actions by the Kaiser. The Kaiser had apparently told Carl von Stumm-Halberg, the industrialist and Free Conservative politician, that he was going to send the Reich Chancellor and the

Reichstag to the devil. According to the State Secretary of the Reich Navy Office, Admiral Hollmann, the Kaiser believed that they could not go on any longer on the present constitutional basis. Under Bismarck the monarchy had been pushed too far into the background, but Wilhelm planned to have 'new leaders and rule as in Russia'. He would get rid of the Reichstag and replace it with delegations from the individual states. Bülow also noted that Götz von Seckendorff, the *Oberhofmeister* and Cabinet Chief of Wilhelm II's mother, Victoria, had said that the Kaiser was unpopular, even among his own family.[168]

Even though Bülow recognised that the Kaiser did not have the nerves to carry out these threats, Bülow's notes of 1897 indicate his profound concern with the Kaiser's volatility and the extent to which Wilhelm was damaging the prestige of the monarchy. Monts recalled that Bülow had told him in a long conversation that he saw his main task as Chancellor as being to help Germany over the rule of Wilhelm II. 'Were this episode overcome, Germany would once again move forward; but for the moment it would mean marking time and paralysing as far as possible the great dangers which sprang from the individuality of this ruler.'[169] Although this perhaps imputes too great a degree of selflessness to Bülow's ambition to attain the Chancellorship, there is no doubt that already in 1897 Bülow conceived that his primary role as State Secretary and later Chancellor would be to manage the Kaiser. Bülow obviously felt that he would be able to manage his impressionable and immature master, even if it meant devoting most of his energies to the task; and in an important letter to Lindenau in November 1897, after his formal appointment as State Secretary of the Foregin Office but before he actually left Rome, Bülow revealed that the cultivation of his relationship with Wilhelm II was a serious political calculation. As State Secretary, he wrote, he would have to make use of his time practically and sensibly.

The main reason is that I will otherwise lose the synoptic view over the broad sweep of our politics and in particular the indispensable composure, freshness and (*last not least*) [English in original] time for His Majesty. But here, given the present relations, lies the centre of my activity. In any other respect I could certainly be easily and advantageously replaced, but not with and *vis-à-vis* His Majesty. If I don't maintain constant (verbal and written) contact with His Majesty, the *status quo*, which was welded together with difficulty, will fall apart at the seams and a change will result, the direction of which, given our general situation and the inner disposition of His Majesty, is easy to predict.[170]

Bülow thus gave expression to his anxieties about the implications of Wilhelm II's rule for German national unity and the Reich Constitution, and to counter such dangers he consciously intended to devote the major part of his working day to nurturing his relationship with the Kaiser. The morning hours were to be left free for the Kaiser or spent on preparation work for

the Kaiser. Audiences were to be limited to the hour between 12 noon and
1.0 p.m., and visits from ambassadors, journalists and other important
personages to the hour between 6.0 p.m. and 7.0 p.m. 'In this way I will
remain fresh for the main things', Bülow argued.

Bülow may well have equated such a role with loyalty to the monarchy,
convinced that it would serve the monarchy's best interests. Nevertheless,
this was not the loyalty of a man determined to execute the Kaiser's every
wish. His criticisms of Wilhelm's personality, his recognition of the dangers
to which Wilhelm's rule might expose Germany, his intimation that he
would not take the Kaiser's words too seriously, his confidence, based on
years of experience, in his ability to manipulate and control friendships, his
conception of a Chancellor in the forefront of politics – all these indicate that
the relationship between Kaiser Wilhelm II and Bernhard von Bülow would
not be so straightforward as that between master and servant, and that as the
Kaiser's 'political Chief of Staff' Bülow would expect considerable freedom
and independence in the way he interpreted royal plans.

Bülow as State Secretary of the Foreign Office, 1897–1900

As State Secretary of the German Foreign Office between 1897 and 1900
Bülow laid much of the basis of his future Chancellorship. It was during this
period that he established a close, personal relationship with Wilhelm II, and
a pattern emerged in their official relations which was to survive virtually
unchanged until 1909. Bülow became the Kaiser's foremost political adviser
and, although he chose not to exploit immediately all the opportunities this
offered to him, a shift in emphasis within the German executive was
perceptible. As the position of the Reich Chancellor, Hohenlohe, grew
progressively weaker and the Kaiser assumed greater control over the
government,[171] the personal influence of Bülow began to extend well beyond
the formal requirements of his office. The State Secretaryship of the Foreign
Office assumed a significance it had not had under Bülow's predecessor and
which it would lose again under his successor. Few doubted that, in the event
of Hohenlohe's resignation, Wilhelm would choose Bülow as the next
Chancellor, and Hohenlohe's Chancellorship was increasingly seen as merely
the vehicle through which his successor should gain experience of government.[172] By October 1900 the terrain was sufficiently prepared and Bülow's
assumption of the Chancellorship was achieved with the minimum of
disruption.

In appointing Bernhard von Bülow State Secretary of the Foreign Office
in October 1897[173] Wilhelm II installed his 'personal, intimate friend' in the
Wilhelmstrasse.[174] The Kaiser's trust in Bülow probably owed something
both to his earlier affection for 'the Contessina'[175] and to his close friendship

with Bülow's brother, Adolf, who was Wilhelm's personal adjutant from 1879 until his death in a riding accident in 1897.[176] Adolf von Bülow, who had been widely regarded as more intelligent than his elder brother[177] and who had been considered by Wilhelm II for the Chancellorship,[178] was responsible for the 'boisterous friendliness' with which Wilhelm greeted Bülow on their first meeting in 1884;[179] and he was also suspected by Holstein of having arranged a correspondence between his brother and the Prince in 1885.[180] Nevertheless, the most important influence in determining the Kaiser's attitude to his new State Secretary in 1897 was Philipp Eulenburg. It was Eulenburg who had drawn Wilhelm's attention to Bülow's political talents and who had represented Bülow's arrival in Berlin as a panacea for the monarchy's problems.[181] Much to Chancellor Caprivi's annoyance, Eulenburg had encouraged Bülow to resume direct correspondence with the Kaiser in 1894 so that Wilhelm would gradually become accustomed to communicating with Bülow.[182] And such was the effectiveness of Eulenburg's patronage that even before Bülow's appointment Wilhelm referred to Bülow in conversation with Szögyényi, the Austrian ambassador to Berlin, as 'the man with my absolute confidence'.[183]

Bülow thus began his official activity in Berlin with an incomparable advantage, and from 1897 he devoted his energies to the assiduous cultivation of his relationship with the Kaiser. Sensitive to Wilhelm's impetuous temperament, from the moment he became State Secretary Bülow was careful not to subject the Kaiser too frequently to long, formal audiences.[184] Instead, he gave Wilhelm every encouragement to seek out his adviser for spontaneous and informal political discussions as often as he wished. In the past, the Kaiser had occasionally paid a visit to the Chancellor or State Secretary of the Foreign Office after his morning walk in the Tiergarten, but this practice had lapsed completely by 1897.[185] Only when Bülow took up residence in the Wilhelmstrasse was it resumed and encouraged to become a habit. In January 1898 Wilhelm began to pay the State Secretary regular, frequently daily visits, and these were supplemented with social invitations. While the Chancellor complained that the Kaiser avoided him,[186] Wilhelm might visit Bülow in the morning, have lunch with him and summon him again in the evening.[187] In the month of February 1898 the State Secretary probably saw the monarch on twice as many days as Chancellor Hohenlohe did in the entire year. While Hohenlohe's personal contact with Wilhelm II was limited to a Crown Council meeting on 15 February 1898, Wilhelm missed only three or four opportunities of seeing Bülow.[188] It is thus not surprising that Bülow's favoured position became ever more apparent and that Alexander Hohenlohe wrote to his father: 'In the newspapers I still miss the news that the Kaiser was with you or you were with the Kaiser, while I am always reading that Bülow was with him or that he was with Bülow.'[189]

Bülow's approach to his relationship with the Kaiser was remarkably successful. 'What a joy to have to deal with someone who is devoted to you body and soul, and also can understand and wants to understand!' Wilhelm wrote rapturously to Eulenburg in 1897.[190] Bülow was 'the absolute magician' whom heaven had sent him quite undeservedly,[191] and from 1897 Wilhelm showered his new favourite with praise, presents and honours, not least promoting him to *Graf* (Count) in 1899.[192] Philipp Eulenburg reaped the rewards of the Kaiser's confidence in Bülow when he accompanied Wilhelm on his North Sea Cruise in July 1898. 'The Kaiser accepts everything that comes from Berlin smoothly and without question as being your work', he wrote to Bülow.[193] Bülow was soon acknowledged as a key figure in influencing the Kaiser.[194] Even the Kaiserin, recognising Bülow's expertise in handling her husband and interpreting imperial moods, sought his advice and made appeals to his influence.[195] Commenting on the friendship between the Kaiser and State Secretary in a private letter to the Austrian Foreign Minister, Goluchowski, in May 1898, Szögyényi cast the usual doubts on Bülow's sincerity and reliability but had to confess that he had shown great skill and pliancy in handling his royal master.[196]

In his memoirs Bülow sought to give the impression that right from the beginning he was prepared to contradict the Kaiser and assert his own views.[197] Contemporaries assessed his character differently. On hearing the news of Bülow's appointment, the perceptive and well-informed Baroness Spitzemberg noted in her diary that Bülow was an 'eminently gifted but highly ambitious and unfortunately very smooth man from whom the Kaiser will never hear a word of contradiction';[198] and General Alfred von Waldersee reported Bülow as saying, 'I did not want to annoy the Kaiser right at the beginning by opposing him, but I wanted first to create my position',[199] a view ominously reminiscent of a similar assertion made by Hohenlohe in 1894.[200] Bülow obviously resorted to all kinds of methods when dealing with Wilhelm II. He had had plenty of advice from Eulenburg about how to handle the Kaiser, and understood that Wilhelm could be contradicted in private and that he would accept an idea if led to believe that the idea was his own.[201] Closer observation of Bülow in the Kaiser's presence led Waldersee to modify his view of Bülow as someone who acquiesced in everything Wilhelm wanted. Bülow, he wrote, said many flattering things to the Kaiser and never said 'no', but he often acted differently afterwards, knowing that Wilhelm made hasty judgements and often forgot what he had said on the spur of the moment.[202] Unlike his predecessors, Bülow was to develop a keen appreciation of 'what is possible with His Majesty and what is not possible or leads to crises'.[203] But his letters to Eulenburg and to Wilhelm himself indicate the sycophantic depths to which he was prepared to plunge. To both he insisted that his only real service was to understand the Kaiser's aims and intentions, and that even his strength in the execution of those intentions lagged far behind the power of Wilhelm's ideas.[204] Moreoever, Bülow was aware of his limitations and unlikely to insist on his views as a matter of principle. As he wrote to Holstein in 1899 in connection with the naval question, 'I cannot consider it useful to make suggestions to His Majesty which have no prospect of actual success and would only make him annoyed with me [*an mir irre machen würden*].'[205] His influence on the Kaiser depended on the successful cultivation of a personal relationship with him, and this in turn depended on Wilhelm's confidence that Bülow was working towards his aims and acting in his interests.

Before Bülow moved to Berlin, he had envisaged devoting several hours each day to the needs of the Kaiser, but in fact this allocation of time to Wilhelm was too generous. In practice, the Kaiser was frequently absent from Berlin and, while this clearly placed a greater burden of correspondence on Bülow, it was only during the winter months, especially from January to March when the Court moved from Potsdam to Berlin, that the emphasis on personal contact with the monarch would involve a daily and substantial sacrifice in time and energy. Nevertheless, the winter months were also the high-point of the German political year, with both the Reichstag and the Prussian Landtag in session, and the priority Bülow gave to the cultivation of his relationship with Wilhelm II was clearly not going to be without negative implications. Three years' experience of Bülow as State Secretary of the Foreign Office prompted Lerchenfeld, the Bavarian envoy in Berlin, to predict in 1900 that as Chancellor Bülow would be too involved in foreign policy and 'the cultivation of his relationship with His Majesty' to follow all the details of domestic policy'[206] and he complained that Bülow would have to learn the art of organising his time more efficiently if he were going to be equal to the demands of the Chancellorship.[207]

Bülow's appointment to the State Secretaryship in 1897 was the precondition for the re-establishment of harmonious relations between the Kaiser and the Foreign Office. Bülow's predecessor, Marschall, had incurred the Kaiser's displeasure during his seven years in office by creating a position for himself in the German Reichstag and by becoming involved in domestic politics. He had exercised a growing influence over the Catholic Centre Party; he had alienated the Conservatives, the traditional supporters of monarchical authority, by becoming closely associated with the more liberal trade policy of the New Course; and in the last months of his State Secretaryship, his relations with the Kaiser had become completely untenable.[208] Marschall left office convinced that his mistake had been to stray outside the bounds of his own department,[209] and Holstein had similar advice for Bülow. 'The Kaiser has the urgent wish that in future the leader of the Foreign Office will devote himself exclusively to foreign affairs',

Holstein wrote in June 1897.[210] Bülow proved only too willing to comply.

Bülow's appointment to the State Secretaryship coincided and was associated with the inauguration of German *Weltpolitik*. At an audience with the Kaiser in June 1897 Bülow had learnt of Tirpitz's grandiose naval programme, which was intended to achieve for Germany world power status, and had agreed to conduct German foreign policy in accordance with the dictates of these plans.[211] Bülow profited from the new spirit which pervaded German foreign policy in 1897. His role in the seizure of Kiaochow in the autumn of 1897 was much less spectacular than he himself later chose to believe,[212] but Germany's success in foreign policy coupled with his brilliant début in the Reichstag in December 1897 provided Bülow with a most auspicious beginning to his Berlin career. Commenting on Bülow's first appearance in the Reichstag, the Württemberg Minister to Berlin, Varnbüler, reported that the new State Secretary had won general sympathy.

Some fortunate phrases in his short, succinct speech – like, for example, 'we don't want to put anyone in the shadow but we too demand our place in the sun' and 'the times when the German left the earth to one of his neighbours, the sea to the other, and reserved for himself the heavens where pure doctrine reigns – these times are over' – have already become almost proverbial and are on everyone's lips.[213]

'No one since Bismarck has had such success as you', Eulenburg wrote to Bülow in February 1898,[214] and success engendered new confidence in Reich policy.[215] After seven years' experience of 'the mediocrities' there was scarcely one dissenting voice in the general acclaim of the new State Secretary in the early months of 1898.[216]

Since he was ambitious and well versed in foreign affairs, Bülow's eligibility for his new post was unquestioned, and it seemed unlikely that he would be willing to adopt a secondary role in the formulation and execution of foreign policy. In a promemoria in July 1896, Bogdan von Hutten-Czapski, a close friend of Hohenlohe's, had recognized that Bülow's character 'is not suitable . . . for an office, the most important affairs of which are in fact directed by the Reich Chancellor personally'.[217] The Chancellor's influence on foreign policy declined rapidly. In April 1898 Szögyényi wrote to Goluchowski that the Chancellor was informed generally of international events, but that decisions concerning foreign policy were usually taken without his foreknowledge. 'Since Herr von Bülow has moved into the Wilhelmstrasse, he is the real Minister of Foreign Affairs of the German Reich and the activity of the Reich Chancellor in foreign questions is limited only to a secondary role.'[218] Nor was Bülow likely to emulate his predecessor and take his lead from Holstein. Holstein too was content to slip more into the background after 1897, convinced that Bülow had assumed office only reluctantly and that he depended on him for advice.[219] The 'highly interesting duel' which Varnbüler had anticipated behind the scenes in the Foreign Office seems to have been averted by Bülow's adept handling of the influential Counsellor.[220] Perhaps appreciating the value of a quieter life Holstein even gave up consulting with foreign diplomats after 1897, except in exceptional circumstances.[221]

Holstein had come to believe that Bülow 'had quite outstanding talent for his position',[222] but despite his willingness to work with Bülow after 1897 he did not wholly acquiesce in the new State Secretary's conduct of affairs. In October 1898 he criticised Bülow for allowing 'a political beginner', Oswald von Richthofen, and then 'a generally recognised cypher', Eduard von Derenthall, to deputise for him, which, Holstein claimed, had encouraged the public to assume that the Chancellor and the Kaiser were directing foreign policy, not the State Secretary.[223] He spoke of resigning twice, in June 1899 after reproaching Bülow for political seasickness and a tendency to yield in the face of counterpressure[224] and in April 1900, after Bülow had accused him of wanting to replace him with Kiderlen-Wächter,[225] the Kaiser's former favourite who had fallen mysteriously from grace shortly after Bülow's appointment.[226] Holstein may also have felt at times that his influence on Bülow was being undermined. He was probably highly suspicious and critical of Bülow's continued correspondence and personal friendship with Herbert Bismarck;[227] and he also suspected Lindenau of agitating against him. 'Amongst the Foreign Ministry staff, it is now Lindenau and Lichnowsky who are most intimate with the State Secretary', Holstein wrote to a friend, not without a hint of jealousy, in April 1900.[228] However, Bülow always extricated himself successfully from disputes with Holstein and convinced him of his good faith. In June 1899 he implored the Counsellor not to 'leave him in the lurch'. 'Quite apart from my admiration for your political genius, I love you much more as a human being than your stony scepticism will allow you to believe'.[229] And again in April 1900 Bülow stressed his trust, respect and consideration for Holstein. 'No one knows better than you how little I want to stay in my present position, which I made no effort to attain.'[230]

Bülow had to proceed with care and consideration in his relations with Holstein if he wanted to preserve the latter's services for the state and avoid creating a dangerous and influential enemy. With the rest of the staff in the Foreign Office he had a free hand and could assert his control as he wished. Eulenburg had written to Bülow in August 1897 that the Kaiser's remarks about him gave him full power, also in personnel questions. 'Build your nest as you *need* it and *want* it, without hesitation or consideration. Bite sharply around you – if it is necessary. One does not get far in the Wilhelmstrasse by being good-natured', Eulenburg advised.[231] But Bülow ultimately found that he did not have to heed Eulenburg's recommendation. Although changes were introduced in the diplomatic corps in August 1897 and there was greater mobility in the Service during Bülow's State Secretaryship,[232] there was no major reorganisation of personnel in the Foreign Office in the wake of Bülow's appointment.[233] Provided he had the Kaiser's support, the new State Secretary did not fear for his authority. But, as he told Eulenburg, he would encounter opposition within the Foreign Office the moment his relations with the Kaiser showed the least sign of strain.[234]

Bülow did, however, select a new Under State Secretary, and his choice of Oswald von Richthofen was warmly applauded by Herbert Bismarck and by Bülow's brother, Alfred. Alfred von Bülow wrote in August 1897 that over the years Richthofen had 'unswervingly cherished the memory of our father', and he did not hesitate to add that Richthofen would also be a suitable State Secretary if Bülow became Chancellor.[235] Herbert Bismarck gave Bülow some practical advice. It was imperative, he told Bülow, that the Under State Secretary saw his primary task as being to unburden the State Secretary.[236] Bülow was to place great confidence and trust in Richthofen, a confidence which continued throughout the first years of Bülow's Chancellorship until Richthofen's unexpected death in 1906. 'Not only will I always allow you to speak freely', he told Richthofen in July 1899, 'but I expressly ask you always to tell me your view without reserve. Rest assured that I not only never misunderstand sincerity [*Aufrichtigkeit*], but I place this above all other qualities.'[237]

Richthofen became one of Bülow's closest advisers, but in many ways he was also the one who was to suffer most the consequences of Bülow's work methods. In general, Bülow proved a very popular State Secretary among the Foreign Office officials, and many later attested to his pleasant style of leadership and his fairness as a chief.[238] Bülow himself admitted that life in the Foreign Office became more relaxed after he became State Secretary,[239] and to begin with it looked as if Bülow's subordinates would find the pressure of work less severe because of Bülow's intention to direct affairs personally. Szögyényi wrote in 1898 that there was general satisfaction with the new chief in the Foreign Office:

the officials in the Wilhelmstrasse have less to do than was the case under the former regime. The new State Secretary wants to maintain for himself exclusive contact with the diplomats and does not like to see mission chiefs turning to anyone but himself, or at most the Under State Secretary.[240]

But Bülow was never able to adhere to the rigid timetable for visits he had outlined to Lindenau in 1897, and he was never able to see all those he had to see within the hours he had allotted. In January 1900 the Baden envoy in Berlin, Jagemann, reported that in the past year Bülow had cancelled twenty-two of the thirty-five diplomatic receptions he should have held on

Tuesday evenings (the other weeks he was absent from Berlin). Of the thirteen he did hold, only three took place at the time originally scheduled. Moreover, only a few diplomats managed to see Bülow during the hour, and most had to leave without seeing the State Secretary because time ran out. Inevitably, therefore, mission chiefs avoided attending these receptions whenever possible and preferred to see Richthofen, who was always approachable and obliging.[241]

From his early days as a diplomat Bülow had been encouraged to cultivate a calm and casual, even careless, attitude towards minor frustrations and irritations[242] (Bülow always boasted that he took things 'indifferently [*pomadig*]'[243]), and the new State Secretary fast developed what has been described as a 'cavalier attitude' towards his work.[244] In his memoirs Bülow claimed he spent the mornings studying official papers and the afternoons walking and mulling over what he had read.[245] Clearly this kind of routine was disrupted by a visit from the Kaiser, but it was not only the cultivation of his relationship with Wilhelm II which ate into his time and consumed his energies. Bülow was obsessively concerned with his health and consequently always ensured that he had sufficient time to eat, sleep, walk and relax.[246] He was a renowned *causeur* who was always prone to chatter on to one caller at the expense of the next.[247] Moreoever he placed a premium on the cultivation of other social contacts, especially in the more intimate atmosphere of *soirées* at his home.[248] Hutten-Czapski recalled:

Bülow's house, after his entry into Berlin politics and society, became a centre for all influential circles. The still young and ambitious State Secretary, who had already directed his sights on the Chancellorship, had come to Berlin with the resolve to base his political position on as many personal connections as possible. His brilliant social talents and the enchanting elegance [*Anmut*] of his wife soon helped him to success.[249]

Bülow proved unable to discipline himself for long periods of sustained hard work. Averse to the more routine, bureaucratic tasks of his office, unwilling to forfeit his hours of recreation and entertainment, inclined to adopt a 'personal' approach to politics, Bülow was not the most efficient State Secretary of the Foreign Office and, not surprisingly, the brunt of the routine and paper work was borne by Richthofen.[250]

Simultaneously with his appointment to the State Secretaryship Bülow was created Prussian Minister without portfolio and was therefore entitled to attend Prussian Ministry of State meetings from 1897. But, as indicated, he did not appear immediately anxious to exploit the opportunitites this gave him. Instead, from the beginning, he made a conscious effort to avoid involvement in domestic affairs. Bülow 'seems to want to concentrate for the time being wholly on the foreign department', Varnbüler reported in February 1898.[251] This tactic can in part be attributed to his desire to avoid repeating Marschall's mistakes, which might have prejudiced his position with the Kaiser. Fears also persisted throughout 1897 that Hohenlohe might resign, and that Bülow would be associated with a reactionary regime intent on domestic repression. Holstein had advised Bülow in June 1897 not to renounce the position of Prussian Minister. Although such a step would have freed him from any co-responsibility for domestic questions, it would also have meant that he would have sunk half a storey down the government hierarchy.[252] Philipp Eulenburg had shared this concern. 'More than ever', he told Bülow, 'it will be necessary for you to keep yourself out of domestic politics and confine yourself *completely* to foreign affairs. His Majesty shares this view and affectionately agrees to everything which concerns you.'[253] Bülow thus had reason as State Secretary to avoid participation in domestic politics, but his real motive was gradually to become clear. Bülow pursued a tactic of non-involvement in domestic policy in order to be able to begin a future Chancellorship with a clean slate, untainted and unscathed by previous political commitments and previous political mistakes.

If he began his State Secretaryship intent on avoiding any official involvement in matters of internal policy, the three years Bülow spent at the Foreign Office were nevertheless his political apprenticeship in domestic affairs. As Prussian Minister he placed great emphasis on being informed exactly about all internal events. 'He also appears very conscientiously in every sitting of the State Ministry, follows the negotiations with interest but consistently refrains from voting', Szögyényi reported in May 1898.[254] Between 1897 and 1900 the State Ministry remained chaotic and disunited under Hohenlohe's weak leadership,[255] but Bülow made no attempt to assume a more dominant role. He expressed views on domestic policy in private and to those people of influence whom he wanted to impress as a Chancellor candidate.[256] He gave partial support to Hohenlohe, for example in feeling that the direction of the *Sammlungspolitik* (the 'policy of collection' which aimed to rally 'national' and anti-socialist forces behind the government) inaugurated by the Finance Minister, Johannes von Miquel, and the State Secretary of Interior, Arthur von Posadowsky-Wehner, was too oriented towards the agrarians;[257] and he was clearly beginning to formulate his ideas on a 'middle course' in commercial policy.[258] But he remained reluctant to participate in any official or overt way in decision-making on domestic issues. 'On principle', he wrote to Holstein in November 1899 after the latter had made various suggestions about domestic policy which included the removal of Miquel,[259] 'I very much dislike interfering in internal problems when I see that the Chancellor is once again zealously at work on the great affairs of state.'[260]

A similar reserve is also evident in Bülow's relations with the Reichstag and the political parties. Although Bülow had made an encouraging par-

liamentary début and although Monts later claimed that Bülow used the
State Secretaryship to prepare the terrain in the parliaments and the press for
his future appointment as Chancellor,[261] the new State Secretary kept his
relations with the Reichstag to the absolute minimum, relying exclusively on
his personal friend and middleman, the Centre Party deputy, Prince Franz
Arenberg. In April 1899 the interpellation of the government in the Reichstag by a leading Pan-German, Dr Adolf Lehr, about the dispute with Britain
over the Samoan islands was widely seen as a badly staged fiasco; and many,
especially in conservative circles, felt that Bülow was to blame because he
should have realised that Lehr was not a suitable person to unite the majority
of the Reichstag behind the government. It was claimed that the State
Secretary had not had sufficient parliamentary experience or contact with the
parliamentary deputies. Jagemann reported that Bülow almost hermetically
sealed himself off from parliamentarians and that this 'principle of seclusion
[*Abschliessungsprinzip*]' was also applied to other circles. Clearly Bülow
wanted to avoid some of the problems other Ministers had experienced after
establishing close relations with parliamentary deputies, but Jagemann found
the practice unwise and wondered whether it derived from Bülow's personal
inclination or whether he simply needed quiet in order to work.[262] It was,
however, the Württemberg ambassador who seems to have gleaned Bülow's
intentions accurately:

I alone have reason to assume that Herr von Bülow, in refraining from closer contact
with the individual Reichstag parties, is pursuing the well-considered intention not
to become involved in the economic and social questions of the state but, as far as
possible, to limit himself and to concentrate on his department of foreign policy –
partly because this alone already lays total claim to his physical and mental powers
[*Arbeitskraft*], partly too in order not to eclipse completely the . . . Reich Chancellor, – last not least, in case he himself is called upon to take his place, in order to
keep himself intact *vis-à-vis* the parliamentary parties and not use himself up
prematurely.[263]

Bülow's apparent concentration on foreign policy, his reluctance to
become officially involved in domestic issues and his passivity in the Prussian
Ministry of State did not necessarily enhance his popularity with his Berlin
colleagues. Miquel's jealousy of Bülow had been detected by Varnbüler as
early as December 1897 after Bülow's success in the Reichstag. Miquel, a
former leader of the National Liberal Party and mayor of Frankfurt, himself
enjoyed a reputation as an orator and, as one of the Kaiser's favourite
Ministers before Bülow's arrival on the scene, he must have sensed immediately that he would no longer be first in line among Prussian Ministers
for promotion to the Chancellorship.[264] In October 1899 Hohenlohe, who
was having his own battle with the independent-minded Finance Minister,[265]
wrote to Bülow that Miquel was intriguing against him because of his
favoured position with the Kaiser.[266] Such hostility to a new *persona grata* was

not unusual. Monts told his friend, Heinrich von Tschirschky und Bögen-dorff, that 'the military, the fawning courtiers [*Schranzen*], the Ministers, everyone resents the new sun which puts them in the shade'.[267] But Miquel and Posadowsky, who together had the most stature in the Prussian Ministry of State, were not only concerned about Bülow because of his favoured position with the Kaiser, or even because he was a prospective rival for the Chancellorship, but also because, behind the façade of non-involvement in domestic issues, Bülow was in fact becoming increasingly influential on internal policy on account of his close contact with Wilhelm II. In May 1898 Szögyényi reported that the Kaiser had complete confidence in Bülow 'and discusses with him, to the great vexation of Herr von Miquel and Count Posadowsky, not only questions of foreign policy but also extensively all domestic affairs which belong to the jurisdiction of the latter'.[268] Even as State Secretary Bülow was already becoming the mediator between the Kaiser and the responsible government. His conversations with Wilhelm embraced the Canal Bill, the Hard Labour Bill, questions of meat inspection and hydraul-ics, and on each occasion Bülow communicated the Kaiser's views to the Chancellor.[269] Charting Bülow's rise, in January 1900 Szögyényi reported that Bülow had 'a dominant influence not only on the foreign affairs of the Reich, but also on domestic affairs'.[270]

Despite Bülow's outward aloofness from domestic affairs,[271] by January 1900 the Chancellor's influence on Reich policy had become purely nominal and Szögyényi clearly regarded Bülow as the unofficial head of the Reich government.[272] Hohenlohe frequently complained about his difficult situa-tion, but such a system, in which the Chancellor enjoyed no authority, obviously suited the Kaiser very well and he had no interest in precipitating Hohenlohe's resignation. During Bülow's State Secretaryship there was much discussion about Hohenlohe's eventual successor. Waldersee, Botho Eulenburg (who had been Prussian Minister-President from 1892 to 1894) and especially Philipp Eulenburg all seemed less probable candidates for the Chancellorship than they had been earlier in the 1890s but, besides Bülow's candidacy there was talk of the *Statthalter* of Alsace-Lorraine, Hermann zu Hohenlohe-Langenburg, and the President of the Prussian Upper House, Prince Wilhelm zu Wied, becoming Chancellor.[273] In July 1898 Bülow had told Eulenburg to make it clear to the Kaiser that he could not stay on as State Secretary under any Chancellor other than Hohenlohe.

A nearly eighty-year-old, tired, sick, completely indolent, totally passive old man, whom I moreover know most intimately from being with him every day for six years in Paris and who has long been accustomed to my leadership, can bear the fact that I have a completely free hand abroad and at home, in the press, in the Office and in the State Ministry, as corresponds to the interests of His Majesty. Any other Reich Chancellor, whatever he might first say or promise, would not find this situation tolerable, [would] very soon become mistrustful and jealous and make it impossible for me to render real service to His Majesty.[274]

Eulenburg had quickly reassured Bülow that the Kaiser only had him in mind as Hohenlohe's successor.[275] In January 1900 Szögyényi, who was closer to Wilhelm II than most other ambassadors, still felt that the Kaiser would choose Bülow as Chancellor, even if he deemed it necessary to resort to an interim Chancellor for a while.[276]

Yet there are signs by 1900 that Bülow himself was becoming impatient and beginning to wonder whether his ultimate goal would elude him. By December 1899 he no longer found it worth while to follow with interest all the debates in the Prussian Ministry of State but stayed at State Ministry meetings only for as long as his department was affected.[277] Between January 1900 and his appointment as Chancellor in late October Bülow attended only eight of the twenty-two State Ministry meetings (by contrast Posadowsky attended fifteen and Miquel sixteen), and even then mostly left early.[278] While his cultivated aloofness and seclusion exasperated his government colleagues, his reserve *vis-à-vis* the Reichstag was fast evaporating. By June 1900 Bülow had thrown caution to the wind and, contrary to Miquel's strategy, the Chancellor's inclinations and Wilhelm II's known opinions, he was openly telling Centre Party deputies that he was in favour of a repeal of the Jesuit Law, the last major relic of the *Kulturkampf* years.[279] To Hohenlohe, Bülow urged the necessity of his remaining in office in the national interest, but it was known that he spoke differently to third persons, and his 'restlessness' was apparent to the Chancellor.[280] Arthur von Huhn, the Berlin correspondent of the *Kölnische Zeitung*, told Hohenlohe shortly before the latter resigned that 'Bülow wants to become Reich Chancellor, even if he acts as though he does not want to'. Moreover Huhn had the impression that Bülow himself was doubting whether the Kaiser would take him,[281] an impression which is confirmed by Bülow's memoir account of the months preceding his appointment as Chancellor.[282] There were a number of frictions between the Kaiser and the State Secretary in the summer of 1900. Bülow, who saw one of his primary tasks as being to encourage Wilhelm to confide in him, was not informed beforehand when the Kaiser appointed Waldersee Commander-in-Chief of the China expedition.[283] He was pained by Wilhelm's 'Hun Speech' in July 1900,[284] and throughout the summer he received perturbing reports from Philipp Eulenburg about the Kaiser's hyper-nervous condition.[285] All this contributed to Bülow's anxiety about his relationship with the Kaiser and gave substance to his fear that 'he would . . . hardly take me as Reich Chancellor'.[286] Only when the two men met again in the autumn was Bülow relieved to find that the Kaiser's attitude towards him was more favourable than he had assumed.[287] When Hohenlohe finally resigned in October 1900 Wilhelm did not hesitate to choose Bülow.[288]

2

The assumption of the Chancellorship, 1900–1901

The new Chancellor and the German political system

On 16 October 1900 Hohenlohe visited Wilhelm II in Homburg and requested his resignation.[1] Although only a few days previously he had conferred with Miquel and Posadowsky about the coming Reichstag session, the senile and asthmatic Chancellor seemed finally to have realised that he was playing a ridiculous role and that he could no longer stand before the Reichstag to defend a policy he had heard nothing about.[2] The Kaiser made no attempt to persuade him to stay, immediately responded, 'I'll doubtless take Bülow' and summoned the Foreign Secretary to Homburg on the same day.[3] Bülow encouraged the view that he was completely surprised by this turn of events,[4] but in all probability he had been expecting a change of Chancellor that autumn. On 7 October he had discussed his candidature for the Chancellorship with Wilhelm II at Hubertusstock and on 15 October he had told Hammann, the Chief of the Foreign Office Press Department, how to handle the eventuality of a change of Chancellor in the press.[5] In October 1900 the appointment of the State Secretary of the Foreign Office to the Chancellorship was regarded by the entire German press as a matter of course[6] and in general the news was greeted with optimism and relief. After ten years of political uncertainty it was felt that Germany had finally found a worthy successor to Bismarck.[7]

The Chancellorship of the German Empire, to which Bülow had long aspired and which he now finally attained, was the highest responsible political office in what was without doubt one of the most complex political systems ever devised.[8] In 1871 a centralised Reich government had been a political impossibility when each of the twenty-five states in the new Empire frequently had its own prince, government and parliament, and was jealously anxious to preserve its own powers and traditions. Thus the Constitution of 1871 had provided for a federal system in Germany and sovereignty theoretically resided in the Bundesrat or federal council, a unique body which represented the various state governments and which combined its executive functions with some of the legislative rights of an Upper Chamber. The Bundesrat met in secret (the plenum met about once a week), each state in theory had the right to initiate legislation, and decisions on most matters were taken on the basis of a simple majority. However, the number of votes each state had in the Bundesrat depended on its size. Prussia, the largest and most populous federal state, had seventeen votes, and no constitutional changes could be passed without its approval.

The Bundesrat never developed into the key decision-making body in the Reich because the representatives of the federal states or Bundesrat plenipotentiaries cast their votes according to the instructions they received from their home governments. No real debate was possible in the Bundesrat, and thus its theoretical sovereignty was widely seen to be a fiction. In practice, policy initiatives in the German Empire rested with the dominant state, Prussia, and especially in the early years legislation was mainly prepared in the Prussian Ministries. The Bundesrat tended to be a vehicle for Prussian domination of the Reich, but its theoretical sovereignty conveniently shielded from criticism the real rulers in Berlin.

The absence of a Reich government and the elusive character of the Bundesrat as a decision-making body made it especially difficult for the other national institution recognised by the Constitution, the Reichstag or parliament, to develop effective parliamentary powers. The Reichstag was the most democratic and representative institution in the Empire, its suffrage being formally equal, direct and secret, and all men over twenty-five years old were eligible to vote. Nevertheless, under the impact of demographic change, it became gradually less representative since constituency boundaries were never adjusted and the distribution of seats came to favour political parties, such as the Conservatives and Catholic Centre Party, whose voters were regionally concentrated and mainly lived on the land. Moreover, the Reichstag's parliamentary powers were strictly curtailed. What political leverage it had stemmed solely from the fact that its approval was necessary for the passage of legislation and, crucially, the budget. There was no system of ministerial responsibility to the Reichstag, the parliament had no influence over the composition of the executive, and it had only a limited right of interpellation. Whole areas of policy-making – notably foreign policy but also those matters still regulated by the federal states – remained beyond its control. In addition, the political parties were not potential governments, and party politicians could not realistically aspire to become statesmen. The parties (which were not officially recognised by the Constitution) did not need to develop practical political programmes and they were widely criticised for their 'irresponsibility' in that they could afford to represent specific sectional or economic interests.

The only 'responsible' Reich Minister – the Constitution did not say how or to whom – was the Reich Chancellor. Article 17 of the Constitution was not very explicit about his role, but his task was generally to ensure the smooth operation of the political system by mediating between the state governments and overseeing the passage of legislation through the Bundesrat and Reichstag. As the pressure of Reich business increased after 1871, a series of Reich Offices were created, each headed by a State Secretary who was subordinate to the Chancellor and whose primary purpose was to ease the burden of work on the single Reich statesman. Increasingly (and especially after 1900) political commentators came to refer to the Chancellor and the State Secretaries as the 'Reich government', but this description, while indicative of the general pressures at work in the Empire for a centralisation of powers, is constitutionally inaccurate and misleading. There was no Reich cabinet around the Chancellor and, since the State Secretaries were strictly his subordinates, there was no possibility of ministerial opposition to the Chancellor in the Reich. It is true that an increasing number of bills came to be prepared in the Reich Offices rather than in the Prussian Ministries. Nevertheless, the State Secretaries – and indeed the Chancellor himself – could only speak in the Bundesrat and Reichstag by virtue of the fact that they were also appointed Prussian delegates to the Bundesrat.

Moreover, as was demonstrated only too clearly in the years 1892–4, when Chancellor Caprivi had sought to separate the offices, the Chancellor's powers were largely illusory if he were not simultaneously Prussian Minister-President and Prussian Foreign Minister.[9] It was this dual role which inspired the confidence of the federal states in his leadership, since any form of Reich government independent of the Prussian government was inconceivable and the existence of Prussia was seen as the best guarantee that the principle of federalism would be upheld in the Reich. Prussia had a crucial part to play in the German Empire, and in Prussia a system of semi-absolutism still obtained where the Prussian King had the right to decide all important matters and the only limitations to his powers were those imposed by the emasculated Constitution of 1851, a remnant of the revolutionary upheavals of 1848. In Prussia the Ministers were appointed by the King and were servants of the Crown. The Prussian Minister-President was only *primus inter pares* in the Ministry of State, a body which lacked the cohesion of a modern Cabinet and in which each Minister was independent, answerable only to the King. The Chancellor and Minister-President could thus face the possibility of defeat by his ministerial colleagues in Prussia and, in an attempt to bolster his position in the Ministry of State, it became common practice for some State Secretaries of the Reich Offices to be appointed Prussian Ministers without portfolio. However, the most effective support the Minister-President could enjoy was the confidence of the King, who could overrule any decisions taken in the Prussian Ministry.

The different circumstances under which the Chancellor and Minister-President had to operate in the Reich and Prussia are further emphasised when one considers the nature of the Prussian legislature, the Landtag, the political composition of which varied greatly from that of the Reichstag. For legislation to be passed in Prussia, it had to be approved by two Houses, an Upper Chamber or House of Lords consisting of princes of royal blood, hereditary nobles, hereditary members and life members appointed by the Crown, and a Lower Chamber or House of Deputies, elected according to a complicated three-class suffrage which heavily favoured the wealthiest sections of the population, who paid the most taxes. The voting system was not direct, equal or secret and, especially since electors cast their votes orally, it was open to considerable abuse and manipulation by government authorities. In particular, the government was able to exert pressure on electors through the system of local government whereby Prussia was divided into provinces (presided over by an *Oberpräsident*), government districts (presided over by a *Reigerungspräsident*) and smaller districts or 'circles' (headed by a *Landrat*). The key appointments in the Prussian bureaucracy, which was very hierarchical and subordinate to the Prussian Ministry, were again made by the King, and many State Ministers were capable bureaucrats who had worked their way up through the provincial administration. The effect of the three-class suffrage and the influence of government officials was to produce a House of Deputies which was far more conservative than its counterpart in the Reich. The Chancellor and Minister-President thus had to work with very different parliamentary majorities in the two legislatures.

All this would have made the task facing a Reich Chancellor one which involved considerable ingenuity even if there had not been a further factor of immense importance in the political equation. The Chancellor was appointed and dismissed by the German Kaiser, who was always the Prussian King, and his position depended far less on the smooth management of the executive and legislature than on his ability to maintain the confidence of the monarch. The German Kaiser was granted enormous powers by the Reich Constitution which he enjoyed alongside his prerogatives as Prussian King. Not the least of these were his sovereignty in matters of foreign policy (including the right to declare war, although this had to be subsequently approved by the Bundesrat), his personal command of the Army and Navy, and his control of personnel appointments. The Chancellor was the Kaiser's first political adviser (though only in civilian matters), and he had to countersign the monarch's orders if they were to assume constitutional validity. While this obligation gave the Chancellor some leverage against the Kaiser in that he could refuse to accept 'constitutional responsibility' for the monarch's proposals, if it came to a clash between Kaiser and Chancellor, the latter really had little option but to resign.

In October 1900 Bülow thus succeeded to a very prestigious but very onerous office. Indeed his successor, Bethmann Hollweg, was to say that 'Only a genius or a man driven by ambition and lust for power can covet

2 Kaiser Wilhelm II

this post.'[10] In 1900 Bülow could feel sure of the Kaiser's confidence but, as a diplomat by profession, he had had relatively little experience of political and parliamentary life in Berlin. While there seemed little likelihood that German foreign policy would be affected by the change of Chancellor since, as one commentator observed, it was already 'completely in the hands of Count Bülow',[11] his attitude to domestic issues and the controversial economic questions on the political horizon remained uncertain.[12] It was also unclear how far the new Chancellor would be able to emancipate himself from foreign policy and carve out a major role for himself in the government decision-making processes.[13] In 1900 Bülow inherited an unenviable situation from his predecessor with respect to the Chancellor's position within the executive, the relationship between Berlin and the federal states and the relationship between executive and legislature. Bülow's main attention during the first months of his Chancellorship would necessarily be focused on increasing the authority of the Reich Chancellor within the government system.

The impact on the executive

Bülow's assumption of the Chancellorship in 1900 was exceptionally smooth. As Eulenburg wrote to Wilhelm II, unlike the two previous Chancellors, who had been born from the convulsions of crisis, Bülow's Chancellorship had a sweet, gentle birth.[14] He was appointed because of his predecessor's voluntary resignation and consequently was able to take over as Chancellor and Prussian Minister-President with no major personnel changes in the highest government departments. The composition of the Prussian Ministry of State remained intact, a clear indication to its more cynical members of how little the Ministers were now going to matter. With respect to the Reich departments, in October 1900 there was discussion of the possible resignations of Thielmann, the State Secretary of the Treasury, who had never got on with Bülow since they had worked together at the Paris embassy seventeen years earlier, and Nieberding, the State Secretary of the Reich Justice Office, who was not *persona grata* to the Kaiser.[15] In the event, however, only Posadowsky requested his resignation as State Secretary of Interior and Deputy Reich Chancellor on hearing the news of Bülow's appointment.[16] Posadowsky was personally antipathetic to Bülow by 1900[17] but, although some claimed he aspired to the Chancellorship, it seems unlikely that he expected to be appointed. Posadowsky was too well aware of the situation not to realise that if the Kaiser were to choose a State Secretary as Hohenlohe's successor, his choice would fall on Bülow.[18] Bülow secured a relatively gracious telegram from the Kaiser to Posadowsky declining the State Secretary's resignation request. 'But Count Posadowsky must not continue with this attitude if he does not want to have a rupture with His Majesty', Bülow told Richthofen.[19]

In the Foreign Office Bülow's promotion meant the appointment of a new State Secretary and Under State Secretary. Richthofen's appointment as State Secretary was not achieved without difficulty. According to Bülow, Wilhelm II disliked the traditional Prussian, bureaucratic mentality and found men like Richthofen rather dull. Thus he was not easily persuaded to accept Richthofen in 1900.[20] Moreover, relations between Richthofen and Holstein had become so antagonistic since 1897 that Holstein had consistently gone on leave or reported sick whenever Richthofen had to deputise for Bülow.[21] A highly successful tactical move by Bülow in October 1900 was his offer of the State Secretaryship to Holstein.[22] It was only a matter of form since there was never any possibility that Holstein would accept a responsible position, involving regular appearances before the Reichstag. But it flattered the Counsellor's vanity and Holstein remained indebted to Bülow for his consideration.[23] Holstein was also more disposed to accept Richthofen as State Secretary after Bülow had agreed to appoint his protégé, Otto von Mühlberg, to the Under State Secretaryship. Mühlberg had hitherto been Director of the Trade Department in the Foreign Office, and it was thought that his extensive commercial knowledge would be of great value during the future trade treaty negotiations.[24]

Both the Kaiser and Holstein therefore acquiesced in Richthofen's appointment to the State Secretaryship in 1900, but Richthofen was himself inclined to impose conditions before he would accept the new post. Lichnowsky telegraphed to Bülow that, although Richthofen was extremely grateful for his nomination and prepared to be conciliatory towards Holstein, he felt his authority would be illusory unless he had complete control over all ciphered communications entering or leaving the Foreign Office.[25] This suggestion was clearly aimed against Holstein, and Bülow replied quite ruthlessly through Lichnowsky that he found Richthofen's attitude timorous and petty. He had had great difficulty in persuading the Kaiser to accept Richthofen, and the latter owed 'this enormous advancement which surpasses everything he could ever have hoped for' to him. In these circumstances Richthofen should neither hesitate nor make conditions. He, Bülow, had not imposed conditions concerning Holstein when he had taken over the State Secretaryship, despite frictions between them both in the past. 'If Baron Richthofen lets himself be stopped from the beginning by petty bureaucratic scruples', Bülow threatened, 'I will have to find another Secretary of State and send Baron Richthofen to some little post abroad.'[26]

Despite Bülow's reference to his own appointment as State Secretary, the situation was clearly very different from what it had been in 1897. In the same telegram to Lichnowsky, Bülow wrote that as far as possible nothing

would be done in the Foreign Office contrary to his intentions. Thus
Richthofen need not fear for his authority since it would derive from
Bülow's confidence. There was no question that Bülow, the professional
diplomat, would be willing to surrender his leadership of German foreign
policy to the same extent as Caprivi and Hohenlohe had done. Like
Bismarck, Bülow would remain *de facto* Minister of Foreign Affairs (he
automatically also became Prussian Foreign Minister in 1900), and the State
Secretary would take second place. Thus the question of a new State
Secretary was seen in October 1900 as an issue of minor importance, and the
mere choice of Richthofen, 'a very clever, capable, completely reliable and
amiable personality, but not the man to conduct German foreign policy
according to his own precepts',[27] confirmed that the position was not going
to have the significance it had had during Bülow's incumbency. Szögyényi
predicted that just as Richthofen had always sought the State Secretary's
advice when Under State Secretary, so too he would now defer to the
Chancellor's decisions on important questions before he could give any
information.[28] This shift back in the Chancellor's favour was further emphasised by the decision not to promote Richthofen to Prussian Minister
without portfolio concurrently with his appointment as State Secretary.
Thus Richthofen suffered the disadvantages of the step down in the government hierarchy which Holstein had advised Bülow against in 1897. In March
1901 Richthofen told the British ambassador in Berlin, Sir Frank Lascelles,
that he could not give an official answer to a question posed by the British
government about German policy towards China. As Lascelles reported to
London 'he could only give me one after consulting with the Chancellor,
who no doubt would take the Emperor's orders on the subject'.[29]

Bülow may have intended to retain his control over German foreign
policy as Chancellor from 1900 but, for the time being at least, he had to
recognise that his priorities lay elsewhere. 'As I now have to turn my
attention mainly to domestic questions and to correspondence with HM',
he informed his Foreign Office subordinates in a telling communication on
19 October, 'I request that until further notice only the most necessary and
most urgent matters be submitted to me from the Foreign Office department.' He went on:

I will of course sign as before the decrees and telegrams in important political
questions. With respect to newspaper cuttings, too, only those of real personal
significance for me are to be submitted to me. Prince Lichnowsky reports to me
directly on personnel matters, *Geheimrat* Hammann likewise on urgent press affairs.
My reception hour remains the time from 6 p.m. to 7 p.m., for important audiences
I a.m. available from noon to I p.m. Before 11 o'clock I want to be disturbed only
in wholly exceptional cases.[30]

Bülow thus had not changed his opinion since 1897 that the preservation of his relationship with the Kaiser was the most indispensable part of his role. However, it remained to be seen whether these rather minor adjustments to his working day would enable him to become equal to the demands of the Chancellorship, and at least one experienced political commentator had serious doubts in October 1900.[31]

One of Bülow's primary concerns from October 1900 was the need to restore the authority of the Reich Chancellor within the German executive as a whole and to establish at least the semblance of government unity in Prussia. Three years of the Kaiser's 'personal rule' and the feebleness of the old Chancellor had had disastrous consequences for the Reich executive, and the Prussian government too was in disarray.[32] Those Ministers who had been appointed since 1897 had been selected according to their readiness to submit to the will of the Crown. The others had either been intimidated by the Kaiser's strong personality and growing interference in the work of their departments or, like Miquel, they had profited from the ensuing governmental disunity and had been able to augment their influence within the executive to an extent which would have been impossible under the leadership of a strong Chancellor. The Ministers and State Secretaries were unable, either individually or collectively, to confront the Kaiser with effective resistance, even in the face of his most extreme demands. As a result, the Ministers had been reduced to mutal recrimination and bickering, and the disagreements within the Prussian Ministry of State, in part a natural consequence of its heterogeneous composition and divisive organisation, had been exacerbated.

On 23 October 1900, within days of becoming Chancellor, Bülow called together the Prussian Ministry of State for its first meeting under his Minister-Presidency and, in an effort to counter the centrifugal tendencies at work in the executive, he outlined the main principles according to which he intended to conduct the affairs of his office and expected the government to operate.[33] The form of Bülow's address to the Prussian Ministers was significant. 'His Majesty must feel that Hohenlohe is *his* representative in the Ministry and that he will, if need be, even go against the majority of the Ministers', Bülow had written to Eulenburg in 1895,[34] and this approach was evident in 1900. Throughout his entire declaration Bülow made it clear that he was voicing the Kaiser's intentions, and he restricted his role to that of a mediator repeating 'the principles . . . which our Kaiser has prescribed to me for the conduct of affairs'.

The Kaiser, Bülow told his ministerial colleagues, placed primary emphasis on a united government. Different views could be expressed during Ministry meetings, but once a decision had been made and had Wilhelm II's approval, it was to be upheld by all members of the Prussian government equally. The widespread assumption that there were different shades of opinion within the State Ministry had to cease. A completely united Ministry was the precondition for that governmental stability and resolution which the country demanded and required, and which was indispensable if the rights of the Crown were to be safeguarded effectively. The Kaiser further emphasised the necessity of complete harmony between Prussian and Reich policy. His Majesty knew that the Prussian monarchy constituted the basis of his position in the Reich and in the world, but he expected the Prussian Ministry of State to do everything in its power to facilitate his role as head of the Reich. The Kaiser would see that nothing was done in the Reich which harmed Prussian interests, but on the other hand Prussian policy had to take account of the needs of the Reich and the political situation in the Reich. Parliamentary bills of political significance had to be represented in the Reichstag first and foremost by the Prussian Ministers concerned.

Bülow went on to express the monarch's expectation that absolute secrecy would be maintained about the course of Ministry meetings. Only the Minister-President had the right to decide whether any aspect of their deliberations should reach the public. Finally, Bülow discussed the coming parliamentary session and warned the Ministers that new legislation in both Reichstag and Landtag was to be kept to a minimum. The Kaiser's conviction was that the government's main task for the time being should be *quieta non movere*. Bülow himself would scrutinise the bills being prepared in each of the Prussian departments and decide whether they were strictly necessary.

Bülow did not present the Prussian Ministry of State (or Reichstag) with a general programme or strategy with respect to domestic affairs in 1900. Indeed, it is clear that he did not really have a domestic policy as such, except the rather vague aim to promote national unity. His address to the Prussian Ministers was concerned with method or tactics, not with policies, and except for the priority he gave to parliamentary bills 'for national reasons' (such as those intended to Germanise Prussia's Polish provinces) he gave no indication of how he would approach specific domestic issues or of any principles to which he personally would adhere in domestic policy. The whole tenor of his address in fact suggested a desire to minimise the importance of domestic issues, reduce the number of contentious domestic problems which only divided the nation, and subordinate domestic affairs to the national imperatives.

Notwithstanding this lack of substance in his address, Bülow's appeal for government unity in October 1900 was ostensibly successful. He concluded his address with a request for the support and confidence of the Prussian Ministers, and there is no doubt that by identifying himself completely with the will of the monarch, Bülow made himself immune to open criticism and temporarily silenced dissident voices within the Prussian Ministry. The effectiveness of his approach was testified to by Thurn, the Austrian *chargé d'affaires*, four days after the meeting: 'Right from the beginning Count

Bülow seems to have understood how to secure for himself such a prepon-
derant position *vis-à-vis* his ministerial colleagues that – at least for the time
being – he need fear no moves from them which are in opposition to his
views.'[35]

It must have been obvious even to Bülow himself, however, that the unity
he imposed on the Prussian Ministry of State in October 1900 was to a large
extent superficial and that it would take more than skilfully worded declarations to eliminate the divisions which had characterised the executive during
Hohenlohe's Chancellorship and which had their roots both in personal
antagonisms and in deeply felt political differences. A major problem con-
fronting Bülow in October 1900 was the bitter disagreement within the
executive over the form and levels of the new tariff duties, which had to be
settled before Germany's commercial treaties came up for renewal in 1906.[36]
The debate over the future Tariff Law was not new, and for many months
the conflict within the executive had been paralleled by a lively controversy
in the German press over the extent to which the agrarians' demands for
greater protection should be accommodated.[37] But Bülow inherited the task
of resolving a potentially explosive issue, the regulation of which would
vitally affect the economic interests of all sectors of the population, and the
tariff question was ultimately to prove the most severe test of his leadership,
both within the executive and in the Reichstag in the early years of his
Chancellorship.

Bülow probably began his Chancellorship with no firm opinion and even
less knowledge about the tariff issue,[38] but he recognised its political importance and its implications for his own position within the executive. The
departments which were most receptive to the demands of the agrarians were
the 'conservative' Prussian Ministries of Agriculture and Finance, and the
Reich Office of Interior. Thus they included Miquel and Posadowsky, who
were urging the adoption of a double tariff, with maximum and minimum
levels, a system which existed in France and other countries and which would
ensure a high degree of protection for German agricultural products. On the
other hand, the Reich Treasury, the Prussian Ministry of Trade and only
belatedly the Foreign Office (probably on Richthofen's advice[39]) were
anxious to retain the old system of a simple tariff, which had promoted
Germany's rapid industrial expansion, and they argued that the new levels
should not be so high that they jeopardised the successful renegotiation of
favourable commercial treaties with Germany's neighbours.[40] Thus the
conflict within the executive over the tariff threatened to become a power
contest between Bülow and his most influential rivals, for it was widely
assumed that a man so closely associated with German *Weltpolitik* and the
Kaiser's naval plans would be unlikely to espouse the self-interested
arguments of the extreme agrarians.[41]

Although Jagemann wondered in October 1900 whether the tariff issue would induce the new Chancellor to rid himself of the inconvenient agrarian elements in the Prussian Ministry of State,[42] Bülow was too flexible in his political views to adhere rigidly to one side in the dispute, and he had never been so committed to a liberal commercial policy as the Baden ambassador assumed. In 1894 Bülow had written to Eulenburg condemning the agitation of the agrarians, but at the same time he claimed that he could not see why Caprivi could not protect the legitimate interests of agriculture, 'the social, political, military significance of which no one rates higher than I do'.[43] Moreover, even in 1899, when he had been looking for a new Director of the Trade Department in the Foreign Office, he had appreciated how important it was to find someone who straddled the middle ground on economic questions and who would not let himself be pulled in either the agrarian or free trade direction.[44] In 1900 Bülow did not suddenly shift to the right, as Jagemann reported,[45] but he approached the tariff issue as he was to approach so many domestic issues with the aim of finding an acceptable compromise between two opposing positions. As late as January 1901 Szögyényi reported that Bülow had adopted no definite position on the big domestic issues on the immediate horizon – the tariff, the trade treaties, the financial reform – but he intended to adopt a pragmatic approach and find the middle ground. 'He will wait for these to come to him and . . . he intends to take a decision only as each case demands [*von Fall zu Fall*].'[46] Less concerned with the specific economic arguments than his governmental colleagues, in October 1900 Bülow subordinated the tariff issue to general political considerations. A *Geheimrat* in the Reich Treasury told Jagemann that Bülow would reconcile himself to the cooperation of Miquel and Posadowsky for domestic reasons and that he wanted to gain the support of the agrarians for his overall policy [*Gesamtpolitik*]. For the agrarians were not only a strong element in the Conservative Party but were also a growing contingent in the Centre and National Liberal parties.[47]

Bülow thus endeavoured to resolve the conflict within the executive over the tariff issue by participating in an interdepartmental conference at the end of October and urging a compromise solution.[48] Bülow's proposal of a minimum duty on certain agricultural products but otherwise adherence to a simple tariff was accepted, partly because his formula was deliberately left vague and ambiguous with no discussion of the specific details,[49] and partly because Miquel completely failed to support Posadowsky, the latter being left to defend the double tariff system virtually on his own. Lerchenfeld interpreted the outcome of the conference as a success for Bülow, the Reich Treasury and the Foreign Office. Moreover, he reported, Bülow had not only effectively countered Posadowsky's demands, but he had also ensured that the State Secretary of Interior would represent the new compromise tariff in the Reichstag since no one in the Reich Treasury or Foreign Office had sufficient authority to do so.[50]

Although the October conference marked the beginning of the emergence of a new compromise tariff, it did not constitute a real solution to the dispute, and Bülow had only glossed over the differences within the executive on the tariff issue. The controversy within the government was not resolved by the outcome of the conference.[51] A blanket had simply been thrown over the main contestants, and opposition to Bülow's proposals still flourished, if not overtly. In November 1900 Hammerstein, the Minister of Agriculture, told Lerchenfeld that the level of the duties on grain would be higher than the latter had assumed from the results of the conference.[52] In December, Miquel accused the Bavarian government of leaving him in the lurch with respect to his agrarian policy.[53] The Reich Treasury was thwarted in its attempt to have the Tariff Bill ready by March 1901 by the Reich Office of Interior because its work for the *Begründung* (justification) proved completely unusable (the friction between the two State Secretaries was less significant in this respect than the continuing disagreement between the officials).[54] Finally, in November 1900 Bülow met with opposition from a more serious quarter. Perhaps under the influence of friends such as Albert Ballin, the head of the Hamburg–America shipping line, Wilhelm II declared that he would not consent to an increase in the grain duties. As Lerchenfeld reported:

The Reich Chancellor will straightaway have to furnish proof of his influence here. Count Bülow does not agree with the standpoint of his imperial master and is in addition too much of a politician to undertake the attempt to step before the Reichstag with a tariff which contains no increase in the existing grain duties.[55]

The tariff issue and the debate within the executive were thus far from resolved, and by December 1900 the Chancellor was already looking for new allies to support the compromise tariff.

Bülow's difficulties within the executive over the tariff issue were an additional factor which prompted him to improve Berlin's relations with the federal states from October 1900. Before he had become Chancellor Bülow had identified particularism as the main evil in the Reich and a growing threat to national unity. Particularist sentiment had certainly increased in the 1890s under the impact of the New Course and the Kaiser's 'personal rule', and there had been considerable concern about the effect of a weak Chancellor on the federalist structure of the Reich.[56] The dwindling authority of Caprivi and Hohenlohe's inability to assert his control over the Prussian Ministers had encouraged the federal states' suspicions of Berlin's intentions. In October 1900 Lerchenfeld reported that the power of the individual State Secretaries had developed too far under Hohenlohe, that he had not provided centralised leadership and that consequently the final decision on Reich matters had frequently rested with the Prussian Ministry of State. He and other South German envoys to Berlin thus hoped and expected 'that on important occasions the new Chancellor will act with greater authority and will emancipate himself more from the opinions of the State Secretaries and majority decisions of the Prussian State Ministry than his predecessors'.[57] Moreover, Bülow was well aware by October 1900 that 'there exists at present especially in Munich and Dresden some ill-feeling over the fact that the federal states are not always informed sufficiently and in good time about the course of Reich political measures and questions'[58] and that the ties, especially between South Germany and the Reich leadership, had become looser in recent years.[59]

Bülow thus began his Chancellorship with the firm intention of emphasising his commitment to federalism and reassuring the more important South German governments that he would respect their constitutional rights.[60] According to Monts, the Prussian Minister in Munich, Bülow's reassurances were primarily motivated by expediency, for he realised that he could not swim against the particularist tide at that time. But with the Berlin executive still disunited, the new Chancellor also recognised how he would need all the allies he could muster if he was to counter oppositional tendencies among the Prussian Ministers or the jealousy of the Kaiser's Court and military entourage.[61] In particular, Bülow was very soon convinced that it would be an advantage if he gained the support of the federal states for his compromise tariff before he had to take it to the Kaiser, the Prussian Ministry of State and the Reichstag, and plans were thus made for a confidential conference of Finance Ministers from the more important states to discuss the tariff before it was finally settled in the Reich Offices.[62]

In December 1900 Bülow followed up his assurances of goodwill to the South German ambassadors by embarking on a tour of the South German states.[63] His visit to South Germany was first and foremost a politeness, but it also ostensibly had a political purpose. As Szögyényi reported, 'Count Bülow wanted to strengthen the connection between the Reich administration and the governments of the federal states and induce them to take a more active part in the settlement of Reich affairs than was the case under the regimes of Caprivi and Hohenlohe.'[64] Bülow proved very successful in persuading the South Germans of his good intentions and his desire to follow in Bismarck's tradition in his dealings with the federal governments. He insisted that he would respect the spirit of the Versailles treaties of 1871 and that they need not suspect him of unitarianism. Indeed, the new Chancellor understood how to win general sympathy and create an excellent impression in all five capitals he visited (Munich, Stuttgart, Karlsruhe, Darmstadt and Dresden).[65] Those who had not previously met Bülow were captivated by his conciliatory manner and his characteristic readiness to agree with whatever was said to him. But even Brauer, the Baden Minister-President, was satisfied with the visit. Brauer knew Bülow better than most (they had met in 1875 in St Petersburg[66]) and admitted that 'Count Bülow is not easy to grasp [*fassen*] in conversations because – while constantly acknowledging what is said to him – he only talks in generalities.'[67] But he had not wanted to hear anything special from the Chancellor, and was left with the impression that Bülow would conduct Reich affairs with circumspection and caution. Above all, Brauer believed, Bülow would promote national unity.

Bülow's assumption of the Chancellorship thus had an immediate impact on the executive in 1900, but it remained unclear whether the changes he introduced – fresh unity in the Reich and Prussian administrations, and a new mood of cooperation between Berlin and the federal states – were anything more than cosmetic. In particular, despite the apparent agreement on the form of the new tariff regulations, Bülow's authority had still to be tested when major political and economic interests were at stake. Bülow had expressed his intention to concentrate on domestic questions in the coming months, but he had no specific political programme and displayed no willingness to immerse himself in the details of domestic policy. The priority he gave to the 'national imperatives' entailed submerging contentious political issues as far as possible and trying to find the middle ground when a decision was unavoidable.

The Chancellor and the Reichstag

Bülow was relatively successful in the autumn of 1900 in restoring harmonious relations with the German Reichstag. During Hohenlohe's Chancellorship the executive had lacked a coherent and practical strategy in relation to the Reichstag.[68] With the Kaiser only concerned about securing his favourite projects – the Navy Bills, the Hard Labour Bill, the Canal Bill – and unwilling to grant concessions to deputies, the government had been unable to create a reliable basis of support for its policies within the parliaments. Miquel's idealistic concept of *Sammlungspolitik* had been seen by his colleagues and by Reichstag deputies as at best unclear and at worst inadequate and artificial, for especially after the elections of 1898 it was politically impossible to exclude the Centre Party from government majorities.[69] Moreover, during the last years of Hohenlohe's Chancellorship, the Reichstag had been forced into the unhappy role of having to counter the Kaiser's wishes because there was no effective resistance to his personal projects within the executive.[70]

Even more unfortunate from Bülow's point of view was the likely effect of the events of the summer on the mood of the new Reichstag session. Bülow himself as State Secretary had advised the Chancellor not to summon the Reichstag to approve credits for the China expedition,[71] but now as Chancellor he had to face the Reichstag's wrath over the *Reichsleitung*'s ostensible lack of regard for its budgetary rights. In addition, the Kaiser's speeches during the summer could be expected to attract severe criticism in the parliament;[72] and a major scandal erupted, perhaps not coincidentally in late October 1900, which threatened to unseat the State Secretary of Interior. All this combined to create a situation of extreme delicacy in the autumn of 1900, and it was scarcely possible to conceive of any alternative to a conciliatory approach by the *Reichsleitung* towards the Reichstag. But it may well have been precisely Hohenlohe's recognition of the need to countenance concessions which had prompted the old Chancellor's resignation. Jagemann reported that Wilhelm II had refused to allow Hohenlohe to request an indemnity with respect to the unapproved credits for the Chinese expedition since he equated such a gesture with a request for forgiveness.[73]

In these circumstances it came as a complete surprise to all concerned when Bülow extricated himself from his first set of difficulties in the Reichstag in November 1900 by requesting an indemnity. 'Above all things no domestic crisis!' the new Chancellor had allegedly remarked shortly after his appointment,[74] and it was characteristic that he used all his influence and dexterity to avert a confrontation between the Crown and the Reichstag. The Crown Speech of 14 November had demonstrated Bülow's desire to be conciliatory and had only just stopped short of asking for an indemnity.[75] But confidential discussions with party leaders and in particular the Centre leader, Lieber, prior to the beginning of the Chinese debate, had finally convinced Bülow that there was no question of the Reichstag's agreeing to a supplementary budget (*Nachtragsetat*).[76] Thus Bülow's first speech as Chancellor to the Reichstag on 19 November won general approval.[77]

While Szögyényi reported that Bülow had ultimately been able to convince Wilhelm II of the necessity of requesting an indemnity,[78] the more general assumption was that the new Chancellor had acted on his own authority and had in fact gone behind the Kaiser's back. The Centre Party deputy, Karl Bachem, understood from Lieber that Bülow had not been able to reveal his intention earlier because he had never been sure that the Kaiser would not telegraph him at the last minute with specific orders. Only when he was on the point of walking into the Reichstag, having still not heard from Wilhelm, could Bülow send word to the Centre leader that he would, after all, request an indemnity.[79] If Bülow had requested an indemnity without the Kaiser's express consent, his first gamble on the monarch's acquiescence was successful. Bülow's friend, Franz Arenberg, later told Bachem that Wilhelm had reacted 'quite well' to Bülow's action and had telegraphed the Chancellor (though only after his second speech on 20 November, when he launched a humorous attack on the

Progressive Party leader, Eugen Richter) congratulating him on his great success.[80]

In general, the debate on China in the Reichstag in November 1900 was exceptionally favourable both for Bülow and the *Reichsleitung*. Jagemann regretted that, contrary to constitutional custom, the Kaiser's speeches had formed the main topic of discussion;[81] and, in justifying the former Chancellor's decision not to summon the Reichstag, Bülow proved only too willing to plead his own innocence.[82] But, on the other hand, Bülow's assertion that he wanted to assume full moral responsibility for all Wilhelm II's speeches (constitutionally he was only responsible for the Kaiser's 'orders and directives') created an excellent impression, even though some doubted how easily he would be able to fulfil his promise.[83]

Bülow still had a second difficulty to face in the Reichstag in November 1900, namely the so-called 12,000 Mark affair, which implicated Posadowsky and the Reich Office of Interior in a propaganda campaign for a bill to restrict strikes.[84] But the prospects for the government already looked more favourable, and the Chancellor achieved yet another parliamentary success. Despite the tense personal relationship between Bülow and Posadowsky, Bülow was not in a position to let Posadowsky fall on account of the scandal. Posadowsky had made himself unpopular in industrialist circles because of his warm support for the double tariff system in the Economic Committee, which had been set up in 1897 to prepare the tariff, and the scandal may have been timed to serve as a warning to Bülow not to give in too much to the agrarians' demands.[85] But Posadowsky's extensive knowledge of domestic affairs really made him indispensable to the Chancellor in 1900, and his resignation would have brought the government into conflict with the agrarians, whose support Bülow hoped to win.[86] Thus Posadowsky's subordinate, the *Ministerialdirektor* in the Reich Office of Interior, Erich von Woedtke, was made the scapegoat for the affair,[87] and Bülow defended his colleague in the Reichstag on 24 November.[88] But Posadowsky had to pay a price for Bülow's support for, as Szögyényi reported, the Chancellor

gave excellent testimony as far as Count Posadowsky's eminent abilities and character were concerned, just as recently on the question of the failure to summon the Reichstag, he also emphasised warmly Prince Hohenlohe's long career as a statesman and his proven constitutional sense; but in both cases the impression nevertheless remained that the brilliant success of Count Bülow had been achieved, to a not insignificant extent, at the cost of these two gentlemen.[89]

Posadowsky's silence did not augur well,[90] and in December 1900 Lerchenfeld reported that the position of the State Secretary of Interior might have suffered more from the affair than he had originally assumed.[91]

By the end of November Bülow's immediate problems in the Reichstag had been overcome, but it is difficult to determine exactly how seriously

Bülow regarded the parliamentary situation in the autumn of 1900. Not-withstanding the problems and the likelihood of a long debate over the China affair, the general view of experienced political observers in October 1900 was that the new Chancellor was certain of the support of the great majority of the Reichstag and had little to fear from the political parties.[92] Moreover, the mistakes of his opponents – in particular the clumsy tactics of the Social Democratic Party over the 12,000 Mark affair – contributed to Bülow's success in late 1900 and there was never any real danger of concerted parliamentary hostility to the *Reichsleitung*.[93] But Bülow himself remained anxious about the situation in the Reichstag and he seems to have linked the parliamentary opposition to the events of the summer with the growing disillusionment of the federal states with the Kaiser's 'personal rule'. 'I have succeeded in two speeches in saving the situation before the Reichstag and the Bundesrat which seemed almost hopeless', he wrote to Eulenburg on 22 November[94] and perhaps, like Eulenburg, alarmed by the degree of animosity displayed by some of the speakers in the China debate,[95] he went on to say that the danger Eulenburg had long anticipated of an alliance between the German parliament and the German princes against the Kaiser was imminent. Bülow urged Eulenburg to use all his influence to restrain the Kaiser and avert a crisis, and Eulenburg responded promptly by resuming his former role and writing to Wilhelm counselling caution.[96] But Eulenburg also had other thoughts about the parliamentary situation. 'How happy this entire Reichstag lot would be to go with you against His Majesty!' he wrote prophetically to Bülow.[97]

Bülow's conciliatory approach towards the Reichstag in the autumn of 1900 averted a major crisis and demonstrated his strong position with the Kaiser. Bülow clearly hoped to continue this policy of showing consideration and respect towards the Reichstag, and his appeal to Eulenburg was not least designed to ensure the Kaiser's docility with respect to parliamentary affairs in the future. For the time being, however, Eulenburg's anxiety that Wilhelm II might take Bülow's successes in the Reichstag amiss[98] proved unfounded. In public Wilhelm spoke with evident delight about his new Chancellor's parliamentary performances[99] and was especially appreciative of Bülow's speech of 12 December against the President of the Pan-German League, Dr Hasse, who had criticised the government for not receiving the South African President Krueger.[100] 'Count Bülow struck exactly the right tone here, was calm and dignified in his speech', Wilhelm told Szögyényi. 'In accordance with his – Kaiser Wilhelm's – direct advice, however, he did not pay certain elements, like for example the Social Democrats and the Pan-Germans, the honour of taking them seriously, and ceremoniously [*förmlich*] overwhelmed them with his caustic derision.'[101] Shortly afterwards Wilhelm II bestowed the Order of the Black Eagle on Bülow 'as a token of my gratitude for the way in which you got me out of the awkward situation in the Reichstag'.[102]

Once the confrontation between the Reichstag and the *Reichsleitung* had been averted in the autumn of 1900 Bülow could devote his attention to preparing the parliamentary terrain for the big domestic issues. As has been indicated, Bülow began his Chancellorship with no comprehensive programme for domestic policy and, as far as the Reichstag was concerned, he primarily hoped to reduce the quantity of legislation with which it had to deal and hence restrict the source of potential domestic conflict. His conviction was that the less the Reichstag had to do, the more apathetic and docile it would become. Nevertheless, his pragmatic approach to domestic policy did entail enlisting the support and sympathy of the 'reasonable' Conservative and moderate parties in the Reichstag. As a 'man of mediation'[103] who hoped to find sufficient middle ground on each issue to effect acceptable compromises, Bülow had a concept of the *Mittellinie* ('middle course') which was essentially fluid and undefined, determined by the nature of each issue and the degree of political polarisation. Thus he ideally did not want to exclude any parties, except the extreme left, from collaboration with the *Reichsleitung*.

By December 1900 there were signs that Bülow was reverting to his preferred personal approach and trying to win over important individual Reichstag deputies psychologically.[104] But, more significantly, within weeks of assuming the Chancellorship an incident in the Reichstag revealed the importance he attached to securing the goodwill of the Centre Party, a party which, with its heterogeneous composition, seemed to Bülow to be a microcosm of German political opinion.[105] Since he had acted on the assumption that he needed the support of the majority of the Centre, Bülow's response to the Centre's Tolerance Motion (which supported the free practice of religion in the federal states) in December 1900 came as a surprise to all concerned.

There was no question of the federal governments' supporting the Centre's initiative in December 1900. The Kaiser had immediately pronounced against it, and for religious and particularist reasons most of the middle and small German states had condemned the proposals.[106] Nevertheless Bülow wanted to exploit this first opportunity to be conciliatory towards the Centre and Catholics in general at apparently little cost and, contrary to constitutional custom, it was agreed in the Bundesrat that he should read out a declaration from the federal governments explaining their rejection of the Motion. The mere fact that the Chancellor responded to a motion initiated from the floor of the Reichstag before a vote had been taken and that the declaration was sympathetic to religious convictions and sensibilities was expected to create a favourable impression.[107]

Bülow's intervention during the first reading of the Tolerance Motion was something new and unusual which departed from the Bismarckian practice and surprised the entire Centre Party.[108] But Bülow had decided to go further. In consultation with Lieber before the debate began, he had decided to read out the Bundesrat declaration and then add a statement of his own to the effect that he personally had no wish to preserve the antiquated, disparate and frequently petty restrictions on the free practice of religion within the individual states and he hoped that they could be removed. Lieber had questioned what the Kaiser would say, but Bülow claimed that he did not consider it feasible simply to read out the Bundesrat declaration on this occasion, even though he knew he had to tread very carefully and that he had 'many enemies'.[109]

Bülow thus made a great concession by deigning to reply in such a conciliatory way to the Centre's initiative, and his action won general applause in the Reichstag. But in going further than the Bundesrat had agreed, the Chancellor attracted criticism from the federal states, some of which were placed in a very difficult position.[110] Even the Prince-Regent of Bavaria had urged Bülow not to support the Motion.[111] To placate the Centre on a relatively minor issue and to take personal credit in the Reichstag, the Chancellor already showed a willingness to assert his independence from a Bundesrat decision and ran the risk of being accused of having acted against the spirit of the Constitution. Not only did he ride roughshod over the rights of the Bundesrat, but he also only acquired the agreement of the Prussian Ministry of State retrospectively, claiming he had not had time to call a meeting beforehand.[112]

Despite his desire from October 1900 to be conciliatory towards the Centre Party and despite his assertion in the summer of 1900 that he personally favoured the repeal of the Jesuit Law, Bülow in fact began his Chancellorship with no intention of making practical concessions to the Centre Party. Aware of the Kaiser's resentment of the Centre's intolerable 'domination' in Prussia and the Reich,[113] he doubtless anticipated the obstacles he would encounter if he embarked on such a course, and in January 1901 he instructed Richthofen to tell the Württemberg ambassador confidentially that although the Centre had to be considered the decisive party in the Reichstag, he would try as far as possible to keep it in a good mood and compliant 'through polite treatment and regard for the consideration which the Centre Party has to pay to its voters', without making material concessions.[114] Bachem suspected this reluctance to follow up his fine-sounding words with deeds as early as October 1900, and he believed that the party would have to be very careful with the new Chancellor.[115] Only gradually would Bülow realise that the reliable support of the Centre could only be won by delivering more tangible results.

For the time being, however, Bülow could afford to feel well satisfied with the response of the Reichstag to his first few weeks as Chancellor. His handling of the China affair had brought him the respect of the majority parties and contributed to his general popularity in the autumn of 1900; and with the general goodwill of the Reichstag and his personal inclination to be conciliatory, the parliamentary prospects for 1901 seemed bright. While his Reichstag triumphs had been achieved at some cost to the appearance of executive unity, this more negative aspect of his procedure was not given undue significance in 1900 and did him no damage among the political parties. Only the Social Democratic Party remained adamantly hostile to him, and in November 1900 its newspaper *Vorwärts* predicted that the new Chancellor would not last long.

He is so much at pains to please everybody that he will ultimately incur everyone's displeasure. No Chancellor before has ever had such a compact majority in the Reichstag behind him, never was the organisation of the claque so comprehensive and spirited [*todesmutig*] – and exactly for that reason we think we can dare to prophesy: Count B[ülow] will also be the one who will one day receive the most unkind, most bitter and most malicious obituaries [*Nachrufe*], when his hour is up.[116]

The imminent crisis: the Prussian Canal Bill, 1901

The *Reichsleitung*'s success in avoiding a confrontation with the Reichstag in the autumn of 1900 may well have encouraged the Prussian government to reintroduce the ill-fated Canal Bill into the Prussian Landtag in January 1901. Discussions with Prussian deputies shortly after he became Chancellor convinced Bülow that he was in a position to break the resistance of the Conservatives and agrarians to one of the Kaiser's favourite projects,[117] and there was no doubt that the prospects for the acceptance of the bill were brighter than they had been in 1899, when the first Canal Bill had been rejected by the Landtag and the Kaiser had suffered a considerable loss of prestige.[118] The new bill was more extensive than its predecessor, and the contentious *Mittellandkanal*, which was to link Dortmund and the Ruhr with the Weser, Elbe and Oder rivers, was now incorporated within a comprehensive system of water transport. Moreover, hopes were high in government circles that the expectation of higher grain duties would pacify the bill's opponents, who primarily feared that the new canal would reduce the cost of transporting imported grain. Thielen, the Minister of Public Works, was reasonably optimistic[119] and, with the future tariff ensuring the good humour and pliancy of the Conservatives, Brefeld, the Minister of Trade, believed that at least a stretch of the canal would be approved.[120] In his first speech to the Prussian Lower House on 9 January Bülow adopted a conciliatory approach, emphasising how he saw the government's main task as being to reconcile the conflicting economic interests and how the new Canal Bill would not only promote the industrial development of the western regions, but also the interests of agriculture in the east. The Canal Bill, he told the House, was economically the most important bill since the nationalisation of the railways, and he expressed his confidence that it would receive the necessary support.[121]

Despite the generally optimistic appraisal of the situation in early January 1901, by the end of the month all the favourable indicators had vanished. Although Bülow must have hoped that he could secure the acceptance of the Canal Bill and thereby strengthen his position with the Kaiser, he cunningly chose not to become involved personally in the canal issue. Instead, from the beginning he declared that the Canal Bill was an issue he had inherited and which had already been entrusted to the Finance Minister and Vice-President of the Prussian Ministry, Miquel. Dependent on the support of the Conservatives, Miquel's parliamentary representation of the bill was so unclear that he was almost immediately judged to be a secret opponent of the canal.[122] And while the activities of the Finance Minister undermined the chances of success, there is no doubt that Bülow himself made matters much worse by committing a grave tactical error. In January 1901 the Chancellor publicly bound himself to an increase in the grain duties and behind the scenes even indicated that he favoured a minimum level of over five Marks per *Doppelzentner*.[123] His declaration alienated liberal opinion and did not satisfy the Conservatives, who wanted the minimum duties on cereals firmly established before they would approve the Canal Bill. Leading Conservative parliamentarians in the Prussian Lower House even began to talk cynically about rejecting the Canal Bill once they had achieved a higher tariff.[124]

There were thus already signs that with the new Canal Bill the Prussian government had embarked on a course which would again end in defeat and humiliation, and by March 1901 Bülow's parliamentary position, not only in the Landtag but also in the Reichstag, had deteriorated considerably. While liberals resented the Chancellor's apparent shift to the right, the sympathy of the Conservatives and agrarians was further forfeited by events in the field of foreign policy. Both Bülow and Philipp Eulenburg were dismayed when, with a sudden display of emotion, the Kaiser departed for England in January 1901 to be at the death-bed of his grandmother, Queen Victoria.[125] Wilhelm's gesture created a good impression in England, but his prolonged absence alienated German public opinion and incensed those pro-Russian Conservatives who were haunted by the spectre of an Anglo-German alliance. At a time when Bülow was seeking to win the sympathy of the agrarians, the Kaiser's sudden demonstration of friendliness towards England threatened to ruin his efforts, and even General Hans von Plessen, who accompanied Wilhelm to England, wrote to Bülow that it was 'terrible that during these very busy and important weeks [*Geschäftswochen*] His

Majesty is not in Berlin'.[126] Wilhelm returned to Germany on 7 February and went straight to Homburg, where Bülow spent a week with the monarch, apparently trying to move him to some kind of similar demonstration in the interests of German relations with Russia.[127] But, as Eulenburg wrote to Bülow with anxious solicitude, the Kaiser's behaviour had already murdered the embryo of agrarian sympathy,[128] and Bülow's defence of German foreign policy in the Reichstag on 5 March 1901 was not favourably received.[129]

The Kaiser was as disenchanted with his people as they were with him, and his pessimism, irritability and anger formed a lurid background to Bülow's efforts to achieve a satisfactory conclusion to the Canal Bill in the spring of 1901. After Bülow's departure from Homburg in February 1901, Wilhelm became extremely excitable and sensitive about the anti-English articles in the German press[130] and, when he returned to Berlin at the end of the month (having spent scarcely a week in the capital that winter), his mood was hardly improved when he was struck with a piece of iron by an epileptic worker in Bremen on 7 March.[131] Although the Kaiser initially took the assassination attempt with great equanimity and still tried to deal with urgent government business despite being forbidden to read or speak,[132] his ill-humour intensified when he perceived what a minor impression the incident had made on the German public, his entourage and his family.[133] In an audience with Szögyényi on 24 March, at which Bülow was also present, the unhappy monarch gave full vent to his feelings:

I have the right and the duty . . . to be the leader of my people. I will also continue not to be deterred from following my conviction and practising the rights bestowed on me by God by the eternal fault-finding and intrigues [*Nörgeleien und Quertreibereien*] I encounter. Yet I must admit openly to you that it often has a very demoralising effect on me when my instructions are criticised *from all sides* in the most malicious way.

The agrarians, he complained, reproached him because he did not provide sufficient protection for agriculture. The Conservatives showed their sentiments only too clearly in their attitude to the canal question. The Centre desired the re-entry of the Jesuits, which he could not concede. The aristocracy maligned him: he did not give enough Court parties, went on expensive travels and encouraged 'Byzantinism' in his attitude at Court. As far as the liberals and Social Democrats were concerned he obviously could do nothing right, but their accusations left him cold. Even the commercial classes were not satisfied with him, though he had given them the Navy and *Weltpolitk*. 'All classes of the population and first and foremost the "high aristocracy", which is supposed to stand closest to the throne, abuses me in the most impermissible way because of my English leanings [*Engländerei*]', Wilhelm continued. 'You see from this presentation [*Darstellung*] that I don't have illusions of being a popular monarch.'[134]

The Kaiser spoke with his usual liveliness, but was clearly emotional and suffering from the shock of recent events. After they withdrew, Bülow did his best to persuade the Austrian ambassador to treat the Kaiser's remarks with the utmost confidentiality. But it was in this mood that Wilhelm II, his voice quivering with excitement, delivered his speech at the beginning of April 1901 to the Alexander-Garde-Regiment.[135] The Kaiser's references to 1848, when the people of Berlin marched against their King, caused embarrassment and prompted the Grand Duke of Baden to write to Bülow 'that the state of our German public relations seems to have reached a high-point of internal danger which compels us to prepare preventive measures for the future'.[136]

Although rumours emanating from the Kaiser's entourage that Bülow handed in his resignation in March 1901 appear to be unfounded,[137] there is no doubt that the Kaiser contributed to Bülow's problems in the spring of 1901. In an effort to win over the Centre, Posadowsky told the Centre deputy, Karl Trimborn, in February 1901 that the government was inclined to grant salaries to Reichstag members if in turn the Reichstag reduced the quorum for a second reading to 100 members.[138] (The passage of legislation was frequently held up by the low number of deputies who attended the sittings.) But one month later Bülow told Bachem that although he personally was convinced that Reichstag salaries were imperative, the Kaiser would not yet agree to them.[139] While Bülow fretted about Germany's relations with Russia, Wilhelm, who was annoyed by Russia's Far Eastern policy, told the British ambassador that he would not mind at all if it came to a break with Russia.[140] While Bülow tried to win the support of the agrarians, the Kaiser allegedly told the two Vice-Presidents of the Prussian Upper House that there was no question of a higher duty on cereals than five Marks and that he would not sign the Tariff Bill before the Conservatives and agrarians had accepted the canal.[141]

Bülow did what he could to exert a moderating influence on the Kaiser and appealed to others to do the same. At the end of April 1901 Bülow urged the Grand Duke of Baden to impress on the Kaiser during his forthcoming visit to Karlsruhe how important it was to pacify German public opinion, and his letter was strewn with familiar sentiments – the need to avoid irritating the Tsar, reduce the quantity of Reichstag legislation, strike a sensible middle course on the tariff issue with as great a degree of protection for agriculture as possible. Bülow was also concerned that the Kaiser should not encourage the conservative 'Bismarck fronde' by refusing to attend the unveiling of the Bismarck memorial statue in Berlin in June 1901.[142] But he no longer mentioned the Canal Bill, for by this time he was already reconciled to its failure.

At the beginning of March 1901 Philipp Eulenburg had written to Bülow

with advice on how he could escape from the difficulties over the Canal Bill
in the Prussian Landtag. The style and content of Bülow's communications
to Eulenburg after he became Chancellor indicate that he was trying to free
himself from the political influence of the royal favourite and not inform him
of events in Berlin.[143] But Eulenburg did not allow himself to be put off by
Bülow's rather curt communiqués and the belittling of his anxieties. Instead,
he wrote the Chancellor a long and sympathetic letter pointing out the
dangers inherent in the situation over the Canal Bill and advising that the bill
be withdrawn.[144]

From the beginning, Eulenburg claimed, he had considered the rein-
troduction of the Canal Bill that winter to be a mistake. Danger threatened
from the left and the right. Eulenburg assumed that Bülow had proposed an
increase in the grain duties in order to win the agrarians for the Canal Bill,
but he had no confidence in the Conservatives' ability to recognise the perils,
for both their party and the state, if they came into conflict with the Crown.
The left was deliberately trying to exploit the rift and encourage the
Conservatives in their foolhardiness. The Kaiser, too, was quite capable of
running headlong into the same trap in which he had been caught before.
Bülow's position would become very difficult if, after he had advocated
higher grain duties in accordance with the Conservatives' wishes, the Conservatives now rejected the canal. The government could not give up the
project, but the Kaiser would have to wait. 'The prestige of the government
is not undermined by the constant return of the bill, for there is no talk of
capitulation, even if the entire German press will sing on this note –
especially if the duties come despite everything.'

Eulenburg's letter attested to his long experience of Berlin political life.
Despite his distance from and his lack of information about what was
happening in the German capital, he had been able to reconstruct Bülow's
predicament and the general situation in the spring of 1901 with a fair degree
of accuracy, even anticipating that 'the old fox', Miquel, might deliberately
have prepared difficulties for the Chancellor. Bülow still refused to be drawn
into a political debate with Eulenburg, merely admitting that he was 'very
harassed but in good spirits'.[145] But he may well have internalised Eulenburg's advice, for this was the very course he was to pursue in May 1901.
Although there is no evidence that Bülow was preparing any action over the
Canal Bill until the end of April, and although he officially still hoped for
a compromise,[146] in an enigmatic note to Hammann, his Press Chief, in the
middle of April, Bülow wrote that, 'The main thing is that the most absolute
silence is observed about the envisaged solution [*Ausweg*] until further
notice.'[147] In May 1901 Bülow told Eulenburg that the crisis had unfolded
in accordance with 'my plans conceived a long time ago and maturely
considered'.[148]

By the end of April, the position of the government with respect to the Canal Bill had become completely untenable and Bülow was virtually forced to act. The Landtag committee was expected to come to a decision at the beginning of May which, though by no means rejecting all the government's wishes, would involve the refusal of the *Mittellandkanal*, which was the main part of the bill.[149] Such a decision would constitute a major defeat for the Prussian government on an issue in which the King of Prussia had become personally engaged; but if the government followed up the defeat by dissolving the Landtag, a very dangerous situation might result. If the government did not bring pressure to bear during the election campaign, the elections might well lead to the return of exactly the same elements which had rejected the canal, and the elections would amount to a plebiscite directed against the Kaiser. But if the government did intervene in the election campaign, a party combination would be returned which would ensure a majority for the canal, but only at the price of decimating the Conservative Party, which was the unshakeable support of monarchical authority in Prussia.

The only alternative was, as Eulenburg had advised, to close the Landtag before things got to this stage, and at the end of April Bülow was advised by several deputies and by the Reichstag President, Count Ballestrem, to follow this course.[150] While discussing the matter with Bülow on 24 April, the Centre deputy, Am Zehnhoff, had the impression 'that Bülow understands nothing at all about the matter and is not even superficially oriented'.[151] But after long discussions with the Kaiser about the Canal Bill after Wilhelm's return to Berlin (after a short absence) on 30 April,[152] Bülow summoned the Prussian Ministry of State to a meeting on 2 May. The Conservatives would not vote for the Canal Bill, he told his colleagues, and Wilhelm II would not agree to accept only part of it. The Kaiser had rejected the idea of a dissolution and therefore the Landtag was to be closed the next day. Miquel alone protested, doubting whether the Kaiser's decision was based on an accurate assessment of the situation and urging the government to await the vote of the Upper House so that it would have at least one Chamber on its side. But Bülow's proposals were accepted,[153] and on 3 May 1901 the Minister-President informed a joint sitting of the two Houses that the Landtag was to be closed.[154]

Bülow's ability to avert a potentially serious crisis over the Canal Bill in 1901 demonstrated the extent to which he could influence Wilhelm and Wilhelm's continued confidence in his Chancellor. When he was confronted with the impossibility of achieving the canal project, the Kaiser's personal inclination had been to dissolve the Lower House and hold new elections, and Szógyényi reported that there had been a hard struggle between Kaiser and Chancellor before Wilhelm had finally agreed that the session should merely be adjourned.[155] Moreover, even then, Wilhelm expected Bülow to deliver a sharp reproof to the Conservative Party. At a small social gathering at the home of Guido Henckel von Donnersmarck before the joint sitting of the Landtag, the Kaiser revealed the extent to which he had internalised Bülow's arguments, but he also indicated his displeasure. He was not thinking in terms of a dissolution, he told the assembled company (which included Varnbüler), but merely of closure. The negotiations in the committee had become so bogged down that it was better to call it a day and leave the Conservatives and agrarians time to reconsider the matter, in all its implications, calmly and maturely at home. But, notwithstanding Wilhelm's unusual patience when he asserted that it had taken him ten years to give Germany a Navy and that he would also achieve the canal, he went on to say that Bülow already had some 'real bullets [*scharfgeladene Patronen*] in his pocket' and that the Conservatives would not be sent on their way without a severe admonition.[156] Thus it came as even more of a surprise to those who had expected the Minister-President to reprimand the majority of the Lower House when Bülow omitted to express the Kaiser's strong displeasure in his brief speech on 3 May.[157] To the immense satisfaction of the Conservatives, Bülow merely spoke in a tone of mild, reproachful regret and restricted himself to a completely impartial justification of the closure.

The closure of the Landtag prompted the liberal press to unleash a storm of indignation against the Chancellor who had prevented the pulverisation of the Conservative Party in a controversial election campaign. On the other hand the Conservatives were now full of respect for the man who had rescued them from an embarrassing situation and had negotiated a comparatively mild truce. As Varnbüler reported, the Conservatives saw in Bülow's avoidance of a crisis 'the first real evidence of his conservative frame of mind, his firmness of character . . . his strength, his influence on the Kaiser [*nach oben*]'. He was now considered to be 'the strong man' they had always wanted. The Conservatives were doubtless deceiving themselves, for just because Bülow had exerted all his influence to avert a domestic conflict, it did not necessarily follow that he would now place that influence at the disposal of the extreme agrarians. Bülow would never be the strong man who with one blow could drive industrialists, Progressives and Social Democrats to the wall.[158] But for the time being the Conservatives were content, and the Chancellor had extricated himself from certain parliamentary defeat.

The ministerial changes of May 1901

The withdrawal of the Canal Bill in May 1901 averted a major political crisis, but the full impact of the Landtag closure was only to become apparent in the following days. During the State Ministry meeting of 2 May 1901 Bülow had expressly communicated the Kaiser's gratitude and satisfaction to those Ministers, namely Miquel and Thielen, who had been directly concerned with presenting the bill. There was no mention of any personnel changes, but Bülow was quick to see how the retreat over the Canal Bill could be combined with the removal of his most powerful opponent in the Prussian Ministry of State, and he clearly expected Miquel to submit his resignation after the meeting. Instead, only Thielen complied, and on the morning of 3 May Bülow was obliged to send Wilmowski, his Chief of Reich Chancellery, to Miquel to tell him that his resignation was desired.[159] Miquel reluctantly submitted a letter of resignation, justifying his decision on grounds of poor health, and his lead was followed by the Ministers of Agriculture and Trade.[160] Miquel, Hammerstein and Brefeld received news of the acceptance of their resignations immediately after the Landtag sitting of 3 May, and the official announcements appeared on 4 May.[161]

The three resignations in May 1901 were altogether only loosely connected with the canal issue. If the Kaiser had really been displeased with his Ministers over the Canal Bill, he would have accepted Thielen's resignation as well, but he rejected it.[162] It had been recognised that Miquel's days as a Minister were numbered from the autumn of 1900,[163] and his position had become untenable after he had gradually lost the confidence of his colleagues and the political parties.[164] Although the Finance Minister had not openly opposed Bülow in the Prussian Ministry of State, he had refused to subordinate himself to Bülow's leadership[165] and Bülow had sought to avoid disagreements with Miquel in the State Ministry by circumventing it when he anticipated opposition and discussing issues directly with the Kaiser.[166] Moreover, Miquel had intrigued against the Chancellor over the tariff issue and had tried to get the Centre Party to commit itself to a high tariff.[167] Thus Bülow welcomed the excuse to remove the main challenge to his authority within the Prussian government. The departure of the Ministers of Agriculture and Trade, Hammerstein-Loxten and Brefeld, had nothing to do with the Canal Bill at all. Hammerstein was old and redundant, and his aims with respect to the Tariff Bill were not compatible with Bülow's since he was committed to a six-Mark duty on cereals.[168] Brefeld's ministerial activity had left much to be desired, and he had made himself unpopular with the big industrialists.[169] Neither man was likely to be an asset to the government during the future tariff negotiations.

In precipitating a ministerial crisis Bülow acted quickly and energetically without consulting his colleagues over the resignations or new appointments. 'A collegiate discussion [*Behandlung*] of these things does not seem to have taken place in the State Ministry', Jagemann reported, 'but His Majesty with the President of the State Ministry and the Chief of the Civil Cabinet brought about a settlement alone.'[170] Although rumours had been circulating in the press about impending ministerial changes for some days[171] and some newspapers announced the three resignations on the evening of 3 May, Posadowsky was still ignorant about the accuracy of the reports on 4 May.[172]

The new ministerial appointments were not fully resolved until 5 May. The new Prussian Finance Minister was the former Minister of Interior, Rheinbaben, who for many years had been Miquel's protégé in the Finance Ministry as a *Vortragender Rat* and who had gained much sympathy during his brief period as Minister since 1899.[173] Rheinbaben resisted accepting the portfolio of finance until the Kaiser made it clear to him that he could not remain Minister of Interior, and his change of post was less because of his special qualifications for the Finance Ministry than because of his 'soft' attitude as Minister of Interior towards the Conservatives. 'They wanted to get rid of him as Minister of Interior without affronting the Conservatives too much by his complete removal. So they let him be kicked upstairs', Varnbüler reported.[174]

The new Minister of Agriculture was the former Postmaster General, Podbielski, who had requested his resignation from the Reich Service in January 1901.[175] Podbielski was regarded as something of a swashbuckler. An ex-General, a man of 'union clubs' and an enthusiastic hunter, he was socially close to the Conservatives and a frequent guest at Wilhelm II's beer evenings and skat parties. But, although he was the owner of a large estate and familiar with the needs and distress of German agriculture, he was in many ways 'the problem child of the agrarians' and did not conform exactly to their wishes. As Varnbüler reported, he was not one of those 'who lose courage and wail for state assistance [*welche die Flinte ins Korn werfen und nach Staatshilfe jammern*]'. By founding subsidiary industrial concerns he had kept his estates productive and profitable, and to the Kaiser he represented a shining example of that self-help which the monarch preached at every opportunity to the impecunious agrarians.[176] Podbielski had not fulfilled expectations at the Reich Post Office and, despite his organisational talents, the Office had lost a lot of money. Nor did Lerchenfeld believe that he would transcend a certain dilettantism in the Ministry of Agriculture.[177] He was replaced at the Post Office by a bureaucrat, Kraetke, who was generally well received.

In order to avoid giving the new Ministry of State too 'feudal' a character, the new Minister of Trade stood further to the left and was seen as a representative of industrial and middle-class interests.[178] Möller was a newcomer to the State Service and a parliamentary deputy on the right wing of the National Liberal Party. A big industrialist and a self-made man, in order to take over the portfolio of Trade he had to give up numerous seats on Boards of Directors and his position as managing director of a factory.[179] It was assumed that Möller would be able to command a number of votes from the middle parties in the Reichstag and Prussian Lower House. He supported commercial treaties but also believed that agriculture should be afforded moderate protection.[180] Too conservative for the Progessives and considered 'another Berlepsch' by the Conservatives, Möller seemed to be the ideal choice for Bülow's *Mittellinie*.[181]

The new Minister of Interior was the former *Bezirkspräsident* of Metz, Hammerstein, who had proved himself a capable administrator during the thirty years he had spent in Alsace-Lorraine[182] and had been considered for a higher post during Bismarck's Chancellorship.[183] The Kaiser had got to know Hammerstein during his frequent visits to the *Reichslanden*,[184] but his promotion was criticised because he was a Hanoverian and not very well informed about Prussian affairs. August Eulenburg believed that Hammerstein was 'much too western' and so stubborn that he would not last long;[185] and this sense of the new Minister's inadequacy was shared by many Conservatives who felt that Hammerstein would not be able to handle the *Landräte* and by Philipp Eulenburg, who hinted as much to Bülow.[186]

The new ministerial appointments in May 1901 were decided exclusively by the Kaiser and Chancellor, and the extent to which Bülow was able to influence Wilhelm is of key significance. The Kaiser's physical presence in Berlin dominated the crisis. Returning to Berlin on 30 April, he stayed a mere three days before departing for Donaueschingen,[187] and Eulenburg confessed to Bülow that 'this sudden arrival and disappearance of the Kaiser to slaughter three Ministers between two grouse love-calls [*Auerhahnbalzen*]' made a rather hectic impression on him.[188] During his time in Berlin, Wilhelm conferred at length with Bülow each day and made an unexpected appearance at Bülow's birthday celebrations on 3 May, at which it seems that the candidates for the various Ministries had individual discussions *en cachette* with the Chancellor.[189] Further, the new appointments smacked of the Kaiser's choice. Both Podbielski and Hammerstein were favourites of the Kaiser, and Bülow cannot have been very happy with either. As Szögyényi wrote privately to Goluchowski,

Count Bülow, who lays claim to the full extent of the Kaiser's favour for himself and does not like to share it with others, did not for this reason greet the appointment of Herr von Podbielski and, as I am assured, also that of Baron von Hammerstein with particular delight.[190]

The Kaiser was also involved in the search for a new Finance Minister and offered the post to Siemens, a favourite with whom he had connections through the Anatolian Railway, and Henckel von Donnersmarck before forcing Rheinbaben to accept it.[191]

But the Chancellor's influence was also evident. As has been indicated, the removal of the Ministers of Finance, Trade and Agriculture was the result of Bülow's successful exploitation of the impending defeat of the Prussian

Canal Bill and only loosely connected with the parliamentary situation. The appointment of the National Liberal deputy, Möller, as Minister of Trade can be attributed to Bülow. Moreover, all three new Ministers in 1901 had to agree to certain conditions imposed by the Chancellor and designed to ensure their support of the moderate economic policy advocated by the Foreign Office. They had to agree in principle to the new trade treaties, they had to support a moderate increase in the grain duties and a minimum level which would not jeopardise the trade treaties, and they had to agree to further adherence to the canal project.[192] However much Bülow disliked the promotion of Podbielski, he could scarcely have agreed to his complete removal. For the departure of Podbielski, like that of Rheinbaben, would have aroused the distrust of the Conservatives, and Bülow depended on his new Minister of Agriculture to influence the agrarians for the *Mittellinie*.[193] Podbielski was one of the first to sign Bülow's pact, and his name was expected to have a pacifying effect on the Conservatives.[194] Finally, Hammerstein's appointment as Minister of Interior can be seen as a compromise between Kaiser and Chancellor. Although it was generally easy to find a replacement for the Ministry of Interior, which was not seen as a major department in Prussia, this post in practice proved the hardest to fill. The Kaiser's original candidate had been the *Oberpräsident* of Potsdam, Bethmann Hollweg, whom he had got to know at Hohenfinow and respected highly. But, too agrarian in his attitude to the grain duties, Bethmann had failed Bülow's 'political exam'[195] and had been inclined to set his own conditions.[196] Thus Bülow had refused to accept his appointment and the question of a new Minister of Interior remained unsettled even after Wilhelm had left Berlin. Only on 5 May did Wilhelm II finally telegraph Bülow from Donaueschingen that he would drop Bethmann's candidacy and summon Hammerstein.[197]

In the days following the ministerial changes in Prussia Bülow was at pains to emphasise the significance of the reshuffle for his own position and future German policy. Above all, the removal of Miquel meant that he was now without rival in the Prussian Ministry of State and the Chancellor's freedom and authority had been enhanced. Bülow's strengthened position was given formal political expression by the decision to leave the Vice-Presidency of the Prussian Ministry vacant. The most senior State Minister (in 1901 this was Thielen) would take over the affairs of the Vice-Presidency.[198] Richthofen told Jagemann that Bülow's main concern had been to create a homogeneous Ministry and put an end to the years of a 'dual economy' under Caprivi and Botho Eulenburg, Hohenlohe and Miquel, and more recently himself and Miquel. 'No Chancellor has ever created his Ministry so much according to his own choice under the present Kaiser', Richthofen asserted, and, clearly on Bülow's instructions, he used the same arguments to Szögyényi a few days later.[199] Bülow himself emphasised the significance of the personnel changes for Germany's future economic policy. On 6 May he told Lerchenfeld that the changes had been made so that a middle of the road tariff policy could be pursued;[200] and at a dinner at Botho Eulenburg's he told Varnbüler to write to his government 'that I believe I have thereby won a sure basis for a moderate and reasonable treatment and solution of the tariff questions'.[201]

Bülow's victory was confirmed by many in 1901, and there was much discussion of the new 'Bülow Ministry' or 'Bülow Cabinet' which would now be able to solve all the important questions of domestic and economic policy.[202] Bülow was felt to have acted not merely as Prussian Minister-President but as Reich Chancellor with Germany's interests as a whole in mind. He had abandoned the Prussian Canal Bill temporarily in order to ensure a more favourable climate for the passage of the tariff and trade treaties; and he had reconstructed the Prussian Ministry according to Reich criteria rather than been guided by purely Prussian affairs. Bülow had removed the only Minister who might have contested 'the place in the sun' and the new Ministry was completely loyal to him, Varnbüler reported appreciatively.[203]

Throughout the ministerial crisis Bülow's personal position had remained secure and there had never for one moment been any question of a change of Chancellor. Eulenburg noted how the canal crisis, because of the personnel changes, seemed but a transitory phase in German domestic policy which in no way touched or could touch Bülow's position. 'You stand too high above such things as guardian of the state – the Ministers must bleed when things don't go as they are supposed to go', he wrote to Bülow.[204] Bülow's strong position with the Kaiser ensured that any crisis would occur beneath him, and even at the height of the crisis Bülow had displayed 'a welcome serenity', displaying more concern about his dachshund's heart-attack than the loss of some ministerial colleagues.[205]

The removal of Miquel must be seen as a personal victory for Bülow. According to Franz Arenberg, in his conciliatory policy towards the Centre, Bülow had only been able to rely on the support of Posadowsky, Gossler (the War Minister) and Tirpitz in the Prussian Ministry of State. All the other Ministers, under Miquel's leadership, had made difficulties for the Chancellor.[206] Nevertheless, the extent of Bülow's victory in 1901 is more ambiguous than some reports suggest and, despite the (frequently government inspired) optimistic press appraisals of the responsible government's future unity and resolve, the Austrian ambassador was clearly not alone in seeing the withdrawal of the Canal Bill as a major defeat for the government and Crown, and one which boded ill for Bülow's prestige. While Varnbüler reported that the Conservatives had been tricked by Bülow and that they had now lost their key card when it came to securing higher grain duties,[207] Szögyényi felt that the Conservatives and the Centre had won a major victory which indicated that they would be able to assert their will again with respect to the tariff and trade treaties. Even Miquel's departure could not compensate for the damage to the authority of both Crown and Chancellor inflicted by the canal affair, Szögyényi reported pessimistically.[208]

Moreover, despite the removal of Miquel, the significance of the personnel changes within the executive in May 1901 can also be questioned. Bülow had not purged the Prussian Ministry of agrarian sympathisers or royal favourites, and the new appointments signified no fundamental reorientation of policy, even over the tariff issue. Since October 1900 Bülow had been concerned to steer a middle course and, as Lerchenfeld recognised, he certainly would have succeeded in gaining the agreement of the previous Ministry of State to his programme because he was sure of the Kaiser's confidence. It was the task of representing the new tariff before the Reichstag which Bülow hoped would be facilitated by the personnel changes. The Reichstag knew the prehistory of the tariff and that opinion within the Prussian Ministry had been divided. At best, there could only have been the appearance of unity with the former Ministry – if that, for while officially supporting the bill, Miquel had made it quite clear behind the scenes that if he had had his way, the agrarians would have got more. 'With the present composition of the State Ministry, currents of this kind with respect to tariff policy are out of the question', Lerchenfeld confidently asserted.[209] But only the future negotiations on the Tariff Bill could reveal whether the new ministerial appointments in 1901 marked a fundamental change and whether Bülow's authority within the executive had really increased as a result of his handling of the canal episode.

3

The Bülow system, 1901–1905

The political context

The four years after the ministerial crisis of May 1901 were the smoothest in Bülow's Chancellorship and remain unique in the constitutional history of Wilhelm II's reign. Despite all the problems which stemmed from the Kaiser's impetuosity and difficult personality, despite the less favourable implications of Bülow's political methods and the perennial difficulties which arose from the Empire's complicated political structure, a semblance of stability was achieved. In large measure this stability derived from the strong and secure position of the Chancellor. The fundamental pillars of the so-called 'Bülow system' – Bülow's relationship with the Kaiser, his domination of the executive and his management of the press and public opinion – will be examined below. Nevertheless, with the benefit of hindsight it is clear that the stability achieved between 1901 and 1905 was more apparent than real and that Bülow's new style of leadership merely helped to mask the underlying political polarisation during these years. The government suffered no major legislative defeats before 1906, but the inherent weaknesses in Bülow's parliamentary approach were visible well before the critical years of his Chancellorship.

Politically the early years of Bülow's Chancellorship were dominated by economic issues. The new tariff legislation was finally passed by the Reichstag in December 1902 despite a major attempt to obstruct the bill by the parties of the left; and, despite fears that new commercial treaties would be impossible given the increased agricultural tariff levels, the executive managed with some difficulty to renegotiate the treaties in 1904–5 which came into force along with the new tariff on 31 December 1906. The Empire's financial problems, already destined to become a critical issue after the passage of the Navy Laws in 1898 and 1900, were aggravated further by the need to crush a colonial uprising in South-West Africa from 1903 and by increases in military expenditure which were approved in 1905. A so-called 'small' Reich financial reform was passed in May 1904 and a more extensive reform, which included a limited form of inheritance tax, was concluded in 1906. Both of these, however, were to prove inadequate, and the Empire's financial deficit continued to accumulate.[1]

Much has been written about the place of economic issues, especially the tariff of 1902, in the government's general political strategy during these years.[2] Drawing on the work of Eckart Kehr, a number of historians such as Hans-Ulrich Wehler and Volker Berghahn have seen the tariff as fundamental in securing the support of the agrarians and Conservatives for a policy of naval expansion and imperialism. According to this view, the domestic alliance between heavy industry and agriculture (or 'iron and rye') which the tariff served to cement was the bedrock of *Sammlungspolitik*, the government's strategy from 1897 of rallying all national and anti-socialist elements behind the throne. It was, therefore, a primary determinant of Reich domestic politics in the period before 1914, ensuring the preservation of the existing social and political order and erecting a formidable barrier to democratic reform. This 'social imperialist' interpretation of government policy has been criticised first and foremost by Geoff Eley, who has pointed out how generalisations concerning the government's strategy have been applied to the period 1897–1909 without a firm basis of detailed research. Eley has argued that the relationship between agricultural protectionism and naval armaments (and, by implication, *Weltpolitik*) was tactical and co-incidental rather than strategic. Indeed, far from facilitating the emergence of a broad basis of government support, Tirpitz's naval plans highlighted the contradictions between industry and agriculture and helped to forge an alternative coalition of forces, hostile to the conservative *Sammlung* and committed to the expansion of the industrial economy. In Eley's view, *Sammlungspolitik* was more an aim or aspiration on the part of the government than a coherent strategy, and the alleged alliance between 'iron and rye' remained inherently unstable, undermined by the clash of economic interests and the fundamental disunity of the political parties which the government was seeking to bring together.

There are further problems in focusing on the tariff legislation of 1902 and drawing conclusions about the government's political strategy before 1914. It is important to remember that the economic issues which dominated the domestic political scene in the early years of Bülow's Chancellorship and which aroused party passions to an unprecedented extent were not initiated by the Reich leadership. The commercial treaties, which had been concluded during Caprivi's Chancellorship and had done much to promote Germany's industrial development, were due to expire in 1903, and since there was widespread acceptance of the need to afford agriculture a greater degree of protection than had been the case in the 1890s, the tariff issue had to be resolved if a worse situation were not to arise. The tariff was passed by a majority of moderate Conservatives, Centre and National Liberals who, by means of the so-called 'Kardorff compromise', voted for the duties *en bloc* and rallied behind the government, but as late as November 1902 this outcome appeared unlikely and the parliamentary situation remained confused right up to the passage of the bill.[3] Moreover, the tariff negotiations left a legacy of bitterness – the agrarians felt they had not achieved enough, the left resented the prospect of higher food prices, the majority parties believed they deserved major concessions as a reward for their support, the federal states were dismayed at their exclusion from the final compromise – and government hopes that it could exploit its tariff victory and that the majority parties would present a united front in the Reichstag elections of 1903 were to be disappointed.[4] Altogether, an examination of the tariff issue creates an impression of the disarray of Wilhelmine party politics and the helplessness of the government in its attempt to produce a genuine consensus. The tariff was far from being the cornerstone of Reich domestic policy. Indeed, it could be argued that the government had no strategy beyond an understandable desire to get a tariff acceptable to moderate opinion through the Reichstag and that it had a considerable amount of luck in getting a tariff accepted at all.[5]

Just how close the Reich leadership came to defeat over the tariff issue and how happy it would have been to jettison the whole issue is clearly revealed by Bülow's changing attitude towards the tariff between May 1901 and December 1902. After the ministerial changes of 1901 Bülow demonstratively assumed at least the formal leadership of the tariff negotiations, mobilising the federal states against those Prussian Ministers (Posadowsky, Podbielski and Rheinbaben) who still supported a more extensive double tariff system.[6] However the Chancellor's self-confidence was soon undermined when publication of the bill in June 1901 led to a storm of public protest and when his speech introducing the tariff in the Reichstag in December 1901 was coolly received.[7] 'Extremely downtrodden and jumpy [*betreten und nervös*]' and accused of pursuing a 'see-saw policy' in trying to reconcile the rival demands of industry and agriculture,[8] Bülow found that he could not rely on his economic advisers, notably Podbielski and Rheinbaben, when it came to representing the new levels in the Reichstag, and he clearly decided that he did not wish to become too closely associated with the fate of the bill. From December 1901 Bülow withdrew into the background, keeping out of the parliamentary debates and, notwithstanding Centre Party complaints, leaving the brunt of the work in the Reichstag committee to Posadowsky,[9] 'Count Bülow is keeping carefully behind the scenes so that the failure of the undertaking cannot appear as a fiasco attributable to him', Jagemann reported astutely in February 1902, and by July the press too was reporting that the Chancellor realised that the tariff could not pass the Reichstag.[10]

Throughout 1902 Bülow demonstrated how intent he was on adhering to his original premise that above all else domestic crises had to be avoided. By the summer he was clearly beginning to face up to the consequences of a probable parliamentary defeat over the tariff in the autumn and the likelihood that the Kaiser, despite his pro-industrial leanings, would espouse a shift to the right if the SPD and liberals brought down the bill.[11] The Chancellor can perhaps be accused of economic ignorance and political naivety, but at his summer retreat in Norderney in 1902 he began to think seriously about abandoning the Tariff Bill altogether. He suggested to Richthofen that he could allow it to fall because of some obstacle or other and then conclude new trade treaties as quickly as possible on the basis of the minimum grain duties of the new tariff and the old industrial duties. These could then be put before the existing Reichstag, which would swallow them, and they would avoid the next elections being dominated by the issue of higher bread prices.[12] The Centre leader, Spahn, visited Bülow in Norderney in September 1902 and 'had the impression that the Chancellor had got used to the idea of negotiating new trade treaties without the new tariff, [treaties] which would then naturally turn out correspondingly worse';[13] and in October 1902 in a letter to his Press Chief, Hammann, Bülow clearly indicated that he favoured a retreat – as in May 1901 – to a full-scale defeat.

Do you really believe that it is in my interest to bring about a speedy decision on the tariff question as the liberals wish? Is it not more advisable for me if the Tariff Bill comes to grief because of the left's obstruction or runs aground in some other way rather than is rejected by the Reichstag? The possible failure [*Nichtzustandekommen*] of the tariff must above all bear as little as possible the character of a political defeat à la canal question 1899 or School Bill 1892. The eventual success of the tariff is naturally preferable to all other outcomes if only because, with the mood HM is in after the foolish attitude of the liberal newspapers during recent months, any crisis this winter could have incalculable consequences.[14]

Bülow was particularly vulnerable to party pressure in the autumn of 1902, especially when his anxieties over the Tariff Bill coincided with the first major upset in his relations with Wilhelm II since 1897.[15] As late as 23 November 1902 he was informed after a meeting of Reichstag deputies that the prospects for the acceptance of the tariff were virtually nil because the Conservatives 'had declared they saw no occasion to abandon their demands; at the final reckoning Count Bülow would nevertheless give in'.[16] In the event, of course, the Chancellor's advisers persuaded him to remain firm, and he was able to reap all the rewards of success as the architect of the new Tariff Law.[17] Nevertheless, his oscillations are both characteristic and revealing. Bülow would have preferred to abandon the bill, with all the economic and political consequences, rather than be saddled with a Reichstag defeat.

With the exception of the Tariff Law, the legislation passed between 1901 and 1905 was relatively uncontroversial, and under Bülow's leadership the German executive seemed to want to pursue a policy of deliberate stagnation. There was very little legislative innovation during these years. Even the government's much-lauded social policy initiatives dried up after 1903, although the Centre Party was able to secure a widows' and orphans' insurance scheme in 1902 in exchange for its support of the tariff.[18] A Canal Bill was successfully steered through the Prussian Landtag in 1904, but the main obstacle to the bills of 1899 and 1901, the connecting strip between Hanover and the Elbe, was silently dropped by the government and the significance of the bill was thus considerably diminished.[19]

Ironically the government measures which aroused the most political controversy between 1903 and 1906 were the concessions made to the Reichstag parties to ensure the safe passage of major legislation such as the trade treaties and the financial reforms. The Chancellor had no organic relationship with the Reichstag and had to find acceptable majorities as best he could. Especially after the Reichstag elections of 1899, it was a political impossibility to secure a parliamentary majority without the support of the pivotal Catholic Centre Party. Bülow's efforts to woo and placate the Centre Party met with growing criticism from those who resented its 'domination' of domestic policy and the Chancellor's apparent compliance with its wishes. Bülow, indeed, became identified with a pro-Centre course, and his enemies regarded this *'do ut des* strategy' as the most pernicious feature of his 'system'.[20]

The Chancellor came to be attacked not only for making concessions to the Reichstag, and the Centre in particular, but also for the manner in which he made them and his sense of timing. In early January 1903 he promised the Reichstag a Polling Booth Law to make voting at Reichstag elections more secret, a measure which had the support of all the political parties except the Conservatives and which he hoped would ensure Centre approval of the Navy Budget and the building of a railway in German East Africa.[21] Bülow believed it was a requirement of a 'realistic policy . . . to comply with the repeated demand of the great majority of the Reichstag' which included the Centre,[22] and he had been told by the Centre Party deputy, Müller-Fulda, that if the Polling Booth Law were accepted by the government, the railway (in which the Kaiser was personally interested) would be approved. However, after his Reichstag statement Spahn told him that the railway could not possibly be approved because of the financial situation.[23] The Chancellor thus exposed himself to criticism for failing to use a concession at an appropriate time and achieving nothing in return. Moreover, his action surprised and displeased Bundesrat circles, for he had made his legislative promise before the Bundesrat had had time to adopt a position, thereby exerting pressure on the federal states.[24]

This incident served as a prelude to the far more serious controversy over the repeal of Paragraph 2 of the Jesuit Law, which arguably caused the biggest public and parliamentary outcry in the years following the conclusion of the tariff issue. Even before he became Chancellor Bülow had held out to the Centre the prospect of some kind of modification to this last major relic of the *Kulturkampf,* and during the tariff negotiations he made repeated promises to Centre leaders that Paragraph 2, which forbade the entry of the Jesuits into Germany, would be repealed.[25] The fulfilment of this promise became especially urgent after December 1902 and on 3 February 1903, without consulting the Prussian Ministry of State or the Bundesrat, the Chancellor declared in the Reichstag that in so far as he had an influence on the Prussian votes in the Bundesrat, he would use it in favour of the repeal of Paragraph 2.[26] Although Bülow secured the agreement of the Prussian Ministry to the repeal eight days later,[27] his hopes that the Bundesrat would be equally compliant were disappointed. The majority of the smaller German states resented a procedure which left them with scarcely the rights of an Upper Chamber. Bülow's behaviour broke with the tradition that the Bundesrat always presented a united front to the Reichstag. It also meant that the Bundesrat only found out what bills it would have to consider or what position Prussia would adopt on certain issues through declarations made by its President in plenary sittings of the Reichstag. Moreover, the smaller states had grave misgivings about the effect of an increasing number of concessions on the covetousness of the political parties.[28] Consequently the Bundesrat vote on the repeal had to be repeatedly postponed since, with only the Prussian and Bavarian votes in favour, a majority for the repeal was by no means assured.[29] Only thirteen months after his original Reichstag declaration was Bülow finally successful in persuading Baden also to support the repeal, and the reform was carried by 29 votes to 25 with 4 abstentions on 8 March 1904.[30]

By this time any political gains Bülow had hoped to make with the concession were largely lost, and the results were decidedly counterproductive. The middle and small German states had effectively registered a protest over Bülow's style of rule in general, for their negative stance was motivated as much by a desire 'to teach the Reich Chancellor a lesson, [namely] that he has to confer with them before he delivers declarations to the Reichstag' as by fundamental objections to the repeal itself.[31] Bülow's policy of concessions to the Centre Party met with growing incomprehension on the part of the federal states, and no one in the Bundesrat seemed to know why the repeal had been promised.[32] Even a Prussian Minister was reported to have said that they could have ruled for ten years with the concessions that were now being given away at one swoop.[33] Moreover, the Centre Party, frustrated by the delay, began to be sceptical about the Chancellor's sincerity and adopted a more coercive approach, for example rejecting minor military and naval demands in the Reichstag budget committee in March and April 1903, which provided fuel to Bülow's opponents and undermined his case.[34] Finally, the news of the repeal in 1904 caused a sensation and even the liberal parties, which had previously supported the repeal of the entire Jesuit Law, went into opposition over the concession to the Centre.[35] 'Absolutely confounded' by the outcry, Bülow was attacked in both the Reichstag and the Prussian Landtag and found himself uncomfortably isolated when even moderate Conservatives expressed their dissatisfaction with his system of government and his 'weak' policy.[36] In April 1904 the entire Reichstag with the exception of the Centre adopted a resolution that the Bundesrat should keep only to decisions of the Reichstag of that session and that it should not adhere to decisions taken during earlier legislative periods, as was the case with the repeal of Paragraph 2. The resolution signified a mild vote of no confidence in the Chancellor, and the new hostility was also evident in subsequent debates.[37]

Thus Bülow increasingly came to be seen and criticised as a 'Centre Party Chancellor' before 1906, especially in the Conservative camp and on the parliamentary left. But for all the problems inherent in his conciliation of the Centre, it should not be overlooked that his Reichstag policy generally worked well for him between 1901 and 1905. Temporarily unsettled by the clamour surrounding the repeal of Paragraph 2, the Chancellor was not deterred from seeking to conciliate the Centre, and in the twelve months after April 1904 (when the financial reform, trade treaties, Army Bill and Canal Bill were passed) his relations with the parliaments were ostensibly very successful. Bülow developed a close political relationship with Spahn, and the Reich leadership discussed its legislative plans at an early stage with Centre leaders who, despite some misgivings, were in the main amicable and cooperative. Nor was Bülow put off from making major concessions. Having frequently expressed his willingness to grant salaries to Reichstag members, despite the Kaiser's well-known opposition, he continued to negotiate with party leaders on this question and was to achieve the concession by 1906 in return for Centre cooperation over the 'big' financial reform and the Navy Bill.[38]

The Centre Party therefore seemed to be a fundamental and integral element in the Bülow system before 1906; nevertheless the harmony between Chancellor and Centre during these years has been grossly exaggerated. Bülow's relationship with the pivotal Reichstag party was never as smooth as his critics and opponents imputed, and consequently his break with the Centre in 1906 was never so sudden or so dramatic as might be assumed. Indeed, the parliamentary dimension to the crisis of 1905–6 is visible well in advance. As one recent study has effectively shown, the internal pressures within the Centre Party made it very difficult for the Reichstag *Fraktion* to cooperate too closely with the Reich leadership after December 1902 or to become simply a 'party of order' in alliance with the Conservatives and National Liberals.[39] The 'bourgeois' leadership of the Centre was forced to take heed of the demands of populist and working-class elements among its voters if it did not wish to witness mass defections from its ranks; and after the elections of 1903 representation of the so-called 'democratic' wing of the Centre was considerably strengthened, which inevitably forced the party to adopt a more radical stance on such issues as suffrage reform in the federal states, tax questions, *Weltpolitik* and the cost of the naval programme, and colonial maladministration.

Moreover, after the death of Lieber in 1902, the Centre Party leadership became collective, and the difficulties this posed for the Reich leadership have already been indicated with respect to the presumed fruits of the Polling Booth Law.[40] While it was relatively easy for Bülow and Posadowsky to do business with 'bourgeois' or aristocratic leaders such as Peter Spahn, Georg von Hertling, Franz von Ballestrem and Cardinal Kopp, whose outlook was basically conservative and pro-government, their views were not nearly so in tune with those of the more radical leaders such as Adolf Gröber, Georg Heim and even Karl Bachem, the last of whom as early as August 1901 attached 'no value at all any more to the favour of the government in Prussia and the Reich' and told Richard Müller-Fulda, 'We have cracked only a few nuts with this system. We will get further if our Centre policy is completely independent.'[41] After 1903, when Erzberger won a seat in the Reichstag and quickly rose to prominence by exploiting his 'democratic' support, the Reich leadership found it had a new, exceptionally gifted and potentially formidable critic among Centre ranks. Erzberger was elected at the age of twenty-nine to the Reichstag budget committee in 1904 and Spahn's prestige began noticeably to decline.[42]

There were thus always elements in the higher echelons of the Centre Party which were less sympathetic to a pro-government course and critical of aspects of government policy. In May 1902 Bülow and Posadowsky were 'very taken aback' when Bachem pointed out to them that the new Polish Bill in Prussia came at a very inopportune time if Centre support was expected for the tariff.[43] In 1903 and 1904 the Centre made difficulties for the Reich leadership over budgetary matters. The Centre's criticisms of the Navy Budget in 1904 were particularly unwelcome to the Chancellor, coming just after the repeal of Paragraph 2, and Bülow had to write to Cardinal Kopp that it was of decisive importance for the future that the Centre

does not adopt too critical and cavilling a standpoint when dealing with questions of defence. If the position of the party on Army and Navy questions is decisive for the attitude of HM, the Kaiser, so the mood of the federal princes depends on the Centre's offering its hand in an understanding on the reorganisation of the Reich finances, which is frankly a question of life and death for the individual states. The

Centre does not need for this reason to be a government party, but it must assume to a higher degree than hitherto the character of a party from which [the] Kaiser and federal states increasingly gain the conviction that the fundamental questions, which have to be solved in the interests of the well-being of the Reich, will be solved in a satisfactory way with its sympathetic cooperation.[44]

In 1905, when the Centre again declared its opposition to the new military estimates, the Chancellor was forced to make a personal appeal to Spahn. 'My situation is a very difficult and serious one', he wrote on 11 March. 'You know, my dear Herr Spahn, from my open explanations what little cause for optimism our present foreign situation affords.' In the case of a Reichstag rejection, he would have to 'draw the consequences' and dissolve the Reichstag. Proposing a compromise, the Chancellor added, 'you can see from this, dear Herr Spahn, how I am prepared to conciliate you and your party as far as is at all possible in the interests of the country and without seriously shattering my position.'[45]

Bülow's appeal to the Centre in 1905 was ultimately successful, but the relatively minor aggravations caused by the Centre's more radical attitude to certain issues assumed growing political significance. The Chancellor's conciliation of the Centre and his apparently 'weak' policy attracted criticism not only from the federal states and the other political parties but also among the Protestant entourage at the Kaiser's Court; and although Bülow was still in a sufficiently strong position to shield the monarch from adverse comments on his policy,[46] the scope for intrigues against the favourite Chancellor widened. As early as 1902 Jagemann reported that the Kaiser could not have been aware of the real nature of the parliamentary constellation, or he would never have agreed to 'such useless sacrifices' as the concessions which finally secured the tariff.[47] In 1903 Lerchenfeld commented on the growing Protestant opposition to Bülow's Reichstag policy.[48] The repeal of Paragraph 2 created, in Holstein's words, 'masses of enemies' for the government,[49] and Bülow recognised in April 1904 that there were intrigues being hatched against him. Since Wilhelm II's attitude towards him could suddenly change, he told Hertling, it was vital that the Centre proved conciliatory and ensured that the Kaiser had no real grounds for complaint.[50] By 1905 former supporters of Bülow, such as Monts, now German ambassador in Rome, were disillusioned with the Chancellor's approach and committed opponents of his friendly policy towards the Catholic Church.[51] Such people were only looking for the opportunity to make their views known to the Kaiser and possibly influence him against Bülow; and at the Kaiser's Court it was said that a barrier was being erected between the monarch and Catholic opinion which was becoming increasingly difficult to penetrate.[52]

Pressure on the Chancellor to defend his political course increased dramatically after the Reichstag elections of 1903, which resulted in the return of

twenty-five more socialist deputies to the parliament.[53] Having been told by
Spahn that the SPD would gain no more than ten seats, Bülow had been
characteristically complacent about the possible outcome before the
elections,[54] but from the summer of 1903 he was constantly worried about
the effects of the growth of the SPD, the general dissatisfaction which
prevailed in Conservative circles in the wake of the elections, and the possible
repercussions on the mood of the Kaiser. Immediately after the results
became known, the monarch reiterated his confidence in the Chancellor,
merely stating that 'things must go on all the same [*es müsse auch so
weitergehen*] and Count Bülow will certainly understand how to cope with
the parties'.[55] But it was impossible for the Kaiser to remain oblivious to
Conservative sentiment for long, and Varnbüler, returning from a trip to
Russia which had perhaps made him excessively pessimistic, wrote a devas-
tating account of the post-election mood and conditions in Germany in 1903.
Conservatives, he reported, directed their rancour first and foremost against
Bülow, whom they accused of being a

smooth diplomat, pussyfooter [*Leisetreter*], master in the art of meaningless phrases,
the man of the middle course and of compromises, of deviation and procrastination
[*Durchlavierens und Hinziehens*], of the skilful little coup and dazzling momentary
successes, the Mecklenburger without heart and understanding for the true nature
of Old Prussia.

The view that force of arms would soon be the only way out was widespread
among agrarian landowners, throughout the Prussian bureaucracy and in the
Army.[56]

 This kind of sentiment was highly dangerous to the Chancellor for, as
Tschirschky had recognised in January 1903, if Wilhelm II also became
convinced that the SPD had to be opposed by force, he would have to find
a new Chancellor.[57] Bülow was, moreover, soon confronted with undeniable
evidence of the Kaiser's growing discontent in July 1903 as Eulenburg,
Eisendecher and Tschirschky all found sailing with the monarch on his North
Sea cruise extremely strenuous.[58] Eulenburg even questioned Wilhelm's
sanity, and in August 1903 witnessed the Kaiser directly criticising the
Chancellor's judgement of parliamentary affairs. Bülow, Wilhelm maintained, had since admitted to him that he had erred in thinking that after the
introduction of a Polling Booth Law voters would have no fear of compulsion and fewer would vote for the SPD. It was now quite clear to him,
Wilhelm, that things could not go on any longer without shooting. Regardless of what Bülow or anyone else said, the gang had to be eradicated root
and branch.[59]

 Bülow was aware of the threat, which persisted into the autumn of 1903.
In September he told Hammann that at a recent meeting the Kaiser had
spoken about the need for a 'sharp crack-down' on Social Democracy, which

was undermining the monarchy and the Army, and that the question whether, when and how to proceed against the socialists ruled the situation behind the scenes. The Chancellor appealed to Hammann to rally press support for a moderate policy.

> If I am against an inopportune action in this direction this is truly not because I consider such an action to be useless, or even particularly difficult. But it is because I believe that the German body politic [*Volkskörper*] is strong and healthy enough, given time, to eject the Social Democratic poison, in so far as it is poison, for itself. It is because I think that such a course corresponds better to the interest of the German people, which is alone decisive for me, than untimely and in any case premature operations. But I must be better supported than hitherto by the reasonable press.[60]

In the same month Bülow confirmed to Spahn that the Kaiser 'had indeed been very alarmed over the increase in the Social Democratic deputies in the Reichstag', and he voiced his concern about the difficulties he would face as Chancellor with Wilhelm II if an SPD deputy were elected Vice-President of the Reichstag.[61] But, while recognising that his performance in the Reichstag during the 1903–4 session would have to take account of the Kaiser's fears about the growth in the SPD,[62] Bülow was also acutely aware that he could not fight on two fronts at the same time.[63] Bismarck had had to make peace with Rome before waging war on Social Democracy, and if the pressures mounted for a more energetic campaign to curb socialist pretensions, this only strengthened the Chancellor in his conviction that it was impossible to rule without the Centre Party and that concessions would have to be granted to ensure its docility.

Thus from 1903 Bülow was more concerned about pressure from above to deal energetically with the socialist threat than he was about criticisms of his pro-Centre parliamentary orientation or the possible danger of a renewed *Kulturkampf*. Throughout 1904 Wilhelm II's anxiety about anarchists and assassins intensified his nervousness about Social Democracy, and in November 1904 he was further agitated by socialist gains in the Italian elections.[64] While Bülow personally continued to have a far more complacent view of the nature and effects of socialist militancy, the Kaiser seemed to be moving in the opposite direction and once again toying with the idea of political repression.

According to Zedlitz, by the end of 1904 Wilhelm had developed the idea of an anti-socialist parliamentary combination which would also permit the government to act independently of the Centre.[65] While this may well have been a recurring notion of the Kaiser's,[66] there is no evidence to suggest that Bülow was thinking along these lines before 1906. Bülow knew that the Kaiser resented the Centre's influence on him,[67] but given the uncompromising opposition of the SPD, it is clear that he saw no alternative policy to the one he was pursuing. A resurrection of the old *Kartell* was patently unrealistic when the National Liberal Party had dwindled to barely half its 1887 strength; and with the left liberals divided into three splinter parties which together commanded only thirty-six seats in the Reichstag, Bülow had no thoughts of a new kind of parliamentary grouping before the crisis of 1906. In January 1904 Bülow told Tirpitz that he did not believe in the possibility of a coalition of the 'bourgeois' parties and that the German people would be politically too immature for such a course for a century.[68] Six months later he conclusively demonstrated his contempt for the left liberals when he remarked that they 'admittedly have many newspapers but have scarcely ten men behind them in the Reichstag; thus [they] are *de facto* completely insignificant or can only make mischief but not achieve anything constructive [*kein Vorspann leisten können*]'.[69]

For all these reasons Bülow adhered to a pro-Centre course and saw no need to steer into unknown waters. He was sensitive to the heightening of confessional tempers and criticisms of his policy, and wary of influences on the Kaiser. But as long as his position with the Kaiser remained secure, the difficulties inherent in his Reichstag policy could be dismissed as a minor, if unpleasant irritation. Pressure may have increased on the Chancellor to pander less to the will of the Centre, especially after the trade treaties were concluded in February 1905. But Bülow's parliamentary approach appeared to have been effective, and the humiliating government defeats of the 1890s had been avoided. A semblance of stability was achieved and even Bülow's critics recognised that his system had its compensations and that a change of Chancellor promised little.[70]

However, despite the fact that he rapidly developed a reputation as 'a more parliamentary Minister' than any of his predecessors as Chancellor,[71] Bülow did not develop a genuine parliamentary strategy between 1900 and 1905 or establish a stable coalition of support in the Reichstag. While this failure must in part be attributed to the volatility of the political parties,[72] it also reflected a fundamental lack of vision and political direction on the part of the Chancellor. As will be examined in the rest of this chapter, Bülow's position was exceptionally strong before 1905. He controlled the executive to an extent unmatched by any other Chancellor after Bismarck, and he successfully restored the prestige and public image of the Chancellorship. Yet once he had established his authority, he emphasised the preservation of stability (and, above all, his own position), having no real political programme and primarily desiring to avoid contentious legislation. At a time of manifest social polarisation, effective political leadership was lacking, for Bülow was uninterested in specific issues of domestic policy unless they threatened to trigger off a political crisis or adversely affect his personal position. Unshaken in his belief that 'The art of governing consists in making the necessary concessions at the right time',[73] the Chancellor soon became preoccupied with parliamentary tactics rather than with issues of substance, devoting an enormous amount of time to the preparation and rehearsal of his parliamentary speeches (which he invariably committed to memory),[74] and courting popularity with the political parties, not least by urging the bestowal of orders and decorations on parliamentarians 'as a method, not to be underestimated, of keeping the gentlemen in a good mood'.[75] 'A Minister who regarded himself as the mediator between Crown and parliamentary majority could offer little more', Jagemann observed in 1903, dismayed at the number of concessions Bülow was granting to the Reichstag and the extent to which he allowed the parties to seize the initiative.[76] Bülow's political approach naturally tended towards compromise and flexibility, but for his critics this amounted to little more than 'trimming and hedging [*Lavieren und Paktieren*]'.[77] The bankruptcy of this approach was revealed in the crisis of 1905–6.

Kaiser and Chancellor

During the first five years of his Chancellorship, Bülow's position remained secure because he was able to retain the full confidence and trust of Wilhelm II. Succeeding where Bismarck, Caprivi and Hohenlohe had all ultimately failed, Bülow established a close, personal relationship with the monarch, the political significance of which can scarcely be exaggerated. It was the Kaiser's benevolent attitude to his new Chancellor from October 1900 which enabled Bülow to embark on a far more conciliatory policy towards the German Reichstag than would otherwise have been possible; and, as we shall see, it was by virtue of Wilhelm's confidence in him that Bülow succeeded in eliminating the main sources of political opposition from the Prussian Ministry of State and reasserted the authority of the Reich Chancellor within the executive. In March 1903 Lerchenfeld reported that with rare skill Bülow had 'created for himself a position and gained an influence with the Kaiser which no one else rivals at the moment'.[78] Despite occasional frictions between Wilhelm and Bülow, the security of the Chancellor's position was repeatedly confirmed.[79]

In establishing a harmonious working relationship with the Kaiser, Bülow built on the foundations he had laid as State Secretary of the Foreign Office. His appointment in 1900 marked no fundamental change in his relations with Wilhelm, and Wilhelm continued to consult personally with Bülow as frequently as his busy schedule would permit. According to the diaries kept by his adjutants, the Kaiser saw Bülow on average about seventy days a year, a figure which may surprise those who had been led by the evidence of contemporary accounts to believe that the two men saw each other daily,[80] but a figure which is realistic given Wilhelm's other interests and commitments. Bülow saw more of the Kaiser in the first three months of the year than in the remaining nine months. Only in 1909 do the diaries indicate a sharp decline in the number of Wilhelm's informal visits to the Reich Chancellery, a decline which must have been as disruptive of the Kaiser's routine as it was of Bülow's. In eleven years the only evidence of change had been the increasing frequency with which Wilhelm had taken the motor car.[81]

The relationship between Wilhelm and Bülow was essentially political, but it also had a personal dimension. Although Wilhelm regularly visited Bülow between 9.0 a.m. and 10.0 a.m. at the Chancellery to discuss the burning political questions of the day, the two men frequently lunched and dined together, and the Kaiser was not an infrequent guest at the Bülows' *soirées*. Socially Bülow and Wilhelm conversed on a wide range of topics and even at Liebenberg, within the circle of the Kaiser's most intimate friends, Varnbüler maintained that Bülow was accepted and had his given place.[82] Valentini, later the Civil Cabinet Chief, recalled how, on the Kaiser's visit to Rome in the spring of 1903, Bülow 'positively bubbled over with *bon mots* and anecdotes, displayed an astonishing knowledge of history, especially of Italian conditions, delighted [everyone] with his descriptions [*Schilderung*] of the Roman personalities at the Quirinal and in the Vatican and in this way bore the main burden [*Hauptkosten*] of conversation'. Valentini 'completely understood the great influence which this exceptional man exerted over the Kaiser'.[83]

However, Bülow's ability to secure for himself a virtually unassailable position with Wilhelm II between 1900 and 1905 was not primarily attributable to his conversational talents. Bülow's skill in managing people was well known and his letters to Wilhelm reveal both the bounds of his Byzantine sycophancy and an understanding of Wilhelm's character. Bülow tailored the content, language and style of his letters to suit the Kaiser's temperament. As an ambitious diplomat, he had sought to attract the monarch's attention by including a liberal quantity of gossip in his political reports;[84] now, as Chancellor, he tried to make his letters to Wilhelm anecdotal and amusing, sometimes even including verses.[85] Bülow expounded policy, but he always kept his expositions concise and interesting and sought to convey the impression that he was following the Kaiser's lead. Quick to inform the Kaiser that he had carried out his orders immediately,[86] Bülow bolstered the monarch's belief in his own chosen policy, asked him questions and deferred to his judgement.[87] Moreover, successes had to be attributed to the Kaiser's political acumen. The Germans could thank the Kaiser, Bülow wrote in 1904, that the danger of a Franco-Russian attack had now receded because of the monarch's 'consistently loyal, friendly and correct attitude towards the Tsar of Russia'.[88]

Bülow shared with Wilhelm an essentially similar view of the Prussian state. In 1903 he was able to endorse fully the monarch's interpretation of why the Rothschilds were disgruntled about their level of acceptance in Berlin society.

The Rothschilds have in Vienna (despite high nobility and clergy), in Paris (despite Dreyfus) and especially in London, a social position which cannot be conceded to them [in Germany] given the structure of our state, which is independent of the plutocracy and based on the Army and bureaucracy, that is, on the concept of honour.[89]

However, the contrived nature of many of the opinions he expressed to Wilhelm is obvious, and the Chancellor displayed a remarkable ability to accommodate and pander to the monarch's prejudices and idiosyncrasies. Bülow adopted a brusque, dismissive tone and a coarseness of language in his allusions to the Reichstag which was quite at variance with the manifest consideration he otherwise displayed. In 1903, amidst criticisms of his failure to provide an election slogan, he wrote to the Kaiser:

Nothing has annoyed the parties more than that the government did not do them the favour of sitting as the eagle on the crows' hut [*Krähenhütte*] in order to let itself be sh- on the head in this position by the party ravens [*Fraktionsraben*]. The same people who raised a hullabaloo when Your Majesty gave a signal on truly vital, national matters [*in wirklichen nationalen Lebensfragen ein Fanal aufsteckten*] now yammered that there was no slogan 'from above'. It is the old experience that the people who are inclined to overestimate themselves are never more humiliated than when you don't take any notice of them.[90]

A similar calculation is evident in Bülow's references to women. In general he both praised the Kaiser's ability to see through women and confirmed him in his suspicion of them.[91] But he also reinforced Wilhelm's confidence in his personal powers of attraction and his capacity to charm members of the opposite sex. Although it is well known that Queen Alexandra disliked the Kaiser intensely,[92] Bülow expressed his confidence in March 1903 that in Copenhagen Wilhelm would be able to captivate both the English Queen and her sister, the Tsar's mother, and transform them from longstanding opponents of German policy into friends of the Reich.[93]

Whenever possible, Bülow sprinkled his letters to the Kaiser with praise and flattery. The Kaiser's telegram to the Tsar was 'splendid', his words to the Russian ambassador 'excellent', his remarks in his last letter 'completely accurate', his political intentions 'quite right'.[94] The Chancellor lauded Wilhelm's personal qualities and played on his desire for greatness. 'The handling of the English is infinitely [*unendlich*] arduous, infinitely difficult, requires an infinite amount of patience and skill', he wrote in 1900.

But just as the Hohenzollern eagle [*Aar*] wiped the two-headed Austrian eagle [*Adler*] off the field and clipped the wings of the Gallic cock, so with God's help and

Your Majesty's strength and wisdom, it will also deal [*fertig werden*] with the English leopard. Its wings are growing [*Seine Fittiche wachsen*].[95]

Bülow also took pains to demonstrate his attentiveness and consideration. His thoughts always accompanied Wilhelm, he sympathised with imperial frustrations and irritations and responded to imperial anecdotes. In April 1902, while in Venice, Bülow was 'terribly amused' to read the Kaiser's description of how he got the unprepared Szögyényi out of bed one morning; and his only regret was to hear that the weather in Berlin was so bad when he was egotistically enjoying the sun.[96] In June 1903 he sent the Kaiser a book, Adolf Kussmaul's ('Youthful Memoirs of an Old Physician') *Jugenderinnerungen eines alten Arztes*, which he thought the monarch might find interesting and suitable for the North Sea cruise.[97]

Bülow's behaviour and approach towards Wilhelm was that of the courtier *par excellence*, the mentality of whom has been brilliantly exposed by Norbert Elias in his study of Court society under Louis XIV.[98] As Elias confirms, 'To lead one's higher-ranking interlocutor almost imperceptibly where one wishes is the prime requirement of this courtly manner of dealing with people', and Bülow's skill in the art of diplomacy, his mastery of the tactics of conversation and his concern for apparent 'externals' – the form of behaviour, the primacy of the 'how' over the 'what' in any procedure, the overriding importance of the relationship and a person's power and status – all attest to this heritage.[99] In 1901 Bülow wrote to the Kaiser responding to the latter's obvious concern about the prevalent mood of anglophobia in Germany, and the passage is worth quoting at some length since it illustrates Bülow's multi-layered manipulation of the monarch.

Only a German can indeed understand the deeper sources of German anglophobia, and never were these better characterised than by Your Majesty a year ago to Chamberlain and Balfour. I have spoken with the Minister of Interior and with the Police President about the journalistic excesses of the present anglophobia and think that that will be of use. An article in the *Reichsanzeiger* would only please the Fronde, which could draw from it new material for polemics. The agitation will run aground on its own inner hollowness when the English treat us with more consideration, namely in African affairs, and the German people become more and more convinced that their Kaiser is led merely by the true, real German interests without predilection or aversion to this or that neighbour, which are all indeed only chess pieces in Your Majesty's political game.[100]

Here one sees yet again Bülow's flattery of the Kaiser's understanding of political issues and how he helped foster Wilhelm's delusions of grandeur and omnipotence by encouraging an essentially one-dimensional view of international relations. At the same time Bülow sought to convey an impression of action on a matter of importance to Wilhelm while he was actually complacent about the issue and preferred to do nothing, relying on the agitation burning itself out. Finally there is a didactic hint in the passage, the suggestion that Germany did have some grounds for anti-English feeling and that the monarch might do well not to display any special preference for England. All this was of course carefully couched in terms that would be acceptable to Wilhelm and in no way affront his self-esteem. At no time did Bülow press the argument or express his view categorically. Rather, his approach echoed that of an earlier courtier, Saint-Simon, who, in conversation with the Dauphin, sought 'to impregnate him gently and thoroughly with my feelings and views on all these matters' while ensuring that the French Crown Prince remained convinced that he had arrived at such views himself.[101]

Bülow's flattery of the Kaiser was blatantly insincere. At a time when Wilhelm's speech-making was subject to increasing criticism, the Chancellor admired the power of Wilhelm's oratory[102] and told him that he possessed the rare gift of always saying the right thing. 'I was really moved by what Your Majesty said about your All-Highest wish if possible to place the right people in the right positions', he wrote in August 1902. 'I tell myself often how far my ability to serve Your Majesty falls short of my desires [Wollen]. But such words repeatedly act as a spur.'[103] His hypocrisy was even more evident in April 1902, when Wilhelm informed Bülow of a proposal he had made to the Austrian Kaiser, Franz Joseph. Bülow responded with an effusive outburst:

This idea is really Ariadne's thread, which can lead us out of an apparently endless labyrinth. May God grant that the old Kaiser [Franz Joseph] possesses sufficient insight – and independence – to seize upon this redeeming idea. At the same time this idea, just like Prince Heinrich's visit to America, is so astonishingly simple that one wonders why others have not hit upon it. But not everyone is a Columbus.[104]

Bülow had not even approved of Prince Heinrich's visit to America, feeling that the christening of a sports yacht was not sufficient cause for such a demonstration.[105] The Chancellor continued to pander to Wilhelm's worst qualities while becoming increasingly critical of him behind his back. Bülow, who insisted to Wilhelm that he had 'nothing else to wish for on this earth but that God may grant me the privilege of serving my dear Master and Kaiser until my last breath',[106] complained to Tirpitz in January 1905 of Wilhelm's 'boundless vanity', his immaturity and his 'abnormal lack of logic'. 'He, the Reich Chancellor, could no longer listen to the incessant boasting.'[107]

Bülow clearly did not have the kind of relationship with Wilhelm that would have enabled him to be very independent when faced with the imperial will. Waldersee maintained that on several occasions Bülow had stated that he could do nothing about a particular measure since it emanated from the Kaiser,[108] and it is highly unlikely that the Chancellor came into conflict with the monarch as frequently during the first five years of his Chancellorship as his memoir account suggests.[109] Bülow failed to censure the Kaiser for inadvisable and impulsive actions, and all too often acquiesced. He bowed to imperial pressure to counteract the 'Polish danger' (the agitation of the Poles in the Prussian provinces) through legislation in the Prussian Landtag in 1902, even though the new Polish Bill came at a very inopportune time when Centre support was expected for the tariff in the Reichstag;[110] and generally Wilhelm's growing hostility to Catholic, Polish and agrarian pretensions complicated Bülow's relations with the political parties.[111] In his memoirs Bülow claimed that he had a serious argument with Wilhelm II in 1902 over his Swinemünde telegram to the Prince-Regent of Bavaria,[112] but the indications are that he vented his anger on his subordinates in the Foreign Office for publishing the telegram (on Wilhelm's instructions) and merely registered his displeasure with the Kaiser by refusing two social invitations.[113] In January 1903 he told Spahn that nothing could be done about Reichstag salaries because of the Kaiser's opposition. 'He always avoids the issue [*er biegt ja immer aus*] as soon as he sees that the Kaiser dislikes the subject of the audience', Bachem concluded.[114]

Nevertheless, it would probably be wrong to conclude (as many did) from his obvious sycophancy and Byzantinism that Bülow always submitted to the Kaiser's wishes and simply executed the monarch's decisions.[115] Bülow himself frequently countered the view that Wilhelm could not be contradicted or insisted obstinately on his own will. He told Varnbüler in 1901 that Wilhelm only tolerated no contradiction when he suspected systematic opposition or personal prejudice. The monarch was always open to objective argument and could be induced to change his view without showing any sensitivity.[116] In 1903 Bülow told Szögyényi that he could contradict Wilhelm when they were alone, provided he formulated it carefully.[117]

Moreover, as we have seen, Bülow excelled in the tactics of the courtier and relied on more covert or subtle methods of getting his own way. Szögyényi claimed that Bülow neither brusquely opposed Wilhelm like Bismarck nor opposed him with passive, morose resistance, like Caprivi and Hohenlohe.

Rather, he knows how to say 'Yes' whenever possible to a suggestion of His Majesty's and then nevertheless achieves through gradual and cautious objections what he wants in most cases, while he leaves His Majesty with the conviction that he himself had not only the first word but also the last word on the matter.[118]

Szögyényi's assessment would harmonise with Holstein's view (in early 1902) that Bülow had on occasion dissuaded the Kaiser from doing something but never directly opposed him.[119] Bülow was in any case a man of conciliation, not confrontation, who relied on persuasion and skilfully chosen arguments to bring Wilhelm round to his opinions. In 1901 he was able to dissuade the Kaiser from making an unfortunate bureaucratic appointment by intimating that the unsuitable candidate had bad drinking habits;[120] and in 1904 he pressured Wilhelm into agreeing to the resignation of the Kaiserin's *Oberhofmeister*, Mirbach, not only by enumerating the political dangers to the Crown if he remained in office, but also by indicating to the monarch (through Lucanus) that all his favourite Ministers ('especially Hammerstein, Rheinbaben and Studt') agreed with the Chancellor on this issue.[121]

Without doubt, Bülow preferred not to have to resort to even the most mildly expressed opposition if at all possible. For, quite apart from the longterm implications of such tactics for the vitality of his 'system', there was always the chance that the Kaiser would not be receptive even to objective political arguments. After discussing the appointment of a new *Oberpräsident* in Silesia with the monarch in 1903, Bülow wrote to Holstein: 'The more decisively I stressed the objective reasons which, according to my dutiful conviction, spoke against Th[iele-Winckler], the more I had the impression that my resistance was being attributed to other considerations.'[122] On this particular occasion Bülow hoped that he would be able to find another candidate whom he could recommend to Wilhelm 'with a good conscience', and he was ultimately successful.[123] But personnel questions were always potentially contentious issues between Kaiser and Chancellor and issues over which, as we shall see, the Chancellor frequently backed down.[124]

Resignations and appointments were difficult for the Chancellor not only because they involved the Kaiser's special prerogative but also because decisions could generally not be long deferred. On other issues Bülow had more scope for manoeuvre and, although his system depended on his immediate submission if it came to a direct confrontation with the monarch, by adroit manipulation he was frequently able to achieve his aim. Bülow had a rich choice of weapons in his armoury. In the Kaiser's presence, the Chancellor could resort to evasive tactics or divert him from a difficult subject by recounting an entertaining anecdote; away from the Kaiser he could pursue delaying tactics or act without his foreknowledge. It was widely suspected that Bülow distorted events to the Kaiser and kept him misinformed about the real state of affairs.[125] After his very unpleasant reception in the Reichstag in December 1901, Bülow told the Kaiser that the sitting had taken the desired course and that the debate had been very calm and boring.[126]

If the Chancellor saw a potential problem looming, he was sometimes able to act in anticipation. In 1904 he effectively preempted the possibility of imperial intervention in the Russian trade treaty negotiations by explaining to the Kaiser that the Russian negotiator, Witte, though he longed to see Wilhelm, could only have the honour of meeting the German monarch as a 'reward' for the successful conclusion of the negotiations.[127] This kind of 'preventive' strategy was also followed by the Chancellor over a longer period, for example with respect to parliamentary affairs. Bülow actively encouraged the Kaiser to leave the management of parliamentary affairs to his Chancellor, and for all his violent utterances against the Reichstag, there was always a side of Wilhelm that was only too pleased to do so. To forestall imperial intervention in Reichstag affairs, Bülow whenever possible nurtured the monarch's belief that the parliaments should be left to their own devices and that they would eventually stew in their own juice. Thus in February 1903 Wilhelm told Szögyényi that he felt the granting of universal suffrage had been a serious mistake. But he went on:

He, Kaiser Wilhelm, had already seriously thought about how it would be possible to effect a change in this respect, but he had to admit that Count Bülow was perfectly right when he objected that an action to limit the suffrage must be initiated not from above but from below, of which there were already some signs at hand. Consequently he, Kaiser Wilhelm, had decided not to stir up this question.[128]

The limitations of this kind of approach have already been seen, and by 1905 the Kaiser was already beginning to voice with growing urgency his own ideas on how the government's parliamentary difficulties could best be solved.[129] But there is also no doubt that between 1900 and 1905 Wilhelm amply demonstrated his confidence in Bülow's conduct of affairs and acted with relative restraint. He agreed to abandon temporarily the Canal Bill in 1901 with the minimum of fuss;[130] he agreed to the parliamentary concessions, some of which he had sworn never to concede;[131] and, in general, he always applauded Bülow's methods – even categorically stating his approval of those of Bülow's speeches considered most injurious to the dignity of the Crown.[132]

The Kaiser's relative restraint is a major feature of German domestic politics during these years. Bülow viewed himself as a Chancellor who possessed Wilhelm II's confidence in high measure and thus had more opportunity to conduct German policy independently,[133] and the Kaiser himself displayed an unusual willingness to acquiesce in Bülow's *faits accomplis* between 1900 and 1905. He made no murmur of protest at the way Bülow handled the China debate in November 1900[134] and the Chancellor, if necessary, was prepared to act independently again. In 1904 the death of the Regent of Lippe renewed the contentious problem of the Lippe succession and a crisis threatened when Wilhelm II, without consulting Bülow, sent a sharp telegram to the late Regent's son, Leopold, claiming that he could not recognise his Regency as the legal situation was not clarified.[135] Bülow boldly seized the initiative and in turn failed to confer with the monarch before releasing a public letter explaining the Kaiser's action in a favourable way and indicating, in the Kaiser's name, that the troops should be sworn in to Leopold immediately. 'That will determine whether I am still Reich Chancellor or not in three days' time', Bülow told his friend, Franz Arenberg.[136] But the Kaiser completely endorsed the Chancellor's action, remarked grumpily that yet again one of his telegrams had been misunderstood, and Bülow remained in office.[137]

Bülow's *démarche* over the Lippe affair indicated how secure he felt in the Kaiser's favour and was not taken amiss by Wilhelm. It was this kind of incident which compared favourably with episodes during previous Chancellorships and, initially at least, the confidence displayed by the Kaiser in Bülow inspired others with renewed confidence in the system. Bülow was probably the only one of Wilhelm's Chancellors who felt that he could 'guarantee that HM will not take any unsuitable decisions' in a particular direction and who could state categorically to Holstein that 'in the present situation HM will not do anything without having consulted me beforehand'.[138] Those close to the Kaiser remained anxious about his autocratic leanings – his assertions that *he* made German foreign policy, that it was *his* right and duty to lead his people, that the Ministers were to carry out *his* orders only.[139] They still looked for symptoms of the monarch's psychological decline and considered that the Kaiser's psychic condition deteriorated rather than improved between 1900 and 1905.[140] Moreover, they all agreed that Bülow's approach reinforced dangerous illusions in Wilhelm and contributed to his enormous over-estimation of his own powers.[141] But even when these doubts did arise, the Bülow system seemed to have one immense advantage over all the previous regimes, namely the deep trust between Kaiser and Chancellor. In November 1901 the suspicion remained in the mind of Varnbüler that Wilhelm still might want to be his own Chancellor. But he was reassured by his observation that the Kaiser always remained in close contact with Bülow. And even if Wilhelm did initiate political moves, he informed the Chancellor immediately afterwards and left to Bülow their further implementation.[142] Bülow thus fulfilled his constitutional role of covering the monarch with his responsibility.

The Kaiser's willingness to confide in the Chancellor and his trust that Bülow was conducting affairs in his interest and according to his precepts between 1900 and 1905 constituted a new phenomenon in post-Bismarckian domestic politics, and one which reflects not only on the adroitness of the Chancellor but also on the personality of Wilhelm II. Bülow's approach to his relationship with the Kaiser was calculating, manipulative and insincere. But there is no doubt that, when looked at from the Kaiser's perspective, it was also an extremely satisfactory one. With a sycophantic and apparently servile Chancellor, Wilhelm was convinced that his personal will would prevail, and in a very real sense Bülow shielded the monarch from all the more onerous and exasperating tasks of government which had previously oppressed him. Many observers pointed out that one of the secrets of Bülow's success was that he never said anything unpleasant to the Kaiser but instead told him each morning that everything was going all right.[143] The Chancellor's (sometimes contrived) optimism and nonchalance, his calmness and complacency in the face of imperial outbursts (provided they were not directed against him), his willingness to subordinate his personal egoism and walk for two hours, 'his head sunk in thought', with an animated monarch who gesticulated wildly,[144] all this seems to have had a pacifying effect on the Kaiser, who consequently felt less compelled to act. On the Mediterranean cruise in March 1904 Valentini observed that the Kaiser closed his eyes to Germany's gloomy domestic situation and left it all to 'his Bülow' to sort out;[145] and in July 1901 Wilhelm even told Eulenburg that he let Bülow rule. 'Since I have him, I can sleep peacefully. I leave things to him and know that everything is all right.'[146]

Wilhelm's words to Eulenburg may well have contained an element of self-deception, but they nevertheless indicate the immense relief which he felt with Bülow as Chancellor. The Kaiser had found a Chancellor who was attentive and responsive, one who was prepared to listen and wanted to understand;[147] and in a peculiar way the Kaiser's growing dependence on his Chancellor became apparent. 'He has a mixture of respect tempered with fear with regard to yourself, for he occasionally has a dim and sometimes a clear feeling that without you, he cannot get any further', Eulenburg told Bülow in 1903.[148] Wilhelm needed and wanted to believe in Bülow, as a political adviser and as a friend. The extent of the Chancellor's influence over the monarch, the Kaiser's relative acquiescence in Bülow's conduct of affairs and, finally, the nature of his disillusionment with his Chancellor in later years[149] can only be appreciated if it is recognised that Wilhelm had as little interest in upsetting their relationship as did his ambitious Chancellor.

Bülow's methods with the Kaiser were thus successful between 1900 and 1905 not least because Wilhelm, too, wanted to ensure the preservation of their intimacy. There was no shortage of possible sources of tension between Kaiser and Chancellor during these years, but both men sought to avoid a confrontation. In the summer of 1901 there were rumours of 'serious differences' between Kaiser and Chancellor,[150] and it was said that Bülow's successors were already at the door.[151] The tension may have been connected with Bülow's speech at the unveiling of the Bismarck memorial[152] or possibly with the appointment of Köller as State Secretary to Alsace-Lorraine (though Bülow's acquiescence in this appointment is more probably a reflection of his insecurity).[153] There was also press discussion of foreign policy differences, and in June 1901 Bülow told Hammann 'to avoid carefully anything which could encourage the (absurd or malicious) comment that I am more anglophile or anti-Boer than HM or even in contrast to HM am an opponent of good relations with Russia'.[154] However, the most likely explanation is that Bülow's compromise Tariff Bill was more agrarian than Wilhelm would have liked,[155] and Wilhelm came to realise that Bülow was steering a rather independent course. Albert Ballin remarked that Wilhelm was too intelligent not to realise that Bülow always agreed with him to his face, but then managed behind his back to achieve *his* way, either by acting through the parties or by other methods. 'The Kaiser was firmly determined to uphold the commercial treaties. The moment these were threatened, Bülow would fall'.[156]

Similar frictions were evident between Kaiser and Chancellor in 1902 over Anglo-German relations, in 1903 over the Social Democratic gains in the Reichstag and in 1904 over foreign policy differences. From 1904 with the outbreak of the Russo-Japanese war and the Herero rebellion in South-West Africa — not to mention the negotiations for an Anglo-French entente — the Kaiser displayed a new interest in foreign affairs[157] and was more likely to interfere with the Chancellor's policy. Bülow, who had officially denied the likelihood of a war in the Far East while secretly doing everything he could to precipitate one,[158] at the end of 1903 had been 'in despair that His Majesty sees the situation in East Asia so blackly and says so'.[159] When the hostilities broke out, he had to justify his apparently erroneous forecast to the Kaiser and the German public,[160] and only gradually was he able to persuade the agitated monarch of the advantages which might accrue to Germany from the conflict.[161] In May 1904 Wilhelm went against the advice of the Chancellor, the Foreign Office, the Prussian War Minister and the Chief of the General Staff in transferring the leadership of the German troops in South-West Africa from the governor, Leutwein, to General Trotha.[162] But, whatever his misgivings, Bülow again acquiesced and defended the Kaiser's decision in the Reichstag.[163]

By far the most serious crisis in the relationship between Kaiser and Chancellor before the crisis of 1905–6 was their confrontation in the autumn of 1902 over their relative responsibility for the deterioration in Anglo-German relations. It had been apparent for some time that the two men entertained very different attitudes towards England, and Holstein later maintained that Bülow tried for years to push the Kaiser on to an anti-English course.[164] Wilhelm's efforts to stabilise good relations with England were constantly undermined by the activities of the German Foreign Office,[165] and in January 1902 he displayed his irritation over the storm of protest which Bülow's famous speech against Joseph Chamberlain provoked in England when he told the English ambassador that he had instructed the Chancellor to make the speech and that anyway,

they should know in England that here not Count Bülow but he, Kaiser Wilhelm, makes foreign policy, and not merely in its broad outlines but in all its details [and] no one can be in doubt of the completely friendly nature of his feelings towards England after the many proofs which he had given of them.[166]

Bülow himself recognised in September 1902 that, given the strength of public feeling in England and Germany, any diplomatic incident between the two countries could have 'incalculable consequences'.[167] Nevertheless, in the same month he persuaded a reluctant Kaiser to agree to receive three touring Boer generals in the interests of pacifying German public opinion.[168] The news of the Kaiser's impending audience unleashed such fury in England that for a time it appeared that Wilhelm would have to give up his planned visit to England in November.[169] Only Holstein's successful exploitation of an unresolved formality enabled the audience to be cancelled without loss of face. Moreover, the Chancellor was spared a public humiliation, for the Kaiser had soon decided that he would refuse to see the generals after all. Deeply impressed by the possibility of a war against England, Wilhelm was convinced that 'It is only my person which prevents the English from attacking us', and his confidence in Bülow was badly shaken.[170] Returning to Berlin on 16 October, the Kaiser aroused general astonishment by staying a week without seeing Bülow, and the Chancellor was finally forced to request an audience which took place on 23 October and lasted three hours.[171] 'It was very lively', Holstein recorded in his diary, and, with the Kaiser complaining that 'he was dissatisfied with the guidance of the semi-official press and with the conduct of affairs in general', the conversation remained unpleasant until Bülow effectively indicated to Wilhelm his personal share of responsibility for the sorry state of Anglo-German relations.[172]

The significance of this episode should perhaps not be exaggerated, for the difference was soon patched up after October 1902 and apparently forgotten. Indeed, in December 1902, after the successful conclusion of the tariff negotiations, Wilhelm spontaneously bestowed on Bülow the title of *Fürst* (Prince), and the Chancellor, professing tears of gratitude, had to prevail upon the monarch to withdraw the honour as he was without sufficient income to fulfil the role.[173] Nevertheless, in marking the first time that Wilhelm openly expressed his anger to Bülow, it may well have had a lasting impact on their relationship. In later years Bülow noted that there were three phases in his relationship with the Kaiser: 1889–1902, 1902–6 and the period from 1906.[174] The confrontation revealed the beginnings of the Kaiser's disillusionment and, however temporary the discord, the issue was never fully resolved.[175]

The 'honeymoon period' of Bülow's Chancellorship was shortlived[176] but, for all the frictions and irritations, Bülow's relations with the Kaiser were harmonious and productive between 1900 and 1905. Recognising the pivotal function the relationship played within the 'Bülow system', observers were quick to monitor its ups and downs and ready to detect a cooling in the friendship. But despite the rumours and gossip that Bülow's position had become insecure, the Kaiser's confidence in the Chancellor was repeatedly confirmed. In June 1905 Wilhelm again conferred on Bülow the title of Prince and, since his Reichstag victories had coincided with the inheritance of a personal fortune, this time the Chancellor displayed no reluctance to accept the promotion.[177] Bülow's Chancellorship was seen to have many disadvantages – his sycophantic and manipulative techniques with the monarch; his malleability and pliancy in the face of parliamentary pressure; the more negative aspects of his system within the executive;[178] his excessive concern with his personal reputation and sensitivity to public opinion.[179] But for all these features of the Bülow system, which in some cases attracted severe criticism, the recognition was widespread that a change of Chancellor promised little better.[180] At least Bülow knew how to restrain and manage the Kaiser, and this was appreciated as no mean feat.

However, in concluding this analysis of Bülow's relationship with the Kaiser, it should be emphasised that Bülow did not manage the Kaiser single-handedly and that the continuation of his influence over the monarch required the cooperation of others. We have already seen how Wilhelm II personally had a vested interest in the preservation of harmonious relations with Bülow, and his determination to believe in Bülow is a vital factor in explaining how highly placed critics of the Chancellor were silenced between 1900 and 1905. But Bülow needed to ensure the loyalty of others who were in a position to exert political influence on Wilhelm II. August Eulenburg, the Kaiser's *Oberhof- und Hausmarschall* and later *Hausminister* (who has been described by the historian of Wilhelm's entourage as 'the only Court functionary who had political influence'[181]) was flattered by the Chancellor and generally on good terms with him, although his approval of certain aspects of Bülow's policy cannot be assumed.[182] More important to the Chancellor was a satisfactory working relationship with Lucanus, the Chief of the Kaiser's Civil Cabinet, whose influence declined after 1897 but by whose cooperation Bülow set great store.[183]

Lucanus's support was invaluable on personnel questions, especially those concerning the Prussian bureaucracy,[184] and Bülow liked to have the Cabinet Chief present at difficult audiences.[185] Moreover, from the beginning Bülow encouraged that atmosphere of confidentiality in his relations with Lucanus which he had cultivated with so many others. 'Of course I will speak to nobody about this combination before I know Your Excellency's opinion', he told Lucanus in June 1901 after seeking his advice about a new *Oberpräsident* in Hanover.[186] Bülow flattered Lucanus by referring to their 'confidential relations', to his 'mastery of style', to the enormous amount he owed to 'Your Excellency's rare knowledge of issues and personnel, your proven advice and (last not least) your friendly goodwill towards me'.[187] In later years Bülow went to great lengths to do Lucanus a favour by promoting his son's career.[188] But although Lucanus rendered 'great services' for Bülow[189] and Bülow's concern about his health (and his possible successors) indicates his lack of interest in precipitating his resignation,[190] there is some evidence of tension between the two men. In May 1901 Szögyényi informed Goluchowski of a rumour that Bülow wanted to remove Lucanus and replace him with the Chief of Reich Chancellery, Wilmowski, who had the Chancellor's special confidence.[191] In 1904 Lucanus's eventual successor, Valentini, accompanied Wilhelm on his Mediterranean cruise and recorded that Bülow had succeeded in driving back Lucanus's influence so that now he was probably not even asked his opinion.[192] But Lucanus remained relatively influential throughout these years and may even have been responsible for the Kaiser's long resistance to the granting of Reichstag salaries.[193] In 1906 Monts claimed that it was Lucanus who was urging Bülow's dismissal.[194]

Above all, the Bülow system depended on vigilance, the need to ensure that there were no other influences on the monarch to rival the Chancellor's and the need to ensure that no one who came into close contact with Wilhelm would seek to undermine Bülow's position. Bülow necessarily had to take an interest in the Kaiser's entourage, keep a watchful eye for signs of treachery and search for methods of neutralising or removing unreliable influences. He promoted Wilhelm's friendships with non-political friends, with professors such as Adolf Harnack and Theodor Schiemann, both masters of the art of flattering the Kaiser and able to divert him from more contentious issues.[195] Schiemann, Bülow later noted, 'owes me everything',[196] and the Chancellor's rage was bitter when both Schiemann and Harnack eventually turned against him.[197] It was said that Bülow gradually wove 'a net around the Kaiser' which few could penetrate.[198] A diplomat who 'made up to HM [*sich an S.M. herangemacht*]' or 'would have sucked up to HM in a disturbing way and achieved a peculiar influence [*hätte sich bedenklich an S.M. herangeschnauffen und merkwürdigen Einfluss erlangt*]' was shunted off to an insignificant post.[199] Others visited and left Berlin without being granted an audience.[200] To parliamentarians Wilhelm was effectively inaccessible. A dinner at Ballestrem's in 1904 was, according to Bachem, the first time the Kaiser had been in company consisting primarily of parliamentarians since the Caprivi era.[201]

But in general Bülow had very little to fear from the men around the Kaiser between 1900 and 1905, and there was no real likelihood of an alternative centre of political influence emerging within the Kaiser's entourage. Although Waldersee claimed in 1902 that 'the unofficial advisers play a greater role than ever, the Ministers as good as none at all',[202] this observation should be interpreted as more indicative of the Kaiser's growing isolation from the responsible government than of the influence of his entourage. In 1903 Lerchenfeld reported that, with very few exceptions, the niveau of the Kaiser's entourage was not very high. 'Probably no one in his entourage has a great, constant influence', he went on, attributing to Bülow a virtual monopoly in this area.²⁰³ Moreover, as Varnbüler reported after the Mediterranean cruise in April 1905, people did not really converse or discuss issues with the Kaiser. Wilhelm II stated his opinions 'with such forceful arguments and with such apodictic certainty' that contradiction was extremely difficult and mainly took the form of silence.²⁰⁴ The Kaiser's preference for surrounding himself with sycophants who displayed little personal initiative, his need for the familiar and dislike of new faces, his choice of companions who mirrored elements in his own personality rather than challenged them²⁰⁵ all ensured that the monarch dominated his entourage to an extent that made even subtle criticism of the favourite Chancellor impossible.

Bülow probably realised this, and that the only possible exception to this generalisation was Philipp Eulenburg. Bülow's role in undermining Eulenburg's position with the Kaiser after 1900 is murky, but there is sufficient evidence to suspect the Chancellor's duplicity towards his former patron and his interest, if not direct involvement, in precipitating the royal favourite's demise. The attacks on Philipp Eulenburg began within months of Bülow's assumption of the Chancellorship,²⁰⁶ and although Holstein was suspected by some to be behind them,²⁰⁷ Bülow assured Varnbüler that he had had Holstein's word of honour that he was not involved in the press campaign.²⁰⁸ Guttenberg, the Bavarian *chargé d'affaires*, heard from a trustworthy source that

> on this occasion it seems, however, not so much to be a question of an intrigue of Herr von Holstein's but rather of a struggle of Count Bülow himself against Prince Eulenburg. The Reich Chancellor is supposed to fear the great personal influence of the Prince on the Kaiser . . . ²⁰⁹

Bülow, Guttenberg went on, had heard that Eulenburg had figured on the list of Chancellor candidates in 1900, and this was an additional reason for his desire to remove his rival 'for all time'. In this connection, it is interesting to note that 'an apparently organised press campaign of the most malicious kind' began against Waldersee at about the same time, and again it was suspected that the motive behind the attacks was to undermine his eligibility for the Chancellorship.²¹⁰

Personal and political reasons played their part in encouraging Eulenburg to press for permission to resign as ambassador to Vienna in 1901 and 1902, and these have been analysed thoroughly elsewhere.²¹¹ Moreover, it was clearly not only Bülow who had an interest in eliminating Eulenburg's influence on the Kaiser.[212] Nevertheless, by December 1901 Wilhelm II was already casting aspersions on Eulenburg's skill as a politician,[213] and his new attitude towards his friend, however inconsistent, suggests the influence of someone in a very strong position. In the spring of 1902 Eulenburg himself suspected that Bülow had fallen under Holstein's influence (whom he saw as his chief opponent),[214] though the Chancellor quickly reassured him.[215] Concerned that he was losing Wilhelm II's confidence, Eulenburg was also reassured by a friendly letter from the Kaiser at the end of May.[216] But within a week of the despatch of this letter, Bülow told Szögyényi confidentially that Wilhelm was 'not nearly so favourably disposed [towards Eulenburg] as earlier'. To the ambassador's great surprise, the Chancellor went on to declare that the Kaiser was against the appointment of a candidate (Count Diller) as Austrian military attaché in Berlin *because* he was Philipp Eulenburg's relation.[217] If Bülow was trying to undermine Eulenburg's position and simultaneously smooth his resignation, he had to tread very carefully, given how drawn Wilhelm was to Eulenburg's personality. On 9 September 1902 the Kaiser suddenly despatched his personal physician to Liebenberg to see whether it would still not be possible for Eulenburg to accompany Wilhelm to Rominten later that month. This prompted Richthofen to remind the Austrian *chargé d'affaires* that Bülow's earlier remarks to Szögyényi on the question of Eulenburg's successor − a conversation which took place without the Kaiser's knowledge and constituted an intrigue on the part of the Chancellor[218] − were to be treated with the strictest confidentiality. 'This was all the more necessary', Richthofen asserted, 'for it was by no means settled that Eulenburg would actually resign, and the Kaiser would only agree to this most unwillingly if Eulenburg's health made such a course imperative.'[219]

Bülow was a jealous guardian of the Kaiser's confidence. However much the influence of the Kaiser's friend had declined after 1897, however badly Bülow kept Eulenburg informed of events in Berlin, however much Eulenburg professed disinterest in politics now that he had fulfilled his mission,[220] there was always the possibility that he could reassert his undeniable power over the Kaiser and resume his political activities. Bülow knew Eulenburg sufficiently well to have plenty of incriminating material against him.[221] Moreover, he was placed in the most advantageous position, able to use an array of channels to destroy Eulenburg's reputation and influence. Although there is no evidence that he used the contact, he was offered a link with Maximilian Harden (the journalist who later spearheaded the campaign against the 'Liebenberg circle') in 1902 by the German Minister in Peking, Mumm von Schwarzenstein. Mumm had met Harden during a visit to Berlin. 'Of course I will never communicate with H[arden] again without express instructions from Your Excellency, be it in writing, orally or through mediators', he told Bülow, but he believed the contact might be useful.[222] Eulenburg resigned as ambassador to Vienna in November 1902 and apparently remained on the best of terms with Bülow.[223] But the spectre of Eulenburg's potential influence on Wilhelm continued to haunt the Chancellor, making him susceptible to the arguments of Eulenburg's enemies and wary of any signs of his restoration to the Kaiser's favour.

The Chancellor within the executive

Within the executive, Bülow's relationship with the Kaiser was of paramount importance. As had been evident during his State Secretaryship, any Minister who enjoyed Wilhelm II's special favour had an insuperable advantage over his colleagues, and as Chancellor Bülow was prepared to create a position for himself that was totally dependent on the Kaiser's confidence. From the very first Prussian State Ministry meeting under his Minister-Presidency, Bülow sought to emphasise the identity of interest between Kaiser and Reich Chancellor. This close identification with the will of the monarch and readiness to mediate between monarch and responsible government proved to be the source of his strength. Bülow exploited his relationship with the Kaiser to increase his authority and stature as Chancellor, and he was able to display autocratic tendencies which few might have suspected. In 1903 Lerchenfeld reported that, as in Bismarck's time, the Chancellor's will was decisive in the *Reichsleitung* and in Prussia.[224]

Although the resignation of Miquel removed the main challenge to his authority within the Prussian government, even after May 1901 Bülow displayed very little interest in the Prussian Ministry of State. He disliked collegiate bodies[225] and he chose to impose his authority on his colleagues from above, making no attempt to gain the personal allegiance of the Ministers or to create a further power base for himself within the executive. He attended only slightly more than half of the meetings of the Prussian Ministry of State between October 1900 and March 1905. Before Miquel's removal he in fact missed only four short, routine meetings, but after May 1901 only Tirpitz had a worse attendance record. In 1904 Bülow attended a mere nine out of twenty-one meetings.[226] (It is also surely not coincidental that the Minister who attended the most meetings between May 1901 and March 1905 was Möller, the new and inexperienced Minister of Trade.[227])

Bülow's absence from such a large number of State Ministry meetings in no way affected the security of his position. From the start he made it easier for Ministers to stay away from routine meetings without special dispensation[228] and no important decisions were taken in his absence.[229] On occasion, the Ministry of State merely gave its formal approval to decisions that had already been made.[230] The decreased significance of the Prussian Ministry during these years is also indicated by the fact that Bülow made no attempt to impose himself on Ministry meetings. He participated little in the discussions, relied on Posadowsky to provide more detailed arguments and preferred to defer decisions (for example until after further discussions between departments or with party leaders) when complications arose.[231] In November 1902 he wrote a letter to Philipp Eulenburg during a State Ministry sitting 'while Budde and Podbielski cannot agree over the question of a water advisory council [*Wasserbeirat*] and before a lecture [*Vortrag*] by Posadowsky on sickness insurance begins which will probably occupy us until 8 o'clock'. Bülow complained that for two hours they had been sitting in an overheated room with closed windows, and he compared the air to that in the barracks.[232] Oppressed by his 'imprisonment' and bored by the proceedings, it is thus clear why Bülow chose to avoid State Ministry meetings if at all possible.

Bülow's lack of interest in Ministry discussions partly stemmed from his determination not to become involved in departmental work but to concentrate on developing a broader, political perspective. Bülow conceived of a Chancellor who, in alliance with the throne, would stand above the government departments. He depended on the Ministers to the extent that his own knowledge of departmental work was limited and superficial, but he saw them as mere experts or specialists who were competent in their own particular area but had no desire to see that area extended. The Chancellor alone commanded a view over the broad sweep of politics, and he alone was guided by longterm aims and political objectives rather than by the partisan or sectional interests of a particular deparment.[233] On many issues which were discussed by the Prussian Ministry of State Bülow clearly had no opinion, and it is frequently not clear from the protocols which way he voted.[234] Pragmatic in his approach and aware of the need to consider what would be acceptable to the political parties or the Reich, the Minister-President often sought genuine compromises,[235] and he had a strong sense of priorities.[236]

Bülow refrained from overt leadership of the Prussian Ministry of State, but there is no question that he was ever outvoted by the other Ministers during these years or that his view did not prevail once he had chosen to commit himself. In some respects the unity he imposed on the Prussian Ministers after May 1901 remained superficial, for there was no real corporate spirit displayed within the Ministry of State and, as we will see, Bülow's political methods did not always gain respect for his authority. In June 1902 the Chancellor had again to appeal to the Prussian Ministers for unity in their representation of parliamentary bills,[237] and by 1904 some Ministers were prepared to criticise directly Bülow's conduct of affairs.[238] There was growing opposition among the Ministers to the Chancellor's conciliation of the Centre. In 1902 Podbielski spoke strongly against the granting of Reichstag salaries;[239] in 1903 he was joined by Rheinbaben in opposing the Polling Booth Law.[240] By January 1904 at least five Ministers out of the eleven present were opposed to a conciliatory reply to a Centre interpellation in the Reichstag on workers' welfare (Hammerstein, Möller, Rheinbaben, Schönstedt, Studt) and, in proposing the partial accommodation of the Centre's wishes, Posadowsky could only rely on the support of Tirpitz and Einem. But once Bülow came out in defence of Posadowsky and indicated that Wilhelm II would also be sympathetic to the Centre's views on this issue, the opposition was muted and Posadowsky was given a free hand in delivering the government's reply.[241]

The Chancellor's approach generally was to smooth over differences where they could not quite be resolved and, as at the tariff conference in June 1901, 'to confirm general agreement in such a conciliatory manner that ultimately no one dared to contradict'.[242] If he did anticipate an unwelcome decision in the State Ministry, he could always inform the Ministers, as he did in June 1905 before they discussed the financial reform, that their decisions were only to be regarded as proposals, as Wilhelm II had reserved a final decision for himself.[243] This was probably only a tactic for, by contrast, in November 1905 Bülow was to insist on secret discussions on the *Volksschulunterhaltungsgesetz* (Maintenance of Primary Schools Law) as Wilhelm had not yet agreed to the introduction of the law.[244]

Bülow's conciliatory manner and polite reserve within the Prussian Ministry contrast with his rather brusque and dismissive treatment of the Ministers outside the meetings. Uninterested in departmental work and inclined to rely on a few close advisers, bypassing official channels and offices where possible, Bülow was prepared to devote only little of his time to his ministerial colleagues. The majority of the Ministers thus rarely saw the Chancellor except during State Ministry meetings, and Bülow was likely to turn down a request for an audience, even from a new Minister, by asking for a written report.[245] There were complaints about the Chancellor's inaccessibility, and Ministers were often deprived of information or not consulted on issues that concerned their departments. During the tariff negotiations in 1902 Jagemann complained that he could get no reliable information from the government except from Bülow and Posadowsky, 'for the other Ministers are either used, like Messrs Podbielski and Möller, only as specialists for individual transactions, or they are completely ignored [*links liegen lassen*] like the Treasury Secretary and the Prussian Finance Minister'.[246] When Bülow summoned Studt on 31 January 1903 to discuss the repeal of Paragraph 2 of the Jesuit Law, the Minister was not prepared for the discussion and the subject came as a complete surprise. Studt reserved the right to submit a written memorandum outlining his objections to the repeal,

which was duly delivered on 2 February.[247] But on 3 February Bülow made
his declaration in the Reichstag, and the Ministry of State was not called to
consider the question until 11 February.[248] During important negotiations the
Chancellor regarded the Ministers as a positive liability and gave strict
instructions that they were to be kept away.[249] When the Prussian Ministers
complained in the Ministry of State about their exclusion from the last stages
of the negotiations for the Russian trade treaty in Norderney in 1904, Bülow
simply expressed his regret that it had not been possible to include the
Prussian departments and clearly felt under no pressure to change his ways.[250]

Such treatment cannot have made Bülow very popular with his colleagues, and the Chancellor's growing isolation was not without serious
political implications. But so long as Bülow had the Kaiser's confidence and
support, opposition was effectively thwarted. Bülow was not the man to
express his dissatisfaction to a Minister openly, but behind his façade of
amiability and conciliatoriness, he was not beyond giving unpleasant assign-
ments to others and he could always appeal to a higher authority. He
mobilised the Kaiser in order to bring Podbielski into line during the tariff
negotiations in 1901–2. The Prussian Minister of Agriculture had avoided
defending the contentious grain duties in the Reichstag during the first
reading of the Tariff Bill and had contrived to be 'away hunting virtually the
whole time'.[251] Bülow prevailed upon Wilhelm II in December 1901 to force
Podbielski to speak out against exaggerated agrarian demands,[252] and when
the Minister again began 'to dodge the tariff negotiations' in 1902, the
Chancellor once more ensured that he toed the line. 'If Podbielski does not
take the first opportunity which presents itself to speak out against the
agrarian demands for increases, I must have recourse to His Majesty', Bülow
told Richthofen in September 1902. 'Who could best say to Podbielski that
it is in his interest to go voluntarily into the fire instead of being forced by
His Majesty?'[253] In February 1903 Wilhelm expressed his lively satisfaction
that the Minister of Agriculture was finally speaking out effectively against
exorbitant agrarian demands.[254] The Chancellor's appeal to the monarch was
clearly not an isolated or exceptional occurrence. In September 1902 Bülow
again threatened 'to go to His Majesty' if Rheinbaben did not incorporate the
Chancellor's proposed changes in his next budget.[255]

The Kaiser placed his full confidence in Bülow, and expected the Minister-
President to ensure that 'the Ministers stand to attention before him'.[256] Most
Ministers, with the exception of Tirpitz, Podbielski and the War Minister,
saw the Kaiser as infrequently as they saw the Chancellor,[257] and when an
audience did become necessary, Bülow was the mediator, giving advice on
how the monarch was to be approached and the kind of arguments to which
he would be susceptible.[258] No Minister could rival Bülow's position with
the Kaiser between 1900 and 1905, and Zedlitz maintained they were all

frightened out of their wits by Wilhelm II.[259] Even Podbielski received a 'proper box on the ears' from the Kaiser for carrying his brash humour too far while in Rominten in 1903. The Minister did not appear unduly chastised by the experience,[260] but his popularity with the Kaiser suffered an, albeit temporary, setback. In January 1904 Waldersee observed that Podbielski too now rarely saw the monarch.[261]

While the Prussian Ministers were technically his equals, Bülow could afford to pay even less consideration to the State Secretaries of the Reich Offices, who were constitutionally his subordinates. Bülow left the brunt of the work to the State Secretaries but, as was evident from his attitude to Richthofen's appointment in 1900,[262] he refused to allow them the independence and influence which he himself had previously enjoyed. From October 1900 the State Secretaries had to be content with short, generally written instructions from the Reich Chancellor and rare personal contact with him.[263] Podbielski, who resented this treatment, submitted his resignation as State Secretary of the Reich Post Office within three months of Bülow's assumption of the Chancellorship. In his letter of resignation he maintained that 'The position of the State Secretaries is at the moment such as to make it impossible for me to remain any longer in this position'.[264] However, he accepted the Prussian Ministry of Agriculture in May 1901.

In 1903 Lerchenfeld reported that, with the exception of Posadowsky, all the State Secretaries, while being very capable and industrious, lacked personal, political authority.[265] He presumably forgot to mention Tirpitz, who, like Posadowsky, was simultaneously a Prussian Minister without portfolio. Bülow consistently supported Tirpitz throughout 'his constant frictions with the Cabinets, with other Admirals [and] above all, with His Majesty',[266] in part out of personal friendship for the Navy Secretary, in part because of his political commitment to the naval programme.[267] Bülow always treated Tirpitz with the utmost respect and made no attempt to interfere in the work of his department during these years.[268] In 1906 the Chancellor wrote that Tirpitz 'is now finally beginning to have the confidence in me which, after my seven years' constant support for him, I indeed have a claim to and which is also in HM's interest'.[269] Unlike most of the State Secretaries Tirpitz enjoyed independent authority and stature within the Reich executive. The State Secretary of the Treasury, Thielmann, was similarly beginning to understand by the spring of 1903 how to bolster his position *vis-à-vis* the other Reich and Prussian departments by seeking the support of the federal states.[270] But ironically, and perhaps not coincidentally, Thielmann was removed from office later that year.

Without doubt, the most influential State Secretary during the first years of Bülow's Chancellorship was the State Secretary of Interior, Arthur von Posadowsky-Wehner, who had attempted to resign in 1900.[271] Bülow placed great reliance upon Posadowsky's extensive knowledge of domestic affairs, and the State Secretary was widely recognised to have a (not always fortunate) influence on the Chancellor. In February 1903 Lerchenfeld maintained that Posadowsky's influence on Bülow was almost unrivalled, both because no one else in the Prussian or Reich administration possessed such independent authority and because the Chancellor tended to shut himself away and see only Posadowsky and Richthofen. 'Thus things are now mostly settled between the Chancellor and the State Secretary of Interior in advance, and after that the Prussian vote [for the Bundesrat] is decided on [*festgestellt*] in the State Ministry.'[272] The Bavarian Minister-President, too, had a similar view of Posadowsky's role. Posadowsky, Podewils asserted, had impressed Bülow with his indispensability almost to the same extent as he had imposed himself on Hohenlohe. 'Count Bülow does not know the domestic legislation well enough and is also not the kind of man who will strain himself by struggling with questions which are alien to him.' Thus Bülow deferred to Posadowsky's superior knowledge, sometimes without complete conviction. Podewils claimed that he had seen with his own eyes how intensively Posadowsky worked on the Chancellor and how Bülow sought to avoid coming into conflict with his views.[273]

Posadowsky bore an enormous burden of work during Bülow's Chancellorship, and it is clear that in some areas, for example social policy, he enjoyed considerable independence and should be seen as the real formulator of policy.[274] While Bülow always ensured that he had sufficient leisure and spent most of the summer at his holiday retreat in Norderney, it was Posadowsky who was considered to be completely indispensable and who was kept in Berlin at work on official business.[275] Nevertheless, although Bülow was aware of Posadowsky's many useful qualities, he also knew his limitations,[276] and it would be completely erroneous to view the Chancellor as some kind of slave to his State Secretary on matters of domestic policy. Posadowsky was committed to a pro-Centre course, but so was Bülow during these years. Moreover, Posadowsky's position may well have suffered permanent damage after the 12,000 Mark affair, and he never quite regained the authority which he had enjoyed during the Hohenlohe era.[277]

Bülow had not paid undue consideration to Posadowsky between 1897 and 1900,[278] nor was he excessively deferential to the State Secretary after he became Chancellor. Posadowsky's previously prominent role as a government spokesman in the Reichstag was circumscribed after 1900,[279] and it is clear that Bülow did not always approve of the tenor of his public statements.[280] Posadowsky was not immune from dismissive treatment at the hands of the Chancellor. Bülow left Posadowsky to fight the 'Podbielski group' in the State Ministry while he kept unobtrusively in the background;[281] he reaped the rewards of Posadowsky's work, most notably after

3 Friedrich Wilhelm von Loebell, Chief of the Reich Chancellery 1904–10 and one of
Bülow's most trusted advisers

the safe passage of the Tariff Law in December 1902, although the State
Secretary would have had to bear the cost of a defeat;[282] and he let Posadowsky find out about important government personnel changes from the
newspapers.[283] In 1905, when Bülow suspected Posadowsky of damaging the
revised Canal Bill's chances in the Prussian Landtag, he told Richthofen to
make it clear tactfully to Posadowsky that he was not only harming the
government's interests, but ultimately his own.[284] Bülow never feared that

the position of the State Secretary might become a threat to his personal position, for Posadowsky had little support from the Crown. The Kaiser, who sent Posadowsky to England every year to broaden his horizons because he was 'too agrarian',[285] always received the Vice-Chancellor with great coolness,[286] and this must have made him a very convenient workhorse for Bülow. The State Secretary of Interior performed all the laborious tasks of Bülow's Chancellorship and could be relied upon in an emergency. Yet he was no rival for the Chancellorship, and if Bülow did desire to adopt a more prominent role on a particular issue, he simply had Posadowsky informed that the Kaiser had left him a free hand in dealing with the affair.[287]

Posadowsky had greater access to the Reich Chancellor than most of the State Secretaries and Prussian Ministers, but he cannot be considered one of Bülow's closest advisers. Moreover, his influence on Bülow's decisions must have declined after Friedrich Wilhelm von Loebell replaced Conrad as Chief of the Reich Chancellery in September 1904. Loebell was well versed in German domestic politics and rapidly became Bülow's foremost political adviser.[288] His main activity was to mediate between the Chancellor on the one hand and the highest Reich Offices, the Prussian Ministries and the party leaders on the other.[289] But his growing indispensability to the Chancellor is indicated by the rapid expansion of his role. Loebell frequently accompanied the Minister-President to State Ministry meetings and came into conflict with the Under State Secretary to the State Ministry because he dealt with Prussian affairs.[290] In 1907 he was appointed deputy plenipotentiary to the Bundesrat (which enabled him to speak in the parliaments), and a few months later he was promoted to Under State Secretary. Loebell claimed that these changes were necessary because of the disputes over competence and rank among the higher state offices, and that the Chancellor and Kaiser stuck to their guns despite considerable opposition to his promotion within the executive.[291] By Loebell's own admission, his relationship with Bülow 'soon became closer and closer', and as everything Bülow saw had to pass through Loebell's office and the two men had daily consultations, the influence of the Chancellery Chief should not be underestimated.[292]

Loebell was one of Bülow's most trusted advisers and one who was immensely impressed by the Chancellor's qualities and abilities.[293] Another was the State Secretary of the Foreign Office, Richthofen, who collaborated closely with the Chancellery Chief after 1904. Bülow kept Richthofen informed about all the major political questions and liked to hear his views not only on matters of foreign policy.[294] Relying on Richthofen's judgement on issues ranging from the tariff and trade treaties to personnel questions and the handling of the political parties,[295] Bülow asked the State Secretary of the Foreign Office to assess the relative merits of Thielmann's and Posadowsky's financial proposals in 1903.[296] And in 1905, when confronted with the divergent views of Stengel, Rheinbaben and Posadowsky on how the military and naval budgets were to be handled in the Reichstag, Bülow wrote to Richthofen: 'I have great confidence in your understanding of matters relating to financial policy as well as in your overall perspective and know that you will advise me [to adopt] that course which corresponds to our political and national interest as a whole'.[297]

Bülow made enormous demands on his closest advisers, and it was partly Richthofen's feeling that he was 'also Head of the Reich Chancellery' which prompted Bülow to find a completely loyal replacement for Conrad in 1904.[298] Loebell rarely had a holiday, and his health deteriorated after 1904.[299] Richthofen, too, found the strain increasingly difficult to bear, and despite Bülow's attempts to off-load the State Secretary and preserve his strength 'for the Service, the country and me',[300] he ultimately died of a heart attack in January 1906.[301] There were others in the Chancellor's closest circle – in particular Hammann, the Press Chief, had the Chancellor's confidence, and his role will be examined more thoroughly below.[302] But, like Holstein, who was constantly at war with Richthofen[303] and who initially had difficulty gaining access to the Chancellor even once a week,[304] their advice was more specialised and less all-pervasive. Holstein heard little and had even less influence with respect to domestic affairs.[305] To his chagrin, it was Richthofen, Loebell and Hammann who were privy to the Chancellor's innermost thoughts.[306]

It was among this small group of advisers that Bülow's most important decisions were taken.[307] Bülow's preference for personal advisers (and for personal secretaries[308]) galled the Ministers and State Secretaries not least because their influence correspondingly declined. In 1903 Jagemann reported that the system of making decisions *en petit comité* and then presenting the official, responsible bodies with a *fait accompli* applied in the internal administration as well as in the Bundesrat.[309] But Bülow's colleagues and subordinates also criticised other aspects of his system within the executive which seemed to have negative implications for the status of their work. Nieberding, Stengel, Posadowsky and, it can safely be assumed, others too complained on occasion because Bülow 'treated the most important questions of his department with such enormous indifference and superficiality'.[310]

As has been indicated, despite his freedom within the executive, the Chancellor displayed very little interest in departmental work. Never bureaucratic by nature, Bülow prided himself on keeping his mind free of the 'trivial imponderables' in politics.[311] Indeed, he insisted on the most meticulous order on his office desk to ensure he saw 'a clear way in front of me ... and for inner peace'.[312] Just as he never appeared before the Kaiser with a briefcase full of papers, so he never sat down at a desk with a pile of documents but obliged Loebell to bring him one at a time if necessary.[313]

Moreover, especially during the first years of his Chancellorship, Bülow could afford to leave affairs to the departments concerned. Hence the criticisms of his indifference, though his approach could also be interpreted more positively: 'The Reich Chancellor with clever and magnanimous restraint restricted his role to giving directives and intervened only at important moments.'[314]

When the Chancellor did take an interest in a particular issue or piece of legislation within the executive, it is difficult to avoid the conclusion that his involvement reflected an interest on the part of the Kaiser. He seized every opportunity to identify himself closely with the Kaiser's will and mediate between the monarch and the responsible government. Bülow took more than usual interest in the Polish question, an issue with which Wilhelm was very concerned and where he expected actions to follow words.[315] He was quick to seize the initiative over the Silesian flood disaster in 1903 after the Kaiser called a Crown Council on the subject. Bülow welcomed the opportunity to accelerate the relief action and to show himself capable of proceeding with the energy the Minister of Interior had lacked.[316] In January 1905, when the Chancellor was preoccupied with the international situation, the trade treaties, the colonial difficulties, the state of the Reich finances and a campaign against the SPD, he informed Hammann that 'In the foreground of interest for me is the strike in the Ruhr.'[317] Again the Chancellor wanted to display his concern about an issue of importance to the Kaiser, and eleven days later a second Crown Council meeting was held to discuss the Ruhr strike.[318]

Bülow also of course had to take action when his credibility with the Kaiser or his personal position depended on it. Having assured the Kaiser that the commercial treaties would not be jeopardised by the conclusion of a tariff more favourable to the agrarians, the Chancellor had a particular stake in securing the successful renegotiation of the treaties and was very susceptible to imperial pressure.[319] But, apart from this, Bülow was happy to admit that he had no head for figures, and left everything to do with financial affairs to his 'excellent and expert colleagues';[320] or that he understood no more about agriculture than that 'a goose had two legs and one cannot milk a bull'.[321] After his thorough analysis of financial policy between 1903 and 1911, Peter-Christian Witt concluded that Bülow was not interested in financial reform until his position was threatened by the prospect of a catastrophic defeat.[322]

Bülow had groaned about the quantity of work with which he was confronted as State Secretary of the Foreign Office.[323] Ministers, State Secretaries, diplomats and others found him an elusive Chancellor who was rarely available for consultation and who did not organise his time efficiently.[324] Uninterested in detailed work, even in major projects, he did not

employ a systematic approach to the business of government, and he found
it convenient and pleasant to take decisions while out walking with
Loebell.[325] Bolstered by the support of Wilhelm II, his intervention could be
decisive within the executive, but his control was not all-pervasive. Unlike
Bismarck, he had no command of the details, and this clearly gave some
departments – and individuals – within the executive a large degree of
autonomy.[326]

Bülow thus restored the authority of the Reich Chancellor, but his
approach undermined cohesion in the executive and exacerbated the centrifugal tendencies built into the system. On one level the departmental
anarchy of the Hohenlohe years continued, for Bülow limited his role to the
sphere of political tactics and mediation and left what he could to the
specialists. His secretive and highly personal methods meant that few were
informed about the general tenor or trend of his political decisions. This lack
of information coupled with the manipulative outpourings of a highly
efficient Press Bureau ensured a 'strict Bülow censorship system'[327] which not
only 'atomised' the Ministers and State Secretaries but also ultimately isolated
the Chancellor.

If we turn, finally, to the top-level personnel changes in the executive
between 1900 and 1905, it is evident that here too Bülow could afford to be
relatively unconcerned. After the ministerial reshuffle of May 1901 there
were relatively few changes in the highest positions during the ensuing four
years, and those that occurred were regulated by Kaiser and Chancellor at
most in consultation with Bülow' closest advisers and the Chief of the Civil
Cabinet. There are too few examples to draw any meaningful conclusions
about the Chancellor's role, but, as was evident in May 1901, he was always
prepared if necessary to submit to the Kaiser's wishes.

The Kaiser continued to guard his prerogative on personnel issues after
May 1901. In August 1901 he replaced Puttkamer by Köller as State
Secretary of Alsace-Lorraine completely on his own initiative. He consulted
neither Bülow nor the *Statthalter* but simply informed Bülow of his decision
when the Chancellor arrived in Kiel. 'On All-Highest orders I had to write
to the *Statthalter* Hohenlohe in this sense', Bülow told Lucanus, and the
Chancellor meekly performed the necessary.[328] A month later, justifying the
personnel change to Lerchenfeld, Bülow maintained that he, the Chancellor,
had suggested it to the Kaiser.[329] In June 1902 Thielen, the Minister of Public
Works, resigned because he had lost the Kaiser's confidence since May
1901,[330] and Bülow played an insignificant role in the choice of Budde as his
successor. Budde, who was the third general (after Gossler and Podbielski)
in the Prussian Ministry, enjoyed Wilhelm's special confidence and was
widely recognised to aspire to a position and influence, qualities which were
anathema to Bülow in a Minister.[331] The Chancellor doubtless also would

have preferred a candidate who was not such a staunch defender of the Canal Bill, for this might have eased his tense relations with the Conservative Party.[332] Rheinbaben, the Minister of Finance, feared that the new Minister of Public Works would be encouraged by Wilhelm II to indulge in costly experiments.[333] For it was expected that Budde 'will always be eager to try and comply with wishes from the highest quarters without consideration for the difficulties in his way'.[334]

Bülow played a similarly insignificant part in the appointment of Einem, whom he considered 'an excellent successor' to Gossler as War Minister in 1903.[335] Wilhelm II's relationship with Gossler had been difficult for some years,[336] and Gossler was also disliked in military circles.[337] His resignation in 1903 was precipitated by his refusal to agree to the military increases demanded by the Kaiser, but in fact Einem, too, refused to accept the ministerial portfolio unless Wilhelm agreed to moderate his demands.[338] Also in the summer of 1903, Bülow may well have hoped to remove Hammerstein, the Minister of Interior, who was seen to have mismanaged the Silesian flood disaster. Relations between Bülow and Hammerstein had never been good and Hammerstein had been unskilful in the parliaments.[339] But if Bülow did have designs of this kind, his efforts were unsuccessful. Hammerstein continued to be *persona grata* to the Kaiser and remained in office until his death in 1905.[340] Finally, in March 1905 Bethmann Hollweg became the new Minister of Interior, and again one can question Bülow's role in promoting this friend of the Kaiser's. Bülow seems to have considered Bethmann 'too agrarian' after his refusal to accept the Chancellor's conditions in May 1901.[341] But, once the canal issue was solved, Bülow could clearly have no political objections to the appointment,[342] and thus, if the suggestion emanated from Wilhelm, the Chancellor acquiesced.

The Kaiser was not prepared to leave the regulation of such matters to others. Nonetheless, he was not unreceptive to Bülow's advice, and the Chancellor did exert some influence on personnel questions. When Bülow had a political reason for wanting to effect a personnel change, he generally seems to have been able to do so. He removed Miquel in 1901, and in the interests of a Reich finance reform, he removed Thielmann from the Reich Treasury in the summer of 1903 and replaced him with Stengel virtually single-handed. The appointment of Stengel was cloaked in secrecy, for Bülow consulted only Richthofen and Conrad and ignored Rheinbaben and Posadowsky, the two Ministers with the greatest interest in the appointment.[343] Bülow was unpleasantly surprised when Holstein got wind of Stengel's nomination,[344] and even Thielmann, who had no plans to resign, was only informed that he should do so two days after Bülow had secured the Kaiser's agreement to Stengel's appointment.[345]

Bülow exasperated his colleagues by such autocratic behaviour,[346] but he was clearly confident that he would be able to execute such changes. In September 1903 he considered replacing Nieberding as State Secretary of the Reich Justice Office because of his poor performance in the parliaments;[347] and in August 1904 he similarly considered replacing the Prussian Minister of Justice, Schönstedt, because his position had been weakened by a number of unfortunate incidents.[348] Unless, like Hammerstein, the Minister enjoyed Wilhelm's special favour, Bülow did not doubt that the Kaiser would allow him to remove inappropriate Ministers, even if the monarch took a more lively interest in the choice of their successors.

The difficulty in drawing any significant conclusion about the Chancellor's role in influencing personnel decisions is also evident in the areas of diplomatic and bureaucratic appointments. There is ample evidence of Wilhelm's arbitrary action on matters concerning diplomatic personnel. (The replacement of Holleben by Speck von Sternburg as ambassador to the United States in 1903 is a notorious example.)[349] But for each of these incidents there were a host of decisions taken by the Chancellor[350] and, as was evident in 1902, when Bülow got the Vienna government to request Wedel as a replacement for Philipp Eulenburg in order to forestall Wilhelm II's appointment of Monts,[351] the Chancellor was prepared to intrigue against the Kaiser to ensure the selection of a particular candidate. With respect to Prussian bureaucratic personnel, the Kaiser was also prepared to leave some appointments completely in Bülow's hands;[352] or he sometimes suggested a number of candidates but left the ultimate choice to the Chancellor.[353] Equally, Wilhelm could display complete independence on these issues and decide against the candidate proposed by Bülow and Lucanus.[354] What is clear is that Wilhelm collaborated closely with Bülow and that the two men sometimes decided on these changes two years in advance.[355] The Chancellor was very sensitive to the Kaiser's moods and views,[356] but also confident in his powers of persuasion. As he told an anxious Hammann in October 1902: 'One must leave things to me and not disturb the threads for me by premature intervention.'[357]

Moreover, how important to Bülow was the appointment of Wilhelm's favourites as Ministers, diplomats and bureaucrats before 1905–6? The whole issue of ministerial appointments assumes less significance if Bülow continued to impose his authority on his colleagues from above. Bülow did not enjoy having 'other Gods'[358] alongside him in the Prussian Ministry, but with Wilhelm's unconditional support during this period, how much were lesser favourites such as Podbielski, Rheinbaben and Hammerstein a threat to the Chancellor's position? In the Prussian Ministry of State Podbielski and Rheinbaben formed what can be described as an agrarian opposition to Bülow. They were vocal but always in a minority. Before 1906 Bülow was never outdone by the 'Podbielski group'. As we have seen, he had methods of dealing with the Minister of Agriculture, and his inclusion in the government was politically desirable to retain the confidence of the Conservatives. His biggest clash with Podbielski before 1906 occurred in January 1905, when Podbielski violently opposed the Austrian trade treaty in the Prussian Ministry of State.[359] Such behaviour was not welcome to Bülow and he described Podbielski's attitude afterwards as contemptible. It was an academic comment, however. Bülow regretted that such a knowledgeable and conscientious man repeatedly showed faults of character, but concluded that they had to use him as he was.[360] As was evident in May 1901, the Kaiser had no coherent plan in choosing personnel beyond selecting favourites. Szögyényi claimed that two more diverse candidates for the Finance Ministry than Siemens, 'a pronounced liberal', and Henckel von Donnersmarck, 'one of the main supports of the Junker party', could scarcely have been found.[361] Finally, Bülow's justification to Lerchenfeld of Köller's appointment indicates his willingness to cover Wilhelm with his responsibility, but it also perhaps suggests the Chancellor's characteristic complacency and nonchalance when confronted with such occurrences.

Bülow's position within the executive was secure during these years, and he had no reason to fear prospective rivals. Thus he could afford to be relatively complacent about personnel issues and this made him, for Wilhelm II, a very convenient Chancellor. Unless outside difficulties arose or political considerations became paramount, the Kaiser could be confident that he would get his way. Bülow had no interest in undermining this confidence. He had painstakingly constructed a system based on the mutual confidence of Kaiser and Chancellor which it would have been folly to put at risk by assuming a determined stance on personnel issues or insisting vigorously on the appointment of his own candidates. Bülow's security within the executive, indeed his whole system, depended on the Kaiser's conviction that his personal will would prevail.

Bülow, the press and 'public opinion'

When Bülow acceded to the Chancellorship in 1900, he had quite a novel conception of his future role. He intended to be a Chancellor in the Bismarckian tradition who promoted national unity and German power, commanded a view over the broad sweep of politics and was not dogmatic in his political beliefs; and he wanted to confirm the vitality of the Bismarckian system by cultivating a close relationship with the Kaiser, whom he could thereby restrain, and by ensuring smooth and harmonious relations between the executive and legislature. In addition, he was convinced that if the monarchy was to survive into the twentieth century, it had to rest on a more popular basis and inspire the confidence of all the more moderate elements in German society. Before 1897, Bülow often talked about strengthening the bonds between the Kaiser and the nation, and as Chancellor he regarded it as a sound political principle to do nothing which did not have the support of the educated classes and the bourgeoisie.[362] Moreover, always fascinated by the appearance as well as the substance of power, he was concerned to promote the correct image as Chancellor and conform as closely as possible to the popular conception of a leading statesman (which again owed much to Bismarck). All this meant that Bülow devoted an inordinate amount of time to the manipulation and wooing of 'public opinion', which for him was largely synonymous with the outpourings of the German press.

Bülow had had early experience of the kind of political uses to which the press could be put. During his first years in the German Foreign Office he had worked for a time in the special press department organised by Bismarck to break Wilhelm I's opposition to the alliance with Austria, and he had composed letters from all parts of Germany which were published in newspapers and then shown to Wilhelm I as evidence of public support for the alliance.[363] Later, in Paris, he had won Holstein's praise by writing numerous articles for political purposes and submitting letters to the editors of French newspapers with the aim of encouraging French colonial ventures.[364] Bülow continued to take a great interest in the press in St Petersburg, writing a fifty-page report on journalistic activities in the city;[365] and he was ultimately to believe that the press had an almost boundless influence on public opinion and on international politics.[366] During his Chancellorship, the Foreign Office Press Bureau under its Chief, Dr Otto Hammann, developed into a powerful and elaborate apparatus with immense scope for patronage and influence. Without doubt this can largely be attributed to Bülow's enormous interest in this realm.

To a certain extent, given the nature of the German political system, some government interference in the affairs of the 'free press' was inevitable. Wilhelmine government technically operated 'above the parties', and consequently the executive lacked its own political press to explain government policy or to float its ideas. Although Bismarck always denied that he had any influence over the press, during his Chancellorship there developed a complex network of 'semi-official' (*offiziös*) newspapers, willing to express unofficially the government's views and dependent in some way or other on government support.[367] When Caprivi tried to reduce government interference in the freedom of the press after 1890, assuming that the executive was not so sensitive as to be unable to bear uninhibited press utterances, he soon ran into difficulties. Most of his ministerial colleagues developed their own press links, the *offiziös* system became increasingly anarchic and the disunity of the administration, indeed the personal enmities in the Prussian State

Ministry, were reflected in the newspapers.[368] Attempts were made to reorganise the semi-official press and to develop a more united government press policy during Hohenlohe's Chancellorship, but again there was little cooperation from the Prussian Ministries.[369] In particular, Miquel's semi-official press, led first and foremost by Viktor Schweinburg's *Berliner Politische Nachrichten*, proved to be a highly dangerous weapon when mobilised against the Chancellor.[370] Thus by October 1900 the situation had become urgent and there were immediate calls for Bülow to clean up the *offiziös* press and end the confusion.[371] Bülow quickly took steps to centralise government relations with the press in the Foreign Office, which was under his direct control, and to restrict other Ministries' contacts with the press. Even though Prussian Ministers were not subordinate to the Chancellor and their relations with the press could not be eliminated altogether, their access to the press was closed where possible, and by 1902 department officials who had previously been willing to divulge information to journalists were clearly forbidden to do so.[372] The Foreign Office Press Bureau aspired to have a monopoly and claimed the right to decide whether to supply or withhold information and material for publication on all major political issues.[373]

Bülow's press directives, which were virtually all handwritten in the form of letters, cards and jottings and which abound in Hammann's private papers in Potsdam, give ample illustration of the numerous functions which the Press Bureau fulfilled. Through its various means of influence over a substantial proportion of the German press (in 1906 Holstein claimed that there were not many 'truly independent' journalists[374]) it explained official policy to the German public and German policy to the world.[375] It was responsible for the publication of official announcements and events.[376] It played a major role in selecting those articles from the press to be shown to Wilhelm II.[377] It denied and circulated press rumours,[378] and it rooted out the instigators of press attacks on the government.[379] The Press Bureau could be used to create diversions from inopportune or unwelcome events.[380] It might sponsor the establishment of a new newspaper to work for a specific purpose, such as a Franco-German alliance.[381] It attacked German articles hostile to official policy[382] and circulated foreign articles which criticised and thereby justified German policy. For example, in 1904 Bülow wanted an article in the *Army and Navy Review*, an English periodical, circulated 'partly to spread understanding for the necessity of the Navy, but partly too so that we cannot be accused of burying our heads in the sand in a difficult situation'.[383] The Press Bureau clamped down on articles of which it – or Kaiser Wilhelm – disapproved, and it attributed 'stupid articles' to the incitement of Germany's enemies.[384] During the Russo-Japanese war, Bülow had anti-Japanese articles in the German press sent to St Petersburg and anti-Russian articles to London, Washington and Tokyo.[385]

Not all the methods used by the Press Bureau were quite so crude or transparent. In 1906 Bülow criticised individual German newspapers for discussing openly the question of an alliance with France, and he maintained 'That is just as stupid as if I start talking immediately of coitus to a respectable woman whom I would like to possess, instead of first sending her flowers and presents and being really nice to her.'[386] Further, Bülow clearly used the Press Bureau in many other ways besides the obvious one of manipulating the German press. In 1902 he exploited a press article as an excuse to act against the counsel of his advisers, including Hammann, and make his 'biting on granite' speech against Joseph Chamberlain. The Chancellor regretted insinuations in the *Berliner Tageblatt* that he was too soft, 'because they will cause me to adopt a sharper tone in the Reichstag, especially about Chamberlain, than I would otherwise have done'.[387] In 1903 he instructed Hammann to collect a list of all the *'epitheta ornantia'* hurled between the Social Democratic press and Harden, and to classify them under the names of the chief protagonists so that the Press Bureau would have a readymade supply of all the 'poisonous darts [*Dreckwürfe*], accusations and insinuations' which each had attracted.[388] Moreover, following in Bismarck's tradition, Bülow clearly found the Press Bureau a useful weapon in bolstering his position with the Kaiser (who was also very sensitive to press views) and convincing him of the correctness of his policies. In 1903, he mobilised the Press Bureau to provide press support for a moderate SPD policy[389] and through his use of press articles, for example to argue the case for the granting of salaries to Reichstag members,[390] he must have sought to influence the Kaiser on other issues. A study of Bülow's Moroccan policy has also indicated the 'astounding importance' of press releases and leaks in informing Wilhelm II.[391] Bülow saw the Press Bureau very much as his own personal weapon, using it to cover policies and actions for which he felt responsible, but not those of other government departments. When Martin Spahn, a Catholic and the son of the Centre Party leader, was appointed to a chair of history at the new University of Strasburg in 1902, Bülow was not prepared to let 'our Press Bureau' do the work of the Ministry of Culture, but expected the latter to 'stay by us in the battle line'. It was the responsibility of the *Ministerialdirektor* in the Ministry of Culture, Friedrich Althoff, to ensure that the standpoint of the Prussian government was represented in those newspapers to which it had access.[392]

Officially Bülow endeavoured to cultivate an attitude of benevolent detachment towards the press. On principle, he maintained, he treated the press with respect,[393] but its attacks on the government left him cold.[394] In an instruction to Hammann he wrote:

I share the opinion of Frederick the Great 'that one must not embarrass [*genieren*] the gazettes'. This view stems not only from my indifference to journalistic attacks and criticism, but also from [my] genuine goodwill towards journalism.[395]

Such an impression, intended for publication, was far removed from the truth. Bülow's personal press enquiries and directives, many of which concerned seemingly very trivial matters, reveal his obsessive interest in his press coverage and his extreme sensitivity to press attacks. The Chancellor took criticism personally, always suspecting ill-wishers, and he was completely unscrupulous in his efforts to curb the freedom of the press. If a newspaper became spiteful, he immediately wanted to know who was behind it.[396] Newspapers had to be drawn 'gradually and inconspicuously into my camp'.[397] Bülow expected good coverage in the press in return for favours,[398] and he was perfectly amenable to representing the interests of a large industrial company during government negotiations, provided that the company prevented 'unpatriotic and clumsy articles' in a newspaper it could influence.[399] 'He must be intimidated', Bülow noted next to the name of a publisher of unpatriotic material in 1905.[400] Reluctant to receive diplomats or Ministers about affairs of state, the Chancellor was frequently prepared to meet with press representatives and captivate them with his charm and presence.[401] When the Austrian *chargé d'affaires* pointed this out, Bülow angrily wondered 'whether a diplomat who says such tactless things can be received at all'.[402] In 1907 Bülow maintained to Hammann, 'In principle ... I am of the view that we must be very eclectic in handling (and influencing) the press. It was precisely in his most successful period that Bismarck sought to make connections with newspapers of all shades, really rebuffed no newspaper and laid his eggs everywhere.'[403]

With the help of Hammann and the Press Bureau, Bülow assiduously cultivated a public image of his Chancellorship which flattered his personal role. To restore confidence in the monarchy, he stressed the close identification between Kaiser and Chancellor, his security in the Kaiser's favour and his readiness to accept full responsibility for Wilhelm II's actions. Paying an almost fastidious attention to detail, the Chancellor's directives to Hammann were designed to emphasise how frequently he saw the Kaiser and how closely the two men collaborated. When Wilhelm saw a Minister, it had to be stressed in the press that the audience took place in the Chancellor's presence;[404] personnel changes in the higher bureaucracy occurred 'in full agreement with the Reich Chancellor and Minister-President'.[405] When Bülow visited Wilhelm in Marienburg in 1902, it had to be announced that this was on Wilhelm's invitation;[406] Wilhelm's speech at Marienburg had to be represented as demonstrating his unconditional support of Bülow's Polish policy and Bülow wanted it reported that Wilhelm afterwards drank to the Chancellor.[407] When Wilhelm invited himself to dinner with Bülow in October 1902 in order to bolster the Chancellor's weakened position, Bülow was very concerned that the press should not interpret it in this light and that it should have no doubts about the harmonious relations between Kaiser and

Chancellor. In a revealing press directive to Hammann the following day, he repeated a request

not to propagate the news of the dinner yesterday as if my position (which in reality was never shaken for a moment or even only threatened) had been consolidated. At the most it can be said here and there how there was no need at all for such external proof of the relations between Kaiser and Chancellor in order to prove the absurdity of those foolish crisis rumours which, besides, no one in serious circles believed and which no earnest politician ever took seriously. That could best be said in those newspapers which directly or indirectly are spreading such fictions.[408]

While nurturing the image of a Chancellor who enjoyed the Kaiser's confidence, Bülow also used the press to enhance his personal position as a Chancellor with far-sighted aims and a sense of purpose whom the nation could trust. Bülow presented himself as a statesman with rare mental gifts and intellectual prowess, who was a cut above other politicians and fully in control of the nation's destiny. His directives to Hammann constantly emphasised his foresight, skill and determination. As many papers as possible had to support 'my energetic national action' over the Polish question.[409] If the tariff were not passed, this would not be the fault of the federal governments 'and least of all von Bülow's!'.[410] The settlement of the Lippe question had to appear to the outside world as the work of the Reich Chancellor. It had to be so conducted that it 'becomes a real success for the Reich Chancellor and secures the confidence of the German people in his devotion to duty, his independence and his conduct of affairs'. (Thus Bülow was pleased that the matter was referred to the *Reichsgericht* and not the *Landesgericht*. 'With the *Reichsgericht*, the Reich Chancellor is also more in the foreground'.)[411] Stengel's appointment as State Secretary of the Treasury in 1903 had to be seen as a fortunate development and as new evidence of Bülow's concern for the federal character of the Reich and of the good relations he had with Munich.[412] In February 1905, when the Canal Bill was passed, Bülow told Hammann that scarcely any other question had caused him more trouble and exposed him to such dangerous attack.

Probably in no other question could I have shown more judgement, composure and caution. It is a victory that is equally significant for our industrial and cultural development as for my personal position in Prussia and at home. It was the result of correct tactics and clever manoeuvering. The departmental Ministers, namely Budde . . . Rheinbaben and Podbielski deserve merit for executing my directives correctly.[413]

Bülow was also at pains to promote an image of diligence. Since he received Ministers so rarely, it was perhaps understandable that he wanted such audiences publicised.[414] 'I am receiving Möller this afternoon who wanted to speak to me, I assume because I have been urging mining legislation reform',

Bülow wrote to Hammann in December 1904. 'I leave it to your discretion whether you want to say in the press that, although I was forced to stay indoors because of my chill, I nevertheless had a lengthy conversation with Möller.'[415] When he left the Reichstag early, Bülow instructed Hammann to justify his departure by saying that he had discussions with the departmental Ministers or an audience with the Kaiser 'or something similar'.[416] An extended stay in Homburg with Wilhelm II could be attributed 'to the international situation or . . . the indispensability of my reports on domestic questions'.[417] Even a few days in the country had to be justified in the press.[418] In September 1905 a brief visit to Berlin was proof 'that the Reich Chancellor is always at his post, in domestic and foreign policy'.[419]

Bülow used the press to try to deflect attention away from less illustrious episodes during his Chancellorship. In 1901, when domestic worries were paramount, he wanted his role in foreign policy to be emphasised more in the press. 'I am not exclusively Tariff Chancellor or the Chancellor of the Kaufmann and Puttkamer-Köller affairs, but above all the leader of German foreign policy', he informed the Press Bureau.[420] He was also prepared to go to quite unscrupulous lengths in order to bolster his position in the public eye. In September 1903 he saw how a 'fairy-tale' in the *Saale-Zeitung*, to the effect that socialist-revisionist Ministers would be a real possibility if only Bülow agreed, could be used by conservative newspapers as evidence that he was not yet the greatest evil;[421] and in 1904 he was quite happy to let a rumour circulate that the arch-conservative Manteuffel would be his successor because 'it would not do any harm at all if that were believed, especially in liberal circles'.[422] His image abroad did not escape his attention either. In 1902, when he was promoted to an *Oberst à la suite* with the *Königs-Husaren-Regiment*, he wanted it mentioned 'in the foreign – not the domestic! – press' that this was a great honour.[423] When he was personally attacked in the foreign press, this merely indicated 'that I know how to preserve our political and economic independence'.[424]

It is difficult to avoid the conclusion that, even by modern politicians' standards, Bülow was exceptionally sensitive to his public image and very easily wounded in his personal vanity. In 1901 it mattered to him when the press reported that he embraced the Italian Minister-President, Zanardelli, for the Chancellor insisted that he had only shaken hands with him.[425] He was concerned when news got out in 1905 (possibly from Althoff in the Ministry of Culture) about an unfortunate incident when he was at school in Halle which reflected ill on his strength of character.[426] And in 1904 Bülow was particularly aggrieved when Karl Schnetzler, the *Oberbürgermeister* of Karlsruhe, made a speech in which, without naming Bülow in person, he in effect drew an unfavourable comparison between the fourth Chancellor and the first.[427] Bülow felt personally injured by the speech after reading the press reports and hearing that the Grand Duke of Baden had apparently given it his full approval.[428] Consequently, the Chancellor was prepared to turn the episode into an unfortunate diplomatic incident by writing to the Baden government and seeking public demonstration of the Grand Duke's confidence in his conduct of affairs.[429] Eventually the Grand Duke expressed his regret that 'Count Bülow could accept completely erroneous press remarks as true',[430] but he complained to Brauer about this 'highly unpleasant affair of Bülow's sensitivity'.[431] Brauer too recognised that Bülow was 'not so insensitive and indifferent to personal press attacks as a Minister these days should be'.[432] The Chancellor later insisted that the speech had left him 'completely cold' and that it was only the Grand Duke's recognition of it which he had found so distressing.[433]

This kind of obsessiveness also extended to the reporting of Bülow's speeches, for the Chancellor saw his oratorical successes as playing a major role in the cultivation of his public image. Bülow believed with Hegel that speeches were 'effective actions [*wirksame Handlungen*]' and that 'speeches from peoples to peoples or to Princes and peoples are integral parts of history'.[434] Thus, like Bismarck, he appreciated the value of having his speeches published extensively in the press the next morning[435] and he participated actively in the publication of all his parliamentary speeches in book form during his Chancellorship.[436] Bülow relied on his closest advisers to furnish much of the material for his speeches, but he personally supervised every draft and scrutinised each detail. On public occasions he was always concerned to 'say something which makes an impression',[437] and sometimes he did not simply want the content of his speech discussed in the press but also 'the manner and way in which I spoke'.[438] On the other hand, he never wanted it stated in the press when he had to read a speech, which he had to do on a particularly tricky occasion.[439] Desiring to win recognition as a skilful orator and to cut an impressive figure at the head of the Reich executive, he almost invariably committed every word of his speeches to memory, and his 'dress rehearsals' in the Foreign Office later attracted considerable notoriety.[440]

In one of his notebooks, Bülow once wrote down a quotation from *Punch* about the English politician Lord Rosebery. 'Lord Rosebery', it read, 'has the indefinable quality of being personally interesting to the multitude'.[441] Bülow aspired to such a quality. In July 1902 he sent Hammann notes for a 'harmless item' in a newspaper about his summer stay in Norderney. The article would focus on what the Chancellor did, the clothes he wore and how he was able to feel a free man on the island – a piece of pure image-making in a style worthy of more modern journalistic exploits.[442] Another article in 1904 also focused on the Chancellor's summer vacation but, with discontent with Bülow's Chancellorship growing, it chose to concentrate more on politics and less on leisure:

It is for him in no way a mere holiday [*Ruheaufenthalt*]. For his life goes on in tireless work. He works almost more than in Berlin, for in the capital his time is frequently taken up by representational duties [*Pflichten der Repräsentation*]. In Norderney, on the other hand, nothing diverts him from his work. He chose this island town for his stay because he can easily reach Berlin from here.[443]

Bülow found the time to write many of his own press releases, no matter how trivial, and the notion that 'politics does not stand still for him while he's at the sea-side' became a recurring theme.[444] He always understood the advantages in cutting a good figure in the press, and in 1902 considered whether they should officially deny a press report that he was guarded by two policemen (*Wachtmeister*) and that amateur photographers were kept well away. 'No photographer is kept at a distance, and the task of the policemen consists of watching out for dogs and occasionally carrying my cape.'[445]

Bülow thus took an enormous interest in press affairs and came to have a very inflated view of the influence the press could exert. With respect to foreign policy, resistance to anti-German press intrigues took on the character of 'national defence', and the Press Bureau was instructed to strengthen its armoury. In 1905 Bülow secured Wilhelm II's agreement to a whole series of measures to increase German influence over the foreign press;[446] and convinced, like Hammann, that 'The times in which Germany did not need to worry about the judgements of the Chinese and Brazilians are over',[447] Bülow instructed all German embassies abroad to cultivate personal connections with representatives of the press and to report on their progress.[448] Certainly the Chancellor's concern to wield a major influence over the foreign and domestic press was inseparably bound up with his personal vanity and not merely a response to the changing times. German embassies were also instructed to send all the caricatures and cartoons in the press about Bülow to Berlin, and these were assiduously collected by the Chancellor's private secretaries.[449] 'Fête the brilliant statesman Bülow abroad and at home and you will fare well on earth', one newspaper complained in 1908.[450]

Bülow's inclination to have each of his actions immediately publicised by the press[451] and his obsession with his public image necessarily made him very reliant on his Press Chief, Otto Hammann. Hammann received a poor mention in Bülow's memoirs. Bülow claimed that the Press Chief eavesdropped and sniffed around everywhere and would have made a good detective,[452] but he criticised his lack of skill in dealing with public opinion and its journalist representatives, his inexperience, tactlessness and ignorance

4 Dr Otto Hammann, Chief of the Foreign Office Press Bureau, with his wife in 1909

about foreign affairs. Bülow gave no indication that Hammann ever exerted any significant political influence on the Chancellor and asserted that he gained under Bethmann Hollweg 'a political influence which he did not have under me'.[453] The whole area of public relations during Bülow's Chancellorship was left untouched, and Hammann was ultimately lumped together with all the inept leaders in Berlin who unwittingly contributed to events in July 1914.

Quite apart from the fact that such a patently hypersensitive Chancellor could never have tolerated as a Press Chief the kind of clumsy tactician which Bülow's portrayal of Hammann suggests, Bülow's assessment of Hammann and his political influence is clearly erroneous on all counts. As Loebell recalled, Hammann was 'a very clever man with a fine sense of political tact', and Bülow 'valued him greatly and did almost nothing without listening to his opinion too'.[454] Along with Richthofen and Loebell, Hammann was one of Bülow's closest advisers, and his influence grew rather than diminished as Bülow's Chancellorship progressed. Bülow's trust in Hammann is demonstrated by the fact that in his first year as Chancellor he ordered that all incoming telegrams could be shown to the Press Chief in confidence, on the assumption that the Press Bureau needed to know the details of international policy as well as what was said in the press if it was to be an effective instrument. Later this order was extended to cover political reports and instructions so that members of the Press Bureau would be better informed when briefing journalists (these orders were quickly rescinded after Bülow's resignation in 1909).[455]

Hammann's role during Bülow's Chancellorship should not be seen as one exclusively confined to matters concerning the press. Rather, he became the Chancellor's public relations man *par excellence*, and Bülow used his talents in a host of ways. Hammann played a major part in the drafting, editing and 'staging' of Bülow's speeches, and Bülow regularly sent him material and arguments around which the speeches were to be composed.[456] In 1905 Bülow sent Hammann an envelope of newspaper articles containing all the main arguments against the Mining Law and expected Hammann to provide the replies;[457] on another occasion, he listed the attacks expected from the right in the Reichstag and wanted Hammann to supply the answers.[458] Bülow asked the Press Chief whether he should attend Reichstag debates,[459] and his confidence in Hammann's political instinct is further demonstrated by the fact that he liked Hammann to sit through Reichstag debates and, if necessary, have him called.[460] Bülow sought Hammann's advice on important policy decisions, tactics and personnel questions;[461] and he informed him of issues of which the responsible Minister knew nothing.[462] In 1902, when Hammann sent Bülow a list of prospective candidates for the police presidency, none of whom suited the Chancellor, Bülow simply requested more.[463] Bülow's demands on his Press Chief grew. 'Please send me your ideas on England before the end of the day' was an unlikely request he made in 1905.[464]

It would have been surprising if Hammann had failed to exploit his privileged position in the Chancellor's confidence yet, for all Holstein's complaints and the rumours that the Press Bureau pursued an independent course during Bülow's Chancellorship, the indications are that he did not abuse his influence or act without Bülow's authorisation.[465] Without doubt, he jealously guarded his position. In 1902 there was a strong possibility that the respected journalist Hugo Jacobi would become Chief Editor of the *Norddeutsche Allgemeine Zeitung*. Hammann clearly influenced Bülow against this appointment by telling him that Jacobi would render greater services in an independent position.[466] Hammann feared that as Chief Editor of the *Norddeutsche Allgemeine Zeitung*, Jacobi would usurp his own coveted position with the Chancellor and, according to Holstein, the Press Chief assured Jacobi of an annual remuneration of 15,000 Marks to deter him from pursuing the post.[467]

During Bülow's Chancellorship the influence of the Foreign Office Press Bureau grew,[468] and it became perhaps the Chancellor's most formidable weapon. Few outsiders can have had any conception of its all-embracing role or of the Chancellor's almost fanatical interest in the German and foreign press and the press coverage he received. In 1906, when Tschirschky moved into the Wilhelmstrasse as the new State Secretary of the Foreign Office, he wrote to Monts in astonishment: 'You have no idea of B[ülow]'s dependence on the press. Hammann is really the "one who leads" [*der "leitende"*].'[469] Between 1900 and 1905 the Press Bureau functioned, as it were, in peacetime. After 1905, as the Chancellor's position became more insecure and any unforeseen circumstances might have unseated him, the Bureau was mobilised for more energetic action, and Bülow's press directives to Hammann became even more urgent, more frenzied in tone. At the height of the international crisis of 1905–6 Bülow wrote to Hammann: 'Everything now depends on my emerging well from the Morocco affair.'[470] Gradually Bülow's concern with his public image and his reliance on the Press Bureau became so obsessive that the appearance superseded everything else in importance. There is probably no more fitting testimony to the personal preoccupations of Germany's fourth Chancellor than the message he sent to Hammann from his sick-bed after his collapse in April 1906: 'My position *vis-à-vis* the German people and in the world for a generation depends on the manner and way in which public opinion is *now* influenced and led.'[471]

4

The crisis of 1905–1906

In the spring and early summer of 1905 the Chancellor's position was exceptionally strong. After he achieved a number of notable parliamentary successes earlier in the year, Bülow's elevation to the status of Prince on 6 June 1905 coincided with the fall of the French Foreign Minister, Delcassé, as a result of Germany's diplomatic initiative over Morocco.[1] Even the Chancellor's conservative critics were noticably impressed by this apparent recognition of Germany, after so many humiliations, as a *quantité appréciable* in world politics, and the diplomatic victory had favourable repercussions on the German domestic situation.[2] Despite the Conservatives' continued misgivings about aspects of Bülow's internal policy, a controversial Mining Law, giving new rights to the miners in the wake of their strike, was passed by the Prussian Landtag in July 1905 without recourse to the dissolution threatened by the government.[3] The Chancellor's Press Bureau fed the optimism[4] and, for all the rumours of imminent war, Bülow himself exuded an air of confidence and self-satisfaction. After nearly five years as Chancellor, his career seemed to have reached a new peak, and even those who minimised his skill had to applaud his luck.[5]

However, within weeks of these successes, the impression was reversed. The Chancellor was faced with a series of protracted crises, affecting all aspects of foreign and domestic policy which shattered the Bülow system of 1900–5 and threatened a speedy end to his political career. The Chancellor suffered a variety of personal and political defeats; his position was precarious throughout most of 1906; and the intrigue and counter-intrigue that characterised German politics intensified and was revealed in all its degeneracy to the public. Only by supreme effort of will and by taking the most audacious gamble of his political career in December 1906 was Bülow able to repair some of the damage. This chapter disentangles the threads of the crisis and illuminates the pressures on the Chancellor which ultimately provoked the 'Bülow Bloc' experiment of 1907–9.

The Kaiser and the conduct of foreign policy

In March 1905 the German Foreign Office launched its diplomatic offensive over Morocco.[6] The initiative was primarily conceived as a means of testing the recently concluded Anglo-French entente, which had recognised France's special interests in Morocco, but from the very beginning it met with difficulties. The Kaiser was ultimately only prepared to land at Tangiers and proclaim a German interest in Morocco under great pressure from the Chancellor; [7] and Bülow had to devote considerable energy to restraining the Kaiser on his return to Germany from making inopportune remarks which might have prejudiced German policy.[8] In addition, the driving force behind the original campaign was undoubtedly Holstein, and, although he initially collaborated 'in the greatest harmony' with Bülow,[9] working conditions in the Foreign Office were tense because the Moroccan affair aggravated the antagonism between Holstein and Richthofen. By May there were rumours that Richthofen wanted to resign and that Holstein sought to replace him with Mühlberg.[10] Holstein's insistence on an international conference, despite the unfavourable diplomatic alignment of powers, and Bülow's failure to impose unity on the conduct of German foreign policy during the critical months after Delcassé's fall were primarily responsible for the deterioration in the German position after June 1905 and Germany's eventual diplomatic defeat at the Algeciras conference in 1906.[11] But, despite the problems inherent in the Moroccan campaign from the beginning, the course of the crisis was marked by a series of twists and turns before the final humiliation, and even in mid-October 1905 Lerchenfeld could report that, having teetered dangerously near the brink of complete disaster, Germany's Moroccan campaign was back on the right road again.[12] It was thus not primarily Morocco which undermined the Kaiser's confidence in the Chancellor's conduct of foreign policy in the second half of 1905; rather, it was the Chancellor's reaction to the Kaiser's renewed attempt to conclude an alliance with Russia which constituted the first step in the erosion of his system.

It has long been a source of puzzlement for historians of Bülow's Chancellorship why Bülow decided to submit his resignation (for the first time in his political career) over the conclusion of a Russo-German defensive alliance by the Kaiser and Tsar at Björkö in the Finnish Straits in July 1905.[13] Bülow did not accompany the Kaiser to Björkö, and ostensibly his anger was over Wilhelm's amendments to the proposed draft treaty, which included limiting the military obligations to Europe.[14] But there is something very unsatisfactory about attempts to explain the episode simply by reference to this issue or even within the wider context of German foreign policy.[15] Bülow without doubt wanted to establish closer relations with Russia; and he had been interested in concluding a defensive alliance at least since the Dogger Bank incident antagonised relations between Britain and Russia in the autumn of 1904.[16] Undoubtedly, too, his delight on hearing the news of the conclusion of the treaty diminished after he learnt of the Kaiser's changes.[17] But it was by no means clear that the 'en Europe' clause significantly detracted from the value of the alliance for Germany – the Kaiser clearly believed that it was in Germany's interest not to have to go to Russia's assistance in Asia,[18] and even Holstein and Bülow still desired to retain the Björkö treaty.[19] Moreover, the delay before Bülow submitted his resignation suggests some kind of calculation on the part of the Chancellor. Bülow learnt of the additional clause on 26 July and spent two days in correspondence with his Foreign Office advisers before he communicated his doubts about it to the Kaiser.[20] Even after the Kaiser had informed Bülow on 30 July that 'It was I who inserted the phrase "en Europe" after mature consideration and most deliberately',[21] Bülow wrote a comparatively conciliatory reply, still adhering to the view that the treaty would be more valuable without the addition, but prepared to praise Wilhelm's general achievement.[22] Only on 2 August did Bülow decide that he could not accept responsibility for the modification, and his resignation was despatched the following day.[23]

It could be argued that Bülow only belatedly became convinced of the gravity of the Kaiser's amendments or that he was finally persuaded to resign by his advisers. According to the diplomat Hermann von Eckardstein, Richthofen told him in October 1905 that he had had great difficulty persuading Bülow to resign in order to cancel the treaty.[24] Richthofen was certainly opposed to a Russo-German treaty of any kind;[25] and, having been on holiday since the middle of July and excluded from the negotiations, he visited Bülow in Norderney on 1 August.[26] Nevertheless, it is extremely unlikely that Bülow would have bowed to the pressure of his advisers on such an issue, and the motives behind his decision can only be appreciated if Björkö is placed within the general context, not only of German foreign policy, but also of the position of the Chancellor in July 1905.

Bülow's position in the early summer of 1905, after his parliamentary victories and the fall of Delcassé, was an exceptionally strong one, and he was secure not least with the Kaiser. Promoted to a Prince in June 1905, Bülow was greeted with three cheers when he arrived to see the Kaiser on the *Hohenzollern* on 9 July, 'a special honour in recognition of the agreement procured from France to a Morocco conference'.[27] The Kaiser still seemed as enamoured of his Chancellor as he had been of his new State Secretary of the Foreign Office in 1897. Moreover, Bülow's inheritance of four million Marks from a recently deceased relative was bound to impress the monarch[28] and seemed to ensure for the Chancellor a material independence which was interpreted as valuable politically.[29] Bülow correctly anticipated that there would be no question of the Kaiser's acceptance of his resignation in July 1905.

At the same time, however, Bülow's exasperation with Wilhelm II was growing. The Kaiser's interference in the Chancellor's conduct of foreign policy had been increasing since 1904, and after a particularly strenuous autumn when Wilhelm had been very preoccupied with the possibility of a war against England,[30] Bülow's patience was at a low ebb. Wilhelm's New Year address to his generals irritated him profoundly. The Chancellor attributed many of Germany's international difficulties, perhaps even the Anglo-French entente, to the Kaiser's treatment of his fellow sovereigns. Bülow complained bitterly to Tirpitz that the most calm people were 'checkmated' after a long period with the Kaiser. Philipp Eulenburg spent three days in bed after an imperial visit; the same applied to Tschirschky.[31] In 1904 the Kaiser had been responsible for the unfortunate choice of General Trotha as commander of the expeditionary force sent to crush the colonial revolt in South-West Africa, where the situation was critical by the summer of 1905.[32] In June 1905 and again later in the year Wilhelm may well have compromised German policy in the Moroccan crisis by making known his peaceful intentions and his desire to gain an understanding with France.[33] Then in July he considered himself to be the best judge of Germany's interests and modified the Björkö treaty without prior consultation with the Chancellor.

The Bülow system was without doubt still politically viable in July 1905. Apart from the occasional lapse or when, as at Björkö, communication with the Chancellor was difficult, Wilhelm continued to demonstrate his confidence in Bülow (as when he landed at Tangiers) and to discuss political issues with him. But Bülow must have looked back nostalgically to the period 1900–4 when foreign policy problems seemed less pressing and the Kaiser had been willing to remain in the background. Moreover, as Bülow's complaints to Tirpitz indicate, the Bülow system was rapidly becoming impossible for the Chancellor to sustain on a personal level. Still the recipient of laudatory telegrams from the Kaiser, perhaps intoxicated by his recent successes and the rhetoric of his own Press Bureau, Bülow was finding it increasingly difficult to truckle to the monarch in the familiar way. After more than seven years of close collaboration, Bülow seems to have become convinced that the Kaiser really was dependent on him. His assumption was to prove erroneous, but it helps to explain Bülow's motives in tendering his resignation. As Hammann later suspected, Bülow wanted 'to teach the Kaiser a lesson and to strengthen the position of the Chancellor against autocratic velleities on the part of Wilhelm II'.[34]

Initially, Bülow's submission of his resignation met with the desired response and did indeed provoke feelings of acute dependence and inferiority in the Kaiser. Wilhelm, who had been so ecstatic over his personal success in concluding the alliance,[35] capitulated completely to the Chancellor and his demands concerning the treaty. 'To be treated like this by the best and most intimate friend that I have – since the death of my poor Adolf [Bülow] – without any valid reason being given, has dealt me such a terrible blow that I have completely collapsed and must fear that I will fall victim to a serious nervous illness [*Nervenkrankheit*].' Reminding Bülow how he had disembarked at Tangiers against his wish merely to please the Chancellor, mounted a strange horse despite his withered arm, ridden through mobs of 'Spanish anarchists' and risked his life for Bülow's policy, the Kaiser claimed that they were 'made for each other, to work and to achieve for our dear German Fatherland' and that Bülow was '100,000 times more valuable to me and our Fatherland than all the treaties in the world'. He could not and would not accept Bülow's resignation and appealed to the Chancellor to speak no more about it. Bülow had to indicate immediately that he would stay. 'For the morning after the receipt of your resignation would fail to find the Kaiser alive! Think of my poor wife and children.'[36]

Yet, however much Wilhelm's shocked reaction and appeals to Bülow's friendship and compassion may have given the Chancellor cause for internal satisfaction, there is no denying that, given the nature of their relationship and the function it fulfilled within the Bülow system, Bülow's resignation request over the Björkö treaty was in the longterm an act of crass stupidity. Even the emotion of Wilhelm's letter cannot conceal the fact that he could not understand the political motives for Bülow's action, especially after the Chancellor's previous encouragement of his initiatives. Moreover, for all his torment, Wilhelm's allusions to Bülow's intention to leave 'your most loyal friend' in the lurch in such a tense and dangerous situation and after all the 'love and honours' he, the Kaiser, had showered on the Chancellor already bore the implication of treachery and betrayal. 'But Bülow, I have not deserved that from you. No, my friend, you will remain in office and by my side and will continue to work in common with me *ad majorem Germaniae Gloriam* . . . You cannot and must not fail me, for you would be disavowing the whole of your policy this year and I would be disgraced [*blamiert*] for ever.'[37]

Bülow's reply was the usual effervescent mixture of flattery, praise and admiration, professing tears of emotion while he insisted that it had been his duty to offer to resign since they both saw the situation differently.[38] Ostensibly the incident seemed closed and relations between Kaiser and Chancellor could resume their former confidentiality. Yet Björkö was to be the most serious assault on Wilhelm II's confidence in Bülow since 1897. Moreover, if Bülow's objective was to force the monarch to adopt a more restrained attitude towards foreign policy and in particular to leave the threads of the Moroccan crisis and the embryonic continental alliance to the Chancellor, he was bitterly disappointed. Wilhelm initially gave in to Bülow's demands, but in the long run his confidence in the Chancellor's judgement and reliability was shaken. The Kaiser was now even less likely to leave everything to Bülow than he had been before.

If Bülow did not realise his mistake immediately, he had done by the autumn of 1905. Coincidentally, it was just at this time that Philipp Eulenburg, who had been in closer contact with the Kaiser again since 1904,[39] re-emerged unequivocally on the German political scene. Eulenburg visited Wilhelm in Rominten in September 1905, and Wilhelm went to Liebenberg the following month.[40] Eulenburg's presence in Rominten assumed a certain political significance since it coincided with the visit there of the Russian Minister, Witte, but as important from Bülow's point of view must have been the shadow that Eulenburg's reappearance cast on his relationship with the Kaiser. On 25 September, while walking with Eulenburg, Wilhelm unburdened his feelings over the whole Björkö episode, justifying again his decision to make the changes in the treaty and revealing quite clearly his continued perplexity over Bülow's response.

I simply don't comprehend Bülow – I don't understand him at all, how he could suddenly become so contrary over this question. For three weeks the torment went back and forth and now everything's fine again. But others too said to me that they had not understood Bernhard: Richthofen and Mühlberg, who had to be called in for the drafting of the treaty. Might Holstein perhaps be behind it? – I don't know. But in any case Bernhard took the matter so seriously that I did not know at all how I was to come out of it. 'I thought that perhaps someone else would manage affairs better than I – in such grave times', he wrote. Yes, well if the times are grave, then surely he cannot desert me or leave me in the lurch. As I said, I truly don't understand why he wanted to go.

As Eulenburg confirmed, the Kaiser's belief that harmony had once again been restored with the Chancellor did not necessarily mean a return to the *status quo ante*. 'Il y a un petit froid', he noted after another walk with the Kaiser, for the monarch had voiced his suspicion that Bülow's gesture of defiance had been the product of 'injured vanity . . . because *he* had not devised the treaty'.[41]

Eulenburg did not hide his anxiety about the relationship between Kaiser and Chancellor from Bülow. In October he wrote to the Chancellor, 'I am dying to see you because a certain lack of clarity in HM's account of Björkö made me think – and frightened me [*mir zu denken – und zu fürchten gibt*].'[42] Moreover, however loyal Eulenburg was to the Chancellor personally and politically,[43] Bülow cannot have welcomed other manifestations of the Kaiser's renewed confidence in his former favourite. One can imagine Bülow's displeasure on reading that the Kaiser told Eulenburg with the old confidentiality about 'the *entire* course of policy' and that Eulenburg had difficulty restraining himself from telling the monarch a few plain truths.[44] Eulenburg made no secret of the fact that he had many opportunities to discuss politics with the Kaiser; and the facility with which he resumed his former role must have shocked Bülow. Although Eulenburg did not conceal anything from Bülow and kept within the Chancellor's instructions on political matters, Bülow cannot have enjoyed having to conduct policy again in the autumn of 1905 through Eulenburg's good offices. This impression is reinforced when one considers that Eulenburg did not believe that there existed the close identity of interest between Kaiser and Chancellor which Bülow had sought to demonstrate but instead, consciously or unconsciously, assumed a certain friction in their relations. Acting as a mediator between Witte and the Kaiser, Eulenburg sent a copy of one of Witte's letters to Bülow explicitly stating that it was without Wilhelm's knowledge. '*You know how he is*', Eulenburg wrote to Bülow, 'and how the thought of an understanding without or apart from him [*ohne oder neben ihm*] fills him with mistrust.'[45] Eulenburg underestimated the Kaiser's confidence in Bülow, for the monarch himself promptly sent the original letter from Witte on to Bülow for his information.[46] But Bülow must have resented the implication that Wilhelm II would have disapproved if he had known about the Chancellor's involvement.

Eulenburg was not the only friend of the Kaiser's to figure prominently in the autumn of 1905. During November Wilhelm also stayed in Donaueschingen and 'surpassed himself' in the kindnesses he displayed towards Max Fürstenberg and his wife.[47] But although it is tempting to conclude that the influence of the Kaiser's personal friends was growing just as Bülow's seemed to be in doubt, it was only Eulenburg who adopted a political role in 1905 and cooperated with the Kaiser and government in the conduct of foreign policy. Bülow successfully concealed any apprehension he felt, and Eulenburg's role as an intermediary between the Kaiser and Witte eventually became redundant when the German hopes for a continental alliance finally evaporated in the spring of 1906 (and Witte resigned in May). But the new uncertainty in Bülow's relationship with the Kaiser may well have affected the Chancellor's conduct of foreign policy in the winter of 1905–6 and his oscillations between a compliant and a more rigorous attitude towards France.[48] Moreover, his suspicions about the political implications of Eulenburg's reappearance were probably reinforced when Eulenburg received the Order of the Black Eagle in March 1906.[49] The Chancellor may have worried about Eulenburg's political aspirations, and it is perhaps not coincidental that in January 1906 he instructed a Reich Chancellery official to look into the constitutional provisions for Alsace-Lorraine and especially the question of the appointment of the *Statthalter*. Since it was widely rumoured that Eulenburg coveted this lucrative position, he cannot have been too happy to have confirmed that Wilhelm II was in no way limited in his choice of *Statthalter*.[50]

Personnel changes within the executive

The Chancellor's weakening position in the autumn of 1905 is reflected in a series of personnel changes within the executive, not all planned or intended,

which together posed a challenge to his authority. After four years of relative
stability in the highest Reich and Prussian departments, there were four new
appointments in as many months, and this new volatility with respect to
government personnel was also indicated by the growing number of
rumours about impending ministerial resignations. Berckheim reported in
October 1905 that scarcely a day passed without news that one Minister or
another wanted to resign,[51] and Budde (who died of a stomach cancer in
April 1906[52]), Podbielski (who was exposed to press attacks from October
1905 but who may have been looking for a 'good departure'[53]) and
Rheinbaben (who, it was said, wanted to exchange his portfolio for an
Oberpräsidium[54]) all figured on this list. In the event the four new appointments affected the Ministries of Trade and Justice, the proposed new Reich
Colonial Office and the State Secretaryship of the Foreign Office, and one
of these – the replacement of Karl von Schönstedt, the 73-year-old Minister
of Justice, by Maximilian von Beseler in November 1905[55] – did not have
any overt political significance. But the other three personnel changes can all
be interpreted as detrimental to the Chancellor's interests and symptomatic
of the Kaiser's growing reluctance to rely exclusively on Bülow's mediation.

Perhaps the only statement that can be made with any certainty about
Möller's resignation in October 1905 is that it was not voluntary. There were
various interpretations put forward about why he was dismissed, all of which
may have contained an element of truth. Möller's performance as Minister
of Trade after his appointment in May 1901 had been disappointing. He had
been criticised by members of the Prussian bureaucracy, by the Reich
Treasury, the agrarians, even his own party, and the Trade Department in
the Foreign Office always considered that he had been more useful to the
government as a National Liberal deputy.[56] But the immediate context of his
dismissal was his clumsy attempt to nationalise the Hibernia mining
company and his behaviour towards the Rhine–Westphalian coal syndicate.[57]

According to press reports, Möller may well have fallen victim to an
intrigue within the Prussian government. Möller, who had initially declared
during the spring parliamentary session that he did not want to nationalise
the Hibernia but who later changed his mind, could not secure the support
of his colleagues, for the more conservative Ministers had always regarded
him as some kind of intruder and in particular resented his promotion of the
Mining Law. Thus Möller's secret enemies in the Prussian government
exploited the Hibernia affair to force his removal; and when Möller denied
press rumours in September 1905 that his resignation was imminent, he was
told by someone in 'not merely a decisive but actually a very decisive
government position' that he could not now initiate the government's
purchase of the Hibernia which he had declared himself against in the spring.
Thus Möller 'finally realised that he had to submit his resignation'.[58]

The possibility that the initiative for Möller's dismissal came from within the Prussian government is supported by a report of the Baden ambassador after a conversation with two well-oriented members of the Prussian Upper House. Berckheim reported that Rheinbaben, whose position was reputedly 'very strong' in late 1905, had been very angry over the failure to acquire the Hibernia earlier in the year (for it had then been purchased by the consortium of Rhenish–Westphalian industrialists) and had convinced both the Kaiser and the Chancellor of the necessity of Möller's replacement.[59] Bülow, too, may have found Möller inconvenient in 1905 because the Minister was personally committed to the Stock Exchange Bill, which was popular with the National Liberals but which the Chancellor was inclined to renounce in order to keep the Reichstag majority in a good mood for the financial reform (of 1906) and the Navy Bill.[60] It took considerable prompting from both Bülow and Lucanus before Möller finally submitted his resignation on 15 October.[61]

Möller's resignation was certainly engineered, and Bülow wanted the new appointment to 'appear as the replacement of a modest by a greater capacity'.[62] The new Minister of Trade was to be the former *Oberpräsident* of West Prussia, Delbrück, who was *persona grata* to the Kaiser.[63] The Bremen ambassador went so far as to report that Möller had been dismissed because Wilhelm II had wanted to install Delbrück,[64] but in fact the monarch had initially opposed removing Delbrück from Danzig, possibly because Delbrück himself doubted his suitability for the Trade Ministry.[65] However, after the Kaiser had conferred with him several times during his stay at Rominten in September 1905 and after Loebell also spent several hours convincing him of his qualifications for the post, Delbrück finally agreed to the appointment.[66]

The installation of another Minister who enjoyed the Kaiser's special favour would not have been so significant if it had remained an isolated case in the autumn and winter of 1905–6. But almost immediately the Kaiser intervened decisively in another personnel issue being discussed by the Chancellor and his advisers, and this time Wilhelm's candidate – the eldest son of the *Statthalter* of Alsace-Lorraine, *Erbprinz* Ernst zu Hohenlohe-Langenburg – gave Bülow far greater cause for concern.

The reorganisation of the colonial administration in Berlin had been the subject of public discussion for well over a year by the autumn of 1905, ever since the inadequacies of the system had been brought into stark relief by the colonial risings in German South-West and East Africa and by the attacks on the government in the press and in the Reichstag.[67] Bülow had concerned himself with the issue of reform in a major speech in the Reichstag in December 1904,[68] and although one alternative would have been to transfer responsibility for colonial affairs from the Foreign Office to the Reich Navy

Office or War Ministry and thereby establish a purely military administration, this kind of solution was resisted by the departments concerned. It was
clear that the most advantageous course was to establish a separate Reich
Office for the colonies under a State Secretary or Under State Secretary
subordinate to the Chancellor.[69] However, the organisational changes were
delayed by the protracted nature of the uprisings. The Colonial Director in
the Foreign Office, Oskar Stübel, wanted to resign, and by September 1905
his position was untenable both inside and outside his department.[70] But his
proposed successor, Adolf von Götzen (who was too young to assume a State
Secretaryship and therefore would have been made an Under State Secretary) was seen as indispensable in East Africa,[71] and eventually the Chancellor
was forced to think of someone else for the post.

In early November 1905 Richthofen approached Heinrich Wiegand, the
Director of the Norddeutsche Lloyd, but received a negative response.[72]
Bülow considered forcing Wiegand to accept the position by mobilising the
Kaiser, but later dropped the idea.[73] The new State Secretaryship was also
offered to Hermann von Pfaff, the Bavarian Foreign Minister, who was
inclined to reject the position.[74] By the middle of the month Bülow seems
to have been thinking of Arthur von Gwinner, the Director of the Deutsche
Bank, when a serious complication arose in the form of the Kaiser's proposal
of Hohenlohe-Langenburg. Richthofen clearly expected Bülow to be able to
dissuade Wilhelm from this choice during an audience on 14 November[75] –
indeed, in the summer of 1905, Bülow had felt sufficiently strong to insist
successfully on the eventual recall of General Trotha from South-West
Africa.[76] Thus the State Secretary already suggested that Gwinner be offered
the temporary leadership of the colonial department in the Foreign Office
until the new State Secretaryship was approved by the Reichstag.[77] But if
Bülow did resist Hohenlohe's candidature, he was ineffective. On 14
November Wilhelm wrote to Hohenlohe that a new, independent Reich
Office for the administration of all colonial affairs was to be created and that
he had him in mind to head the new department.[78]

Hohenlohe thus replaced Stübel in late November 1905 and it was
confirmed that he would be the new State Secretary of a Reich Colonial
Office, subject to parliamentary approval, from 1 April 1906.[79] Hohenlohe
was a complete novice in colonial matters;[80] his appointment met with
surprise in government circles and he could expect difficulties in the Reichstag after the government's refusal to recall the Reichstag in the summer
when it despatched reinforcements to South-West Africa.[81] More significantly, Hohenlohe's appointment was highly embarrassing to the Chancellor and
seemed to be a glaring example of the Kaiser's 'personal rule'. Hohenlohe
was on *Du* terms with the Kaiser[82] – they were related both by marriage and
by blood – and doubtless would not decline to exploit his favoured position.

As State Secretary he was unlikely to subordinate himself to the Chancellor and, after a meeting with Bülow in November 1905, he wanted written confirmation of some of the points they had discussed. Hohenlohe stressed that it was of 'decisive significance' for him that he had full independence in organising the new office and executing a new colonial programme; he stipulated conditions about his assumption of the State Secretaryship, the financial arrangements for the post and the responsibility of the new office. He regarded the provisional period as Colonial Director as 'an especially difficult sacrifice for me' since the Kaiser had never mentioned this lower status to him before.[83] Bülow responded predictably with ostensibly excessive conciliatoriness, instructing Richthofen to reply in a most friendly manner and assure him of the Chancellor's full support. But his displeasure at the attempts of the Kaiser's favourite to impose conditions was also evident. 'At the same time', Bülow wrote,

> let it drop – again in a really conciliatory way – that the State Secretary of the Colonies will enjoy the same independence and responsibility as all the State Secretaries, whose independence is indeed only constitutionally restricted by their position with respect to the Reich Chancellor. In the first place his task would be to carry out my programme of 5 December last year, which we can enclose.[84]

Bülow thus recognised the threat and made it quite clear to Hohenlohe that he was the Chancellor's subordinate. But he must also have been aware that any problems with his new colleague would arise not so much from the day-to-day conduct of colonial affairs but from Hohenlohe's personal access to Wilhelm II. As Szögyényi heard, even before Hohenlohe took over the business of the colonial department,

> Prince Bülow seems . . . to fear that Kaiser Wilhelm selected the *Erbprinz* as State Secretary of the new Colonial Office which is to be established, chiefly in order to have him near him so that he, the Kaiser, at the given time will have an appropriate Reich Chancellor candidate at his disposal.[85]

However unfounded these fears were, Bülow's suspicion would grow in the ensuing months. Nor were they lost on the wary Holstein, who wrote to Brauer in December 1905: 'Bülow has a cold and, what is more, is nervous as a result of the interpretation which individual newspapers have put forward with respect to the appointment of the *Erbprinz* of Hohenlohe-Langenburg as Colonial Secretary, for they described the latter as the coming Chancellor.'[86]

It was customary for important government personnel changes to take place in the early autumn, before the opening of the new parliamentary sessions. Thus Bülow must have hoped that no further incidents of this kind would arise for a few months, especially as he was beginning to feel under pressure from a variety of directions. The Kaiser still had plenty of scope for intervention in diplomatic appointments and, annoyed since the spring about the performance of German diplomats in St Petersburg ('Had I known how things were in reality, we would have stood long ago in Warsaw', he told Varnbüler in April 1905[87]), in October 1905 he replaced Friedrich von Alvensleben as ambassador with Wilhelm von Schön, 'a personal intimate friend of mine having my fullest confidence for many years'.[88] Clearly any further government personnel changes were likely to be in a direction not necessarily welcomed by the Chancellor. Thus Bülow hoped to ride out his difficulties in late 1905 and, perhaps by means of a satisfactory conclusion to the Moroccan affair, rehabilitate himself completely in the Kaiser's favour.

But it was at a most critical juncture of the Moroccan crisis that a new State Secretary of the Foreign Office had to be found. There had been persistent rumours about Richthofen's imminent resignation from early 1905, both on account of his alleged weariness with office and his difficulties with Holstein;[89] and from May 1904 the State Secretary had been feeling under increasing strain because of the complicated diplomatic situation and the reliance placed on him by the Chancellor.[90] In August 1905 Bülow had even instructed him to examine thoroughly the situation in East Africa, to have all the relevant material shown to him and 'to take colonial affairs completely into your hands'.[91] On 31 December Richthofen wrote to his son that he found the burden of work and the responsibility more difficult to bear and that he did not sleep well. 'If I could only get a few free hours a day for myself.'[92] Apparently distraught because an important document on the Moroccan question was missing,[93] he suffered a heart attack at a dinner in early January 1906 and died some days later on 17 January.[94]

Richthofen's death intensified the difficulties in the German Foreign Office, for Holstein had been on the verge of resigning since the summer of 1905.[95] Earlier in January 1906 he had written Bülow a long letter criticising the Chancellor's policy and complaining about the influence of Hammann.[96] Although there was now no question (if there ever had been) that he would actually carry out his threat and submit his resignation, he secured his promotion to Director of the Political Department, partly in order to bolster his position under a new State Secretary.[97] More importantly Richthofen's death gave the Kaiser another opportunity to intervene in personnel questions and choose his successor. For, as Szögyényi recognised right from the beginning, 'The decision will of course be made by Kaiser Wilhelm himself.'[98]

Although both Monts and Brauer were seen as suitable and independent-minded candidates for the State Secretaryship, and although Brauer maintained that Bülow favoured his candidacy in January 1906,[99] there is no doubt that the most desirable successor to Richthofen from Bülow's point of view was Mühlberg, the Under State Secretary, who was competent and popular in diplomatic circles.[100] Mühlberg was also supported by Holstein, and his appointment would have ensured continuity in the work of the Foreign Office as well as Bülow's personal control. Szögyényi was assured from a very well-informed source that Bülow did his utmost to secure Mühlberg's appointment, but the ambassador never believed that Mühlberg would be the new State Secretary as he had never been *persona grata* to the Kaiser. Mühlberg had risen through the consular service and had never held a diplomatic post; moreover, he came from a middle-class background and a recently ennobled Jewish family. Szögyényi knew that Wilhelm II would never choose such a man.[101]

The Kaiser's candidate was Heinrich von Tschirschky, the Prussian Minister to Hamburg, who regularly accompanied Wilhelm II on his travels (he had been with him at Björkö[102]) and who had Wilhelm's confidence and friendship. Berckheim heard from two members of the Court that there were 'serious differences of opinion' between the Kaiser and the Chancellor over Tschirschky's appointment,[103] but if Bülow did make timid objections they were disregarded by the monarch, and Bülow did not let the issue further sour their relationship.[104] Tschirschky was appointed State Secretary on 22 January and, as well as reflecting Wilhelm II's personal initiative,[105] the appointment also seemed to have broader, political implications. Berckheim reported that the energetic policy pursued by Bülow and Holstein over Morocco had not had the Kaiser's approval and that Tschirschky had been appointed to pursue a conciliatory and peaceful policy, even if it entailed the loss of German prestige.[106] Brauer, on the other hand, maintained that Wilhelm wanted to reassume the direction of German foreign policy person-ally by appointing Tschirschky. The lesson of Germany's diplomatic defeats was that he, Kaiser Wilhelm, did not conduct affairs sufficiently himself.[107]

It would probably be fair to say that nobody was particularly happy with the appointment except the Kaiser himself. Tschirschky felt it would have been cowardly to refuse his promotion, but he did not like his new position, having earlier been angling for the Russian embassy.[108] He wrote to Monts, 'HM, B.B. and Holstein! Each alone would be enough to make one tremble, despite all the talents and qualities which all three of them have.'[109] Mühlberg immediately submitted his resignation, claiming that after twenty-five years he merely wanted peace and quiet, but clearly having no inclination to work under the younger man.[110] Bülow went to great lengths to persuade Mühlberg to remain at his post, even if only for a few more weeks, and held out to him the prospect of an eventual diplomatic appointment.[111] But although the Chancellor appealed to Mühlberg's conscience in the name of the Kaiser, Wilhelm himself attached little significance to Mühlberg's re-maining in office, and on 23 January Bülow wrote to Hammann that the press rumours of Mühlberg's intention to resign were 'very unwelcome' as they would 'annoy HM and prejudice the future of Mühlberg'.[112]

Above all, Tschirschky's appointment was a severe blow to Bülow's authority. Although Tschirschky maintained to Monts that he would be loyal to the Chancellor,[113] and although he intended, unlike Richthofen, to restrict himself exclusively to foreign affairs,[114] he was seen by all to be the Kaiser's favourite and, as events were to prove, his conception of Germany's interests did not quite harmonise with Bülow's perception of his own. Bülow resented the interpretations of Tschirschky's appointment by the press and complained to Hammann that 'It is useful neither for Tsch[irschky] nor especially for HM that the former is made out to be [*frisiert wird*] only the favourite of the latter.'[115] He could also have added that it was equally detrimental to his own position, but characteristically, rather than adopt any direct tactics aimed at ousting Tschirschky, the Chancellor chose to resort to intrigue to undermine the position of his new subordinate. As he told Hammann:

I would consider it useful if it were said here and there in the press – but so that it is circulated further – that Tschirschky made his début as the intimate colleague of Herbert Bismarck. It can also (discreetly) be said that Tsch[irschky] is the brother-in-law of Count Friedrich Vitzthum (Pres. of the Saxon I Chamber, Saxon *Oberhof-marschall*), who was very close to the Bismarck family.[116]

Presumably Bülow hoped thereby to prejudice Tschirschky's popularity with the Kaiser, but the Chancellor faced an uphill struggle.

If one surveys the personnel changes in the autumn and winter of 1905–6 they certainly represented an impairment of the Chancellor's position, quite apart from the difficulties the new State Secretaries of the Foreign Office and the proposed Colonial Office, in particular, would introduce into the conduct of policy. Taken in conjunction with other isolated reports of shifts within the executive – for example the strong position of the Finance Minister and the growing reputation of Bethmann Hollweg, both of whom reportedly discussed affairs with the Kaiser beyond the immediate concerns of their departments by late 1905[117] – they attest to Wilhelm II's growing impatience with the capabilities and reliability of his Chancellor and his intention to play a more dominant role in government affairs. Bülow had never set great store by a loyal band of followers within the executive, but the list of the Kaiser's known favourites by January 1906 was formidable. Rheinbaben, Podbielski, Budde, Einem, Bethmann, Studt and Delbrück had been hand-picked as Prussian Ministers by Wilhelm II; Tschirschky, Hohenlohe-Langenburg and Tirpitz (who had his disagreements with the Kaiser but was nevertheless indispensable to him) held, or it was believed soon would hold, important Reich Offices. Only Posadowsky, Nieberding, Stengel and possibly Beseler cannot be considered imperial favourites, and yet even they felt no particular loyalty to Bülow.

It would of course be a mistake to attach too great a significance to the composition of the Prussian Ministry *per se*. The Kaiser still adhered to no consistent political objectives in selecting personnel, beyond his desire to install his favourites; and when the confrontation between Kaiser and Chancellor came in the autumn of 1906 over the Podbielski affair, the issue determined that the Ministers supported Bülow. Bülow was still able to secure the Ministers' consent to Reichstag salaries in February 1906, even though he had to work unusually hard to do so.[118] But the changing complexion of the executive added to Bülow's anxieties in the spring of 1906 and further encouraged his predilection for personal advisers, unofficial methods and intrigue. Moreover, in February 1906 Wilhelm II summoned another Crown Council meeting which, unlike its two predecessors during Bülow's Chancellorship, was prompted not by some exceptional circumstance – the flood disaster or the miners' strike – but took the form of a regular State Ministry meeting with a variety of issues on the agenda. The protocol suggests Bülow's customary passivity, perhaps even redundancy, when confronted with the Kaiser's presence in such a forum;[119] and perhaps he feared that the meeting would serve as a precedent for Wilhelm's renewed involvement in Prussian affairs as in 1897–1900. Fortunately for Bülow, the Kaiser would not be tempted to play such an active role for long (perhaps Bülow's management had spoiled the Kaiser, who disliked routine work even more than the Chancellor,[120] for there was only one more Crown Council meeting – in February 1909 – during Bülow's Chancellorship). But there were some rumours of an 'open discussion' between Kaiser and Chancellor after the meeting in February 1906 'which did not take a completely harmless course'.[121] And the Chancellor's problems in the executive were without doubt one element in the multiplicity of issues which contributed to his physical collapse in April 1906.

Bülow's collapse

In the early months of 1906 the pressures on the Chancellor were immense. Germany's abysmal diplomatic predicament at the Algeciras conference which opened on 16 January was the focus of constant concern and threatened to have major implications for Bülow's personal position. But he also faced difficulties in other areas, with personnel in the Foreign Office and with the political parties, and all these problems made demands on his time and consumed his energy. In addition, there were less tangible anxieties – worries about the Kaiser's waning confidence in him, the rumours that his position was precarious, the discussion of his successor, the possible influence of Eulenburg. All these factors combined to place great mental and physical strain on the Chancellor and contributed to his collapse in the Reichstag in April 1906.

From the beginning of the deliberations at Algeciras, Bülow's primary concern was that he personally should emerge from the Moroccan episode as well as possible.[122] But throughout February 1906 the French adhered resolutely to their demands, confident of international support, and the Chancellor soon abandoned his belief that the failure of the conference would be preferable to German capitulation.[123] Unwilling to support a policy of firmness *vis-à-vis* France when 'neither public opinion, parliament, princes or even the army will have anything to do with a war over Morocco',[124] and perhaps under imperial pressure (though this is not entirely proven),[125] he decided on a course of compromise and retreat, hoping to salvage what he could from an unenviable situation.

Thus from February 1906 the Chancellor was preoccupied with a massive campaign of deception. Concerned now merely with the appearance of victory, he hoped to obscure the German humiliation at Algeciras and counter the impression that the whole Morocco crisis had ended in a German diplomatic defeat. In December 1905 Bülow had instructed Hammann to enrol two more colleagues to help him,[126] and his press directives in February and March 1906 reflected the overwhelming priority of portraying the Moroccan crisis as a German and a personal success. 'The main thing now is that the impression does not arise in our public opinion that we were excessively compliant in Algeciras or allowed ourselves to be humiliated', he told Hammann in the middle of March.[127] But even now the Chancellor's approach was not wholly consistent, for one day he urged Hammann to emphasise the government's intransigence, ruthlessness and severity throughout the crisis so that it would not appear to have capitulated to the French position,[128] but a few days later he wanted Germany's reasonableness to be accentuated in the face of unpredictable and fantastic French demands.[129] Bülow was also perfectly aware of his personal shortcomings, which had dogged the Moroccan initiative from the start. As he wrote in another instruction: 'After agreement has been reached, the impression must be aroused that from the beginning I had in mind a definite goal – and indeed achieved exactly that – which, however, could not be revealed immediately. Without proposals and exorbitant demands [*Überfordern*], no compromise.'[130]

Germany's isolation at Algeciras was no compliment to German diplomacy, and it doubtless further undermined Wilhelm II's confidence in Bülow's conduct of affairs.[131] Wilhelm had not approved of the Foreign Office's policy throughout all stages of the Moroccan campaign[132] and, already resentful about his 'Statistenrolle' (minor role) in the landing at Tangiers,[133] he was beginning to express the view that he had only landed against his better judgement and on the express wish of the Chancellor, who in turn was advised by Holstein.[134] If Wilhelm had any remaining illusions about Germany's international position, these were quickly dispelled in late March 1906 by Tschirschky, who informed Monts that he had 'told HM the complete truth about our situation'.[135] Moreover, since the new State Secretary presumably did not hide from the Kaiser his belief in the need for some kind of rapprochement with Britain, it cannot have strengthened Bülow's position with Wilhelm II that, as in 1902, the Chancellor was rumoured to be the main obstacle to an improvement in Anglo-German relations. It was believed at the German embassy in Paris that Bülow's position was threatened by the English dislike of him;[136] and even Metternich, the German ambassador in London, informed Berlin that no one in England could believe in the Kaiser's peaceful intentions until he had a new Chancellor.[137] In early 1906 the press of St Petersburg, Paris and London made numerous personal attacks on the German Chancellor, circulating the alleged view of the late Chancellor Hohenlohe that Bülow had a 'superficial and indolent disposition which . . . was precisely the defect that the chief counsellor of Wilhelm II ought not to possess'.[138] Such criticisms of Bülow cannot have escaped the Kaiser's attention, although the Chancellor did what he could to minimise their political impact. 'The personal relations between Kaiser and his Reich Chancellor – and this is indeed the main thing in Germany – are, as before, extremely good [*die allerbesten*]', Szögyényi maintained in March 1906. But the ambassador's grounds for this optimism were but evidence of his own gullibility, for he continued:

and just recently it has been announced ostentatiously by the newspapers that Kaiser Wilhelm visits the Reich Chancellery daily and invited the Prince and Princess to a family dinner, indeed even on the occasion of a theatre performance at Court. Given this excellent, personal relationship, it is unthinkable that serious official differences could exist between the Kaiser and his Chancellor.[139]

If the Algeciras conference and its unfavourable conclusion had repercussions on the position of the Chancellor, it also had implications for the position of Holstein within the Foreign Office. With the Kaiser disposed to blame Holstein for the mismanagement of German policy and with Tschirschky increasingly convinced that the Counsellor would have to go,[140] Holstein began to be discussed with growing prominence in the German press, and the articles assumed more and more the character of an officially inspired campaign.[141] In the press, in parliamentary circles, at the stock exchange, Holstein was seen as the bogey-man who had wanted to embroil Germany in a war against France and, although he no longer played the same role as earlier, many well-informed people believed 'that it will soon be him who, given the changed situation, will be sacrificed as the scapegoat and will soon be resigning'.[142] Holstein's thoughts indeed hinged on resignation, for he surmised that Tschirschky's cool attitude towards him reflected the Kaiser's hostility.[143] But there seems little doubt that it was really Bülow who influenced the Kaiser and Tschirschky against Holstein and sought to blame Holstein for the failure of his own conduct of foreign policy.[144] Bülow spent five hours with Holstein on 2 April, attempting to dissuade him from persisting with his resignation request,[145] but the whole episode was quite clearly a charade. Bülow was only looking for the opportunity to ditch his difficult subordinate.[146]

Bülow was preoccupied with Algeciras and with Holstein's resignation in the days immediately preceding his collapse. Tschirschky told Monts un-equivocally later in April 1906 that all those who worked closely with the Chancellor had no doubt that Holstein was primarily responsible for Bülow's mental and physical exhaustion.[147] But there were also other issues which made demands on the Chancellor and must have taken their toll. On 4 April Tirpitz tendered his resignation to Wilhelm II. It was immediately rejected, but was another attempt by the Navy Secretary to safeguard his fleet building programme against imperial encroachments.[148] Bülow had been involved in the discussions on the shape of the new Navy Bill of 1906 and, seeing the advantages of a big national issue, he had earlier supported the idea of exploiting the unfavourable international situation to shorten the lifetime of the battleships.[149] But Bülow was ultimately convinced by Tirpitz of the need to resist Wilhelm's desire to increase further the naval demands.[150] Moreover, the disagreement between Kaiser and Chancellor after the Crown Council meeting on 13 February in all probability concerned the naval issue, for the Kaiser was very aggrieved that he would not get his ships.[151]

Bülow may also have been under pressure from the Kaiser and the more conservative Ministers to take energetic action against the SPD. Mass de-monstrations had been planned against the Prussian three-class suffrage in January 1906,[152] and on New Year's Eve Wilhelm II had written his famous letter to the Chancellor, rejecting the possibility of a war against France and Britain partly because of the threat of Social Democracy at home. 'First fire on the socialists, decapitate [them] and render [them] harmless, if necessary by means of a bloodbath, and then war abroad', the Kaiser had declared,[153] and this was a theme he also developed at the Crown Council meeting when he urged the government to take preventive measures against Social Demo-cratic infiltration of the Army.[154] But, although Bülow adopted a more militant tone in his speeches in late 1905 and early 1906 and his references to the *Revolutionspartei* contrasted sharply with the conciliatory approach of his State Secretary of Interior,[155] Bülow seems to have resisted any pressure to resort to violent methods. In January 1906 he argued in the Prussian Ministry of State that it was still important to ensure that the educated classes were behind the government and that the latter kept within the bounds of the law.[156] Moreover, although Bülow saw Posadowsky in December 1905, partly to discuss 'the future tone of the Count towards Social Democracy',[157] it is not clear whether he wanted Posadowsky to moderate his defence of his social welfare legislation or to ignore the apparent change in attitude of the Chancellor. Posadowsky continued to pursue his policy and maintained that there were no differences between himself and the Chancellor.[158]

Finally, in early 1906 Bülow found himself in renewed difficulties with the Centre Party in the Reichstag. In January, after an imprudent declaration defending duelling in the officer corps by the War Minister, Einem, which 'had an effect on the Centre and on the Social Democrats like a red rag on a herd of bulls',[159] there were fears that the Centre would retaliate by adopting a negative attitude towards important legislation such as the financial reform and the Military Pensions Law.[160] Bülow, who had lent the declaration his authority (though, probably through overwork, he had not read it), worked himself up into a state of 'great agitation and consternation' in private with Centre leaders, reminding them of all his efforts on behalf of their party and threatening to resign.[161] But, for all his references to his financial independence and his wife's concern that he should avoid Richthofen's fate, Bülow's performance was mainly for effect and, indeed, was initially successful. Only in March 1906 did the Centre really threaten to disrupt the government's plans and, although the party had not forgotten its anger over the duelling declaration, other considerations were of paramount importance.[162]

The bill to create a Reich Colonial Office had been well received in the Reichstag when it had first been introduced but, by the middle of March, the mood of the Centre, now influenced more than ever by its more democratic and populist wing, had undergone a change, and the prospects of Reichstag approval of the new office were definitely bleak.[163] Although Hohenlohe-Langenburg had proved to be a more skilful Director of the Colonial Department than many had expected, it was widely known that he was only prepared to continue conducting affairs if placed at the head of an independent Reich Office. It had also been a tactical mistake to announce that Hohenlohe would be the future State Secretary before the Reichstag had approved the new position.[164] The wrath of the Centre Party seemed to be directed against Hohenlohe personally.[165] His Protestant confession, hostility to Catholics, princely rank, inexperience in colonial affairs and favoured position with the Kaiser all played a role in prompting the Reichstag budget committee's rejection of the new post on 21 March.[166]

Hohenlohe himself had anticipated a negative decision and still found his provisional status intolerable. On 5 March he had written to the Chancellor requesting a holiday after he had represented the colonial budget during the second reading.[167] But the budget committee's rejection placed Bülow in an acute dilemma. On the one hand he was forced to defend the reform of the colonial administration, and the rejection of the Kaiser's favourite, especially at the hands of the Centre, would be a personal defeat for the Chancellor. The Kaiser might hold him personally responsible for the failure to approve the new office.[168] On the other hand, Bülow cannot really have wanted to support his rival and may have seen the opportunity to remove him. As Szögyényi reported, it was Bülow himself who maintained that there were personal reasons why he wanted the Reichstag to approve the bill,[169] a singularly uncharacteristic confession if his personal position had really been threatened by the defeat.

Bachem, too, remained in doubt as to whether Bülow actually wanted the Colonial Office approved, after a hint from the Chancellor that it was more important to get on with the financial reform. Bachem was convinced 'that Bülow's general position would be made more difficult if Hohenlohe remained and became State Secretary'. Although Bülow had to appear diligent in his support of Hohenlohe's candidature, the Centre Party deputy scarcely believed that Bülow had welcomed the Kaiser's choice, for Hohenlohe would have direct access to the monarch and assume an exceptional position *vis-à-vis* the Chancellor on account of his close family relations with Germany's ruling houses. Bachem believed that Hohenlohe would create difficulties for Bülow's policy, quite apart from the threat he posed as Bülow's potential successor. The new State Secretary might make exorbitant colonial demands which would bring the Kaiser into conflict with the Reichstag; and Bachem also noted that Hohenlohe's wife would take precedence over Marie von Bülow at all Court ceremonies by virtue of her birth. 'These are all reasons why neither we nor Bülow could wish that Hohenlohe become State Secretary', he concluded,[170] but his musings may well have contained an element of wishful thinking. In no position to influence the majority of his party on this issue, Bachem may well have been trying to justify a decision he felt he could do little about.

Bülow's position in the early months of 1906 with respect to the colonial budget was ambiguous. Though rumours that the Kaiser had given the Chancellor an ultimatum on this question were discounted,[171] his position might well have been equally endangered if Hohenlohe were formally installed. If Bülow did hope to remove Hohenlohe, it is unlikely that a parliamentary defeat over the second reading of the colonial budget would have seemed the best moment. Here, as with Holstein's resignation, the Chancellor's illness seemed to come at a most propitious time, and it is difficult to assess what his original intentions were.[172] Throughout March the Chancellor committed himself to an energetic campaign to secure the safe passage of the colonial budget,[173] and the fight for the Reich Colonial Office became inflated into 'a state affair of the first degree'.[174] Bülow's major speech on 29 March made a big impression,[175] and the following day the office was approved by 127 votes to 110.[176] The absence of a large number of Centre deputies (influenced by the Chancellor) from the debate and a last-minute conversion by the Progressive liberals helped to provide this narrow government victory,[177] and for the time being the Chancellor could afford to feel satisfied.

In March 1906 Berlin abounded with rumours that Bülow's position was shattered and that he would soon fall. If they were not connected with Germany's diplomatic defeat at Algeciras, they were linked to Hohenlohe's appointment and the plans for a Reich Colonial Office.[178] Bülow remained ostensibly composed, although perhaps in rather philosophical mood. 'Like snowflakes, the fates of men and peoples swirl around each other', he wrote to Holstein on 25 March.[179] A few days before his collapse he told Hertling that his position with the Kaiser was such that he could expect to remain Chancellor for as long as he wanted.[180]

However, in reality the Chancellor was fatigued and nervous, and in early April he complained to Hammann that 'The entire non-German press is swarming with the news of my alleged resignation.' He went on: 'We must prevent in future that fatuous inventions of this kind become so widespread. From all sides (Paris, London, Rome) I am being asked whether there is any truth in them. In future such agitation [*Treibereien*] must really be countered more quickly and energetically.' Bülow instructed Hammann to have it said in the foreign press that the Chancellor's position was much stronger at Court, in the parliament and in the country than was assumed abroad and that any rumours of crisis probably came from insubordinate intriguers. The idea that he was to be replaced by Hohenlohe-Langenburg was, he asserted, especially ridiculous.[181] But the Chancellor remained highly sensitive to apparent shifts in attitude towards him, worrying in early April that Ballin had turned against him.[182] Philipp Eulenburg's receipt of the Order of the Black Eagle was but another reminder of the variety of challenges he faced.

Bülow collapsed during the Reichstag debate on 5 April, after he had made a short speech on Algeciras but before he had delivered his more important reply to the members' interpellations.[183] The leader of the Social Democrats, August Bebel, was making an attack on German foreign policy at the time, and Mühlberg, who was standing next to Bülow, recalled later 'how his face went pale, a yellow mucus ran out of his mouth and he collapsed'.[184] The Chancellor had been suffering from a severe cold, but he had given no impression of being a sick man;[185] yet the burden of work during the previous weeks, the unusual conditions in the Foreign Office and the uncertainties with respect to his personal position had clearly left their mark. The Kaiser had cancelled his Mediterranean cruise because of the Algeciras conference, and thus the Chancellor had been deprived of the usual period of calm he enjoyed in March and April. The Kaiser's prolonged presence in Berlin had undoubtedly contributed to the strain but, although Mühlberg and Lerchenfeld attributed the Chancellor's exhaustion to the demands made on his time by the Kaiser,[186] this was something which Bülow was generally used to and which, in different circumstances, might have given him cause for satisfaction. In March 1906 Wilhelm saw Bülow twice as frequently as during the same month in the two previous years. But in early April 1906 the diaries of the Kaiser's adjutants explicitly state that the Kaiser's morning visits were to Tschirschky, not the Chancellery next door, a development which may have produced more anxiety in the Chancellor than the visits to himself.[187] However problematic relations between Kaiser and Chancellor were in early 1906, the Kaiser interrupted his engagements immediately on hearing of Bülow's collapse and promptly drove to the Reichstag to enquire personally how he was.[188] But although Bülow's doctor confirmed that there were no signs of paralysis and that the Chancellor would be able to go home in a few hours, few doubted that his collapse would signify a protracted convalescence.[189] The future of both Bülow and his Chancellorship was an open question.

The watershed of Bülow's Chancellorship

For most of April 1906 Bülow was confined to his bed. Although he had probably only fainted, he was ordered to rest as if he had had a heart attack.[190] Suffering from persistent neuralgic pains, he received no visitors except for close relatives until 23 April, when Loebell and Tschirschky were permitted a brief visit.[191] In part, this precaution was necessary to keep the Kaiser away,[192] and the monarch did not see the Chancellor until his birthday on 3 May.[193] Later in May, Bülow moved to Norderney, where he was to remain, except for a few brief excursions, until 16 October.[194]

Bülow's prolonged absence from Berlin was bound to have grave implications for his personal position, and the months following his collapse can aptly be described as a watershed in his Chancellorship. Bülow wrote later that in 1906 he suffered from an acute depression only comparable to an earlier despondency in 1882–3.[195] In the early days of his convalescence he certainly found the rest imposed on him irksome, worried about political matters and could not be consoled that he had not delivered his second speech in the Reichstag.[196] But he also soon recognised the crossroads he had reached and within a couple of weeks could write to Hammann that 'such a moment will never return again and what we make of it [*was wir ihm ausschlagen*] no eternity will bring back to us'. The guidance of public opinion at this time would shape his reputation for a generation, and he also envisaged more practical and immediate results. If they succeeded, he, the Chancellor, would emerge from this test as Siegfried in the legend emerged from the dragon's blood: 'unassailable and we will have a free hand in domestic (social!) policy and in foreign policy'.[197]

Bülow's references to his preoccupations during these crucial months are oblique, but notwithstanding his justifiable concern about the opportunity his illness gave to his enemies and the loyalty of all those close to the Kaiser,[198] the Chancellor had the time to reflect more positively about his future plans and strategy. Bülow had no thoughts of resignation; rather, he searched for ways to bolster his personal position and place his system on a more secure footing. At the end of May he wrote to Hammann that he felt more rested than he had been for a long time and that consequently he was as full of ideas and intentions 'as a poodle [is] full of fleas'.[199]

One such idea which Bülow toyed with in the early summer of 1906 was the practicality of constitutional changes and in particular the possibility of a Reich Upper House or responsible Reich Ministries. This was a reform which had long appealed to Posadowsky[200] and, despite the serious objections to such constitutional amendments, Bülow was not put off by the idea. He instructed Loebell to write a memorandum on the attitude of the parties to the creation of Reich Ministries, its possible effects and, above all, whether it would strengthen or weaken the Chancellorship.[201] Loebell, however, a former Conservative politician, considered the idea very dangerous and advised against any restrictions on the authority of the Reich Chancellor or greater independence for the State Secretaries. He argued that only the left and perhaps the democratic wing of the Centre would wholeheartedly support the change while it would be unacceptable also to the federal states.

The Reich Chancellor can never in my view support something which would considerably limit his influence and position. He should not be allowed to become *primus inter pares* like the Minister-President in Prussia, but must rule absolutely [*uneingeschränkt herrschen*]. Only his will can decide in big questions; in small departmental questions the State Secretaries can conduct affairs independently as hitherto. That the State Secretaries desire greater independence is understandable; the Reich Constitution does not permit such [independence] with good reason.[202]

Loebell did not consider in his memorandum how the creation of responsible Reich Ministries might affect the Kaiser's position or whether the Chancellor, by forfeiting some of his freedom of manoeuvre within the executive and Reichstag, might have gained by having greater authority *vis-à-vis* the monarch. Nevertheless, after receiving the advice from his Chancellery Chief, Bülow abandoned any plans he entertained in this direction, plans which might have drastically curtailed the power of the Kaiser, if he had agreed to them, but which also would have placed restrictions on his own position.

Bülow also wrote a long letter to the Kaiser in July 1906 which was concerned with events in Russia but in which his main aim was to express his views about Germany's historical development. He discussed the growth of democratic ideas in Europe since the French Revolution and the 'massive reversal [*ungeheuere Umschwung*]' of this trend in 1866 and 1870. But significantly he continued in the past tense:

Since then the view was widespread that a strong monarch and a skilful Minister were more valuable than liberal institutions, democratic tendencies and parliamentary games. Through a chain of mistakes, omissions and precipitate moves [*Übereilungen*] the good old gentleman on the Danube and the kind young gentleman on the Neva have determined [*fertig bekommen*] that now it is widely believed again that salvation still lies rather on the left than on the right. A number of things which Your Majesty's powerful personality and noble efforts would have achieved for the monarchical principle have thereby been spoiled [*verdorben*]. That must be a warning to us to be firm and wise abroad and at home and, for the rest, [it] is but an invitation to go on bravely, confident in the old *Preussen-Gott*.[203]

In his stress in this letter on the Germans' love of freedom and equality, the differences between the Russian autocratic and the German political traditions, the need to recognise the signs of the time and to make opportune concessions, the effects of an unsuccessful war on a 'personal and absolutist government system', the rising tide of democracy and the decline of the European autocracies, and the loss of confidence in simply a strong monarch and a skilful Minister, Bülow was without doubt trying to impress on Wilhelm the dangers of a reactionary course, the perils of 'personal rule' and the crossroads which Germany had now reached in her domestic development.

The ideas Bülow hatched in Norderney were, for the time being at least, mainly academic, although it is not impossible that the Chancellor was behind the growing press criticism of the Kaiser by the late summer. As Holstein recognised, if Bülow was behind the new attitude expressed in the pro-government newspapers, it was because he had come round to the view that, if he were replaced, it would be with a 'hard' Chancellor who would be less convenient for the Kaiser and potentially disastrous for Germany.[204] Bülow was also concerned to extract the maximum political capital he could from his illness with respect to government personnel and policy issues, and again he resorted to the manipulation of the press to bolster his position. He rapidly exploited his absence to remove Holstein from office in a way that convinced the Privy Counsellor of the Chancellor's innocence;[205] and he was guilty of complicity in the subsequent press campaign against Holstein, conducted primarily by Harden.[206] Moreover, when at the end of May the Reichstag rejected the establishment of a Reich Colonial Office and a colonial railway on the third reading, the defeat was far from critical for the Chancellor but indeed was almost a welcome occurrence.[207] Bülow wrote to Hammann:

That is one of those cases which you very rightly anticipated during my convalescence when one can and should observe exactly how things go when I am not there or don't give everything my support [*mich für alles einsetze*]! This discrepancy between the brilliant result of the second reading, when I myself intervened, and the result as soon as I don't place myself in front of the rift, must be emphasised and broadcast [*breitgetreten*] in every way and in as many places as possible.[208]

With respect to colonial affairs Bülow clearly pursued a policy of ensuring maximum chaos in order to be able to pose as the eventual redeemer. Admitting to Wilhelm II that 'In all probability things have happened [in the colonial department] which cannot be hushed up but must be burnt out *ferro et igni*',[209] he urged Hammann to pursue an energetic campaign in the press. 'That is the right tone!' he wrote enthusiastically at the end of June. 'The task is not to burn nonentities and weaklings white but to make it clear to Reichstag, people, public opinion and all whom it concerns that *in colonialibus* everything is in a muddle [*verfahren*] and if things in future are to go better again, this will only be thanks to the Reich Chancellor.' All articles which bespoke this theme were to be passed on to the Kaiser, and Bülow relied on Hammann to see that this 'important task' was fulfilled.[210]

Bülow thus tried to exploit his illness and absence to strengthen his political position. But of more significance for the future was the impact of his collapse on the government system in Berlin and the Chancellor's relations with the Kaiser. Although it had generally been felt in April 1906 tht Bülow would not be able to resume his official activities for some time and the idea of appointing Joseph Maria von Radowitz, the German ambassador in Madrid, as a deputy Chancellor was mooted,[211] the decision was taken not to appoint a special deputy during Bülow's absence (in which case Posadowsky would have resigned) but to leave to the Vice-Chancellor and State Secretary of Interior the general representation of the Chancellor and to Tschirschky the conduct of foreign policy.[212] Although Bülow sought in his memoirs to give the impression that the government machine completely ground to a halt,[213] in some respects, given the nature of his leadership, Bülow's absence was not sorely felt in 1906. At the end of April Szögyényi reported that Posadowsky represented the Chancellor in the Reichstag and Bundesrat; for the rest, the State Secretaries were conducting the affairs of their offices quite independently.[214] But in Prussia the consequences of Bülow's absence were more serious and Rheinbaben, who was mentioned as a Chancellor candidate in April 1906,[215] took steps to tighten up State Ministry procedure. Evidence is scant, but in general the State Ministry in May and June 1906 was able to reassert some of the authority it had previously lost.[216]

Bülow was not unaware of the erosion of his personal authority and the need to maintain at least the semblance of control. Although the general representation of the Chancellor continued, as early as 10 May he informed

5 The Kaiser visitng Bülow on the island of Norderney in 1906. Bülow's wife is on the left.

the State Secretaries that he had resumed the conduct of affairs and that henceforth all important material was to be shown to him once again.[217] In August 1906 he deliberately returned to Berlin to chair a State Ministry meeting. He was primarily concerned with the appearance of his authority, for the subjects on the agenda mattered little to him.[218]

Despite the Chancellor's efforts, his personal position continued to be undermined throughout 1906. In April 1906 Baroness Spitzemberg wrote that he was losing control,[219] and, if it had not done so already, the conduct of foreign policy passed unequivocally to the Kaiser and Tschirschky. The Kaiser shifted his visits and attentions from Bülow to Tschirschky,[220] and although the State Secretary, at least in the beginning, did not deliberately work against Bülow, he disagreed with the Chancellor on questions of policy and involved the monarch in the controversies.[221] Tschirschky was no more successful than Bülow in restraining the Kaiser from impulsive gestures[222] and he also admitted to difficulties with 'irresponsible' advisers.[223] But, most significantly, he confessed to Monts in August 1906 that Bülow was politically 'really completely excluded [*ausgeschaltet*]';[224] and Holstein too heard that Tschirschky was 'handling foreign policy and especially personnel questions directly with the Kaiser'.[225] The political differences between the Chancellor and State Secretary became more acute in the autumn when Bülow was planning a major speech on foreign policy of which Tschirschky strongly disapproved;[226] and when Tschirschky visited Hungary and Italy and was treated as the real architect of German foreign policy.[227] Bülow must have been aware of the real state of play. Nevertheless, he remained ostensibly on good terms with Tschirschky and praised him to the Kaiser.[228] Yet Tschirschky also disapproved of the pro-Centre course at home,[229] and once he recognised that the Kaiser's attitude to the Chancellor had changed, it is quite possible that here too he exerted an influence on the monarch.

It was on his relations with the Kaiser that Bülow's absence made the greatest impression. The tensions had been evident before Bülow's collapse, but in the early days of his illness, there may even have been a rapprochement.[230] In May 1906, after the acceptance of the financial reform, Wilhelm sent Bülow a public telegram emphasising his continuing confidence in the Chancellor, a gesture which was well received, though it might have been made at Bülow's request.[231] But soon new complications arose to sour the relationship, and it is clear that the Chancellor could no longer exert his old influence on the monarch. The Kaiser was incensed by the 'shameful' rejection of the colonial budget (and especially the railway). He complained to Bülow that the mask had been ripped off the Centre, revealing that it was arm in arm with Social Democracy, but that did not surprise him at all, for he had long suspected the alliance.[232] Moreover, Wilhelm held Bülow responsible for the defeat because salaries 'were approved too soon', without securing the project.[233] The Chancellor attempted to defend himself, pointing out once more that

When I myself spoke up for [the colonial railway and the Reich Colonial Office] in the Reichstag a few weeks ago, the business was passed with a big majority. I would have very much liked to have stayed in Berlin now to speak personally for these demands, which lie close to my heart, in the third reading too. However, I truly needed to relax and [breathe] the pure sea air after all the troubles and struggles of the winter. In my absence the affair then went wrong.[234]

Bülow stressed that after a 'huge Tax Bill', the Military Pensions Law and the Navy Bill had all been passed by the Reichstag, it would be a political mistake to show too much displeasure over 'an organisational and personnel matter'. But the following day the Kaiser despatched another letter to the Chancellor attacking the Centre,[235] and by July his indignation reached new heights under the impact of attacks made by Erzberger ('the professional back-stairs creeper, calumniator and slanderer') on the colonial administration.[236]

The Chancellor's inability to exploit the defeat of the colonial budget to remove Hohenlohe-Langenburg was further evidence of Bülow's declining influence over Wilhelm. On hearing the news of the Reichstag defeat, he wrote to Hammann that the Kaiser's favourite was not to appear a martyr. Hohenlohe was 'not to become too big, for reasons we have discussed',[237] and, in agreement with Loebell, Bülow issued instructions that the question of Hohenlohe's resignation should be discussed with the Kaiser.[238] But even now Wilhelm resisted letting Hohenlohe fall to the Centre and be replaced by Götzen, whom he described as 'finished physically and completely incapable of holding the office',[239] and Bülow capitulated to the monarch's will. In a letter to the Kaiser, Bülow explained that he had only suggested Götzen when he heard from Berlin that Hohenlohe did not wish to stay in office, but that for personal and political reasons he considered Hohenlohe's remaining to be the best solution.[240] Bülow tried to play down the significance of this 'irrelevant personnel matter' in the press,[241] but he must have been disappointed. At the end of June Lerchenfeld reported that the Kaiser had forced Hohenlohe to stay.[242]

Bülow also clashed with the Kaiser over the question of a political amnesty in the summer of 1906 on the occasion of the birth of the monarch's first grandchild. The suggestion had the approval of the Ministry of State, but Wilhelm was outraged by the proposal and declared that the Ministry had to wait until the sovereign sent it *his* suggestions.[243] Then, at an audience in Wilhelmshöhe in August 1906, Bülow came under pressure from the monarch to take energetic measures against anarchism and the SPD.[244] Already concerned about the Kaiser's greatly increased antagonism to the Centre Party,[245] Bülow proved willing to respond and began to think in terms of an anti-socialist campaign as the focus for the Reichstag elections anticipated in 1908.[246] By September 1906 Wilhelm II was clearly considering Bülow's dismissal, although Tschirschky counselled awaiting the course of the political campaign in the winter and first deciding on a suitable successor. The Foreign Secretary's recommendation that Wilhelm should appoint a Prussian with Prussian roots at the very least was an implied criticism of Bülow, and the open discussion of his successor boded ill for the Chancellor.[247]

Meanwhile the rumours persisted in the press that Bülow no longer had Wilhelm's confidence and that his position was shattered. The Chancellor endeavoured to fight a rear-guard action. When the Kaiser included in his speech at Cuxhaven on 19 June 1906 a sentence praising Bülow as the man who had done most to preserve peace, the message from Norderney to the Foreign Office Press Bureau was clear:

Leitmotiv for the discussion of the Kaiser speech in Cuxhaven: services of His Excellency in preserving the dignity and security as well as the peace of Germany greater than hitherto known by the public but will doubtless become more apparent. Only after R[eich] Chancellor ensured dignity, security, interests of nation, i.e. ship in harbour, does he collapse, now however back to rights, world situation doubtless improved by him. Confidence of Kaiser in R[eich] C[hancellor] in foreign and domestic policy naturally greater than ever. End of Uhland's poem 'King Charles's Sea Voyage' is suitable as characterisation of the months February and March. Submit article in this sense.[248]

The odds seemed stacked against the Chancellor, however, especially when the intriguers were closing in. Initially Bülow's growing number of enemies had been silenced by his collapse, and criticism of his policies had diminished in the face of a conspicuous absence of appropriate successors.[249] But some were already adjusting to the idea of Hohenlohe-Langenburg as Chancellor in the autumn[250] and there was much discussion of methods by which the Chancellorship could be dismantled, perhaps by the creation of a Diplomatic Cabinet akin to the Military, Naval and Civil Cabinets.[251] By early May it was evident that Bülow either had enemies very close at hand or that he himself was playing an exceptionally devious game. Despite all the signs of his steady recovery, rumours began to circulate about a deterioration in his physical condition which 'came from such official circles that one could scarcely doubt their correctness'.[252] At this stage Bülow probably still had no interest in feeding these fears. In late May he instructed Hammann to intimate repeatedly in the press 'that my illness was exploited by intriguers and self-seekers [*Streber*] to shatter my position or install some *non valeur* or other in my place. These attempts have, however, failed miserably.'[253] A few months later, having returned to Berlin and been witness to a further erosion of his authority rather than its restoration, Bülow would see new uses for this kind of press discussion and exploit the spectre of a Kaiser's camarilla to prevent his removal from office.

The Podbielski crisis

Before Bülow returned to Berlin in October 1906, a crisis developed which inflicted more damage on his relationship with the Kaiser than any other during his Chancellorship before 1908 and which finally convinced him that there could be no return to his previous system if he wanted to survive in office. For a long time it had been rumoured that the Minister of Agriculture, General von Podbielski, intended to resign. He was allegedly weary of office,[254] constantly at loggerheads with Posadowsky,[255] and, despite the public outcry, had adopted an uncompromising position over the so-called 'meat crisis' from 1905, refusing to countenance a relaxation of border controls on meat imports despite spiralling meat prices at home.[256] All this had convinced observers as early as October 1905 that he was merely looking for an appropriate exit,[257] and he was expected to resign in the spring of 1906.[258] But Podbielski remained throughout the summer, by which time the press attacks on his involvement with the Tippelskirch firm (which had

6 General Viktor von Podbielski, Prussian Minister of Agriculture 1901–6

begun in the autumn of 1905[259]) had succeeded in placing the Minister at the
centre of a major colonial scandal.

The scandal arose when Major Fischer, who was in charge of the clothing
depot, was accused of accepting bribes from the Tippelskirch firm which was
the main supplier for the troops in the colonies. Fischer was arrested on
charges of corruption, and Podbielski, too, was attacked by the liberal press
because he was a shareholder in the firm. To a certain extent, the persecution
of Podbielski was unjustified. Podbielski had invested 10,000 Marks in the
Tippelskirch firm which he had not withdrawn on becoming State Secretary

of the Post Office in 1897 because this would have ruined the company. But he had informed the government of his relations with the firm, and it was not seen as an obstacle to his appointment. Moreover, as Lerchenfeld reported, there was no evidence that Podbielski's relations with the firm influenced his ministerial activity in the way the press maintained. The chief weapon of Podbielski's critics was that he transferred his shares in the firm to his wife.[260]

In early August 1906 Szögyényi reported that the government seemed intent on standing firm over the press attacks and that it would not allow itself to be bullied into dismissing Podbielski until the Fischer affair had been fully investigated.[261] Nevertheless, once the scandal broke, Bülow assumed that Podbielski would submit to him a report on his relations with the Tippelskirch firm, a report which he eventually had to order from the Minister and which was submitted on 13 August. According to the Bavarian *chargé d'affaires*, at the end of this report Podbielski unmistakably requested his resignation,[262] and it was this piece of information which Bülow passed on to the *Norddeutsche Allgemeine Zeitung* shortly afterwards.[263]

Bülow may well have hoped to create a *fait accompli*, but to his dismay Podbielski subsequently denied his intention to resign in the *Berliner Lokalanzeiger*, a gesture which aroused sharp disapproval in government circles.[264] Moreover, when Bülow visited the Kaiser in Wilhelmshöhe in the middle of August, he was unable to persuade either the monarch or the Chief of the Civil Cabinet of the necessity of Podbielski's resignation. Given Podbielski's apparent refusal to resign voluntarily, Bülow had been planning to give him a further push in this direction. But, as he told Hammann,

Lucanus remained convinced that HM should not intervene in this affair either pro or contra, and the resignation of Podbielski was not to occur before the facts behind the affair have been clarified. HM shared this view, and so in my letter to Podbielski, the addition you suggested about the fundamental inadmissibility [*Unstatthaftigkeit*] of business connections between a Minister and a firm involved in state deliveries had to be omitted as too broad a hint [*als zu direkter Wink mit dem Zaunpfahl*].[265]

Bülow thus could do little but attempt to speed up the investigation into the affair, but even at this stage a consensus was beginning to develop in government circles in Berlin (and in Podbielski's own Ministry) that the Minister of Agriculture would have to go.[266]

The conclusion of the investigation did not resolve the affair but instead occasioned its transformation into a full-scale government crisis. The findings were not sufficient to convince Wilhelm II or Lucanus of Podbielski's culpability. Loebell had a long discussion with Lucanus on 3 September during which he tried to exert all his influence as a former Conservative parliamentarian. But the Cabinet Chief merely deemed it expedient for Podbielski to sever his connections with the firm and altogether seemed rather reserved about the affair.[267] Wilhelm II had an audience with Podbielski, in the presence of Lucanus, on 4 September and came to the conclusion that the Minister had no reason to resign. The government had known about Podbielski's connections with the firm and he, Wilhelm, refused to submit to public pressure. He instructed Podbielski to sever his links with the firm, but the Minister could remain in office.[268]

Far from standing firm, the Chancellor was now quite prepared to accept a situation in which he had demonstrably come out second best.[269] He may still have hoped that Podbielski would resign. But, as he told Hammann, the Kaiser regarded the matter as settled, and 'Whether Podbielski will resign or not in the autumn is in these circumstances difficult to say.' He did not consider his own resignation, but already turned his attention to how he could handle the affair during the next parliamentary session. As he continued to Hammann:

A statement by me on the Podbielski affair in the Reichstag would therefore have to be formulated very carefully. At best probably in the form that I leave it to Podbielski to defend himself against attacks made against him and for my part only indicate that the dismissal of Ministers is a matter for the Crown; however, at the same time justify my own behaviour and especially the publications in the 'NAZ', and describe the assertion of divergencies between myself and Podbielski as a legend. Naturally I'll only touch on the Podbielski theme in the Reichstag if it is brought up by someone else or if I am personally attacked because of the affair.[270]

Bülow's response to the Kaiser's decision reflected either extraordinary naivety or his remoteness from Berlin and ignorance about the level of public feeling aroused by the scandal. For in conservative and ministerial circles in Berlin it was already felt that Bülow could not appear before the Reichstag in the autumn if Podbielski remained in office.[271] Bülow might have been able to regulate the affair more successfully if he had been in closer contact with the Kaiser.[272] But after Wilhelmshöhe Bülow only saw the Kaiser once more before his return to Berlin; and in Berlin they only met at one social lunch in October and were not to see each other again until after the crisis was over.[273] It was thus virtually impossible for the Chancellor to discuss the question of Podbielski's resignation directly with the monarch;[274] nor was he able to influence Podbielski personally since the latter spent most of October on his estate.[275] Podbielski's physical condition was deteriorating and he had to miss two State Ministry meetings at the end of October because of gout.[276] Nevertheless Berckheim saw the Minister in October, and he showed every inclination to cling to office. He laughingly dismissed rumours of his resignation as fictions, and the ambassador was forced to conclude 'that the position of Herr von Podbielski is more secure than ever and that he possesses the All-Highest confidence in the most extensive measure'.[277]

By the end of October even Posadowsky admitted to Bachem that the

Podbielski affair was 'exceptionally bad'.[278] In the Foreign Office one had only to mention the Minister's name to detect a certain nervousness,[279] and when Eisendecher reported a vague reference by the Grand Duke of Baden to 'the crisis before which we stand' and his 'worries about the future', Bülow clearly demonstrated his own.[280] Although in the struggle between Chancellor and Minister, it seemed inevitable that the latter would have to be the loser, it was striking how long the Kaiser hesitated before he made a decision, and the time to effect the personnel change was rapidly running out. The Reichstag was due to meet on 13 November, and an interpellation on the meat crisis was expected in the first few days. It seemed scarcely possible that Podbielski could reply to such an interpellation when the Conservative and Centre parties denied him active support and the left would not allow him to speak.[281] Holstein advised Bülow to consult the State Ministry and find out whether Podbielski could count on the support of his colleagues, and especially Posadowsky, in fending off parliamentary attacks. After Bülow had proceeded against Podbielski in the *Norddeutsche Allgemeine Zeitung* the Minister's remaining in office would be a severe blow to the Chancellor's position, Holstein warned.[282] Széchényi, the Austrian *chargé d'affaires*, judged the issue even more critically. 'If the Minister of Agriculture remains at his post beyond the 13th of this month, then the Prince's own authority *vis-à-vis* the Reich deputies would be so profoundly shattered that the question of his own continuance in office could be raised.'[283]

The monarch was certainly receptive when Podbielski explained his 'misunderstanding' with the Chancellor over the question of his resignation by referring to the fact that, as a Prussian Minister, he could only request his resignation from the King.[284] Bülow may have been able to rehabilitate himself partially in the Kaiser's favour in early November, as Eulenburg maintained, through his successful handling of the Brunswick question.[285] Nevertheless, it was during the first week of November that the Podbielski crisis reached its dramatic climax. Twice the Kaiser ordered Podbielski to remain at his post, even though this brought him into direct conflict with the Chancellor and the entire Prussian Ministry.[286] Only on 11 November was the imperial order for Podbielski's dismissal finally sent to the Chancellor for his counter-signature – to the not inconsiderable relief of the Minister himself.[287] On 8 November Bülow had sent Bethmann Hollweg on a special mission to Podbielski's estate, a mission that ultimately proved unnecessary as Podbielski's formal resignation request had arrived later that day.[288]

However, Bülow had won a pyrrhic victory. Despite the fact that Wilhelm demonstratively dined with the Bülows on 10 November to stifle the crisis rumours,[289] the Podbielski crisis had exacerbated the tension between Kaiser and Chancellor. Unwilling to heed parliamentary pressure or public opinion (which reproached Podbielski for hiding behind the Crown in the Tippelskirch affair[290]), Wilhelm could not easily forgive this encroachment on his prerogative to appoint and dismiss Ministers as he pleased.[291] If he had been considering a new Chancellor earlier in the autumn, the Podbielski crisis made the prospect of change even more attractive. Realising that he would have little influence on the appointment of Podbielski's successor, Bülow suggested to Lucanus that the Cabinet Chief propose, on his own initiative, Otto von Manteuffel as the new Minister of Agriculture[292] (who would have gone some way to calm Conservative anxieties that Podbielski's removal would signify a return to the economic policies of the Caprivi era[293]). But if Lucanus did propose Manteuffel, the suggestion was rejected. By mid November the choice was between Bernhard von Arnim-Kriewen and Hermann von Arnim-Boitzenburg, and both the Chancellery and Lucanus considered the latter impossible.[294] Wilhelm II approved the appointment of Arnim-Kriewen on 18 November[295] (Bethmann Hollweg had temporarily assumed leadership of the Ministry of Agriculture between Podbielski's resignation and Arnim's appointment[296]), and two days later the decision was confirmed by the Prussian Ministry of State after an unusually open discussion of Arnim's suitability for the post.[297] But by this time the Podbielski crisis had been submerged in the general crisis which loomed in late 1906, for the Reichstag was once again in session and it presented Bülow with both new dilemmas and new opportunities.

The 'dénouement'

If the Kaiser could not forgive the Chancellor for forcing Podbielski's resignation,[298] it was probably no accident that public attention was immediately diverted from that conflict by the storm over the Kaiser's 'personal rule' and the alleged 'secret camarilla' in the same month. At the height of the Podbielski crisis in early November, Wilhelm II had visited Liebenberg, Eulenburg's *Schloss*, where it was widely rumoured that he was reinforced in his intransigent attitude to the affair.[299] The visit certainly fuelled the crisis rumours and focused public attention on possible 'irresponsible advisers'. Almost immediately a lively discussion began in the press about the plans hatched during the hunting trip to replace Bülow as Chancellor by the Chief of the General Staff, Helmuth von Moltke, or by another Moltke.[300] The camarilla's strategy, it was claimed, was ostensibly to show great concern for the Chancellor's health, insist that he was 'spared' too much work and gradually ease him out of office, to begin with by the appointment of a special Vice-Chancellor.[301]

The belief in a secret camarilla, or at least pernicious influences on the monarch, was widespread in late 1906. Lerchenfeld reported that Bülow's illness 'seems to have given certain circles the desired opportunity to work against him' and that now Bülow's position with the Kaiser was shaky, these people were closing in on the Kaiser.[302] Berckheim had the rumours confirmed by a safe source in the Kaiser's entourage and by the War Minister, Einem. Philipp Eulenburg, he reported on 8 November, wanted to remove Bülow, who was the chief obstacle to his appointment to the lucrative post of *Statthalter* of Alsace-Lorraine.

Prince Bülow rightly considers any further use of Prince Eulenburg in a high state office impossible, and indeed for a reason the sparrows are, so to speak, twittering from the roof tops but which no one dares to say even by way of a hint to the Kaiser; the Prince is namely alleged to indulge in passions which are admittedly tolerated in the Orient and in Russia, but which in our country are punished by the criminal judge [*Strafrichter*].[303]

Later in November Maximilian Harden, whom even Varnbüler regarded as the most talented, skilful, unscrupulous and hence also most dangerous journalist of the time,[304] renewed his campaign against Philipp Eulenburg to free the monarchy from his influence, and he asserted that the Kaiser's friend was responsible for Bülow's appointment as State Secretary, Moltke's appointment as Chief of the General Staff and Tschirschky's appointment as State Secretary. Acting primarily as an independent patriot, Harden aimed to neutralise Eulenburg's influence and force him to keep away from the Kaiser.[305]

Nevertheless, as Monts recognised, the alleged intrigues of Eulenburg and others in the autumn of 1906 were substantiated by very few facts.[306] Varnbüler, a member of the Liebenberg circle, did indeed defend the candidacy of Helmuth von Moltke for the Chancellorship to Baroness Spitzemberg in November 1906, claiming that his (hostile) attitude to universal suffrage was 'the main thing';[307] and he had looked forward to the Liebenberg visit (and been disappointed when it had been temporarily cancelled) because of the 'political booty' he expected to obtain there. A few hours in an intimate circle with the Kaiser was, he reported, worth more than what he got from officials in the Foreign Office in a whole year.[308] But Varnbüler later maintained that the visit to Liebenberg in November 1906 did not even give him sufficient material for a political report,[309] and Zedlitz, too, confirmed that politics was not discussed.[310] Moreover, it is highly unlikely that Philipp Eulenburg worked to undermine Bülow's position in the way that was alleged, not least because the Chancellor knew too much about his private life.[311] One cannot discount the recognition that if there was an intrigue against Bülow in late 1906 the chief protagonists were naturally careful to leave little trace of their activities; nor is it impossible that Bülow himself was suspicious of Eulenburg's influence and believed in the existence of a camarilla.[312] But in April 1907 Tschirschky maintained that Bülow had been wrong to see Eulenburg as his main opponent, that there were many others as well and that it was chiefly the Kaiser who, confronted with the mood of the country and Bülow's apparent physical apathy, came to the conclusion that the Chancellor could not long remain in office.[313] Press attacks on irresponsible advisers were a sure way to strengthen the responsible government,[314] relieve the position of the Chancellor and, by whipping up public fears of the Kaiser's 'personal rule', ensure that it would be politically impossible for Wilhelm to remove Bülow at least for the time being. The political situation in late 1906 was highly confused and the Chancellor was suddenly attacked by newspapers which had previously supported him.[315] It is certainly well within the bounds of possibility to suspect that Bülow himself played a major role in the orchestration of the furore over 'personal rule' in late 1906 as a temporary expedient to prevent his own dismissal.[316]

The public discussion of a secret camarilla reached its climax on 14 November when the National Liberal leader, Bassermann, interpellated Bülow on the international situation.[317] In his second contribution to the debate Bülow directly confronted the issues of 'personal rule' and camarilla politics. Defending the role of a 'flesh and blood Kaiser' and reminding the Reichstag that the Ministers were the representatives of the Crown, Bülow went on to say that, provided the Kaiser kept within the bounds of the Constitution, all complaints about personal rule and absolutism were exaggerated. A camarilla was 'an ugly, alien, poisonous plant' which no one had ever tried to plant in Germany without inflicting great harm on the German people and princes. The Kaiser, he concluded, was too upright a character and had too clear a head to take advice from irresponsible elements.[318] But the Chancellor's equivocal words – and his subsequent intimation in the *Norddeutsche Allgemeine Zeitung* that he believed in the existence of a camarilla – did little to pacify the public mood or clarify the confused political atmosphere.[319] According to Bülow, the Kaiser too was dissatisfied with his public pronouncements, embroidering the report of the sitting with 'irritable and mistrustful marginal notes'. Bülow maintained that he told the Kaiser that even the best-contrived press campaign could not have produced the current level of public discontent if it had not had something to build on. The majority of the German people were monarchist, but they were extraordinarily sensitive to anything that smacked of absolutism.[320]

Bülow had saved the situation temporarily, but there is no doubt that his position with the Kaiser remained precarious. With Bülow in danger of becoming 'Chlodwig II' (another Prince Chlodwig zu Hohenlohe-Schillingsfürst) with respect to the conduct of foreign policy,[321] Tschirschky's reference to Wilhelm's perception of Bülow's physical apathy in 1906 is revealing. Eulenburg too warned Bülow that energy was becoming an obsession with the Kaiser;[322] and the Brunswick question had been seen by Wilhelm II as a kind of test-case for the Chancellor, when he had the opportunity to prove that he was as energetic as before.[323] Wilhelm II had finally recognised the growing hostility, since at least 1903, in conservative circles to the Chancellor's course in domestic politics, and, like Bülow's critics, wanted to see the trimming and hedging replaced by vigorous action. The Grand Duke of Baden was affected by gloomy assessments of Germany's internal problems and encouraged the Chancellor to take legislative action against the socialists.[324] A member of the royal family, Prince Friedrich Wilhelm of Prussia, lamented the 'red' and 'black' dangers in domestic politics and wrote to Franz von Rottenburg, 'often one would indeed like to see some more energy: in the long run the government surely cannot get along with this policy of wanting to avoid every struggle'.[325] There is no evidence that the Kaiser personally put any great pressure on the Chancellor to act in late 1906, but then he was already considering Bülow's removal. Nevertheless it is only within this general context of the prevailing pessimism about Germany's domestic situation and the personal insecurity of the Chancellor that the final *dénouement* of the crisis of 1905–6, the Reichstag dissolution in December 1906, can be understood. Bülow's willingness to dissolve the Reichstag represented a final attempt to rehabilitate himself in the Kaiser's favour, by the one method which carried any prospect of success, and it was undertaken in full recognition of the dangers involved but also in the knowledge that there could be no return to the system of 1900–5.

Bülow had been reluctantly groping towards a more energetic strategy since at least the summer of 1906 in order to appease the Kaiser and his critics. He had recognised that sooner or later he would have to embark on a more militant policy against the socialists, and by early November 1906 he was either unable to oppose the conservative exponents of such a course in the Prussian Ministry of State and at Court or he had become reconciled to an anti-socialist campaign. On 2 November Posadowsky urged Bachem to ensure that the Centre press made as much noise as possible in defence of the social welfare legislation since otherwise, given the strong opposition in the Prussian Ministry and the intense dislike of all social measures, the programme would come to a standstill. One could not direct policy in the Reichstag according to the instincts of the majority of the Prussian Lower House, the State Secretary asserted disbelievingly, but he implied that this was exactly what Bethmann Hollweg, the representative of the East Elbian agrarians, and Rheinbaben, the representative of 'big industry', wanted to do. It was imperative that Bülow personally was made aware that such a course was impossible.[326]

The appointment of Bernhard Dernburg in September 1906 as successor to Hohenlohe-Langenburg in the colonial department also signified Bülow's awareness that there could be no half-measures. Once the passions following the parliamentary defeat of the colonial budget had cooled, Bülow and Loebell had easily persuaded a disillusioned Hohenlohe-Langenburg to submit his resignation and, with Lucanus's help, the request had been accepted by the Kaiser.[327] Loebell was primarily responsible for the decision to offer the leadership of the colonial department to Dernburg, the director of the Darmstädter Bank für Handel und Industrie and a man of left liberal political persuasion.[328] The remarkable aspect of Dernburg's appointment was the ease with which a 'hustling financier' of Jewish descent was accepted by both Chancellor and Kaiser. Wilhelm II and Bülow agreed to this appointment without a prior meeting with the candidate.[329] According to Loebell, the Kaiser became highly interested in Dernburg and prepared to accept him as Colonial Director after Bülow told him that he owned his own car.[330] On the other hand, given Dernburg's personal qualities and character, it was an open question how he would collaborate with Bülow. Dernburg was known to be exceptionally gifted, ambitious, radical and energetic, just the man to undertake a fundamental reorganisation of the colonial administration.[331] It was this dynamism which must have seemed an obvious asset to Bülow at a time when his Chancellorship conveyed an impression of uncertainty, hesitancy and transitoriness.

One interpretation of the Reichstag dissolution in December 1906, which later gained some popularity, was that it was Dernburg who virtually forced Bülow to adopt an uncompromising stance over the colonial estimates.[332] The government introduced supplementary estimates into the Reichstag in November 1906 to finance the military expedition in South-West Africa and the colonial railway; but the attacks of the Centre Party's radical wing on individual abuses in the colonial administration had not abated and, after several days of stormy debate, the confrontation came to a head when Dernburg and the Centre deputy, Roeren, clashed with unprecedented acerbity on 3 December.[333] Spahn was later told by Adolf Stöcker, the founder of the anti-Semitic Christian-Social Party who had close connections with the Court, that Dernburg had been victorious over Bülow and, by winning over the Kaiser, forced the Chancellor on to a drastic course.[334] Karl Bachem, convinced that Bülow 'quite certainly did not go along with this policy willingly as it contradicted the entire programme he had pursued hitherto', believed the Chancellor decided on a dissolution so as not to be ousted from the saddle by Dernburg. 'He therefore came to Dernburg's aid, if at first only in a guarded form.' [335]

But there is no evidence to suggest that Bülow was forced to dissolve the Reichstag in 1906 either by Dernburg or the Kaiser. The varying interpretations of Bülow's parliamentary predicament in 1906 have been fully discussed elsewhere,[336] and the Chancellor wanted a dissolution and new elections, even if it is not completely clear when he came to this decision. Bülow had been toying with the idea of elections inspired by some national issue for some months before December 1906.[337] But, on the other hand, he supported Dernburg in the Reichstag on 4 December in a markedly more moderate tone, which seems to counter the interpretation that he deliberately raised the temperature.[338] Moreover, in a letter to Holstein on 4 December he wrote that he had decided 'to place myself unequivocally and emphatically on the side of Dernburg', but he implied that his main aim was still to distinguish the majority of the Centre Party from its more radical and democratic wing.[339] As usual, Bülow did not commit himself to a definite decision until the very last moment; and if he did envisage an eventual Reichstag dissolution early in December, he kept his cards very close to his chest, for surprise would be a vital ingredient in his strategy.

The Reichstag budget committee rejected the estimates by a big majority on 11 December. That very morning Bülow had denied any truth in the dissolution rumours to the Reichstag President, Ballestrem,[340] and only shortly before the decision did Szögyényi report that the Chancellor was definitely considering the possibility of a dissolution.[341] At a State Ministry meeting in the Reichstag building on the evening of 11 December, Bülow informed the Prussian Ministers of his plans and, with Loebell's assistance, put forward the case for a dissolution, even though he acknowledged that there was still a slim chance that a left liberal compromise motion might be accepted. Posadowsky (and possibly Tirpitz, though this is not borne out by the protocol[342]) voiced strong opposition to the idea of a dissolution and subsequent 'patriotic' elections against the Centre and SPD. But Bülow disregarded the objections and was clearly in no mood to negotiate a compromise with the Centre Party leaders.[343] Posadowsky told the Bundesrat the next day that the vote in the State Ministry for a dissolution had been unanimous, so he must have ultimately suppressed his doubts. He had also become convinced that the government would obtain a majority for the estimates and that the dissolution order would prove superfluous.[344] But on 13 December, after Bülow had studiously avoided the Centre leaders for two days,[345] the supplementary estimates were defeated on the second reading by a mere ten votes. Amidst great excitement, the Chancellor read out the imperial order for the dissolution of the Reichstag, which he had brought to the Reichstag in a white envelope instead of the customary red as a further disguise of his intention.[346]

Without doubt Bülow forced a conflict in December 1906, a conflict which almost immediately was recognised to have been unnecessary. The majority parties, including the Centre, had shown a willingness to compromise, and an acceptable formula could probably have been found if Bülow had not insisted on a rapid tempo and the resolution of the issue before Christmas.[347] But the mood of the country and his own personal position were such that the Chancellor felt compelled to act. The dissolution of the Reichstag was immediately seen as a liberating act from the tyranny of the Centre Party,[348] and the personal motives behind Bülow's espousal of a radical policy are not difficult to identify. Although not completely aware of the consequences of a dissolution, the Kaiser was delighted by this sudden display of energy[349] and the Chancellor's position in Wilhelm's favour seemed strengthened anew.[350]

In this sense one of Bülow's main aims in the dissolution was already achieved. Although he had displayed an interest in the changing attitude of the Progressive liberals towards the government throughout 1906[351] and counted on their patriotism on national issues, it is unlikely that at this stage Bülow envisaged a new longterm strategy beyond the hope for a strong national majority and a personal victory. As Bülow's brother intimated to the Bavarian Minister in Bern, the Kaiser had become critical of the Chancellor's domestic policy, had lost patience with the skilful manoeuvres which only achieved what was strictly necessary, and had wanted the *Reichsleitung* to adopt a 'categorical attitude' to the Reichstag.[352] Thus in striking a blow against the Centre Party, Bülow had gone a long way to rehabilitate himself in Wilhelm's favour, regardless of the results of the new elections.[353]

Bülow's dissolution of the Reichstag in December 1906 must be seen as an act of weakness, not strength, and placed squarely within the context of his precarious personal position and growing disillusionment with his Reichstag policy since 1903. His version of *Sammlungspolitik*, which had accorded the Centre a pre-eminent role, had manifestly failed by 1906 and the Chancellor was left with no alternative.[354] Bewildered and resentful of the Chancellor's sudden *volte-face*, Karl Bachem returned repeatedly to the notion that Bülow had seized on a 'desperate measure [*Verzweiflungsmittel*]' to stay in office, driven by the mood of the Kaiser and by his interest in 'personal policy, not sensible Reich policy'.[355] In June 1907 Varnbüler reported that the Reichstag dissolution had constituted an attempt by the Chancellor to repair his shattered position at Court.[356] Bülow intimated as much to Lerchenfeld in 1908 when he admitted that in the long run the Kaiser would not have supported a pro-Centre policy.[357] Bülow took a major gamble in December 1906 for, even given the Kaiser's renewed confidence, it was not clear what kind of system could be constructed on the ruins of the old. But since in the event of a compromise with the Centre in December 1906 the duration of his Chancellorship would have been short, the dissolution was a risk which Bülow was compelled to take.

5

Government with the Bloc, 1907

The inauguration of 'Blockpolitik'

Despite the euphoria in some circles after the Reichstag dissolution in 1906, most political observers were pessimistic in the early weeks of the election campaign about the chances of a change in the relative strengths of the political parties and the likelihood of a more favourable parliamentary constellation as a result.[1] Posadowsky, in particular, warned Bülow the day after the dissolution that the Centre would still be sufficiently strong in the new Reichstag to make successful defence, colonial and economic policies impossible without its willing collaboration;[2] and he repeated his doubts about whether the new elections would result in a different majority to Bundesrat plenipotentiaries on 17 December, advising the federal governments 'not to alienate permanently elements which have repeatedly rendered excellent services to the government and which in all probability will be needed again'.[3] In some respects, the *Reichsleitung* was fortunate in 1906–7 in the double-edged nature of its election campaign. Since the dissolution had been effected against both the Centre and the SPD, it was possible to shift the emphasis of the campaign to suit different purposes.[4] Nevertheless, with the Centre mindful of its support in industrial districts and the radicals within the party enjoying the upper hand, there was also a real danger that the Centre and the SPD would make electoral pacts, especially in South Germany, and that an oppositional majority would be returned.[5]

In addition, the diversity of interest among the parties on which the government now relied created new difficulties and new pressures. From December 1906 Conservative opinion hoped and expected that Bülow would be the 'strong man' who would fight the SPD with iron resolution; and although the government certainly did not want to be responsible for a confessional *Kulturkampf* against its Catholic citizens, there was considerable liberal pressure to strike out in this direction and anti-clerical agitation was fuelled by the nationalist pressure groups which played a major role in the campaign.[6] Within a week of the dissolution Bülow was already coming under pressure to remove Ministers such as Studt who, in the Progressives' view, had been too conciliatory to ultramontane demands. Bülow proved willing to discuss this question with Loebell[7] and to prepare Wilhelm II for the eventual removal of Posadowsky.[8]

Bülow was no less aware than his colleagues of the difficulties inherent in any attempt to bring together the Conservative parties, the National Liberals and the Progressives on a national issue when they had such different political and especially economic programmes and when they were primarily united in their hatred of 'Centre domination'. For this reason he was prepared to heed the example of the 1887 elections over the Army Bill and to bang the nationalist drum. Advised that a victory for the SPD and the Centre would not only bring about a serious internal crisis but also endanger European peace,[9] he told Hammann that they would have to pay close attention to the international situation as the elections approached. All foreign expressions of opinion had to be carefully collected and distributed widely throughout Germany, from which it followed 'that the English, French, Russians – all our enemies in the world – desire the triumph of the Black–Red alliance because this would signify the end of German unity, power and greatness. Then our enemies would have an easy game in attacking us and making Germany again into the handmaid of the others.'[10] At the same time, to prevent the emergence of a Centre–socialist bloc, Bülow endeavoured to keep the election campaign free of certain contentious issues – the renewal of the *Kulturkampf*, the threat of a *Staatsstreich*, the possibility of changes in the election suffrage and the question of 'personal rule'.[11] But if anything, the Chancellor became more gloomy about the election prospects as the campaign progressed. Initially inspired with renewed confidence after the events of 13 December, he soon once again displayed feelings of insecurity and became very preoccupied with the consequences of the dissolution.[12] Injured by personal and political attacks in the press, Bülow mobilised the Press Bureau to defend him, frequently with little finesse. On 23 December the *Norddeutsche Allgemeine Zeitung* officially denied news from Vienna that the Kaiser was intending to visit Lichnowsky the following year in Schloss Grätz. As Szögyényi told Aehrenthal, the entire world was asking 'cui bono?', and he reluctantly concluded that Bülow had ordered the denial to suppress rumours in certain circles that Lichnowsky was to be his successor.[13]

How clear a conception did Bülow have of a future Conservative–liberal 'Bülow Bloc' before the election results were known, and to what extent did he intend to sever his links with the Centre Party? With respect to both these issues, it is necessary to disentangle Bülow's public pronouncements and political behaviour after the election results from his more cautious and ambivalent position during the weeks of the election campaign. The government launched a serious and energetic campaign in December 1906 to rally the electorate against the political predominance of the Centre and the Social Democrats and to mobilise previously apathetic voters (of whom there were approximately three million in 1903) for the national cause.[14] But there is no doubt that the campaign assumed an unusual and unexpected vindictiveness, not least because of the determined agitation of the radical nationalist pressure groups, to which the government was generous with its funds.[15] Bülow himself, who had not had any contact with the future Bloc parties before the dissolution, was more inclined to appeal to the political responsibility of the electors and to the general necessity of an alliance of the 'bourgeois parties', a strategy which was perfectly in line with his political recommendations almost twenty years before and with his parliamentary approach from 1900.[16] Moreover, he also did not suddenly break with his earlier conviction that the Centre remained of key significance as a 'state-supporting' party, and Szögyényi perceived a discrepancy between the remarks of the Chancellor and the anti-Centre outbursts, even of the government newspapers.[17]

In the early stages of the election campaign Bülow by no means shared the public eagerness to relegate the Centre to a less significant oppositional role; and he probably hoped 'to teach the Centre a lesson', not in order to earn its lasting hostility, but to make it more compliant and less disposed to join the SPD and Poles in opposing national bills.[18] In his New Year's letter to General von Liebert, the President of the Reichsverband gegen die Sozialdemokratie, Bülow contrasted the Centre's behaviour in 1906 with its commendable support of national bills before, and he expressed his hope that 'the parties of the right, the National Liberal Party and the radical groups farther to the left, with methodical action in the election campaign, could win enough ground so as to build a majority from time to time'.[19] This intimation that he intended to work with different majorities offended the very parties the government now hoped to win,[20] and consequently in his next major public pronouncement, at a banquet of the Action Committee on Imperialism, the Chancellor went further and spoke of a 'pairing of Conservative and liberal spirits', suggesting a programme around which these parties could unite.[21] However, Bülow did not yet envisage a permanent rupture with the Centre, and it was only after the election of the new Reichstag, in which ironically the Centre was to adopt a more restrained attitude and no longer be so receptive to the demands of its radical wing,[22] that the Chancellor modified his earlier attitude to the events of 1906 and for various reasons resolved to break with the Centre completely.

If Bülow's attitude during the election campaign was necessarily cautious, the Kaiser's view of the elections and their significance was unequivocal. Wilhelm II attributed the entire crisis of December 1906 to the unpatriotic and anti-monarchist stance of the Centre Party; and he explained to Szögyényi at a dinner in January 1907 that, despite the fact that Germany's Catholic citizens had been better treated by government and Crown than in countries where Catholics were in the majority, their representatives were now daring to oppose him on questions affecting national honour and dignity.[23] The Kaiser's anti-Centre sentiment had the effect of placing Bülow in limbo during the weeks of the election campaign. Although after the Court moved to Berlin in early January the Kaiser's morning visits to Bülow and Tschirschky were resumed and Wilhelm in fact saw more of Bülow in January 1907 than in any other month of his State Secretaryship or Chancellorship,[24] it may well have been the Kaiser who gradually pushed the Chancellor on to an anti-Centre course. Contrary to the opinon of many, Bülow was probably not dependent, from the point of view of his relationship with the Kaiser, on favourable election results.[25] Szögyényi was convinced 'that Kaiser Wilhelm, if it should appear necessary, would empower the Reich Chancellor, who still stands high in his favour, to [undertake] even a second Reichstag dissolution'.[26] But unfavourable election results would have weakened the Chancellor's political position and undermined his ability to recommend restraint. The implications of a government defeat in the elections, if not actually prompting Bülow's resignation, would have been such as to drag him on to a course which he had opposed since 1890. It is difficult to imagine that he would have survived this new direction for long.

Bülow's confidence increased enormously after the results of the first round of elections on 25 January became known. Nearly 85 per cent of those eligible to vote had gone to the polls, and it was clear that the pro-government parties had won a victory against the SPD if not against the Centre.[27] No one had expected the loss of some twenty SPD seats[28] and in the remaining days of the campaign Bülow shifted his attention to the fight against the socialists. Concerned not to antagonise the Catholics unduly, on Hammann's advice he sought to bring pressure to bear on the Centre from the Vatican to prevent where possible its cooperation with the SPD in the final round.[29] Immersing himself in such details as whether it would create a bad impression if the Kaiser attended a fancy dress ball on the day of the final ballot and already beginning preparations for the Crown speech at the opening of the new Reichstag (which he maintained had to be 'short, lively, very national [and] pervaded by a (in the best sense) liberal and progressive spirit'),[30] Bülow told Szögyényi on 28 January that he had been sure they would drive back the SPD significantly and that he had been confident about the expediency and ultimate success of the election campaign all along, an assertion the ambassador immediately doubted.[31] With Hammann Bülow planned an article on 'my position after the elections', at the end of which he wanted emphasised, though not too obtrusively,

How completely different after six years' Reich Chancellorship the position of the present Reich Chancellor is, compared to that of his two predecessors, of whom

Caprivi was finished even after barely two years (1892, Zedlitz School Law) and Hohenlohe after three years (1897 resignation of Bötticher and Marschall).

After six years in office, Bülow wrote, the present Reich Chancellor was more secure than ever before.[32]

The government victory was confirmed by the final round of elections on 5 February, from which it emerged that the SPD had lost thirty-eight seats. The Centre had in fact gained five seats,[33] but its decisive position in the Reichstag had been undermined by the socialist defeat and neither Bülow nor the Kaiser was prepared to allow this minor detail to cloud the impression of success. As Szögyényi privately informed Aehrenthal after a long conversation with the Kaiser even before the results were confirmed:

In accordance with his impulsive temperament Kaiser Wilhelm believes that now the Social Democrats have been dealt such a smarting blow on the head [*so empfindlich aufs Haupt geschlagen worden sind*], they can look forward to a completely new, propitious era. The fact that the Centre will move into the new Reichstag not weakened, indeed even *numerically* strengthened, is now silently passed over by Kaiser Wilhelm, just like his Reich Chancellor, and he does not remember that he assured me only recently that the real, main purpose of the Reichstag dissolution consisted in teaching the Centre a painful [*empfindlich*] lesson and pillorying its unpatriotic behaviour. The Highest Person seems to want to ignore completely that there ever was a campaign against the Centre and would like to portray the situation as if the entire election campaign had really been directed only against Social Democracy.[34]

Szögyényi recognised that the Centre might now be less inclined to combine with the socialists and the Poles against the government but, like most political observers in the wake of the election results, he tended to believe that the new Reichstag would make German domestic politics even more complicated than before. Considering that there was no question of the Bloc's becoming a permanent support of government policy, Szögyényi had reported at the end of January that the question was whether Bülow would succeed in working with two kinds of parliamentary majority – the Conservative–liberal combination for so-called national questions and the Conservative–Centre combination on economic matters.[35] Baroness Spitzemberg already saw the Chancellor caught between an aggravated but in no way weakened Centre Party and liberal demands for a less conservative government. Bülow, she wrote, would have to make liberal concessions if he was to secure a majority for government bills.[36] So unnatural did the new situation appear to some that Bülow was compared to Cardinal Wolsey, forced by Henry VIII into the notorious marriage affair and ultimately ruined by the consequences.[37] Others described the Chancellor as 'a child of good fortune', in no way conceiving of a permanent parliamentary 'Bülow Bloc' but instead anticipating a return to the lofty ideal of a genuine 'government above the parties'.[38]

As the crowds thronged to the Chancellor's palace on 5 February, it was thus apparent that the election results had clarified little. In the early weeks of 1907 Bülow was counselled from all sides not to alienate the Centre Party permanently but if possible to draw it into the national Bloc.[39] But, if he had lacked a clear vision of the future before the election results, the Chancellor was now encouraged by the victory over the SPD, the weakening of the Centre's pivotal position and the Kaiser's evident satisfaction with his new display of toughness to ally himself more firmly with the Conservatives and liberals and to embark on a more rigid course than the circumstances seemed to warrant. The new Reichstag opened on 19 February and, under pressure from Bülow, immediately broke with the tradition that the President was always elected from the strongest party. The Conservative Udo zu Stolberg-Wernigerode replaced Ballestrem as President with a National Liberal, Hermann Paasche, and a Progressive, Johannes Kaempf, as the two Vice-Presidents.[40] The unity of the new Bloc was thus symbolically underlined, and on 25 and 26 February Bülow made two speeches against the Centre and the SPD which Holstein believed were designed to please the Kaiser but which seemed to signify the Chancellor's further alienation from the Centre.[41] Bülow blamed the Centre Party for the failure to create a united bloc of all the bourgeois parties against Social Democracy in previous years and expressed his intention to work with the new Reichstag majority elected by the German people.[42]

Bülow's attitude towards the Centre during the first five months of 1907 was not politically damaging. The government deliberately avoided introducing contentious legislation of awkward budget details during the first session of the new Reichstag, and by the time the Reichstag was closed on 14 May the government could look back with some satisfaction on what had been achieved. The Reich budget, the credits for South-West Africa and the new State Secretaryship for the colonies were voted through without any difficulty. The budget debate had not been so smooth for years, and only the SPD, Poles and part of the Centre had opposed the new office.[43] The Progressive liberals had shown a willingness to compromise with the Conservatives in order to frustrate the Centre,[44] and, while the Bloc had held together well, the Centre seemed to have become relatively contrite. It was almost more moderate in opposition than it had been as a 'government party'; its behaviour in the first months of 1907 was interpreted as an attempt to effect a reconciliation with the government.[45]

But it was the Chancellor's hardening attitude towards the Centre which made such a reconciliation appear increasingly unlikely. He exploited the unexpected defeat of the SPD to treat the Centre in a peremptory manner,[46] and despite all the advice he received to the contrary, Bülow dissociated himself more and more from the Centre. As early as March he seemed 'to have come to the view that the possibility does indeed exist of ruling with right and left'.[47] Lerchenfeld understood Bülow's policy in so far as, after his attitude during the election campaign, the Chancellor would have appeared inconsistent if he had immediately dropped his programme of a Conservative and liberal 'pairing'. But, in reporting that 'the Reich Chancellor is sticking to the idea of ruling with the Bloc', the ambassador voiced his fear 'that the Prince, after the first successes, is deluding himself about the possibility of keeping the Conservatives and the left together indefinitely'.[48] The Chancellor's illusions about the durability of the Bloc were shared by the Kaiser. After a conversation with Wilhelm II, who stressed how important it was that the new Reichstag had time to settle down and get to know itself before being confronted with major bills, Lerchenfeld gained the impression that 'the High Lord is reckoning with the possibility that the Bloc parties will stay together'.[49]

Such expectations were incomprehensible to experienced political observers such as Lerchenfeld, Szögyényi and Berckheim. For they were convinced that in the autumn 'questions will and must come which will break the Bloc and then the Reich Chancellor will certainly be faced with the necessity of trying [to rule] again with the Centre'.[50] However much they applauded Bülow's professed intention to practise more reserve *vis-à-vis* parliamentary deputies and never again to have such an intimate relationship with one party as he had had with the Centre between 1900 and 1906, the re-establishment of some kind of *modus vivendi* with the Centre was judged to be inevitable and any behaviour which precluded this eventuality a political mistake.[51] Lerchenfeld believed that practical politics would ultimately outweigh personal rancours, but by March 1907 some already considered that a resurrection of the old Conservative–Centre cooperation would be impossible under Bülow. Rumours began to circulate once again that the Chancellor's days in office were numbered, this time because he had broken with the Centre and would be at the end of his governmental strength when the Bloc collapsed.[52]

For Berckheim, the alternative facing Bülow was clear. The Bloc could not survive; thus the question was whether Bülow could appease the Centre with promises and concessions in the six months between May and the reopening of the Reichstag in November, or whether the Chancellor himself would have to be sacrificed so that peace between the government and the Centre could be restored.[53] The Centre was ultimately indispensable; the Chancellor, it appeared, was not. But within a month of Berckheim's gloomy report on the domestic predicament of the Chancellor, Bülow demonstrated categorically that he rejected both these solutions. Heedless of the warnings about the durability of the Bloc, he chose to identify himself further with the course on which he had embarked in January 1907. Far from convinced that the Bloc would ultimately be his undoing and that he would have to be personally sacrificed to the Centre, Bülow jettisoned two colleagues for the sake of the Bloc and thereby underlined his commitment to the new strategy.

Victims of the Bloc

Almost immediately after the election results were known, the German press began to discuss the probability of ministerial changes. The Bavarian-born State Secretary of the Treasury, Stengel, read news of his impending resignation procured from a 'well-informed source' and, aware of how Bülow used the press as a sounding board on such matters, he promptly offered to resign if the new political situation made this desirable. Bülow, however, had no wish at this stage to remove Stengel, who had the confidence of the great majority of the Reichstag, and rejected the offer.[54] Rumours concerning the imminent resignations of Posadowsky and Studt were to have more foundation, and both men were dismissed in June 1907 as a direct consequence of the Chancellor's new strategy in the Reichstag.

The resignation of the Minister of Culture had been expected and, by Bülow's own admission, delayed for several months, and Studt's departure was certainly the less controversial of the changes in June 1907.[55] Even so, Studt had hoped and expected to be able to stay on as Minister over the summer in order to conclude unfinished business and was unpleasantly surprised by a visit on 22 June from Lucanus, who informed him otherwise.[56] As Minister of Culture Studt had been disliked by the entire German left because he had conducted the affairs of his office completely in accordance with the wishes of the Conservative–Centre majority in the Prussian Lower House. In particular, the Prussian School Law, which had only been passed in June 1906 with the cooperation of the National Liberals after great pressure had been put on Studt by the Kaiser, Chancellor and Ministry of State (Wilhelm II especially feared a similar *débâcle* to that of 1892 if the National Liberals were not participants),[57] had alienated liberal opinion and encouraged a systematic press campaign against Studt.[58] Wilhelm II, always an admirer of Studt's imperviousness to the dictates of public opinion,[59] supported him throughout 1906, which perhaps explains Bülow's exceptional friendliness towards him.[60] But especially after the Reichstag dissolution, Bülow must have found Studt an inconvenient colleague, and the left liberals hoped that the Minister's removal would be one of the first fruits of their collaboration in the Bloc.[61] From February 1907 it became increasingly clear that Studt's ministerial activities (which attested to the difficulty of working even with the National Liberals in Prussia, let alone the Bloc) and his public pronouncements in the Landtag were completely at variance with the Chancellor's new policy and that the Minister would indeed be sacrificed to the Bloc.[62]

The expectation of Studt's resignation provoked all kinds of anxieties, especially among German Catholics, about organisational changes in the Prussian Ministry of Culture and the appointment of a new, liberal Minister. There certainly were government plans (initiated by the *Ministerialdirektor*, Althoff) to divide the Ministry into separate departments, and a new Ministry of Religion might have constituted a step in a liberal or anti-clerical direction.[63] But Bülow ultimately became hostile to the idea of separating religious and educational affairs, at the most envisaging an independent department for art, science and technology or the transfer of matters concerning medicine to the Prussian Ministry of Interior. He was prepared to leave the examination of such questions to the new Minister[64] and by the end of the year, especially after Althoff's resignation, the issue had lost political significance.[65] Of more concern to Conservatives and Catholics alike was the possibility of a new, liberal Minister of Culture, appointed to defy the Centre and prepared to inaugurate a new *Kulturkampf*. Again Bülow sought to reassure those such as Cardinal Kopp who had these fears, insisting that he personally would be strong enough to prevent any moves in this direction. But Kopp despatched letters to the Chancellor, Lucanus and Studt, warning that German Catholics would not hesitate to support the SPD – as they had done in the Bismarck era – if attacked by the government and that such an eventuality would be more dangerous to the state than to the church.[66]

Kopp's arguments may well have impressed Bülow sufficiently to influence his choice of a completely innocuous successor to Studt. Ludwig Holle, a former Under State Secretary in the Ministry of Public Works and an alleged specialist in hydraulics,[67] was an unknown quantity politically and certainly not liberal in his political views. As Bülow told the Prussian Ministry, he was 'an official without pronounced political direction . . . who, in the leadership of his department, will have to keep to the middle way'.[68] Holle's appointment may have satisfied German Catholics that a new *Kulturkampf* was not about to commence, but such an insignificant figure could scarcely be a potential bridge to the Centre.[69] Liberals were also disappointed by the choice of Holle, though their main object had been achieved.[70] In April 1907 Studt had told Bülow that the liberals attacked his 'system', knowing very well 'that as head of department I make a personal decision on every matter of some importance and that all the declarations of my subordinates are dependent on my inspection and approval'.[71] Thus his removal was a major victory for liberals of all shades and went some way to convince them of Bülow's sincere commitment to the Bloc.

The major surprise in June 1907 was the ostensibly abrupt dismissal of Posadowsky, but here too it is evident that Bülow had been planning Posadowsky's departure for some time and that the State Secretary had in fact (unknown to him) been granted a brief reprieve. From the moment he dissolved the Reichstag and launched an anti-Centre election campaign, Bülow probably regarded the removal of his Vice-Chancellor as only a matter of time, and one of the first indications of the Chancellor's intentions was provided early in 1907 by the Kaiser who, in conversation with Szögyényi, unconsciously revealed the influence of his adviser. Repeating an interpretation, voiced a few days earlier by Bülow, of how the foreign press had formed an erroneous conception of the Reichstag dissolution,[72] Wilhelm asserted that Posadowsky, 'an otherwise exceptionally capable and good, high German state civil servant', had contributed to the political gossip which had led foreign diplomats astray.

In particular, this quite excellent departmental official, but bad politician, had raised objections to the dissolution of the Reichstag and in this respect had perhaps lent his fears all too loud expression; the wife of the State Secretary, a lady as tactless as she is ambitious, even went so far as to declare to the most various of people that in her opinion the fall of Prince Bülow was inevitable and that her husband, Count Posadowsky, was destined to assume the Prince's difficult inheritance.

Such 'Tartar stories', Wilhelm claimed, had inexplicably been believed even by some serious people abroad, and 'even the generally known fact that he – Kaiser Wilhelm – paid his Chancellor a long visit every day in a demonstrative way had not opened the people's eyes'.[73]

Bülow worked systematically in the press and with the Kaiser in early 1907 to remove Posadowsky, and by March the State Secretary was at the centre of a lively press discussion.[74] Lerchenfeld seemed to sense the way the wind was blowing and asserted that it would only need a word from the Chancellor, given his strong position once more, to dispense with an inconvenient colleague. But, while knowing that Posadowsky did not agree with Bülow's policy, Lerchenfeld considered it 'unthinkable that Prince Bülow wants to be rid of him', for the State Secretary did not directly oppose the Chancellor and understood as no other how to subordinate himself to Bülow.[75] In fact Bülow was planning to seek Wilhelm II's agreement to Posadowsky's resignation on the very morning that Lerchenfeld wrote his report. But the unexpected defence of Posadowsky in many German newspapers ultimately made the Chancellor baulk at pushing through his dismissal in March 1907, and for reasons of expediency he temporarily shelved his plans. As Bülow complained to Hammann, the Germans allowed the major political issues, 'necessary homogeneity of the government, domestic policy which the Bloc represents, etc. to recede behind what are without doubt trivial and sentimental personal considerations'. Thus he suggested 'that in

7 Arthur von Posadowsky-Wehner, State Secretary of the Reich Office of Interior
1897–1907

these circumstances we had better postpone Posadowsky's departure *until the
summer holidays* in order to prepare public opinion better than has been done,
as far as I can see, up to now'.[76] Shortly afterwards he agreed to Posadowsky's
releasing an official denial of the rumours of his impending resignation,
though he carefully avoided any personal involvement in the *démenti*.[77]

The press attacks on Posadowsky continued until June, and he was luridly
portrayed as the decisive opponent of the Reichstag dissolution and the man

who had prophesied that the SPD would return to the Reichstag with 114 seats. Posadowsky later claimed that he gradually came to realise that the attacks were systematic and that newspapers close to the Chancellor had intentionally fed the rumours; and, bitter about his humiliation, he claimed that he personally decided to resign when after weeks of this exposure he had finally been linked to the 'Liebenberg round table' and his influence had been compared to that of irresponsible advisers.[78] But, in reality, the State Secretary was completely surprised when Lucanus appeared before him on 22 June (the same day the Cabinet Chief spoke to Studt) to demand his resignation.[79] As Loebell wrote to Bülow afterwards, 'Count von Posadowsky, greatly excited, spoke of intrigues and press campaigns [and] refuses any other state office.'[80] In effect Posadowsky was ungraciously dismissed, and only eight days after the announcement of his resignation (which occurred even before he had an official reply to his request) did the presentation of the Kaiser's marble bust and an imperial letter slightly soften the bad impression created.[81] Varnbüler compared these methods to those used against Podbielski and the 'camarilla', though as a staunch Conservative he believed that the State Secretary's Reichstag policy completely justified Bülow's action.[82]

Bülow's motives in removing Posadowsky in June 1907 were both personal and political. The two men had never liked each other, though it was not simply a desire 'to make hay while the sun shines' which drove Bülow to dispense with his colleague now that his position was strengthened once more.[83] Einem told Berckheim that 'for a long time and not merely recently there has existed a latent conflict between Prince Bülow and Count Posadowsky',[84] but they had not clashed openly on foreign and domestic questions[85] and it is unlikely that Posadowsky's independent initiatives, which the Chancellor occasionally resented, were a major factor in contributing to his fall.[86]

The key issue was Posadowsky's commitment to a Reichstag policy hinging on the Centre Party and his attitude to Bülow's *Blockpolitik*. But even so, Posadowsky's association with 'the naked domination of the Centre' and excessive leniency towards the SPD was to be much exaggerated, not least by Bülow.[87] Posadowsky maintained that the political conflict construed by the press between him and the Chancellor over the Reichstag dissolution was completely inaccurate. He admitted that he had submitted an objective memorandum on the prospects of the new elections and that he had not predicted such a favourable result; but he also claimed that Bülow had probably not expected the result either[88] and that, when he had been asked his opinion in the Prussian Ministry of State, he had maintained that it was for the Chancellor to decide. The election campaign itself had been conducted by 'the Reich Chancellor and his people', and there had never been a conflict or even open dissension between himself and Bülow.[89]

Since Bülow decided to remove Posadowsky so quickly after the Reichstag dissolution, it does seem that the State Secretary's main failing was his fundamental inability to comprehend the real nature of the crisis in 1906. Varnbüler claimed that Posadowsky simply had not understood the Chancellor's predicament in December 1906 and therefore had no conception of the compulsion Bülow was under to act as he did. 'For a long time nobody has believed any more that the Prince systematically prepared to break with the Centre long in advance [*von langer Hand*], as his semi-official press [*Offiziösen*] have since broadcast', Varnbüler reported. Even Bülow's warmest supporters now contented themselves with the recognition that the Chancellor had skilfully and successfully exploited the opportunity offered to him by Dernburg's impudence as a new Minister. For, the ambassador continued, Bülow had really no choice but 'to ride into the attack with this dare-devil'. His position with the Kaiser was so precarious that he could not have sacrificed Dernburg to the Centre without falling himself. Thus Bülow's motive in dissolving the Reichstag was to stay in office, and it was understandable that Posadowsky, 'who personally was not in such a predicament [and who] had been raised [*grossgezogen*] in obedience to the Centre, did not immediately comprehend this sudden boldness of his master and through his hesitation came into a certain conflict with him'.[90]

The rift between Bülow and Posadowsky over the events of December 1906 had widened after the election results when Bülow began to entertain notions of governing exclusively with the Bloc. Posadowsky expected that the 1907 Budget would be passed with the help of the Centre, and his Reichstag speech in February 1907 was interpreted as incompatible with the *Blockpolitik*. It was clear that Bülow wanted his principal subordinate in domestic policy to support his new strategy more actively. Moreover, Bülow recognised that Posadowsky no longer suited the direction of German policy and that his removal would facilitate the task of working with the Bloc.[91] Although Posadowsky's social policy had been popular with the left in the Reichstag, his collaboration with the Centre made him suspect. For the Conservatives, his ideas had always smacked of 'state socialism' and they would be more inclined to make the moderate concessions to liberalism which were necessary if the Bloc were to stay together if they were asked of them by a less progressive personality than Posadowsky.[92]

It may well have been his greater suitability as a mediator between left and right which determined the choice of Bethmann Hollweg as Posadowsky's successor in June 1907. The Prussian Ministry of Interior, made vacant by Bethmann's promotion, was transferred to the former *Oberpräsident* of East Prussia and brother of the Chief of the General Staff, Friedrich von Moltke.[93] Bethmann Hollweg scarcely had liberal views, though Conservatives judged him to have a 'modern' orientation,[94] and he had initially adopted a rather cautious, even apprehensive, position on the Reichstag dissolution in 1906.[95] By June 1907 he had developed into a professed supporter of Bülow's new strategy; he was 'convinced of the possibility of executing the *Blockpolitik*' and believed he represented the Conservative–liberal pairing.[96] Bethmann had clearly been selected as Posadowsky's successor many weeks before the changes were effected.[97]

The appointment of Bethmann as State Secretary of Interior was significant in underlining the government's commitment to the Bloc and Bülow's firm intention to continue on the path he had taken in December 1906. It also had lesser implications for domestic policy within the executive and in particular the work of the Reich Office of Interior. Although some doubted whether Bethmann would be equal to the demands of his new office, for he certainly could not match Posadowsky's indefatigable capacity for hard work,[98] Lerchenfeld maintained that Bethmann, who was 'undoubtedly one of the most significant personalities in Prussia', would be at least as successful as Posadowsky, since his predecessor had neglected the affairs of his office and devoted his energies to the Reichstag.[99] It was rumoured that Bethmann only agreed to accept the Reich Office of Interior if the office was divided, and there was much discussion of organisational changes, also affecting the Reich Offices of Justice and Treasury, in association with the personnel changes in June 1907.[100] But hopes of paring down the business of the Reich Office of Interior or creating new State Secretaryships remained unrealised because of the practical difficulties involved, and Bethmann told Berckheim at the end of June that he was taking over the work of his predecessor in its entirety.[101] What was clear from June 1907 was that Bethmann's appointment signified a brake on the speed of the social welfare reforms associated with Posadowsky. Bülow indicated his awareness of financial imperatives, but he also told Lerchenfeld that Posadowsky had become too much of a theoretician and that Bethmann would conduct affairs more practically.[102] Posadowsky found it incomprehensible that the introduction of social welfare legislation was to be halted at a time when the Bloc majority necessitated concessions to the left, and he could only conclude that the Kaiser was incorrectly informed about domestic relations.[103]

The political importance of Bethmann's appointment primarily arose from his simultaneous promotion to Vice-President of the Prussian Ministry of State, a position Posadowsky had aspired to for many years but never attained.[104] Bethmann himself had attached great weight to the Vice-Presidency, which not least ensured that he would continue to be directly informed of Prussian domestic politics by the *Oberpräsidenten*,[105] and in presenting the filling of the position as necessary for the future unity and homogeneity of Reich and Prussian policy, Bülow ironically used arguments exactly like those he had used against the appointment of a Vice-President in 1901. In May 1901 Bülow had hoped to end the years of a 'dual economy' and ensure unity between the highest departments in the Reich and Prussia; in 1907 Bethmann told Berckheim that through his appointment the Kaiser and Bülow intended to express the full unity of German policy,[106] and the Chancellor stressed in the Ministry of State how, without mechanically transferring the *Blockpolitik* to Prussia, Prussian policy could not remain unaffected by the new constellation in the Reich.[107] Szögyényi doubted the efficacy of Bethmann's promotion. After Miquel's departure, he reported, the homogeneity of the German government could in no way be reconstructed, and he expected little improvement with the new Vice-President.[108]

Bethmann's promotion to the Vice-Presidency was clearly the most sensitive political issue within the executive in June 1907, and one over which Bülow must have expected some opposition from his Prussian colleagues. Aware that Bethmann's appointment rode roughshod over the possible claims of longer-serving Prussian Ministers, Bülow took care to justify his decision for political reasons to Tirpitz and Einem,[109] though it is unlikely that they were much disturbed by Bethmann's promotion. The chief affront was ostensibly to Rheinbaben, to whom Bülow formally apologised in the Prussian Ministry of State on 25 June when he informed it of the personnel changes.[110] Loebell had advised Bülow to see Rheinbaben personally before the meeting,[111] and the Finance Minister was deliberately appeased by the bestowal of the Order of the Black Eagle for his services. In Varnbüler's opinion Bülow's behaviour 'shows again that the Reich Chancellor does not let the trees grow to the heavens, tolerates no other gods alongside him'.[112] It was said that there was no disagreements between Bülow and the Finance Minister,[113] but Bethmann's promotion to the Vice-Presidency doubtless aggravated their antagonism, and Rheinbaben did not forget the apparent slight.[114] Significantly Bethmann Hollweg excluded both Rheinbaben and Arnim when he listed the Prussian Ministers on whom he could now rely.[115]

All in all, the personnel changes of June 1907 and their accompanying commitment of the government to the Bloc made personal rather than political sense for Bülow. Apparently Bülow had regained the Kaiser's favour and now emerged with enhanced authority and prestige; and few doubted his personal achievement in effecting the personnel changes and the decisive importance of his personal motives. Varnbüler reported that the *revirement* appeared as 'a trial of strength and a confirmation of [the] power of Prince Bülow', a warning to all who should dare to cross his path.[116] Szögyényi maintained that Bülow now seemed set on removing all his enemies and that this was the most sure indication 'of how secure the Chancellor now feels in the saddle'.[117] Berckheim placed the personnel changes in the same context as the removal of another, allegedly pernicious, political influence from the German domestic scene. Bülow, he reported, had 'exploited the opportunity extremely skilfully to remove two rivals who could possibly have become dangerous to him personally; first, Prince Eulenburg via Holstein-Harden, and then Count Posadowsky by portraying him as unreliable and friendly towards the Centre. Was the latter really that? I scarcely believe it.'[118]

Such observers were probably right to accentuate Bülow's personal motives, but their conception of the Chancellor's new-found omnipotence proved essentially erroneous. Bülow was not so secure in the saddle as the removal of Posadowsky seemed to indicate. He may only have been able to effect the personnel changes in June 1907 because Bethmann, Holle (who had been involved in the canal project) and Moltke were all popular with the Kaiser, and there were already many other symptoms of the Chancellor's growing political bankruptcy.[119] Bülow's commitment to the Bloc and his determination to stand or fall with it were greeted by some as a welcome clarification of the domestic situation.[120] But the old doubts about the durability of the Bloc remained despite some improvement in its prospects, and Bülow's conduct in June 1907 can be judged as another step on the road to political suicide. It is not only with the benefit of hindsight that one can see how limited were the government's chances of success with the Bloc, and even contemporaries recognised Bülow's lack of realism if he believed certain issues could be regulated satisfactorily with the new combination. As Lerchenfeld reported:

There must be at least the possibility of solving certain questions with the earlier majority of Conservatives and Centre. Count Posadowsky, who always represented this view, would have been in a position to restore the torn links with the Centre again. His successor who is sworn in to the *Blockpolitik* will find this difficult. The Reich Chancellor admittedly told me that the new Minister of Culture was chosen with a view to maintaining good relations with the Catholics. But this will not satisfy the Centre as a political party.[121]

If it was, as Szögyényi believed, 'scarcely thinkable' that Bülow really hoped to work with right and left for any length of time,[122] immediately the question arises whether he intended to remain as Chancellor much longer. Some said that Bülow promoted Bethmann Hollweg in order to use up an heir presumptive,[123] but others were already reporting that Bülow had lost his former drive and enthusiasm for his work and was beginning to be drawn by the idea of a quiet life in his recently acquired Italian villa.[124] As the Württemberg *chargé d'affaires* reported:

In the closest entourage of the Prince one makes no secret of the fact that already for some time he has wanted to shake off the dust of the Wilhelmstrasse and is kept from his intention by love of the Fatherland. The driving force in this direction is the Princess herself, who is worried about the health of her husband [and] besieges him more and more with the request finally for once to live exclusively for himself and his family.[125]

How far Bülow shared these rather uncharacteristic desires of his wife and how far this was simply a pose is a moot point. But some of Bülow's personal friends also told Szögyényi that he fully identified himself with his new policy and that if it proved unworkable, he would leave the political stage in all glory, as a man fallen victim to his convictions. Such behaviour scarcely seemed loyal to the Kaiser. But then, Szögyényi added, 'consideration of his own position has always played a very predominant role in the political life and work of Prince Bülow'.[126]

Problems within the executive

Bülow's position appeared very strong in June 1907 after the removal of Posadowsky and Studt, but he was by no means as secure as he had been between 1900 and 1905. His commitment to the Bloc posed all kinds of questions about the loyalty of the political parties to the Chancellor and the Bloc's vitality as a parliamentary majority. Moreover, the events of 1906 had shattered the public image of Bülow's Chancellorship; no longer did his position appear impregnable and, although rumours about a Chancellor crisis were temporarily silenced in early 1907, they soon recurred and multiplied in all possible forms.[127] In May 1907 Bülow had recourse to an official announcement in the *Norddeutsche Allgemeine Zeitung* denying differences between the Kaiser and Chancellor and the imminence of another period of convalescence.[128] But the rumours did not die, and the presagers of the collapse of Bülow's Chancellorship were not finally placated until his resignation in 1909.

Behind the façade of his restored authority, there were also indications that Bülow's position within the executive and his relationship with the Kaiser rested on rather shaky foundations. How serious these various symptoms of weakness were is debatable, for there were some observers in the early summer of 1907 who believed that the preconditions existed for a permanent strengthening of the Chancellor's position.[129] The main question was whether Bülow would prove willing or able to exploit the opportunities open to him in 1907 to restructure his system anew. But if such preconditions existed, they were soon dissipated. By 1907 Bülow lacked both the political vision and the personal determination to find radical solutions for either the new or the more familiar problems. Grappling with the parliamentary implications of the Reichstag dissolution in 1906 and having no new prescriptions for handling his imperial master, Bülow neglected his power position within the executive and sustained the appearance of his control only imperfectly. Without personal conviction, with no far-sighted political plans and often at a disadvantage when confronted with less gifted people who knew what they wanted, Bülow muddled along and his public face increasingly came to conceal the hollowness of his position.[130]

Bülow's commitment to the *Blockpolitik* created problems not only in the Reichstag but also in the executive. In 1903 Lerchenfeld had observed that if Bülow had really wanted to pursue a liberal course, he would have had to change the entire Prussian bureaucracy.[131] Despite the removal of Posadowsky and Studt, the new strategy aggravated the persistent tensions between Prussia and the Reich, and liberal hopes that Rheinbaben, 'the head of the Prussian fronde', would soon follow his two colleagues into retirement were disappointed. Rheinbaben's continued control of the Prussian Ministry of Finance, especially with a major financial reform looming on the horizon, constituted an important limitation to the Chancellor's victory in 1907 and one which contributed significantly to the Bloc crisis later in the year. Moreover, as the Württemberg *chargé d'affaires* reported, Studt's resignation alone was not sufficient to pave the way for the Bloc in the Prussian parliament. With the Conservatives exceptionally reluctant to extend their ties of friendship with the liberals to the Prussian Lower House, Bülow could expect little success if he tried to encourage the emulation of the Bloc experiment in the Prussian Landtag. 'Rheinbaben's star will continue to shine here alongside Bülow and the resolution of this dualism cannot be foreseen for the time being', Speth concluded.[132]

The position of the State Secretaries was also scarcely easier after the Reichstag dissolution, because they were largely saddled with the practical difficulties inherent in the attempt to work with right and left. Bülow informed his subordinates that, given the new situation in the Reichstag, the political implications of all bills had to be closely scrutinised and, in particular, consideration had to be paid to the prospects of success a bill might have with the new majority. He made it clear that when necessary the State Secretaries should sound out the party leaders about the future legislation before presenting the relevant bill to the State Ministry or Bundesrat; and the department chiefs were instructed to discuss their plans with the new State Secretary of Interior, Bethmann Hollweg, and seek Bülow's personal approval if this seemed desirable.[133] These guidelines, however, were bound to be followed only with difficulty by State Secretaries, not to mention bureaucrats and officials, accustomed to working with the Conservative–Centre parliamentary grouping. Stengel, confronted with the Reich's serious financial problems and reluctant to break with the Centre, was not permitted by Bülow to resign in the summer of 1907, and his position became increasingly untenable.[134] Tirpitz, too, who was preparing a major amendment to the Navy Laws, found the new relationship with the Centre problematic. Although the approval of the *Novelle* depended, as he recognised, first and foremost on the Bloc, it was difficult to negotiate with the Progressives who had numerous, rival leaders fighting for influence in the party,[135] and it was tempting to approach the Centre leaders, if only to put pressure on the Progressives. Moreover, as Tirpitz made clear to Bülow, 'the most knowledgeable and hence most dangerous experts on the true significance of the Navy Law, which at the moment is still not completely understood by most politicians and politickers [*Politikastern*] sit in the Centre Party'.[136] The pitfalls involved in making enemies of former friends were numerous.

Perhaps the most serious indictment of Bülow's system within the executive and his apparent obliviousness to the predicament of his subordinates was the letter of resignation submitted by the State Secretary of the Reich Justice Office, Nieberding, in July 1907.[137] Bülow had considered Nieberding's dismissal in the past, but had no desire to see him go in 1907. Nevertheless Nieberding felt that the Chancellor misunderstood the motives behind his decision and therefore submitted a long memorandum outlining his problems which is worth examining at some length.

Nieberding, like other State Secretaries, had been the victim of press attacks throughout 1907 and, like Posadowsky, had received very little support from the Chancellor in trying to suppress rumours of his imminent departure. He was assailed from all sides by questions about his future; his position in the Reich Justice Office had gradually become uncomfortable and his authority undermined. Especially after the resignation of Posadowsky, with whom he had often been associated, Nieberding was forced in the face of continued press criticism to conclude that his departure might be welcomed by the Kaiser and Chancellor.

Nieberding recognised that his position was essentially weakened because he did not enjoy the favour of the Kaiser. He had reconciled himself to the lack of imperial appreciation as far as his personal feelings were concerned. 'I know HM finds my performance in the Reichstag insufficiently "dashing" [*schneidig*]', he wrote, but he did not agree with the monarch's criticisms and believed that a conciliatory approach, which masked the absence of substantive concessions, was more effective than brusque rebuffs from the government. But the interests of the state were, he asserted, a different matter, and the Kaiser's confidence was clearly a necessity if he was to sustain his official authority. After nearly fifteen years as State Secretary of the Reich Justice Office and as the oldest and longest-serving head of a department, Nieberding had to confess that when it came to imperial favours, he virtually did not exist for the Kaiser and that this neglect damaged the prestige of his position in the public eye and, above all, in the bureaucracy.

The circles of the federal governments, in which a State Secretary primarily has to work, are more than sensitive to the extent to which HM the Kaiser's interest and goodwill are directed towards a Reich Office and its representative. The consideration which is paid to one of the Reich Offices corresponds very considerably to the attention which HM deigns to display towards the office. The less this is, the greater becomes the task to which the office has to do justice. And some observations have already made me doubt whether I am not injuring the prestige of the Reich Justice Office and the duties it has to perform if, despite everything, I remain in my position.

The lack of confidence displayed in Nieberding by Kaiser and Chancellor contributed to the impression that the State Secretary was merely a 'technical bureau chief' and that he had no influence on political questions. Nieberding's recent experiences in the Reichstag had confirmed the doubts of the political parties about whether he even had much political influence on questions within his own department. In particular, during the debate on the Reich Justice Office budget, Nieberding had been forced to explain away the delay in the reform of criminal procedures (for which he had not been responsible), and had been unable to tell the deputies when the justice bills would be introduced. Immediately after the debate, the bills had been introduced into the Reichstag, and the left liberal parties especially had concluded with satisfaction that Nieberding no longer had any contact with the Reich Chancellor. Disliked by the Progressives, Nieberding found that his activity was increasingly represented as incompatible with the Chancellor's policy. 'Frequently repeated and never denied, these misrepresentations have encouraged the view that I no longer enjoy the confidence of the Reich Chancellor. Without this confidence I consider my activity in office useless.'

Finally, Nieberding pointed out that the opposition to the criminal procedure reform in the Prussian government came primarily from Bethmann Hollweg and Rheinbaben, both of whom had recently been honoured by the Kaiser. Both men were also hostile to some of the provisions in the new legislation designed specifically to win liberal support in the Reichstag. 'For someone in my weak position it is difficult to stand up to such favoured opponents', he complained. The federal states gave him no support and he could only rely on the Prussian Justice Minister. If the reform failed there would be no doubt that he personally would bear the cost of the parliamentary campaign.

All in all, Nieberding's memorandum of July 1907 attested to the difficulty of being a State Secretary during Bülow's Chancellorship, without support from the Kaiser and especially once the Chancellor had committed the government to a parliamentary course which forced his subordinates to work with both right and left in an unnatural alliance. But perhaps even more damning was the Chancellor's response. After informing Nieberding that Bülow still did not desire his resignation, Loebell went on to say that Bülow did not consider the reasons Nieberding had given for his decision (the lack of confidence of the Kaiser, Chancellor, Prussian Ministry, Bundesrat,

Reichstag and public opinion) 'valid . . . to warrant resignation'. Rather weakly Loebell pointed out that 'The influence of official channels on the press is very small and is much overestimated' and that Bülow wanted Nieberding to stay in the office which he had headed successfully for so many years.[138] Bülow's dismissive and insincere attitude was apparent only one month later when the National Liberal leader, Bassermann, impressed on the Chancellor in Norderney that Nieberding was spent and would have to go. Bülow told Loebell he would discuss this question with him at their next meeting,[139] but in fact the State Secretary was to survive the Chancellor in office, if only by a few months.[140]

A State Secretary with whom Bülow continued to have a difficult relationship was Tschirschky. Once the Chancellor crisis rumours began to recur, the continuing disagreements between Bülow and the State Secretary of the Foreign Office were a persistent theme.[141] The resignation of Paul von Below, who had replaced Lichnowsky as the head of the Foreign Office Personnel Department and who regularly accompanied Bülow on his travels 'as a kind of Cabinet Chief', was attributed to the frictions arising from Below's formal subordination to Tschirschky.[142] Baroness Spitzemberg heard in April of 'a very violent scene' between the Chancellor and State Secretary 'which very nearly led to a conflict'.[143] There was alleged to be a 'Bülow camp' and a 'Tschirschky circle', with Bülow trying to circumnavigate Tschirschky's area of competence.[144] Such allegations were denied categorically by Tschirschky, but confirmed by such well-informed people that Lerchenfeld could not vouch that they were completely without foundation.[145]

Lerchenfeld observed that 'the Reich Chancellor and the State Secretary associate together in the same intimate way as before',[146] and certainly if there was friction between the two men, Bülow characteristically ensured that outwardly harmonious relations prevailed. Moreover, with Holstein convinced of Tschirschky's culpability in bringing about his resignation and Harden erroneously depicting the State Secretary as 'Eulenburg's creature'[147] it is clear that there were influences outside the government trying to stir up enmity between Bülow and his subordinate. Tschirschky's inadequate parliamentary performances as well as his condemnation as the Kaiser's favourite also created enemies for the State Secretary in certain circles.[148] Nevertheless Bülow remained highly suspicious of Tschirschky, and his suspicions were not completely without foundation, for the State Secretary did constitute a threat to his authority. Tschirschky continued to be highly critical of the Chancellor's influence on foreign policy, denying that Bülow had ever had a 'productive, positive idea';[149] and if he had considered a new Chancellor a possibility in the previous autumn, there is no evidence that he had abandoned this view in 1907.[150] Tschirschky was prepared to conduct foreign

8 Bülow with his wife, Marie, and their poodle, Mohrchen, on the island of Norderney in 1907

policy independently of Kaiser and Chancellor, informing both of a treaty with Denmark in January 1907 only when it was ready to be signed. (Curiously on this occasion Tschirschky initiated Bethmann Hollweg into the negotiations, which is perhaps indicative of the latter's authority within the executive.)[151] According to Holstein, in April 1907 Bülow and Tschirschky also disagreed over the disarmament question and the incident was 'significant in showing up the position of Bülow' since the Kaiser had backed the State Secretary.[152]

Tschirschky was primarily suspect to the Chancellor because of his relationship with the Kaiser, and in Italy in April 1907 Bülow persistently sought Monts's reassurance about Tschirschky's personal loyalty.[153] Tschirschky himself still insisted that he had never intrigued against Bülow, and he told Monts,

In so far as he [Bülow] considers it at all possible that someone who does not stand on the top step does not strive to topple the person above, he trusts me. I don't understand why he finds my position with the Kaiser inconvenient. For, as he correctly assumes, this intimate position damages me in the parliament and with the people; as he sees things, that can only be a good thing.[154]

It is unlikely that Bülow saw Tschirschky as a potential successor, but he must have worried that the State Secretary would influence the monarch against him. The diaries of the Kaiser's adjutants in the first three months of 1907 indicate Wilhelm II's renewed confidence in the Chancellor, who he saw more frequently than at any other time since 1897; but they also indicate no corresponding diminution in Wilhelm's esteem of Tschirschky, and many of the Kaiser's visits were to the Chancellor and State Secretary together. When Bülow was away for part of March and April, the Kaiser continued to visit the Foreign Office to see Tschirschky alone.[155] Only in July 1907 is there any evidence of a weakening of Tschirschky's position, and then this was because of his mismanagement of the Cambon affair. His readiness to agree to French representation at a number of other German Courts (those of Dresden, Karlsruhe and Stuttgart) without consulting the Kaiser or Bülow incurred Wilhelm II's disapproval, and Varnbüler heard that the position of the State Secretary was now endangered.[156]

It is clear that in 1907 Bülow did not recover the authority to lead German foreign policy which he had lost in 1905–6, and the evidence suggests his relative lack of influence, possibly even exclusion from the conduct of foreign affairs. Holstein maintained that 'No policy whatever is being formulated any longer in the Foreign Ministry' and that 'in so far as B[ülow]'s allowed to do anything at all about foreign policy, he is probably holding his anti-English inclinations because he is afraid that a genuine rapprochement would bring about his removal'.[157] In fairness to Bülow he was probably preoccupied with parliamentary affairs and the cementing of the Bloc. But Lascelles too complained that Bülow had long ceased to lead and exert an influence on policy, doing nothing except prepare his speeches;[158] and even Tschirschky criticised the Chancellor's lack of activity. 'B.B. does less than ever', he wrote to Monts in May 1907, 'so that even Hammann asked me recently whether I really knew what B. did the whole day.'[159]

This apathy was not just a feature of Bülow's involvement in the Foreign Office but characterised his approach to all government work within the executive by 1907. Even if he was not actually looking for a 'good exit' from 1907, he had not emerged from the events of 1906 unscathed. His illness and shattered authority had left personal as well as political scars, and whenever he was in an intimate circle with the Chancellor, Varnbüler observed

An elegiac trait which did not go with his usual joviality, with the contented 'dimpled smile' [*behaglichen 'Grübchenlächeln'*]. Less self-confident assurance than earlier – a certain despondency or rather weariness, something like disappointment, resignation, *dépit*, over the inadequacy of human ability and work – more the nature of a withdrawn [*weltabgekehrt*] philosopher than of a statesman [*Staatslenker*] rejoicing in struggle and practical work.

Bitter and disillusioned, Bülow argued at a dinner that if Bismarck had died in 1866, his genius would never have been recognised and that if Napoleon III had left the world stage in 1859, he would have been considered one of the greatest rulers in history. Both Varnbüler and Harnack had the impression that the Chancellor was not speaking academically but subjectively, resentful that despite all his eloquence and skill, he still had not achieved decisive successes or won full recognition from even one political party.[160]

Bülow's new listlessness and pessimism reinforced his personal inclination to be highly selective, even lackadaisical about his involvement in executive affairs. His isolation within the executive increased and 'he hardly saw anybody but Hammann and Loebell'. With stories circulating about the way his speeches were drafted, Holstein advised him 'to see his Ministers more often and get material for his speeches from memoranda prepared in the Ministries'.[161] In effect Bülow appeared to be reducing the Chancellorship to the kind of less significant, mediatory role accorded to it by the letter of the Reich Constitution. But even this function Bülow fulfilled imperfectly. Ministers and State Secretaries felt deprived of genuine political influence, but the Chancellor had no real understanding of their work and devoted his attention exclusively to the needs of the Kaiser and Reichstag. He was unable to ensure a united political will within the executive, and the Chancellor's role became increasingly superfluous. While the centrifugal tendencies within the system were aggravated, the more Bülow withdrew, the less he appeared to be needed.

It was in his relations with the Kaiser that Bülow had hoped for the greatest improvement after December 1906; but here, too, he was to be disappointed, for the old confidentiality of the years 1900–5 was never restored. The Kaiser's enthusiasm in the wake of the election results was already waning by the summer of 1907 and a number of issues arose to cloud his relationship with the Chancellor, none of which was to go away quickly. First, there were the Moltke and Eulenburg scandals, which will be discussed in more detail below but which profoundly affected the Kaiser and seemed to implicate the Chancellor. Then there were the growing criticisms of Germany's diplomatic position, for which Bülow was held responsible. The Kaiser was excessively optimistic about the prospects of a Franco-German entente in May, but the implications of England's entente with Russia, concluded in August 1907, cannot have escaped him.[162] Finally, there was the whole question of the Bloc and Bülow's relations with the political parties which began to place a strain on the relationship between Kaiser and Chancellor once the initial euphoria had passed. Not only did Bülow have to scrutinise Wilhelm's public utterances and actions in the summer of 1907 more than ever 'this year in view of the new Reichstag and the demands of the national *Blockpolitik*',[163] but he also had to ensure that Wilhelm continued to maintain a positive attitude to the Bloc and that he did not misinterpret the Chancellor's increased involvement in parliamentary affairs – a task which was by no means easy when the Reichstag dissolution in 1906 had been represented as a move to free the government from excessive deference to a political party. Never fully aware of the implications of the *Blockpolitik*, Wilhelm II probably neither understood nor condoned Bülow's extensive discussions with parliamentarians in the summer of 1907. Negotiations with the political parties must have seemed irrelevant and demeaning to an autocratically inclined monarch who was convinced that the Reichstag counted for little, but Bülow attempted to explain the necessity of these preparations for the next parliamentary session in a letter to Wilhelm in September 1907. The talks with Reichstag deputies were irritating, he admitted, 'but necessary so that we hold the Bloc together'; and the Bloc had already had the good effect of making the Centre Party more modest and aware of its national duty. Deliberately choosing an issue the importance of which Wilhelm could readily appreciate, the Chancellor went on:

With the left liberals I have especially worked to effect that they must support the naval and military demands unconditionally, and Payer has promised me this. He is a Swabian, the leader of the South German People's Party. Anyone who had prophesied forty, twenty or even ten years ago that a Württemberg member of the People's Party would agree to the Army and naval demands would have risked being admitted to a *maison de santé* as someone of unsound mind. That is also a consequence of the fresh breeze which blows from the high sea, but it took a long time before 'the resistance of the dull world' ['*der Widerstand der stumpfen Welt*'] was overcome.[164]

Bülow admitted in some notes that the Kaiser's attitude towards him began to change again from the summer of 1907 and that, under the impact of Centre and clerical intrigues, Wilhelm began to sneer at the Bloc. The anti-Bülow agitation continued, he wrote, in Highcliffe that autumn and persisted throughout 1907–8 until it finally exploded into the open after the *Daily Telegraph* affair in November 1908.[165] There is some evidence of a press campaign from October 1907, possibly inspired by Erzberger, to disturb Bülow's relations with the Kaiser and thus bring about his fall.[166] The Centre's parliamentary machinations in late 1907 and exploitation of the Moltke-Harden scandal may also have been a complicating factor. Moreover, Bülow did not accompany Wilhelm to England in November 1907 – a fact which aroused widespread speculation in Berlin despite Bülow's official and hollow excuses – because he had not been invited.[167] The Chancellor was justifiably concerned about the influences on the Kaiser during his long stay in England, though by this time his own performances in the Reichstag (his speech on the Moltke-Harden scandal as well as his handling of the Bloc crisis) had further damaged their relationship.

But even before all the political scandals and upheavals of the autumn, the appointment of Schön as Tschirschky's successor in September 1907 demonstrated how much less Bülow could now influence the Kaiser than in the early years of his Chancellorship. Tschirschky's resignation as State Secretary of the Foreign Office and his transfer to the Vienna embassy as part of a more extensive diplomatic *revirement* arguably represented a major victory for the Chancellor, even though it would have been personally and politically damaging for him to acknowledge it as such. Tschirschky had never felt very comfortable in his position as State Secretary under Bülow,[168] and in the summer of 1907, as we have seen, he may have suffered a relative loss of the Kaiser's favour. On 2 September he asked the Kaiser directly if he could replace Wedel as ambassador to Vienna.[169] Wedel was to move to Strasburg as *Statthalter* since the departure of Hohenlohe-Langenburg had become inevitable once he had lost the Kaiser's confidence.[170]

Tschirschky's personal inclinations seemed curiously to coincide with Bülow's political aims in September 1907, but it is clear that the Chancellor had played an underhand role in encouraging the State Secretary's decision. Flotow, the official in the Foreign Office responsible for personnel matters, wrote to Bülow at the end of the month that 'There will be no lack of people who recognise or suspect the real state of affairs with this change.' He continued:

Even now I hear that unfortunately the parliamentary deputy Bassermann is supposed to have said that Your Excellency would no longer permit the State Secretary to stand before the Reichstag. If such voices multiply, the quiet work with which I brought the State Secretary quite painlessly to [agree to] this change will have been in vain. I also have the impression from conversations with Herr von Tschirschky that HM is in fact more disposed towards him than I had believed. Everything which makes an honourable change possible will therefore also suit His Majesty.[171]

Whether political or personal considerations had weighed uppermost in Bülow's decision to work to oust Tschirschky is a moot point. Berckheim reported that Bülow backed Tschirschky's request for Vienna 'not because of his inadequate gifts as a speaker but because, as became evident in the course of time, he was too independent in the formulation and execution of the details of foreign policy, which the Chancellor once regarded as his exclusive, private domain'.[172]

Bülow therefore supported Tschirschky's transfer to Vienna and wrote to the Kaiser to this effect on 9 September, even telling Wilhelm that 'When I suggested Tschirschky to Your Majesty as State Secretary, he told me right from the start that he did not think his health would be equal to this post'.[173]

(Bülow may have been relying on the Kaiser's forgetfulness, but his assertion proves beyond doubt that he never resisted Tschirschky's appointment in 1906.) The Chancellor had already been informed by Tschirschky that Wilhelm agreed in principle to his new appointment but awaited a list of candidates for the State Secretaryship before making a definite decision.[174] This list, Bülow admitted to the monarch, had been a considerable headache for him, but he proposed in his letter three possible candidates. The Chancellor's brief description of their respective qualities is indicative of the methods and approach he adopted when seeking to influence Wilhelm.

SCHÖN: An experienced diplomat, skilful in society, of pleasant manners, intelligent, active. How far he would be equal to the work of the central office cannot be predicted with certainty. It would also be a shame to take him away from St Petersburg, where he is doing really well.

MÜHLBERG: Has conducted the office, when entrusted with its provisional leadership, to Your Majesty's satisfaction. Sure capacity for work, experience, at the same time really clever.

KIDERLEN: Is the best political mind in Your Majesty's diplomacy despite some faults. His faults have also improved during the ten years he has been in the shadows. That his talents have remained the same, he has shown now in leading the embassy in Constantinople. He has the great advantage of knowing the Orient thoroughly, which will definitely be much more in the foreground again in the next years.[175]

Bülow must have been told by Tschirschky that Wilhelm II was considering Schön. Hence the inclusion of this 'courtier and society man of the worst kind'[176] in the Chancellor's list even though Bülow skilfully tried to discourage the Kaiser from making this choice. Mühlberg had been Bülow's candidate in 1906, and though the Chancellor probably expected the Kaiser to reject him again, his appointment certainly would have involved the least disruption in the work of the Foreign Office. Mühlberg subsequently resigned when he was passed over a second time and Rotenhan had to make way for him as Minister to the Vatican.[177] The most interesting candidate proposed by the Chancellor was Kiderlen-Wächter, the Kaiser's former favourite whose fall from grace in the late 1890s was certainly on account of Bülow's influence. Bülow's recommendation of Kiderlen in the difficult circumstances of 1907 not only indicated his preoccupation with domestic politics and the Bloc, but also his recognition that, especially after Holstein's departure, he personally was not in a position to raise Germany from the international quagmire in which she found herself. It was high time that such a talented diplomat returned to Berlin.

The Kaiser's response to this list of candidates, however, revealed the limits to Bülow's influence by 1907 and the hollowness of the Chancellor's victory in removing Tschirschky. Wilhelm was not sensitive to Bülow's subtle inferences and promptly settled for Schön. 'In accordance with Your Majesty's decision I wrote today to Schön', Bülow informed him on 16 September. He also applauded the choice of Pourtalès, whom he found 'really suitable' as Schön's successor in St Petersburg.[178] The Austrian *chargé d'affaires* later claimed that Pourtalès was one of Bülow's protégés and came from the coterie of men blindly devoted to the Chancellor.[179] But Baroness Spitzemberg maintained that Bülow did not really like him.[180] Pourtalès himself, who had complained to Bülow in July 1907 about his slow promotion up the diplomatic ladder, was astounded by his appointment to a post once occupied by such men as Bismarck, Reuss and Schweinitz.[181]

Bülow was clearly acutely embarrassed by Schön's appointment, not only because it was so obvious to whom he owed it, but also because he was likely to be even less impressive in the Reichstag than Tschirschky had been.[182] In the press Bülow encouraged the view 'that Herr von Schön will have no other ambition but to be the sympathetic assistant and representative of the Reich Chancellor' and that, given the Chancellor's conduct of foreign policy, the personality of the State Secretary was not very important.[183] To Holstein he omitted to mention that he had suggested Schön at all, simply explaining that he had proposed Mühlberg and Kiderlen but that Wilhelm II had wanted an ambassador selected.[184] Holstein's criticism was characteristically acerbic. 'Once again you have subordinated your sound common sense to the decisions – or let us say the whims – of the Kaiser', he wrote to Bülow, insisting that people would soon lose confidence in 'this manner of ruling'.

By your present, most recent system of *optima voluisse sat est*, that is of simply letting things take their course, our country not only loses the advantages of your many and versatile talents, but in addition you become the cover for things for which you can hardly answer, or for which you should not answer.[185]

Bülow's only defence was to relate the extraordinary story that he would have preferred to send Tschirschky to Rome (where Holstein thought he would be 'least bad'), but Tschirschky had secured a medical certificate testifying that he would not be able to stand the climate there. Furthermore, Bülow intimated, Tschirschky had really wanted Paris; thus he had not got his way. By implication, of course, Bülow indicated that he had saved the career of Holstein's friend, Radolin, who was ambassador in Paris.[186]

In the last analysis Bülow had no new strategy for dealing with Wilhelm II in 1907, and the one that he had was wearing increasingly thin. The political circumstances changed, but a letter written to the Kaiser by Bülow during the Bloc years was not appreciably different from one written in the early years of his Chancellorship or during his State Secretaryship. Bülow remained the sycophant, praising the Kaiser for his 'beautiful, deeply felt speech in Memel, equally excellent in content and in form'[187] or for his achievement in building the German Navy.[188] 'What can we do?' Bülow wrote to Loebell after the Kaiser had taken exception to a proposed tax on automobiles in September 1907, claiming that it would cost the country 'millions' through 'artificially' suppressing the burgeoning sport in automobiles.[189] Bülow could do little but write to the Kaiser that this issue (and a proposed tax on railway tickets) would be examined anew and a solution found which protected this young industry and corresponded to His Majesty's intentions.[190]

The repercussions of the Eulenburg scandals

For all the political uncertainties surrounding the Chancellor's position within the executive, his ability to influence Wilhelm II and the viability of government with the Bloc, perhaps the most damage was done to Bülow's Chancellorship in 1907 with the eruption of the public scandals involving members of the Kaiser's closest entourage. The abrupt dismissals in May and June 1907 of Kuno Moltke, the Military Commandant of Berlin (along with other members of the Kaiser's military entourage), and Philipp Eulenburg as a result of Harden's renewed press campaign focused public attention on the alleged homosexuality and pernicious political influence of some of Wilhelm II's most intimate associates, and the monarchy itself was heavily implicated. Revelations at the subsequent trials seemed to confirm the existence of a degenerate and deleterious camarilla, jealously guarding its influence over the Kaiser and thwarting constitutional government. Though the full force of public disgust with the system of rule was held in check until the political crisis of 1908, the public image of Bülow's Chancellorship was further eroded and his last years in office were badly tarnished.

Bülow himself was not an innocent onlooker with respect to the Moltke and Eulenburg scandals, and the aim here is not so much to recount the history of the trials as to focus on the Chancellor's role in the proceedings and the political repercussions of the affair.[191] Bülow initially had as great an interest as Harden in neutralising irresponsible influences on the Kaiser, but the scandals ultimately assumed proportions far beyond anything he might have originally envisaged or been able to control.

Bülow was undoubtedly guilty of complicity in Harden's campaign against Eulenburg in that he fed the journalist with material and encouraged fears of a secret camarilla in the autumn of 1906 to bolster his weakened position with the Kaiser. Nevertheless, how far Bülow believed in Harden's allegations about Eulenburg's continued political influence is difficult to establish. Szögyényi reported categorically in June 1907 that Eulenburg had been intriguing against Bülow since he was removed from Vienna in 1902 and that Bülow had long realised 'that it was not only in his own interest but also in the Crown's to render Philipp Eulenburg harmless'.[192] Like Harden, Bülow tried to persuade Eulenburg to stay away from Berlin in January 1907, but Eulenburg did not heed this advice and shortly after his return, Harden's attacks on him were renewed.[193] In May 1907 Eulenburg assured Bülow of his loyalty 'towards the only person whom I consider possible as Reich Chancellor',[194] and if Bülow did suspect his friend's influence, he had little evidence except for Eulenburg's involvement in foreign policy in late 1905. Varnbüler was probably accurate when he reported that Bülow could not seriously believe in Eulenburg's alleged machinations. But, the ambassador went on, 'he has too sceptical and cautious a disposition to trust even good friends . . . unconditionally, is too much of an opportunist not to dissociate himself from them when they could make difficulties for his official position'.[195] From May 1907 any letters Bülow wrote to Eulenburg in a private capacity were undated, written in pencil and probably posted while out walking.[196]

Bülow was sufficiently anxious to see the demise of the Kaiser's best friend to be prepared to put up with the inconvenience of personal attacks in the first months of 1907. More than concern about his health or his relations with Tschirschky, the agitation about the irresponsible advisers fuelled the rumours of a Chancellor crisis, but Bülow did nothing to calm public fears or stifle the attacks. As Varnbüler reported in May 1907, the peaceloving citizen's recurring nightmare was 'the Court camarilla – the secret government [*Nebenregierung*] – the irresponsible advisers who allegedly excite mistrust and conflict between Kaiser and Chancellor, strengthen the autocratic regime, frustrate constitutional government'. But the real purpose of the attacks was not completely clear, for

Sometimes they are cloaked more in the form of warning the Chancellor of those intrigues and secret influences, to make him tough [*scharf*] against them, to mobilise public opinion to defend him against the encroachments of the Crown. Sometimes they seem directed more against the Chancellor himself, wanting to portray his weakness and incapacity in order to preserve the independence of the responsible government. Or should two birds be killed with one stone, imperial prestige be discredited [and] Bülow toppled because he does not limit the power [*Machtstellung*] of the Crown sufficiently or defends it too effectively – in order to make way for the 'strong man' – the great unknown who could then dictate his terms to the Kaiser and gain a free hand?[197]

This lack of clarity in Harden's campaign against Eulenburg was without doubt a result of the journalist's personal ambivalence towards the responsible government, his reluctance to see his attacks through to their logical conclusion and his patriotic desire not to damage the monarchy irreparably.[198] Harden had no respect for Bülow, whom he considered 'the most dangerous type of propper-upper . . . on whose authority and with whose aid everything is falsified';[199] and Bülow's efforts to effect through Holstein a more favourable attitude towards him on the part of the journalist were unsuccessful.[200] But, on the other hand, Harden was never willing to press unequivocally for Bülow's removal. His chief targets were elsewhere, and he was warned by Holstein that 'an attack on the entire political world – Government, Parliament and the irresponsibles – would not be successful'.[201] Harden's reluctance was turned to Bülow's advantage, and in the early months of 1907 their aims curiously coincided.

The resignations of Moltke and Eulenburg were of such obvious benefit to the Chancellor that from the summer of 1907 Bülow's complicity in Harden's campaign was widely suspected. The Chancellor's alleged enemies were removed and, as Harden himself recognised with satisfaction, everything savouring of camarilla had been made much more difficult.[202] Szögyényi concluded that the whole affair had been carefully planned to bring about Eulenburg's fall and that Bülow had been involved.[203] Others went further, claiming 'that Harden's entire manoeuvre has been arranged by the Reich Chancellor, who imported this Italian method of combat from the home of his wife'.[204] Contemporaries tended to see only Harden's friendship with Holstein and the latter's continued relationship with Bülow for them to conclude that the Chancellor stood behind the journalist.[205] Bülow, of course, was not responsible for Harden's campaign against Eulenburg, and suspicions in 1907 about the Chancellor's involvement were intuitive rather than based on a factual knowledge of his role.

The growing number of rumours about Bülow's complicity in the Eulenburg affair cannot have escaped the Kaiser's attention, and the monarch had adequate grounds for criticising his adviser's behaviour on several counts, if he were capable of a rational assessment of the circumstances. During the six months of Harden's attacks on the Kaiser's associates from November 1906 to May 1907, Bülow did nothing to enlighten the monarch about the allegations. He even refused to inform the Kaiser when asked by the Crown Prince,[206] and there is no doubt that Wilhelm was particularly aggrieved to hear the news about his friends from his son.[207] Bülow defended himself against accusations about this neglect in the Reichstag in November 1907 and maintained that a responsible Minister could not go to the Kaiser about such matters without concrete evidence.[208] Wilhelm was justifiably furious with his military entourage for keeping him in the dark about the *Zukunft* attacks, but Szögyényi also reported in June 1907 that he was especially annoyed with Bülow over the affair, though the Chancellor tolerated this *cura posterior* and was content with Eulenburg's disgrace.[209]

Even once the Kaiser knew about the allegations, Bülow failed to present the case frankly to the monarch[210] and may even have been responsible for

Wilhelm's precipitate decision to dismiss the individuals before their guilt had been confirmed.[211] It has been suggested that the Chancellor was behind the initial rejection of Moltke's suit by the public prosecutor.[212] Bülow also claimed that he disagreed openly with the Kaiser and Lucanus over the way Eulenburg should proceed,[213] though this seems unlikely. The Kaiser was shocked and repulsed by the insinuations about his friends' homosexuality, but Bülow probably made no attempt to prevent him from escalating the scandal by forcing Moltke and Eulenburg to clear their honour through the law courts.

From June 1907 the interest of Bülow, Harden and Harden's victims was to see the affair buried as quickly and quietly as possible with a minimum of publicity. With Berlin society buzzing with the news of the scandals and all kinds of people alleged to be homosexual, it was clear that if behind-the-scenes efforts to achieve a compromise were unsuccessful, 'the most unpleasant things' would necessarily come to light.[214] Bülow's position was ambiguous for he could not fail to truckle to the Kaiser's wishes, but he had no personal interest in seeing Harden convicted of libel and his victims rehabilitated.[215] Obsessed by the Eulenburg affair even before the scandals became the focus of public attention,[216] Bülow forced a reluctant Varnbüler to mediate with Eulenburg and involved him in hour-long conversations about the origins and future development of the affair as well as the mood of the Kaiser and his entourage. Despite his persistence, Bülow never quite succeeded in convincing Varnbüler that his only desire was to save his 'friend'. Quite apart from his belief that it was Bülow's duty to sacrifice Eulenburg if the interests of the Kaiser and the state required it, Varnbüler was highly suspicious of Bülow's activities throughout 1907 and always assumed a wide gulf between his words and deeds.[217]

Bülow's position weakened perceptibly from June 1907 as it became clear that the scandals could not be contained and as political repercussions became more likely. However anxious Bülow had been to discredit Eulenburg, his political career had been too interlaced with Eulenberg's influence for the Chancellor to view the prospect of public trials with equanimity. Bülow kept out of Berlin for most of the summer, but the public reaction to Harden's allegations and their apparent confirmation when his victims were banned from Court largely determined his decision to prosecute Adolf Brand. Brand, 'a known pederast' who had been sentenced to one year's imprisonment in 1900 for insulting the Centre Party leader, Dr Lieber,[218] had independently accused the Chancellor of homosexual acts with a subordinate, Scheefer. This was not the only instance of libellous accusations about the Chancellor, and Bülow's name was also linked with another subordinate, Seeband. But Bülow was advised to proceed only against Brand,[219] and though he realised that his attacks were not connected with the Liebenberg

circle and wanted no parallels drawn with the *Zukunft*'s campaign, he came
to his decision not, as he insisted to Loebell, 'on account of myself, for I stand
above such filthy accusations [*Dreckwürfe*], but in the interests of public
purity'.[220]

The Bülow–Brand trial was destined to become something of a show-
piece in the autumn of 1907, for there was never any likelihood that Bülow
would be found guilty. At the trial, which took place on 6 November,
Bülow denied any familiarity with his officials, and especially with Scheefer
or Seeband, either in Berlin or in Rome.[221] The following day the *Berliner
Tageblatt* reported that nobody even half in their right minds could have
believed that Bülow was really a homosexual.[222]

Bülow had always understood the homoerotic nature of the Liebenberg
circle (his brother Alfred had been a member for years, and Karl Ulrich von
Bülow, another brother, was also a homosexual[223]) and was doubtless not so
repelled by homosexuality as he made out. In September 1907 he curiously
felt the need to defend himself to Loebell, insisting 'that all my life I have
found every homosexual inclination not only disgusting but simply incomprehensible. I have never experienced repulsive drives of this kind in any
form at all or to any degree, even in my thoughts.'[224] In 1908 he went to great
lengths to have Scheefer and Seeband removed from office, and it is clear that
the removal of Scheefer, who acted as Bülow's private secretary and had an
apartment in the Chancellery, presented the Chancellor with a far more
difficult and delicate task than the dismissal of a Minister or State Secretary.[225]
The whole affair smacked of blackmail, with Scheefer suggesting to Bülow
that Seeband, who was 'the intimate friend of Kistler [Eulenburg's private
secretary], *auf Du und Du und Kuss und Kuss*' (on a *Du* and *Du* and a kiss and
kiss basis with him) owed his position to Eulenburg, who had wanted this
private link with the Chancellor, just as he had placed his intimate friend,
Moltke, close to the Kaiser. Eulenburg, Scheefer maintained, had forced
Seeband on Bülow in Berlin 'even though (or because I?) was in Berlin'.[226]
Bülow succeeded in having Scheefer appointed Consul in Trieste and,
although his resignation from Bülow's private secretariat (which the Chancellor consequently dismantled) was not voluntary, an order was deliberately
bestowed on him by the Kaiser in order to ensure that his departure was not
misinterpreted.[227]

The Bülow–Brand trial was but a minor interlude in the greater drama
which occupied Berlin in the autumn of 1907. Bülow carefully avoided being
called as a witness in the first Moltke–Harden trial (23–9 October 1907) by
staying away from the capital.[228] His absence at such a time was commented
upon unfavourably,[229] but Loebell kept him informed in Klein-Flottbeck of
all the unsavoury details. On the very first day of the trial, the Chancellery
Chief wrote to Bülow:

The Harden trial has gone extremely unfavourably for Count Moltke. The scenes from the married life of the Count, discussed in the most public forum, make his abnormality seem proven and completely destroy him as a person. Also grave evidence has been furnished for the political influence of the [Liebenberg] Round Table. Among other things constant reports from Moltke to Eulenburg about all the events at Court of a political and personal nature, remarks in letters: 'We form a tight circle around the Kaiser, no one comes to him without us', etc. were read out. Established that Count Moltke knew of Lecomte's perversion[230] when he introduced him to the Kaiser and he was invited to Liebenberg.[231]

The second day of the trial went scarcely better and again, Loebell informed Bülow, the evidence touched now and again on political matters.[232] By 26 October Loebell believed that Bülow's return was highly desirable the next day and that

Even now it is perhaps advisable for Your Excellency to express your indignation [to the Kaiser] over the course of the trial, the intrusion into personal relationships, etc. and announce yourself for an audience. The latter is recommended by Hammann and Flotow especially. The Kaiser noted today on an English report on the trial submitted to him: 'Why didn't the cowardly [*schlappe*] Kuno defend his honour straight away as a dashing [*schneidig*] officer? Then this dreadful business would never have happened.'[233]

Bülow acknowledged the Chancellery Chief's concern about the mood of the Kaiser and promptly wrote the same day to Wilhelm about the 'scandalous' conduct of the Moltke–Harden trial and the need for the military authorities 'to cauterise *ferro et igni* such filthy abscesses wherever they may be discovered'.[234] But he did not return to Berlin until 29 October,[235] by which time the trial had ended with Harden's acquittal.

The Kaiser was incensed by the verdict of the trial and was primarily responsible for its immediate revocation and the transfer of the case to the public prosecutor.[236] In his telegram on 26 October, Bülow had given no hint that he would not accept Harden's acquittal, but the Kaiser was primarily concerned to confirm the innocence of his friends.[237] Bülow's only method of calming Wilhelm was to agree with everything he said, and thus when the Kaiser interpreted the whole affair as a campaign by Social Democracy and Jewry against his person and the Army, he could assure his interlocutors that the Chancellor shared this view.[238] While Wilhelm expressed the expectation that the public prosecutor would now proceed without delay against 'Herr Harden and Consorts', Bülow as well as Bethmann, Dernburg and the former Minister, Podbielski, were involved in efforts in November and December 1907 to find an acceptable compromise which would settle the matter out of court.[239] 'Only when HM spoke out with the greatest resolution and in telegraphic form against *any* compromise in the Moltke–Harden trial'[240] did Bülow finally abandon his efforts. Shortly after the opening of the second Moltke–Harden trial (19 December 1907 to 3 January 1908), which found Harden guilty of libel and placed the Chancellor in a 'quite peculiar' position,[241] Bülow issued an official denial in the press that he had ever worked for a compromise and professed a 'completely correct' attitude throughout the entire affair.[242]

By this time, however, the political repercussions of the scandals were evident, with widespread disgust at Harden's system of personal attacks but also growing revulsion with the system of rule.[243] With even the Austrian *chargé d'affaires*, Prince zu Hohenlohe-Waldenburg-Schillingsfürst, convinced that many in the Kaiser's military entourage should be dismissed immediately and replaced with new people – though even he recognised that Wilhelm II's personality primarily determined the quality of the entourage[244] – it was clear that awkward questions would be posed once the Reichstag reopened and that enemies of the government would be quick to exploit this windfall.

There is no evidence that Bülow's position with the Kaiser was seriously weakened by the conclusion of the first Moltke–Harden trial or by growing public criticism of the Chancellor's failure to inform the Kaiser earlier. Bülow successfully had the verdict revoked by the Prussian Ministry of Justice, and in early November Wilhelm saw Bülow daily, giving no hint of any displeasure. As Hohenlohe reported,

It indeed lay in the realm of possibility that the Reich Chancellor's position would be shaken by the trial, but *de facto* this was not the case; on the contrary, HM – since Prince Bülow has returned to Berlin – has let no opportunity pass of showing that the Chancellor still enjoys his confidence. Two days ago HM dined at the Reich Chancellor's, the next day he invited him and the Princess to the palace and yesterday afternoon he paid the Prince a long visit in the Wilhelmstrasse.[245]

On 8 November Wilhelm left for England and was not to return until 13 December. Although he had wanted to cancel the official visit to London and Windsor, his decision to spend an additional three weeks on the Isle of Wight was criticised in Germany. As Lerchenfeld reported, it was assumed that the Kaiser wanted to escape for as long as possible from the recent, painful experiences in Berlin.[246]

But once the Kaiser was away, the scandals were subsumed into the general political crisis which threatened in December 1907. To the dismay of the more moderate members, radical elements in the Centre Party exploited the scandals to attack the Chancellor and to undermine his position with respect to the Bloc.[247] Rumours circulated that Bülow's position with the Kaiser had been shattered by the Moltke–Harden trial and that Goltz or Fürstenberg would soon replace him.[248] By the time Wilhelm returned to Berlin, Bülow's position had indeed deteriorated, not least because the Kaiser 'reproached the Chancellor with want of energy and skill' in not preventing the open discussion of the scandals in the Reichstag.[249] But the Bloc crisis also had serious implications for the relationship between Kaiser and Chancellor, and even in early November Hohenlohe had written that if Bülow's days in office were numbered, this could be attributed 'not so much to the recent scandal affairs as to the general domestic situation'.[250]

The Bloc crisis of December 1907

Throughout the summer of 1907 Bülow had to conduct extensive negotiations with the leaders of the Bloc parties in an attempt to ensure agreement on the main pieces of legislation on the agenda in the autumn. The Chancellor had discussed specific issues with party leaders in previous years, but never before had it been necessary to undertake preparations for a new Reichstag session which encompassed all aspects of the parliamentary programme and which in many cases required simultaneous negotiations and trade-offs on different questions in order to appease the various interests. The problems were compounded by the balance of power between the parties in the Bloc, the differing importance each attached to the maintenance of the Bloc and their long-standing allegiance to conflicting loyalties and principles, none of which could easily be sacrificed without considerable loss of face and damage to party interests. In addition, some consideration of Prussian affairs, where the party political relationships remained essentially different, constantly intruded into the calculations of the Bloc parties and spilled over into the negotiations with the government on Reich legislation. By early October Bethmann was convinced 'that the inclination exists among the party leaders not to pitch their aspirations too high in order to facilitate cooperation between Conservatives and liberals'.[251] But, despite Bülow's hopes in the summer to ensure complete agreement between the Bloc parties on all government bills *'before* the parliamentary session begins',[252] a mood of uncertainty and pessimism prevailed right up to the reopening of the Reichstag, and on some issues the prospects for collaboration seemed remarkably slim.[253]

Bülow deliberately invited Conservative and liberal leaders of all shades to Norderney in August and September 1907 in order to maintain a certain parity of treatment, but the tractability of the Bloc parties varied enormously. As the representatives of moderate liberalism, the National Liberals occupied a pivotal position within the Bloc and Bülow told their leader, Bassermann, in August that the government departments would prepare the winter's legislation in agreement with the Bloc parties 'and especially with him'.[254] Bülow's close collaboration with Bassermann in the last years of his Chancellorship dates from this time, and in all his dealings with the National Liberal leader he proved conciliatory and receptive, though his sincerity cannot always be assumed.[255] The various left liberal parties were apparently the most unpredictable elements in the Bloc, but given their inexperience in negotiating with the government and their anxiety not to precipitate a return to the Centre, Bülow was probably able to conclude pacts with each of them.[256] After the publication of Friedrich Naumann's July 1907 article in the *Berliner Tageblatt*, demanding the Reichstag suffrage for Prussia, the government feared that the left liberals might make the introduction of universal suffrage in Prussia the precondition for their continued adherence to the Bloc.[257] But, although Bülow discussed the question of a reform of the Prussian suffrage *and* a simultaneous reform of the Reichstag suffrage, which would benefit the bourgeois parties, with the Prussian Minister of Interior, Friedrich von Moltke, in September 1907,[258] he was convinced 'that the ardent wish exists among the great majority of the National Liberals and even among many Progressives *dans leur for intérieur* that the government does not follow the South German example and permits no radicalisation of the Prussian election suffrage'.[259] Though vociferous in their radical demands, the liberals were not in a strong position within the Bloc and in practice were willing to 'negotiate' on an issue which would have destroyed their relative strength in Prussia.[260]

The strongest elements in the Bloc were undoubtedly the Conservative parties, which together had eighty-four seats (the National Liberals had fifty-four)[261] and which always had the alternative of working with the Centre. Determined to defend their power base in Prussia and completely hostile to the idea of Prussian suffrage reform, the Conservatives and especially the agrarians impressed on the Chancellor the need 'to do something for East Prussia'[262] and were particularly reluctant to make economic concessions to liberalism. Already anticipating that the Centre would be the first to reproach them if they abandoned the interests of the German *Mittelstand*,[263] the Conservatives created the most problems for Bülow's *Blockpolitik* because of their reluctance to conciliate the liberals over the proposed new Stock Exchange Law (which lifted many of the previous restrictions on stock market transactions) and Law of Association (which replaced a multiplicity of state laws and, in particular, removed the numerous restrictions on political associations). Bülow was 'willing to do everything for the agrarians which is compatible with the maintenance of the Bloc',[264] but agrarian intransigence over the Stock Exchange Law involved Loebell and the Minster of Trade, Delbrück, in a trip to Klein-Flottbeck to see the Chancellor in the middle of October.[265]

Conservative discontent within the Bloc was dangerous to Bülow not only because the Conservatives had a strong parliamentary position, but also because they enjoyed support within the executive and the sympathy of the federal governments. Bülow told Loebell to ensure that Rheinbaben did everything to convince the Conservatives of the need for a more liberal Stock Exchange Law.[266] In early October 1907 in the Prussian Ministry of State, Bülow, reiterating his commitment to the Bloc, explained why he felt that the Law of Association was an appropriate area where concessions could be made to the liberals.

He did not come to the *Blockpolitik* as a brainwave overnight. It became a political necessity. The Centre increasingly failed [to support the government] and frankly forced the government to dissolve the Reichstag. The present situation arose from the results of the elections. It has as little prospect of lasting for ever as anything else, but it probably does have a chance of continuing for some time. Not only HM but also the interest of the country demands that a serious attempt [is made to govern] with the *Blockpolitik*.

Bülow went on to say that in such difficult and dangerous times the monarchy could no longer look merely to the Conservatives and Centre for support. It had to broaden its base to include the liberals and, if economic concessions to liberalism were impossible, the government could break with the principle of exaggerated paternalism (*Bevormundung*) with the Law of Association.[267] How far Bülow succeeded in convincing all his Prussian colleagues is not clear, but Bülow and Bethmann ensured their views prevailed in the Ministry of State. The draft Law of Association, which was to apply throughout the Reich, then immediately ran into opposition in the Bundesrat from the non-Prussian states, though it was not finally to be modified until the Reichstag debates. Intended as a concession to the liberals but in many respects not going far enough, it has variously been seen as both a liberal and a conservative law.[268]

By far the most contentious problem which had to be resolved remained the financial question, especially after the announcement of the new naval demands.[269] A major financial reform was a particularly difficult issue for the Bloc to regulate. The Conservatives opposed all taxes which would hit property owners and were ardent believers in the merits of indirect taxation and state monopolies. The liberals opposed indirect taxation on principle because it placed the financial burden on the mass of the population, and supported the introduction of direct Reich taxes – a wealth tax or the extension of the existing inheritance tax.[270] Conservative interests were reinforced by the resistance of the federal governments to direct Reich taxation, which circumscribed their powers, and by their hostility to other possible solutions, such as an increase in their matricular contributions.[271] The State Secretary of the Treasury, Stengel, who had been selected to work with the Centre and who, as a Bavarian, was alleged to have particularist leanings,[272] was also unsympathetic to liberal demands.[273] Above all, Rheinbaben was highly unlikely to agree either to some kind of income tax or an extension of the inheritance tax (which he had only reluctantly conceded in

1905),[274] and some heard that Bülow had promised the left liberals that he would remove the Prussian Finance Minister before a major reform was undertaken.[275]

Bülow's inadequacy in dealing with the financial problem has been well illustrated elsewhere.[276] He tried to avoid involvement in the controversies within the executive and gave insufficient support to Stengel in his struggles with Rheinbaben; but he expected agreement to be reached on the financial proposals with the political parties in advance of the parliamentary negotiations so as not to endanger the Bloc, and he made personal promises to party leaders which he could not hope to fulfil. During his discussions with parliamentarians in the summer of 1907, Bülow deliberately tried to keep the financial question in the background, and it is clear that he did not envisage its introduction in the winter session of 1907–8, or at least not until the Stock Exchange and Association Laws were concluded. This reluctance to introduce new tax bills was unrealistic, and the Chancellor's 'eternal evasion and procrastination' meant that the Reich's financial problems became more complicated each year.[277]

The financial problem could not be evaded altogether in late 1907, for the Reichstag negotiations on the Budget and the need to find immediate finance for a deficit of over 100 million Marks brought the whole issue into the centre of political debate at the end of November and precipitated the Bloc crisis in the following month.[278] Bülow had to attend most of the first reading and made three speeches on aspects of the foreign and domestic situation.[279] But the third speech, on the future of the Bloc, revealed his unwillingness to grapple with the problems of practical politics. He asserted that the Bloc, like the Centre Party, would stay together if it always sought the 'middle way', and dismissed the clash of economic interests within the Bloc with a joke about whether the inheritance tax was direct or indirect.[280] It was left to Rheinbaben to aggravate the differences between right and left when he categorically rejected direct taxation and forced Bassermann to rise to the bait.[281]

The antagonism between government and liberals prompted by the financial question came to a head on 3 December when the National Liberal, Paasche, attacked the War Minister, Einem, for his alleged misrepresentation of the trial proceedings against Counts Hohenau and Lynar, two members of the royal entourage, both Army officers, accused of homosexuality.[282] Paasche's unqualified attacks caused Bülow to summon the leaders of the Bloc parties to a conference on 4 December, at which he made it quite clear that the necessary unity between the parties was lacking and that unless they declared their willingness to cooperate with the government, he would resign. Einem subsequently repudiated Paasche's attacks with ease, and the Reichstag was adjourned for twenty-four hours while the Chancellor awaited a firm commitment from the Bloc parties.[283] On 5 December Normann, Basserman and Wiemer declared in the name of their respective parties their resolve to participate loyally and honestly in the Bloc. As Bülow telegraphed to Wilhelm II in England, 'The declaration was received with stormy applause from the majority, violent protest from the Centre and Social Democracy.'[284] The Bloc crisis was thus ostensibly over with an apparent vote of confidence in the Chancellor.

Nevertheless, the implications of this seemingly trivial incident were profound for the position of the Chancellor, and the parliamentary crisis had scarcely been resolved in a way which promised greater cooperation between the parties in the future. The parties' expression of their willingness to work with the Bloc could not necessarily outweigh their party interests, and no practical solutions or compromises had been arranged to ensure the passage of Reich legislation. The Conservatives and liberals still disagreed over aspects of the Stock Exchange Law, the Association Law and the financial reform, and even after 5 December business in the Reichstag committees continued to be hampered by trivial bickering among the Bloc parties.[285] Bassermann admittedly proved willing to drop the idea of a direct Reich tax for the time being in December 1907, but this conciliatoriness and receptiveness to Bülow's pressure was interpreted as weakness by the Conservatives and may have encouraged their later intransigence over the issue.[286] Szögyényi believed that the prospects of a financial reform acceptable to the Bloc had improved as a result of the crisis,[287] but it remained highly doubtful whether the liberals would feel able to concede to Conservative demands on all the contentious issues.[288]

Just a glance at the government's simultaneous difficulties in the Prussian Landtag, where Conservatives and liberals were locked in conflict over the anti-Polish Expropriation Law (which gave the government the right to expropriate Polish estates in Posen and West Prussia), is sufficient to indicate the continued strains on the Bloc. At the State Ministry meeting on 6 December Bülow tried to separate this Prussian problem from the *Blockpolitik* and expressed the hope that, with care, the Reich's financial difficulties would be surmounted with the Bloc.[289] But four days later at another meeting, Bülow was considering whether to dissolve the Prussian Landtag and fight the Conservatives.[290] It is scarcely possible that he believed such a course would have no impact on the party constellation in the Reich.

More important than the continued political uncertainties surrounding the Bloc were the implications of the parliamentary crisis for Bülow's position as Chancellor. From the moment he had indicated to the party leaders his readiness to resign if the necessary declarations were not forthcoming, the crisis in the Reichstag contained the seeds of a Chancellor crisis.[291] Szögyényi interpreted Bülow's gesture as a clear tactic to bring the political parties into

line and belatedly to convince the Kaiser of his energy in repulsing parliamentary attacks on the Army as a result of the scandals.[292] But Bülow had
now publicly stated his intention to stand or fall with the Bloc and his refusal
to collaborate again with the Centre. As Lerchenfeld reported on 5
December:

At any rate, through his action yesterday, the Prince has assumed a position which
each of his predecessors had hitherto rejected, namely that of a parliamentary
Minister, whose continuation in office depends on the majority. That seems to me
a more than dubious step because it not only binds the present Reich Chancellor but
will also constitute a very inconvenient precedent for each successor. The step was
not taken yesterday. It only became evident to all yesterday. The principle of always
taking a majority according to the circumstances, wherever one could find it, was
abandoned from the moment Prince Bülow identified himself with the Bloc. At the
beginning of this session there would also have been the opportunity to ensure
freedom of manoeuvre. But after the repeated, clear rejection of the Centre, which
rang out of all the Reich Chancellor's speeches, his fate was sealed.[293]

What had long been an assumption of the Chancellor, namely that he could
not continue in office without the support of the Bloc, had thus become a
fact of German political life. This was not necessarily in the logic of events
since the Reichstag dissolution of 1906, for it was Bülow's attitude subsequent to the elections which had precluded the possibility of a rapprochement with the Centre. Nevertheless, in December 1907 Bülow linked his
fortunes publicly and exclusively to those of the Bloc. A return to the
parliamentary system of 1900–6 would now be impossible under his Chancellorship.

Bülow's resolution of the Bloc crisis made the Chancellor more dependent
on the political parties and personally vulnerable in the event of attempts to
shatter the Bloc. Moreover, many in government circles continued to doubt
the durability or wisdom of the Bloc strategy,[294] and the question arose how
far Bülow intended his commitment to the Bloc to apply to all the other
Ministers and State Secretaries within the executive. Since both Bülow and
Bethmann had been present at the conference of 4 December and Bülow had
not specifically excluded his colleagues when he expressed his intention to
work only with the Bloc, it was easy to conclude, as did the Bavarian
military plenipotentiary, that 'We thus no longer have a constitutional
government system but really a parliamentary system!'[295] Bülow probably
had no intention of limiting the sphere of action of his colleagues (or even
his own options if his attitude towards the Centre in 1908 is an indicator),
and he did not expect them to follow his lead. Bethmann had already made
it clear to Berckheim that there were issues over which the division of the
Bloc parties would not be seen as irreparable;[296] and, as on most occasions,
Bülow spoke only for himself with few thoughts about the subsequent

predicament of his associates. In the following months some of Bülow's subordinates continued to maintain political links with the Centre, sometimes even with the Chancellor's blessing.[297] But this anomalous situation further undermined unity within the executive and the Chancellor's overall political control.

The Bloc crisis also restricted Bülow's freedom of manoeuvre within the executive and made him less able to make arbitrary decisions by increasing his dependence on Ministers whom he had not appointed and now had even less scope to remove. If Bülow had hoped eventually to replace Rheinbaben, he was soon to realise that such a move was now politically impossible given the Conservatives' refusal to work without him;[298] at the same time the removal of Stengel seemed potentially difficult when the second largest federal state had already been disturbed by the rupture with the Centre.[299] Political considerations had always intruded into the regulation of personnel questions, but the scope for an *ad hoc* settlement of such issues between Kaiser and Chancellor had appreciably diminished. Bülow's commitment to a specific coalition implied a new attentiveness to such factors as a Minister's popularity with a political party, the representative nature of the government in parliamentary terms and the support each member of the executive could muster in the Reichstag.

Szögyényi grasped the implications of this new situation when he reported that a major difficulty was 'that Prince Bülow cannot rely completely on any of his colleagues in the State Ministry and at the same time is not in a position to effect a personnel change without kicking major parties in the teeth [*vor den Kopf stossen*]'. He admitted that in ten years Bülow had never been able to establish confidential relations with his colleagues, and in this respect the Chancellor seemed to be about to reap the consequences of years of neglect in the executive. His fear of possible successors and tendency to set himself up on Olympian heights had left him relatively isolated in government and society circles, and with few personal friends. Ministers like Rheinbaben and Einem understandably mistrusted a man who often treated his most capable colleagues with scant consideration and who had no scruples in disposing of Miquel or Posadowsky.[300]

Above all, Bülow's personal commitment to the Bloc in December 1907 constituted a marked shift away from the period when the relationship between Kaiser and Chancellor had been the pivot of Bülow's system, and the implied demotion of the Kaiser's confidence and his prerogative to appoint and dismiss the Chancellor introduced a new element into imperial domestic politics. Bülow may have exaggerated Wilhelm II's hostility to the Centre and believed that the monarch too would never again countenance a strategy of collaboration with this party.[301] Nevertheless, Wilhelm's enthusiasm about the Bloc was on the wane, and there is no evidence that he saw the new combination as anything more than a parliamentary convenience. The potential repercussions of the Bloc crisis on Bülow's relationship with the Kaiser were enormous. Contrary to all his previous declarations on German political traditions and the system of rule, the Chancellor had now asserted that the Kaiser's confidence alone was not sufficient to permit his remaining in office. In informing Wilhelm of the Reichstag adjournment in December 1907, Bülow omitted to mention his threat to resign;[302] and in so far as he understood the crisis, Wilhelm undoubtedly approved of the Chancellor's procedure for, on his authority, the Kaiserin had demonstratively visited the Bülows after the vote of confidence in the Reichstag.[303] But Bülow's refusal to continue conducting affairs unless he were sure of the majority of the Reichstag constituted an attempt to strengthen his position 'from below', and it remained to be seen how the Kaiser would react to this apparent concession to parliamentarism.[304] More than ever Bülow had sandwiched himself between the will of the monarch and the needs of the parliamentary situation, and his continuance in office depended on his ability to reconcile the two.

The collapse of the system, 1908–1909

Bülow's decline

At the beginning of 1908 the political prospects for Bülow and his Chancellorship were by no means promising. The previous months had already supplied ample evidence of his declining influence on the Kaiser, his inability to assert his political leadership within the executive and the fundamental weakness of the Bloc. Despite the resolution of the parliamentary crisis in December 1907, the political situation remained confused, with persistent rumours of a Chancellor crisis (Bethmann, Marschall and Einem were all now being named as possible successors),[1] and little confidence among Bülow's subordinates and colleagues about the vitality of the Bloc. The prestige of Bülow's Chancellorship had been irreparably damaged by the scandal trials, and even Varnbüler had formed a rather macabre picture of the Berlin government from his occasional glimpses behind the scenes. It was difficult, he reported, to view Germany's government system with equanimity when what one saw was

a game of intrigue without parallel – nobody trusting anyone else an inch – the initiated, the deceived, the betrayed in all sorts of gradations [*Eingeweihte, Hintergegangene, Betrogene in den verschiedensten Abstufungen*] – a secret war of all against all – camarilla everywhere, perhaps even the most harmless [are] those now being pilloried, precisely to divert attention from more dangerous [elements].[2]

Holstein wrote to Bülow in January 1908 that he would resign if he were Chancellor[3] but, after a visit to the capital in the same month, the diplomat and later Foreign Secretary, Jagow, was depressed and dismayed to find that Bülow was not thinking of leaving at all.[4] The Chancellor remained in office but, until the domestic crisis of the autumn, he visibly did less and less, subordinating national interests to the needs of his own personal reputation[5] and seeking to extract as much as possible from his parliamentary creation before their mutual demise. Though conscious of the Kaiser's growing disenchantment and not oblivious to the fragility of the Bloc, in the early months of 1908 Bülow scarcely anticipated the storms which awaited him or the humiliation of his fall. The Chancellor was primarily preoccupied with ensuring for himself what the opposition press maliciously described as 'a departure into eternity',[6] and the manuscripts on his desk counted for little in his bid to shape the judgements of future generations.

Bülow's weakening position with the Kaiser was evident on a number of fronts before the *Daily Telegraph* affair finally ruptured their relations in November 1908. Ostensibly Wilhelm II continued to place his confidence in the Chancellor and, though the bumper year of 1907 was not to be repeated and the Kaiser's visits to the Wilhelmstrasse may have been as much to see Schön as Bülow, the regularity of their discussions was not appreciably different from those of earlier years.[7] Yet Bülow displayed less ability or will to act independently, less conviction when he sought to influence Wilhelm, less skill in evading the monarch's instructions.[8] In January 1908 his handling of the suffrage question (when he brusquely rejected the Reichstag suffrage for Prussia) and the Expropriation Law in the Prussian Landtag can only be ascribed to imperial pressure since it contradicted so patently his strategy of reconciling left and right in the Reichstag.[9]

The Kaiser too was more suspicious of the Chancellor's activities, less trusting in his good faith and more reluctant to confide in him. His letter to Lord Tweedmouth, the First Lord of the British Admiralty, in February 1908 (which tried to convince him of the harmlessness of Germany's naval armaments programme),[10] his interference in the appointment of a new American ambassador to Berlin in March,[11] and his Döberitz speech in May (when he discussed Germany's 'encirclement' in a belligerent tone in the presence of the Russian and Japanese military attachés)[12] all occurred without prior consultation with the Chancellor and created awkward *faits accomplis*. Bülow admittedly expressed his 'regret' about the effects of the Döberitz speech in a letter to Wilhelm,[13] and Lerchenfeld used this as evidence 'that the Chancellor, if he has to, does not omit to tell his imperial master the truth'.[14] But in all probability Bülow was only prepared to make his feelings known to the Kaiser because their relationship was already strained and he had little to lose. Moreover, the Chancellor did not emerge from the incident well, because Wilhelm remained convinced that he had not made a political speech and subsequently forced Bülow to issue an official denial to this effect in the *Norddeutsche Allgemeine Zeitung* of 19 June which was manifestly untrue.[15]

The Kaiser was indignant when he was not officially informed about the Navy League crisis in late 1907,[16] and, before Harden reopened the Eulenburg case in April, he had just cause to believe that Bülow was not sincere in sharing his jubilation at the outcome of the second Moltke–Harden trial.[17] Bülow's public utterances on the affair were extremely cautious, but nevertheless Szögyényi reported that the Chancellor could not conceal how much it would have vexed him if the Kaiser's favourite had succeeded in rehabilitating himself.[18] Varnbüler, too, had doubts about Bülow's role and attitude in the affair which he 'would hardly like to express, let alone write down',[19] and it would be very surprising if the Kaiser had remained insensitive to Bülow's ambivalence. Wilhelm discussed Bülow's relations with Holstein, Tschirschky, Frau von Lebbin (Holstein's friend) and Mühlberg with members of his entourage in July 1908,[20] and he must have been particularly suspicious about the Chancellor's continued friendship with Holstein.

In his presentation of personnel issues the Kaiser also found the Chancellor more transparent and was consequently less inclined to respond to Bülow's suggestions. In February 1908 Stengel finally resigned as there was no question of getting his tax proposals through the Reichstag and aspects of the financial reform were still opposed by Rheinbaben and the federal states.[21] Bülow supported the State Secretary's decision even though it came at rather an inconvenient time and he explained in his letter to Wilhelm that Stengel was resigning for personal reasons.[22] Moreover, Bülow only informed the Kaiser three days after the resignation was generally known to be a fact,[23] and the monarch was not at all pleased to receive such belated confirmation of the press reports. When the Chancellor recommended Adickes, the *Oberbürgermeister* of Frankfurt, as a possible successor and requested permission to negotiate with him, the Kaiser responded, 'He's already put this in the newspapers! It says in all the papers that he's going to be asked!' Describing Adickes as ambitious and indiscreet, Wilhelm claimed that he would become a second Miquel and that he did not like him.[24] Bülow consequently had to extricate himself from his negotiations with Adickes[25] and it is not clear whether the appointment of Sydow, the former Under State Secretary in the Reich Post Office, was after a recommendation by another candidate (Müller, the Director of the Dresdner Bank)[26] or on the suggestion of the Kaiserin.[27] Bülow succeeded in having Sydow appointed Prussian Minister without portfolio in order to strengthen his hand against Rheinbaben,[28] but the personnel change was hardly a success for the Chancellor and cannot have confirmed his credentials to the Kaiser.

Bülow was able to execute a diplomatic change which Wilhelm had adamantly opposed by delaying it until the autumn of 1908.[29] But in July 1908 the Kaiser appointed Valentini as his new Chief of the Civil Cabinet without discussing the question with Bülow at all. Bülow, who had been expecting some kind of exchange of views, would in fact have recommended Valentini, for Loebell admitted that he had been working on the Chancellor for weeks to support the candidacy of his 'Duzfreund'. For Loebell, the Kaiser's appointment of Valentini only demonstrated anew that the monarch always made the right decision on important questions.[30]

Above all, by the summer of 1908 the deteriorating international situation intruded into the relations between Kaiser and Chancellor, and each seems to have held the other primarily responsible for Germany's plight.[31] It is unlikely that Bülow was quite so determined to curb naval armaments and to improve Anglo-German relations as he indicated to Holstein and in his memoirs,[32] but he certainly discussed the naval issue on several occasions with the Kaiser in the summer of 1908 in connection with British attempts to reach an understanding, and he had a particularly unpleasant audience with Wilhelm at Wiesbaden in the middle of May.[33] The Kaiser had conversations with others, such as Admiral von Müller and Treutler (the Minister who accompanied Wilhelm to Swinemünde in 1908 and apparently begged the Chancellor not to raise the naval issues again[34]), about the Chancellor – on one occasion Bülow was discussed in connection with Metternich, who was pressing for a naval agreement, on another the monarch came on to the subject of the Chancellor after criticising 'the timidity of the diplomats'.[35] In the summer of 1908 Bülow was not yet prepared to risk his position by asserting unwelcome opinions to the Kaiser, though he may have been working through the press to create a more favourable climate for an eventual understanding with England, an attempt which he abandoned once the Kaiser proved intransigent. According to Müller, at the end of July Wilhelm and Bülow had an open discussion which apparently satisfied the monarch.[36] In August Bülow refused to meet Lloyd George about a reduction in the naval tempo as 'it would awaken hopes in England which could not yet be fulfilled at the moment';[37] and he instructed the Foreign Office Press Bureau not to allow the semi-official press to touch on the question of a naval understanding with England at all until further notice.[38]

Bülow's record in foreign policy and his relationship with Holstein certainly gave intriguers the opportunity to undermine his position with the Kaiser. In July 1908 Bülow was informed by the journalist Eugen Zimmermann (who was 'Harden's mouthpiece') of the plans of the 'Henckel group' of Silesian magnates to discredit the Chancellor, in part by bringing to the Kaiser's or public attention some unflattering remarks Bülow had made about Wilhelm but also by exploiting these grievances.[39] Bülow dismissed inferences about his brother Karl's alleged 'modern vices' as infamous and absurd slander, but he admitted to Hammann that there might in general be some truth in Zimmermann's revelations.[40] Prussian Conservatives already had ample political reasons to welcome a change of Chancellor, and Wilhelm's willingness to discuss the Chancellor with his entourage opened up many opportunities for Bülow's enemies.

Bülow's other main concern throughout the first nine months of 1908 was still the Bloc, for after the crisis of December 1907 his personal position depended not only on the Kaiser's continued confidence but also on the survival of his parliamentary experiment. In some respects the chances of the Bloc's survival were more favourable in early 1908 once Stengel had resigned and the Reich finance reform had definitely been postponed until the autumn.[41] In April 1908 both the Law of Association and the Stock Exchange Law ('the big Bloc laws' in Bülow's estimation) were passed by the Reichstag,[42] and when the session was closed in early May the Kaiser, on Bülow's request, sent the Chancellor a telegram praising his skill and applauding the patriotic attitude of the majority.[43] Szögyényi, at least, was confident about the future and reported that, despite criticism of Bülow's foreign policy, 'In fact Prince Bülow now completely commands the situation in domestic policy for the time being, and if unexpected incidents don't occur, he will be in a position to deal with the big tasks which still stand before him and which include, first and foremost, the reform of the Reich's finances.'[44]

Nevertheless, it was widely believed in government circles that Reich affairs would stagnate if they had to continue with this 'artificial' majority,[45] and Berckheim bemoaned that 'We are pursuing purely personal politics and living from hand to mouth'.[46] The Chancellor certainly allowed the nature of the parliamentary combination to determine policy. While on holiday in Venice in April 1908 he decided that the reform of criminal procedure (which he had first mentioned in a speech in November 1907[47]) would be an excellent field of activity for the Bloc and one in which 'in particular a healthy conservatism and the most radical liberalism can . . . collaborate'. Convinced that the country wanted 'practical Bloc fruits, practical and modern measures' and that the Bloc laws of April had had an impact far beyond their material significance, Bülow even turned his attention to replacing Nieberding, whose resignation he had rejected the previous year but whose departure now seemed opportune if the legal reforms were to be made with the Bloc.[48]

Bülow hoped to maintain the Bloc throughout 1908, though he was not oblivious to the problems this posed. In April he was informed that some twenty members of the Progressive Party who were unhappy with the Law of Association and the government's position on Prussian suffrage reform had announced their secession from the liberal *Wahlverein*, apparently with the intention of forming a new party with the SPD revisionists.[49] In June a new Prussian Lower House was elected, but after Bülow had ordered 'a really boring election campaign',[50] the relationships between the parties were little different and the government still had to work with a Conservative–Centre majority in Prussia.[51] Above all, the Chancellor's relations with the Centre in the Reichstag remained problematic, for it scarcely seemed possible that the financial reform could be regulated without the Centre's cooperation. But here a shift of attitude on the part of the Chancellor is perceptible. Underestimating the effect of his brusque behaviour since December 1906 even on the conservative elements within the Centre Party and almost in defiance of his commitment to the Bloc parties in December 1907, Bülow began to believe that a rapprochement with the Centre would be possible under his Chancellorship and that the Centre would collaborate with the government in the financial reform.

Ostensibly Bülow scarcely modified his intransigent attitude towards the Centre in the early months of 1908, and in the press he continued to emphasise and exacerbate the rift between the party and the government as a means of cementing the Bloc.[52] A persistent theme which he exploited to the full in securing the safe passage of the Bloc laws in April was that the collapse of the Bloc would mean the restoration of the Centre's hegemony;[53] and, while the Centre deliberately played a waiting game throughout 1908 and concentrated its attacks on official policy,[54] Bülow, who well knew that the collapse of the Bloc was synonymous with his political demise, urged Hammann to exploit all the remarks of the Centre press which were directed against him. 'The Bloc, the Reichstag and the German people must feel precisely now that the Centre wants to bring about my fall', Bülow wrote in February 1908 when he was searching for a new State Secretary of the Treasury.[55] It was 'doubly necessary' in March when the parties were making difficulties in the Reichstag that the press made it clear that the Centre's aim was the Chancellor's resignation.[56]

How far Bülow believed in his own propaganda is questionable, and the evidence suggests that, if anything, he underestimated the personal animosity which the Centre felt towards him. He was extremely bitter about the behaviour of his former allies to whom he had made so many concessions and who, as he complained in April 1908, now attacked a statesman who had been more considerate towards the Catholic Church and Catholic sentiments 'than probably any other Minister in Europe'.[57] But it was no secret that 'some high Reich civil servants' wanted to restore normal relations with the Centre, and in February 1908 Bülow told a surprised Lerchenfeld that in certain circumstances (and notably in the financial reform) he would be prepared to work again with the Centre. Lerchenfeld immediately concluded that the Kaiser had become convinced that nothing positive could be achieved with the Bloc,[58] but it is clear that the new State Secretary of the Treasury also appreciated that the financial reform could not be concluded without the Centre and that he may even have made Bülow's acceptance of the Centre's involvement a precondition of his appointment.[59] After the Centre's support of the Navy Bill in March 1908 (support which was intended to demonstrate to the Conservatives that they did not need to depend on the liberals in matters of national defence)[60] the Chancellor's optimism visibly increased. Fully endorsing Sydow's initiatives in re-establishing links with the Centre, in May Bülow openly expressed the hope that a great party like the Centre could not fail to support a vital Reich issue merely for motives of spite.[61]

Bülow displayed very little interest in the Reich reform itself,[62] but he aimed in 1908 to turn it into a national rather than a political issue and elevate it above party political squabbles. In Venice in April 1908 the Chancellor had already had the leisure to think about his speech on the subject in the autumn (he had maintained the fiction in the press that he still conducted affairs while away, but in fact Schön complained that he had heard little from him),[63] and he instructed Loebell to produce a draft with Hammann by the end of May so that he would have time 'to see roughly what the tone will be and then on this basis think about further ideas and ripostes in the quiet of summer'. Bülow was thinking of a speech which was 'in no way factual, let alone detailed, but completely political'. It had to be fresh, natural, and comprehensive to the mass of the population and include historical illustrations of the consequences of a neglected deficit for a country's political fate and national prestige. At the same time the Germans had to be reminded of 'what other countries (France, England, Italy) have imposed on themselves in the way of taxes and sacrifices. The more I can elevate the question to a high niveau, the better.'[64]

Bülow secured Wilhelm II's agreement to the main aspects of Sydow's financial proposals in June 1908,[65] and imperial support was vital if unity was to be ensured within the executive after the earlier disagreements over the reform.[66] For the rest, Bülow pinned his hopes on 'effective negotiations with influential personalities and skilful influencing of the press during the summer' to win parliamentary approval of the reform.[67] Correct presentation of the reform in the press was all-important to the Chancellor's strategy, and Bülow planned to create a great wave of public enthusiasm which would ultimately pressurise the Reichstag into accepting the necessary taxes and drown any resistance to individual proposals.[68] For Bülow, the national significance of the reform had to outweigh the personal economic interests of individual citizens or parties and, as in the past, he proved adept at harnessing most other issues to the principal cause. Though he was careful not to allow the reform to fuel demands for disarmament or naval cuts,[69] those who wailed about encirclement were to be told categorically that only the financial reform could ameliorate the situation. 'Tout est là', Bülow wrote to Hammann in June 1908.[70] Foreign embassies were instructed to collect any material which could serve the task of popular agitation for the reform, notably all remarks in the foreign press which drew unfavourable conclusions about Germany's international position from the state of her finances.[71]

Bülow's emphasis on the national significance of the reform was not least a tactic to encourage the Centre's collaboration. As Bülow further told Hammann in June 1908 and reiterated in the Prussian Ministry of State, the reform was not to be presented to the public as a Bloc reform or a Bloc bill, and in this respect was not similar to the Bloc laws of the previous winter. 'It must not look as if we are running after the Centre', he instructed. 'But we need now not to irritate it unnecessarily; it should not look as if we wanted to exclude it'.[72] Bülow explained to the Prussian Ministers that they would ultimately ensure the participation of the Centre in the financial reform if the Centre continued to believe that the government reckoned on the success of the reform even without its help. Although the radical Erzberger–Gröber wing in the Centre party enjoyed its new freedom of manoeuvre, the Chancellor believed that the more conservative elements favoured cooperation with the government. The main task therefore was 'to avoid everything which could damage the pro-government current in the Centre'.[73]

Bülow's hopes for public support of the financial reform of a kind reminiscent of the 1907 election campaign were sadly disappointed. In August a brief visit to Berlin confirmed his impression 'that the agitation for the Reich financial reform has as good as fallen asleep [*eingeschlafen*] – if it ever really got going briskly at all'. Anticipating that unless the German people recognised the moral and material significance of the reform as a question of 'life or death', the political parties would find all kinds of 'excuses and pretexts' in the autumn and fail to support the proposals, Bülow wrote to Hammann that 'If things remain this quiet, we are heading for a fiasco with the reform.' The Chancellor urged the launching of an attack against 'cowardice, pig-headedness [*Eigenmut*], stupidity and wickedness', and suggested that Hammann involved the professors and *haute finance* in the cause.[74] Hammann was scarcely flattered by the criticism of his 'sleepy agitation', but Bülow pleaded the 'paramount importance' of the reform's success 'for Reich and people' which made it 'perhaps forgivable if I appear insatiable with respect to the agitation for this project'. And as if to forestall Hammann's suspicion that another factor was also involved, he added: 'In this my personal position really matters less to me. The failure of the reform would give me *une très belle sortie*. But for our country, its domestic well-being and its external prestige, it would be a blow from which it would be difficult to recover.'[75]

Bülow's personal stake in the reform explains his persistence, and by the autumn of 1908 his dependence on the success of the reform was becoming increasingly apparent. The issue had clearly not been elevated above party political considerations and, with the left liberals piqued about Sydow's negotiations with the Centre, which implied 'that for him the Bülow Bloc does not exist',[76] and with the Centre already showing signs of being guided primarily by tactical considerations and the desire to shatter the Bloc,[77] by

September there were already indications that the financial reform might well develop into a vote of confidence in Bülow's Chancellorship. In their discussions with Sydow all the Bloc parties and the Centre expressed a willingness to collaborate in the reform, but their motives varied and a majority emerged against each tax proposal.[78]

Clearly if the reform was to succeed, it would require a supreme effort and all the skill and influence of a strong Reich Chancellor. Bülow had the Kaiser's support, which was not to be underestimated, especially with the Conservatives, and in September 1908 he told Holstein that he was 'up to his ears' in the financial reform.[79] But the Chancellor continued to see domestic politics in terms of speeches and appearances, concerned to say something on public occasions 'which makes an impact'[80] and anxious to preside over the Bundesrat 'at least once' when it was discussing the financial reform and to have this emphasised in the press.[81] On 18 September his press directive to Hammann conveyed an impression of diligence. He had had (in his own, and alternative, words) a 'long discussion' with Sydow, had opened a Bundesrat sitting with a 'lengthy (thorough) exposition (or address)', and the duration of the sitting was to be recorded.[82] But the notes taken at the sitting by Weizsäcker, the Minister-President of Württemberg, make it clear that Bülow's opening remarks were conspicuously short, that the Chancellor made no mention of the need to cut expenditure and that the subsequent, well-prepared speech given by Podewils, the Bavarian Minister-President, made a comic impression 'as it was conceived as the echo of a speech which the Reich Chancellor had not given'. Bülow, Weizsäcker noted, 'behaves like a viceroy, honours ostentatiously only Podewils with his favour, has not the slightest interest in the issue, at least apparently'.[83]

Bülow's increasingly leisurely work methods, as well as his almost exclusive preoccupation with parliamentary tactics and his own personal position, inspired little optimism about the prospects of the financial reform. Moreover, in the autumn of 1908 new complications arose to consume his limited energy before the *Daily Telegraph* affair finally shattered his power position within the executive and destroyed even the semblance of his effective leadership. In late September the Chancellor had to turn his attention once again to the Eulenburg case, which Harden had reopened in April by staging a libel trial in Munich, out of reach of the Prussian authorities. The testimony of a Starnberg fisherman, Jakob Ernst, who admitted to having had sexual relations with Eulenburg in the 1880s, had prompted Eulenburg's immediate arrest in May 1908, and the Kaiser's favourite had been forced to stand trial, accused of perjury, until the proceedings were suspended in July on account of his health. In September 1908 Eulenburg was released on bail but, after the Supreme Court had

9 A drawing of Bülow by Olaf Gulbransson

declared the second Moltke–Harden trial invalid in May, the Moltke–Harden case was still pending and the Chancellor recognised the need to prevent a third Moltke–Harden trial before the Eulenburg case was concluded.[84] As Bülow told Loebell, it would be totally unjust if Eulenburg walked around free while Harden was put on trial.[85] But the Chancellor found it difficult to enforce his views even in the face of opposition from the Prussian Ministry of Justice. Bülow blustered and threatened to make the issue into a 'Cabinet question' (that is, he would have resigned) if he did not get his way.[86] But the threat had to be repeated and he still failed to achieve results.[87] Angrily criticising the Prussian Ministries of Interior and Culture as well (which he had found remiss in the summer in their influencing of the press[88]), Bülow wrote to Loebell in early October that, at a time when the foreign and domestic situation was very difficult, he was sick and tired of encountering 'the narrow-mindedness or malevolence of the Prussian departments' wherever he went. The scandal trials had finally to end, he continued. 'I can think of no other incident in years which has affected me so unpleasantly. And that at a time when I must keep my head clear for big questions of foreign and domestic policy'.[89]

The Chancellor's irritation was profound, for only two days before, Austria had annexed the provinces of Bosnia and Herzegovina.[90] In an attempt to reassert his control of foreign policy and doubtless also to ameliorate the impression of the Morocco fiasco, Bülow adopted a determined policy of support for Austria in the Bosnian crisis, fearing that otherwise she might become disenchanted with the German alliance.[91] Bülow insisted on this course despite the misgivings of the Foreign Office, which had not been informed of Aehrenthal's intentions.[92] Moreover, he had to disregard the sensibilities of the Kaiser, who described Aehrenthal's action as a 'terrible stupidity' and wanted to stand by the Turks.[93]

But even the developing international crisis did not completely shake the Chancellor's complacency. Neither Bülow nor Schön returned to Berlin for several days and at a critical time the leadership of the Foreign Office was entrusted to the Under State Secretary.[94] Once the Chancellor did return to Berlin, his actions were primarily tailored for effect. Indeed, he was soon to hand the whole foreign policy problem over to Kiderlen-Wächter, who was recalled to the Foreign Office and compared his conditions of work to those of slave labour.[95] Bülow justified this move to the Kaiser, saying: 'In the present difficult situation it is absolutely essential that foreign affairs are led by an official completely equal to his tasks.'[96] Bülow himself had numerous short interviews with foreign ambassadors[97] and on 18 October delivered a short speech in which he referred to events in the Near East at the Rathaus in Regensburg. 'I believe it will have a good effect!' he had told Loebell when ordering the draft.

It demonstrates that the Reich Chancellor is on the alert. It corresponds to what the Ministers in England, France [and] Italy have done. The longer I am Reich Chancellor, the more I see how it is above all a question of the Chancellor holding his ground [*sich behauptet*], standing in the foreground and not letting himself be effaced.[98]

Two weeks later Bülow faced the most severe domestic crisis of his career.

The 'Daily Telegraph' crisis

In all probability Bülow never read the text of the Kaiser's interview with Colonel Sir Edward James Montagu Stuart-Wortley before it was published in the *Daily Telegraph* on 28 October 1908.[99] The interview, which comprised various remarks made by the Kaiser on different occasions during his stay in England in late 1907, had been approved by Wilhelm and was intended to demonstrate his friendship towards England.[100] But the Kaiser's assertion, among other things, that he had sent the British a plan of campaign for the Boer war which 'ran very much on the same lines as that which was actually adopted by Lord Roberts and carried by him into successful operation'[101] was greeted with disbelief and some amusement in Britain, and aroused feelings of humiliation and indignation in Germany.[102] Immediately regarded as but the latest in a long series of imperial indiscretions, the incident made political guarantees against such irresponsibility in the future seem imperative. The *Daily Telegraph* affair rapidly developed into a major domestic crisis which focused public criticism on the Kaiser's 'personal rule', precipitated his nervous collapse and shattered his remaining confidence in the Chancellor. Bülow seemed to survive the experience, but from November 1908 his resignation could not long be delayed.

In some respects the *Daily Telegraph* affair was symptomatic of Bülow's style of work within the executive and could have happened at any time during his Chancellorship. It indicated his increasingly nonchalant attitude towards everything but the most major issues and ultimately destroyed the Kaiser's belief that the Chancellor always carried out his orders faithfully. Having been sent the text of the interview with express instructions from Wilhelm not to pass it on to the Foreign Office, Bülow disregarded his wishes and delegated the matter to his subordinates with inadequate directives in late September or early October.[103] Bülow was not so busy at this time with the financial reform and the Bosnian crisis as he subsequently made out, though the text was returned to him a day after the Austrian annexation.[104] Only after his return to Berlin later in October did Bülow complain to others about his work-load,[105] and even at the height of the crisis the Chancellor lamented that he was 'exceeding the normal working day now by 2–3 hours',[106] an admission which would have gained him little sympathy from Kiderlen, who was kept at his desk until the small hours of the morning.[107]

Bülow was officially responsible for the publication of the interview; indeed, the Kaiser had acted in complete accordance with the Constitution, and his belief in his own innocence was to be reinforced by the initial handling of the affair. Once the storm broke, Bülow at first did not heed the advice of those, such as Holstein, who saw the chief grievance as the content of the interview and the Kaiser's indiscretion.[108] Instead, he tried to deflect criticism from the monarch and himself by placing the blame on the Foreign Office officials who had apparently been negligent in their examination of the text. To the Kaiser he admitted that he had not checked the manuscript personally 'through pressure of business' and offered to resign because of 'the lack of circumspection displayed by the Foreign Ministry'.[109] Wilhelm apparently did not take amiss this confession which contradicted Bülow's earlier assertion that he had acted in accordance with the monarch's instructions.[110] He rejected the offer of resignation and in the early days of November even seemed to enjoy the Chancellor's discomfiture, confident that this time he personally could not be faulted.[111] Bülow's official explanation of the affair in the *Norddeutsche Allgemeine Zeitung* also confirmed a 'regrettable chain of negligence [*bedauerliche Verkettung von Nachlässigkeiten*]' in the Foreign Office,[112] and Bülow maintained that if he had read the text of the interview in advance, he naturally would not have permitted its publication.[113] The implications of this statement inevitably led back to the Kaiser once the outcry over the seemingly anarchic conditions and lack of leadership in the Foreign Office had died down.[114] But, in the short term, the declaration in the *Norddeutsche Allgemeine Zeitung* 'only added to the tragedy the curse of ridicule', for it now became clear that four times the text of the interview had been shunted back and forth and never once had it been stopped.[115]

Bülow's initial interpretation of the affair was, as one historian has written, 'a characteristic manoeuvre, shifting the blame for his own negligence and moral cowardice on to others',[116] and was certainly not appreciated by his subordinates. Schön, who had been on holiday during the decisive weeks, spent several hours trying to dissuade the Chancellor from 'uncovering the guilt of the Foreign Office' and then sank into a nervous depression in early November, which necessitated Kiderlen's deputyship.[117] Stemrich, the Under State Secretary, was deeply wounded by Bülow's behaviour and became preoccupied with thoughts of resignation until finally persuaded to stay in early December.[118] Klehmet, the official who (like Müller in Norderney) had only been asked to examine the historical accuracy of the text and not its suitability for publication,[119] was ultimately made the scapegoat of the affair and transferred as Consul General to Athens.[120] Klehmet's sense of grievance against the Chancellor was strong, and in early 1909 he was to enter into an ominous correspondence with Valentini about his future rehabilitation.[121]

Bülow clearly did not anticipate the public reaction to his version of events. In the early days of the crisis, the Chancellor was the main target of press criticism and the demand for his resignation was widespread. Although the Kaiser continued to take the affair lightly, Loebell could not deny to Varnbüler the existence of a Chancellor crisis,[122] and the Austrian *chargé d'affaires* reported that there was little hope that Bülow could remain in office.[123] It was probably the possibility that in these circumstances Wilhelm would be influenced against him which prompted Bülow to encourage the monarch not to change his plans but to leave Berlin on a hunting trip on 3 November.[124] The Kaiser's absence at such a time was to create a very bad impression and many, even in his closest entourage, believed that he had been ill advised.[125] However, Bülow undoubtedly wanted Wilhelm out of the way in November 1908 so that he could handle the crisis as he saw fit. The Kaiser departed in good humour and only later did the Chancellor recognise the disadvantages of his absence, especially when Wilhelm had not experienced at first hand the full severity of public feeling.[126]

Even before the Kaiser left Berlin there were signs that the direction of public criticism was changing, and Bülow displayed every intention to tack with the new wind. The damage to the Reich was increasingly seen in the fact that the Kaiser's words had been spoken rather than in the fact of their publication, and the Chancellor's guilt seemed relatively trivial when the root cause of the crisis was seen to rest with the ruler.[127] On 2 November Varnbüler reported that the judgement of the Chancellor in the Reichstag would be relatively moderate since no party, except perhaps the extreme right wing of the Conservatives (who opposed the inheritance tax and electoral reform), had any interest in precipitating his fall over the affair.[128] In subsequent days Bülow, with customary skill, exploited the new mood to strengthen his personal position, and by the time the Reichstag debate on the *Daily Telegraph* crisis began on 10 November the attitude of the Bloc parties was favourable to the Chancellor.[129]

Bülow successfully postponed the Reichstag debate for as long as possible, which contributed to a certain cooling of parliamentary passions and allowed Bethmann Hollweg to bring influence to bear on individual deputies.[130] In a short speech on 10 November, which Bülow had intended to be '*very* serious, brief [and] forceful' with 'no excuse at all, no humility, no jokes!',[131] he accepted responsibility for the publication of the interview but barely defended the Kaiser and expressed the expectation that the monarch would exercise greater restraint in future.[132] Bülow had abandoned a speech drafted earlier in November which had defended the Kaiser more explicitly[133] and, given the unprecedented attacks on the monarch during the two-day debate, he undoubtedly committed a grave political error when he failed to speak again on 11 November and left the defence of the Foreign Office to

Kiderlen.[134] At a State Ministry meeting immediately after the debate it was recorded that the unanimous opposition of all the parties to 'personal rule' had made it impossible to deflect parliamentary criticism from the Kaiser's person, as was usual.[135] But Bülow quickly recognised his mistake and was on the defensive in the press. 'It was correct of the Reich Chancellor that he did not speak a second time', he told Hammann. Everything now depended on actions, not words, and whether the Kaiser identified himself with the Chancellor's declaration of 10 November.[136]

Bülow was supported by the majority of the Reichstag and the press by the middle of November, and he also secured the unanimous approval of the Prussian State Ministry and the Bundesrat in his intention to exact firm guarantees from the Kaiser. On 11 November the State Ministry agreed that the Chancellor and Minister-President 'in the name of the State Ministry' should discuss the gravity of the situation with the Kaiser (hence Bülow's dismissal would have entailed the resignation of the entire Ministry).[137] In his memoir on the *Daily Telegraph* affair, written in the winter of 1909–10, Bülow recalled that the Ministers spoke very openly and, at times, agitatedly, and that at their request the content of their discussions had not been minuted. He enumerated some of their suggestions – that it would create a better impression if the Kaiser were more involved in the day-to-day business of government; that there should be less talk in the press of his hunting trips and other pleasures and more attention paid to when he saw Ministers; that the Kaiser should spend some months in Berlin or Potsdam without a break and perhaps for once do without his annual North Sea cruise or visit to Corfu; that he should devote a 'truly major part of the day' to work and not look as if he were dissipating his powers; that he should see parliamentarians more frequently and listen rather than talk himself.[138] Such proposals were arguably little more than palliatives which could not attack the root cause of the problem, but Bülow declared himself satisfied with the course of the meeting and informed Hammann, 'I have the entire State Ministry behind me. It senses the great gravity of the situation'.[139] His new mood was also evident at a long overdue meeting of the Bundesrat Committee on Foreign Affairs on 12 November. In a lengthy speech he protested that he could not read everything the Kaiser sent him and that he was reluctant to dismiss capable officials. The Foreign Office procedure was peripheral to the main issue. The Kaiser's remarks were well known in England and, if the *Daily Telegraph* interview had been prevented, they would have achieved publicity through other channels.[140]

With the Bundesrat, State Ministry, Reichstag and press all basically behind him, Bülow thus assembled an impressive array of support in November 1908, but the remarkable aspect of the *Daily Telegraph* crisis is how little he used it. After the Reichstag debate public attention was focused on the impending audience between Kaiser and Chancellor, which was anticipated first in Donaueschingen, then in Kiel, and finally took place in Potsdam on 17 November.[141] Supported by all the main political institutions, it seemed scarcely possible that Bülow would fail to exploit the advantage this gave him and not return from the encounter with effective constitutional safeguards. Yet he proved curiously naive about the effects of the crisis on his personal relationship with Wilhelm II and reluctant to place the government of Germany on a new footing which might have limited his own position. Bülow went to Potsdam, convinced that the pivot of government could continue to be the mutual confidence between Kaiser and Chancellor; and, although he exploited the support of the State Ministers in the press[142] and told them afterwards that it had been invaluable in helping him to carry out his intentions, Bülow deemed it best 'in the interests of a good relationship between HM and the State Ministry' not to mention this support to the Kaiser.[143] Bülow deliberately handled his audience with the Kaiser on a personal level and avoided any intimation that the Kaiser had been placed in the kind of 'position of constraint' which had angered him so much during the constitutional struggles of the 1890s.[144] Bülow's behaviour contributed to the transformation of the Daily Telegraph affair from a political crisis into a personal crisis between Kaiser and Chancellor and did much to ensure that its only lasting consequence would be Bülow's fall.

By 17 November the Kaiser's mood had changed considerably since the early days of the crisis. Bülow himself had played a significant role in this, for he had acted on Holstein's advice and instructed his cousin, Martin von Rücker-Jenisch, who had accompanied Wilhelm to Austria, to convert the Kaiser from the initial view of the semi-official press that the Foreign Office was primarily to blame.[145] After being convinced that he personally did not need to reproach himself, Wilhelm had been told by Jenisch, Hülsen and others that the main grievance was his readiness to conduct political conversations with foreigners, that he had been responsible for the original indiscretions and that Bülow could not possibly have condoned the content of the Kaiser's interview.[146] Wilhelm had not accepted this new interpretation of events without first contradicting it, but Bülow had argued his case through Jenisch.[147] On 13 November Jenisch had informed the Chancellor that the Kaiser was sad but calm and composed. With skilful handling Valentini was convinced that he would give Bülow the necessary guarantees.[148]

There is no doubt that Bülow was misled about the Kaiser's mood before their audience on 17 November, though this was probably unintentional. Jenisch had admitted to the Chancellor that Wilhelm continued to believe that he had not been sufficiently defended in the Reichstag, and he had advised Bülow to raise this question with Wilhelm at their audience.[149] He had also relayed to the Chancellor the view of Valentini that the Kaiser was suffering emotionally and that Bülow would do best not to be too heavy-handed with him. It would be 'very dangerous' if Bülow tried to exact programmatic declarations from the Kaiser at their audience or make him say some kind of public *pater peccavi*.[150] Nevertheless, in general Jenisch managed to convey the impression of Wilhelm's fragility and vulnerability as a result of the crisis, which was based in part on the observations of the Chief of the Civil Cabinet, but which is not in harmony with Valentini's personal account of his conversations with Wilhelm. In reality it seems that Wilhelm was already acutely aggrieved by Bülow's behaviour. He was convinced that Bülow had approved of everything he had said and done in England in 1907 (perhaps an indication of the Chancellor's sycophancy), he was indignant that Bülow had not read the script of the interview despite his instructions, and he believed that the Chancellor had abandoned him in the Reichstag. Moreover, it is clear that the *Daily Telegraph* crisis had already triggered all kinds of other associations in his mind and in particular reopened the old wounds of 1905–6. He had implored the Chancellor to leave him out of the Moroccan adventure, he told Valentini on 13 November, but Bülow and the Foreign Office had forced him to land.[151]

Bülow also, like Varnbüler, may have believed that the death of Hülsen, the Chief of the Military Cabinet, on 14 November in bizarre circumstances would have seemed like an omen to the Kaiser and made him more susceptible to the Chancellor's demands.[152] He was thus surprised on 17 November to find the mood of the Kaiser 'more irritated, opposition more stubborn, conversation more difficult than I had assumed from the infor-mation of Jenisch and Valentini, who had seen me beforehand'.[153] Although in his memoirs Bülow sought to give the impression of a depressed and despondent monarch who was astonished and grateful to the Chancellor that he came out of the affair so well,[154] all the indications suggest that the audience was far from smooth and that Wilhelm remained convinced both that the criticism was exaggerated and that an injustice had been committed against him.[155] Bülow told Holstein that he 'held firmly to all the demands listed in my notebook, without toning anything down' and that he 'left no doubt that I would otherwise resign at once'.[156] But he clearly rejected a course of 'brutal pressure' on the Kaiser and instead heeded Valentini's advice that 'The world must implicitly conclude from the fact that you remain Reich Chancellor that HM gave you the assurances demanded in your Reichstag speech'.[157] The announcement in the *Norddeutsche Allgemeine Zeitung* on 17 November represented only a verbal assurance to the Chancel-lor on the part of the Kaiser and came as a disappointment to all those who had expected firmer constitutional guarantees.[158]

Bülow believed that he had achieved what he wanted without extending the powers of government institutions, and in the next few days he professed complete satisfaction with the course of the audience, insisting that the Kaiser had received him with exceptional amiability.[159] He was generally congratulated on solving the crisis in a way which ensured his continuance in office[160] and, indeed, in the short term, his dismissal had been made politically impossible. When Bülow introduced the financial reform in the Reichstag on 19 November, Varnbüler reported that the bearing of the Chancellor had changed completely.

Instead of the tragic pose, the at times too elegiac tone of a deeply worried patriot and political martyr who had taken the sins of others upon himself, Prince Bülow now displayed the assurance and confidence of a statesman who commands the situation and has the way free to solve real tasks. In fact he has emerged from this recent crisis in a stonger and more secure position *vis-à-vis* the Kaiser and nation than a Reich Chancellor has ever had before him since Bismarck's times – and even the latter [did not have] under the 'new master'.[161]

In late 1908 Bülow even felt sufficiently strong to launch an offensive on the naval question, an offensive which brought no positive results but gave Tirpitz cause for concern.[162]

Nevertheless, Bülow's procedure in November 1908 brought no long-term advantages either to the position of the Chancellor or to the cause of constitutional government, and any personal benefits he reaped from the crisis were quickly dissipated. Bülow told Lerchenfeld after his audience with the Kaiser that the only effective guarantee against personal rule was 'a Reich Chancellor who has the confidence of the federal governments and the Reichstag and, supported by that confidence, can stand up to HM'. But he remained hostile to constitutional changes, such as the introduction of responsible Reich Ministers, and sought to influence the parties against such aspirations before the Reichstag debate on the Constitution in early December.[163] Bülow did not want the Chancellor to be more accountable to parliament, nor was he prepared to head a more collective form of government. He was not alone in failing to exploit the *Daily Telegraph* crisis, and the debate on the Constitution in the Reichstag (2–3 December), which he did not attend, revealed the fundamental disunity of the political parties, their inability to exert effective parliamentary pressure and their tendency to try to weaken rather than strengthen the Chancellor's position.[164] But Bülow gained nothing tangible from the affair, and his hopes 'that from now on there will be a different kind of rule and a good many things can get better' were illusory.[165] As became clear in the ensuing weeks the only permanent achievement of the Chancellor was the Kaiser's hostility.

Kaiser and Chancellor

In late November 1908, while Bülow was in confident mood and convinced that he had the majority of the German people behind him,[166] the Kaiser suffered a nervous collapse and languished in depression. Bülow described Wilhelm's illness as a 'severe cold' and 'completely insignificant',[167] but Max Fürstenberg, the Kaiser's close friend with whom he had stayed in Donaueschingen and who arrived in Berlin for Hülsen's funeral, revealed that the monarch conveyed the impression of a broken man.[168] He scarcely went out, refused to work or to see anybody and on 24 November he even made up his mind to abdicate, though his intention was thwarted by his entourage.[169] Wilhelm was convinced that he had become 'the greatest martyr of his time',[170] and not even Fürstenberg could lift him from his despondency. Fürstenberg, who recognised that he was 'perhaps the first and only person who, through Your Majesty's confidential grace, was initiated into the secret of this terrible hour' when the Kaiser had received the Chancellor,[171] wrote to Wilhelm at the end of November how much it had distressed him to hear that he was still suffering from the impact of recent events. Wilhelm, he asserted, did not need to see too blackly into the future. 'Your Majesty's heroic decision to listen to the Chancellor's exposition [Vortrag] calmly and accept his proposals calmly – that has opened the eyes of thousands and thousands of Your Majesty's misled, loyal subjects and aroused admiration inside and outside the German Fatherland.' The Kaiser must not despair, for 'enlightenment and repentance' would soon follow.[172]

The Kaiser ultimately emerged from his depression within a few months, but the Daily Telegraph crisis had dealt a critical blow to the relationship between Kaiser and Chancellor. Although there were occasions when an experienced political observer like Lerchenfeld could report that 'the Reich Chancellor's relationship with his imperial master seems at least outwardly satisfactory'[173] and despite a brief reconciliation in March 1909, the Kaiser's disillusionment with the Chancellor was never really in doubt and it undermined Bülow's political effectiveness during the last months of his Chancellorship. 'The intimate, personal, friendly relationship between Kaiser Wilhelm and Prince Bülow can never again be resurrected', Szögyényi reported as early as 25 November, and since he was convinced that no other kind of relationship could inspire the necessary confidence, he predicted 'that sooner or later we will have to reckon with a change of Chancellor'.[174] From November 1908 Bülow's system declined rapidly, and his loss of the Kaiser's trust was fundamental to the process of disintegration.

The Kaiser's anger with the Chancellor did not abate in the wake of the crisis, though to some extent he succeeded in deflecting it into a reproachful but patient detachment. Fürstenberg told Szögyényi about the difficult times he had experienced with Wilhelm in Donaueschingen. 'From the very beginning he was firmly convinced of the need to keep the Reich Chancellor under the given "compelling" circumstances', the ambassador was informed, 'yet he was extremely displeased that Prince Bülow did not find the right tone in his Reichstag speech to defend correctly his imperial master who had showered him with so many proofs of his confidence'.[175] Szögyényi himself had the opportunity to gauge the Kaiser's mood during a two-hour audience with him on 3 December. Wilhelm 'poured his heart out' and complained bitterly about the behaviour of the Chancellor.[176] He swore that Bülow had always approved of his remarks either before or immediately afterwards, he was outraged that he had not even troubled to read the text and he claimed he had been made the 'scapegoat' for the affair while 'my Reich Chancellor innocently washed his hands'. 'Despite this method of behaviour I could do nothing but insist that Bülow remain in office', Wilhelm maintained. 'I had to suppress my personal feelings and keep in mind only the well-being of the Fatherland.' When the financial reform was concluded with the Bloc, Bülow could be removed. In the meantime he, the Kaiser, had resolved to practise extreme reserve in all foreign and domestic questions and then see 'whether the affairs of the Reich are looked after any better'. It was Bülow who had made all the significant mistakes in foreign policy, and again the monarch returned to the theme of Morocco and how he had known from the beginning that German policy was wrong-headed.[177]

Bülow knew of the Kaiser's fury[178] but could do little about it. August Eulenburg impressed on him 'how immensely important the constant, *personal* contact between Your Excellency and HM is, and especially now – when HM seems inclined to withdraw completely – more than ever'.[179] But on the two occasions Bülow and Wilhelm met in December 1908, the Kaiser acted with calculated and cool correctness, which may have gone some way to reassure the Chancellor about the security of his position but which scarcely signified that Wilhelm was any less convinced that he had been 'left in the lurch'.[180] Bülow incensed the Kaiser when he warmly defended Holstein in the Reichstag in December 1908,[181] and in the first week of January the press discussion of Wilhelm's approval of an article written by Schlieffen provoked an argument between Kaiser and Chancellor. Holstein believed that the Kaiser's behaviour constituted 'a reversion to the practices of the past' and that Bülow should resign;[182] Wilhelm, by contrast, was outraged that the press criticism was tolerated, and his suspicions of a systematic campaign were fuelled by Fürstenberg.[183]

As Holstein wrote to Bülow in January 1909, the only question was 'whether you can hope to win over the Kaiser again merely by patience and forbearance'.[184] But, however much Wilhelm II disliked change and found Bülow's submissiveness convenient, however much he could not 'bear the thought of having to do without the daily reports of Bülow on politics and other matters',[185] too many anti-Bülow influences coalesced in late 1908 and sought to feed the Kaiser's resentment.[186] Criticism is not synonymous with intrigue, but even in government circles it was felt that Bülow's handling of the Kaiser during the *Daily Telegraph* crisis lacked an 'educational element'. Many of the growing number of complaints about the Chancellor hinged on the belief that he was primarily responsible for the steady growth in Wilhelm's self-esteem since 1900 because he had failed to oppose the Kaiser energetically at the right time. Thus Bülow was blamed for the development of 'personal rule' from 1900.[187] But Bülow was accused of being too hard as well as too soft. Conservative opinion, already unhappy with what it regarded as the Chancellor's miserable defence of the Prussian King in the German Reichstag,[188] was particularly susceptible to the widely propagated view that Bülow had read the *Daily Telegraph* interview and deliberately orchestrated the November crisis in order to free his policy from the limitations imposed by 'personal rule'.[189] The 'great awakening of the people' was not on the scale which Fürstenberg predicted,[190] but a conservative backlash began to develop in November 1908 and gathered momentum in the ensuing weeks.[191] Although the Kaiser believed that he did not need the assistance of others and that when the time came he could 'let himself off the hook' and dismiss the Chancellor,[192] he was certainly influenced by anti-Bülow propaganda which also prejudiced the opinions of others in his entourage.[193]

Intrigues against the Chancellor proliferated in late 1908 and a characteristic feature of them was the openness in which they were hatched.[194] Bülow recognised that his position was being undermined from more than one quarter and told Holstein in January 1909 that he would have to operate with great caution.[195] He heard about an intrigue planned at Donaueschingen during the Kaiser's stay to return to the kind of 'Bismarckian' programme implemented before 1890 and propose Radowitz as a possible 'Vice-Chancellor under a Chancellor Wilhelm'.[196] The foreign press carried articles portraying the influential Max Fürstenberg as the fifth Reich Chancellor.[197] Bülow was also fully aware of hostile interpretations of the *Daily Telegraph* affair and of subversive activities 'in certain circles which are close to HM'.[198] The mood at Court and in the Army was unfriendly towards the Chancellor,[199] and Bülow suspected that members of the military entourage, the ambitious Crown Prince, the Scherl press and even Szögyényi were all under the influence of the 'Upper Silesians'.[200] He was told that 'retired Ministers with wide-ranging connections and magnates' were involved in the agitation against him[201] and was wary of the support in the executive and the Reichstag for Bethmann Hollweg as Chancellor.[202] Parliamentary (especially Centre) machinations to destroy his position depended less on the Kaiser's receptiveness, but it was predictably the press campaigns which most intensified

Bülow's nervousness.[203] In January 1909 Varnbüler reported that the Chancellor's position was weaker than it had been during the November days and that all the rumours, allegations and conjectures ultimately culminated in the question how the relationship between Kaiser and Chancellor would develop.[204]

Bülow certainly considered again the possibility of resignation in January 1909, but it was generally recognised that despite the apparent conflict with the Kaiser, his position was at least temporarily secure.[205] The Chancellor's dismissal before the conclusion of the financial reform would have been highly dangerous for the Kaiser,[206] and Bülow himself told Holstein that though he had earlier very much wanted to resign, 'I would like to choose the moment of my resignation myself and not slip and fall on some dirty piece of orange peel'.[207] Lerchenfeld reported that Bülow had recently spoken as if he were weary of office and that he too might have set the termination of the financial reform as the date of his departure. 'But I have still never known a statesman to go earlier than he must, and that will also be so in this case', the ambassador mused.[208] In the following weeks Bülow tried to exploit his brief period of reprieve to strengthen his position, and on 19 January he even made a belated attempt to justify his behaviour in November both to the Kaiser and to the Conservatives by speaking out against 'the exaggerated criticism, the *médisance* of bourgeois and upper-class circles, naive and perfidious newspaper articles, gossip and talk of camarilla' in the Prussian Lower House.[209] The speech revealed his sensitivity to the dangers inherent in Conservative attacks against him but failed to confirm his conservative credentials and constituted a severe miscalculation on the part of the Chancellor. The result of the speech was 'ill-will everywhere and an increase in the agitation against Bülow'.[210] Even the Kaiser 'expressed strong disapproval' of the speech and maintained 'that it was quite superfluous to drag in the affair of the *Daily Telegraph* of last November'.[211]

The antagonism between Kaiser and Chancellor continued until the middle of March and exacerbated the impression of disunity within the executive. Despite Bülow's efforts to resurrect the old confidentiality and familiarity in his communications to the Kaiser,[212] Wilhelm took an unmistakable delight in influencing his uncle, King Edward VII, against the Chancellor in February 1909 and ensured that 'King Edward simply "cut" the Chancellor' and spoke no word of politics to him during the royal visit to Germany.[213] With almost childish glee the Kaiser relayed to Bülow the King's alleged displeasure at Bülow's handling of the *Daily Telegraph* affair and responded with 'Pharisee!' when Bülow took issue with the criticisms.[214] Further disunity was evident when Wilhelm II sent a telegram *en clair* to Radolin in February 1909 indicating that he, and not the Chancellor, was responsible for the recent Moroccan agreement.[215] The Kaiser also abandoned his relative restraint on 18 February to preside over a Crown Council meeting on the reorganisation of the Prussian administration, a meeting which Bülow maintained had long been intended but which he doubtless did not welcome.[216] Though the protocol does not reveal the cause of the dissension, both Berckheim and Lerchenfeld reported that there was considerable discord at the Crown Council between Wilhelm and Bülow and that the former was ill with excitement and anger for two days afterwards.[217]

Meanwhile, the Kaiser's routine had changed drastically for the first time since Bülow's assumption of the Chancellorship. No longer did he pay daily, informal visits to the Chancellery. Wilhelm saw Bülow on merely three or four occasions in January and February 1909 and he kept their relations to the minimum, official level.[218] To alleviate the impression this created, the Court made an unusual winter move to Potsdam, but observers of the Kaiser's polite coolness towards the Chancellor on public occasions sensed immediately 'that in their personal relations something has been torn in two which can never heal again'.[219] The Kaiser's attendants despaired of his new lethargy[220] while Varnbüler, deprived of the early morning spectacle from his balcony window of the lively discussions between Kaiser and Chancellor, believed that Bülow's policy might gain in consistency. The problem was, he recognised, that hostile influences and the camarilla, which Bülow publicly denied but secretly fought, would have greater freedom of manoeuvre 'if the leading statesman is no longer daily in a position to nip them in the bud'.[221]

The lack of mutual confidence in their personal relationship inevitably intruded into official relations between Kaiser and Chancellor and undermined Bülow's authority to bring the financial reform to a successful conclusion. By early March the Chancellor was finally convinced that he could no longer conduct affairs in these circumstances.[222] Since time had not conspired to bring about an improvement in their relations, Bülow exploited Loebell's close links with Valentini and Wilhelm's esteem for his wife to arrange an audience with the Kaiser which he hoped would clear the air.[223] The audience took place on 11 March and lasted two and a half hours.[224] Like its predecessor in November, it constituted a private conversation between the two men which was subject to considerable retrospective embellishment. In his memoirs Bülow glossed over his defence against Wilhelm's criticisms and stressed the completeness of their reconciliation afterwards. He admitted that Wilhelm sent a telegram to his brother later on 11 March in which he claimed he had 'just forgiven Bülow after he begged my pardon in a paroxysm of tears'. But Bülow maintained that this was pure invention and simply Wilhelm's way of explaining the reconciliation. The general impression of the account is that the Kaiser reiterated his confidence in the Chancellor and received little in exchange. The idea that Bülow achieved the reconciliation by repeating the interpretation of the crisis he had held to since November is far from convincing.[225]

Despite Bülow's account, there seems little doubt that the probable course of the audience was highly unflattering to the Chancellor. Bülow certainly repeated his offer of resignation, which Wilhelm again rejected because of the financial reform.[226] But, in the face of Wilhelm's continued hostility, the Chancellor capitulated completely to the monarch. Even allowing for some exaggeration in Wilhelm's later descriptions of the audience,[227] the Kaiser's story was remarkably consistent and confirmed that the Chancellor had apologised for the *Daily Telegraph* affair. Zedlitz noted that Bülow had declared that if he had remembered his previous conversations with Wilhelm he would never have adopted the position he had in November 1908;[228] and on 12 March the Kaiser told Lerchenfeld:

Yesterday the Reich Chancellor was with me and asked me for forgiveness. He explained to me that certain things had disappeared from his memory then. Otherwise he would not have undertaken the action. I told him my opinion without qualification. It cost tears and the Chancellor was very crushed. But I have forgiven him and the matter is over.[229]

Bülow had previously professed tears of emotion in his correspondence with Wilhelm.[230] On 11 March, according to Wilhelm, 'Bülow howled like a dog in a yard', Baroness Spitzemberg wrote in her diary.[231]

On this basis it is understandable that Wilhelm was extremely satisfied with the outcome of the audience, and the reconciliation seemed complete.[232] Notwithstanding some alleged remarks that he was 'finished' with Bülow,[233] the Kaiser invited himself to dinner with the Chancellor on 12 March, staying into the small hours, and the daily walks in the Tiergarten and visits to Bülow were resumed for the rest of the month.[234] Relations between Kaiser and Chancellor seemed fully back to normal;[235] and Germany's apparent diplomatic victory in the Bosnian crisis soon further sweetened Wilhelm's mood.[236]

Nevertheless Bülow's admission of guilt ensured that Wilhelm now had 'no idea of what the November revolution really signifies or should signify'[237] and that the Chancellor was dependent on the Kaiser's continued grace, unable to counter hostile interpretations of the crisis if they were voiced to Wilhelm. By indicating his error in November, Bülow had paid an enormous price for the reconciliation. As Lerchenfeld reported,

My impression of the affair is not a happy one. It is indeed good if Bülow stays – and he must stay because of foreign policy – that his position is secure, but if the reconciliation took place in the form which HM told me yesterday, the Reich Chancellor will have less authority *vis-à-vis* the Kaiser than before the conflict and the entire action will have been virtually in vain.

Lerchenfeld's only hint of optimism stemmed from his belief that Bülow had not acted on his own in November 1908 but with the support of the Prussian Ministry, Bundesrat and Reichstag. 'I say virtually', he went on, 'as the warning came not from Bülow alone but also from other authorities which have not asked for forgiveness.'[238] Lerchenfeld could not have known that Bülow had scarcely mentioned the 'other authorities' to the Kaiser the previous autumn. Wilhelm had seen the entire crisis as one which arose from the wrongs of his Chancellor and which had no other consequences after he had 'forgiven' Bülow.[239]

Perhaps if Bülow's relationship with the Kaiser had existed in a vacuum, the Chancellor's tactic in March 1909 might have been successful and his position (and subservience) assured. In spite of all his bombast, Wilhelm II was lazy by nature, seeking to avoid personal conflict and the rigours of day-to-day political activity. For reasons of convenience and habit, he would have preferred not to have to remove Bülow and would have happily cherished the illusion that Bülow was sincere and loyal. On many occasions the Kaiser had turned a blind eye to Bülow's apparent misdemeanours, and even after the Moroccan crisis he had always liked to hear that it had constituted a German success.[240]

But the reconciliation of March 1909 proved short-lived and never convinced the press that Bülow's position was once again secure.[241] Despite Bülow's misgivings, Wilhelm left on his Mediterranean cruise at the beginning of April,[242] and when the two men met again in Venice on 14 April, Bülow recalled that the Kaiser's mood had changed completely and that he was 'less expansive, touchy and visibly ill-humoured and mistrustful'. His enemies at Court and especially Fürstenberg had influenced Wilhelm against the Chancellor,[243] and Holstein too warned Bülow that the Kaiser was again talking of Bülow's treachery and his later 'convulsions of tears'.[244] Wilhelm complained to Eisendecher in Karlsruhe in May that Bülow had 'treated him shamefully in November'. He, the Kaiser, 'gave it to him soundly on that long walk; never in his life [had he] spoken his mind so thoroughly and made him say *pater peccavi*'. Bülow had admitted to his sins and become quite small. He now understood that Wilhelm had him where he wanted him and 'must do what I want'.[245] On another occasion the Kaiser was alleged to have said that he had 'Bernhard now completely in his hand'.[246]

Bülow's behaviour in March 1909 ensured that the November experiences left few personal scars on the Kaiser and that the political results of the recent crisis were paltry. The Chancellor gained nothing of value in return. Indeed, after April 1909 he was only to see the Kaiser on a handful of occasions before the decisive audience on 26 June.[247] To the outside world Bülow continued the pretence that all was well between Kaiser and Chancellor, but Wilhelm once again treated Bülow with unmistakable coolness[248] and initiated a wider and wider circle of people into his true opinions.[249] The high expectations of some that a new system of rule would follow after the recent upheavals gave way to profound disappointment and disillusionment.[250] A depressed and fatalistic mood pervaded Berlin politics and predetermined the response to the final *débâcle* in June.

The collapse of the Bloc

Bülow's last months as Chancellor were lived out against the background of a highly confused domestic situation, dominated by the concluding negotiations over the Reich financial reform, and in the face of repeated evidence that he had forfeited imperial support through his handling of the *Daily Telegraph* affair. Preoccupied with his problems with the Kaiser and in the Reichstag, Bülow allowed his position and authority within the executive to be further eroded and in late 1908 proved unable to prevent a third Moltke–Harden trial because of opposition in the Justice Ministry, where officials openly declared that the political interests of the Reich Chancellor were immaterial.[251] With respect to foreign policy, in the wake of the November crisis Bülow scarcely attempted to conceal the chaos in the Foreign Office and his inability to provide effective leadership, admitting to Holstein that the machine no longer functioned as efficiently as in the years before 1906.[252] Although he continued to pursue the possibility of a naval agreement with England throughout 1909 (an attempt which, even if it had been successful, could not have obliterated later historical assessments of his warm support for German naval armaments since 1897),[253] the Chancellor bothered himself little with international affairs, and in April 1909 he claimed the credit for Germany's apparent success in the Bosnian crisis even though Kiderlen had directed German policy.[254] Once Kiderlen's assignment in Berlin was completed, the old conditions in the Foreign Office quickly reasserted themselves.[255] The supposition in July 1909 that it was Bülow's primary interest in diplomacy which led him to misjudge and neglect the financial reform is but further evidence of the complete bankruptcy of his 'system' by the time the Chancellor resigned.[256]

The political prospects for a successful conclusion of the financial reform with the Bloc had been bleak even before the *Daily Telegraph* affair intervened.[257] The November crisis further aggravated the differences between the Bloc parties by highlighting Conservative isolation on the question of constitutional reform.[258] Although Bülow proved unwilling to make constitutional concessions to the liberals to secure their agreement to the financial reform,[259] his promise of a reform of the Prussian suffrage and the belief that Bülow hoped to move in the direction of parliamentary rule fuelled Conservative suspicion of the Chancellor, and this anxiety was brought to the

Kaiser's attention by Valentini in December 1908.[260] The crisis also had repercussions on the attitude of the Centre to the reform, for once the Kaiser's loss of confidence in Bülow was proven, the Centre could realistically hope to dislodge him by precipitating the collapse of the Bloc. Bülow was bitter about Centre tactics throughout 1909, even though he was largely responsible for its enmity.[261] The Centre initially aimed at obstruction of the reform but soon recognised the opportunity to restore its parliamentary pre-eminence and avenge the dissolution of 1906 by supporting the Conservatives.[262] Numerous tactical considerations and extraneous political questions complicated the machinations of the political parties with respect to the financial reform in 1909,[263] and the repercussions of the *Daily Telegraph* affair were fundamental in transforming the reform into a judgement on Bülow's Chancellorship.

Bülow introduced the Reich financial reform in the Reichstag on 19 November 1908 with a short speech which was received rather coolly,[264] and the first reading altogether produced a very negative impression.[265] The left liberals vociferously opposed the indirect taxation, for example on drink and tobacco, which accounted for approximately four-fifths of the 475 million Marks which the reform was to generate. But the chief problem remained Conservative intransigence over the inheritance tax, which was now extended to include children and spouses and rendered undivided estates liable for taxation instead of individual legacies.[266] The collaboration of the liberals in the financial reform was scarcely conceivable without some form of direct taxation, but the National Liberals also strongly opposed the inheritance tax, which they feared would adversely affect their popularity among the electorate.[267] The liberals' preferred wealth tax was even more unacceptable to the Conservatives and, since it constituted a greater invasion of the federal states' sovereign rights, would never have secured approval in the Bundesrat.[268] Thus the inheritance tax seemed crucial and the whole reform centred around the question whether the right would support government policy when their economic interests were threatened. National Liberal hostility to the inheritance tax may well have encouraged Conservative opposition, but even Holstein told Bülow that his support of the reform contradicted his claim to be a Conservative and that he was 'putting the axe to the roots of the estates of the landed gentry and the peasantry' with the inheritance tax.[269]

Bülow's efforts to ensure the success of the financial reform undoubtedly suffered from his diminished popularity and authority in the wake of the *Daily Telegraph* affair and the vulnerability of his personal position, which encouraged doubts about the durability of the Bloc. Nevertheless, there was a general feeling that the government failed to exploit all the cards at its disposal in 1909, for, although the parties deliberately pitched their demands high so as not to prejudice their position if the Bloc collapsed, none of them had any real interest in a return to the system of fluctuating majorities and Centre hegemony, and no Bloc party wished to incur the odium for destroying the coalition.[270] Bülow claimed in January 1909 that 'The further development of the domestic situation depends primarily on the attitude of the Conservatives' and that the Reich financial reform was probably the most difficult problem 'next to squaring the circle'.[271] But even he recognised that though the Conservatives were the least committed to the *Blockpolitik* they stood to lose much in the long run if the Bloc collapsed.

Yet Bülow's attempt to bring the financial reform to a satisfactory conclusion during the last months of his Chancellorship was marred by errors of judgement which confirmed the impression of his isolation within the executive and his reliance on limited advice. His untimely Landtag speech on 19 January (the first part of which concerned the financial reform) was motivated by a desire to regain Conservative sympathy, but the Chancellor undoubtedly misjudged the likely impact of the speech because be had deliberately left the negotiations with the political parties to Bethmann Hollweg and then conferred only with the Reich Chancellery.[272] Lerchenfeld reported that the appeal to the Conservatives had come too early, and opposition to both the Chancellor and the inheritance tax was only nourished by Bülow's performance.[273] Bülow continued to rely heavily on Hammann's press propaganda to create a general climate favourable to the reform, though this support was lost in April 1909 when Hammann went on leave because of legal proceedings against him.[274] Above all, Bülow depended on Loebell, whose personal loyalty to the Chancellor cannot be faulted but who maintained close links with Valentini, who suspected Bülow's activities.[275] Loebell may not have fully appreciated the Chancellor's predicament in 1909 and, since he was not worried about alienating the Progressives if sufficient support was forthcoming among the Conservatives, Centre and National Liberals, he can at best be described as more 'flexible' than Bülow about the possible parliamentary majorities which could conclude the reform.[276]

Bülow seemed unable to stand firm in the face of party pressure in 1909. Despite his apparent commitment to the Bloc and his famous skill in wheeling and dealing, there were persistent fears that he would waver and give in to left or right in the coalition, and his ambiguous statements tended to heighten the general political uncertainty.[277] Bülow assured the federal states that he would not agree to a wealth tax, but he adopted a more positive attitude when discussing the issue with Bassermann and gave qualified support to a Reichspartei compromise proposal on a wealth tax (which was abandoned in March 1909).[278] In this way Bülow further encouraged party intransigence and aroused enormous suspicion about his possible intentions. Even Hammann told the Chancellor in March 1909 that the press agitation for the reform, which had successfully ensured that all the political parties were convinced of its national importance, had come to a standstill because of a fundamental lack of clarity over the government's aims. If the agitation were to be renewed in grand style, the press had 'to be clear about the government position on the individual questions which are alone still of interest', namely whether the government was determined to keep to the inheritance tax or whether it had in mind some other form of property tax. Even if there were still doubts about the inheritance tax because of the confused party situation (or, he might have added, because of Bülow's tendency to lead from behind), Hammann insisted that they must 'above all try to stifle the growing impression that the government authorities, in attempting to solve the problem of the property tax, have surrendered the leadership to the individual states and to the party leaders'.[279]

In his memoirs Bülow suggests that, given Conservative opposition to the inheritance tax (and Prussian suffrage reform) and the attitude of the Centre, the Bloc could only have been upheld if the Crown had supported him firmly.[280] The Chancellor's position was apparently strengthened after his reconciliation with the Kaiser on 11 March, and the prospects for a successful conclusion of the financial reform with the Bloc improved. The Chancellor's freedom of manoeuvre was increased once it appeared that he might survive in office even if the Bloc collapsed,[281] and Bethmann became confident that the inheritance tax would be passed in one form or another.[282] Bülow's speeches during the budget debate at the end of March were generally regarded as politically effective even though the domestic situation was not greatly clarified,[283] and Lerchenfeld reported that Bülow was once again firmly in the saddle.[284] After Kaiser and Chancellor had departed for their Easter vacation, Berckheim went so far as to record that 'Prince Bülow's lucky star shines more brightly than it has for years: even the greatest pessimists are also beginning to believe in the possibility of a success for him in the financial reform question'.[285]

Nevertheless the reconciliation could not paper over the cracks in the Bloc for long, and by March 1909 the new Conservative–Centre majority was in fact crystallising in the finance committee. After the Centre made a tactical decision to support the right, the Conservatives announced on 24 March that they would conclude the reform with whichever party best served their interests.[286] In effect this anouncement signified the termination of the *Blockpolitik*, though the liberals were still to hope for an understanding for a few more weeks. Bülow maintained his pressure on the Conservative Party and at the end of April he openly told Conservative leaders that he would not conclude the financial reform without them or against the liberals. In an effort to encourage greater party responsibility, he asked them to consider what alternative strategy they preferred, on what parties they hoped to rely and who they would like to see leading the government in order to achieve their aims.[287] This apparent submission to parliamentary practices cannot have endeared him to the Conservatives, and his opponents were unlikely to be much influenced by his threat to resign.[288] Moreover, the Chancellor's assertion that he would not dissolve the Reichstag against the Conservative Party was a tactical error. Henceforward the Conservatives had even less inclination or reason to support the controversial inheritance tax.[289]

During the last weeks of negotiations on the financial reform it became clear that the Bloc was cracking at all its joints,[290] and the political situation was so complex that Varnbüler gave up trying to follow all the daily fluctuations for his political reports. Bethmann admitted that the prospects for the reform were bleak, and with the Conservatives and liberals mutually suspicious, government reassurances to one side inevitably provoked panic on the other.[291] The Conservatives and Centre, together with a few smaller groups, secured a majority against the inheritance tax in the finance committee and, to the government's dismay, the liberals and SPD walked out of the committee on 27 May, finally shattering even the semblance of Bloc unity and further relaxing the pressure on the Conservatives to agree to the inheritance tax at the final count.[292] There remained some doubts as to whether Bülow and the government would work with the new majority, but Bülow exuded weariness and reiterated his commitment to the liberals.[293] Szögyényi reported that the Chancellor continued to negotiate with party leaders and believed that he would still succeed in winning over at least part of the Conservative Party for the inheritance tax. But 'one of the most influential members of the government' (presumably Bethmann Hollweg) recognised that the reform would have to be concluded with the Centre.[294]

Although there is a fundamental lack of clarity about Bülow's intentions in the last weeks of his Chancellorship, and the question arises whether he wanted to resign or not in the summer of 1909. Bülow made an uncharacteristic series of tactical errors in the negotiations over the Reich financial reform, and it was later recognised that at times he had operated unskilfully.[295] Varnbüler lamented in May 1909 that the Chancellor simply did not act, making as if to intervene decisively and then failing to do so, constantly unravelling the threads of the negotiations only to let them become entangled again.[296] Bülow certainly missed several opportunities to break the parties' resistance to aspects of the reform,[297] and it is also curious that, even after the reconciliation with the Kaiser, he never sought any kind of imperial admonition to the Conservatives to bring them into line. It has been argued that in the wake of the *Daily Telegraph* affair Wilhelm II had not the necessary prestige to intervene effectively[298] and he probably had no great inclination to rescue a treacherous Chancellor.[299] But he was certainly unimpressed by Conservative intransigence and later inveighed against

Junker defiance. If all other means failed, Valentini told Loebell in May 1909, the Kaiser was not at all averse to the idea of a dissolution to put an end to Conservative opposition.[300]

Bülow may have gambled on the Kaiser's reluctance to submit to the will of a parliamentary majority when he weighed the alternatives open to him in the spring of 1909. Given that he had lost the Kaiser's confidence, his Conservative and Centre opponents undoubtedly believed that the failure of the Reich financial reform was the best way to oust him.[301] But it can be argued that Bülow was by no means certain that the failure of the reform would mean his resignation. Contemporaries, at least, did not credit him with the necessary resolve and integrity to resign in the event of the financial reform's defeat in the Reichstag.[302] In the wake of the reconciliation with the Kaiser there is evidence to suggest that he considered sacrificing Sydow and postponing the reform further over the summer, a prospect which was most unwelcome to the federal states, among whom Bülow's position was said to be insecure.[303] Furthermore, although in his memoirs Bülow claims that he advised the Kaiser in Wiesbaden on 18 May not to undertake a Reichstag dissolution over the financial reform, he recognised that Wilhelm II was equally reluctant to dismiss a Chancellor on account of a parliamentary defeat,[304] and Weizsäcker heard in July 1909 that Bülow had seriously considered a dissolution for a long time.[305] Hertling was told by the Silesian Centre deputy, Praschma (who in turn had been given the information by 'a well-known South German Prince' – probably Fürstenberg – who had been with Wilhelm II) that at Wiesbaden Bülow had in fact warned Wilhelm not to dismiss him if the reform failed as this would look like a capitulation to the Conservative–clerical majority. Instead the Chancellor had *recommended* a dissolution of the Reichstag, a proposal that the Kaiser had laughingly compared to Bülow's attempt in November to impose a parliamentary regime upon him.[306] It is scarcely conceivable that Bülow contemplated almost Bismarckian tactics in 1909 and deliberately tried to sabotage the financial reform in order to create such a confused and dangerous situation that his dismissal would be impossible.[307] Nevertheless the rumours and suspicions about Bülow's intentions clouded his activities during the final weeks so that even after his trip to Kiel to see the Kaiser in June 1909 it was reported that Bülow's entourage had believed that the Chancellor merely wanted to strengthen his position and gain the Kaiser's support before making a new attempt to convert the Conservatives.[308]

The simplest explanation of Bülow's behaviour in 1909 is undoubtedly that he was weary of office and slowly losing his grip on the conduct of affairs. Indifference rather than ambition determined his attitude to the fate of the financial reform. If the Bloc passed the reform, he hoped for a 'good exit'; if the coalition collapsed, his refusal to continue as Chancellor with a

10 Bülow's last speech in the Reichstag on 16 June 1909

different parliamentary majority could serve as a declaration of principle and earn him public respect as a man of conviction. Lerchenfeld believed Bülow had long wanted to resign by June 1909,[309] but, despite everything, Bülow himself only seems to have become finally reconciled to this course after the Wiesbaden audience in May when the Kaiser blocked the other options. Wilhelm himself later maintained that Bülow had favoured the adjournment of the reform, but the monarch insisted on its immediate conclusion.[310] What is clear is that Bülow gradually ran out of options in the spring of 1909, and his attitude subsequent to his resignation indicates that his final decision was not wholly voluntary.

From late May Bülow was preoccupied with what he recognised would be his 'swan song', a speech delivered on 16 June and one which has been seen as one of his best.[311] In his last Reichstag performance Bülow chastised the political parties for their political irresponsibility and individual failings, and he confirmed his intention to resign if the inheritance tax were rejected. Yet the speech was devoid of real, practical value when it came to boosting the chances of a successful reform. It was almost provocative to the Centre and too docile to have an effect on the Conservatives.[312] Indeed, Bülow had softened certain passages in the original draft in which his bitterness against the political parties was given fuller expression, and his primary preoccupation was with his personal reputation rather than the outcome of the reform. With an almost detached fatalism, Bülow had written to Loebell: 'I believe I should not give the impression of being irritated, annoyed or even "piqued". Even less should I appear depressed or sorry for myself! At this of all times I must appear superior, distinguished and self-assured, as a statesman.'[313]

On 24 June the inheritance tax was rejected on its second reading by a majority of Conservatives, Centre and Poles against the votes of the Reichspartei, liberals and SPD.[314] Even before the second reading the Bavarian members of the Centre Party had indicated to the Chancellor that they would vote for the inheritance tax at the third reading if Bülow gave them a kindly word, but Bülow had deemed this beneath his dignity and displayed no desire to work again with a majority which included the Centre.[315] The Centre had thus voted en bloc against the inheritance tax and, though Bülow doubtless could have achieved a majority for the inheritance tax in 1909 (he needed only five votes), it would not have been a Bloc majority. Bülow preferred to sacrifice the reform. On 25 June he left for Kiel to request his resignation from the Kaiser.[316] But even now the circumstances of his departure from office were to be completely different from what he had envisaged.

Bülow's fall

When Bülow went to Kiel in June 1909 he must have realised that his resignation at such a time was politically impossible. The outcome of the financial reform was still in doubt and the domestic situation remained highly confused. A change of Chancellor would have entailed the postponement of the reform and presented Bülow's successor with a very difficult task.[317] Bülow was advised from at least one quarter (the Saxon Minister, Rüger) to remain in office, delay the reform until the autumn and then if necessary dissolve the Reichstag;[318] and once there was no danger that this course would be adopted, Bülow received assurances also from Karlsruhe and Stuttgart that they would have supported a dissolution if it had been contemplated though the 'psychological moment' had now passed.[319] Moreover, the Kaiser's initial reaction to the rejection of the inheritance tax was that the vote was a farce; if necessary he would impose the tax law by force.[320] Even though it was later stressed that the final events in June 1909 had run a course desired by the Chancellor, the uncertainty surrounding Bülow's intentions thus prevails to the last. While Lerchenfeld concluded that Bülow had long intended to resign and the rejection of the inheritance tax was little more than an excuse,[321] Szögyényi maintained that when Bülow first entered into a correspondence with Wilhelm on the parliamentary situation, he had formed no such resolve. But the correspondence quickly led to the trip to Kiel. 'Whether then Prince Bülow immediately drew conclusions from the mood of the Kaiser, [or] whether he himself had come to the conviction that his resignation would have to be definite, will probably never be possible to establish.'[322]

The Kaiser accepted Bülow's resignation in principle at their audience on 26 June, but to avoid the impression that monarch, government and Bundesrat had capitulated to the will of the Reichstag, he insisted that Bülow remain in office until the reform was finally settled.[323] On the Chancellor's return to Berlin, it was announced in the *Norddeutsche Allgemeine Zeitung* of 27 June that Bülow's resignation was imminent, pending the conclusion of the Reich finance reform (a far more explicit statement than had originally been envisaged by the Prussian Ministers),[324] and on 29 June, at a confidential meeting on the Reich financial reform with members of the executive and representatives from the federal states, Bülow explained that there were situations where a Minister was no longer in a position to continue conducting affairs, even though he was far from recognising the principle that the Chancellor's position depended on parliamentary decisions.[325]

From 26 June Bülow virtually withdrew from any active involvement in government affairs though he was not to resign officially as Chancellor until 14 July. Bethmann Hollweg conducted the concluding negotiations with the Conservative–Centre majority on the financial reform[326] and, with the

prospects for a satisfactory settlement considered good at the end of June, the
new taxes were voted speedily in the Reichstag and a compromise was
reached with the Bundesrat which ensured that the financial reform was
passed on the third reading on 10 July.[327] Bülow refused to countersign the
law and left this to his successor, a gesture which was later criticised by
Sydow but which was consistent with his argument that he would only
conclude a reform with the Bloc and with the inheritance tax.[328]

Even though Bülow remained in office for a few short weeks after 26 June,
his position was thus a peculiar one and it is scarcely possible that he had
conceived of this rather inglorious 'interregnum'.[329] Szögyényi reported that
the Chancellor's situation seemed like 'a weak last scene in a massively staged
final act'.[330] Bülow continued to conduct affairs officially while openly
disclaiming all responsibility for them,[331] but all his efforts to ensure that his
departure would be regretted and lamented met with scant success. 'Prince
Bülow is said to be very discouraged and disgusted', Szögyényi reported on
6 July, but

nevertheless he allows public opinion to be saturated with semi-official communiqués
which are supposed to secure for him a good departure. At the same time he lets
it be emphasised again and again that his relations with the Kaiser are the very best
and that the decision to resign from his office is solely attributable to his initiative.[332]

The following day the ambassador himself saw the Chancellor, who justified
his decision to resign but again complained about the perfidy of the parties.
In Kiel the Kaiser had only accepted his resignation after long discussions and
'with a heavy heart', Bülow emphasised, and he assured Szögyényi that all
the stories circulating that Wilhelm had seized the opportunity to remove
him with alacrity were completely erroneous.[333]

Bülow's last audiences and meetings were all characterised by a certain
sentimentality, and he was acutely sensitive to the historical finality of his
official actions. On 13 July he presided over his last State Ministry meeting,
at which Bethmann Hollweg assured him that his political effectiveness
would not prove a transitory phenomenon and that history and public
opinion too would recognise the full impact of his work.[334] It was recorded
in the protocol that Bethmann had hoped 'that the awareness of loyal services
which he rendered to HM and the Fatherland . . . would lead him to forget
all the bitterness connected with his departure'.[335] This open admission of
Bülow's disillusionment in 1909 at least reflects his disappointment with the
nature of his fall, but also suggests his fundamental disbelief that the Kaiser
had ultimately let him go.

Bülow had one brief, final audience with the Kaiser on 14 July which was
a mere formality, and the Kaiser and Kaiserin dined with the Bülows on 15
July as a final gesture to the departing Prince.[336] On 18 July Bülow left for

Norderney and all the members of the Prussian State Ministry and Reich executive assembled at the Berlin station to see the couple off.[337] The ministerial changes had been formalised on 14 July with Delbrück becoming State Secretary of Interior, Sydow becoming Prussian Minister of Trade, and Wermuth, the former Under State Secretary in the Reich Office of Interior, assuming responsibility for the Treasury.[338] The new Chancellor, Bethmann Hollweg, had been supported by Bülow and accepted the office only after a certain hesitation and reluctance.[339] Other Chancellor candidates had been considered and rejected (Wedel, Goltz, Schorlemer, Rheinbaben, Botho Eulenburg, Tirpitz and Monts were all candidates of varying suitability),[340] but Bülow had intended to recommend Bethmann even before the audience in Kiel.[341]

Bülow's final audience with Wilhelm II on 14 July was officially described as exceptionally friendly,[342] but on the same day Wilhelm received the ambassadors of Bavaria, Saxony and Württemberg and for three-quarters of an hour delivered 'annihilating criticism' (Lerchenfeld) of Bülow's character. Unhappily, Bülow learnt of Wilhelm's remarks through his friend, Friedrich Vitzthum, and along with the attacks of the conservative press in the summer of 1909, the episode served to prolong the acrimony in the wake of his departure.[343] In his political report on the audience, Lerchenfeld softened the harsher statements and deliberately recorded only the broad outlines of the Kaiser's exposition. Varnbüler recognised no such constraints and in an extensive private letter to Weizsäcker leant full colour to the extraordinary reception.[344]

The Kaiser's exposition is interesting because it provides further evidence of Wilhelm II's acute sense of Bülow's betrayal in November 1908 and his consequent complete disillusionment with the friendship he had enjoyed with the Chancellor since before 1900. In discussing the parliamentary situation in the wake of the financial reform, Wilhelm displayed his great reluctance to accept a reform dictated by the Conservative–clerical majority, but he rejected all the other options (including the postponement of the reform recommended by the Chancellor at Wiesbaden) and preferred what he recognised was a humiliating outcome to any course which would have enabled the retention of the Chancellor. Wilhelm betrayed no hint of the suspicion of Bülow's *Blockpolitik* which Valentini had alleged to the Chancellor in June 1909;[345] indeed, he recognised that after the government had repeatedly declared the proposals of the new 'Blue-Black Bloc' unacceptable, its acquiescence in the reform constituted not only a portentous capitulation to the Reichstag majority but also the abandonment of the political direction embarked on in December 1906, which the majority of the German people had greeted with enthusiasm. He acknowledged that three-quarters of the Centre Party had recognised the utility of the inheritance tax but had only been interested in Bülow's fall; and he chastised the Conservatives, who had tried to represent their behaviour as an attempt to liberate the monarch from an unfaithful Chancellor. The Conservatives, Wilhelm declared, had adopted an unprecedented stance against the Kaiser and King, and he did not need their help to protect the privileges of the Crown and his right to appoint and dismiss Ministers.

The Kaiser thus bowed to the dictates of the new parliamentary constellation, but his willingness to do so stemmed essentially from his experiences in November 1908. The Kaiser's complaints about Bülow's behaviour are too familiar to bear further repetition, but his continued emotion is not difficult to discern, and the very confidentiality of his former relations with the Chancellor determined the violence of his response.

Betrayed and surrendered by his own Chancellor, slandered by the Reichstag, abandoned by the Bundesrat, disgraced before his people and the whole world – in his imperial role, not in a position like any other private man could have done, to justify himself publicly by clarifying the facts – perhaps also in too weak a frame of mind because of the shattering impact of the death of his friend Hülsen – he submitted, confident that truth and right would prevail on their own – and thus signed that declaration which was submitted to him on his return from Donaueschingen.

Since then he still had not really understood all that had happened or why Bülow had betrayed him. He had 'often thought everything was only a bad dream, not known whether he himself or Bülow was crazy'.[346] He had to acknowledge the enormous cleverness and talents of the Prince who, like no one else, had a command over affairs and knew and could judge people of importance. 'It was never so easy to work with anyone as with Prince Bülow. He knew every thought of the Kaiser.' But the character of the Prince had not matched his talents, Wilhelm declared. Among other things Bülow had been too sensitive to attacks in the press, had 'surrounded himself much too much with journalists' and had been too intimate with them.[347]

The Kaiser's bitterness over the attacks on his 'personal rule' in November 1908 was also nourished by his belief that he had been an impeccable constitutional monarch since 1900. In general, Wilhelm prefaced his remarks,

His personal and official relations with Prince Bülow since his assumption of office were so intimate and confidential that for this reason alone surprise occurrences [*Überraschungen*], an autocratic regime which circumnavigated the Reich Chancellor, were out of the question. Every day he had conferred with the Prince for hours . . . before every political trip had talked through all the eventualities with him, during that [trip] been in continuous contact with him by letter and telegraph.

But, the Kaiser suggested, Bülow himself had lost control in the end. The Chancellor had been too intimate with Holstein, who had wanted to embroil Germany in a war with France, and his aunt, the Grand Duchess of Baden, had warned him that Holstein had been the *spiritus rector* of the whole campaign in November. Holstein, Wilhelm asserted, had been the tool of Maximilian Harden, and the police had since confirmed that the handling of the *Daily Telegraph* affair had been discussed and decided upon in the salon of Holstein's friend, Frau von Lebbin. 'In reality', the Kaiser declared blackly, 'for two years neither the Kaiser nor the Chancellor had ruled Germany, but that sinister consortium.' He had just made all these revelations to the new Chancellor, who had been flabbergasted. If they were true, Bethmann had declared, then Bülow had 'led the entire State Ministry . . . astray'.

Oscillating between this appraisal of Bülow's impotence and his conviction of his treachery, the Kaiser maintained that now the time had come to part from the Prince.

Such an imaginative [*geistreich*], well-educated, pleasing *causeur* and *charmeur*, such a compelling speaker and quick-witted debater, such a smooth and skilled diplomat, versed in all the personalities, cancans and intrigues of all the cabinets and courts in the world, he would doubtless never again have as a Chancellor – but also he hoped never again such an – unreliable – HM used a much sharper expression – character.

Now they had to face the future, not dwell on the past. The authority of the *Reichsleitung* and the federal governments would have to be restored and, after such a success, the Reichstag would inevitably try to encroach further on the prerogatives of the Bundesrat. The boundary would have to be more sharply delineated, perhaps, Wilhelm hinted, by increasing the power or use of the imperial veto. But there were to be no changes overnight, passions would have to be allowed to cool and there were to be no dangerous experiments. The Bloc had collapsed, but the idea of gathering the state-supporting 'middle' parties in the face of the growth of the SPD and Centre hegemony would still be upheld. The Conservative–Centre coalition had to realise that it could not impress its reactionary stamp on the new government. Sydow's inclusion in particular in the Prussian government as Minister of Trade was intended to show that the parliamentary system did not operate in Germany and that he, Wilhelm, would not have his Ministers forced on him by the Reichstag majority.[348]

With these depressing indicators of the future, the ambassadors were dismissed. Bülow's long Chancellorship was over, but already it seemed a mere interlude. The man who had hoped to stay in power for twenty years and to match Bismarck's achievements was pronounced 'finished' by the Kaiser, having forfeited the confidence of the monarch, 'all his colleagues and recently . . . *all* the important elements of public life in Germany'.[349] Bülow would soon seek refuge from painful memories in Rome, a city of antiquity which he believed would provide an environment conducive to philosophical reflection and the study of history.[350] But, as one observer remarked gloomily in July 1909, 'a time will come when one will recognise the fateful effect of this man'.[351]

Conclusion

Bernhard von Bülow was born into a privileged and aristocratic North German family with a long tradition of political service to the state. He did not have to prove his credentials as a leader by rising through a political party, standing for election and excelling in the cut and thrust of political debate. Bülow faced no such hurdles, being groomed for a high government position from childhood, and he never questioned his future except when he briefly flirted with the idea of devoting his energies to service in that other quintessentially Prussian institution, the Army. Within the framework of the German Diplomatic Service, which was largely characterised by its rigid recruitment methods, narrow social composition and élitist tendencies, Bülow was widely regarded as superior to most of his contemporaries in intelligence, skill and judgement. Nevertheless, he further dispensed with the more official channels through which he might have eventually expected promotion and instead resorted to conspiratorial (though scarcely less traditional) methods in order to fulfil his ambitions. His meteoric rise in the 1890s – to the ambassadorship in Rome, the State Secretaryship and, finally, the Chancellorship – was primarily attributable to the influence of the Kaiser's favourite, Philipp Eulenburg, whose favour Bülow in turn courted. Bülow thus attained the Chancellorship in 1900 through the back door, and the story of his early successes is simultaneously the story of the progressive emasculation of the 'responsible government'.

Bülow acceded to the Chancellorship in 1900 with a clearer vision of what he hoped to achieve than how he hoped to achieve it. In his own words he desired to preserve the '*status quo*' in Germany, to ensure the stability and durability of the Bismarckian Empire centred on Prussia, which incorporated the traditional values and privileges of the Prussian King, Prussian Army and the landowning Junker class. In marked contrast to other elements in the top echelons of the government and military hierarchies, who became convinced in the 1890s that the government system could not function under the new Kaiser, Wilhelm II, without substantial modification, Bülow and Philipp Eulenburg were confident that their programme for 'personal rule in the good sense' would serve as the remedy for Germany's ills. Bülow intended to neutralise the worst features of Wilhelm II's rule as displayed in the 1890s, restrain the monarch from making precipitate moves and avoid the kind of confrontation between Crown and 'responsible government' and parliament that might have hastened the disintegration of the Reich. To some extent Bülow was also aware of the fragility of the government's support if the policy-makers in Berlin allowed themselves to be guided exclusively by the narrow sectional interests of one particular class. He hoped to broaden the basis of Reich domestic politics, strengthen national unity and popularise the monarchy by cultivating the friendly cooperation of the federal states, consolidating the centre ground and appealing to German nationalism.

Bülow was ambitious for the highest office and clearly desired personal and political success. Yet there is scant evidence that his hunger for power was motivated by any deep moral or political imperatives. Notwithstanding the sweeping historical surveys, the literary allusions and his general insistence on the need for 'integrative' measures, Bülow's political correspondence before 1900 reveals a remarkable paucity of ideas, and the substance of 'personal rule – in the good sense' remained significantly ill defined. Bülow began his Chancellorship with few concrete political proposals and nothing that resembled a practical programme. In so far as he looked to Bismarck's achievements as a model, he was impressed as much by public perceptions of Bismarck's contribution to German greatness as by the political reality of his legacy, and he was critical of aspects of Bismarck's foreign and domestic policy. Dismissing the promises and pledges made by new governments in parliamentary countries, he declared his intention to win confidence gradually through his actual conduct of affairs.[1] But the new Chancellor's diagnosis of the Reich's problems was always more sophisticated than his cure.

The stumbling-block of successive Chancellors before 1900 was Wilhelm II, and Bülow's major success, which distinguished him from his predecessors and was appreciated by everyone in Court, government and political circles, was his ability to establish and maintain a close relationship with the Kaiser. As Monts wrote in 1901, Bülow was 'the best man we have, and the only one who to a certain extent understands how to manipulate HM'.[2] Bülow's early political career had already provided ample evidence of his manifest ability to 'deal with people', and even as State Secretary of the Foreign Office he consciously regarded the cultivation of his relationship with the monarch as his most important task, the 'centre of gravity' of his activities. He demonstrated a keen appreciation of Wilhelm's personality and he exploited all his social skills and psychological insights to win the monarch's friendship and trust. Well versed in the art of pleasing, appreciating how appearances could often be more important than reality and ready to assume a studied nonchalance when it served his political purposes, Bülow proved adept at playing the role of courtier and his mentality and approach, indeed his position within the Wilhelmine government system, cannot be understood without reference to the existence of the Kaiser and his Court. Bülow was not a party man and he should not be exclusively judged as if he were a contemporary Prime Minister or politician. His survival in office as Wilhelm II's longest-serving Chancellor was attributable to qualities, skills and behaviour not primarily explicable in political terms.

As Chancellor, Bülow intentionally based his entire system of government on harmonious relations between Kaiser and Chancellor – indeed, this proved to be the essence of 'personal rule – in the good sense' and the single, most important factor underlying the new stability after 1900. Wilhelm's confidence was the source of the Chancellor's strength, authority and security within the executive, and allowed him considerable freedom of manoeuvre in the first half of his Chancellorship. The Kaiser jealously guarded his royal prerogatives, for example in military and personnel issues, and he continued to take a lively, though not constant, interest in certain aspects of policy. But Bülow successfully ensured that the monarch acted with relative restraint and was receptive to his advice. Wilhelm II displayed a remarkable trust in Bülow's judgement and repeatedly left to him the conduct of affairs. With only minor lapses he acted constitutionally from 1900 and was not, in any strict sense of the term, 'his own Chancellor' as he had been in the late 1890s. Even after 1906, when his confidence in Bülow was severely shaken, Wilhelm II continued to find him an extremely convenient Chancellor. Bülow shielded the monarch from the more onerous tasks of government and was ostensibly pliant and affable. Captivated also by his chief Minister's skill as a conversationalist, which far exceeded anything that the majority of his personal entourage could offer, it was only with reluctance, when he really had no alternative but to accept the fact of Bülow's perfidy, that Wilhelm abandoned the belief that Bülow operated according to his (the Kaiser's) precepts and served his interests.

Bülow's approach to his relationship with the Kaiser was essentially manipulative, and in the short term it brought the Chancellor many advantages. Nevertheless, his success in restraining the Kaiser, his relative freedom of manoeuvre and the new confidence which their harmonious relationship engendered in the system in the early years were only achieved at a terrible cost. Imperial Germany was not a pre-industrial society under royal monopoly rule and, while the Chancellor may not have been blind to the dangers inherent in staking his position on one man or oblivious to the challenges posed by the growth of new élites and rival power centres, his muddled attempt to play the role of King's Minister involved a fundamental disregard for and denigration of the other important institutions in Wilhelmine political life. Moreover, the Kaiser did not rule personally on a day-to-day basis between 1900 and 1909, but he still presided over a 'personal regime' and enjoyed immense political and military privileges. After the power struggles of the 1890s Bülow made no attempt to redress the balance which had swung in the monarch's favour. Indeed, rather than try to claw back some of the power the Chancellor had lost, Bülow chose to base his personal position on the Kaiser's authority and confidence, and he constructed his system on an identity of interest between Kaiser and Chancellor. Bülow was acutely sensitive to the fact that Wilhelm II alone had the power to dismiss him – hence his determination to sustain their friendship, his obsequious and ingratiating approach and predisposition to submit to the monarch in a direct confrontation. All Bülow's energies were harnessed to the overriding need to avoid a conflict with the Kaiser. In 1906, when he was forced by his colleagues and by political considerations to stand firm over the Podbielski crisis, this course ran counter to the Chancellor's personal inclinations and to the kind of relationship with the monarch he had aimed to achieve.

Again, in 1908, the Chancellor's ineptitude and impotence were glaringly apparent when circumstances forced him to try to resolve a crisis in which the identity of interest between Kaiser and Chancellor had broken down. Bülow ultimately was not merely content to play the role of courtier but actually reduced the position of the Chancellor to that of a courtier, imprisoned within a web of fawning praise and Byzantine servility. As Zedlitz maintained in 1908, the explanation for his abrupt break with the Centre and the Bloc policy with the liberals (as well as for his subsequent alienation of the liberals by his rejection of universal suffrage in the Prussian Lower House and his sharp action against the Poles with the Expropriation Law) can only be found in 'his personal relationship with the Kaiser'.[3] Indeed his position with the Kaiser eventually 'weighed him down like lead'.[4] 'Do not forget, Your Excellency, that you are not Court Chancellor but Reich Chancellor [*nicht Hof- sondern Reichskanzler*]', Bethmann Hollweg implored Bülow before his decisive audience with the Kaiser on the *Daily Telegraph* affair.[5] But Bülow had invested so much in his relationship with the Kaiser that his short-term manipulation and 'management' of Wilhelm counted for little in a real crisis. So long as he clung desperately to office, Bülow remained (as he once described himself) the little lucky charm on the Kaiser's watchchain.[6] When he incurred the Kaiser's lasting enmity, his system was moribund. He had no further political reserves on which he could draw.

For what exactly did Bülow achieve, given that he enjoyed the Kaiser's confidence for so much of his Chancellorship? To what extent did he prove able or willing to exploit (or risk) the security of his position to tackle Germany's serious political problems which he was always so ready to enumerate? For political reasons, but above all for personal ones, Bülow thwarted the evolution of a more collective form of government after 1900 and, especially before 1906, when his position with the Kaiser was unassailable, he made no attempt to create the kind of consensus within the highest echelons of the government that might have facilitated reform. On the contrary, Bülow's autocratic methods, his dismissive attitude to ministerial work, his willingness to rely exclusively on the Kaiser's confidence, his preference for personal advisers, above all his intoxication with the trappings of power, and with his personal position and reputation, ensured that a genuine 'Bülow Ministry' never emerged between 1900 and 1905 and that consequently there was no possibility of collective government thinking; instead, the Chancellor became progressively more aloof from his colleagues and ultimately forfeited their respect. Too jealous of Wilhelm II's favour and mindful of potential threats to his position, Bülow excluded the Ministers from his deliberations and encouraged them to become submissive bureaucrats, most of whom he could ignore with impunity. As Tirpitz suggested in 1909, the majority of the Ministers and State Secretaries never knew the Chancellor's thoughts, and none had any clear conceptions of the aims he was working towards.[7] The Chancellor's isolation and inaccessibility encouraged disillusionment within the executive, and Ministers became imbued with a helpless fatalism in the face of events they believed they could not influence.

Bülow's style of leadership was divisive and encouraged fragmentation within the executive. His concentration on the 'broad sweep of politics' in practice meant that his role became progressively more vacuous, and the historian must ultimately sympathise with Tschirschky, who wondered what the Chancellor did all day. While Bülow devoted his energies to his relationship with the Kaiser, parliamentary tactics and public relations, adopting the functions of a political manager rather than a leading statesman who was capable of making the political choices, serious government work during his Chancellorship was delivered by his subordinates and by the bureaucracy;[8] and since he placed few programmatic difficulties in the way of the Ministers and State Secretaries, each was left to regulate the affairs of his department much as he wished. Even during the Bloc period Bülow was able to work with conservative Prussian Ministers who for the most part were left to their own devices. Executive unity proved to be a chimera when the Chancellor always wanted to shine and take the credit at the expense of his colleagues. While Bülow was supported by the Crown, he had little difficulty in asserting his authority, although his control was never all-pervasive. Once he forfeited the Kaiser's confidence, the centrifugal tendencies, immanent in the system, were exacerbated and allowed to develop unchecked. During his last months in office, Bülow conveyed the impression of an increasingly lonely man, one who expected little sympathy from his colleagues and only turned to them sporadically and reluctantly for support. When he lost the Kaiser's trust, he simultaneously lost his self-confidence and vitality, becoming increasingly weary of his duties and politically ineffectual.

Bülow's relations with the federal states followed a similar pattern, for, having professed an intention to strengthen the bonds between the Reich administration and the federal governments, he effectively excluded the Bundesrat from its legitimate role in decision-making, as in the tariff compromise, and provoked the remarkable confrontation over the Jesuit Law in 1903–4. His secretive methods conspired against a greater degree of participation in Berlin affairs on the part of the federal states and, especially with respect to foreign policy (when the existence of the Bundesrat Committee on Foreign Affairs was consistently ignored and the most fatuous excuses were provided for the failure to convene it), the federal governments repeatedly complained that they knew less about government policy than the Reichstag.[9] Such treatment by the Chancellor was scarcely conducive to promote national unity in the way that Bülow had always believed necessary, and the Bundesrat if anything became even less influential during Bülow's Chancellorship, ultimately having to accept a humiliating role in the conclusion of the Reich financial reform. If the spectre of particularism became weaker after 1900, this was despite the policies pursued in Berlin rather than a consequence of them. Bülow himself merely paid lip-service to the federal idea.

Given the importance Bülow attached to his relations with the Kaiser and the Reichstag, it was in the executive's dealings with the legislature that one might have expected the most 'movement' during Bülow's Chancellorship. Bülow professed a desire to broaden the basis of imperial domestic politics by harnessing the Centre Party and moderate liberals behind government policy, and he was without doubt unfortunate, coming to power at a time when traditional party alignments were in a state of flux, when new social pressures were necessitating new political responses and German political life was becoming increasingly polarised. But Bülow had no coherent strategy behind which the forces of moderation could rally, and during his Chancellorship the time-honoured concept of *Sammlungspolitik* was in practice little more than a reaffirmation of the old adage that the government had to seek majorities wherever it could find them.

Bülow began his Chancellorship with essentially negative aspirations – the avoidance of confrontations with the parliaments, the avoidance of extremes in domestic policy, a moratorium on contentious legislation. He made little attempt to direct German domestic policy and, in so far as he considered domestic issues, he assessed them purely in terms of the party constellation in the Reich and Prussia and their legislative feasibility. The important domestic issues of Bülow's Chancellorship were confronted because they had to be (the financial reforms) or because they necessitated renewal (the tariff and the trade treaties). Even the Tariff Law, which has been seen by some historians as the cornerstone of Reich domestic politics in the early years of the century, might have been abandoned if Bülow had been able to follow his personal inclinations. The Tariff Law was passed, but it was very nearly rejected. Thus there was a fine line between success and failure, even during the early years of Bülow's Chancellorship.

The only sense in which Bülow did launch a new initiative in the executive's relations with the legislature from 1900 was his attempt to create a new parliamentary climate favourable to government legislation. His verbal assurances to the political parties soon proved ineffective, but Bülow expended considerable energy trying to achieve the parliamentary concessions he deemed necessary, and he ultimately dissipated his powers in the pursuit of tactics which at most maintained a semblance of stability. The Polling Booth Law, the repeal of Paragraph 2 of the Jesuit Law, the granting of salaries to Reichstag members were scarcely more than palliatives and could not provide a reliable basis for support in the Reichstag. But they created enemies for the Chancellor, especially on the right, and some of the most critical episodes between 1900 and 1909 were provoked by Bülow's constant attempts to demonstrate his conservatism. Bitter about the 1903 elections, resentful of the salaries which radicalised their party and brought in 'the little people with narrower concerns'[10] and later antagonised by Bülow's promise of Prussian suffrage reform and an inheritance tax which undermined the economic basis of their political power, traditional Conservatives became the most formidable opponents of Bülow's Chancellorship and proved uncompromisingly hostile even to the most piecemeal and cosmetic reforms.

From 1900 onwards Bülow concentrated on making the system work without substantial modifications. This was the essence of his adherence to the 'status quo', and his Chancellorship was devoid of genuine reformist initiatives. For all his intelligence, Bülow was too imprisoned within the value system of his own class, ignorant of the real political alternatives arising out of the clash of economic interests or class antagonisms, and naive about the fundamental sources of political power to confront Germany's domestic problems with great vision, imagination or effectiveness. His credentials as a reformer were also essentially limited when, as in 1906, he was motivated by the desire to strengthen his personal position and survive in office rather than by the need to strengthen the Chancellorship as an institution. Bülow's refusal to tolerate any restriction on his personal freedom of manoeuvre made an increase in the powers of the State Secretaries unacceptable, let alone a shift of the balance in favour of the legislature.

Bülow had no plans for a 'parliamentarisation' or 'democratisation' of German political life before 1906, and any moves in this direction were even less feasible and realistic when his authority had been undermined by the crisis of 1905–6 and his personal position was less secure. The Bloc of 1907–9 was an ingenious piece of improvisation, a makeshift arrangement dictated by political expediency. As an alliance between Conservatism and liberalism, its political foundations were weak. Given the nature of its inception, the need to search for legislation it could pass and the impossibility of reconciling it with Prussian policy, it is difficult to see the Bloc as anything more than a tactical experiment. It was repeatedly asserted during the Bloc years that Bülow lacked a clear direction, that he did not know what he wanted and that he had no coherent plans.[11] In particular, his bitter and ambivalent attitude towards the Centre after 1906 precluded the possibility that the Bloc would really serve to broaden the basis of imperial domestic politics or place the government on a new footing. The Bloc experiment cannot be divorced from the steady erosion of Bülow's personal authority during these years. The Chancellor's main concern was his survival in office, and he was not in a position to spearhead a programme of reform even if he had displayed a greater willingness to do so.

Long after his dismissal Bülow insisted on his royalism and his continued devotion to the monarchy,[12] an expression of opinion which cannot be dismissed as an attempt to preserve his personal reputation and the chances of his eventual recall.[13] In 1910 he told Loebell (whom he still regarded as his 'political conscience'[14]) that he had 'always regarded the maintenance of the traditional position of the Crown in Prussia and the Reich as one of my most important tasks' and that no one knew better than he 'that the parliamentary system is neither desirable nor even possible in our country'.[15] His conception of what it would take to 'modernise' German conservatism, 'revise' the bureaucracy and 'politicise' German liberalism was fundamentally limited, despite the aura of 'progress' which these phrases convey, given that he remained convinced 'that Prussian values [*Preussenthum*], Army and agriculture are the firmest foundations of Germany's power position, our unity and our future'.[16] Indeed, it was only after the Kaiser's abdication and the establishment of the Weimar Republic that Bülow perceptibly shifted his ground and argued that he had intended to prepare Germany progessively for a system of parliamentary government. He was responsible for the appointment of only one parliamentary deputy to a ministerial position (Möller in 1901), an experiment which was widely regarded as a failure, and there was more of a trend towards appointing generals than parliamentarians as Prussian Ministers during his Chancellorship. The idea that Bülow's dismissal had prevented 'a slow, methodical evolution' towards democracy and stacked the odds in favour of a revolution was a myth propagated not least by Bülow's own memoirs.[17] At best Bülow hoped to 'mark time' over Wilhelm II's rule,[18] but even this is probably to credit him with too great a degree of selflessness.

Of course, it is legitimate to question whether, given the weakness of

German liberalism and in the face of strong monarchical authority, Bülow was ever in a position to bolster the Chancellor's independent authority or significantly reform the system. He was not alone responsible for the failure to achieve substantial constitutional reforms in the wake of the *Daily Telegraph* affair of 1908, and it may well be that any individual in his position would have proved equally impotent. In 1917 Philip Eulenburg questioned how far Bülow or any other Chancellor under Wilhelm II could claim to have an independent policy, and he insisted that what Bülow was unable to achieve – whether through lack of courage, inaction or because the Kaiser opposed it – told its own story. Bülow, he maintained, was only 'responsible' for German policy in that he did not resign when his political convictions did not harmonise with the Kaiser's aims.[19] Dernburg, in 1927, painted a similar picture of Bülow's impotence while adopting a broader perspective. There was no doubt, he argued, that the servility and Byzantinism of the Kaiser's advisers contributed much to Wilhelm II's unfortunate development, but the blame did not lie with the personalities alone. Instead, the fault lay with what he regarded as the antiquated structure of the Prussian state. Dernburg claimed that Germany before the First World War was largely an appendix of Prussia and that the King and Kaiser, influenced by his closest entourage, appointed Prussian Ministers from the same narrow, conservative class which dominated the Prussian Landtag through the three-class suffrage. These Ministers 'had no political support among the people and only the choice between obedience or dismissal [*zwischen Sichfügen und fortgejagt werden*]'. They had no means of opposing the monarch if they were simultaneously determined to keep their privileges. 'Given the nature of the ruler it was completely insignificant who was Minister at any one time', for each 'was equally as powerless and dependent [*angewiesen*] on "handling the King"' as any of his predecessors if [Germany] was to be ruled *at all*'. This subservience to the 'All-Highest Lord' was not merely a feature of the central government but permeated the entire political system to the smallest electoral district where each 'lord' expected a similar degree of servility and Byzantinism from the mass of the electorate.[20] Clearly Bülow's mentality needs to be set within the wider context of the ideology of Prussian monarchism and the prevalence of patriarchal tradition; and this book shows that both Bülow's personality and the more general outlook of the German governing élite are subjects worthy of further historical investigation. The ruling élite was internally divided and characterised by contradictions. For, as was evident during the canal crisis in 1901, it could not proceed against Prussian conservatism and destroy the constraints from which it suffered without simultaneously destroying privilege, monarchical authority and the foundations of its own social and political existence.

To deny the impulse of creative reform during Bülow's Chancellorship and question his general effectiveness does not mean that one has to embrace theories of 'permanent crisis' in Germany before the First World War. Indeed, although a major conclusion of this book is that the scope for constitutional reform 'from above' was severely circumscribed between 1900 and 1909 and that Bülow had neither the inclination and ability nor the determination and vision to surmount the obstacles, it should be emphasised that in his own terms Bülow probably achieved what he wanted until 1909 – the working of the system with himself in the highest office. Bülow may have desired to stabilise the imperial system, but he certainly did not see the central dilemma of government as the extent to which it should permit a parliamentarisation of German political life. Primarily interested in his own political survival and increasingly oblivious to the long-term implications of his style of management, Bülow even, quite misleadingly, suggested to Loebell in August 1909 that his only misfortune was that the Conservatives rejected the inheritance tax and hence precluded the possibility that 'I could have conducted foreign and domestic policy for many years to come.'[21] One can chastise Bülow for his complacency; but if, in retrospect, the response of the men at the top to the problems of the *Kaiserreich* seems imperfect, this is only further confirmation that despite Germany's economic dynamism and growing socialist militancy, the pressure exerted on her rulers to make substantial reforms was inadequate.

'History will judge him more justly than the present day', Loebell wrote to Valentini in 1910, convinced that Bülow had been 'the most successful statesman since Bismarck' in domestic policy and that he had conducted German foreign policy during a difficult time with skill and occasional brilliance.[22] The position of the Reich Chancellor, the sole Reich Minister, in Wilhelmine Germany was scarcely an enviable one. Nevertheless, it is precisely Bülow's obliviousness to everything except the needs of his personal position and reputation which makes him such an unsympathetic and unattractive personality from the point of view of the historian. In order to retain the Chancellorship for nine years Bülow was prepared to base his position on the goodwill of an autocratically inclined and emotionally unstable Kaiser and to acquiesce in playing a specific and, in the last analysis, subordinate role in a military monarchy. Bülow not only failed to change the system: he did not even attempt to do so. Content with the appearance rather than the substance of power, he became obsessed with public relations and 'modern' techniques to ensure his political survival within the existing framework. His propaganda machine projected an image of the Chancellor which was increasingly at variance with his actual role in the government system. In public he posed as the man who could manage both the Kaiser and the Reichstag and he thus became, in Harden's phrase, the 'most dangerous propper-upper' who prevented the real contestants in the power struggle from appreciating the fundamental incompatibility of their interests. The impression of order, control and stability which Bülow cultivated may have satisfied the Chancellor's arrogance and vanity, but it belied reality. Ultimately the historian is struck by the essential emptiness and superficiality of this man who had no plans for the direction of German policy, who had no conception of Germany's long-term interests or possible political objectives, and who, in the final analysis, only sought to cut an imposing figure in the history books. Ironically, as Philipp Eulenburg realised, the fourth Chancellor, far from being Kaiser Wilhelm II's 'Bismarck', was destined to take his place in history 'wedged between Bismarck and the World War, with the Hohenlohes and Caprivis'.[23] But even this unflattering verdict scarcely conveys the full implications and effect of his mismanagement.

For Bülow's Chancellorship was disastrous for Germany, and by any criterion represented nine misspent years. In 1909 Germany found herself 'encircled' by hostile powers, and the international outlook was bleaker than at any time since Bismarck's dismissal. In domestic politics Bülow left a legacy of bitterness and turmoil in the Reichstag, and his successor's freedom of manoeuvre was seriously curtailed. The government had become no more democratic, no more efficient, no more popular and, with the potential power of the Kaiser (and his generals) unchecked, Bülow's constant pandering to the monarch's self-image had exacerbated the precarious nature of the system over which he presided. Bülow's 'system' had ultimately become a 'non-system', the absence of government, and the impression it conveyed was one of total disorganisation at the highest level. The most powerful, dynamic country in Europe, renowned for the efficiency of its administration, lacked all direction and was perilously short of options. Political power had slipped even further out of the hands of the 'responsible' civilian politicians towards the generals at the Kaiser's Court. As early as November 1901 Varnbüler, oppressed by doubt and worry, had lamented, 'Everything is so dark, all relations, political, social, economic so chaotic – even the men at the helm whom I watch are voyaging blindly into the fog.'[24] Eight years later, Philipp Eulenburg wrote to Bülow shortly after the latter's resignation, 'I now have the feeling that I am voyaging aboard a ship on which the captain is an actor, the helmsman an alpinist . . . The moment has come which we both often saw coming, not without trepidation.'[25] Within five years Germany was at war.

Appendix 1

Holders of government office, 1900–1909

German Kaiser and King of Prussia	Wilhelm II	1888–1918
Chief of Civil Cabinet	Hermann von Lucanus	1888–1908
Chief of Military Cabinet	Rudolf von Valentini	1908–1918
	Wilhelm von Hahnke	1888–1901
	Dietrich von Hülsen-Haeseler	1901–1908
	Moritz von Lyncker	1908–1918
Chief of Naval Cabinet	Gustav von Senden-Bibran	1889–1906
	Georg von Müller	1906–1918

THE PRUSSIAN MINISTERS

Minister-President and Foreign Minister	Bernhard von Bülow	1900–1909
Minister of Agriculture	Ernst von Hammerstein-Loxten	1894–1901
	Viktor von Podbielski	1901–1906
	Bernhard von Arnim-Kriewen	1906–1910
Minister of Culture (Ecclesiastical Affairs, Education and Medicine)	Konrad von Studt	1899–1907
	Ludwig Holle	1907–1909
Minister of Finance	Johannes von Miquel	1890–1901
	Georg von Rheinbaben	1901–1910
Minister of Interior	Georg von Rheinbaben	1899–1901
	Hans von Hammerstein	1901–1905
	Theobald von Bethmann Hollweg	1905–1907
	Friedrich von Moltke	1907–1909
Minister of Justice	Karl von Schönstedt	1894–1905
	Maximilian von Beseler	1905–1917
Minister of Public Works	Karl von Thielen	1891–1902
	Hermann von Budde	1902–1906
	Paul von Breitenbach	1906–1918
Minister of Trade	Ludwig Brefeld	1896–1901
	Theodor Möller	1901–1905
	Clemens von Delbrück	1905–1909
Minister of War	Heinrich von Gossler	1896–1903
	Karl von Einem	1903–1909

THE HEADS OF THE REICH OFFICES

Reich Chancellor	Bernhard von Bülow	1900–1909

Chief of Reich Chancellery	Kurt von Wilmowski	1894–1901
	Alfred von Conrad	1901–1904
	Friedrich von Loebell	1904–1910
Foreign Secretary	Oswald von Richthofen	1900–1906
	Heinrich von Tschirschky und Bögendorff	1906–1907
	Wilhelm von Schön	1907–1909
Secretary of Interior	Arthur von Posadowsky-Wehner	1897–1907
	Theobald von Bethmann Hollweg	1907–1909
Secretary of Justice	Arnold Nieberding	1893–1909
Navy Secretary	Alfred von Tirpitz	1897–1916
Postmaster-General	Viktor von Podbielski	1897–1901
	Reinhold Kraetke	1901–1917
President of Railway Office	Friedrich Schulz	1890–1909
Secretary of the Treasury	Maximilian von Thielmann	1897–1903
	Hermann von Stengel	1903–1908
	Reinhold von Sydow	1908–1909
Secretary of Colonial Office (established 1907)	Bernhard von Dernburg	1907–1910

Appendix 2

The composition of the Reichstag, 1887–1912

Party	1887	1890	1893	1898	1903	1907	1912
Conservatives	80	73	72	56	54	60	43
Reichspartei[a]	41	20	28	23	21	24	14
National Liberals	99	42	53	46	51	54	45
Liberal Vereinigung	32	66	13	12	9	14	42
Progressives			24	29	21	28	
Volkspartei	—	10	11	8	6	7	
Centre	98	106	96	102	100	105	91
Guelphs	4	11	7	9	6	1	5
SPD	11	35	44	56	81	43	110
Poles	13	16	19	14	16	20	18
Danes	1	1	1	1	1	1	1
Alsatians	15	10	8	10	9	7	9
Anti-Semites	1	5	16	13	11	16	13
Others	2	2	5	18	11	17	6
Total	397	397	397	397	397	397	397

[a] The Reichspartei was called the Free Conservative Party in Prussia.

Notes

Introduction

1 Norman Rich and M. H. Fisher (eds.), *The Holstein Papers*, 4 vols. (Cambridge, 1955–63), II, p. 188.

2 See for example Rudolf Vierhaus (ed.), *Das Tagebuch der Baronin Spitzemberg. Aufzeichnungen aus der Hofgesellschaft des Hohenzollernreiches* (Göttingen, 1960), 16 January 1906, p. 455.

3 Whereas most major and many minor British politicians have been seen as worthy of historical investigation, German Reich Chancellors such as Caprivi and Hohenlohe as well as Bülow have still not found their serious biographer. A notable exception to this observation is the recent spate of Bismarck biographies. See especially Lothar Gall, *Bismarck. The White Revolutionary*, 2 vols. (English edition, London, 1986) and Ernst Engelberg, *Bismarck. Urpreusse und Reichsgründer* (Berlin, 1985). Otherwise most recent scholarly biographies of men in German public life have been written by non-Germans. See, for example, Margaret Lavinia Anderson, *Windthorst. A Political Biography* (Oxford, 1981); Norman Rich, *Friedrich von Holstein. Politics and Diplomacy in the Era of Bismarck and Wilhelm II*, 2 vols. (Cambridge, 1965); and K. H. Jarausch, *The Enigmatic Chancellor. Bethmann Hollweg and the Hubris of Imperial Germany* (New Haven, 1973). For a useful survey of recent West German historical writing, see Georg Iggers (ed.), *The Social History of Politics. Critical Perspectives in West German Historical Writing Since 1945* (Leamington Spa, 1985).

4 Interest in Wilhelmine Germany was largely kindled by the 'Fischer controversy' on the origins of the First World War. See especially Fritz Fischer, *Griff nach der Weltmacht* (Düsseldorf, 1961) and *Krieg der Illusionen* (Düsseldorf, 1969). The implications of the controversy are considered by John Moses, *The Politics of Illusion* (London, 1975).

5 New studies range from an analysis of the role of the Kaiser and kingship to explorations of everyday life, from agricultural history to the ideology of imperialism. See, for example, John C. G. Röhl, *Kaiser, Hof und Staat. Wilhelm II und die deutsche Politik* (Munich, 1987); R. J. Evans and W. R. Lee (eds.), *The German Family* (London, 1981); Robert G. Moeller (ed.), *Peasants and Lords in Modern Germany* (London, 1986); Woodruff D. Smith, *The Ideological Origins of Nazi Imperialism* (Oxford, 1986).

6 It is impossible to survey recent writing on aspects of Wilhelmine politics here, but see in particular James N. Retallack, *Notables of the Right. The Conservative Party and Political Mobilisation in Germany 1876–1918* (London, 1988); Stanley Suval, *Electoral Politics in Wilhelmine Germany* (Chapel Hill, 1985); Geoff Eley, *Reshaping the German Right. Radical Nationalism and Political Change after Bismarck* (London, 1980); David Blackbourn, *Class, Religion and Local Politics in Wilhelmine Germany. The Centre Party in Württemberg before 1914* (London, 1980); Wilfried Loth, *Katholiken im Kaiserreich. Der politische Katholizismus in der Krise des Wilhelminischen Deutschlands* (Düsseldorf, 1984).

7 Geoff Eley, 'The British Model and the German Road: Rethinking the Course of German

History before 1914', in David Blackbourn and Geoff Eley, *The Peculiarities of German History* (Oxford, 1984), p. 153. See also Geoff Eley, 'The View From the Throne: the Personal Rule of Kaiser Wilhelm II', *Historical Journal*, 28/2 (1985), 474f.

8 See for example Eley, 'The British Model', p. 107.

9 See Peter Winzen, *Bülows Weltmachtkonzept. Untersuchungen zur Frühphase seiner Aussenpolitik 1897–1901* (Boppard am Rhein, 1977); Volker R. Berghahn, *Der Tirpitz-Plan. Genesis und Verfall einer innenpolitischen Krisenstrategie unter Wilhelm II* (Düsseldorf, 1971); Derek M. Bleyberg, 'Government and Legislative Process in Wilhelmine Germany. The Reorganisation of the Tariff Laws under Reich Chancellor von Bülow, 1897 to 1902', D.Phil. thesis, University of East Anglia, 1979, microfilm.

10 In the 1970s historians' views of the *Kaiserreich* were dominated by a very pessimistic and rigid interpretation of Germany's development in the nineteenth century which drew its inspiration from the work of Eckart Kehr and presented a picture of Imperial Germany as incapable of adapting to the modern world and in a state of political paralysis or permanent crisis by 1914. See Eckart Kehr, *Schlachtflottenbau und Parteipolitik 1894–1901* (Berlin, 1930) and *Der Primat der Innenpolitik* ed. Hans-Ulrich Wehler (Berlin, 1965). Kehr's essays have been edited and translated into English by Gordon Craig, *Economic Interest, Militarism and Foreign Policy* (Berkeley, 1977). The most powerful exponent of this view is Hans-Ulrich Wehler, *Das Deutsche Kaiserreich 1871–1918* (Göttingen, 1973); now translated as *The German Empire 1871–1918* (Leamington Spa, 1985). Wehler's thesis that Imperial Germany was a 'pseudo-constitutional semi-absolutism' which was dominated by an agrarian, pre-industrial power élite, determined to preserve the social and political status quo, was very influential but has always had its critics and has now come under attack from all directions. See, for example, Geoff Eley, 'Die "Kehrites" und das Kaiserreich: Bemerkungen zu einer aktuellen Kontroverse', *Geschichte und Gesellschaft*, 4 (1978), 91–107; Thomas Nipperdey, 'Wehlers "Kaiserreich": Eine kritische Auseinandersetzung', *Geschichte und Gesellschaft*, 1 (1975), 539–60 and '1933 und Kontinuität der deutschen Geschichte', *Historische Zeitschrift*, 227 (1978), 86–111; Hans-Günther Zmarzlik, 'Das Kaiserreich in Neuer Sicht?', *Historische Zeitschrift*, 222 (1976), 105–26.

11 See especially Wehler, *German Empire*; cf. Manfred Rauh, *Die Parlamentarisierung des Deutschen Reiches* (Düsseldorf, 1977) and *Föderalismus und Parlamentarismus im Wilhelminischen Reich* (Düsseldorf, 1973), who argues that Germany was in fact experiencing a 'quiet parliamentarisation' before 1914 and that especially during Bülow's Chancellorship the Reich executive approximated more and more to a 'normal', constitutional government. See also Dieter Langewiesche, 'Das Deutsche Kaiserreich – Bemerkungen zur Diskussion über Parlamentarisierung und Demokratisierung Deutschlands', *Archiv Sozialgeschichte*, 19 (1979), 628–42. For a wider (and more heated) discussion of Germany's alleged 'backwardness', see Blackbourn and Eley, *Peculiarities of German History*; Hans-Ulrich Wehler, '"Deutscher Sonderweg" oder allgemeine Probleme des westlichen Kapitalismus? Zur Kritik an einigen "Mythen deutscher Geschichtsschreibung"', *Merkur* (1981), 478–87; Hans-Jürgen Puhle, 'Deutscher Sonderweg. Kontroverse um eine vermeintliche Legende', *Journal für Geschichte*, 4 (1981), 44–5; Gordon Craig, 'The German Mystery Case', *New York Review of Books* (30 January 1986), 20–3; Paul Kennedy, review of *Mythen deutscher Geschichtsschreibung*, *Journal of Modern History*, 54/1 (1982), 177–9; Robert G. Moeller, 'The Kaiserreich Recast? Continuity and Change in Modern German Historiography', *Journal of Social History*, 17 (1984), 655–83. See also the review of Eley's *Reshaping the German Right* by Heinrich August Winkler, *Journal of Modern History*, 54/1 (1982), 170–6.

12 The 'Kehrite' view of Wilhelmine domestic politics saw *Sammlungspolitik* – the alliance between the government, the agrarians and big industry against the threat from the left

– as the cornerstone of the government's strategy before 1914. See especially Wehler, *German Empire*, pp. 94ff. and Dirk Stegmann, *Die Erben Bismarcks. Parteien und Verbände in der Spätphase des Wilhelminischen Deutschlands: Sammlungspolitik 1897–1918* (Cologne, 1970). A growing number of historians have since countered this view by arguing that the alleged alliance was shaky, contradictory and transitory, at best applying for a very limited period, and that the so-called alliance parties had different priorities, preferences and indeed notions of what *Sammlung* meant. See especially Geoff Eley, 'Sammlungspolitik, Social Imperialism and the Navy Law of 1898', in Geoff Eley, *From Unification to Nazism. Reinterpreting the German Past* (London, 1986), pp. 110–53 and *Reshaping the German Right*, p. 242; Volker Hentschel, *Wirtschaft und Wirtschaftspolitik im Wilhelminischen Deutschland: Organisierter Kapitalismus und Interventionsstaat?* (Stuttgart, 1978), p. 190; Michael Geyer, *Deutsche Rüstungspolitik 1860–1980* (Frankfurt am Main, 1984), p. 81.

13 Johannes Haller, *Die Aera Bülow. Eine historisch-politische Studie* (Stuttgart and Berlin, 1922).

14 A considerable role in creating this consensus was played by his colleagues and contemporaries. See especially Hermann von Eckardstein, *Lebenserinnerungen und politische Denkwürdigkeiten*, 3 vols. (Leipzig, 1919–21); Anton Graf Monts, *Erinnerungen und Gedanken des Botschafters Anton Graf Monts*, ed. K. Nowak and F. Thimme (Berlin, 1932); Robert von Zedlitz-Trützschler, *Zwölf Jahre am deutschen Kaiserhof* (Berlin, 1924); Friedrich von Thimme (ed.), *Front Wider Bülow. Staatsmänner, Diplomaten und Forscher zu seinen Denkwürdigkeiten* (Munich, 1931); or more recently, Karl Georg von Treutler, *Die Graue Excellenz. Zwischen Staatsräson und Vasallentreue. Aus den Papieren des kaiserlichen Gesandten Karl Georg von Treutler*, ed. Karl-Heinz Janssen (Frankfurt and Berlin, 1971), pp. 170–2. Bülow receives more sympathetic treatment in Johann Heinrich Bernstorff, *Erinnerungen und Briefe* (Zürich, 1936) and Hugo Graf Lerchenfeld-Koefering, *Erinnerungen und Denkwürdigkeiten, 1843 bis 1925* (Berlin, 1935).

15 See Bogdan von Hutten-Czapski, *Sechzig Jahre Politik und Gesellschaft*, 2 vols. (Berlin, 1936), I, p. 568.

16 Bernhard von Bülow, *Denkwürdigkeiten*, 4 vols. (Berlin, 1930–1).

17 Lewis Namier, 'The Men who Floundered into the War', in *Vanished Supremacies. Essays on European History 1812–1918* (Harmondsworth, 1962), p. 100.

18 The storm of public protest culminated in the publication of Thimme, *Front Wider Bülow*. See also Friedrich Hiller von Gaertringen, *Fürst Bülows Denkwürdigkeiten. Untersuchungen zu ihrer Entstehungsgeschichte und Kritik* (Tübingen, 1956).

19 Ian F. D Morrow, 'The Foreign Policy of Prince von Bülow 1898–1909', *Cambridge Historical Journal*, 4 (1932–4), 93. For similar reactions see Jules Cambon, 'Bülow and the War', *Foreign Affairs*, 10 (1932), 402–16; Walter Frank, 'Bernhard von Bülow', *Historische Zeitschrift*, 147 (1933), 349–67; and Siegfried A. Kaehler, 'Legende und Wirklichkeit im Lebensbild des Kanzlers Bernhard von Bülow', in *Studien zur deutschen Geschichte des 19 und 20 Jahrhunderts* (Gottingen, 1961), pp. 220–40.

20 See for example Morrow, 'Foreign Policy', and Cambon, 'Bülow and the War'; Frank, 'Bernhard von Bülow', 362f. and Wolfgang Neumann, 'Die Innenpolitik des Fürsten Bülow von 1900–1906', Ph.D. thesis, University of Kiel, 1950, especially 267f.; Theodor Eschenburg, *Das Kaiserreich am Scheideweg. Bassermann, Bülow und der Block* (Berlin, 1929), especially pp. 282–3; Hans-Georg Hartmann, 'Die Innenpolitik des Fürsten Bülow 1906–9', Ph.D. thesis, University of Kiel, 1950, especially 188f. A fuller survey of the literature on Bülow can be found in the introductions to Katharine A. Lerman, 'Bernhard von Bülow and the Governance of Germany', D.Phil. thesis, University of Sussex, 1983 and Peter Winzen, *Bülows Weltmachtkonzept*.

21 Cambon, 'Bülow and the War', 415.

22 See for example Bülow, *Denkwürdigkeiten*, II, pp. 69, 211f.

23 Karl Erich Born, *Staat und Sozialpolitik seit Bismarcks Sturz* (Wiesbaden, 1957), pp. 182f.

24 Paul R. Duggan, 'Currents of Administrative Reform in Germany 1907–1918', D.Phil. thesis, Harvard University, 1968, especially 3, 25.

25 Bernhard Karl Dehmelt, 'Bülow's Moroccan Policy 1902–5', Ph.D. thesis, University of Pennsylvania, 1963, especially 422, 427.

26 Rich, *Holstein*, II, especially pp. 551, 609f., 744f.

27 Sebastian Haffner, 'Der letzte Bismarckianer. Zur politischen Korrespondenz Eulenburgs', *Merkur* (November 1977), 1103.

28 John C. G. Röhl, *Germany Without Bismarck. The Crisis of Government in the Second Reich 1890–1900* (London, 1967) and (ed.), *Philipp Eulenburgs politische Korrespondenz*, I, *Von der Reichsgründung bis zum neuen Kurs, 1866–1891* (Boppard am Rhein, 1976); II, *Im Brennpunkt der Regierungskrise, 1892–1895* (Boppard, 1979); and III, *Krisen, Krieg und Katastrophen, 1895–1921* (Boppard, 1983).

29 Röhl, *Germany Without Bismarck*, pp. 158, 192.

30 Erich Eyck, *Das persönliche Regiment Wilhelms II* (Zurich, 1948); Rich, *Holstein*, II, pp. 846ff.

31 Röhl organised a colloquium on Kaiser Wilhelm II in Corfu in 1979 and the papers were published in John C. G. Röhl and Nicolaus Sombart (eds.), *Kaiser Wilhelm II. New Interpretations* (Cambridge, 1982); in 1987, with the support of the Historisches Kolleg, he organised another colloquium in Munich on Kaiser Wilhelm II's place in German history. See also Röhl, *Kaiser, Hof und Staat*.

32 Konrad H. Jarausch, review of *Kaiser Wilhelm*, *International History Review*, 5/2 (1983), 304.

33 Röhl, *Kaiser, Hof und Staat*, p. 11, See also Norbert Elias, *The Court Society* (English edition, Oxford, 1983), p. 21.

34 See especially Röhl's introduction to *Kaiser Wilhelm*, pp. 14ff.; and 'Der "Königsmechanismus" im Kaiserreich', in Röhl, *Kaiser, Hof und Staat*.

35 Both John Röhl and Lamar Cecil are currently preparing biographies of the Kaiser. See also Isabel V. Hull, *The Entourage of Kaiser Wilhelm II, 1888–1918* (Cambridge, 1982); and Thomas A. Kohut, *Mirror Image of the Nation: Wilhelm II, His Parents, and the Germans* (Oxford, forthcoming). For one of the numerous reviews of *Kaiser, Hof und Staat* which addressed the issue of the Kaiser's political role, see Thomas Nipperdey, 'Ein Fabeltier unserer Zeit', *Frankfurter Allgemeine Zeitung*, 22 (27 January 1988), 88.

36 Eley, 'The View From the Throne: The Personal Rule of Kaiser Wilhelm II', *Historical Journal*, 28, 2 (1985), 469–85 (quotes on pp. 475 and 483). For one attack on Röhl's 'personalistic approach', see Stegmann, *Die Erben Bismarcks*, p. 14; see also Richard J. Evans, 'From Hitler to Bismarck: "Third Reich" and Kaiserreich in Recent Historiography', in *Rethinking German History. Nineteenth Century Germany and the Origins of the Third Reich* (London, 1987), pp. 55ff, for a glaring example of how some historians dismiss any discussion of the central Berlin executive, the symbolic and actual importance of the Kaiser, and the mentality of the ruling élite. Incredibly, for a social historian, Evans dismissed Hull's book as a 'political irrelevance' since it contained no discussion of 'real political issues, at least in the domestic sphere' and it ignored 'the areas in which such issues were actually decided – the vast Wilhelmine bureaucracy, the *Reichstag*, the *Länder*, the political parties and the pressure groups' (p. 60).

37 See especially Elias, *Court Society*, pp. 265ff., who emphasises the interdependence of groups and individuals within every society and the resultant 'circulation of constraints'. To gain a full picture, he argues, one must not only study the constraints to which the less powerful are exposed but also the constraints to which the upper strata – and indeed

the absolute monarch – are subjected. In this sense 'personal regime', the phrase preferred by Hull, may be a more acceptable translation of 'persönliches Regiment' than 'personal rule'.

38 Hull, *Entourage*, p. 7, See also Röhl, *Kaiser Wilhelm*, p. 14.
39 Röhl and Sombart, *Kaiser Wilhelm*, p. 16; Wehler, *German Empire*, pp. 62ff.
40 Hans-Ulrich Wehler, *Aus der Geschichte lernen? Essays* (Munich, 1988), p. 206.
41 See especially the review of *Germany Without Bismarck* by Elisabeth Fehrenbach in *Historische Zeitschrift*, 212 (1971), 185–8.
42 Hull, *Entourage*, p. 7.
43 Barbara Vogel, *Deutsche Russlandpolitik. Das Scheitern der deutschen Weltpolitik unter Bülow 1900–1906* (Düsseldorf, 1973).
44 Peter Winzen, *Bülows Weltmachtkonzept*, p. 427. Winzen provides no evidence to support his contention that Bülow had a comprehensive programme covering all aspects of domestic policy. Nor can he substantiate his claim that the major factor in prompting Bülow's resignation in 1909 was the realisation that his ambitious *Weltmachtpolitik* had ended in a fiasco (p. 434). One reviewer of Winzen's book felt that Bülow's 'Konzept' in foreign policy was rather to grab what he could get. See Gregor Schöllgen, 'Wer machte im Kaiserreich Politik? Zwischen "persönlichem Regiment" und "polykratischem Chaos"', *Neue Politische Literatur*, 25 (1980), 90. See also Winzen's article 'Prince Bülows Weltmachtpolitik', *Australian Journal of Politics and History*, 22 (1976), 227–42.
45 W. Koch, *Volk und Staatsführung vor dem ersten Weltkrieg* (Stuttgart, 1935), p. 1.
46 See Eschenburg, *Kaiserreich am Scheideweg*, pp. 282–3.
47 Terry Cole, 'Kaiser versus Chancellor: The Crisis of Bülow's Chancellorship 1905–6', in Richard J. Evans (ed.), *Society and Politics in Wilhelmine Germany* (London, 1978), pp. 40–70 (quotations on pp. 41 and 67); Terence F. Cole, 'The *Daily Telegraph* Affair and its Aftermath: the Kaiser, Bülow and the Reichstag, 1908–1909', in Röhl and Sombart *Kaiser Wilhelm*, pp. 249–68 (quotations on pp. 261, 264 and 266).
48 An exception to this among the reviewers of *Kaiser Wilhelm* was David Blackbourn, who recognised that Cole established 'a dissenting line' within the volume. See 'The Kaiser and his Entourage', in David Blackbourn, *Populists and Patricians. Essays in Modern German History* (London, 1987), p. 50.
49 See for example Stegmann, *Die Erben Bismarcks*, who devotes remarkably little attention to the Bülow years.

1 The political rise of Bernhard von Bülow 1849–1900

1 Bülow, *Denkwürdigkeiten*, IV, p. 7.
2 ZSA Merseburg, Althoff Papers, 108, 'Zeugnis der Reife' (Halle), 12 August 1867.
3 Bülow, *Denkwürdigkeiten*, IV, p. 261. See also the summary of Bülow's career in ZSA Merseburg, Althoff Papers, 108.
4 Bülow, *Denkwürdigkeiten*, IV, pp. 548–53; Rich and Fisher, *Holstein Papers*, III, Herbert Bismarck to Holstein, 24 June 1884, p. 119.
5 Chlodwig zu Hohenlohe-Schillingsfürst, *Memoirs*, ed. Friedrich Curtius, 2 vols. (English edition, London, 1906), II, 23 October 1881, p. 282.
6 Rich and Fisher, *Holstein Papers*, III, Kiderlen-Wächter to Holstein, 2 March 1886, p. 159.
7 Alfred von Waldersee, *Denkwürdigkeiten*, ed. H. O. Meisner, 3 vols. (Stuttgart and Berlin, 1922–3), II, 22 March 1890, p. 122; Röhl, *Eulenburg*, I, Holstein to Philipp Eulenburg (hereafter Eulenburg), 26 March 1890, pp. 511f.
8 Rich, *Holstein*, I, p. 113; Bülow, *Denkwürdigkeiten*, IV, p. 547.
9 Rich and Fisher, *Holstein Papers*, II, 27 August 1884, p. 156 and III, Bülow to Holstein, 1 March 1884, p. 106.

10 Ibid., III, Bülow to Holstein, 7 November 1881, p. 57 and 29 December 1881, p. 58. See also Bülow to Holstein, 11 June 1883, p. 83.

11 Röhl, *Eulenburg*, I, Bülow to Eulenburg, 28 August 1890, pp. 564f.

12 Rich and Fisher, *Holstein Papers*, III, Bülow to Holstein, 7 November 1881, p. 57.

13 Ibid., Bülow to Holstein, 29 December 1881, p. 58 and 27 January 1883, p. 77.

14 Ibid., Bülow to Holstein, 11 June 1886, p. 83.

15 See below. After a rift in their relations, 1885–7, Holstein and Bülow resumed their correspondence briefly in 1888–9 and again from 1893.

16 Bülow, *Denkwurdigkeiten*, IV, p. 646.

17 Walther Bussmann (ed.), *Graf Herbert von Bismarck. Aus seiner politischen Korrespondenz* (Göttingen, 1964), Herbert Bismarck to Otto Bismarck, 28 March 1883, p. 168.

18 Rich and Fisher, *Holstein Papers*, III, Bülow to Holstein, 28 June 1884, p. 120.

19 See the correspondence between Bülow and Herbert Bismarck in Bussmann, *Bismarck*. Herbert was clearly very influenced by Bülow's views and valued their private correspondence as a means of directing policy without recourse to official channels. Herbert defended Bülow against criticism of his reports in late 1886. See Röhl, *Eulenburg*, I, Eulenburg to Bülow, 28 February 1887, p. 220.

20 Röhl, *Eulenburg*, I, Bülow to Eulenburg, 2 March 1890, p. 467.

21 Ibid., Bülow to Eulenburg, 29 May 1886, p. 165.

22 Bussmann, *Bismarck*, Prince Wilhelm to Herbert Bismarck, 10 February 1885, p. 272.

23 Röhl, *Eulenburg*, I, Bülow to Eulenburg, 29 May 1886, p. 166; Rich and Fisher, *Holstein Papers*, II, 4 April 1885, pp. 184–5; BA Koblenz, Bülow Papers (BP), 99, Bülow to Lindenau, 1 August 1887.

24 Bussmann, *Bismarck*, Bülow to Herbert Bismarck, 12 April 1887, pp. 435f.

25 BA Koblenz, BP, 99, Bülow to Lindenau, 17 June 1887.

26 Ibid., Bülow to Lindenau, 17 October 1883.

27 Röhl, *Eulenburg*, I, Eulenburg to Bülow, 28 February 1887, p. 219.

28 Bussmann, *Bismarck*, Bülow to Herbert Bismarck, 5 April 1883, pp. 169f.

29 Röhl, *Eulenburg*, I, Bülow to Eulenburg, 29 May 1886, p. 166.

30 BA Koblenz, BP, 99, Bülow to Lindenau, 20 July 1887.

31 Rich and Fisher, *Holstein Papers*, II, 8 April 1885, pp. 186–9 and 12 May 1885, p. 198.

32 From early 1884 Holstein began to see Bismarck's diplomacy as dangerously pro-Russian. See Rich, *Holstein*, I, pp. 174–211. Holstein felt that Bülow was painting a rosy picture from St Petersburg and accused him of 'political romancing'. See Rich, *Holstein Papers*, III, Holstein to Hatzfeldt, 10 November 1886, pp. 194f.

33 Bussmann, *Bismarck*, Herbert Bismarck to Otto Bismarck, 14 April 1887, pp. 436f.

34 Ibid., Herbert Bismarck to Wilhelm Bismarck, 29 April 1888, p. 516.

35 Bismarck commented in March 1890 that Bülow was 'a not very reliable [originally: completely unreliable] man'. See Röhl, *Eulenburg*, I, p. 512, n. 5.

36 Rich and Fisher, *Holstein Papers*, II, Hatzfeldt to Holstein, 11 November 1886, p. 311.

37 Röhl, *Eulenburg*, I, Bülow to Eulenburg, 2 March 1890, p. 474.

38 Bülow, *Denkwürdigkeiten*, IV, p. 617.

39 BA Koblenz, BP, 99, Bülow to Lindenau, 1 August 1887; P. Eulenburg, *Aus 50 Jahren*, ed. J. Haller (Berlin, 1925), note of 11 June 1887, p. 139; Bussmann, *Bismarck*, Bülow to Herbert Bismarck, 12 April 1887, pp. 434–6.

40 BA Koblenz, BP, 99, Bülow to Lindenau, 20 July 1887.

41 Röhl, *Eulenburg*, I, Bülow to Eulenburg, 7 August 1888, p. 303 and 10 July 1889, pp. 341f.

42 Ibid., Bülow to Eulenburg, 23 December 1890, p. 615.

43 Ibid., Bülow to Eulenburg, 28 May 1891, p. 686; BA Koblenz, BP, 99, Bülow to Lindenau, 13 October 1892 and 17 October 1892.

44 Röhl, *Germany Without Bismarck*, pp. 106f. and *Eulenburg*, I, p. 24. See also HSA Stuttgart, E73 12e, Varnbüler's Report, 4 July 1897.

45 BA Koblenz, BP, 99, Bülow to Lindenau, 9 April 1890 and 6 October 1892; Rich and Fisher, *Holstein Papers*, III, Bülow to Holstein, 2 May 1894, p. 473; Monts, *Erinnerungen*, Bülow to Monts, 5 July 1894, p. 330 and 3 May 1895, p. 337.

46 Bülow, *Denkwürdigkeiten*, IV, p. 338.

47 Rich and Fisher, *Holstein Papers*, III, Bülow to Holstein, 18 April 1884, pp. 110–13.

48 Ibid., See also BA Koblenz, BP, 99, Bülow to Lindenau, 21 November 1884 and SA Köln, Bachem Papers, 119, note of 16 March 1901. Cf. Bülow, *Denkwürdigkeiten*, IV, especially pp. 399–402, 528–38, 589–92. Bülow suggests that he only became involved with the Countess after her divorce in 1883 and he claims that, while in Vienna in 1876, he was still having an affair with a 'Princess Y' which his father made him terminate. Monts, however, claims that Bülow's strict and pious father had him transferred to Athens (in December 1876) because he had heard of Bülow's affair with Marie von Dönhoff (Monts, *Erinnerungen*, p. 153). In general Bülow's accounts of his amorous exploits in his early life (and suggestion of an illegitimate child) are somewhat fanciful (IV, pp. 140–2, 199f., 250).

49 Rich and Fisher, *Holstein Papers*, II, 5 November 1885, p. 262. Bülow attributed Dönhoff's reluctance to agree to a divorce as evidence of his belief that Marie would aid his career under the Crown Prince. See BA Koblenz, BP, 99, Bülow to Lindenau, 21 November 1884.

50 BA Koblenz, BP, 173, Prince Wilhelm to Contessina Dönhoff, 13 November 1878 and 1 January 1879.

51 Ibid., Prince Wilhelm to Contessina Dönhoff, 4 December 1878 and 12 February 1879.

52 See for example HSA Stuttgart, Weizsäcker Papers, Varnbüler's Report, 14 July 1909 and PA Bonn, IA, Deutschland, 122, no. 13, Bd. XVI, Marie von Bülow to Wilhelm II, 24 October 1909, It is, however, interesting to note that a reason put forward against Bülow's appointment to the State Secretaryship in 1890 was that his wife would not be acceptable to the Kaiserin – presumably because she was a Catholic. See Röhl, *Eulenburg*, I, Holstein to Eulenburg, 26 March 1890, p. 512 and August Eulenburg to Eulenburg, 27 March 1890, p. 515. There is no evidence that this was an issue after 1897.

53 Rich and Fisher, *Holstein Papers*, III, Bülow to Holstein, 18 April 1884, p. 112.

54 Ibid., p. 111.

55 Röhl, *Eulenburg*, I, Eulenburg to Herbert Bismarck, 14 May 1885, pp. 152f.

56 Eulenburg, *Aus 50 Jahren*, 27 December 1885, p. 121, n. 1.

57 Rich and Fisher, *Holstein Papers*, III, Herbert Bismarck to Holstein, 17 July [1885], p. 148.

58 See for example Hutten–Czapski, *Sechzig Jahre*, I, p. 328; HSA Stuttgart, Varnbüler's Report, 4 July 1897; BA Koblenz, Loebell Papers, 27, unpublished memoirs, pp. 65f.

59 Röhl, *Eulenburg*, I, Bülow to Eulenburg, 29 May 1886, p. 164; Bülow, *Denkwürdigkeiten*, IV, p. 179.

60 Bussmann, *Bismarck*, Bülow to Herbert Bismarck, 18 April 1890, pp. 569f.

61 Röhl, *Eulenburg*, I, Bülow to Eulenburg, 28 August 1890, pp. 564f.

62 For the constitutional crisis in the 1890s, see Röhl, *Germany Without Bismarck*.

63 See Bülow, *Denkwürdigkeiten*, IV, pp. 486–8. Bülow's portrayal of his relationship with Eulenburg in his memoirs is highly inaccurate, but he nevertheless includes Eulenburg among his four closest friends (p. 487). The others were Friedrich Vitzthum, Franz Arenberg and Herbert Bismarck.

64 Röhl, *Eulenburg*, I, Eulenburg to Bülow, 28 February 1887, p. 220.

65 Ibid., Bülow to Eulenburg, 2 March 1890, pp. 466–74 and 23 December 1890, pp. 615f.

66 See Bülow's letters to Eulenburg in Röhl, *Eulenburg*, I, II and III.

67 See for example Röhl, *Eulenburg*, I, Bülow to Eulenburg, 16 February 1891, pp. 635f. See also Hull, *Entourage*, pp. 86ff.

68 Röhl, *Eulenburg*, II, Eulenburg to Bülow, 28 February 1893, p. 1035 and Bülow to Eulenburg, 13 March 1893, pp. 1046f.

69 BA Koblenz, BP, 127, Vitzthum to Bülow, 24 March 1890 and 4 July 1890.

70 See ch. 1, pp. 22ff. below. See also Röhl, *Germany Without Bismarck*; Hull, *Entourage*, pp. 89ff.

71 See especially Röhl, *Germany Without Bismarck*, pp. 106f.

72 Ibid., pp. 134f., 158ff., 221f.

73 See ch. 1, pp. 29f. below. Bülow got Eulenburg to vet his letters to Wilhelm II. See for example Röhl, *Eulenburg*, III, Bülow to Eulenburg, 13 October 1895, p. 1571 and 20 October 1896, p. 1742.

74 See Bülow's correspondence with Holstein from 1893 in Rich, *Holstein Papers*, III, Bülow's personal and political reassurances to Holstein were frequently rather hollow and are not substantiated by Bülow's correspondence with Eulenburg. See J. Haller, *Aus dem Leben des Fürsten Philipp zu Eulenburg-Hertefeld* (Berlin, 1924), pp. 197ff. See also Röhl, *Germany Without Bismarck*, pp. 234f. for Holstein's sudden aversion to Marschall in 1897.

75 Röhl, *Germany Without Bismarck*, pp. 103f., 235.

76 BA Koblenz, BP, 76, Eulenburg to Bülow, 24 April 1897.

77 See Röhl, *Germany Without Bismarck*, pp. 217–22.

78 ZSA Merseburg, Zivilkabinett, 2.2.1, 12926, Imperial Order of 20 October 1897. See also Lamar Cecil, *The German Diplomatic Service 1871–1914* (Princeton, 1976), p. 280.

79 BA Koblenz, BP, 6, Bülow to Marie Bülow, 8 April 1897 and 90, Bülow to Holstein, 11 June 1897. Bülow's wife was in tears because they had to leave Rome. See Rich and Fisher, *Holstein Papers*, IV, Eulenburg to Holstein, 22 June 1897, p. 42; Vierhaus, *Spitzemberg*, 30 June 1897, pp. 356f. See also Monts, *Erinnerungen*, pp. 154f., who believed Bülow wanted to stay in Rome until he could assume the Chancellorship.

80 HSA Stuttgart, Varnbüler's Report, 4 July 1897.

81 See for example Eulenburg, *Aus 50 Jahren*, Eulenburg to Bülow, 29 January 1890, pp. 288–90.

82 Henry Kissinger, *The White House Years* (London, 1979), pp. 27, 54.

83 Monts, *Erinnerungen*, p. 152.

84 See for example Röhl, *Eulenburg*, I, Bülow to Eulenburg, 15 April 1890, p. 532.

85 Ibid., Bülow to Eulenburg, 25 December 1887, p. 257.

86 Bülow, *Denkwürdigkeiten*, IV, p. 529.

87 Rich and Fisher, *Holstein Papers*, III, Bülow to Holstein, 5 February 1888, p. 257.

88 Röhl, *Eulenburg*, I, Bülow to Eulenburg, 10 July 1889, p. 342.

89 Bülow, *Denkwürdigkeiten*, IV, p. 460.

90 BA Koblenz, BP, 99, Bülow to Lindenau, 11 November 1885 and 24 June 1890.

91 Monts, *Erinnerungen*, Bülow to Monts, 30 April 1896, p. 342.

92 See Winzen, 'Prince Bülow's *Weltmachtpolitik*', pp. 227f. and *Bülows Weltmachtkonzept*, pp. 25–35. Winzen omits Bismarck's speeches when he quotes Bülow on his intellectual influences (p. 34).

93 Bülow, *Denkwürdigkeiten*, I, p. 228.

94 Bernhard von Bülow, *Deutsche Politik* (Berlin, 1916), p. 13.

95 Bülow, *Denkwürdigkeiten*, IV, pp. 95, 171. Bülow, like some historians, was inconsistent in his appraisal of Bismarck's statecraft and oscillated between judging him to be a statesman with 'far-sighted plans' (p. 85) and an opportunist who exploited situations as they arose (pp. 97f.).

96 Bussmann, *Bismarck*, Bülow to Herbert Bismarck, 5 April 1883, pp. 169f.

97 Ibid., Bülow to Herbert Bismarck, 8 July 1884, pp. 243f.

98 See for example Bülow, *Denkwürdigkeiten*, I, p. 5.

99 Röhl, *Eulenburg*, I, Bülow to Eulenburg, 2 March 1890, p. 472.

100 Monts, *Erinnerungen*, p. 155.

101 Based on Bülow's letters to Holstein and Herbert Bismarck, and on his political despatches in *Die Grosse Politik der Europäischen Kabinette, 1871–1914*, ed. J. Lepsius, A. Mendelssohn-Bartholdy and F. Thimme, 40 vols. (Berlin, 1922–7), especially III–VI.

102 Röhl, *Eulenburg*, I, Bülow to Eulenburg, 2 March 1890, p. 471.

103 As for example, 'all Romanians suffer from megalomania'. See Rich and Fisher, *Holstein Papers*, III, Bülow to Holstein, 28 October 1889, p. 321.

104 Ibid., Bülow to Holstein, 10 December 1887, p. 237.

105 Bülow at various times advocated a rapprochement with France (Bussmann, *Bismarck*, Bülow to Herbert Bismarck, 11 August 1884, pp. 247f.); a Russo-German alliance (ibid., Bülow to Herbert Bismarck, 20 November 1886, pp. 406f.)' a pro-Austrian policy of standing up to Russia (Rich and Fisher, *Holstein Papers*, III, Bülow to Holstein, 10 December 1887, pp. 236–40); a free hand policy between England and the Dual Alliance (ibid., Bülow to Holstein, 30 October 1895, pp. 552–4); and a continental alliance against England (ibid., Bülow to Holstein, 3 January 1896, pp. 582f.).

106 Röhl, *Eulenburg*, I, Bülow to Eulenburg, 2 March 1890, p. 470. For an explanation of this policy, see Rich, *Holstein*, I, pp. 174f., 322f.

107 Bussmann, *Bismarck*, Bülow to Herbert Bismarck, 26 August 1885, pp. 295–7 and 6 October 1886, pp. 389f. See also Monts, *Erinnerungen*, pp. 152f.

108 Bussmann, *Bismarck*, Herbert Bismarck to Bülow, 31 October 1885, p. 331.

109 Bülow, *Denkwürdigkeiten*, IV, p. 455.

110 Ibid., pp. 10, 57.

111 Monts, *Erinnerungen*, Bülow to Monts, 3 May 1895, p. 336.

112 Bussmann, *Bismarck*, Bülow to Herbert Bismarck, 4 December 1885, p. 349.

113 Ibid., Bülow to Herbert Bismarck, 12 February 1888, p. 508.

114 Ibid., Bülow to Herbert Bismarck, 13 April 1888, p. 513.

115 Röhl, *Eulenburg*, I, Bülow to Eulenburg, 2 March 1890, p. 468.

116 Ibid., Bülow to Eulenburg, 28 May 1891, p. 685 and II, Bülow to Eulenburg, 8 February 1892, p. 759.

117 Ibid., II, Bülow to Eulenburg, 30 May 1893, p. 1080.

118 Ibid., Bülow to Eulenburg, 9 July 1892, pp. 909f.

119 Ibid., I, Bülow to Eulenburg, 28 May 1891, p. 685.

120 Ibid., II, Bülow to Eulenburg, 9 July 1892, p. 908.

121 BA Koblenz, BP, 122, note of 14 April 1897.

122 Röhl, *Eulenburg*, I, Bülow to Eulenburg, 25 December 1887, p. 258.

123 Ibid., Bülow to Eulenburg, 23 December 1889, p. 388.

124 Ibid., Bülow to Eulenburg, 2 March 1890, p. 468.

125 Ibid., Bülow to Eulenburg, 28 August 1890, p. 561f.

126 Ibid., Bülow to Eulenburg, 23 December 1890, p. 615.

127 Ibid., Bülow to Eulenburg, 28 May 1891, p. 685.

128 Ibid., II, Bülow to Eulenburg, 15 December 1894, p. 1432.

129 See Röhl, *Germany Without Bismarck*, pp. 103f.

130 Ibid., p. 194. See also Röhl, *Eulenburg*, III, Bülow to Eulenburg, 23 July 1896, p. 1714.

131 Röhl, *Eulenburg*, II, Bülow to Eulenburg, 9 July 1892, p. 908.

132 Ibid., Bülow to Eulenburg, 6 February 1895, p. 1454.

133 Ibid., Bülow to Eulenburg, 6 April 1892, p. 843.

134 Ibid., Bülow to Eulenburg, 2 May 1894, p. 1296.

135 Ibid., Bülow to Eulenburg, 15 December 1894, p. 1433.
136 Ibid., p. 1432.
137 Ibid., Bülow to Eulenburg, 6 February 1895, p. 1453.
138 Ibid., I, Bülow to Eulenburg, 2 March 1890, p. 471.
139 Ibid., p. 473.
140 Monts, *Erinnerungen*, Bülow to Monts, 25 July 1895, p. 338.
141 Röhl, *Eulenburg*, II, Bülow to Eulenburg, 13 March 1893, p. 1048.
142 Ibid., Bülow to Eulenburg, 8 February 1892, p. 760.
143 Ibid., Bülow to Eulenburg, 6 February 1895, p. 1453; Winzen, 'Prince Bülow's *Welt-machtpolitik*', p. 229.
144 Röhl, *Eulenburg*, I, Bülow to Eulenburg, 2 March 1890, pp. 471f. Bülow often used the same phrases and metaphors in his correspondence with Lindenau. See BA Koblenz, BP, 99, Bülow to Lindenau, 24 June 1890.
145 Röhl, *Eulenburg*, II, Bülow to Eulenburg, 16 February 1891, p. 636.
146 Ibid., Bülow to Eulenburg, 9 January 1893, p. 1007.
147 See, for example, Monts, *Erinnerungen*, Bülow to Monts, 3 May 1895, p. 336; BA Koblenz, BP, 99, Bülow to Lindenau, 24 June 1890; Rich and Fisher, *Holstein Papers*, III, Bülow to Holstein, 15 January 1895, p. 490.
148 BA Koblenz, BP, 151, Notebook A (1879), pp. 46, 18, 34b.
149 Röhl, *Eulenburg*, I, Bülow to Eulenburg, 28 May 1891, p. 684. See also Monts, *Erinnerungen*, Bülow to Monts, 13 October 1895, p. 339.
150 Hull, *Entourage*, p. 88.
151 Röhl, *Germany Without Bismarck*, p. 158.
152 Röhl, *Eulenburg*, II, Bülow to Eulenburg, 15 June 1892, p. 898 and 15 December 1894, pp. 1431f.
153 BA Koblenz, BP, 155, notes of 1916–21, p. 46; Bülow, *Denkwürdigkeiten*, IV, p. 638.
154 Röhl, *Eulenburg*, I, Bülow to Eulenburg, 2 March 1890, p. 472.
155 Ibid., II, Bülow to Eulenburg, 15 December 1894, p. 1431.
156 Ibid., I, Bülow to Eulenburg, 2 March 1890, p. 472 and II, Bülow to Eulenburg, 30 May 1893, p. 1080. See also BA Koblenz, BP, 151, Notebook A (1879), p. 24.
157 Ibid., III, Bülow to Eulenburg, 30 October 1895, p. 1581.
158 Ibid., II, Bülow to Eulenburg, 15 June 1892, pp. 897f.
159 Ibid., Bülow to Eulenburg, 13 March 1893, pp. 1047f.
160 Röhl, *Germany Without Bismarck*, p. 194.
161 Röhl, *Eulenburg*, III, Bülow to Eulenburg, 25 December 1895, p. 1622.
162 See for example BA Koblenz, BP, 75, Eulenburg to Bülow, 6 December 1895.
163 See ZSA Potsdam, Reichskanzlei, 798/2, Bülow to Loebell, 10 October 1908. See also ch. 3., pp. 119ff. below.
164 Röhl, *Eulenburg*, II, Bülow to Eulenburg, 6 October 1894, p. 1371.
165 Ibid., Bülow to Eulenburg, 6 February 1895, p. 1455.
166 Ibid., Bülow to Eulenburg, 9 February 1895, p. 1457.
167 BA Koblenz, BP, 112, note of 14 April 1897.
168 Ibid., 30, note of 1897. See also Röhl, *Eulenburg*, III, Monts to Eulenburg, 20/21 March 1897, p. 1805 and Eulenburg to Wilhelm II, 8 April 1897, p. 1813. See also Röhl, *Germany Without Bismarck*, pp. 210ff.
169 Monts, *Erinnerungen*, p. 155.
170 BA Koblenz, BP, 99, Bülow to Lindenau, 20 November 1897; see Kathy Lerman, 'The Decisive Relationship: Kaiser Wilhelm II and Chancellor Bernhard von Bülow, 1900–1905', in Röhl and Sombart, *Kaiser Wilhelm II*, p. 233. See also Johann Bernstorff, *Memoirs* (American edition, New York, 1936), p. 59.

171 See especially Röhl, *Germany Without Bismarck*, pp. 241–70.

172 See, for example, Chlodwig zu Hohenlohe-Schillingsfürst, *Denkwürdigkeiten der Reichs-kanzlerzeit*, ed. K. A. von Müller (Stuttgart, 1931), Statthalter Hohenlohe to Prince Hohenlohe, 14 July 1897, p. 370.

173 Bülow was appointed provisional State Secretary on 26 June 1897 but was not officially appointed State Secretary and Prussian Minister until 20 October 1897. See Bülow, *Denkwürdigkeiten*, I, p. 170.

174 Hohenlohe, *Denkwürdigkeiten der Reichskanzlerzeit*, Wilhelm II to Hohenlohe, 9 March 1896, p. 195.

175 Bülow, *Denkwürdigkeiten*, I, p. 15.

176 Ibid., pp. 180–4.

177 Rich and Fisher, *Holstein Papers*, II, 6 January 1884; Hutten-Czapski, *Sechzig Jahre*, I, p. 337.

178 BA Koblenz, BP, 75, Eulenburg to Bülow, 3 December 1895.

179 Bülow, *Denkwürdigkeiten*, IV, p. 567.

180 Rich and Fisher, *Holstein Papers*, II, 22 August 1885, p. 233.

181 See Röhl, *Germany Without Bismarck*, pp. 134ff.

182 Ibid., p. 107.

183 BA Koblenz, BP, 76, Eulenburg's note of 20 April 1897. After Szögyényi's ennoblement, his name was spelt Szögyény. For the sake of consistency, the original spelling is used throughout this book.

184 Bülow, *Denkwürdigkeiten*, I, p. 56.

185 For this and following details see ZSA Merseburg, Hausarchiv, Rep. 53F IIIb, Diaries of the Kaiser's Adjutants, 1896–1909, Vols. 7–13. See also Rich and Fisher, *Holstein Papers*, III, Holstein to Bülow, 15 February 1895, p. 496.

186 Hohenlohe, *Denkwürdigkeiten der Reichskanzlerzeit*, 7 January 1900, p. 554 and 17 October 1896, pp. 268f.

187 ZSA Merseburg, Hausarchiv, Adjutants' Diaries, 8, 19 February 1898.

188 Ibid. Wilhelm II saw Bülow on at least twenty days. Of the remaining eight days, three were Sundays and on one the Kaiser was away from Berlin all day. See also Hohenlohe, *Denkwürdigkeiten der Reichskanzlerzeit*, pp. 424–76 and especially 15 February 1898, p. 428.

189 Hohenlohe, *Denkwürdigkeiten der Reichskanzlerzeit*, Alexander Hohenlohe to Prince Hohenlohe, 10 January 1899, pp. 478ff.

190 Haller, *Aus dem Leben*, Wilhelm II to Eulenburg, 20 August 1897, p. 252. See also Bülow, *Denkwürdigkeiten*, I, p. 139.

191 BA Koblenz, BP, 153, note. 293, Wilhelm II to Bülow, 12 September 1898.

192 Ibid., 5, Imperial Order of 22 June 1899; Bülow, *Denkwürdigkeiten*, I, p. 287.

193 BA Koblenz, BP, 76, Eulenburg to Bülow, 20 July 1898.

194 Walther Peter Fuchs (ed.), *Grossherzog Friedrich I von Baden und die Reichspolitik 1871–1907. Bd. 4. 1898–1907* (Stuttgart, 1980), Brauer to Jagemann, 30 April 1898, pp. 37f.

195 BA Koblenz, BP, 109, Kaiserin Auguste Viktoria to Bülow, 18 August 1899; Bülow, *Denkwürdigkeiten*, I, p. 295.

196 HHSA Wien, PA III, 151, Szögyényi to Goluchowski, 21 May 1898.

197 See for example Bülow's professed preference for cruisers rather than battleships when discussing the Navy Bill with Wilhelm II in 1897, Bülow, *Denkwürdigkeiten*, I, pp. 115f.

198 Vierhaus, *Spitzemberg*, 30 June 1897, pp. 356f.

199 Waldersee, *Denkwürdigkeiten*, II, 29 January 1899, pp. 426f.

200 Hohenlohe, *Denkwürdigkeiten der Reichskanzlerzeit*, 31 December 1894, p. 27.

201 Bülow, *Denkwürdigkeiten*, I, p. 5 and IV, p. 687. See also ch. 3, pp. 86ff. below. Norbert

Elias has seen this as an essential skill of the courtier. See Elias, *Court Society*, pp. 106ff.

202 Waldersee, *Denkwürdigkeiten*, II, 14 September 1899, pp. 432f.

203 Röhl, *Eulenburg*, II, Bülow to Eulenburg, 6 October 1894, p. 1371.

204 ZSA Merseburg, Zivilkabinett, 12926, Bülow to Wilhelm II, 7 December 1897; BA Koblenz, BP, 159, Bülow to Eulenburg, 15 February 1898.

205 BA Koblenz, BP, 91, Bülow to Holstein, 24 November 1899.

206 HSA München, 1071, Lerchenfeld's Report, 25 October 1900.

207 Ibid., 20 October 1900.

208 Röhl, *Eulenburg*, III, Eulenburg to Bülow, 8 March 1897, pp. 1797f.; BA Koblenz, BP, 76, Eulenburg to Bülow, 31 May 1897. See also Röhl, *Germany Without Bismarck*, pp. 201–4, 231f.

209 Bülow, *Denkwürdigkeiten*, I, Marschall to Bülow, 4 June 1897, pp. 52–4.

210 BA Koblenz, BP, 90, Holstein to Bülow, 9 June 1897.

211 Bülow, *Denkwürdigkeiten*, I, pp. 56–60; Winzen, *Bülows Weltmachtkonzept*, pp. 63ff. See also ZSA Potsdam, Rath Papers, 9, Bülow to Rath, 12 February 1912. For a stimulating new discussion of the meaning and significance of *Weltpolitik*, see Smith, *Ideological Origins*, especially ch. 4.

212 Winzen, *Bülows Weltmachtkonzept*, pp. 130–9; Bülow, *Denkwürdigkeiten*, I, pp. 184ff., 210ff. See also BA–MA Freiburg, Diederichs Papers, 6, Otto Diederichs to Friedrich Diederichs, 4 April 1898.

213 HSA Stuttgart, Varnbüler's Report, 24 December 1897; *Reichstag*, 6 December 1897, p. 60. See also Bernhard von Bülow, *Reden*, ed. J. Penzler and O. Hötzsch, 3 vols. (Berlin, 1907–9), I, 6 December 1897, pp. 5–8.

214 BA Koblenz, BP, 76, Eulenburg to Bülow, 11 February 1898; Bülow, *Denkwürdigkeiten*, I, p. 224.

215 See, for example, BA Koblenz, BP, 58, Grand Duke Friedrich von Baden to Bülow, 16 February 1898; Bülow, *Denkwürdigkeiten*, I, p. 215.

216 See, for example, Waldersee, *Denkwürdigkeiten*, II, 1898, p. 408 and 10 February 1898, p. 410; Vierhaus, *Spitzemberg*, 11 February 1898, p. 365; Bülow, *Denkwürdigkeiten*, I, pp. 194ff.

217 Hohenlohe, *Denkwürdigkeiten der Reichskanzlerzeit*, 'Promemoria über die Besetzung einiger Aemter', July 1896, p. 243.

218 HHSA Wien, 151, Szögyényi to Goluchowski, 9 April 1898. See also Hohenlohe, *Denkwürdigkeiten der Reichskanzlerzeit*, p. 582.

219 BA Koblenz, BP, 76, Eulenburg to Bülow, 9 June 1897; Rich and Fisher, *Holstein Papers*, IV, Holstein to Bülow, 26 June 1899, p. 134 and Holstein to Pietro Blaserna, 11 April 1900, p. 180.

220 HSA Stuttgart, Varnbüler's Report, 4 July 1897.

221 HHSA Wien, 161, Szögyényi's Report, 7 April 1904. For Holstein's position after 1897, see especially Rich, *Holstein*, II, pp. 547ff.

222 Rich, *Holstein*, II, p. 552.

223 Rich and Fisher, *Holstein Papers*, IV, Holstein to Bülow, 2 October 1898, p. 96.

224 Ibid., Holstein to Bülow, 24 June 1899, p. 131.

225 Ibid., Holstein to Pietro Blaserna, 11 April 1900, pp. 178f.

226 HHSA Wien, 151, Szögyényi to Goluchowski, 9 April 1898. For Bülow's suspected role in the affair, see Vierhaus, *Spitzemberg*, 25 September 1910, p. 524.

227 Rich and Fisher, *Holstein Papers*, IV, Holstein to Bülow, 24 June 1899, p. 131. See also Herbert Bismarck's letters to Bülow in BA Koblenz, BP, 66 and Bülow, *Denkwürdigkeiten*, I, p. 23.

228 Rich and Fisher, *Holstein Papers*, IV, Holstein to Pietro Blaserna, 11 April 1900, p. 180.
229 Ibid., Bülow to Holstein, 24 June 1899, p. 132.
230 Ibid., Bülow to Holstein, 20 April 1900, p. 182.
231 Röhl, *Eulenburg*, III, Eulenburg to Bülow, 23 August 1897, p. 1861; Haller, *Aus dem Leben*, p. 253.
232 Hohenlohe, *Denkwürdigkeiten der Reichskanzlerzeit*, Alexander Hohenlohe to Prince Hohenlohe, 14 August 1897, p. 375; Cecil, *German Diplomatic Service*, p. 289.
233 Rich, *Holstein*, II, p. 552.
234 See Röhl, *Eulenburg*, III, Bülow to Eulenburg, 22 August 1897, p. 1858.
235 BA Koblenz, BP, 14, Alfred Bülow to Bülow, 6 August 1897.
236 Ibid., 66, Herbert Bismarck to Bülow, 12 December 1897.
237 BA Koblenz, Oswald Richthofen Papers, 5, Bülow to Richthofen, 26 July 1899. See also Bülow, *Denkwürdigkeiten*, I, pp. 217f.
238 Cecil, *German Diplomatic Service*, p. 289; Bernstorff, *Memoirs*, p. 45.
239 Bülow, *Denkwürdigkeiten*, I, p. 7.
240 HHSA Wien, 151, Szögyényi to Goluchowski, 15 January 1898.
241 Fuchs, *Grossherzog Friedrich*, Jagemann to Brauer, 8 January 1900, p. 222.
242 See especially the advice given to Bülow by his father and Hatzfeldt in Bülow, *Denkwürdigkeiten*, IV, pp. 289f., 292.
243 ZSA Potsdam, Hammann Papers, 7, Bülow to Hammann [1902].
244 Cecil, *German Diplomatic Service*, p. 302.
245 Bülow, *Denkwürdigkeiten*, I, p. 25.
246 See Bülow's notes on his health and diet in BA Koblenz, BP, 150, Notebook entitled 'Kant. Macht des Gemuthes' (1903) and BP, 32. See also Bülow, *Denkwürdigkeiten*, IV, pp. 41, 115; Cecil, *German Diplomatic Service*, p. 302.
247 Peter Rassow and Karl-Erich Born (eds.), *Akten zur staatlichen Sozialpolitik in Deutschland 1890–1914* (Wiesbaden, 1959), Lerchenfeld to Podewils, 28 March 1903, p. 141.
248 See BA Koblenz, BP, 152, Losungen, for an indication of how frequently the Bülows entertained. See also BA Koblenz, Loebell Papers, 27, unpublished memoirs, pp. 65f.
249 Hutten-Czapski, *Sechzig Jahre*, I, pp. 327f.
250 See also ch. 3, pp. 109f. below.
251 HSA Stuttgart, Varnbüler's Report, 23 February 1898.
252 BA Koblenz, BP, 90, Holstein to Bülow, 9 June 1897. The political system is discussed in detail in ch. 2, pp. 41ff. below.
253 Röhl, *Eulenburg*, III, Eulenburg to Bülow, 7 July 1897, p. 1840.
254 HHSA Wien, 151, Szögyényi's Report, 24 May 1899 (no. 25E).
255 Röhl, *Germany Without Bismarck*, especially pp. 267f.; Waldersee, *Denkwürdigkeiten*, II, 1898, p. 408 and 22 August 1899, p. 432.
256 See, for example, Fuchs, *Grossherzog Friedrich*, Bülow to Grand Duke Friedrich, 17 April 1899, p. 142 and 31 December 1899, p. 218.
257 HHSA Wien, 151, Szögyényi to Goluchowski, 18 June 1898. Bülow was also aware of the need for Centre support, especially because of the naval issue. See BA Koblenz, BP, 76, Eulenburg to Bülow, 23 August 1897 and Winzen, *Bülows Weltmachtkonzept*, pp. 108ff. For the inauguration of *Sammlungspolitik*, see Röhl, *Germany Without Bismarck*, pp. 246ff. See also the literature listed under n. 12 of the introduction above.
258 See BA Koblenz, O. Richtofen Papers, 5, Bülow to Richthofen, 26 July 1899, in which he outlines his criteria for the selection of a new Director of the Trade Department.
259 BA Koblenz, BP, 91, Holstein to Bülow, 26 November 1899. This is the letter which Rich and Fisher were unable to find, *Holstein Papers*, IV, p. 167, n. 4.
260 BA Koblenz, BP, 91, Bülow to Holstein, 28 November 1899, pp. 167f.

261 Monts, *Erinnerungen*, pp. 155f.
262 Fuchs, *Grossherzog Friedrich*, Jagemann to Reck, 18 April 1899, pp. 143f. For the interpellation on Samoa, see *Reichstag*, 14 April 1899, pp. 1754ff. The Samoan issue is discussed by Paul Kennedy, *The Rise of the Anglo-German Antagonism 1860–1914* (London, 1980), pp. 237ff. See also Paul Kennedy, *The Samoan Tangle. A Study in Anglo-German-American Relations, 1878–1900* (Dublin and New York, 1974).
263 HSA Stuttgart, Varnbüler's Report, 16 April 1899.
264 Ibid., 24 December 1897.
265 Fuchs, *Grossherzog Friedrich*, Jagemann to Brauer, 1 March 1899, p. 120 and 3 October 1899, p. 173.
266 BA Koblenz, BP, 89, Hohenlohe to Bülow, 27 October 1899; Bülow, *Denkwürdigkeiten*, I, p. 362.
267 Monts, *Erinnerungen*, Monts to Tschirschky, 7 January 1899, p. 405.
268 HHSA Wien, 151, Szögyényi to Goluchowski, 21 May 1898.
269 Hohenlohe, *Denkwürdigkeiten der Reichskanzlerzeit*, Bülow to Hohenlohe, 26 June 1899, p. 508; Wilmowski to Hohenlohe, 23 October 1899, p. 533; Bülow to Hohenlohe, 15 March 1900, p. 568; PA Bonn, IA, Deutschland, 122, no. 2f, Bd. II, Bülow to Hohenlohe, 27 June 1898.
270 HHSA Wien, 153, Szögyényi's Report, 3 January 1900.
271 Fuchs, *Grossherzog Friedrich*, Jagemann to Brauer, 1 December 1899, p. 209; HHSA Wien, 154, Thurn's Report, 19 October 1900; HSA München, 1071, Lerchenfeld's Report, 20 October 1900. Cf. Karl Bachem, *Vorgeschichte, Geschichte und Politik der Deutschen Zentrumspartei*, 9 vols. (Cologne, 1927–32), VI, p. 98.
272 HHSA Wien, 153, Szögyényi's Report, 3 January 1900.
273 Fuchs, *Grossherzog Friedrich*, Jagemann to Reck, 6 June 1898, p. 43.
274 Röhl, *Eulenburg*, III, Bülow to Eulenburg, 20 July 1898, p. 1911.
275 Ibid., Eulenburg to Bülow, 29 July 1898, p. 1918.
276 HHSA Wien, 153, Szögyényi's Report, 3 January 1900.
277 Fuchs, *Grossherzog Friedrich*, Jagemann to Brauer, 1 December 1899, p. 209.
278 ZSA Merseburg, Staatsministerium, Rep. 90a, BIII, 2b, no. 6, 140–1
279 SA Köln, Bachem Papers, 27, note of 13 June 1900.
280 Fuchs, *Grossherzog Friedrich*, Jagemann to Reck, 17 September 1900, p. 260; Röhl, *Germany Without Bismarck*, pp. 269f.
281 Hohenlohe, *Denkwürdigkeiten der Reichskanzlerzeit*, 15 October 1900, p. 591.
282 Bülow, *Denkwürdigkeiten*, I, pp. 358ff.
283 See Röhl, *Germany Without Bismarck*, pp. 268f.
284 Fuchs, *Grossherzog Friedrich*, Brauer to Grand Duke Friedrich, 5 August 1900, p. 257. For the 'Hun speech', see Bernd Sösemann, 'Die sog. Hunnenrede Wilhelms II. Textkritische und interpretatorische Bemerkungen zur Ansprache des Kaisers vom 27 Juli 1900 in Bremerhaven', *Historische Zeitschrift*, CCXXII (1976), 342–58.
285 Röhl, *Eulenburg*, III, Eulenburg to Bülow, 14 July 1900, pp. 1983f., 24 September 1900, pp. 1992ff., and 1 October 1900, pp. 2001ff. See Röhl, *Germany Without Bismarck*, pp. 268f. and Bülow, *Denkwürdigkeiten*, I, p. 455ff.
286 Bülow, *Denkwürdigkeiten*, I, p. 360.
287 Ibid., p. 371.
288 HHSA Wien, 154, Szögyényi's Report, 14 November 1900.

2 The assumption of the Chancellorship, 1900–1901

1 BA Koblenz, Eulenburg Papers, 56, August Eulenburg to Philipp Eulenburg, 17 October 1900, p. 284.

2 HHSA Wien, 154, Thurn's Report, 19 October 1900; GLA Karlsruhe, 233/34807, Jagemann's Report, 25 October 1900 (no. 139).

3 HHSA Wien, 154, Szögyényi's Report, 14 November 1900.

4 HSA Stuttgart, Varnbüler's Report, 24 October 1900.

5 Bülow, *Denkwürdigkeiten*, I, pp. 371ff.; BA Koblenz, BP, 152, Losungen, 7 October 1900; PA Bonn, AA, IA, Deutschland, 122, no. 2f, Bd. IV, Bülow to Hammann, 17 October 1900.

6 HHSA Wien, 154, Thurn's Report, 19 October 1900.

7 HSA München, 1071, Lerchenfeld's Report, 20 October 1900; BA Koblenz, BP, 108, Hugo Jacobi to Bülow, 19 October 1900; BA Koblenz, Rottenburg Papers, 10, Prince Friedrich Wilhelm to Franz von Rottenburg, 14 December 1900; HHSA Wien, 155, Szögyényi's Report, 16 January 1901.

8 For recent but flawed treatments of the political system, see H. W. Koch, *A Constitutional History of Germany in the Nineteenth and Twentieth Centuries* (London and New York, 1984) and Ernst R. Huber, *Deutsche Verfassungsgeschichte seit 1789. Bd. IV. Struktur und Krisen des Kaiserreichs* (Stuttgart, Berlin, Cologne and Mainz, 1969). See also Suval, *Electoral Politics* for the electoral system. Some of the older works are more informative. See, for example, A. Lawrence Lowell, *Governments and Parties in Continental Europe*, 2 vols. (Boston, New York and Chicago, 1896).

9 See Röhl, *Germany Without Bismarck*, especially pp. 85ff.

10 Jarausch, *Enigmatic Chancellor*, p. 66.

11 HHSA Wien, 154, Thurn's Report, 19 October 1900.

12 Ibid., 155, Szöygényi's Report, 2 January 1901.

13 See, for example, Fuchs, *Grossherzog Friedrich*, Jagemann to Brauer, 18 October 1900, pp. 263f; HSA München, 1071, Lerchenfeld's Report, 25 October 1900.

14 BA Koblenz, Eulenburg Papers, 56 Eulenburg to Wilhelm II, 22 October 1900, pp. 228f.

15 GLA Karlsruhe, 34807, Jagemann's Report, 31 October 1900; Hutten-Czapski, *Sechzig Jahre*, I, p. 84; Fuchs, *Grossherzog Friedrich*, Jagemann to Brauer, 20 October 1900, p. 264.

16 BA Koblenz, BP, 22, Posadowsky to Wilhelm II, 18 October 1900; Bülow, *Denkwürdigkeiten*, I, pp. 386f.

17 Hohenlohe, *Denkwürdigkeiten der Reichskanzlerzeit*, 16 October 1900, p. 592.

18 HSA München, 1071, Lerchenfeld's Report, 25 October 1900; cf. Peter-Christian Witt, *Die Finanzpolitik des Deutschen Reiches von 1903–1913* (Lübeck, 1970), p. 63.

19 BA Koblenz, BP, 98, Bülow to Richthofen, 19 October 1900.

20 Bülow, *Denkwürdigkeiten*, I, p. 393.

21 Fuchs, *Grossherzog Friedrich*, Jagemann to Brauer, 20 October 1900, p. 265; HSA Stuttgart, Varnbüler's Report, 24 October 1900.

22 HHSA Wien, 154, Szögyényi's Report, 14 November 1900 (no. 54E). See also Rich, *Holstein*, II, p. 552.

23 See for example A. von Brauer, *Im Dienste Bismarcks*, ed. H. Rogge (Berlin, 1936), Holstein to Brauer, 7 December 1905, p. 410.

24 HHSA Wien, 154, Szögyényi's Report, 14 November 1900 and Thurn's Report, 20 October 1900.

25 BA Koblenz, BP, 98, Lichnowsky to Bülow, 18 October 1900.

26 Ibid., Bülow to Lichnowsky, 19 October 1900.

27 HSA München, 1071, Lerchenfeld's Report, 25 October 1900. See also HHSA Wien, 154, Thurn's Report, 19 October 1900.

28 HHSA Wien, 154, Szögyényi's Report, 14 November 1900.

29 PRO London, FO 64, 1520, Lascelles's Report, 8 March 1901.

30 PA Bonn, IA, Deutschland, 122, no. 13, Bd. I, Bülow to Foreign Office, 19 October 1900.

31 HSA München, 1071, Lerchenfeld's Reports, 20 October 1900 and 25 October 1900.
32 See especially Röhl, *Germany Without Bismarck*, pp. 241ff. for following.
33 ZSA Merseburg, Staatsministerium, 141, 23 October 1900.
34 Röhl, *Germany Without Bismarck*, p. 174.
35 HHSA Wien, 154, Thurn's Report, 27 October 1900.
36 See Witt, *Finanzpolitik*, pp. 63ff.; Hentschel, *Wirtschaft und Wirtschaftspolitik*, pp. 174ff.
37 Fuchs, *Grossherzog Friedrich*, Jagemann to Brauer, 27 October 1900, p. 267.
38 SA Köln, Bachem Papers, 170, 'Bei Nieberding', 29 October 1900.
39 Fuchs, *Grossherzog Friedrich*, Jagemann to Brauer, 27 October 1900, p. 267.
40 See Witt, *Finanzpolitik*, p. 66.
41 HHSA Wien, 154, Thurn's Report, 19 October 1900.
42 Fuchs, *Grossherzog Friedrich*, Jagemann to Brauer, 18 October 1900, p. 263.
43 Röhl, *Eulenburg*, II, Bülow to Eulenburg, 2 May 1894, p. 1297.
44 BA Koblenz, O. Richthofen Papers, 5, Bülow to Richthofen, 26 July 1899.
45 Fuchs, *Grossherzog Friedrich*, Jagemann to Brauer, 27 October 1900, p. 267.
46 HHSA Wien, 155, Szögyényi's Report, 2 January 1901.
47 Fuchs, *Grossherzog Friedrich*, Jagemann to Brauer, 27 October 1900, p. 267.
48 See also Witt, *Finanzpolitik*, pp. 67f.
49 Bleyberg, 'Government and Legislative Process', pp. 89f.
50 HSA München, 1071, Lerchenfeld's Report, 31 October 1900.
51 See also Witt, *Finanzpolitik*, pp. 67f.; Hans Herzfeld, *Johannes von Miquel*, 2 vols. (Detmold, 1938), II, pp. 617f.
52 HSA München, 1071, Lerchenfeld's Report, 5 November 1900.
53 Ibid., 10 December 1900.
54 Ibid. and 31 October 1900.
55 Ibid., 6 November 1900.
56 See especially Röhl, *Germany Without Bismarck*, pp. 98ff., 217ff.
57 HSA München, 1071, Lerchenfeld's Report, 25 October 1900.
58 PA Bonn, IA, Deutschland, 122, no. 13, Bd. II, Eisendecher to Bülow, 27 October 1900.
59 Ibid., Wilmowski to Hammann, 21 December 1900.
60 Rassow and Born, *Akten zur staatlichen Sozialpolitik*, Lerchenfeld's Report, 7 December 1900, p. 133.
61 Monts, *Erinnerungen*, Monts to Tschirschky, 14 January 1901, p. 410.
62 Fuchs, *Grossherzog Friedrich*, Brauer to Bodmann, 14 January 1901, pp. 286f.
63 Bülow, *Denkwürdigkeiten*, I, pp. 476ff.
64 HHSA Wien, 155, Szögyényi's Report, 2 January 1901.
65 Fuchs, *Grossherzog Friedrich*, Bodmann to Brauer, 18 December 1900, p. 279; PA Bonn, IA, Deutschland, 122, no. 13, Bd. II, Bülow to Wilhelm II, 20 December 1900, Wilmowski to Hammann, 21 December 1900 and Monts's Report, 19 December 1900.
66 Bülow, *Denkwürdigkeiten*, I, p. 392.
67 Fuchs, *Grossherzog Friedrich*, Brauer to Jagemann, 24 December 1900, p. 280.
68 See especially ibid., Jagemann to Brauer, 17 June 1898, p. 47.
69 Ibid., Jagemann to Brauer, 7 May 1898, p. 41.
70 Röhl, *Germany Without Bismarck*, pp. 263f.
71 ZSA Merseburg, Hausarchiv, Rep. 53J Lit. B, 16a, Bd. II, Bülow to Wilhelm II, 22 August 1900. Cf. the advice of Posadowsky. See PA Bonn, IA, Deutschland, 125, Generalia, Bd. I, Posadowsky to Bülow, 2 July 1900 and Bülow to Foreign Office, 24 August 1900.
72 Bülow, *Denkwürdigkeiten*, I, pp. 358ff.; Fuchs, *Grossherzog Friedrich*, Brauer to Grand Duke Friedrich, 5 August 1900, p. 257.

73 Fuchs, *Grossherzog Friedrich*, Jagemann to Brauer, 18 October 1900, p. 263.

74 HHSA Wien, 155, Szögyényi's Report, 2 January 1901.

75 HSA Stuttgart, Varnbüler's Report, 17 November 1900; Reichstag, 14 November 1900, pp. 1f.

76 HHSA Wien, 154, Szögyényi's Report, 20 November 1900; SA Köln, Bachem Papers, note of 21 November 1900.

77 Reichstag, 19 November 1900, pp. 11ff.; Bülow, *Reden*, I, pp. 126ff.

78 HHSA Wien, 154, Szögyényi's Report, 20 November 1900.

79 SA Köln, Bachem Papers, 116, note of [19 November] 1900.

80 SA Köln, Bachem Papers, 116, note of 23 November 1900; Reichstag, 20 November 1900, pp. 61ff.

81 Fuchs, *Grossherzog Friedrich*, Jagemann to Brauer, 20 November 1900, p. 273.

82 Reichstag, 20 November 1900, pp. 61f.; Bülow, *Reden*, I, pp. 143f.; HHSA Wien, 154, Szögyényi's Report, 20 November 1900 (P.S. of 21 November 1900).

83 HHSA Wien, 154, Szögyényi's Report, 20 November 1900.

84 See Bülow, *Denkwürdigkeiten*, I, pp. 467f.; Born, *Staat und Sozialpolitik*, p. 181.

85 Rassow and Born, *Akten zur staatlichen Sozialpolitik*, Lerchenfeld's Report, 26 October 1900, pp. 131ff.

86 GLA Karlsruhe, 34807, Jagemann's Report, 25 October 1900; HHSA Wien, 154, Thurn's Report, 27 October 1900.

87 Fuchs, *Grossherzog Friedrich*, Jagemann to Brauer, 29 November 1900, pp. 275ff.

88 Reichstag, 24 November 1900, pp. 138f.; Bülow, *Reden*, I, pp. 154ff.

89 HHSA Wien, 154, Szögyényi's Report, 25 November 1900.

90 Rassow and Born, *Akten zur staatlichen Sozialpolitik*, Lerchenfeld's Report, 27 November 1900, p. 132.

91 Ibid., 7 December 1900, p. 133.

92 HSA München, 1071, Lerchenfeld's Report, 20 October 1900; HHSA Wien, 154, Thurn's Report, 24 October 1900.

93 Rassow and Born, *Akten zur staatlichen Sozialpolitik*, Lerchenfeld's Report, 17 January 1900, p. 134.

94 BA Koblenz, Eulenburg Papers, 56, Bülow to Eulenburg, 22 November 1900.

95 BA Koblenz, BP, 77, Eulenburg to Bülow, 21 November 1900. See also Bülow, *Denkwürdigkeiten*, I, p. 499.

96 BA Koblenz, Eulenburg Papers, 56, Eulenburg to Wilhelm II, 22 November 1900.

97 BA Koblenz, BP, 77, Eulenburg to Bülow, 21 November 1900; Bülow, *Denkwürdigkeiten*, I, p. 499.

98 Bülow, *Denkwürdigkeiten*, I, p. 499.

99 BA Koblenz, BP, 23, Metternich to Bülow, 25 November 1900.

100 Reichstag, 12 December 1900, pp. 473ff.; Bülow, *Reden*, I, pp. 169f. See too Roger Chickering, *We Men Who Feel Most German. A Cultural Study of the Pan-German League, 1886–1914* (Boston, 1984), pp. 67f. and 212ff.

101 HHSA Wien, 154, Szögyényi to Goluchowski, 18 December 1900.

102 Bülow, *Denkwürdigkeiten*, I, p. 492.

103 HSA München, 1071, Lerchenfeld's Report, 25 October 1900.

104 GLA Karlsruhe, 34807, Jagemann's Report, 8 December 1900.

105 See Bülow, *Denkwürdigkeiten*, I, p. 531.

106 SA Köln, Bachem Papers, 165, 'Zum Toleranzantrag', 5 December 1900. See also Bachem, *Zentrumspartei*, VI, pp. 101ff.

107 GLA Karlsruhe, 34807, Jagemann's Report, 6 December 1900.

108 Reichstag, 5 December 1900, pp. 301f.; Bülow, *Reden*, I, pp. 159f.

109 SA Köln, Bachem Papers, 165, 'Zum Toleranzantrag', 5 December 1900.

110 GLA Karlsruhe, 34807, Jagemann's Report, 6 December 1900.

111 SA Köln, Bachem Papers, 165, note of 29 April 1901.

112 ZSA Merseburg, Staatsministerium, 141, 8 December 1900.

113 Fuchs, *Grossherzog Friedrich*, Jagemann to Brauer, 15 March 1899, p. 128.

114 HSA Stuttgart, Varnbüler's Report, 16 January 1901.

115 SA Köln, Bachem Papers, 170, Bachem to Dahlmann, 27 October 1900.

116 ZSA Potsdam, Hammann Papers, 6, *Vorwärts*, 29 November 1900; Otto Hammann, *Zur Vorgeschichte des Weltkrieges: Erinnerungen aus den Jahren 1897–1906* (Berlin, 1918), p. 103.

117 HHSA Wien, 156, Szögyényi to Goluchowski, 6 May 1901.

118 For the failure of the Canal Bill in 1899, see Röhl, *Germany Without Bismarck*, p. 264. See also Hannelore Horn, *Der Kampf um den Bau des Mittellandkanals* (Cologne, 1964). For an assessment of the Bill's prospects in 1901, see HHSA Wien, 155, Szögyényi's Report, 16 January 1901.

119 GLA Karlsruhe, 34807, Jagemann's Report, 13 January 1901.

120 Ibid., 31 December 1900.

121 Landtag, 9 January 1901, 1–6; Bülow, *Reden*, I, pp. 176ff.

122 Fuchs, *Grossherzog Friedrich*, Jagemann to Brauer, 1 May 1901, p. 310.

123 Ibid., Jagemann to Brauer, 29 January 1901, pp. 288f. A *Doppelzentner* is 100 kilograms or approximately two hundredweight. Thus the new level would have been over 50 Marks a ton.

124 Ibid., Jagemann to Brauer, 18 February 1901, p. 290.

125 See especially Winzen, *Bülows Weltmachtkonzept*, pp. 296ff.

126 BA Koblenz, BP, 22, Plessen to Bülow, 1 February 1901.

127 HHSA Wien, 155, Szögyényi's Report, 15 February 1901.

128 BA Koblenz, Eulenburg Papers, 57, Eulenburg to Bülow, 23 February 1901.

129 MA Stuttgart, M/2, 24, Schaefer to War Minister, 6 March 1901. See also FCO London, Holstein Papers, 30, Holstein to Bülow, 8 March 1901.

130 See, for example, BA Koblenz, BP, 109, Kaiserin Viktoria to Bülow, 23 February 1901.

131 See Bülow, *Denkwürdigkeiten*, I, pp. 518f.

132 HHSA Wien, 155, Szögyényi's Report, 13 March 1901.

133 HSA München, 1073, Lerchenfeld's Report, 17 March 1901.

134 HHSA Wien, 155, Szögyényi's Report, 26 March 1901.

135 HSA München, 2679, Lerchenfeld's Report, 4 April 1901; HHSA Wien, 155, Szögyényi's Report, 4 April 1901. See Bülow, *Denkwürdigkeiten*, I, pp. 519f.

136 Fuchs, *Grossherzog Friedrich*, Grand Duke Friedrich to Bülow, 31 March 1901, p. 301.

137 Ibid., Jagemann to Brauer, 31 March 1901, p. 302.

138 SA Köln, Bachem Papers, 170, note of 27 February 1901.

139 Ibid., 'Bei Bülow', 8 March 1901.

140 HHSA Wien, 155, Szögyényi's Report, 14 April 1901.

141 Ibid., 4 April 1901.

142 Fuchs, *Grossherzog Friedrich*, Bülow to Grand Duke Friedrich, 26 April 1901, p. 306.

143 See, for example, BA Koblenz, BP, 77, Bülow to Eulenburg, 24 February 1901; Bülow, *Denkwürdigkeiten*, I, p. 499.

144 Röhl, *Eulenburg*, III, Eulenburg to Bülow, 1 March 1901, pp. 2016ff.

145 BA Koblenz, Eulenburg Papers, 57, Bülow to Eulenburg, 6 March 1901.

146 Fuchs, *Grossherzog Friedrich*, Bodmann to Brauer, 11 April 1901, p. 304.

147 ZSA Potsdam, Hammann Papers, 7, Bülow to Hammann, 18 April 1901.

148 BA Koblenz, Eulenburg Papers, 57, Bülow to Eulenburg, 16 May 1901.

149 Fuchs, *Grossherzog Friedrich*, Jagemann to Brauer, 1 May 1901, p. 309.

150 SA Köln, Bachem Papers, 124, note of 7 May 1901.
151 Ibid., note of 4 May 1901.
152 ZSA Merseburg, Hausarchiv, Adjutants' Diaries, 9, 30 April 1901 to 3 May 1901; BA Koblenz, BP, 152, Losungen, 30 April 1901.
153 ZSA Merseburg, Staatsministerium, 142, 2 May 1901.
154 Landtag, 3 May 1901, 4125–6; Bülow, *Reden*, I, pp. 220f.
155 HHSA Wien, 155, Szögyényi's Report, 6 May 1901.
156 HSA Stuttgart, Varnbüler's Report, 5 May 1901.
157 HSA München, 1073, Lerchenfeld's Report, 4 May 1901.
158 HSA Stuttgart, Varnbüler's Report, 5 May 1901.
159 SA Köln, Bachem Papers, 124, note of 7 May 1901; Bülow, *Denkwürdigkeiten*, I, pp. 522f.
160 ZSA Merseburg, Zivilkabinett, 3697, resignation requests of 3 May 1901.
161 SA Köln, Bachem Papers, 124, note of 7 May 1901; HHSA Wien, 155, Szögyényi's Report, 4 May 1901.
162 HSA München, 1073, Lerchenfeld's Reports, 2 May 1901 and 5 May 1901; HSA Stuttgart, Varnbüler's Report, 5 May 1901.
163 Fuchs, *Grossherzog Friedrich*, Bodmann to Brauer, 23 November 1900, p. 275.
164 HSA München, 1073, Lerchenfeld's Report, 5 May 1901.
165 HSA Stuttgart, Varnbüler's Report, 5 May 1901.
166 SA Köln, Bachem Papers, 165, note of 29 April 1901 . See also ch. 3, pp. 104f. below.
167 Ibid., 124, note of 7 May 1901.
168 HSA München, 1073, Lerchenfeld's Report, 5 May 1901.
169 HSA Stuttgart, Varnbüler's Reports, 5 May 1901 and 8 May 1901.
170 Fuchs, *Grossherzog Friedrich*, Jagemann to Brauer, 4 May 1901, p. 314.
171 HSA München, 1073, Lerchenfeld's Report, 2 May 1901.
172 Fuchs, *Grossherzog Friedrich*, Jagemann to Brauer, 4 May 1901, p. 314.
173 HHSA Wien, 155, Szögyényi's Report, 6 May 1901.
174 HSA Stuttgart, Varnbüler's Report, 8 May 1901.
175 BA Koblenz, Reichskanzlei, 1644, Podbielski to Bülow, 18 January 1901.
176 HSA Stuttgart, Varnbüler's Report, 8 May 1901; HHSA Wien, 156, Szögyényi to Goluchowski, 6 May 1901.
177 HSA München, 1073, Lerchenfeld's Report, 5 May 1901.
178 HSA Stuttgart, Varnbüler's Report, 8 May 1901.
179 Fuchs, *Grossherzog Friedrich*, Jagemann to Brauer, 8 May 1901, p. 318.
180 HSA München, 1073, Lerchenfeld's Report, 5 May 1901.
181 HSA Stuttgart, Varnbüler's Report, 8 May 1901. Hans Hermann von Berlepsch was Prussian Minister of Trade from 1890 to 1896 and associated with a 'progressive' social policy.
182 HHSA Wien, 155, Szögyényi's Report, 6 May 1901 (no. 22B).
183 HSA Stuttgart, Varnbüler's Report, 8 May 1901.
184 HHSA Wien, 155, Szögyényi's Report (Tel.), 6 May 1901.
185 BA Koblenz, Eulenburg Papers, 57, August Eulenburg to Philipp Eulenburg, 16 May 1901. See Röhl, *Eulenburg*, III, Eulenburg to Bülow, 14 May 1901, p. 2019, n. 6.
186 HSA Stuttgart, Varnbüler's Report, 8 May 1901; Röhl, *Eulenburg*, III, Eulenburg to Bülow, 14 May 1901, p. 2019.
187 ZSA Merseburg, Hausarchiv, Adjutants' Diaries, 9, April–May 1901.
188 Röhl, *Eulenburg*, III, Eulenburg to Bülow, 14 May 1901, p. 2019.
189 ZSA Merseburg, Hausarchiv, Adjutants' Diaries, 9; Fuchs, *Grossherzog Friedrich*, Jagemann to Brauer, 5 May 1901, p. 315.
190 HHSA Wien, 156, Szögyényi to Goluchowski, 6 May 1901; HSA Stuttgart, Varnbüler's Report, 8 May 1901.

191 HSA München, 1073, Lerchenfeld's Report, 5 May 1901; HHSA Wien, 156, Szögyényi to Goluchowski, 6 May 1901.

192 Fuchs, *Grossherzog Friedrich*, Jagemann to Brauer, 5 May 1901 and 8 May 1901, pp. 315–18.

193 HSA München, 1073, Lerchenfeld's Report, 7 May 1901.

194 Fuchs, *Grossherzog Friedrich*, Jagemann to Brauer, 5 May 1901, p. 316.

195 HSA Stuttgart, Varnbüler's Report, 8 May 1901. As *Oberpräsident* of Brandenburg, Bethmann Hollweg also refused to punish the recalcitrant *Landräte* who had opposed the *Mittellandkanal*. See Jarausch, *Enigmatic Chancellor*, p. 44.

196 Fuchs, *Grossherzog Friedrich*, Jagemann to Brauer, 8 May 1901, p. 318.

197 HHSA Wien, 156, Szögyényi to Goluchowski, 6 May 1901; ZSA Potsdam, Reichskanzlei, 2038, Wilhelm II to Bülow, 5 May 1901.

198 HSA München, 1073, Lerchenfeld's Report, 5 May 1901.

199 Fuchs, *Grossherzog Friedrich*, Jagemann to Brauer, 8 May 1901, p. 318; HHSA Wien, 155, Szögyényi's Report, 10 May 1901.

200 HSA München, 1073, Lerchenfeld's Report, 7 May 1901.

201 HSA Stuttgart, Varnbüler's Report, 8 May 1901.

202 BA Koblenz, Eulenburg Papers, 57, Eulenburg to Bülow, 14 May 1901; HHSA Wien, 155, Szögyényi's Report, 10 May 1901.

203 HSA Stuttgart, Varnbüler's Report, 8 May 1901.

204 BA Koblenz, Eulenburg Papers, 57, Eulenburg to Bülow, 14 May 1901.

205 HSA Stuttgart, Varnbüler's Report, 5 May 1901.

206 SA Köln, Bachem Papers, 165, note of 7 May 1901.

207 HSA Stuttgart, Varnbüler's Report, 8 May 1901.

208 HHSA Wien, 155, Szögyényi's Report, 6 May 1901. The British ambassador also reported that although Bülow had cleverly tided over a difficult situation, his prestige had not been increased. See PRO London, FO 64, 1521, Lascelles's Report, 10 May 1901.

209 HSA München, 1073, Lerchenfeld's Report, 7 May 1901.

3 The Bülow system, 1901–1905

1 A good political history of the Wilhelmine Empire is still lacking. The Empire's financial difficulties are examined thoroughly in Witt, *Finanzpolitik*; for the navy, see Berghahn, *Der Tirpitz-Plan*; for the colonies, see Woodruff D. Smith, *The German Colonial Empire* (Chapel Hill, 1978).

2 For the following see especially Eckart Kehr, 'Englandhass und Weltpolitik', in *Der Primat der Innenpolitik*, pp. 149ff.; Wehler, *German Empire*, pp. 46, 94ff.; Berghahn, *Der Tirpitz-Plan*, pp. 15ff., 592ff.; Stegmann, *Die Erben Bismarcks*, pp. 80ff.; cf. Eley, '*Sammlungspolitik*', pp. 110ff. See also Hentschel, *Wirtschaft und Wirtschaftspolitik*, p. 190; Geyer, *Deutsche Rüstungspolitik*, p. 81. For a full but flawed discussion of the tariff issue, see Bleyberg, 'Government and Legislative Process'.

3 See especially PA Bonn, IA, Deutschland, 172 secr., Bd. IV, Hammann's memorandum, 29 November 1902.

4 Rassow and Born, *Akten zur staatlichen Sozialpolitik*, Lerchenfeld to Podewils, 28 March 1903, p. 145. See also ZSA Potsdam, Hammann Papers, 7, Bülow to Hammann, 28 December 1902 and James Retallack, 'Conservatives *Contra* Chancellor: Official Responses to the Spectra of Conservative Demagoguery from Bismarck to Bülow', *Canadian Journal of History*, 20 (1985), 218.

5 Cf. Stegmann, *Die Erben Bismarcks*, pp. 14, 89ff.; Wehler, *German Empire*, p. 97. See also Hentschel, *Wirtschaft und Wirtschaftspolitik*, pp. 174, 176f., 183ff. and 190f.

6 GLA Karlsruhe, 34807, Jagemann's Reports, 3 June 1901 and 5 June 1901; HHSA Wien, 155, Szögyényi's Report, 21 May 1901 and 156, Szögyényi to Goluchowski, 2 June 1901.

7 See Witt, *Finanzpolitik*, pp. 70f.; Hentschel, *Wirtschaft und Wirtschaftspolitik*, pp. 188f.; *Reichstag*, 2 December 1901, pp. 2883f.

8 SA Köln, Bachem Papers, 173, note of 2 December 1901; HHSA Wien, 156, Szögyényi to Goluchowski, 3 December 1901.

9 BA Koblenz, O. Richthofen Papers, 6, 'Zolltarifkommission-Sitzung', 26 February 1902.

10 Fuchs, *Grossherzog Friedrich*, Jagemann to Brauer, 21 February 1902, p. 384; Witt, *Finanzpolitik*, p. 70.

11 FCO London, Holstein Papers, 35, Bülow to Holstein [1902]. On the widening gulf between Bülow and the Conservatives, see HHSA Wien, 157, Szögyényi's Report, 18 June 1902 and HSA Stuttgart, Varnbüler's Report, 8 July 1902.

12 BA Koblenz, BP, 22, Bülow to Richthofen, 14 September 1902.

13 SA Köln, Bachem Papers, 170, note of 16 September 1902.

14 ZSA Potsdam, Hammann Papers, 7, Bülow to Hammann, 3 October 1902. See also Rich and Fisher, *Holstein Papers*, IV, Bülow to Holstein, 4 October 1902, pp. 265ff.

15 See chapter 3, pp. 96f. below.

16 BA Koblenz, BP, 107, memorandum of 23 November 1902. See also PA Bonn, IA, Deutschland, 172 secr., Bd. IV, Hammann's memorandum, 29 November 1902.

17 Rich, *Holstein Papers*, IV, diary entry, 11 November 1902, p. 272; BA Koblenz, BP, 112, Wilhelm II to Bülow, 14 December 1902; HHSA Wien, 158, Szögyényi to Goluchowski, 16 December 1902.

18 See Born, *Staat und Sozialpolitik*, pp. 183f.; Witt, *Finanzpolitik*, p. 71. See also Loth, *Katholiken im Kaiserreich*, p. 116.

19 See Horn, *Mittellandkanal*, pp. 114ff.

20 See especially HSA Stuttgart, Varnbüler's Report, 21 October 1903.

21 *Reichstag*, 20 January 1903, p. 7431; Fuchs, *Grossherzog Friedrich*, Jagemann to Foreign Minister, 30 January 1903, p. 472. See also Suval, *Electoral Politics*, p. 39.

22 ZSA Merseburg, Staatsministerium, 17 January 1903.

23 SA Köln, Bachem Papers, 183, note of 1 February 1903.

24 Fuchs, *Grossherzog Friedrich*, Jagemann to Foreign Minister, 30 January 1903, p. 472 and 4 February 1903, p. 473.

25 See especially HHSA Wien, 157, Szögyényi's Report, 12 February 1902; SA Köln, Bachem Papers, 170, note of 16 September 1902. The repeal of Paragraph 2 would allow individual Jesuits to enter Germany, but Jesuit communities would still be forbidden.

26 *Reichstag*, 3 February 1903, p. 7640.

27 ZSA Merseburg, Staatsministerium, 146, 17 January 1903.

28 Fuchs, *Grossherzog Friedrich*, Jagemann to Foreign Minister, 4 February 1903, p. 473; HSA Stuttgart, Varnbüler's Report, 4 February 1903; Rassow and Born, *Akten zur staatlichen Sozialpolitik*, Lerchenfeld's Reports, 11 February 1903 and 28 March 1903, especially pp. 136, 143.

29 HSA Stuttgart, Varnbüler's Report, 7 March 1903; BA Koblenz, O. Richthofen Papers, 6, Richthofen to Bülow, 14 April 1903. See also Rauh, *Föderalismus und Parlamentarismus*, pp. 255ff.

30 Fuchs, *Grossherzog Friedrich*, Berckheim to Marschall, 8 March 1904, p. 542. See also SA Köln, Bachem Papers, 227, 'Parl. Geschichte des Jesuiten-Ge-Antrages 1890–1900–1903'.

31 Fuchs, *Grossherzog Friedrich*, Bodmann to Brauer, 26 February 1903, p. 490.

32 Ibid., Jagemann to Brauer, 12 February 1903, p. 479.

33 Ibid., Jagemann to Brauer, 15 February 1903, pp. 481ff.

34 GLA Karlsruhe, 34809, Jagemann's Reports, 1 March 1903 and 25 April 1903; HSA München, 1075, Lerchenfeld's Report, 13 March 1903; Monts, *Erinnerungen*, Monts to Tschirschky, 26 January 1903, p. 437.

35 HHSA Wien, 161, Szögyényi's Report, 11 March 1904. Bülow called the liberals' attitude 'childish . . . ridiculous . . . unpolitical and unpatriotic . . .'. See ZSA Potsdam, Hammann Papers, 16, Bülow to Hammann, undated. See also *Reichstag*, 12 April 1904, pp. 2021f.

36 GLA Karlsruhe, 2037, Berckheim's Report, 19 March 1904; HHSA Wien, 161, Szögyényi's Reports, 23 March 1904 and 17 May 1904; BA Koblenz, BP, 107, Bülow to Ballestrem, 6 April 1904.

37 *Reichstag*, 16 April 1904, especially pp. 2148ff., 2166; HHSA Wien, 161, Szögyényi's Report, 19 April 1904.

38 SA Köln, Bachem Papers, 183, notes of 16 January 1902 and 19 January 1902; ibid., 244, note of 16 January 1906. See also Bachem, *Zentrumspartei*, VI, pp. 304ff.

39 See Loth, *Katholiken im Kaiserreich*, especially pp. 81ff.

40 See also PA Bonn, IA, Deutschland, 125, no. 1 Bd. VI, Rotenhan's Report, 12 September 1905.

41 SA Köln, Bachem Papers, 170, Bachem to Müller-Fulda, 20 August 1901.

42 Loth, *Katholiken im Kaiserreich*, pp. 98, 110f.; Klaus Epstein, *Matthias Erzberger and the Dilemma of German Democracy* (Princeton, 1959), especially chapter 3.

43 SA Köln, Bachem Papers, 161, note of 4 May 1902. See also BA Koblenz, BP, 22, Bülow to Richthofen, 26 September 1902.

44 SA Köln, Bachem Papers, 218, Bülow to Kopp, 13 March 1904; Loth, *Katholiken im Kaiserreich*, p. 114. See also BA Koblenz, BP, 107, Bülow to Ballestrem, 6 April 1904.

45 BA Koblenz, BP, 107, Bülow to Spahn, 11 March 1905.

46 See for example HSA München, 2682, Lerchenfeld's Report, 19 May 1904 and ch. 3, pp. 98ff. below.

47 Fuchs, *Grossherzog Friedrich*, Jagemann to Brauer, 21 November 1902, p. 443.

48 Rassow and Born, *Akten zur staatlichen Sozialpolitik*, Lerchenfeld to Podewils, 28 March 1903, pp. 146f.

49 Rogge, *Holstein*, Holstein to Stülpnagel, 10 April 1904, p. 231.

50 Karl von Hertling, 'Bülow, Hertling, Zentrum', in Thimme, *Front Wider Bülow*, p. 139 (Hertling's letter of 25 April 1904).

51 Monts, *Erinnerungen*, Monts to Tschirschky, end of May 1904, pp. 414f. See also Bülow, *Denkwürdigkeiten*, II, pp. 99f.; ZSA Potsdam, Hammann Papers, 16, Bülow to Hammann [1905]; BA–MA Freiburg, Waldersee Papers, 17, Waldersee to Bartenwerffer, 20 January 1904.

52 SA Köln, Bachem Papers, 205a, note of February 1913.

53 HSA Stuttgart, Varnbüler's Report, 1 July 1903; Witt, *Finanzpolitik*, p. 78. For details of the Reichstag elections, see appendix II.

54 BA Koblenz, BP, Bülow to Richthofen, 14 September 1902; ZSA Merseburg, Rep. 53J, Lit. B. no. 16a, II, Bülow to Wilhelm II, 19 June 1903.

55 BA Koblenz, O. Richthofen Papers, 16, Tschirschky to Richthofen, 22 June 1903.

56 HSA Stuttgart, Varnbüler's Report, 1 July 1903. See also his views in Vierhaus, *Spitzemberg*, 26 July 1903, pp. 432f.

57 Monts, *Erinnerungen*, Tschirschky to Monts, 26 January 1903, p. 437.

58 Röhl, *Eulenburg*, III, Eulenburg to Bülow, 21 July 1903, pp. 2090f. and 26 July 1903, p. 2093; BA Koblenz, O. Richthofen Papers, 13, Eisendecher to Richthofen, 22 July 1903; BA Koblenz, BP, 23, Tschirschky to Bülow, 2 August 1903.

59 BA Koblenz, Eulenburg Papers, 74, 'Ein Zwiegespräch', 29 August 1903, p. 38.

60 ZSA Potsdam, Hammann Papers, 8, Bülow to Hammann, 27 September 1903; O. Hammann, *Zur Vorgeschichte des Weltkrieges* (Berlin, 1918), p. 118. See also Klaus Saul, *Staat, Industrie, Arbeiterbewegung im Kaiserreich* (Düsseldorf, 1974), pp. 15f., 34.

61 SA Köln, Bachem Papers, 218, note of 3 December 1903.

62 See, for example, Bülow's attack on Bebel in December 1903, which was very popular. *Reichstag*, 10 December 1903, pp. 54ff.; BA Koblenz, BP, 22, Pourtalès to Bülow, 14 December 1903; BP, 60, Ballin to Bülow, 11 December 1902; Waldersee, *Denkwürdigkeiten*, III, 13 December 1903, p. 223.

63 Fuchs, *Grossherzog Friedrich*, Berckheim to Brauer, 17 October 1903, p. 519.

64 Zedlitz, *Zwölf Jahre*, 14 November 1904, pp. 92f. See also BA Koblenz, BP, 153, 1904, note 6.

65 Zedlitz, *Zwölf Jahre*, 14 November 1904, p. 92.

66 See for example Rich and Fisher, *Holstein Papers*, IV, Holstein to Bülow, 17 February 1897, p. 18.

67 Rassow and Born, *Akten zur staatlichen Sozialpolitik*, Lerchenfeld's Report, 2 March 1908, pp. 328f.

68 BA–MA Freiburg, Tirpitz Papers, 20, notes of 1 January [1904].

69 BA Koblenz, O. Richthofen Papers, 7, Bülow to Richthofen, 3 July 1904.

70 See for example Monts, *Erinnerungen*, Monts to Tschirschky, 14 January 1901, p. 411; Fuchs, *Grossherzog Friedrich*, Brauer to Grand Duke Friedrich, 27 September 1904, p. 559.

71 Fuchs, *Grossherzog Friedrich*, Jagemann to Foreign Minister, 4 February 1903, p. 472.

72 See Dieter Grosser, *Vom monarchischen Konstitutionalismus zur parlamentarischen Demokratie: Die Verfassungspolitik der deutschen Parteien im letzten Jahrzehnt des Kaiserreiches* (The Hague, 1970). There is an abundance of literature on the political parties. See, for example, G. A. Ritter and M. Niehuss (eds.), *Deutsche Parteien vor 1918* (Cologne, 1973); Thomas Nipperdey, *Die Organisation der deutschen Parteien vor 1918* (Düsseldorf, 1961); D. Fricke (ed.), *Die bürgerlichen Parteien in Deutschland, 1830–1945*, 2 vols. (Leipzig, 1968 and 1970). See also Loth, *Katholiken im Kaiserreich*; James J. Sheehan, *German Liberalism in the Nineteenth Century* (Chicago, 1978); Retallack, *Notables of the Right*; Evans, *Society and Politics*. For a useful, recent bibliography, see Wehler, *German Empire*, pp. 275ff.

73 ZSA Potsdam, Hammann Papers, 10, Bülow to Hammann, 16 April 1905.

74 Hammann, *Zur Vorgeschichte des Weltkrieges*, pp. 106ff.; Cecil, *German Diplomatic Service*, p. 303.

75 BA Koblenz, Reichskanzlei, 1391, Conrad to Lucanus, 29 December 1903. For further examples of how Bülow tried to ingratiate himself with parliamentarians, see Katharine Lerman, 'Bernhard von Bülow and the Governance of Germany, 1900–1909', D.Phil. thesis, University of Sussex, 1983, 160ff.

76 Fuchs, *Grossherzog Friedrich*, Jagemann to Foreign Minister, 4 February 1903, p. 473.

77 Monts, *Erinnerungen*, Monts to Tschirschky, 17 January 1903, p. 413; see also HSA Stuttgart, Varnbüler's Report, 1 July 1903.

78 Rassow and Born, *Akten zur staatlichen Sozialpolitik*, Lerchenfeld to Podewils, 28 March 1903, p. 142.

79 See for example HSA München, 2682, Lerchenfeld's Report, 19 May 1904.

80 Cf. Hutten-Czapski, *Sechzig Jahre*, I, p. 394.

81 ZSA Merseburg, Hausarchiv, Adjutants' Diaries, 8–13, 1900–9.

82 HSA Stuttgart, Varnbüler's Report, 17 November 1901.

83 BA Koblenz, Valentini Papers (KE, 341), 'Aus meinem Leben', p. 35.

84 See L. Raschdau, 'Meine Beziehungen zu Fürst Bülow', in Thimme, *Front Wider Bülow*, pp. 21f.; Rich and Fisher, *Holstein Papers*, IV, Holstein to Radolin, 12 December 1901, pp. 241f.

85 ZSA Merseburg, Rep. 53J, Lit. B. no. 16a, III, Bülow to Wilhelm II, 7 September 1903.

86 Ibid., II, Bülow to Wilhelm II, 28 May 1903; Zivilkabinett, 3584, Bülow to Wilhelm II, 17 February 1901.

87 ZSA Merseburg, Rep. 53J, Lit. B. no. 16a, II, Bülow to Wilhelm II, 31 March 1903 and III, 7 September 1903, 2 August 1904 and 10 April 1905.

88 Ibid., III, Bülow to Wilhelm II, 2 August 1904.

89 Ibid., II, Bülow to Wilhelm II, 25 May 1903.

90 Ibid., Bülow to Wilhelm II, 19 June 1903. See also letter of 3 December 1901.

91 Ibid., Bülow to Wilhelm II, 6 August 1900.

92 Lamar Cecil, 'History as Family Chronicle: Kaiser Wilhelm II and the Dynastic Roots of the Anglo-German Antagonism', in Röhl and Sombart, *Kaiser Wilhelm*, p. 103.

93 ZSA Merseburg, Rep. 53J, Lit. B. no. 16a, II, Bülow to Wilhelm II, 31 March 1903. See also Lamar Cecil, 'William II and his Russian "Colleagues"', in Carole Fink, Isabel V. Hull and Macgregor Knox (eds.), *German Nationalism and the European Response, 1890–1945* (Norman and London, 1985), pp. 101, 119ff.

94 ZSA Merseburg, Rep. 53J, Lit. B. no. 16a, II, Bülow to Wilhelm II, 6 August 1900, 31 March 1903, 25 May 1903 and III, 10 April 1905.

95 Ibid., II, Bülow to Wilhelm II, 6 August 1900.

96 Ibid., Bülow to Wilhelm II, 2 April 1902.

97 Ibid., Bülow to Wilhelm II, 19 June 1903.

98 Norbert Elias, *The Court Society*, trans. Edmund Jephcott (Oxford, 1983).

99 Ibid., pp. 108f.

100 ZSA Merseburg, Zivilkabinett, 3584, Bülow to Wilhelm II, 17 February 1901.

101 Elias, *Court Society*, pp. 107ff.

102 ZSA Merseburg, Rep. 53J, Lit. B. no. 16a, III, Bülow to Wilhelm II, 24 June 1903.

103 Ibid., Bülow to Wilhelm II, 31 August 1903.

104 Ibid., II, Bülow to Wilhelm II, 2 April 1902.

105 HHSA Wien, 157, Szögyényi's Report, 26 February 1902.

106 BA Koblenz, BP, 112, Bülow to Wilhelm II, 14 December 1902.

107 BA–MA Freiburg, Tirpitz Papers, 21, note of 4 January [1905].

108 Waldersee, *Denkwürdigkeiten*, III, 19 October 1902, pp. 191f.

109 Bülow, *Denkwürdigkeiten*, I, pp. 528, 541f. and II, pp. 75f.

110 HHSA Wien, 158, Szögyényi to Goluchowski, 29 January 1902; SA Köln, Bachem Papers, 161, note of 4 May 1902; BA Koblenz, BP, 22, Bülow to Richthofen, 26 September 1902.

111 BA Koblenz, Eulenburg Papers, 58, Eulenburg to Bülow, 24 July 1901; HSA Stuttgart, Varnbüler's Report, 14 December 1901.

112 Bülow, *Denkwürdigkeiten*, I, pp. 582ff.

113 HSA München, 76080, Guttenberg's Report, 27 August 1902.

114 SA Köln, Bachem Papers, 183, note of 16 January 1902.

115 Cf. Zedlitz, *Zwölf Jahre*, Zedlitz to his father, 15 September 1907, pp. 168ff.

116 HSA Stuttgart, Varnbüler's Report, 17 November 1901.

117 HHSA Wien, 159, Szögyényi's Report, 27 January 1903.

118 HHSA Wien, 157, Szögyényi's Report (no. 4D), 29 January 1902.

119 Rich and Fisher, *Holstein Papers*, IV, diary entry, 11 January 1902, p. 246.

120 ZSA Merseburg, Zivilkabinett, 3584, Bülow to Lucanus, 5 July 1901. The candidate in question for the post of *Oberpräsident* in Königsberg was Brandenstein, since 1895 *Regierungspräsident* in Hanover, who was seen as the Kaiser's special protégé. In the end, the *Regierungspräsident* in Cologne was promoted to the post. See PA Bonn, IA, Preussen, no. 13, Bd. II, Richthofen to Bülow, 28 June 1901 and Fischer to Richthofen, 28 June 1901.

121 ZSA Merseburg, Zivilkabinett, 3584, Bülow to Lucanus, 28 July 1904; Rep. 53J, Lit. B. no. 16a, III, Bülow to Wilhelm II, 2 August 1904.

122 FCO London, Holstein Papers, 30, Bülow to Holstein, 7 July 1903.
123 Bülow, *Denkwürdigkeiten*, II, pp. 102f.
124 See ch. 3, pp. 112ff. below.
125 BA Koblenz, Valentini Papers (KE, 341), I, 'Reise nach dem Mittelmeer', March 1904; Fuchs, *Grossherzog Friedrich*, Jagemann to Brauer, 21 November 1902, p. 443.
126 SA Köln, Bachem Papers, 173, note of 2 December 1901; ZSA Merseburg, Rep. 53J, Lit. B. no. 16a, II, Bülow to Wilhelm II, 3 December 1901.
127 BA Koblenz, O. Richthofen Papers, 7, Bülow to Wilhelm II, 2 July 1904.
128 HHSA Wien, 160, Szögyényi to Goluchowski, 2 February 1903.
129 See ch. 3, pp. 83f. above.
130 The Kaiser instructed the Minister of Public Works to reintroduce the Canal Bill into the Prussian Landtag in early 1902, but Bülow successfully achieved a postponement. See ZSA Merseburg, Staatsministerium, 143, 20 December 1901; SA Köln, Bachem Papers, 173, note of 2 December 1901; HHSA Wien, 157, Szögyényi's Report, 15 January 1902.
131 See HHSA Wien, 155, Szögyényi's Report, 26 March 1901 for Wilhelm's opposition to the re-entry of the Jesuits. The Kaiser was also the main obstacle to the concession of salaries. See HSA Stuttgart, Varnbüler's Report, 14 December 1901; SA Köln, Bachem Papers, 123, 'Diätenantrag' [1901]; Fuchs, *Grossherzog Friedrich*, Jagemann to Brauer, 15 March 1902, p. 388.
132 HHSA Wien, 158, Szögyényi to Goluchowski, 29 January 1902. Wilhelm applauded Bülow's speech of 16 January 1902 (Bülow, *Reden*, I, pp. 279ff; Landtag, 16 January 1902, 293–7).
133 Rich and Fisher, *Holstein Papers*, IV, Bülow to Holstein, 1 August 1902, p. 260.
134 See above ch. 2, pp. 56f.
135 Bülow, *Denkwürdigkeiten*, II, pp. 55ff.
136 SA Köln, Bachem Papers, 218, note of 2 November 1904; BA Koblenz, BP, 153, note 20 [1904].
137 Ibid. See also Fuchs, *Grossherzog Friedrich*, Brauer to Bodmann, 2 December 1904, pp. 572f.
138 Rich and Fisher, *Holstein Papers*, IV, Bülow to Holstein, 16 May [1903], p. 275.
139 HHSA Wien, 157, Szögyényi's Report, 15 January 1902 (no. 2B); 158, Szögyényi to Goluchowski, 29 January 1902; and 155, Szögyényi's Report, 26 March 1901.
140 See especially Röhl, *Eulenburg*, III, Eulenburg to Bülow, 21 July 1903, pp. 2090ff. and 9 August 1903, pp. 2096ff.; Zedlitz, *Zwölf Jahre*, 30 January 1905, pp. 107f. See also J. C. G. Röhl, 'The Emperor's New Clothes: A Character Sketch of Kaiser Wilhelm II', in Röhl and Sombart, *Kaiser Wilhelm*, especially pp. 36ff.
141 Waldersee, *Denkwürdigkeiten*, III, 16 November 1903, p. 220.
142 HSA Stuttgart, Varnbüler's Report, 17 November 1901.
143 BA Koblenz, Valentini Papers (KE, 341), I, 'Reise nach dem Mittelmeer', March 1904.
144 HSA Stuttgart, Varnbüler's Report, 17 November 1901.
145 BA Koblenz, Valentini Papers (KE, 341), I, 'Reise nach dem Mittelmeer', March 1904.
146 Röhl, *Eulenburg*, III, Eulenburg to Bülow, 24 July 1901, p. 2025.
147 Haller, *Aus dem Leben*, p. 252.
148 Röhl, *Eulenburg*, III, Eulenburg to Bülow, 9 August 1903, p. 2096; Bülow, *Denkwürdigkeiten*, I, p. 616.
149 See ch. 6, pp. 228ff. below.
150 FCO London, Holstein Papers, 30, Bülow to Foreign Office (Holstein), 3 August 1901; Rich and Fisher, *Holstein Papers*, IV, Holstein to Bülow, 4 August 1901, pp. 234ff.
151 SA Köln, Bachem Papers, 170, Kopp to Trimborn, 15 August 1901.
152 See HHSA Wien, 155, Szögyényi's Report, 11 July 1901; HSA Stuttgart, Varnbüler's Report, 17 November 1901.

153 See ch. 3, p. 112 below.
154 PA Bonn, IA, Deutschland, 122, no. 13, Bd. III, Bülow to Hammann, 25 June 1901.
155 For Wilhelm's hostility to greater protection of agriculture, see SA Köln, Bachem Papers, 173, note of 2 December 1901.
156 Rich and Fisher, *Holstein Papers*, IV, Holstein to Bülow, 4 August 1901, pp. 234f.
157 BA Koblenz, Valentini Papers (KE, 341), I, 'Reise nach dem Mittelmeer', March 1904.
158 HSA München, 2681, Lerchenfeld's Report, 27 October 1903 and 2682, Lerchenfeld's Reports, 5 January 1904, 5 February 1904; cf. Rich and Fisher, *Holstein Papers*, IV, Bülow to Holstein, 16 January [1904], p. 277. See also Vogel, *Deutsche Russlandpolitik*, p. 161.
159 BA–MA Freiburg, Tirpitz Papers, 20, note on State Ministry meeting of 31 December 1903.
160 For Wilhelm II's reaction to the outbreak of war, see HSA Stuttgart, Varnbüler's Report, 8 February 1904. For Bülow's attempts at self-justification, see ZSA Potsdam, Hammann Papers, 9, Bülow to Hammann, 9 February 1904 and 22, Holstein to Bülow, 29 February 1904.
161 See for example Wilhelm II's attitude as expressed to Varnbüler in HSA Stuttgart, Varnbüler's Report, 1 March 1904.
162 HSA München, 2682, Lerchenfeld's Report, 12 May 1904.
163 Reichstag, 9 May 1904, pp. 2787f.
164 Rogge, *Holstein*, Holstein to Ida von Stülpnagel [end of November 1902], p. 214.
165 HHSA Wien, 157, Szögyényi's Report, 12 February 1902.
166 Ibid., 15 January 1902 (no. 2B). For Bülow's speech, see Reichstag, 8 January 1902, pp. 3209f. and Bülow, *Reden*, 8 January 1902, pp. 241ff. See also Winzen, *Bülows Weltmachtkonzept*, pp. 378ff.
167 BA Koblenz, BP, 22, Bülow to Richthofen, 24 September 1902.
168 HHSA Wien, 158, Thurn's Report, 11 October 1902. See also *Grosse Politik*, XVII, pp. 218ff.
169 Rich and Fisher, *Holstein Papers*, IV, diary entry 7 November 1902, pp. 268ff.; Rogge, *Holstein*, Holstein to Stülpnagel [end of November 1902], pp. 214ff.
170 Rich and Fisher, *Holstein Papers*, IV, diary entry, 7 November 1902, p. 269.
171 Ibid.; see also ZSA Merseburg, Hausarchiv, Adjutants' Diaries, 9, entries for 16–23 October 1902.
172 Rich and Fisher, *Holstein Papers*, IV, diary entry, 7 November 1902, p. 269.
173 See BA Koblenz, BP, 112, Wilhelm II to Bülow, 14 December 1902 and Bülow to Wilhelm II, 14 December 1902. See also Bülow, *Denkwürdigkeiten*, I, pp. 594f.
174 BA Koblenz, BP, 153, note 196.
175 See for example Rich and Fisher, *Holstein Papers*, IV, diary entries, 11 November 1902, pp. 271f. and 13 November 1902, pp. 272f.
176 HSA Stuttgart, Varnbüler's Report, 17 November 1901.
177 See Bülow, *Denkwürdigkeiten*, II, pp. 89 and 121; ZSA Potsdam, Hammann Papers, Bülow to Hammann, 6 June 1905; HSA Stuttgart, Varnbüler's Report, 25 June 1905.
178 See ch. 3, pp. 102ff. below.
179 See ch. 3, pp. 115ff. below.
180 See for example Fuchs, *Grossherzog Friedrich*, Brauer to Grand Duke Friedrich, 27 September 1904, p. 559.
181 Hull, *Entourage*, p. 23.
182 BA Koblenz, BP, 74, Bülow to August Eulenburg, 18 September 1907. August Eulenburg did not support the Bülow tariff.
183 For the position of Lucanus, see Hull, *Entourage*, pp. 27ff.
184 See for example ZSA Merseburg, Zivilkabinett, 3584, Bülow to Lucanus, 3 June 1901 and 5 July 1901; BA Koblenz, Reichskanzlei, 1644, Bülow to Lucanus, 11 October 1903.

185 BA Koblenz, BP, 22, Bülow to Richthofen, 27 September 1902.
186 ZSA Merseburg, Zivilkabinett, 3584, Bülow to Lucanus, 3 June 1901.
187 Ibid., Bülow to Lucanus, 5 July 1901 and 5 November 1901. In 1897 Eulenburg had told Bülow that Lucanus was '*very* vain' and that he would become Bülow's 'willing tool'. See Röhl, *Eulenburg*, III, Eulenburg to Bülow, 24 April 1897, p. 1821.
188 BA Koblenz, BP, 15, Bülow to Karl von Bülow, 20 May 1907; ZSA Merseburg, Zivilkabinett, 667, Bülow to Lucanus, 8 August 1907.
189 Hull, *Entourage*, p. 28. See also ZSA Merseburg, Zivilkabinett, 3584, Bülow to Lucanus, 28 July 1904.
190 See for example FCO London, Holstein Papers, 30, Bülow to Holstein, 1 August 1902.
191 HHSA Wien, 156, Szögyényi to Goluchowski, 6 May 1901.
192 BA Koblenz, Valentini Papers (KE, 341), I, 'Reise nach dem Mittelmeer', March 1904.
193 See Neumann, 'Innenpolitik', p. 166.
194 Monts, *Erinnerungen*, p. 158.
195 Waldersee, *Denkwürdigkeiten*, III, 19 January 1903; HSA Stuttgart, Varnbüler's Report, 12 April 1905; Bülow, *Denkwürdigkeiten*, I, p. 144.
196 BA Koblenz, BP, 153, note 93 [1903].
197 Bülow, *Denkwürdigkeiten*, II, pp. 454ff.
198 Waldersee, *Denkwürdigkeiten*, III, May 1903, pp. 214f.
199 BA–MA Freiburg, Tirpitz Papers, 20, note of 31 December 1903.
200 Vierhaus, *Spitzemberg*, 10 November 1903, p. 435.
201 SA Köln, Bachem Papers, 218, note of 4 February 1904.
202 Waldersee, *Denkwürdigkeiten*, III, 4 May 1902, p. 185.
203 Rassow and Born, *Akten zur staatlichen Sozialpolitik*, Lerchenfeld to Podewils, 28 March 1903, p. 141.
204 HSA Stuttgart, Varnbüler's Report, 12 April 1905.
205 See especially Hull, *Entourage*, pp. 15ff. In 1897 Bülow told Eulenburg that the Kaiser's entourage was predominantly made up of good, honest people. 'They are not blind to the dangers lying in the individuality of our dear Kaiser, but accept (and in this they are right) His Majesty as something given and believe (this is more dubious) that the Good Lord must take care of everything else.' See Röhl, *Eulenburg*, III, Bülow to Eulenburg, 22 August 1897, p. 1857.
206 GLA Karlsruhe, 34807, Jagemann's Report, 4 July 1901.
207 Röhl, *Eulenburg*, III, Eulenburg to Bülow, 11 September 1901, pp. 2027f.; HSA München, 1073, Guttenberg's Report, 18 September 1901.
208 HSA Stuttgart, Varnbüler's Report, 25 October 1902.
209 HSA München, 1073, Guttenberg's Report, 18 September 1901.
210 Waldersee, *Denkwürdigkeiten*, III, end of December 1901, pp. 171ff.
211 See Hull, *Entourage*, pp. 117ff. and Röhl, *Eulenburg*, I, pp. 34ff.
212 Hull, *Entourage*, pp. 118ff.
213 Rich and Fisher, *Holstein Papers*, IV, Holstein to Radolin, 12 December 1901, p. 242.
214 BA Koblenz, Eulenburg Papers, 59, Eulenburg's note of 12 May 1902 on his letter to Bülow of 21 March 1902 (BP, 77).
215 Röhl, *Eulenburg*, III, Bülow to Eulenburg, 29 March 1902, pp. 2062f.
216 BA Koblenz, BP, 77, Augusta Eulenburg to Bülow, 10 April 1902; Röhl, *Eulenburg*, III, Eulenburg to Wilhelm II, 23 May 1902, pp. 2066ff.
217 HHSA Wien, 158, Szögyényi to Goluchowski, 25 May 1902.
218 Ibid., Szögyényi to Goluchowski, 29 August 1902.
219 Ibid., Thurn to Goluchowski, 9 September 1902.
220 Röhl, *Eulenburg*, III, Eulenburg to Bülow, 23 August 1902, pp. 2073f.

221 See for example Hutten-Czapski, *Sechzig Jahre*, I, p. 466; Monts, *Erinnerungen*, p. 184.

222 BA Koblenz, BP, 22, Mumm to Bülow, 26 October 1902. See also Rich, *Holstein*, II, pp. 774f., who confirms that Bülow supplied Harden with material.

223 See Hull, *Entourage*, pp. 124f.

224 Rassow and Born, *Akten zur staatlichen Sozialpolitik*, Lerchenfeld to Podewils, 28 March 1903, p. 142.

225 GLA Karlsruhe, 34806, Jagemann's Report, 17 October 1899.

226 ZSA Merseburg, Staatsministerium, 140–50. Bülow attended 59 of the 104 meetings between October 1900 and March 1905 (48 out of 89 after May 1901).

227 Möller attended 80 of the 89 meetings. Hammerstein, Schönstedt and Rheinbaben all attended over 70 meetings; Podbielski attended 60, Posadowsky attended 55 and Tirpitz attended 33.

228 ZSA Merseburg, Staatsministerium, 141, 3 November 1900 (copy in Reichskanzlei, 2024).

229 Ibid., 149, 12 October 1904.

230 Ibid., 146, 11 February 1903.

231 Ibid., 144, 10 February 1902.

232 BA Koblenz, Eulenburg Papers, 59, Bülow to Eulenburg, 18 November 1902, pp. 107f.

233 Monts, *Erinnerungen*, Monts to Tschirschky, 1 July 1910, pp. 432–4. See also Röhl, *Eulenburg*, III, Eulenburg to Bülow, 14 May 1901, p. 2019.

234 See for example ZSA Merseburg, Staatsministerium, 148, 2 July 1904.

235 Ibid., 144, 22 April 1902.

236 Ibid., 8 February 1902.

237 ZSA Potsdam, Reichskanzlei, 2021, Bülow to State Ministry, 29 June 1902.

238 ZSA Merseburg, Staatsministerium, 148, 27 July 1904.

239 Fuchs, *Grossherzog Friedrich*, Jagemann to Brauer, 15 March 1902, p. 388.

240 ZSA Merseburg, Staatsministerium, 146, 8 January 1903.

241 Ibid., 148, 26 January 1904.

242 HSA Stuttgart, Varnbüler's Report, 6 June 1901.

243 ZSA Merseburg, Staatsministeriuim, 151, 9/10 June 1905.

244 Ibid., 4 November 1905.

245 ZSA Potsdam, Reichskanzlei, 2050, Budde to Bülow, 25 July 1905 and Conrad's note of 29 July 1904. See also Rassow and Born, *Akten zur staatlichen Sozialpolitik*, Lerchenfeld to Podewils, 28 March 1903, pp. 141f.

246 GLA Karlsruhe, 34808, Jagemann's Report, 22 November 1902.

247 ZSA Merseburg, Studt Papers, 18, note of 31 January 1903; see also Studt to Bülow, 22 February 1903.

248 See ch. 3, pp. 78f. above.

249 BA Koblenz, O. Richthofen Papers, 7, Bülow to Richthofen, 3 July 1904.

250 ZSA Merseburg, Staatsministerium, 148, 27 July 1904.

251 HHSA Wien, 157, Szögyényi's Report, 15 January 1902.

252 Witt, *Finanzpolitik*, pp. 70f.

253 BA Koblenz, BP, 22, Bülow to Richthofen, 24 September 1902.

254 HHSA Wien, 160, Szögyényi to Goluchowski, 2 February 1903.

255 BA Koblenz, BP, 22, Bülow to Richthofen, 27 September 1902.

256 BA Koblenz, Eulenburg Papers, 74, 'Ein Zwiegespräch', 29 August 1903, p. 37.

257 Waldersee, *Denkwürdigkeiten*, III, end of 1901, pp. 174f.; SA Köln, Bachem Papers, 170, 'Bei Nieberding', 29 October 1900.

258 ZSA Potsdam, Hammann Papers, 7, Bülow to Hammann, 22 June 1902; ZSA Merseburg, Studt Papers, 18, Bülow to Studt, 9 September 1902; BA Koblenz, Richthofen Papers, 17, Bülow to Richthofen, 16 January [1904].

259 Zedlitz, *Zwölf Jahre*, 24 November 1903, p. 54.
260 BA Koblenz, Eulenburg Papers, 74, 'Ministerbesuch', 4 October 1903.
261 Waldersee, *Denkwürdigkeiten*, III, 31 January 1904, pp. 228f.
262 See ch. 2, pp. 47f. above.
263 Fuchs, *Grossherzog Friedrich*, Jagemann to Brauer, 5 May 1902, p. 316.
264 BA Koblenz, Reichskanzlei, 1644, Podbielski to Bülow, 18 January 1901.
265 Rassow and Born, *Akten zur staatlichen Sozialpolitik*, Lerchenfeld to Podewils, 28 March 1903, p. 142.
266 BA Koblenz, Loebell Papers, 9, Bülow to Loebell, 17 June 1924.
267 Ibid. See also BA–MA Freiburg, Tirpitz Papers, 23, Tirpitz to Capelle, 14 August 1906.
268 Based on an examination of the files of the Reich Navy Office, Admiralty Staff and Naval Cabinet in BA–MA Freiburg. See also Bülow, *Denkwürdigkeiten*, I, pp. 108ff.
269 PA Bonn, IA, Deutschland, 122, no. 9, Bd. II, Bülow to Hammann, 7 July 1906.
270 Rassow and Born, *Akten zur staatlichen Sozialpolitik*, Lerchenfeld to Podewils, 28 March 1903, p. 144.
271 See ch. 2, pp. 46f. above.
272 Rassow and Born, *Akten zur staatlichen Sozialpolitik*, Lerchenfeld's Report, 11 February 1903, p. 136.
273 HSA München, 876, Podewils's essay on his visit to Berlin, 2 June 1903.
274 See Born, *Staat und Sozialpolitik*, pp. 142ff. Loebell claimed that Bülow gave lively support to Posadowsky's social policy, BA Koblenz, Loebell Papers, 27, memoirs, p. 65.
275 GLA Karlsruhe, 34809, Jagemann's Report, 4 May 1903.
276 Rassow and Born, *Akten zur staatlichen Sozialpolitik*, Lerchenfeld to Podewils, 28 March 1903, p. 144.
277 Ibid., Lerchenfeld's Report, 7 December 1900, p. 133 and for the continuing effect of the 12,000 Mark affair on Posadowsky, see for example BA Koblenz, BP, 22, Bülow to Richthofen, 24 September 1902.
278 BA Koblenz, O. Richthofen Papers, 5, Bülow to Richthofen, 3 August 1899.
279 Fuchs, *Grossherzog Friedrich*, Jagemann to Foreign Minister, 16 January 1902, p. 375.
280 BA Koblenz, BP, 22, Bülow to Richthofen, 24 September 1902.
281 See for example ZSA Merseburg, Staatsministerium, 150, 11 January 1905.
282 HHSA Wien, 158, Szögyényi to Goluchowski, 16 December 1902; Fuchs, *Grossherzog Friedrich*, Jagemann to Foreign Minister, 21 December 1902, p. 549, and Jagemann to Brauer, 21 February 1902, p. 384.
283 Fuchs, *Grossherzog Friedrich*, Jagemann to Brauer, 4 May 1901, p. 314; BA Koblenz, Reichskanzlei, 1622, Bülow to Posadowsky, 11 August 1903.
284 BA Koblenz, O. Richthofen Papers, 17, Bülow to Richthofen [1904–5].
285 HSA Stuttgart, Varnbüler's Report, 14 December 1901.
286 GLA Karlsruhe, 49/2037, Berckheim's Report, 5 January 1904.
287 BA Koblenz, O. Richthofen Papers, 14, Bülow to Richthofen, 12 October 1904.
288 BA Koblenz, Loebell Papers, 27, memoirs, pp. 53f.
289 Ibid., p. 59.
290 Ibid., p. 93. For Loebell's attendance at State Ministry meetings, see ZSA Merseburg Staatsministerium, 149–58.
291 BA Koblenz, Loebell Papers, 27, memoirs, p. 60. The chief difficulties appear to have been with Posadowsky. See Reichskanzlei, 49, on Loebell's promotion in July 1905.
292 BA Koblenz, Loebell Papers, 27, memoirs, pp. 61f. For Bülow's praise of Loebell, see Bülow, *Denkwürdigkeiten*, II, p. 276.
293 BA Koblenz, Loebell Papers, 27, memoirs, p. 70.
294 BA Koblenz, O. Richthofen Papers, 4, Bülow to Richthofen, 18 December [1904].

295 BA Koblenz, BP, 22, Bülow to Richthofen, 14 September 1902 and 26 September 1902; BA Koblenz, O. Richthofen Papers, 17, Bülow to Richthofen, 1 March 1904.
296 BA Koblenz, O. Richthofen Papers, 6, Bülow to Richthofen, 20 July 1903.
297 Ibid., 17, Bülow's response to Richthofen to Bülow, 12 February [1905].
298 Rich and Fisher, *Holstein Papers*, IV, Holstein to Bülow, 25 June 1904, p. 290. Conrad had replaced Wilmowski as Chief of Reich Chancellery in 1901.
299 BA Koblenz, Loebell Papers, 27, memoirs, pp. 64f.; Loebell Papers, 6, Bülow to Loebell, 9 September 1906.
300 BA Koblenz, O. Richthofen Papers, 4, Bülow to Richthofen, 18 December [1904].
301 See ch. 4, p. 138 below.
302 See ch. 3, pp. 123ff below.
303 HHSA Wien, 161, Szögyényi's Report, 7 April 1904; Rich, *Holstein*, II, pp. 685ff.
304 Rich and Fisher, *Holstein Papers*, IV, Holstein to Bülow, 26 December 1900, p. 216.
305 Monts, *Erinnerungen*, Holstein to Monts, 10 July 1898, p. 356.
306 Rich and Fisher, *Holstein Papers*, IV, Holstein to Pourtalès, 29 August 1904, p. 303.
307 BA Koblenz, Loebell Papers, 27, memoirs, p. 64.
308 See ch. 5, pp. 198f. Scheefer was promoted in June 1904.
309 Fuchs, *Grossherzog Friedrich*, Jagemann to Brauer, 12 February 1903, p. 479.
310 SA Köln, Bachem Papers, 287, 'Besuch bei Nieberding anlässlich seines Abschiedes', 26 October 1909.
311 BA Koblenz, Loebell Papers, 27, memoirs, p. 70.
312 Ibid., 6, Bülow to Loebell, 27 April 1908.
313 Ibid., 27, memoirs, pp. 63f.; see also Eulenburg Papers, 77, 'Path. Politik', p. 80.
314 BA Koblenz, Loebell Papers, 27, memoirs, p. 73.
315 BA Koblenz, BP, 22, Bülow to Richthofen, 26 September 1902. See also Monts, *Erinnerungen*, Holstein to Monts, 10 July 1898, p. 356.
316 HHSA Wien, 159, Thurn's Report, 12 August 1903; ZSA Merseburg, Kronrat, 6, 14 August 1903. A Crown Council was a meeting of the Prussian State Ministry over which the monarch presided. There were only two between 1900 and 1905, which again indicates Wilhelm II's confidence in Bülow's conduct of affairs.
317 ZSA Potsdam, Hammann Papers, 10, Bülow to Hammann, 17 January 1905.
318 ZSA Merseburg, Kronrat, 6, 28 January 1905.
319 BA Koblenz, O. Richthofen Papers, 17, Bülow to Richthofen, 17 January 1905.
320 Bülow, *Denkwürdigkeiten*, IV, p. 111.
321 Ibid., p. 76.
322 Witt, *Finanzpolitik*, pp. 100f.
323 Monts, *Erinnerungen*, Monts to Tschirschky, 21 April 1899, p. 405.
324 HHSA Wien, 154, Szögyényi to Goluchowski, 18 December 1900; Rassow and Born, *Akten zur staatlichen Sozialpolitik*, Lerchenfeld to Podewils, 28 March 1903, p. 141.
325 BA Koblenz, Loebell Papers, 27, memoirs, p. 64.
326 Rassow and Born, *Akten zur staatlichen Sozialpolitik*, Lerchenfeld to Podewils, 28 March 1903, p. 142. See for example the influence of Althoff in the Ministery of Culture, BA Koblenz, Hertling Papers, 32, Arenberg to Hertling, 26 August 1901 and 19 November 1901. See also Bernhard von Brocke, 'Hochschul- und Wissenschaftspolitik in Preussen und im deutschen Kaiserreich 1882–1907: das "System Althoff"', *Preussen Geschichte*, 1 (1980), 9–118.
327 HSA Stuttgart, Varnbüler's Report, 17 November 1901.
328 ZSA Merseburg, Zivilkabinett, 3584, Bülow to Lucanus, 5 July 1901; HSA München, 1073, Lerchenfeld's Reports, 30 July 1901 and 7 August 1901. All kinds of difficulties ensued from this appointment, and Bülow had to prevent Hohenlohe from resigning. See

espcially the correspondence between Bülow and Holstein in PA Bonn, IA, Deutschland, 122, no. 9, Bd. II.

329 HSA München, 1073, Lerchenfeld's Report, 13 August 1901.

330 HSA München, 1074, Guttenberg's Report, 24 June 1902.

331 Ibid., 1 July 1902; HHSA Wien, 158, Szögyényi's Report, 8 July 1902.

332 HHSA Wien, 158, Szögyényi's Reports, 18 June 1902 and 8 July 1902.

333 HSA München, 1074, Guttenberg's Report, 24 June 1902.

334 Ibid., 1 July 1902. The *Berliner Tageblatt* reprinted an article written by a Free Conservative for the *Hamburger Nachrichten*, drawing attention to the role of Army men, used to carrying out the King's orders, in the State Ministry. The article differentiated between the Kaiser's 'systematic personal rule' and the personal rule of eighteenth-century rulers, claiming Wilhelm II saw his responsible advisers in the Reich and Prussia as mere executive organs of his will. See PA Bonn, IA, Preussen, no. 9, Bd. III, *Berliner Tageblatt*, 26 June 1902, no. 319.

335 ZSA Potsdam, Reichskanzlei, 2047, Bülow to Lucanus, 12 May 1903.

336 Fuchs, *Grossherzog Friedrich*, Jagemann to Brauer, 9 January 1898, p. 3.

337 GLA Karlsruhe, 34807, Jagemann's Report, 8 December 1900.

338 SA Köln, Bachem Papers, 221, note of 23 March 1905; HHSA Wien, 159, Szögyényi's Report, 20 May 1903; HSA München, 1075, Lerchenfeld's Report, 24 May 1903.

339 HHSA Wien, 159, Thurn's Report, 12 August 1903; HSA München, 1075, Report of Bavarian *chargé d'affaires*, 25 August 1903.

340 HSA München, 2681, Lerchenfeld's Report, 29 September 1903.

341 BA Koblenz, BP, 22, Bülow to Richthofen, 14 September 1902.

342 See Bülow, *Denkwürdigkeiten*, II, p. 103.

343 HSA München, 1075, Report of Bavarian *chargé d'affaires*, 31 August 1903; BA Koblenz, O. Richthofen Papers, 6, Bülow to Richthofen, 20 July 1903 and 1 August 1903; BA Koblenz, Reichskanzlei, 1622, Bülow to Posadowsky (draft), 11 August 1903.

344 BA Koblenz, O. Richthofen Papers, 6, Bülow to Richthofen, 20 July 1903.

345 BA Koblenz, Reichskanzlei, 1622, Bülow to Thielmann, 15 August 1903 and Thielmann to Bülow, 17 August 1903; HSA München, 1075, Report of Bavarian *chargé d'affaires*, 31 August 1903.

346 HSA München, 1075, Report of Bavarian *chargé d'affaires*, 13 August 1903.

347 BA Koblenz, O. Richthofen Papers, 17, Bülow to Richthofen, 7 September 1903 and 11 September 1903.

348 Ibid., 7, Bülow to Richthofen, 19 August 1904. Bülow was thinking primarily of the Königsberg trial in June 1904 when Schönstedt had initiated legal proceedings against German SPD members accused of smuggling revolutionary material into Russia. The accused were subsequently cleared, and the trial represented a moral defeat for the Prussian and Russian governments. See especially M. M. Gol, 'Der Koenigsberger Prozess von 1904 – Ein Beispiel des proletarischen Internationalismus', *Beiträge Geschichtlicher Arbeiterbewegung*, 31 (1979).

349 HHSA Wien, 159, Szögyényi's Report, 25 February 1903; PA Bonn, Eisendecher Papers, 2/4, Holleben to Eisendecher, 17 January 1903 and 5 February 1903.

350 Cecil, *German Diplomatic Service*, p. 219.

351 HHSA Wien, 158, Szögyényi to Goluchowski, 29 August 1902.

352 BA Koblenz, BP, 22, Bülow to Richthofen, 24 September 1902; ZSA Potsdam, Hammann Papers, 7, Bülow to Hammann, 5 October 1902.

353 BA Koblenz, BP, 22, Bülow to Richthofen, 14 September 1902.

354 ZSA Potsdam, Zivilkabinett, 3584, Bülow to Lucanus, 5 July 1901.

355 FCO London, Holstein Papers, 30, Bülow to Holstein, 4 October 1902. See also PA Bonn, IA, Preussen, no. 13, Bd. II, Wilhelm II to Bülow, 2 October 1902.

356 BA Koblenz, BP, 22, Bülow to Richthofen, 27 September 1902.
357 ZSA Potsdam, Hammann Papers, 7, Bülow to Hammann, 5 October 1902.
358 HSA Stuttgart, Varnbüler's Report, 23 June 1907.
359 ZSA Merseburg, Staatsministerium, 150, 11 January 1905.
360 BA Koblenz, O. Richthofen Papers, 17, Bülow to Richthofen, 12 January [1905].
361 HHSA Wien, 156, Szögyényi to Goluchowski, 6 May 1901.
362 BA Koblenz, BP, 151, Notebook A, p. 346 and Notebook D, pp. 166f. See also ZSA Merseburg, Staatsministerium, 152, 8 January 1906 and 3 March 1906.
363 Bülow, *Denkwürdigkeiten*, IV, p. 508.
364 Rich and Fisher, *Holstein Papers*, III, Bülow to Holstein, 1 March 1884, p. 106.
365 BA Koblenz, BP, 99, Bülow to Lindenau, 21 November 1884.
366 PA Bonn, IA, Deutschland, 126a, secr. Bd. II, Bülow to Wilhelm II, 15 November 1905.
367 See especially ibid., 126, Generalia, Bd. II, article entitled 'Regierung und Presse' in *St. Petersburger Zeitung*, 6 November 1900.
368 Ibid., Bd. I, State Ministry protocol of 5 April 1890 (extract); article entitled 'Die offiziöse Presse' in *Berliner Börsen-Courier*, 17 April 1890; Deutschland, 122, no. 3, vol. 3, Gabriel's memorandum, 25 October 1892.
369 Ibid., 126 Generalia Bd. II, Köller to Hohenlohe, 24 November 1894; State Ministry meeting protocols (extracts) of 30 November 1894, 19 December 1895, 15 February 1896 and *Votum* of Minister of Interior, 1 April 1898.
370 Ibid., Bd. II, *St. Petersburger Zeitung*, 6 November 1900, 'Regierung und Presse'; *Freisinnige Zeitung*, 5 January 1901, 'Miquels Leitung der offiziösen Presse'.
371 See for example ibid., *Münchener Allgemeine Zeitung*, 25 October 1900, 'Deutsches Reich. Amtliche Information der Presse'; *Deutsche Tageszeitung*, 26 October 1900, 'Die offiziöse Presse'.
372 Ibid., Bülow to State Secretaries, 16 January 1901; *Staatsbürger Zeitung*, 27 September 1902. Tirpitz continued to have more autonomy in this area than the other State Secretaries. See ibid., Tirpitz to Foreign Office, 26 February 1901 and Wilhelm Deist, *Flottenpolitik und Flottenpropaganda. Das Nachrichtenbüro des Reichsmarineamts, 1897–1914* (Stuttgart, 1976).
373 PA Bonn, IA, Deutschland, 126, Generalia, Bd. II, *Staatsbürger Zeitung*, 18 December 1903, 'Aus der offiziösen Pressküche'. As State Secretary Bülow had insisted that he approve all *offiziös* announcements concerning foreign policy before publication. As Chancellor he reserved this right and expected the State Secretary to submit communiqués for the press to him. See ibid., 126, no. 2b, Bd. II Bülow to Lauser, 17 February 1899 and Bülow to Richthofen, 16 May 1901.
374 Monts, *Erinnerungen*, Holstein to Monts, 16 September 1906, p. 366.
375 ZSA Potsdam, Hammann Papers, 9, Bülow to Hammann, 9 February 1904.
376 Ibid., 7, Bülow to Hammann, 22 June 1902.
377 Ibid., 12, Below to Hammann, 4 July 1906.
378 Ibid., 7, Bülow to Hammann, 18 September 1902 and 10, Bülow to Hammann, 12 November 1905.
379 Ibid., 7, Bülow to Hammann, 5 January 1902.
380 Ibid., 16, Bülow to Hammann, undated [1905].
381 Ibid., 12, Below to Hammann, 2 July 1906.
382 Ibid., 9, Bülow to Hammann, 11 February 1904.
383 Ibid., Bülow to Hammann, 18 November 1904.
384 Ibid., Bülow to Hammann, 11 February 1904.
385 Ibid., Bülow to Hammann, 9 February 1902.
386 Ibid., 12, Below to Hammann, 2 July 1906.

387 Ibid., 7, Bülow to Hammann, 5 January 1902 and Hammann's memorandum of 5 January 1902; Winzen, *Bülows Weltmachtkonzept*, p. 382. For Bülow's speech, see Reichstag, 8 January 1902, pp. 3209ff.

388 ZSA Potsdam, Hammann Papers, 8, Bülow to Hammann, 4 October 1903.

389 See ch. 3, pp. 83f. above.

390 ZSA Potsdam, Hammann Papers, 7, Bülow to Hammann, 12 November 1902.

391 Dehmelt, 'Bülow's Moroccan Policy', 422.

392 ZSA Potsdam, Hammann Papers, 7, Bülow to Hammann, 29 September 1902 and 2 October 1902. See also Brocke, 'Hochschul- und Wissenschaftspolitik', 100ff.

393 ZSA Potsdam, Hammann Papers, 7, Bülow to Hammann, 21 March 1903.

394 Ibid., Bülow to Hammann, 27 September 1902.

395 Ibid., Bülow to Hammann, 18 April 1902.

396 Ibid., Bülow to Hammann, 4 July 1903.

397 Ibid., Bülow to Hammann, 1 January 1902.

398 Ibid., 8, Bülow to Hammann, 17 November 1903.

399 Ibid., 9, Bülow to Hammann, 20 October 1904.

400 PA Bonn, IA, Deutschland, 126, no. 2, Bd. XI, Bülow's marginalia on Hammann's memorandum, 23 November 1905.

401 ZSA Potsdam, 7, Bülow to Hammann, 3 October 1902.

402 PA Bonn, IA, Deutschland, 126, no. 3, Bd. IV, Bülow's marginalia on Mühlberg's memorandum of 26 September 1898.

403 Ibid., Bd. VIII, Bülow to Foreign Office, 11 September 1907.

404 ZSA Potsdam, Hammann Papers, 7, Bülow to Hammann, 22 June 1902.

405 Ibid., Bülow to Hammann, 5 October 1902.

406 Ibid., Bülow to Hammann, 4 June 1902.

407 Ibid., Bülow to Hammann, 6 June 1902.

408 Ibid., Bülow to Hammann, 27 October 1902.

409 Ibid., Bülow to Hammann, 24 May 1902.

410 Ibid., Bülow to Hammann [1902].

411 BA Koblenz, O. Richthofen Papers, 7, Bülow to Richthofen, 20 October 1904.

412 PA Bonn, IA, Deutschland, 122, no. 9, Bd. II, Bülow to Hammann, 23 August 1903.

413 ZSA Potsdam, Hammann Papers, 10, Bülow to Hammann, 8 February 1905.

414 Ibid., 7, Bülow to Hammann, 21 March 1902.

415 Ibid., 9, Bülow to Hammann, 30 December 1904.

416 Ibid., Bülow to Hammann, 18 January 1904. See also BA Koblenz, Reichskanzlei, 1722, Bülow to Wilmowski, 12 February 1901.

417 PA Bonn, IA, Deutschland, 122, no. 13, Bd. III, Bülow to Wilmowski, 12 February 1901.

418 ZSA Potsdam, Hammann Papers, 8, Bülow to Hammann, 27 September 1903.

419 PA Bonn, IA, Deutschland, 122, no. 13, Bd. IX, Bülow to Foreign Office, 23 September 1905.

420 Ibid., 172, secr. Bd. II, Bülow to Foreign Office, 3 September 1901. On the Kaufmann affair, see ibid., 122, no. 13, Bd. III, correspondence between Bülow and Hammann, July 1901 and *Kölnische Volkszeitung*, 14 July 1901, 'Moderne Ministersorgen'. The liberal press was enraged when the Minister of Interior's proposal of Kaufmann as second Bürgermeister of Berlin was rejected by the Crown. The press used the opportunity to attack Bülow (who claimed he never discussed the matter with Wilhelm II) and ponder whether his will carried as little weight as that of the other Ministers. For Puttkamer's replacement by Köller as State Secretary of Alsace-Lorraine, see ch. 3, p. 112 above.

421 ZSA Potsdam, Hammann Papers, 8, Bülow to Hammann, 27 September 1903.

422 Ibid., 9, Bülow to Hammann, 27 September 1904.

423 Ibid., 7, Bülow to Hammann, 20 June 1902.
424 PA Bonn, IA, Deutschland, 122, no. 13, Bd. V, Bülow to Hammann, 31 March 1902.
425 Ibid., Bd. III, Bülow to Hammann, 7 April 1901.
426 ZSA Potsdam, Hamman Papers, 10, Bülow to Hammann, 5 July 1905. The article in *Deutschland. Monatschrift für die gesamte Kultur*, no. 34 of 10 July 1905 is in ZSA Merseburg, Althoff Papers, 108. Althoff had details of Bülow's early career and his school report.
427 Monts, *Erinnerungen*, Monts to Tschirschky, 11 July 1904, p. 416.
428 BA Koblenz, O. Richthofen Papers, 17, Bülow to Richthofen, 21 July 1904, pp. 554f.
429 Fuchs, *Grossherzog Friedrich*, Brauer to Grand Duke Friedrich, 28 July 1904.
430 BA Koblenz, O. Richthofen Papers, 7, Brauer to Richthofen, 8 August 1904, pp. 554f.
431 Fuchs, *Grossherzog Friedrich*, Grand Duke Friedrich to Brauer, 4 August 1904, p. 555.
432 Ibid., Brauer to Grand Duke Friedrich, 8 August 1904, p. 556.
433 Ibid., Brauer to Grand Duke Friedrich, 27 September 1904, p. 559.
434 BA Koblenz, BP, 150, Notebook, 1876.
435 Ibid., 151, Notebook C (1892), p. 81.
436 ZSA Potsdam, Hammann Papers, 8, undated note [1903].
437 Ibid., 14, Bülow to Hammann, 31 July 1908.
438 Ibid., 7, Bülow to Hammann, 4 July 1903.
439 Ibid., Bülow to Hammann, 18 January 1904.
440 See Cecil, *German Diplomatic Service*, p. 303.
441 BA Koblenz, BP, 151, Notebook D (1909), p. 130.
442 ZSA Potsdam, Hammann Papers, 7, Bülow to Hammann, 19 July 1902.
443 BA Koblenz, BP, 149, *Neue Freie Presse*, 21 August 1904, 'Graf Bülow in Norderney'. See also Hiller, *Fürst Bülows Denkwürdigkeiten*, p. 129, n. 45.
444 PA Bonn, IA, Deutschland, 122, no. 13, Bd. IX, Bülow to Foreign Office, 21 July 1905.
445 BA Koblenz, BP, 22, Bülow to Richthofen, 27 September 1902.
446 PA Bonn, IA, Deutschland, 126a secr., Bd. I, Bülow to Wilhelm II, 15 November 1905.
447 Ibid., 126, Generalia, Bd. IV, Hammann's memorandum 'Über Pressepolitik im Ausland', 27 March 1908.
448 Ibid., Bd. II, Bülow to German embassies in Europe and Washington, 8 July 1902; ibid., Bd. IV, Bülow to all the embassies, 13 October 1908.
449 Ibid., 122, no. 2f, Bd. III, Bülow to Vienna embassy, 3 May 1900; ibid., no. 13, Bd. XIII, Seeband to Hammann, 27 November 1900.
450 Ibid., 122, no. 3, Bd. XIX, *Die Welt am Montag*, 12 October 1908, 'Ein Vertrauensmann unserer Regierung'. The article attacked Adolf Stein, who enjoyed Bülow's great confidence and who, as editor of *Der Deutsche*, was able to show potential backers of the paper secret documents with Bülow's marginalia in order to convince them that his paper could not go under. See ibid., 126, no. 2, secr. Bd. I, Adolf Stein to Hammann, 18 November 1907.
451 Neumann, 'Innenpolitik', 53 (quoting Körner).
452 Bülow, *Denkwürdigkeiten*, II, p. 207.
453 Ibid., p. 443. See also *Denkwürdigkeiten*, III, p. 96.
454 BA Koblenz, Loebell Papers, 27, memoirs, p. 90.
455 PA Bonn, IA, Deutschland, 122, no. 2, secr. Bd. I, Hammann's memorandum, 23 March 1914. For a brief account of Hammann's career and growing influence under Bülow, see Friedrich Heilbron, 'Nekrolog auf Otto Hammann', *Deutsches Biographisches Jahrbuch*, 10 (Berlin, 1931), 93–108.
456 ZSA Potsdam, Hammann Papers, 12, Bülow to Hammann, 17 September 1906. See also ibid., 7, Bülow to Hammann, 4 February 1902 and 25 December [1902?].

457 Ibid., 10, Bülow to Hammann, 16 April 1905.
458 Ibid., Bülow to Hammann, 19 March 1903.
459 Ibid., Bülow to Hammann, 22 January 1905.
460 Ibid., 9, Bülow to Hammann, 10 December 1904.
461 Ibid., 7, Bülow to Hammann, 3 October 1902; ibid., 8, Bülow to Hammann, 19 October 1903; ibid., 7, Bülow to Hammann, 2 October 1902.
462 Ibid., 10, Bülow to Hammann, 28 January 1905.
463 Ibid., 7, Bülow to Hammann, 5 October 1902.
464 Ibid., 10, Bülow to Hammann, 17 January 1905.
465 See also Rich, *Holstein*, II, pp. 703f.
466 ZSA Potsdam, Hammann Papers, 7, Bülow to Hammann, 3 October 1902. The difficult negotiations about Jacobi's contract can be followed in PA Bonn, IA, Deutschland, 126, no. 2b. Bd. II, correspondence of September and October 1902. They foundered also on Bülow's reluctance to allow Jacobi genuine editorial freedom and independence.
467 Monts, *Erinnerungen*, Holstein to Monts, 16 September 1906, p. 365.
468 See for example Rich and Fisher, *Holstein Papers*, IV, Holstein to Bülow, January 1906, pp. 382f.
469 Monts, *Erinnerungen*, Tschirschky to Monts, 28 March 1906, p. 441.
470 ZSA Potsdam, Hammann Papers, 11, Bülow to Hammann, 17 January 1906.
471 Ibid., 12, Bülow to Hammann, 21 April 1906.

4 The crisis of 1905–1906

1 Rich, *Holstein*, II, pp. 706ff.
2 HSA Stuttgart, Varnbüler's Report, 25 June 1905.
3 Ibid. See also ZSA Potsdam, Zivilkabinett, 3584, Bülow to Wilhelm II, 25 May 1905 and Bülow to Lucanus, 24 May 1905. In the event of the Landtag's rejection of the Mining Bill, Bülow preferred a dissolution and new elections to the idea of summoning the Reichstag and embarking on Reich legislation. As he told Lucanus, the latter course would have limited Prussia's independence and implied 'recognition of the democratic principle represented in the Reichstag'. Cf. Born, *Staat und Sozialpolitik*, pp. 186f., although Bülow never seriously considered Reich legislation.
4 ZSA Potsdam, Hammann Papers, 6, article entitled 'Der Reichskanzler', June 1905.
5 HSA Stuttgart, Varnbüler's Report, 25 June 1905.
6 See especially Rich, *Holstein*, II, pp. 691ff.; Heiner Raulff, *Zwischen Machtpolitik und Imperialismus: die deutsche Frankreichpolitik 1904–6* (Düsseldorf, 1976); E. N. Anderson, *The First Moroccan Crisis 1904–6* (Chicago, 1930).
7 See for example HSA Stuttgart, Varnbüler's Report, 12 April 1905.
8 HHSA Wien, 161, Szögyényi to Goluchowski, 2 May 1905.
9 Rich and Fisher, *Holstein Papers*, IV, Holstein to Radolin, 8 May 1905, p. 341.
10 HHSA Wien, 161, Szögyényi to Goluchowski, 2 May 1905; GLA Karlsruhe, 34810, Berckheim's Report, 25 May 1905.
11 See especially Rich, *Holstein*, II, pp. 699ff. and 744f.
12 HSA München, 2683, Lerchenfeld to Podewils, 13 October 1905.
13 See for example Walther Klein, *Der Vertrag von Björkoe. Wilhelm II, Bülow und Holstein im Kampf gegen die Isolierung Deutschlands* (Berlin, 1931); Thimme, *Front Wider Bülow*, pp. 16f.
14 Bülow, *Denkwürdigkeiten*, II, pp. 137–50.
15 Cf. Cole, 'Kaiser versus Chancellor', p. 52; Rich, *Holstein*, II, p. 716. Barbara Vogel's interpretation that Bülow's response must be set within the wider context of Germany's

Moroccan policy and aims with respect to France (for in her view Bülow saw Björkö not as 'an escapade of imperial *Privatpolitik*' but as the cornerstone of Germany's continental and world policy) is also unconvincing. See Vogel, *Deutsche Russlandpolitik*, pp. 224 and 233.

16 Vogel, *Deutsche Russlandpolitik*, pp. 204ff.; Rich, *Holstein*, II, pp. 688ff.

17 See *Grosse Politik*, XIX, Bülow to Foreign Office, 26 July 1905, pp. 467f. and 28 July 1905, pp. 476f. See also Frederic Whyte (ed.), *Letters of Prince von Bülow* (London, undated), pp. 158ff.

18 *Grosse Politik*, XIX, Bülow to Foreign Office, 30 July 1905, pp. 477ff.

19 Ibid., Holstein to Bülow, 26 July 1905, pp. 468ff.; Rich, *Holstein*, II, pp. 716f.

20 *Grosse Politik*, XIX, pp. 467ff., 476ff.

21 Ibid., Bülow to Foreign Office, 30 July 1905, p. 477.

22 Ibid., pp. 480f. See also Whyte, *Letters*, pp. 163f.

23 *Grosse Politik*, XIX, Bülow to Foreign Office, 2 August 1905, p. 481.

24 Eckardstein, *Lebenserinnerungen*, III, *Die Isolierung Deutschlands*, pp. 166f.

25 Vogel, *Deutsche Russlandpolitik*, p. 208.

26 *Grosse Politik*, XIX, pp. 481f., n. 3.

27 BA–MA Freiburg, Müller Papers, 3, diary entry of 9 July 1905. For once, Bülow did not want this reported in the press. See PA Bonn, IA, Deutschland, 122, no. 13, Bd. IX, Bülow to Foreign Office, 9 July 1905.

28 Vierhaus, *Spitzemberg*, 2 April 1905, p. 447.

29 HSA Stuttgart, Varnbüler's Report, 25 June 1905.

30 BA–MA Freiburg, Müller Papers, 3, diary entry, 9 December 1904. See also FCO London, Holstein Papers, 35, Bülow to Holstein, 10 January [1905].

31 BA–MA Freiburg, Tirpitz Papers, 21, note of 4 February 1905.

32 See HSA München, 2683, Lerchenfeld's Report, 6 August 1905. See also Smith, *Colonial Empire*, pp. 63ff.

33 Rich, *Holstein*, II, p. 709; HSA München, 1077, Lerchenfeld's Report, 26 May(?) 1905; Rich and Fisher, *Holstein Papers*, IV, Holstein to Radolin, 15 September 1905, pp. 370–2.

34 Otto Hammann, *The World Policy of Germany 1890–1912* (English edition, London, 1927), p. 165.

35 *Grosse Politik*, XIX, Wilhelm II to Bülow, 25 July 1905, pp. 458ff.; Spectator, *Prince Bülow and the Kaiser* (London, 1931), pp. 174–85.

36 *Grosse Politik*, XIX, Wilhelm II to Bülow, 11 August 1905, pp. 496ff.; Bülow, *Denkwürdigkeiten*, II, pp. 145–7; Spectator, *Prince Bülow*, pp. 192–5.

37 *Grosse Politik*, XIX, Wilhelm II to Bülow, 11 August 1905, p. 498.

38 ZSA Merseburg, Rep. 53J, Lit. B. no. 16a, III, Bülow to Wilhelm II, 12 August 1905. Cf. Bülow's paraphrasing of this letter, *Denkwürdigkeiten*, II, pp. 149f.

39 Waldersee, *Denkwürdigkeiten*, III, 31 January 1904, pp. 228f.; BA Koblenz, O. Richthofen Papers, 7, Tschirschky to Richthofen, 10 September 1904.

40 ZSA Merseburg, Hausarchiv, Adjutants' Diaries, 11, entries for September and October 1905.

41 BA Koblenz, Eulenburg Papers, 77, 'Spaziergang mit dem Kaiser am 25 September 1905'; Röhl, *Eulenburg*, III, Eulenburg's essay, 25 September 1905, pp. 2118f.

42 BA Koblenz, Eulenburg Papers, 77, Eulenburg to Bülow, 17 October 1905.

43 See Hull, *Entourage*, pp. 120f.; Rich, *Holstein*, II, pp. 725–7.

44 Röhl, *Eulenburg*, III, Eulenburg to Bülow, 23 September 1905, pp. 2113f.

45 BA Koblenz, Eulenburg Papers, 77, Eulenburg to Bülow, 17 October 1905.

46 Ibid., Wilhelm II to Eulenburg, 19 October 1905.

47 HHSA Wien, 161, Szögyényi to Goluchowski, 28 November 1905. For Wilhelm's relationship with Fürstenberg, see Hull, *Entourage*, pp. 147ff.

48 Rich, *Holstein*, II, pp. 744f.

49 Ibid., p. 750.

50 BA Koblenz, Reichskanzlei, 158, memorandum of 27 January 1906. See also Bülow, *Denkwürdigkeiten*, I, pp. 381ff.

51 Fuchs, *Grossherzog Friedrich*, Berckheim to Marschall, 30 October 1905, pp. 606f.

52 HSA München, 2684, Lerchenfeld's Report, 2 May 1906; Bülow, *Denkwürdigkeiten*, II, p. 96.

53 GLA Karlsruhe, 34810, Berckheim's Report, 16 October 1905; HSA München, 2683, Lerchenfeld's Report, 14 October 1905.

54 Fuchs, *Grossherzog Friedrich*, Berckheim to Marschall, 30 October 1905, pp. 606f.

55 HHSA Wien, 162, Szögyényi's Report, 18 October 1905; ZSA Merseburg, Zivilkabinett, 3698, Schönstedt to Wilhelm II, 13 November 1905.

56 GLA Karlsruhe, 34807, Jagemann's Report, 7 October 1901; HHSA Wien, 162, Szögyényi's Report, 18 October 1905; Bülow, *Denkwürdigkeiten*, II, p. 91.

57 HHSA Wien, 162, Szögyényi's Report, 18 October 1905.

58 ZSA Potsdam, Reichskanzlei, 2044, *Berliner Tageblatt*, no. 534, 19 October 1905, 'Möllers Fall'.

59 GLA Karlsruhe, 34810, Berckheim's Report, 19 October 1905.

60 HHSA Wien, 162, Szögyényi's Report, 18 October 1905 (no. 31c).

61 Ibid.; GLA Karlsruhe, 34810, Berckheim's Report, 19 October 1905; ZSA Potsdam, Reichskanzlei, 2044, Möller to Wilhelm II, 15 October 1905.

62 PA Bonn, IA, Preussen, no. 9, Bd. III, Bülow to Richthofen, 8 September 1905.

63 HHSA Wien, 162, Szögyényi's Report, 18 October 1905 (no. 31c).

64 Neumann, 'Innenpolitik', p. 175 (quoting report of Bremen ambassador to Berlin of 10 October 1905, no. 124).

65 PA Bonn, IA, Preussen, no. 9, Bd. III, Bülow to Richthofen, 8 September 1905.

66 HHSA Wien, 162, Szögyényi's Report, 18 October 1905 (no. 31c); BA Koblenz, O. Richthofen Papers, 7, Loebell to Richthofen, 13 October 1905.

67 For the problems of the Berlin colonial administration, see the useful summary in HSA München, 2684, Lerchenfeld's Report, 27 June 1906. See also ZSA Potsdam, Hammann Papers, 10, Bülow to Hammann, 22 January 1905; Crothers, *German Elections*, pp. 18ff.

68 Reichstag, 5 December 1904, pp. 3371ff.; Bülow, *Reden*, II, 5 December 1904, pp. 111–35.

69 HHSA Wien, 162, Szögyényi's Report, 6 September 1905.

70 BA Koblenz, O. Richthofen Papers, 14, Stübel to Richthofen, 1 September 1905.

71 HSA München, 2683, Ortenburg's Report, 17 September 1905; HSA Stuttgart, Moser's Report, 18 September 1905. See also PA Bonn, IA, Deutschland, 122, no. 2 secr., Bd. I, Bülow to Götzen, 12 July 1905 and Götzen to Bülow, 16 July 1905.

72 BA Koblenz, O. Richthofen Papers, 4, Wiegand to Richthofen, 3 November 1905.

73 ZSA Potsdam, Hammann Papers, 10, Bülow to Hammann, 6 November 1905 and 16, Steinthal to Hammann, 6 November 1905.

74 PA Bonn, IA, Deutschland, 122, no. 2 secr., Bd. II, Richthofen to Pourtalès's, 11 November 1905 and Pourtalès's Report, 12 November 1905.

75 BA Koblenz, O. Richthofen Papers, 14, Richthofen, 'Zum eventl. Immediatvortrag bei Sr. Maj.', 13 November [1905].

76 Ibid., Helfferich to Richthofen, 14 August 1905; HHSA Wien, 161, Szögyényi to Goluchowski, 18 August 1905; HSA–KA München, D4, II, Report of the Bavarian military plenipotentiary, 26 November 1905.

77 BA Koblenz, O. Richthofen Papers, 14, Richthofen, 'Zum eventl. Immediatvortrag', 13 November [1905].
78 ZSA Merseburg, Rep. 53J, Lit. H. no. 6, Wilhelm II to Ernst zu Hohenlohe-Langenburg, 14 November 1905.
79 HHSA Wien, 162, Szögyényi's Report, 16 November 1905.
80 See BA Koblenz, O. Richthofen Papers, 4, Richthofen, 'Betr. Erbprinz zu Hohenlohe-Langenburg', 16 November [1905].
81 HHSA Wien, 161, Szögyényi to Goluchowski, 21 November 1905 and 162, Szögyényi's Report, 28 November 1905; HSA München, 2683, Lerchenfeld's Report, 6 August 1905.
82 See for example ZSA Merseburg, Rep. 53J, Lit. H, no. 6, Wilhelm II to Hohenlohe-Langenburg, 14 November 1905.
83 ZSA Potsdam, Reichskanzlei, 1662, Hohenlohe-Langenburg to Bülow, 19 November 1905.
84 Ibid., Bülow to Richthofen, 21 November 1905.
85 HHSA Wien, 161, Szögyényi to Goluchowski, 21 November 1905.
86 Brauer, *Im Dienste Bismarcks*, Holstein to Brauer, 7 December 1905, pp. 410–13.
87 HSA Stuttgart, Varnbüler's Report, 12 April 1905.
88 W. Goetz (ed.), *Briefe Wilhelms II an den Zaren, 1894–1914* (Berlin, 1920), Wilhelm II to Nicholas II, 26 September 1905, pp. 379–83; HHSA Wien, 161, Szögyényi to Goluchowski, 24 October 1905.
89 HSA Stuttgart, Moser's Report, 26 August 1905.
90 BA Koblenz, Hartmann von Richthofen Papers, 4, O. Richthofen to H. Richthofen, 27 May 1904.
91 PA Bonn, IA, Deutschland, 122, no. 2g, Bd. II, Bülow to Richthofen, 22 August 1905.
92 BA Koblenz, H. Richthofen Papers, 4, O. Richthofen to H. Richthofen, 31 December 1905.
93 SA Köln, Bachem Papers, 228, note of 15 February 1906; Bachem, *Zentrumspartei*, VI, p. 289.
94 HHSA Wien, 162, Szögyényi to Goluchowski, 16 January 1906; Rich, *Holstein*, II, p. 746.
95 HHSA Wien, 162, Szögyényi to Goluchowski, 10 January 1906; Rich, *Holstein*, II, pp. 724f., 731f.
96 Rich and Fisher, *Holstein Papers*, IV, Holstein to Bülow, January 1906, pp. 379–83.
97 Rich, *Holstein*, II, pp. 746f.
98 HHSA Wien, 162, Szögyényi to Goluchowski, 16 January 1906.
99 See Fuchs, *Grossherzog Friedrich*, Brauer to Berckheim, 12 January 1906, p. 616; GLA Karlsruhe, 34811, Berckheim's Report, 12 January 1906; Brauer, *Im Dienste Bismarcks*, January 1906, pp. 416–19.
100 HSA München, 2684, Lerchenfeld's Report, 22 January 1906.
101 HHSA Wien, 162, Szögyényi to Goluchwoski, 23 January 1906.
102 Bülow, *Denkwürdigkeiten*, II, p. 137.
103 Fuchs, *Grossherzog Friedrich*, Berckheim to Marschall, 25 January 1906, p. 619.
104 Ibid.; Brauer, *Im Dienste Bismarcks*, January 1906, pp. 416–19.
105 HSA München, 2684, Lerchenfeld's Report, 22 January 1906; HHSA Wien, 162, Szögyényi to Goluchowski, 23 January 1906.
106 Fuchs, *Grossherzog Friedrich*, Berckheim to Marschall, 25 January 1906, p. 619.
107 Brauer, *Im Dienste Bismarcks*, January 1906, pp. 416–19.
108 PA Bonn, Eisendecher Papers, 3, Tschirschky to Eisendecher, 31 January 1906; BA Koblenz, O. Richthofen Papers, 7, Tschirschky to Richthofen, 18 November 1905.
109 Monts, *Erinnerungen*, Tschirschky to Monts, 30 January 1906, p. 440.
110 HSA München, 2684, Lerchenfeld's Report, 22 January 1906.
111 HHSA Wien, 162, Szögyényi to Goluchowski, 23 January 1906.

112 ZSA Potsdam, Hammann Papers, 11, Bülow to Hammann, 23 January 1906.
113 Monts, *Erinnerungen*, Tschirschky to Monts, 30 January 1906, p. 440.
114 PA Bonn, Eisendecher Papers, 3, Tschirschky to Eisendecher, 31 January 1906.
115 ZSA Potsdam, Hammann Papers, 11, Bülow to Hammann, 23 January 1906.
116 Ibid., Bülow to Hammann, 23 January 1906 (letter headed 'zu verbrennen').
117 Fuchs, *Grossherzog Friedrich*, Berckheim to Marschall, 30 October 1905, p. 607.
118 ZSA Merseburg, Staatsministerium, 152, 12 February 1906 and 13 March 1906; Zivilkabinett, 170, Bülow to Wilhelm II, 3 April 1906.
119 ZSA Merseburg, Kronrat, 6, 13 February 1906.
120 Zedlitz, *Zwölf Jahre*, 27 February 1905, p. 115 and 14 February 1910, pp. 229ff.; Hull, *Entourage*, pp. 15ff.
121 SA Köln, Bachem Papers, 228, note of 15 February 1906.
122 ZSA Potsdam, Hammann Papers, 11, Bülow to Hammann, 17 January 1906.
123 HSA München, 1078, Lerchenfeld's Report, 18 February 1906.
124 Rich and Fisher, *Holstein Papers*, IV, Bülow to Holstein [22 February 1906], p. 397. See also HSA–KA München, D4, III, Report of Bavarian military plenipotentiary, 22 December 1905; cf. BA Koblenz, H. Richthofen Papers, 3, 'Unterredung mit dem Fürsten Bülow', 28 August 1914, during which conversation Bülow claimed that he and Richthofen would have been prepared to fight in 1905.
125 See Rich, *Holstein*, II, pp. 740f.
126 ZSA Potsdam, Hammann Papers, 10, Bülow to Hammann, 16 December 1905.
127 Ibid., 11, Bülow to Hammann, 18 March 1906.
128 Ibid., Bülow to Hammann, 7 March 1906.
129 Ibid., Bülow to Hammann, 15 March 1906.
130 Ibid., Bülow to Hammann, 18 March 1906. Loebell claimed that it was Bülow's 'greatest rhetorical achievement' that he presented the result of the Moroccan crisis as a success. See BA Koblenz, Loebell Papers, 27, memoirs, p. 77.
131 See HSA Stuttgart, Varnbüler's Report, 5 November 1905.
132 HHSA Wien, 163, Szögyényi's Report, 20 March 1906; Rich, *Holstein*, II, pp. 709ff.
133 Monts, *Erinnerungen*, Monts to Tschirschky, 10 January 1906, p. 420.
134 HHSA Wien, 163, Szögyényi's Report, 20 March 1906.
135 Monts, *Erinnerungen*, Tschirschky to Monts, 28 March 1906, p. 441.
136 HSA München, 697, Report of Bavarian Minister in Paris to Podewils, 19 December 1905.
137 Brauer, *Im Dienste Bismarcks*, Holstein to Brauer, 7 December 1905, p. 413.
138 PA Bonn, IA, Deutschland, 122, no. 13, Bd. x, *The Times*, 6 January 1906 and Schön's Report, 7 January 1906.
139 HHSA Wien, 163, Szögyényi's Report, 20 March 1906.
140 Monts, *Erinnerungen*, Tschirschky to Monts, 28 March 1906, p. 441.
141 FCO London, Holstein Papers, 32, Holstein to Bülow, 23 March 1906.
142 HHSA Wien, 163, Szögyényi's Report, 20 March 1906.
143 Rich and Fisher, *Holstein Papers*, IV, Holstein to Bülow, 31 March 1906, p. 406.
144 See especially Rich, *Holstein*, II, pp. 748f.
145 Brauer, *Im Dienste Bismarcks*, Holstein to Brauer, 2 April 1906, p. 417.
146 See Rich, *Holstein*, II, pp. 746–53 for further details.
147 Monts, *Erinnerungen*, Tschirschky to Monts, 13 April 1906, pp. 442f.
148 BA–MA Freiburg, Reichsmarineamt, RM3, 6, Tirpitz to Chief of Naval Cabinet, 4 April 1906 and Wilhelm II to Tirpitz, 5 April 1906.
149 Ibid., Tirpitz's dictated notes of 7 February 1906 and Senden's memorandum of 6 February 1906.
150 Ibid., Tirpitz's dictated notes of 13 February 1906.

151 Ibid.; SA Köln, Bachem Papers, 228, note of 15 February 1906. For further details, see Alfred von Tirpitz, *Politische Dokumente. Bd. 1. Der Aufbau der deutschen Weltmacht* (Berlin, 1924), pp. 25–33.

152 ZSA Merseburg, Staatsministerium, 152, 8 January 1906. The demonstrations took place on 21 January and were without incident. See Vierhaus, *Spitzemberg*, 21 January 1906, p. 455; Hansjoachim Henning (ed.), *Die Sozialpolitik in den letzten Friedensjahren des Kaiserreichs (1905 bis 1914). 2 Band. Das Jahr 1906* (Stuttgart, 1987), pp. 34ff.

153 Bülow, *Denkwürdigkeiten*, II, p. 198.

154 ZSA Merseburg, Kronrat, 6, 13 February 1906. See also Einem's memorandum of 28 December 1905 in PA Bonn, IA, Europa Generalia, 82, no. 1, no. 1 secr., Bd. VIII.

155 Reichstag, 9 December 1905, pp. 191ff.; Bülow, *Reden*, II, 14 December 1905, pp. 276–90 and 25 January 1906, pp. 290–3. Cf. BA Koblenz, Reichskanzlei, 1608, *Konservative Korrespondenz*, no. 12, 12 February 1906, 'Abgeordneter und Minister'.

156 ZSA Merseburg, Staatsministerium, 152, 8 January 1906.

157 BA Koblenz, O. Richthofen Papers, 7, Loebell to Richthofen, 20 December 1905.

158 BA Koblenz, Reichskanzlei, 1608, *Konservative Korrespondenz*, no. 12, 12 February 1906, 'Abgeordneter und Minister'.

159 HSA–KA München, D4, II, Report of Bavarian military plenipotentiary, 15 January 1906; Reichstag, 15 January 1906, pp. 550ff.

160 HSA München, 1078, Lerchenfeld's Report, 16 January 1906; SA Köln, Bachem Papers, 235, note of 17 January 1906.

161 SA Köln, Bachem Papers, 235, note of 26 January 1906. See Cole, 'Kaiser versus Chancellor', p. 43.

162 SA Köln, Bachem Papers, 244, note of 21 March 1906.

163 HHSA Wien, 163, Szögyényi's Report, 20 March 1906; Loth, *Katholiken im Kaiserreich*, pp. 111ff.

164 See HSA München, 2684, Lerchenfeld's Report, 27 June 1906; GLA Karlsruhe, 34811, Berckheim's Report, 19 March 1906.

165 HHSA Wien, 163, Szögyényi's Report, 20 March 1906.

166 HSA München, 2684, Lerchenfeld's Report, 22 March 1906.

167 ZSA Potsdam, Reichskanzlei, 1662, Hohenlohe-Langenburg to Bülow, 5 March 1906.

168 HHSA Wien, 163, Szögyényi's Report, 20 March 1906; HSA München, 2684, Lerchenfeld's Report, 22 March 1906.

169 HHSA Wien, 163, Szögyényi's Report, 20 March 1906.

170 SA Köln, Bachem Papers, 244, note of 21 March 1906. See also Loth, *Katholiken im Kaiserreich*, p. 112, n. 75.

171 SA Köln, Bachem Papers, 238, note of 21 March 1906; HHSA Wien, 163, Szögyényi's Report, 27 March 1906. Cf. Cole, 'Kaiser versus Chancellor', p. 46, who bases his argument on an article in the *Schlesische Volkszeitung* which Bachem considered 'absolutely wrong'.

172 See Rich, *Holstein*, II, p. 751.

173 HSA München, 2684, Lerchenfeld's Reports, 22 March 1906 and 24 March 1906; Cole, 'Kaiser versus Chancellor', pp. 47f.

174 HHSA Wien, 163, Szögyényi's Report, 27 March 1906.

175 Reichstag, 29 March 1906, pp. 2417ff.; HHSA Wien, 163, Szögyényi's Report, 30 March 1906.

176 ZSA Potsdam, Reichskanzlei, 1662, Bülow to Hohenlohe-Langenburg, 30 March 1906.

177 HHSA Wien, 163, Szögyényi's Report, 30 March 1906.

178 ZSA Potsdam, Hammann Papers, 6, articles from *Berliner-Börsenzeitung* of 7 March 1906, *Ostpreussische Zeitung* of 11 March 1906 (on Algeciras) and *Kölnische Volkszeitung* of 14 March 1906 (on Colonial Office).

179 Rich and Fisher, *Holstein Papers*, IV, Bülow to Holstein, 25 March 1906, p. 403.
180 SA Köln, Bachem Papers, 244, note of 7 April 1906.
181 ZSA Potsdam, Hammann Papers, 12, Bülow to Hammann, 1 April 1906.
182 Ibid., Bülow to Hammann, 3 April 1906.
183 Reichstag, 5 April 1906, p. 2633; Bülow, *Reden*, II, 5 April 1906, pp. 303–6.
184 Sigmund Münz, *Fürst Bülow. Der Staatsmann und Mensch. Aufzeichnungen, Erinnerungen und Erwägungen* (Berlin, 1930), p. 182.
185 HSA München, 2684, Lerchenfeld's Report, 5 April 1906.
186 Ibid.; SA Köln, Bachem Papers, 244, note of 7 April 1906.
187 ZSA Merseburg, Hausarchiv, Adjutants' Diaries, 11, entries for March and April 1906.
188 Ibid., entry for 5 April 1906.
189 HSA München, 2684, Lerchenfeld's Report, 5 April 1906.
190 Münz, *Fürst Bülow*, p. 182; Bülow, *Denkwürdigkeiten*, II, pp. 213f.
191 HHSA Wien, 162, Szögyényi to Goluchowski, 24 April 1906 (copy in BA Koblenz, BP, 164).
192 Vierhaus, *Spitzemberg*, 22 April 1906, p. 460.
193 ZSA Merseburg, Hausarchiv, Adjutants' Diaries, 11, 3 May 1906.
194 See BA Koblenz, BP, 152, Losungen, 1906.
195 Ibid., 151, Notebook D, p. 172.
196 HSA Stuttgart, Varnbüler's Report, 10 April 1906.
197 ZSA Potsdam, Hammann Papers, 12, Bülow to Hammann, 21 April 1906.
198 See for example ibid., Bülow to Hammann, 17 June 1906.
199 Ibid., Bülow to Hammann, 27 May 1906.
200 BA Koblenz, BP, 25, Hugo Jacobi to [Loebell], 28 June 1906 and enclosed article in *Grenzboten*.
201 Ibid., Bülow to Loebell, 30 June 1906.
202 Ibid., Loebell's memorandum of 9 July 1906.
203 ZSA Merseburg, Rep. 53J, Lit. B. no. 16a, III, Bülow to Wilhelm II, 17 July 1906; Bülow, *Denkwürdigkeiten*, II, pp. 238–42. Cf. Cole, 'Kaiser versus Chancellor', p. 55 who interprets this letter as an attempt by Bülow to reassure the Kaiser of his belief in the value of a strong monarchy.
204 Monts, *Erinnerungen*, Holstein to Monts, 30 August 1906, p. 361.
205 Rich, *Holstein*, II, pp. 746–53. See also BA Koblenz, Thimme Papers, 49, Hammann to Thimme, 12 January 1924. Bülow commissioned Tschirschky to discuss the question with the Kaiser by sending a message through his brother, Karl-Ulrich.
206 ZSA Potsdam, Hammann Papers, 12, Bülow to Hammann, 27 May 1906; Rich, *Holstein*, II, pp. 760ff.
207 Cf. Cole, 'Kaiser versus Chancellor', pp. 48f.
208 ZSA Potsdam, Hammann Papers, 12, Bülow to Hammann, 27 May 1906.
209 ZSA Merseburg, Rep. 53J, Lit. B. no. 16a, III, Bülow to Wilhelm II, 17 July 1906.
210 ZSA Potsdam, Hammann Papers, 12, Bülow to Hammann, 30 June 1906.
211 Vierhaus, *Spitzemberg*, 22 April 1906, pp. 459f.; Rich and Fisher, *Holstein Papers*, IV, diary entry, 17 February 1907, p. 454.
212 Monts, *Erinnerungen*, Tschirschky to Monts, 13 April 1906, p. 442; HHSA Wien, 163, Szögyényi's Report, 16 May 1906.
213 Bülow, *Denkwürdigkeiten*, II, p. 218.
214 HHSA Wien, 162, Szögyényi to Goluchowski, 24 April 1906.
215 HSA Stuttgart, Varnbüler's Report, 10 April 1906.
216 ZSA Potsdam, Reichskanzlei, 2024, extract from State Ministry meeting of 4 May 1906; Rheinbaben to State Ministers, 15 June 1906 and Studt to President of State Ministry, 10 August 1906.

217 BA Koblenz, Reichskanzlei, 1715, Bülow to State Secretaries, 10 May 1906.
218 Ibid., 2024, Bülow to Günther, 9 August 1906 and Loebell to Bülow, 9 August 1906. Bülow presided over a meeting on 31 August 1906.
219 Vierhaus, *Spitzemberg*, 22 April 1906, pp. 459f.
220 ZSA Potsdam, Hausarchiv, Adjutants' Diaries, entries from April 1906; HHSA Wien, 162, Szögyényi to Goluchowski, 2 May 1906.
221 Monts, *Erinnerungen*, Tschirschky to Monts, 13 April 1906, pp. 442–4.
222 Ibid., Tschirschky to Monts, 19 April 1906, p. 428; HHSA München, 2684, Lerchenfeld's Report, 28 April 1906.
223 PA Bonn, Eisendecher Papers, 3, Tschirchky to Eisendecher, 27 July 1906.
224 Monts, *Erinnerungen*, Tschirschky to Monts, 5 August 1906, p. 444.
225 Rich and Fisher, *Holstein Papers*, IV, Holstein to Pascal David, 29 August 1906, p. 434.
226 ZSA Potsdam, Hammann Papers, 12, Bülow to Hammann, 25 August 1906, 17 September 1906, 5 October 1906; Monts, *Erinnerungen*, Tschirschky to Monts, 25 September 1906, pp. 445f.
227 Rich and Fisher, *Holstein Papers*, IV, Holstein to Harden, 21 October 1906, pp. 440f.
228 ZSA Merseburg, Rep. 53J, Lit. B. no. 16a, III, Bülow to Wilhelm II, 31 May 1906.
229 Monts, *Erinnerungen*, Tschirschky to Monts, 25 September 1906, p. 445.
230 BA Koblenz, BP, 152, Losungen, 15 April 1906.
231 HHSA Wien, 162, Szögyényi's Report, 22 May 1906.
232 PA Bonn, IA, Deutschland, 122, no. 2 secr., Bd. II, Bülow to Foreign Office, 29 May 1906.
233 HSA Stuttgart, Varnbüler's Report, 3 November 1906.
234 PA Bonn, IA, Deutschland, 122, no. 2 secr., Bd. I, Bülow to Foreign Office, 29 May 1906. See also ibid., no. 2, Bd. II, Bülow to Hammann, 30 May 1906, in which Bülow assumes Wilhelm has been shown press cuttings in the sense of his instruction of 27 May.
235 PA Bonn, IA, Deutschland, 122, no. 2 secr., Bd. II, Wilhelm II to Bülow, 30 May 1906.
236 Ibid., Bülow to Foreign Office (Tschirschky), 3 July 1906.
237 ZSA Potsdam, Hammann Papers, 12, Bülow to Hammann, 27 May 1906.
238 ZSA Potsdam, Reichskanzlei, 1663, Loebell to Bülow, 28 May 1906.
239 PA Bonn, IA, Deutschland, 122, no. 2 secr., Bd. I, Wilhelm II to Bülow, 30 May 1906.
240 ZSA Potsdam, Reichskanzlei, 1663, Loebell to Bülow, 28 May 1906.
241 PA Bonn, IA, Deutschland, 12, no. 2, Bd. II, Bülow to Foreign Office, 29 May 1906.
242 HSA München, 2684, Lerchenfeld's Report, 27 June 1906.
243 BA–MA Freiburg, Tirpitz Papers, 9, Bülow to Wilhelm II, 1 August 1906 and the Kaiser's marginalia; Bülow, *Denkwürdigkeiten*, II, pp. 250f.
244 ZSA Merseburg, Zivilkabinett, 3584, Bülow to Wilhelm II, 31 August 1906 and Bülow to Lucanus, 3 October 1906; Staatsministerium, 153, 30 October 1906.
245 ZSA Merseburg, Rep. 53J, Lit. B. no. 16a, III, Bülow to Wilhelm II, 17 July 1906.
246 ZSA Merseburg, Staatsministerium, 153, 30 October 1906.
247 Monts, *Erinnerungen*, Tschirschky to Monts, 25 September 1906, p. 445.
248 PA Bonn, IA, Deutschland, 122, no. 13, Bd. XI, Below to Foreign Office, 20 June 1906. The poem, 'König Karls Meerfahrt', by Ludwig Uhland, relates to Charlemagne and the twelve peers of France, who are all mentioned by name in order and who all express their fears in the storm. The concluding verse is:

Der König Karl am Steuer sass,
Der hat kein Wort gesprochen,
Er lenkt das Schiff mit festem Maass,
Bis sich der Sturm gebrochen.

[King Charles beside the rudder sat,

No word his lips would vent;
With sure control the ship he steered
Until the storm was spent.]
See Ludwig Uhland, *Gedichte*, 5th edn (Stuttgart and Tübingen, 1831), pp. 387–9
(English translation by W. W. Skeat in *The Songs and Ballads of Uhland* (London, 1864),
pp. 350–2).

249 HSA Stuttgart, Varnbüler's Report, 10 April 1906.
250 Neumann, 'Innenpolitik', p. 175 (quoting Report of Bremen ambassador of 9 April
   1906).
251 HSA Stuttgart, Varnbüler's Report, 10 April 1906; HHSA Wien, 162, Szögyényi to
   Goluchowski, 24 April 1906.
252 HSA München, 2684, Lerchenfeld's Report, 7 May 1906.
253 ZSA Potsdam, Hammann Papers, 12, Bülow to Hammann, 27 May 1906.
254 HHSA Wien, 162, Szögyényi to Goluchowski, 7 February 1906.
255 SA Köln, Bachem Papers, 228, note of 15 February 1906.
256 HSA München, 2683, Ortenburg's Report, 17 September 1905; HSA Stuttgart, Moser's
   Reports, 18 September 1905 and 29 September 1905.
257 GLA Karlsruhe, 34810, Berckheim's Report, 16 October 1905.
258 SA Köln, Bachem Papers, 228, note of 15 February 1906.
259 GLA Karlsruhe, 34810, Berckheim's Report, 30 October 1905.
260 HSA München, 2684, Lerchenfeld's Report, 9 November 1906. See also Cole, 'Kaiser
   versus Chancellor', pp. 55–7.
261 HHSA Wien, 163, Szögyényi's Report, 6 August 1906.
262 HSA München, 2684, Ortenburg's Report, 24 August 1906.
263 BA–MA Freiburg, Tirpitz Papers, 9, Boy-Ed's memorandum, 22 August 1906. See also
   PA Bonn, IA, Preussen, no. 9, Bd. III, Bülow to Foreign Office, 22 August 1906.
264 HSA München, 2684, Ortenburg's Report, 24 August 1906.
265 ZSA Potsdam, Hammann Papers, 12, Bülow to Hammann, 25 August 1906.
266 HSA München, 2684, Ortenburg's Report, 24 August 1906.
267 ZSA Potsdam, Reichskanzlei, 1663, Loebell to Bülow, 3 September 1906.
268 ZSA Merseburg, Hausarchiv, Adjutants' Diaries, 11, 4 September 1906; HSA München,
   2684, Ortenburg's Report, 5 September 1906.
269 Rich and Fisher, *Holstein Papers*, IV, Monts to Holstein, 11 September 1906, p. 438. Cf.
   Cole's interpretation, 'Kaiser versus Chancellor', p. 56.
270 ZSA Potsdam, Hammann Papers, 12, Bülow to Hammann, 5 October 1906.
271 Vierhaus, *Spitzemberg*, 6 October 1906, p. 464.
272 See HSA München, 2684, Lerchenfeld's Report, 9 November 1906.
273 ZSA Merseburg, Hausarchiv, Adjutants' Diaries 11, entries from August to November
   1906.
274 HHSA Wien, 163, Szögyényi's Report, 3 November 1906.
275 SA Köln, Bachem Papers, 244, note of 3 November 1906.
276 ZSA Merseburg, Staatsministerium, 153, 27 October 1906 and 30 October 1906.
277 GLA Karlsruhe, 34811, Berckheim's Report, 13 October 1906.
278 SA Köln, Bachem Papers, 244, note of 3 November 1906.
279 HHSA Wien, 163, Széchényi's Report, 3 November 1906.
280 PA Bonn, Eisendecher Papers, 5, Bülow to Eisendecher, 13 October 1906; ZSA Potsdam,
   Reichskanzlei, 1691, Eisendecher to Bülow, 15 October 1906.
281 HHSA Wien, 163, Széchényi's Report, 3 November 1906.
282 FCO London, Holstein Papers, 32, Holstein to Bülow, 30 October 1906.
283 HHSA Wien, 163, Széchényi's Report, 3 November 1906.
284 HSA Stuttgart, Varnbüler's Report, 3 November 1906.

285 Ibid. The Regent of Brunswick, Prince Albrecht von Preussen, had died in September 1906, thus reopening the question of the succession. See Bülow, *Denkwürdigkeiten*, II, pp. 248–50.

286 GLA Karlsruhe, 34811, Berckheim's Reports, 8 November 1906 and 10 November 1906; Fuchs, *Grossherzog Friedrich*, pp. 660–2; Cole, 'Kaiser versus Chancellor', p. 57.

287 ZSA Potsdam, Reichskanzlei, 2054, Lucanus to Loebell, 11 November 1906; Podbielski to Bülow, 12 November 1906 and 13 November 1906.

288 Ibid., Bülow to Lucanus, 8 November 1906.

289 GLA Karlsruhe, 34811, Berckheim's Report, 10 November 1906; BA Koblenz, BP, 152, Losungen, 10 November 1906.

290 PA Bonn, IA, Preussen, no. 9, Bd. III, Hohenlohe's Report, 15 November 1906.

291 HSA München, 2684, Lerchenfeld's Report, 9 November 1906.

292 ZSA Potsdam, Reichskanzlei, 2054, Bülow to Lucanus, 8 November 1906.

293 HSA München, 2684, Lerchenfeld's Report, 9 November 1906; SA Köln, Bachem Papers, 244, *Kölnische Volkszeitung*, 9 November 1906, 'Der Rücktritt des Ministers v. Podbielski'.

294 ZSA Potsdam, Reichskanzlei, 2054, Loebell's memorandum, 17 November 1906.

295 Ibid., Loebell's memorandum, 18 November 1906.

296 Ibid., *Reichs- und Staatsanzeiger*, 12 November 1906.

297 ZSA Merseburg, Staatsministerium, 153, 20 November 1906.

298 Rogge, *Holstein*, Holstein to Stülpnagel, 17 November 1906, p. 268.

299 Fuchs, *Grossherzog Friedrich*, Berckheim to Marschall, 8 November 1906, p. 661.

300 Vierhaus, *Spitzemberg*, 9 November 1906, p. 466.

301 Fuchs, *Grossherzog Friedrich*, Berckheim to Marschall, 8 November 1906, pp. 660f.; HSA München, 2684, Lerchenfeld's Report, 9 November 1906. See also Bülow, *Denkwürdigkeiten*, II, pp. 261f.

302 HSA München, 2684, Lerchenfeld's Report, 9 November 1906.

303 Fuchs, *Grossherzog Friedrich*, Berckheim to Marschall, 8 November 1906, p. 661.

304 HSA Stuttgart, Varnbüler's Report, 19 May 1907.

305 Ibid., 30 May 1905; Rich, *Holstein*, II, pp. 763ff.; Hull, *Entourage*, pp. 133ff.

306 Monts, *Erinnerungen*, Monts to Tschirschky, 27 November 1906, p. 430.

307 Vierhaus, *Spitzemberg*, 12 November 1906, p. 467.

308 HSA Stuttgart, Varnbüler's Report, 3 November 1906.

309 Ibid., 19 May 1907.

310 Zedlitz, *Zwölf Jahre*, 7 June 1907, pp. 159ff. and 26 November 1907, pp. 173f. Cf. Hull, *Entourage*, pp. 121ff.

311 Monts, *Erinnerungen*, Monts to Tschirschky, 27 November 1906, p. 431.

312 Bülow, *Denkwürdigkeiten*, II, pp. 262f.; Hull, *Entourage*, pp. 122ff.

313 Monts, *Erinnerungen*, Tschirschky to Monts, 18 April 1906, p. 448.

314 Rich and Fisher, *Holstein Papers*, IV, Holstein to Pascal David, 13 May 1906, p. 425.

315 HSA München, 2684, Lerchenfeld's Report, 9 November 1906.

316 See also Helmuth Rogge (ed.), *Holstein und Harden: Politisch-publizistisches Zusammenspiel zweier Aussenseiter des Wilhelminischen Reichs* (Munich, 1959), pp. 102f.; Cole, 'Kaiser versus Chancellor', p. 61.

317 Vierhaus, *Spitzemberg*, 15 November 1906, p. 467; Reichstag, 14 November 1906, pp. 3619ff.

318 Reichstag, 14 November 1906, pp. 3649f.; Bülow, *Reden*, II, 14 November 1906, pp. 341–4.

319 Vierhaus, *Spitzemberg*, 15 November 1906, p. 467; Monts, *Erinnerungen*, Tschirschky to Monts, 18 November 1906, p. 446. For the intimation in the *NAZ*, see HHSA Wien, 165, Szögyényi to Aehrenthal, 5 June 1907.

320 Bülow, *Denkwürdigkeiten*, II, pp. 265f.

321 Rich and Fisher, *Holstein Papers*, IV, Holstein to Bülow, 31 October 1906, pp. 446f.

322 Bülow, *Denkwürdigkeiten*, II, p. 261.

323 Ibid., p. 250.

324 Fuchs, *Grossherzog Friedrich*, Grand Duke Friedrich to Bülow, [27] June 1906, pp. 635–7 and 23 August 1906, pp. 641f.

325 BA Koblenz, Rottenburg Papers, 10, Prince Wilhelm to Rottenburg, 8 November 1906.

326 SA Köln, Bachem Papers, 244, note of 3 November 1906.

327 ZSA Potsdam, Reichskanzlei, 1663, Loebell to Bülow, 3 September 1906. Hohenlohe was later awarded 13,845M as compensation for not receiving the State Secretaryship he had been promised. See ibid., Stengel to Bülow, 14 February 1907.

328 BA Koblenz, Loebell Papers, 27, memoirs, p. 99. See also Dernburg's acknowledgement that he would never forget 'that I am "your" Colonial Secretary', ibid., 10, Dernburg to Loebell, 2 January 1909.

329 Ibid., 27, memoirs, pp. 99f.; HHSA Wien, 163, Trautmansdorff's Report, 12 September 1906.

330 BA Koblenz, Loebell Papers, 27, memoirs, p. 100.

331 HSA München, 2684, Ortenburg's Reports, 4 September 1906 and 5 September 1906.

332 SA Köln, Bachem Papers, 259, note of 15 December 1906; HSA München, 1080, Lerchenfeld's Report, 28 February 1908.

333 Zeender, *German Centre Party*, p. 78; Cole, 'Kaiser versus Chancellor', p. 64.

334 SA Köln, Bachem Papers, 259, note of 15 December 1906.

335 Ibid., note of 20 December 1906.

336 Crothers, *German Elections*, especially pp. 95–102.

337 Bülow had been considering the possibility of an anti-socialist campaign. See ZSA Merseburg, Staatsministerium, 153, 30 October 1906.

338 Reichstag, 4 December 1906, pp. 4124f.; Bülow, *Reden*, II, 4 December 1906, pp. 353–6; Crothers, *German Elections*, pp. 81f. Cf. Cole, 'Kaiser versus Chancellor', pp. 64f.

339 FCO London, Holstein Papers, 35, Bülow to Holstein, 4 December 1906. See also ibid., 32, Holstein to Bülow, 4 December 1906.

340 SA Köln, Bachem Papers, 259, note of 20 December 1906.

341 HHSA Wien, 163, Szögyényi's Report, 11 December 1906.

342 Eschenburg, *Kaiserreich am Scheideweg*, p. 42. Cf. BA–MA Freiburg, Tirpitz Papers, 9, Bülow to Tirpitz [June 1907], in which Bülow explicitly states that Tirpitz agreed to the dissolution.

343 ZSA Merseburg, Staatsministerium, 153, 11 December 1906.

344 Fuchs, *Grossherzog Friedrich*, Berckheim to Marschall, 12 December 1906, pp. 671–3.

345 SA Köln, Bachem Papers, 259, note of 20 December and note on a conversation with Ballestrem on 28 August [1909].

346 Crothers, *German Elections*, p. 99; Reichstag, 13 December 1906, p. 4381; Bülow, *Reden*, II, 13 December 1906, p. 361.

347 Fuchs, *Grossherzog Friedrich*, Berckheim to Marschall, 14 December 1906, pp. 673f.; Eschenburg, *Kaiserreich am Scheideweg*, p. 44.

348 Vierhaus, *Spitzemberg*, 14 December 1906, p. 468.

349 Ibid., 16 December 1906, p. 469. See also Kaiser Wilhelm II, *Ereignisse und Gestalten aus den Jahren 1878–1918* (Leipzig, 1922), pp. 95f.

350 Fuchs, *Grossherzog Friedrich*, Berckheim to Marschall, 14 December 1906, p. 674.

351 Crothers, *German Elections*, p. 101.

352 HSA München, 76140, Bavarian Minister in Bern to Podewils, 31 December 1906. Cf. Zedlitz's explanation in *Die Zeit* of 8 June 1907, quoted in Bachem, *Zentrumspartei*, V, pp. 391f.

353 HHSA Wien, 165, Szögyényi to Aehrenthal, 23 January 1907.
354 See Loth, *Katholiken im Kaiserreich*, especially p. 114.
355 SA Köln, Bachem Papers, 259, note of 20 December 1906; Loth, *Katholiken im Kaiserreich*, p. 119, n. 90.
356 HSA Stuttgart, Varnbüler Papers (P10), 746, Varnbüler's Report, 16 June 1907.
357 HSA München, 1080, Lerchenfeld's Report, 28 February 1908.

5 Government with the Bloc, 1907

1 HHSA Wien, 163, Szögyényi's Report, 19 December 1906.
2 PA Bonn, IA, Deutschland, 125, no. 3, Bd. XVIII, Posadowsky to Bülow, 14 December 1906.
3 Fuchs, *Grossherzog Friedrich*, Berckheim to Marschall, 17 December 1906, p. 678.
4 HSA Stuttgart, Weizsäcker Papers, Bülow to Hatzfeldt-Trachenberg, 22 December 1906.
5 PA Bonn, IA, Deutschland, 125, no. 3, Bd. XVIII, Posadowsky to Bülow, 14 December 1906; ibid., Asch's memorandum, 14 December 1906; Loth, *Katholiken im Kaiserreich*, pp. 121ff.
6 See Crothers, *German Elections*, pp. 119ff. See also PA Bonn, IA, Deutschland, 125, no. 1, Bd. VI, Würzburg to Wilke, 20 February 1907; Eley, *Reshaping the German Right*, p. 272.
7 ZSA Potsdam, Reichskanzlei, 2041, Schmidt-Elberfeld to Loebell, 18 December 1906 including marginalia by Bülow and Loebell.
8 HHSA Wien, 165, Szögyényi to Aehrenthal, 5 February 1907.
9 PA Bonn, IA, Deutschland, 125, no. 3, Bd. XVIII, Asch's memorandum, 14 December 1906.
10 ZSA Potsdam, Hammann Papers, 12, Bülow to Hammann [end of 1906].
11 HSA Stuttgart, Weizsäcker Papers, Bülow to Hatzfeldt-Trachenberg, 22 December 1906.
12 HHSA Wien, 162, Szögyényi to Aehrenthal, 26 December 1906.
13 Ibid.
14 See BA Koblenz, Boetticher Papers, Wilmowski to Boetticher, 6 January 1906; PA Bonn, IA, Deutschland, 125, no. 3, Bd. XVIII, Posadowsky to Bülow, 14 December 1906.
15 HSA Stuttgart, Weizsäcker Papers, *Der Beobachter*, 12 February 1907, 'Briefe, die kompromittieren'. See also Crothers, *German Elections*, pp. 113–19; Eley, *Reshaping the German Right*, pp. 254–60.
16 ZSA Potsdam, Hammann Papers, 13, Bülow to Hammann, 5 January 1907.
17 HHSA Wien, 164, Szögyényi's Report, 1 January 1907.
18 Ibid. See also Crothers, *German Elections*, p. 120.
19 PA Bonn, IA, Deutschland, 125, no. 3, Bd. XVIII, Bülow to Liebert [31 December 1906]; Crothers, *German Elections*, pp. 249–53.
20 HHSA Wien, 164, Szögyényi's Report, 8 January 1907.
21 Crothers, *German Elections*, pp. 159ff.
22 See especially Loth, *Katholiken im Kaiserreich*, pp. 132ff.; HSA München, 1079, Lerchenfeld's Report, 24 March 1907.
23 HHSA Wien, 165, Szögyényi to Aehrenthal, 23 January 1907.
24 ZSA Merseburg, Hausarchiv, Adjutants' Diaries, 11, entries for January 1907; HHSA Wien, 165, Szögyényi to Aehrenthal, 16 January 1907
25 Cf. HSA München, 76140, Bavarian Minister in Bern to Podewils, 31 December 1906.
26 HHSA Wien, 165, Szögyényi to Aehrenthal, 23 January 1907.

27 Crothers, *German Elections*, pp. 165–84.
28 Vierhaus, *Spitzemberg*, pp. 469f.; HHSA Wien, 164, Szögyényi's Report, 29 January 1907.
29 ZSA Potsdam, Hammann Papers, 13 Bülow to Hammann [January 1907] and Hammann's memorandum of 29 January 1907.
30 Ibid., Bülow to Hammann, 29 January 1907 and his marginalia on Hammann's memorandum of 29 January 1907.
31 HHSA Wien, 164, Szögyényi's Report, 29 January 1907.
32 ZSA Potsdam, Hammann Papers, 13, Bülow to Hammann [January 1907].
33 See appendix II. It lost four seats in Prussia. See PA Bonn, IA, Deutschland, 125, no. 3, Bd. XXI, Bethmann Hollweg to Wilhelm II, 6 February 1907.
34 HHSA Wien, 165, Szögyényi to Aehrenthal, 5 February 1907.
35 HHSA Wien, 164, Szögyényi's Report, 29 January 1907.
36 Vierhaus, *Spitzemberg*, 27 January 1907, pp. 469f.
37 BA Koblenz, Hertling Papers, 36, Stefan Ehses to Hertling, 8 February 1907.
38 See for example Rich and Fisher, *Holstein Papers*, IV, Holstein to Bülow, 8 February 1907, pp. 452f.
39 Ibid., diary entry of 3 March 1907, p. 456; HSA München, 1079, Lerchenfeld's Report, 9 March 1907.
40 Reichstag, 20 February 1907, pp. 5ff; HHSA Wien, 164, Szögyényi's Report, 20 February 1907. See also Loth, *Katholiken im Kaiserreich*, p. 136.
41 Reichstag, 25 February 1907, pp. 33ff. and 26 February 1907, pp. 63ff.; Rich and Fisher, *Holstein Papers*, IV, diary entry of 3 March 1907, p. 456; Crothers, *German Elections*, pp. 191f.
42 See also Bülow, *Reden*, III, pp. 9, 18.
43 GLA Karlsruhe, 34812, Berckheim's Report, 13 May 1907; HHSA Wien, 164, Széchényi's Report, 15 May 1907.
44 HSA München, 1079, Lerchenfeld's Report, 9 March 1907.
45 Ibid., 24 March 1907; HHSA Wien, 164, Széchényi's Report, 15 May 1907. See also Loth, *Katholiken im Kaiserreich*, pp. 132ff.
46 See HHSA Wien, 164, Szögyényi's Report, 12 March 1907.
47 HSA München, 1079, Lerchenfeld's Report, 9 March 1907.
48 Ibid., 24 March 1907.
49 HSA München, 2685, Lerchenfeld's Report, 13 March 1907.
50 HSA München, 1079, Lerchenfeld's Report, 9 March 1907.
51 HHSA Wien, 164, Szögyényi's Report, 12 March 1907.
52 HSA München, 1079, Lerchenfeld's Report, 9 March 1907.
53 GLA Karlsruhe, 34812, Berckheim's Report, 13 May 1907.
54 BA Koblenz, Reichskanzlei, 1622, Guenther's memorandum, 1 March 1907.
55 HHSA Wien, 164, Szögyényi's Report, 23 June 1907; ZSA Merseburg, Staatsministerium, 154, 25 June 1907.
56 HSA München, 1079, Lerchenfeld's Report, 1 July 1907; PA Bonn, IA, Preussen, no. 9, Bd. III, Loebell to Bülow, 22 June 1907.
57 ZSA Merseburg, Studt Papers, 13, notes of 14 May 1906 and 24 May 1906; ZSA Potsdam, Reichskanzlei, 2041, Bülow to Loebell, 8 July 1906. The Prussian School Bill crisis of 1892 is discussed in Röhl, *Germany Without Bismarck*, pp. 79–84, and J. Alden Nichols, *Germany After Bismarck. The Caprivi Era 1890–1894* (New York, 1968), pp. 97–101. The Zedlitz School Bill, which gave the churches a greater degree of control over the educational system and was intended to conciliate the Centre, had to be withdrawn in 1892 because it was not acceptable to the anti-clerical National Liberals,

whose support was indispensable in South Germany. As a result of the crisis, Caprivi gave up the Minister-Presidency of Prussia.

58 ZSA Merseburg, Studt Papers, 19, Studt to Althoff, 14 July 1906.

59 Röhl, *Germany Without Bismarck*, p. 267.

60 ZSA Merseburg, Studt Papers, 13, note of 14 May 1906 and 19, Studt to Althoff, 14 July 1906. See also Zedlitz, *Zwölf Jahre*, 7 June 1907, p. 162.

61 HSA München, 1079, Lerchenfeld's Report, 9 March 1907.

62 Ibid., 24 March 1907; ZSA Merseburg, Studt Papers, 18, Studt's note on his audience with Bülow, 6 March 1907.

63 ZSA Merseburg, Althoff Papers, 8, 1, Studt to Althoff, 31 March 1907; ZSA Potsdam, Reichskanzlei, 2040, Althoff to Loebell, 10 April 1907 and Loebell to Althoff, 13 April 1907.

64 ZSA Potsdam, Reichskanzlei, 2040, Bülow to Kopp, 20 May 1907.

65 Althoff's resignation was made inevitable by Holle's appointment, and although Bülow anticipated Wilhelm II's opposition, it was effected smoothly in September 1907. See ZSA Merseburg, Zivilkabinett, 18726, Bülow to Lucanus, 2 September 1907 and 667, Bülow to Lucanus, 8 August 1907. In a letter to Wilhelm II on 21 September 1907, Holle recommended the division of the Ministry of Culture into two.

66 ZSA Merseburg, Studt Papers, 20, Kopp to Studt, 21 May 1907; BA Koblenz, BP, 45, Kopp to Bülow, 14 April 1907; ZSA Merseburg, Zivilkabinett, 18726, Studt to Lucanus, 21 May 1907.

67 HSA Stuttgart, Varnbüler's Report, 23 June 1907.

68 ZSA Merseburg, Staatsministerium, 154, 25 June 1907.

69 HSA München, 1079, Lerchenfeld's Report, 28 June 1907; Rassow and Born, *Akten zur staatlichen Sozialpolitik*, p. 268.

70 HHSA Wien, 165, Szögyényi to Aehrenthal, 25 June 1907.

71 ZSA Merseburg, Studt Papers, Studt to Bülow, 30 April 1907.

72 HHSA Wien, 164, Szögyényi's Report, 29 January 1907.

73 HHSA Wien, 165, Szögyényi to Aehrenthal, 5 February 1907.

74 See the articles in BA Koblenz, Reichskanzlei, 1608, e.g. *Deutsche Tageszeitung* and *Berliner Tageblatt* of 8 March 1907, and *Der Deutsche* of 9 March 1907.

75 HSA München, 1079, Lerchenfeld's Report, 9 March 1906; Rassow and Born, *Akten zur staatlichen Sozialpolitik*, p. 264.

76 ZSA Potsdam, Hammann Papers, 13, Bülow to Hammann, 8 March 1907.

77 BA Koblenz, Reichskanzlei, 1608, Bülow to Posadowsky, 24(?) March 1907.

78 HSA Stuttgart, Varnbüler's Report, 23 June 1907.

79 Rassow and Born, *Akten zur staatlichen Sozialpolitik*, Lerchenfeld's Report, 1 July 1907, p. 269; Fuchs, *Grossherzog Friedrich*, Berckheim to Marschall, 25 June 1907, pp. 717f.

80 PA Bonn, IA, Preussen, no. 9, Bd. III, Loebell to Bülow, 22 June 1907.

81 HHSA Wien, 164, Szögyényi's Report, 29 June 1907.

82 HSA Stuttgart, Varnbüler's Report, 23 June 1907.

83 HHSA Wien, 164, Szögyényi's Report, 29 June 1907.

84 Fuchs, *Grossherzog Friedrich*, Berckheim to Marschall, 26 June 1907, p. 719.

85 HHSA Wien, 164, Szögyényi's Report, 29 June 1907.

86 HSA Stuttgart, Speth's Report, 1 July 1907.

87 See for example BA Koblenz, Loebell Papers, 7, Bülow to Loebell, 29 January 1912.

88 HSA Stuttgart, Varnbüler's Report, 23 June 1907.

89 Rassow and Born, *Akten zur staatlichen Sozialpolitik*, Lerchenfeld's Report, 28 June 1907, p. 265.

90 HSA Stuttgart, Varnbüler's Report, 23 June 1907.

91 Rassow and Born, *Akten zur staatlichen Sozialpolitik*, Lerchenfeld's Report, 28 June 1907, p. 267. For Posadowsky and the Centre in 1907, see Loth, *Katholiken im Kaiserreich*, p. 133. For Posadowsky's Reichstag speech, see Reichstag, 28 February 1907, pp. 139f. and Eschenburg, *Kaiserreich am Scheideweg*, pp. 73f.

92 HSA Stuttgart, Varnbüler's Report, 23 June 1907.

93 BA Koblenz, Reichskanzlei, 1608, Wilhelm II to Bethmann Hollweg, 24 June 1907.

94 HSA Stuttgart, Varnbüler's Report, 23 June 1907.

95 BA Koblenz, BP, 64, Bethmann Hollweg to Bülow, 11 December 1907. See also Bülow, *Denkwürdigkeiten*, II, pp. 270f.

96 Fuchs, *Grossherzog Friedrich*, Berckheim to Marschall, 26 June 1907, p. 719.

97 Rassow and Born, *Akten zur staatlichen Sozialpolitik*, Grunelius's Report, 24 June 1907, p. 265.

98 HHSA Wien, 165, Szögyényi to Aehrenthal, 25 June 1907.

99 Rassow and Born, *Akten zur staatlichen Sozialpolitik*, Lerchenfeld's Report, 1 July 1907, p. 270.

100 Ibid.; HHSA Wien, 164, Szögyényi's Report, 23 June 1907.

101 Fuchs, *Grossherzog Friedrich*, Berckheim to Marschall, 26 June 1907, p. 719.

102 Rassow and Born, *Akten zur staatlichen Sozialpolitik*, Lerchenfeld's Report, 28 June 1907, p. 266.

103 HSA Stuttgart, Varnbüler's Report, 23 June 1907.

104 HHSA Wien, 164, Szögyényi's Report, 29 June 1907.

105 HSA München, 1079, Grunelius's Report, 24 June 1907.

106 Fuchs, *Grossherzog Friedrich*, Berckheim to Marschall, 26 June 1907, p. 719.

107 ZSA Merseburg, Staatsministerium, 154, 25 June 1907.

108 HHSA Wien, 165, Szögyényi to Aehrenthal, 25 June 1907.

109 BA–MA Freiburg, Tirpitz Papers, 9, Capelle to Tirpitz, [25] June 1907 and Bülow to Tirpitz [June 1907].

110 ZSA Merseburg, Staatsministerium, 154, 25 June 1907.

111 PA Bonn, IA, Preussen, no. 9, Bd. III, Loebell to Bülow, 22 June 1907.

112 HSA Stuttgart, Varnbüler's Report, 23 June 1907.

113 HSA München, 1079, Grunelius's Report, 24 June 1907.

114 In August 1909 Rheinbaben submitted his resignation because he had again been denied the Vice-Presidency. See ZSA Merseburg, Zivilkabinett, 3698, Rheinbaben to Valentini, 23 August 1909.

115 Fuchs, *Grossherzog Friedrich*, Berckheim to Marschall, 26 June 1907, p. 720.

116 HSA Stuttgart, Varnbüler's Report, 23 June 1907.

117 HHSA Wien, 164, Szögyényi's Report, 23 June 1907.

118 Fuchs, *Grossherzog Friedrich*, Berckheim to Marschall, 26 June 1907, p. 720. Bülow's role in the Eulenburg scandal is discussed below.

119 Hartmann, 'Innenpolitik', 29f.

120 Fuchs, *Grossherzog Friedrich*, Berckheim to Marschall, 26 June 1907, p. 720.

121 Rassow and Born, *Akten zur staatlichen Sozialpolitik*, Lerchenfeld's Report, 28 June 1907, p. 268.

122 HHSA Wien, 164, Szögyényi's Report, 29 June 1907.

123 Ibid.

124 HSA Stuttgart, Varnbüler's Report, 19 May 1907.

125 HSA Stuttgart, Speth's Report, 1 July 1907.

126 HHSA Wien, 164, Szögyényi's Report, 29 June 1907.

127 HSA Stuttgart, Varnbüler's Report, 19 May 1907.

128 HHSA Wien, 164, Szögyényi's Report, 9 May 1907; Jäckh, *Kiderlen-Wächter*, I, Holstein to Kiderlen-Wächter, 9 May 1907, p. 228.

129 HSA Stuttgart, Varnbüler's Report, 19 May 1907; Jäckh, *Kiderlen-Wächter*, I, Holstein to Kiderlen-Wächter, 9 May 1907, p. 228.

130 Monts, *Erinnerungen*, Monts to Jagow, 11 April 1907, p. 20 and 13 May 1907, p. 21. Cf. the interpretation of the Bloc years suggested by Cole, 'Kaiser Versus Chancellor', who believes the Reichstag dissolution of 1906 was 'the beginning of Bülow's campaign to place the government of Germany on a new footing' (p. 67).

131 Rassow and Born, *Akten zur staatlichen Sozialpolitik*, Lerchenfeld's Report, 28 March 1903, p. 146.

132 HSA Stuttgart, Speth's Report, 1 July 1907. See also Eschenburg, *Kaiserreich am Scheideweg*, pp. 72ff., who claims Bülow told Friedberg that the personnel changes were to facilitate an understanding between Conservatives and liberals in Prussia.

133 PA Bonn, IA, Deutschland, 125, Generalia, Bd. IV, Bülow to the State Secretaries, 4 July 1907.

134 See Bachem, Zentrumspartei, VII, pp. 13, 44f.; FCO London, Holstein Papers, 32, Bülow to Holstein, 11 July 1907. See also Hartmann, 'Innenpolitik', 168ff.

135 BA–MA Freiburg, Tirpitz Papers, 9, Capelle to Tirpitz, 17 August 1907.

136 Ibid., Tirpitz to Bülow, 14 August 1907 (also in RM3/7).

137 BA Koblenz, Reichskanzlei, 1616, Nieberding to Loebell, 11 July 1907 and enclosed memorandum of 11 July 1907.

138 Ibid., Loebell to Nieberding, 11 July 1907.

139 BA Koblenz, BP, 178, Bülow to Loebell, 9 August 1907.

140 Nieberding resigned on 25 October 1909. See Huber, *Deutsche Verfassungsgeschichte*, p. 328.

141 HSA Stuttgart, Varnbüler's Report, 19 May 1907.

142 BA Koblenz, Reichskanzlei, 1605, *Berliner Tageblatt*, 17 April 1907, 'Der Rücktritt des Herrn v. Below'.

143 Vierhaus, *Spitzemberg*, 21 April 1907, p. 472.

144 BA Koblenz, Reichskanzlei, 1605, *Berliner Tageblatt*, 17 April 1907, 'Der Rücktritt des Herrn v. Below'; cf. *Deutsche Tageszeitung*, 18 April 1907, 'Der Rücktritt des Geh. Legsrat. v. Below'.

145 HSA München, 1079, Lerchenfeld's Report, 22 April 1907.

146 Ibid.

147 Ibid.; see also Hull, *Entourage*, pp. 52f., 122f.

148 Monts, *Erinnerungen*, Tschirschky to Monts, 18 April 1907, p. 449.

149 Ibid., Tschirschky to Monts, 23 May 1907, p. 450.

150 See Jäckh, *Kiderlen-Wächter*, I, Holstein to Kiderlen-Wächter, 9 May 1907, p. 228.

151 Monts, *Erinnerungen*, Tschirschky to Monts, 10 January 1907, pp. 447f.

152 Rich and Fisher, *Holstein Papers*, IV, diary entry, 17 April 1907, p. 459.

153 Monts, *Erinnerungen*, Monts to a close friend [1907], p. 579.

154 Ibid., Tschirschky to Monts, 18 April 1907, p. 449.

155 ZSA Merseburg, Hausarchiv, Adjutants' Diaries, 11 and 12, entries for January–April 1907.

156 HSA Stuttgart, Weizsäcker Papers, Varnbüler to Weizsäcker, 8 July 1907.

157 Rich and Fisher, *Holstein Papers*, IV, diary entry, 5 March 1907, pp. 456f.

158 Vierhaus, *Spitzemberg*, 12 April 1907, p. 472.

159 Monts, *Erinnerungen*, Tschirschky to Monts, 23 May 1907 (P.S. of 25 May), p. 451.

160 HSA Stuttgart, Varnbüler's Report, 19 May 1907.

161 Rich and Fisher, *Holstein Papers*, IV, Holstein to Bülow, 17 February 1907, p. 454.

162 See for example Monts, *Erinnerungen*, Monts to Jagow, 13 May 1907, p. 21.

163 ZSA Merseburg, Zivilkabinett, 661, Bülow to Lucanus, 8 August 1907.

164 ZSA Merseburg, Rep. 53J, Lit. B. no. 16a, IV, Bülow to Wilhelm II, 9 September 1907.
165 BA Koblenz, BP, 153, note 294 (1907).
166 SA Köln, Bachem Papers, 268b, Bachem to Porsch, 5 October 1907.
167 HHSA Wien, 165, Hohenlohe's Report, 4 November 1907. Bülow told Holstein that Hardinge had tried hard to persuade him to go too as it would please King Edward. See ZSA Potsdam, Holstein Papers, 4, Bülow to Holstein, 18 August 1907.
168 See HSA München, 1079, Lerchenfeld's Report, 4 October 1907.
169 PA Bonn, IA, Deutschland, 122, no. 2 secr., Bd. I, Tschirschky to Bülow, 2 September 1907.
170 HSA Stuttgart, Speth's Report, 17 August 1907; ZSA Potsdam, Holstein Papers, 4, Bülow to Holstein, 18 August 1907. It required two letters from the Kaiser and a hint at the funeral of the Grand Duke of Baden before Hohenlohe handed in his resignation.
171 PA Bonn, IA, Deutschland, 122, no. 2 secr., Bd. I, Flotow to Bülow, 30 September 1907.
172 GLA Karlsruhe, 34812, Berckheim's Report, 17 October 1907.
173 ZSA Merseburg, Rep. 53J, Lit. B, no. 16a, IV, Bülow to Wilhelm II, 9 September 1907.
174 PA Bonn, IA, Deutschland, 122, no. 2 secr., Bd. I, Tschirschky to Bülow, 2 September 1907.
175 ZSA Merseburg, Rep. 53J, Lit. B, no. 16a, IV, Bülow to Wilhelm II, 9 September 1906.
176 Vierhaus, *Spitzemberg*, 9 October 1907. p. 475.
177 HHSA Wien, 164, Hohenlohe's Report, 9 October 1907 and 165, Szögyényi's Report, 26 November 1907. Mühlberg was replaced by Stemrich.
178 ZSA Merseburg, Rep. 53J, Lit. B, no. 16a, IV, Bülow to Wilhelm II, 16 September 1907.
179 HHSA Wien, 164, Hohenlohe's Report, 9 October 1907.
180 Vierhaus, *Spitzemberg*, 9 October 1907, p. 475.
181 PA Bonn, IA, Deutschland, 122, no. 2 secr., Bd. I, Pourtalès to Bülow, 24 July 1907; HHSA Wien, 164, Hohenlohe's Report, 9 October 1907.
182 HSA München, 1079, Lerchenfeld's Report, 4 October 1907. Cf. Freiherr von Schön, *Erlebtes* (Stuttgart and Berlin, 1921), p. 52.
183 BA Koblenz, Reichskanzlei, 1604, *Deutsche Tageszeitung*, 10 October 1907, 'Der "neue Herr" im Auswärtigen Amte'.
184 Rich and Fisher, *Holstein Papers*, IV, Bülow to Holstein, 22 September 1907, p. 495.
185 Ibid., Holstein to Bülow, 26 September 1907, pp. 495f.
186 Ibid., Bülow to Holstein, 29 September 1907, p. 497.
187 ZSA Merseburg, Rep. 53J, Lit. B, no. 16a, IV, Bülow to Wilhelm II, 26 September 1907.
188 Ibid., Bülow to Wilhelm II, 9 September 1907.
189 BA Koblenz, BP, 178, Bülow to Loebell, 17 September 1907.
190 ZSA Merseburg, Rep. 53J, Lit. B, no. 16a, IV, Bülow to Wilhelm II, 22 September 1907.
191 For more light on the trials, see Rich, *Holstein*, II, pp. 757–97; Rogge, *Holstein und Harden*, pp. 1–73; Hull, *Entourage*, pp. 136ff.
192 HHSA Wien, 165, Szögyényi to Aehrenthal, 5 June 1907.
193 HSA Stuttgart, Varnbüler Papers, 746, Varnbüler to Weizsäcker, 30 May 1907.
194 Röhl, *Eulenburg*, III, Eulenburg to Bülow, 12 May 1907, p. 2148.
195 HSA Stuttgart, Varnbüler's Report, 19 May 1907.
196 BA Koblenz, Eulenburg Papers, 75, Eulenburg's note on Bülow to Eulenburg [17 May 1907].
197 HSA Stuttgart, Varnbüler's Report, 19 May 1907.
198 See Rich, *Holstein*, II, pp. 795–7; Hull, *Entourage*, pp. 135ff.
199 Rich and Fisher, *Holstein Papers*, IV, Harden to Holstein, 7 May 1907, p. 468.
200 Ibid., diary entry, 17 February 1907, pp. 454f.
201 Ibid., Holstein to Harden, 4 May 1907, p. 468.
202 Ibid., Harden to Holstein, 15 June 1907, p. 484.

203 HHSA Wien, 165, Szögyényi to Aehrenthal, 26 June 1907.
204 HSA Stuttgart, Varnbüler Papers, 750, S. von Uexkull to Varnbüler, 20 June 1907.
205 See for example HHSA Wien, 165, Hohenlohe's Report, 6 November 1907.
206 Monts, *Erinnerungen*, Tschirschky to Monts, 23 May 1907, p. 451.
207 HHSA Wien, 165, Szögyényi to Aehrenthal, 26 June 1907.
208 Reichstag, 28 November 1907, pp. 1880f.
209 HHSA Wien, 165, Szögyényi to Aehrenthal, 11 June 1907.
210 See for example Rich and Fisher, *Holstein Papers*, IV, Harden to Holstein, 3 June 1907, p. 483.
211 ZSA Merseburg, Studt Papers, 19, Althoff's memorandum, 17 June 1907.
212 See Rich, *Holstein*, II, pp. 781f.
213 HSA Stuttgart, Varnbüler Papers, 746, Varnbüler's Report, 16 June 1907.
214 HHSA Wien, 165, Szögyényi to Aehrenthal, 11 June 1907.
215 See ZSA Merseburg, Studt Papers, 19, Althoff's memorandum, 17 June 1907.
216 Monts, *Erinnerungen*, Tschirschky to Monts, 18 April 1907, p. 449.
217 HSA Stuttgart, Varnbüler Papers, 746, Varnbüler to Weizsäcker, 30 May 1907; BA Koblenz, BP, 152, Losungen, 28 May 1907, 31 May 1907, 3 June 1907.
218 PA Bonn, IA, Deutschland, 122, no. 3, Bd. XIV, Lindig's memorandum, 26 November 1905; ibid., Bd. VIII, *Welt am Montag*, 29 April 1901.
219 ZSA Potsdam, Reichskanzlei, 798/1, memoranda of 1 October 1907 and 5 October 1907.
220 ZSA Potsdam, Hammann Papers, 13, Bülow to Loebell, 27 September 1907. Cf. Harden, who suspected Liebenberg inspiration. See Rich and Fisher, *Holstein Papers*, IV, Harden to Holstein, 11 September 1907, p. 491.
221 See stenographic report of the trial of 6 November 1907 in PA Bonn, IA, Deutschland, 122, no. 3, Bd. XVII; ZSA Merseburg, Zivilkabinett, 3579, *Vossische Zeitung*, 6 November 1907, 'Prozess Bülow-Brand'.
222 GLA Karlsruhe, 34812, *Berliner Tageblatt*, 7 November 1907, 'Das Urteil im Brand-Prozess'.
223 See Hull, *Entourage*, pp. 61f.; Rich, *Holstein Papers*, IV, Harden to Holstein, 9 July 1908, p. 542.
224 ZSA Potsdam, Hammann Papers, 13, Bülow to Loebell, 27 September 1907.
225 BA Koblenz, Loebell Papers, 6, Bülow to Loebell, 16 August 1908.
226 BA Koblenz, BP, 61, Scheefer to Bülow, undated.
227 ZSA Merseburg, Zivilkabinett, 3579, Bülow to Wilhelm II, 27 November 1908 and Loebell to Valentini, 27 November 1908; Wilhelm II to Bülow, 12 December 1908. See also BA Koblenz, Reichskanzlei, 1605, Schwartzkoppen to Loebell, 15 February 1909.
228 ZSA Potsdam, Reichskanzlei, 798/2, Loebell to Bülow, 19 October 1907 and Bülow to Loebell, 24 October 1907.
229 HHSA Wien, 165, Hohenlohe to Aehrenthal, 30 October 1907.
230 Lecomte was French Secretary of Embassy in Berlin, 1895–1907.
231 ZSA Potsdam, Reichskanzlei, 798/2, Loebell to Bülow, 23 October 1907.
232 BA Koblenz, BP, 178, Loebell to Bülow, 24 October 1907.
233 ZSA Potsdam, Reichskanzlei, 798/2, Loebell to Bülow, 26 October 1907.
234 Rich and Fisher, *Holstein Papers*, IV, Bülow to Wilhelm II, 26 November 1907, p. 501.
235 HHSA Wien, 165, Hohenlohe to Aehrenthal, 30 October 1907.
236 See Rich, *Holstein*, II, pp. 784f.
237 See Hull, *Entourage*, pp. 143ff.
238 HHSA Wien, 165, Hohenlohe's Report, 5 November 1907.
239 ZSA Potsdam, Reichskanzlei, 798/2, Loebell to Podbielski, 7 December 1907; Hammann Papers, 12, Bülow to Hammann, 25 December [1907], Bl. 67; BA Koblenz, BP, 32, Dernburg to Loebell, 14 December 1907.

240 ZSA Potsdam, Hammann Papers, 12, Bülow to Hammann, 25 December [1907], Bl. 66.
241 HHSA Wien, 165, Szögyényi's Report, 8 January 1908.
242 ZSA Potsdam, Hammann Papers, 12, Bülow to Hammann, 25 December [1907], Bl. 66.
243 HSA München, 2685, Lerchenfeld's Report, 8 November 1907.
244 HHSA Wien, 165, Hohenlohe to Aehrenthal, 30 October 1907.
245 Ibid., Hohenlohe's Report, 6 November 1907.
246 Ibid., 5 November 1907.
247 SA Köln, Bachem Papers, 268b, note of 29 October 1907. See also Loth, *Katholiken im Kaiserreich*, pp. 139ff.
248 GLA Karlsruhe, 34812, Berckheim's Report, 2 December 1907.
249 Zedlitz, *Zwölf Jahre*, 18 December 1907, p. 181.
250 HHSA Wien, 165, Hohenlohe's Report, 6 November 1907.
251 HSA München, 1079, Lerchenfeld's Report, 3 October 1907.
252 BA Koblenz, BP, 178, Bülow to Loebell, 9 August 1907.
253 HHSA Wien, 164, Hohenlohe's Report, 23 October 1907.
254 BA Koblenz, BP, 178, Bülow to Loebell, 9 August 1907.
255 See especially Eschenburg, *Kaiserreich am Scheideweg*, ch. 3; BA Koblenz, Loebell Papers, 27, memoirs, p. 63. Cf. R. von Sydow, 'Fürst Bülow und die Reichsfinanzreform 1908–9', in Thimme, *Front Wider Bülow*, p. 128, for a more cynical view. Loebell told Valentini in 1910 that the view that Bülow 'let himself be influenced by such a dull and insignificant person as Bassermann is absurd'. BA Koblenz, Schwertfeger Papers, 207, Loebell to Valentini, 15 January 1910.
256 HHSA Wien, 164, Hohenlohe's Report, 18 September 1907.
257 Ibid. See also Eschenburg, *Kaiserreich am Scheideweg*, pp. 77–80.
258 BA Koblenz, BP, 178, Bülow to Loebell, 11 September 1907; Rich and Fisher, *Holstein Papers*, IV, Bülow to Holstein, 29 September 1907, p. 497.
259 ZSA Potsdam, Holstein Papers, 4, Bülow to Holstein, 27 August 1907.
260 HHSA Wien, 164, Hohenlohe's Report, 18 September 1907.
261 See appendix II.
262 BA Koblenz, BP, 178, Bülow to Loebell, 17 September 1907 and 18 September 1907.
263 Ibid. Cf. strategy adopted at a conference of Centre parliamentarians at München-Gladbach on 22 and 23 July 1907. See BA Koblenz, Herold Papers, 2.
264 BA Koblenz, BP, 178, Bülow to Loebell, 17 September 1907.
265 Ibid., Wahnschaffe to Bülow, 14 October 1907 and 177, 'Notiz für die Hamburger Presse', 17 October 1907.
266 Ibid., 178, Bülow to Loebell, 11 September 1907.
267 ZSA Merseburg, Staatsministerium, 155, 5 October 1907.
268 See Born, *Staat und Sozialpolitik*, pp. 216–24; Eschenburg, *Kaiserreich am Scheideweg*, p. 99; Bachem, *Zentrumspartei*, VII, pp. 14–16; Loth, *Katholiken im Kaiserreich*, p. 140. The Law introduced many improvements and, for example, allowed women to become members of political associations and to participate in political meetings for the first time. However, it also excluded all people under eighteen years old and it denied freedom of coalition to agricultural workers. The stipulation that German had to be spoken at all public meetings, a measure directed primarily against the Poles, was particularly controversial.
269 HHSA Wien, 164, Hohenlohe's Report, 23 October 1907.
270 HHSA Wien, 165, Szögyényi's Report, 26 November 1907.
271 See the reports of the Prussian Ministers in the federal states in PA Bonn, IA, Deutschland, 103, Bd. XI.
272 Hartmann, 'Innenpolitik', 168.

273 HSA Stuttgart, Varnbüler's Report, 25 November 1907.
274 HSA Stuttgart, Speth's Report, 1 July 1907. For the opposition of Rheinbaben and other Ministers to the tax in 1905, see PA Bonn, IA, Deutschland, 103, Bde. x and xi, memoranda of April and May 1905.
275 Hartmann, 'Innenpolitik', 33.
276 See especially Witt, *Finanzpolitik*, pp. 172–91.
277 HHSA Wien, 164, Hohenlohe's Report, 23 October 1907.
278 HHSA Wien, 165, Szögyényi's Report, 26 November 1907.
279 GLA Karlsruhe, 34812, Berckheim's Report, 2 December 1907; Reichstag, 28 November 1907, pp. 1880f.; 29 November 1907, pp. 1921ff.; and 30 November 1907, pp. 1935ff. See also Bülow, *Reden*, III, pp. 65–94.
280 Reichstag, 30 November 1907, p. 1937.
281 Reichstag, 29 November 1907, pp. 1895ff.; HSA München, 1079, Lerchenfeld's Report, 4 December 1907.
282 Reichstag, 3 December 1907, pp. 2008ff.
283 Reichstag, 4 December 1907, pp. 2024ff. See also HSA–KA München, D4, II, Report of Bavarian military plenipotentiary, 4 December 1907.
284 ZSA Merseburg, Zivilkabinett, 667, Bülow to Wilhelm II, 5 December 1907; Reichstag, 5 December 1907, pp. 2033f.; HHSA Wien, 165, Szögyényi's Report, 5 December 1907.
285 HSA München, 1079, Lerchenfeld's Report, 12 December 1907.
286 See Eschenburg, *Kaiserreich am Scheideweg*, pp. 96f.
287 HHSA Wien, 165, Szögyényi's Report, 10 December 1907.
288 HSA München, 1079, Lerchenfeld's Report, 5 December 1907.
289 ZSA Merseburg, Staatsministerium, 155, 6 December 1907.
290 Ibid., 10 December 1907. The Expropriation Law of 1908 is discussed in William W. Hagen, *Germans, Poles and Jews. The Nationality Conflict in the Prussian East, 1772–1914* (Chicago, 1980), pp. 186–91. The Conservatives opposed expropriation because they were committed to the principle of the legal inviolability of land ownership, but they ultimately accepted it in the form of an anti-Polish exceptional law.
291 HSA München, 1079, Lerchenfeld's Report, 4 December 1907.
292 HHSA Wien, 165, Szögyényi's Report, 5 December 1907.
293 HSA München, 1079, Lerchenfeld's Report, 5 December 1907.
294 Ibid., 12 December 1907.
295 HSA–KA München, D4, II, Report of Bavarian military plenipotentiary, 5 December 1907.
296 GLA Karlsruhe, 34812, Berckheim's Report, 4 December 1907.
297 See next chapter. Sydow, Tirpitz and Dernburg all relied on Centre cooperation in preparing legislation.
298 HSA München, 1079, Lerchenfeld's Report, 5 December 1907; HSA–KA München, D4, II, Report of Bavarian military plenipotentiary, 4 December 1907.
299 HHSA Wien, 165, Szögyényi's Report, 10 December 1907.
300 Ibid. See also the Report of the Bremen ambassador, Klügmann, of 21 December 1908 in Hartmann, 'Innenpolitik', 276.
301 See for example BA Koblenz, BP, 153, notes 5, 10, 16 and especially 22.
302 ZSA Merseburg, Zivilkabinett, 667, Bülow to Wilhelm II, 4 December 1907.
303 HHSA Wien, 165, Szögyényi's Report, 10 December 1907.
304 See PA Bonn, Weitz Papers, 5, Kiderlen-Wächter to Weitz, 8 January 1908.

6 The collapse of the system, 1908–1909

1 HHSA Wien, 165, Szögyényi's Reports, 7 January 1908 and 22 January 1908; Vierhaus, *Spitzemberg*, 14 January 1908, p. 480; HSA–KA München, D4, II, Report of Bavarian

military plenipotentiary, 15 February 1908.

2 HSA Stuttgart, Varnbüler's Report, 14 December 1907.

3 Rich and Fisher, *Holstein Papers*, IV, Holstein to Bülow, 6 January 1908, p. 613.

4 PA Bonn, Brockdorff–Rantzau Papers, 2/3, Wedel to Rantzau, 16 February 1908.

5 See for example Berckheim's assertion, 'We are pursuing purely personal politics and living from hand to mouth.' See GLA Karlsruhe, 34813, Berckheim's Report, 23 January 1908.

6 HHSA Wien, 165, Szögyényi's Report, 7 January 1908.

7 ZSA Merseburg, Hausarchiv, Adjutants' Diaries, 12, entries for 1908. On 10 February 1908 Schön wrote to Wilhelm that he had to be in the Reichstag at 10.0 a.m. on the following day and that if the Kaiser intended to come as usual to talk to him in the morning, he would be grateful if he would choose a time which would still enable him to be at the sitting. See PA Bonn, IA, Deutschland, 122, no. 2i, Bd. I.

8 See for example Zedlitz, *Zwölf Jahre*, 18 January 1908, pp. 185ff.

9 Ibid.; HSA München, 1080, Lerchenfeld's Report, 28 February 1908; Bülow, *Reden*, III, pp. 94–115.

10 HSA München, 2686, Lerchenfeld's Report, 11 March 1908; HHSA Wien, 166, Szögyényi's Report, 3 March 1908. The letter of 16 February 1908 is published in *Grosse Politik*, XXIV, pp. 32–5.

11 On the advice of Tower, the resigning American ambassador to Berlin, the Kaiser informed Washington that the arranged successor, Hill, was unsuitable. HSA München, 1080, Lerchenfeld's Reports, 27 March 1908 and 30 March 1908; HSA Stuttgart, Varnbüler's Report, 1 April 1908; GLA Karlsruhe, 34813, Berckheim's Report, 30 March 1908. See also Schön, *Erlebtes*, pp. 91–3.

12 HSA München, 1080, Lerchenfeld's Report, 16 June 1908; Bülow, *Denkwürdigkeiten*, II, p. 317.

13 BA Koblenz, BP, 33, Bülow to Wilhelm II, 17 June 1908.

14 HSA München, 1080, Lerchenfeld to Podewils, 19 June 1908.

15 Ibid.; Zedlitz, *Zwölf Jahre*, pp. 193ff.

16 HSA Stuttgart, Weizsäcker Papers, Varnbüler to Weizsäcker, 30 January 1908. For the crisis, see especially Geoff Eley, 'The German Navy League in German Politics 1898–1914', D.Phil. thesis, University of Sussex, 1974, 286–318 and *Reshaping the German Right*, pp. 275ff. The crisis resulted from a conflict within the Navy League between the moderates and the radical nationalists. The radicals were led by Major-General August Keim, to whom Bülow was indebted after the 1907 election campaign and who had come to have a symbolic importance for the Bloc. In December 1907 the Presidium of the League elected Keim as Executive Chairman, but the League's Bavarian patron, Prince Rupprecht, resigned. An emergency General Assembly was called which met in January 1908 and expressed its confidence in Keim and the leadership. Keim, however, left the Navy League later in the year and joined the Pan-German League.

17 See Rich, *Holstein*, II, pp. 787f.

18 HHSA Wien, 165, Szögyényi's Report, 8 January 1908.

19 HSA Stuttgart, Weizsäcker Papers, Varnbüler to Weizsäcker, 11 March 1908.

20 BA–MA Freiburg, Müller Papers, 3, diary entry, 20 July 1908.

21 HHSA Wien, 165, Szögyényi's Report, 7 January 1908; Eschenburg, *Kaiserreich am Scheideweg*, pp. 180ff.

22 BA Koblenz, Reichskanzlei, 1622, Bülow to Wilhelm II, 7 February 1908. See also Witt, *Finanzpolitik*, pp. 172–91.

23 HSA Stuttgart, Varnbüler's Report, 4 February 1908; ZSA Potsdam, Hammann Papers, 14, Bülow to Hammann, 4 February 1908.

24 BA Koblenz, Reichskanzlei, 1622, Wilhelm's marginalia on Bülow's letter of 7 February 1908; Witt, *Finanzpolitik*, p. 200. Miquel had also been *Oberbürgermeister* of Frankfurt (1879–90).

25 BA Koblenz, Reichskanzlei, 1622, Bülow to Adickes (draft), February 1908.

26 See Witt, *Finanzpolitik*, p. 200.

27 See Bachem, *Zentrumspartei*, VII, pp. 46–9.

28 See Rich and Fisher, *Holstein Papers*, IV, Holstein's memorandum, 29 April 1908, p. 527.

29 FCO London, Holstein Papers, 33, Bülow to Holstein, 9 August 1908. The appointment in question was Tattenbach's transfer to Madrid.

30 BA Koblenz, Schwertfeger Papers, 206, Loebell to Valentini, 21 July 1908.

31 Zedlitz, *Zwölf Jahre*, 18 January 1908, pp. 185ff.; Bülow, *Denkwürdigkeiten*, II, especially ch. 21.

32 See Rich, *Holstein*, II, pp. 813–16; Bülow, *Denkwürdigkeiten*, II, pp. 319–21.

33 Ibid.; FCO London, Holstein Papers, 33, Bülow to Holstein [21 May 1908].

34 Bülow, *Denkwürdigkeiten*, II, p. 321.

35 BA–MA Freiburg, Müller Papers, 3, diary entries of 20 July 1908 and 29 July 1908. See also Zedlitz, *Zwölf Jahre*, 18 March 1909, pp. 225f.

36 BA–MA Freiburg, Müller Papers, 3, diary entry of 30 July 1908.

37 BA Koblenz, BP, 182, Bülow to Foreign Office, 22 August 1908; V. R. Berghahn, *Germany and the Approach of War in 1914* (London, 1973), p. 68.

38 BA Koblenz, BP, 182, Flotow to Foreign Office, 21 August 1908. See also A. von Tirpitz, *Politische Dokumente. I. Der Aufbau der deutschen Weltmacht* (Berlin and Stuttgart, 1924), pp. 72ff.

39 Rogge, *Holstein und Harden*, Zimmermann to Bülow, 11 July 1908, pp. 309f. See also Rich and Fisher, *Holstein Papers*, IV, Harden to Holstein, 9 July 1908, pp. 541f.

40 ZSA Potsdam, Hammann Papers, 14, Bülow to Hammann, 13 July 1908.

41 HHSA Wien, 166, Szögyényi's Report, 3 March 1908.

42 BA Koblenz, BP, 152, Losungen, 8 April 1908. See Eschenburg, *Kaiserreich am Scheideweg*, pp. 100–5; Born, *Staat und Sozialpolitik*, pp. 216ff.

43 ZSA Merseburg, Zivilkabinett, 213, Wilhelm II to Bülow, 14 May 1908 (published in *Reichsanzeiger*).

44 HHSA Wien, 166, Szögyényi's Report, 19 May 1908.

45 HSA München, 1080, Lerchenfeld's Report, 28 February 1908.

46 GLA Karlsruhe, 34813, Berckheim's Report, 23 January 1908.

47 Bülow, *Reden*, III, 30 November 1907, pp. 88ff.

48 BA Koblenz, Loebell Papers, 6, Bülow to Loebell, 27 April 1908.

49 BA Koblenz, BP, 178, Loebell to Bülow, 23 April 1908; cf. Naumann Papers (KE, 325), Naumann to Seyffarth, 13 February 1908. The group, under the leadership of Theodor Barth, was unhappy with the Law of Association and the government's position on Prussian suffrage reform.

50 ZSA Potsdam, Hammann Papers, 14, Bülow to Hammann, 25 April 1908.

51 HHSA Wien, 166, Szögyényi's Report, 9 June 1908; see also Eschenburg, *Kaiserreich am Scheideweg*, pp. 111f.

52 Cf. HSA München, 1080, Lerchenfeld's Report, 28 February 1908.

53 ZSA Potsdam, Hammann Papers, 14, Bülow to Hammann, 20 February 1908 and 25 April 1908.

54 HSA München, 1080, Lerchenfeld's Report, 28 February 1908; see also BA Koblenz, Herold Papers, 2, conference protocol of 22–3 July 1908 (München-Gladbach).

55 ZSA Potsdam, Hammann Papers, 14, Bülow to Hammann, 19 February 1908.

56 Ibid., Bülow to Hammann, 11 March 1908.

57 Ibid., Bülow to Hammann, 25 April 1908.
58 HSA München, 1080, Lerchenfeld's Report, 28 February 1908.
59 Sydow, 'Fürst Bülow', p. 110; Witt, *Finanzpolitik*, p. 215.
60 Eschenburg, *Kaiserreich am Scheideweg*, p. 104.
61 HSA München, 1080, Lerchenfeld's Report, 21 May 1908.
62 See for example Sydow, 'Fürst Bülow', p. 112.
63 BA Koblenz, BP, 180, press release of 30 April 1908; HHSA Wien, 167, Szögyényi to Aehrenthal, 22 April 1908.
64 BA Koblenz, Loebell Papers, 6, Bülow to Loebell, 27 April 1908. Bülow also wanted to take with him to Norderney his draft speech for the Prussian Landtag in the autumn.
65 FCO London, Holstein Papers, 34, Bülow to Holstein, 19 June 1908.
66 See for example ZSA Merseburg, Staatsministerium, 156, 26 June 1908, at which meeting Bülow made it clear that the Kaiser expected united government representation of the Bill.
67 Ibid., 12 June 1908.
68 Ibid. See especially Witt, *Finanzpolitik*, pp. 217–26.
69 ZSA Potsdam, Hammann Papers, 14, Bülow to Hammann, 31 July 1908.
70 Ibid., Bülow to Hammann, 14 June 1908.
71 PA Bonn, IA, Deutschland, 103, Bd. XII, Bülow to German embassies, 18 June 1908.
72 ZSA Potsdam, Hammann Papers, 14, Bülow to Hammann, 14 June 1908; Witt, *Finanzpolitik*, p. 215.
73 ZSA Merseburg, Staatsministerium, 156, 14 June 1908; Witt, *Finanzpolitik*, p. 215.
74 ZSA Potsdam, Hammann Papers, 14, Bülow to Hammann, 3 August 1908; Witt, *Finanzpolitik*, p. 226.
75 ZSA Potsdam, Hammann Papers, 14, Bülow to Hammann, 14 August 1908; Witt, *Finanzpolitik*, p. 226.
76 HSA Stuttgart, Haussmann Papers, 1/2, 116, Naumann to Haussmann, 22 September 1908.
77 ZSA Merseburg, Staatsministerium, 157, 21 September 1908.
78 Sydow, 'Fürst Bülow', p. 116. The Centre was planning to bring about the rejection of the spirits monopoly by combining with the left and the rejection of the inheritance tax by combining with the right.
79 Rich and Fisher, *Holstein Papers*, IV, Bülow to Holstein, 11 September 1908, p. 565.
80 ZSA Potsdam, Hammann Papers, 14, Bülow to Hammann, 31 July 1908.
81 Ibid., Bülow to Hammann, 21 August 1908.
82 Ibid., Bülow to Hammann, 18 September 1908.
83 HSA Stuttgart, Weizsäcker Papers, note of 18 September 1908; see also Witt, *Finanzpolitik*, p. 247.
84 Rich and Fisher, *Holstein Papers*, IV, Bülow to Holstein, 25 September 1908, p. 573. See especially Rich, *Holstein*, II, pp. 789ff.; Hull, *Entourage*, pp. 138f.
85 ZSA Potsdam, Reichskanzlei, 798/2, Bülow to Loebell, 29 September 1908.
86 Rich and Fisher, *Holstein Papers*, IV, Bülow to Holstein, 7 October 1908, p. 576.
87 BA Koblenz, BP, 32, Wahnschaffe to Bülow, 7 October 1908 and Bülow to Loebell, 8 October 1908.
88 Ibid., 177, Bülow to Bethmann Hollweg, 11 August 1908.
89 ZSA Potsdam, Reichskanzlei, 798/2, Bülow to Loebell, 8 October 1908.
90 BA Koblenz, BP, 184, Stemrich to Bülow, 5 October 1908 and Bülow to Foreign Office, 6 October 1908. See Rich, *Holstein*, II, pp. 816–18.
91 BA Koblenz, BP, 184, Bülow to Jenisch, 6 October 1908.
92 HSA München, 2686, Lerchenfeld's Report, 6 October 1908.

93 BA Koblenz, BP, 184, Jenisch to Bülow, 8 October 1908.
94 HSA München, 2686, Lerchenfeld's Report, 6 October 1908.
95 Jäckh, *Kiderlen-Wächter*, II, Kiderlen-Wächter to Hedwig Kypke, 10 November 1908, pp. 12f.; Rich, *Holstein*, II, p. 827.
96 PA Bonn, IA, Deutschland, 122, no. 2, Bd. III, Bülow to Wilhelm II, 1 November 1908.
97 BA Koblenz, BP, 184, Bülow to Foreign Office, 10 October 1908.
98 ZSA Potsdam, Reichskanzlei, 798/2, Bülow to Loebell, 10 October 1908.
99 See especially Hiller, *Fürst Bülows Denkwürdigkeiten*, pp. 119ff.; Rich, *Holstein*, II, pp. 818ff.; Rogge, *Holstein und Harden*, pp. 359ff.
100 HSA München, 2686, Lerchenfeld's Report, 3 November 1909.
101 Bülow, *Denkwürdigkeiten*, II, *Daily Telegraph* of 28 October 1908 (p. 11), p. 353.
102 Vierhaus, *Spitzemberg*, pp. 488f.
103 Hiller, *Fürst Bülows Denkwürdigkeiten*, especially pp. 131, 142ff.
104 BA Koblenz, BP, 33, Stemrich to Bülow, 7 October 1908; Bülow to Jenisch, 11 October 1908.
105 Rich and Fisher, *Holstein Papers*, IV, Bülow to Holstein, 20 October 1908, p. 585.
106 FCO London, Holstein Papers, 34, Bülow to Holstein, 7 November 1908.
107 Jäckh, *Kiderlen-Wächter*, II, Kiderlen-Wächter to Hedwig Kypke, 24 November 1908, p. 16.
108 Rogge, *Holstein und Harden*, Holstein to Bülow, 29 October 1908, pp. 361–3; Rich, *Holstein*, II, p. 819.
109 *Grosse Politik*, XXIV, pp. 168f., 179ff.; Rich, *Holstein*, II, p. 820.
110 BA Koblenz, BP, 33, Bülow to Jenisch, 11 October 1908.
111 HSA Stuttgart, Varnbüler's Report, 2 November 1908.
112 HHSA Wien, 166, Flotow's Report, 2 November 1908.
113 HHSA Wien, 167, Flotow to Aehrenthal, 10 November 1908.
114 Ibid.; Vierhaus, *Spitzemberg*, 1 November 1908, pp. 489f.
115 HSA Stuttgart, Varnbüler's Report, 2 November 1908.
116 Rich, *Holstein*, II, p. 820.
117 HHSA Wien, 167, Szögyényi to Aehrenthal, 10 November 1908.
118 BA Koblenz, BP, 33, note on Stemrich's resignation request, undated; FCO London, Holstein Papers, 34, Holstein to Bülow, 24 November 1908 and 26 November 1908; Rich and Fisher, *Holstein Papers*, IV, Bülow to Holstein, 4 December 1908, p. 600.
119 Hiller, *Fürst Bülows Denkwürdigkeiten*, pp. 131, 142f. See also BA Koblenz, BP, 33, Bülow to Müller, 22 December 1908.
120 HSA München, 1080, Lerchenfeld's Report, 6 December 1908. See also the correspondence pertaining to Klehmet's transfer in BA Koblenz, Reichskanzlei, 1605.
121 ZSA Merseburg, Valentini Papers, 23, Klehmet to Valentini, 17 February 1909; BA Koblenz, Schwertfeger Papers, 207, Klehmet to Valentini, 24 January 1908 (copy).
122 HSA Stuttgart, Varnbüler's Report, 2 November 1908.
123 HHSA Wien, 166, Flotow's Report, 2 November 1908.
124 ZSA Merseburg, Hausarchiv, Adjutants' Diaries, 12, 3–17 November 1908; Zedlitz, *Zwölf Jahre*, Zedlitz to his father, 30 November 1908, pp. 196f.
125 BA–MA Freiburg, Müller Papers, 3, Hülsen to Müller, 8 November 1908; BA Koblenz, Recke Papers (KE, 455), Lange to Recke, 20 November 1908.
126 BA Koblenz, BP, 34, 'Denkschrift Bülows über die Novemberereignisse', 1909–10. Einem told the Bavarian military plenipotentiary that Bülow feared the 'unavoidable daily personal discussions' with the Kaiser would complicate the situation. See report in HSA–KA München, D4, II, 13 December 1908.
127 HHSA Wien, 167, Flotow to Aehrenthal, 10 November 1908.
128 HSA Stuttgart, Varnbüler's Report, 2 November 1908. For the attitude of the Centre

during the affair, see also Loth, *Katholiken im Kaiserreich*, pp. 143–53.

129 HHSA Wien, 166, Flotow's Report, 5 November 1908 and 167, Flotow to Aehrenthal, 10 November 1908. Some importance can also be attached to the Conservative decision also to recommend imperial restraint on 5 November 1908. See Witt, *Finanzpolitik*, pp. 239f.

130 HHSA Wien, 167, Flotow to Aehrenthal, 10 November 1908; HSA Stuttgart, Varnbüler's Report, 3 November 1908; HSA München, 2686, Lerchenfeld's Report, 3 November 1908.

131 ZSA Potsdam, Hammann Papers, 14, Bülow to Hammann, 3 November 1908. See also Ralph R. Menning and Carol Bresnahan Menning, '"Baseless Allegations": Wilhelm II and the Hale Interview of 1908', in *Central European History*, 16 (1983), 383.

132 Reichstag, 10 November 1908, pp. 5395ff.

133 Eschenburg, *Kaiserreich am Scheideweg*, pp. 139, 289ff.

134 HHSA Wien, 166, Flotow's Report, 12 November 1908. See also BA Koblenz, Loebell Papers, 27, memoirs, pp. 105ff.; Bülow, *Denkwürdigkeiten*, II, p. 372; Reichstag, 11 November 1908, pp. 5432f.

135 ZSA Merseburg, Staatsministerium, 157, 11 November 1908.

136 ZSA Potsdam, Hammann Papers, 14, Bülow to Hammann, 11 November 1908 (Bl. 58).

137 ZSA Merseburg, Staatsministerium, 157, 11 November 1908. According to the Bavarian military plenipotentiary (HSA–KA München, D4, II, 13 December 1908), Einem implored Bethmann to secure the unanimous support of the State Ministry for the Chancellor and hence ensure that Bülow's dismissal would mean the resignation of the entire Ministry.

138 BA Koblenz, BP, 34, 'Denkschrift', 1909–10.

139 ZSA Potsdam, Hammann Papers, 14, Bülow to Hammann, 11 November 1908 (Bl. 57).

140 HSA München, 2686, Lerchenfeld's Report, 15 November 1908. For complaints about the failure to convene the Diplomatic Committee, see HSA München, 1079, Lerchenfeld to Podewils, 5 November 1907; HSA Stuttgart, Varnbüler's Report, 14 December 1907.

141 HHSA Wien, 166, Flotow's Report, 12 November 1908; HSA Stuttgart, Varnbüler's Report, 16 November 1908.

142 See for example ZSA Potsdam, Hammann Papers, 14, Bülow to Hammann, 11 November 1908 (Bl. 57).

143 ZSA Merseburg, Staatsministerium, 157, 17 November 1908; Sydow, 'Fürst Bülow', p. 121.

144 See especially Röhl, *Germany Without Bismarck*, pp. 144ff. Bülow later claimed that he wanted to teach Wilhelm II a lesson during the crisis and make him 'more reasonable', but he believed he could do this on his own. See BA Koblenz, BP, 33, 'Ad November-Krise 1908'.

145 See Rogge, *Holstein und Harden*, Holstein to Bülow, 6 November 1908, p. 377.

146 BA Koblenz, BP, 33, Jenisch to Bülow, 4 November 1908; BA–MA Freiburg, Müller Papers, 3, Hülsen to Müller, 8 November 1908.

147 BA Koblenz, BP, 33, Bülow to Jenisch, 12 November 1908.

148 Ibid., Jenisch to Bülow, 13 November 1908.

149 Ibid.

150 Ibid., Jenisch to Bülow, 14 November 1908.

151 ZSA Merseburg, Zivilkabinett, 667, Valentini's memorandum on his conversation with the Kaiser on 13 November 1908 (signed on 20 November 1908).

152 HSA Stuttgart, Varnbüler's Report, 16 November 1908. Hülsen had a heart attack after dancing for the Kaiser wearing a tutu.

153 Rich and Fisher, *Holstein Papers*, IV, Bülow to Holstein, 17 November 1908, p. 596.

154 Bülow, *Denkwürdigkeiten*, II, pp. 377–81.
155 HSA München, 1080, Lerchenfeld's Report, 17 November 1908.
156 Rich and Fisher, *Holstein Papers*, IV, Bülow to Holstein, 17 November 1908, p. 596.
157 BA Koblenz, BP, 33, Jenisch to Bülow, 14 November 1908; cf. Holstein's advice in Rich, *Holstein*, II, pp. 824f.
158 Rich, *Holstein*, II, p. 825; Vierhaus, *Spitzemberg*, 17 November 1908, p. 493.
159 HHSA Wien, 166, Szögyényi's Report, 17 November 1908; HSA München, 1080, Lerchenfeld's Report, 18 November 1908.
160 HSA München, 1080, Lerchenfeld's Report, 19 November 1908; BA Koblenz, BP, 60, Ballin to Bülow, 17 November 1908.
161 HSA Stuttgart, Varnbüler's Report, 19 November 1908.
162 See Tirpitz, *Politische Dokumente*, especially pp. 92ff.; Wilhelm Deist, *Flottenpolitik und Flottenpropaganda. Das Nachrichtenbüro des Reichsmarineamts 1897–1914* (Stuttgart, 1976), pp. 250ff.; Hammann, *Bilder aus der letzten Kaiserzeit*, pp. 147ff.; Ivo Nikolai Lambi, *The Navy and German Power Politics 1862–1914* (London, 1984), pp. 295ff.
163 HSA München, 1080, Lerchenfeld's Report, 19 November 1908.
164 HSA München, 2686, Lerchenfeld to Podewils, 28 November 1908 and 1080, Lerchenfeld's Report, 4 December 1908; HSA Stuttgart, Varnbüler's Report, 4 December 1908. See also Dieter Grosser, *Vom monarchischen Konstitutionalismus zur parlamentarischen Demokratie: Die Verfassungspolitik der deutschen Parteien im letzten Jahrzehnt des Kaiserreiches* (The Hague, 1970); W. Frauendienst, 'Der Reichstag im Zeitalter des persönlichen Regiments Wilhelms II 1890–1914', in Ernst Deuerlein (ed.), *Der Reichstag* (Bonn, 1963), pp. 70f.; Eschenburg, *Kaiserreich am Scheideweg*, pp. 158–75; Elisabeth Fehrenbach, *Wandlungen des deutschen Kaisergedankens 1871–1918* (Munich and Vienna, 1969), pp. 138–51.
165 Rich and Fisher, *Holstein Papers*, IV, Bülow to Holstein, 17 November 1908, p. 596.
166 HHSA Wien, 166, Szögyényi's Report, 28 November 1908 and 167, Szögyényi to Aehrenthal, 9 December 1908.
167 HHSA Wien, 166, Szögyényi's Report, 28 November 1908.
168 HHSA Wien, 167, Szögyényi to Aehrenthal, 18 November 1908.
169 Zedlitz, *Zwölf Jahre*, 26 November 1908, pp. 194f.; BA Koblenz, BP, 33, August Eulenburg to Bülow, 25–6 November 1908.
170 Zedlitz, *Zwölf Jahre*, Zedlitz to his father, 30 November 1908, p. 197.
171 ZSA Merseburg, Rep. 53J, Lit. F. no. 3, Fürstenberg to Wilhelm II, 21 November 1908.
172 Ibid., Fürstenberg to Wilhelm II, 29 November 1908.
173 HSA München, 1081, Lerchenfeld's Report, 8 January 1909.
174 HHSA Wien, 167, Szögyényi to Aehrenthal, 25 November 1908.
175 Ibid., Szögyényi to Aehrenthal, 18 November 1908.
176 HHSA Wien, 166, Szögyényi's Report, 3 December 1908.
177 HHSA Wien, 167, Szögyényi to Aehrenthal, 9 December 1908.
178 FCO London, Holstein Papers, 34, Holstein to Bülow, 9 December 1908.
179 BA Koblenz, BP, 74, August Eulenburg to Bülow, 18 December 1908.
180 ZSA Merseburg, Hausarchiv, Adjutants' Diaries, 13, 9 and 19 December 1908; Zedlitz, *Zwölf Jahre*, 22 December 1908, p. 198; Cole, '*Daily Telegraph* Affair', p. 259. See also Bülow's claim that Wilhelm 'cloaks himself in silence towards me' in FCO London, Holstein Papers, 34, Bülow to Holstein [November–December 1908].
181 Reichstag, 10 December 1908, p. 6106; HHSA Wien, 166, Szögyényi's Report, 11 December 1908; PA Bonn, Eisendecher Papers, 1/7, notes on the Kaiser's remarks, 16 May 1909.
182 Rich and Fisher, *Holstein Papers*, IV, Holstein to Bülow, 6 January 1909, p. 613. Cf. ZSA

Merseburg, Rep. 53J, Lit. B. no. 16a, IV, Bülow to Wilhelm II, 11 January 1909. The article, 'Der Krieg in der Gegenwart', appeared in *Deutsche Revue* (Stuttgart and Leipzig, 1909), I, pp. 13–24. See also Rich and Fisher, *Holstein Papers*, I, pp. 159ff.

183 ZSA Merseburg, Rep. 53J, Lit. F. no. 3, Fürstenberg to Wilhelm II, 9 January 1909.

184 FCO London, Holstein Papers, 34, Holstein to Bülow, 9 January 1909.

185 Zedlitz, *Zwölf Jahre*, 12 March 1909, p. 224.

186 See HSA München, 2686, Lerchenfeld to Podewils, 28 November 1908.

187 HSA München, 1080, Lerchenfeld's Report, 18 November 1908; PA Bonn, Brockdorff–Rantzau Papers, 2/3, Wedel to Rantzau, 28 December 1908.

188 HHSA Wien, 166, Flotow's Report, 12 November 1908.

189 Rogge, *Holstein und Harden*, Holstein to Harden, 5 November 1908, p. 373 and Holstein to Bülow, 21 November 1908, pp. 401f. See also HSA Stuttgart, Varnbüler's Report, 19 November 1908; Vierhaus, *Spitzemberg*, 29 November 1908, pp. 494f.

190 ZSA Merseburg, Rep. 53J, Lit. F. no. 3, Fürstenberg to Wilhelm II, Christmas Eve, 1908.

191 HHSA Wien, 166, Flotow's Report, 12 November 1908.

192 HSA München, 2687, Lerchenfeld's Report, 10 February 1909.

193 PA Bonn, Eisendecher Papers, 1/1, Eisendecher's notes of 7–19 February 1909.

194 BA Koblenz, BP, 33, Eugen Zimmermann to Bülow, 6 December 1908.

195 FCO London, Holstein Papers, 34, Bülow to Holstein, 8 January 1909.

196 BA Koblenz, BP, 33, Zimmermann to Bülow, 6 December 1908; Rich and Fisher, *Holstein Papers*, IV, Bülow to Holstein, 16 November 1908, pp. 594f.; FCO London, Holstein Papers, 34, Bülow to Holstein, 25 November 1908.

197 PA Bonn, IA, Deutschland, 122, no. 6, Bd. VII, Buttmann's Report, 19 October 1908.

198 BA Koblenz, BP, 33, Zimmermann to Bülow, 6 December 1908; Rich and Fisher, *Holstein Papers*, IV, Bülow to Holstein, 7 December 1908, p. 601.

199 HSA München, 1081, Lerchenfeld's Report, 8 January 1909.

200 FCO London, Holstein Papers, 34, Bülow to Holstein, 17 December 1908, 28 December 1908 and 25 November 1908.

201 BA Koblenz, BP, 33, Zimmermann to Bülow, 6 December 1909.

202 Ibid., 91, Holstein to Bülow, 3 November 1908; HSA Stuttgart, Varnbüler's Report, 12 December 1908.

203 HSA München, 2687, Lerchenfeld to Podewils, 18 January 1909.

204 HSA Stuttgart, Varnbüler's Report, 22 January 1909. For other individual opponents of Bülow after 1908, see Huber, *Deutsche Verfassungsgeschichte*, pp. 312–14.

205 HSA München, 1081, Lerchenfeld's Report, 2 February 1909; HHSA Wien, 168, Szögyényi to Aehrenthal, 21 January 1909.

206 See Karl von Hertling, 'Bülow, Hertling, Zentrum', in Thimme, *Front Wider Bülow*, 17 November 1908, p. 147; HSA München, 2687, Lerchenfeld to Podewils, 22 January 1909.

207 FCO London, Holstein Papers, 34, Bülow to Holstein, 8 January 1909.

208 HSA München, 2687, Bülow to Podewils, 22 January 1909.

209 HSA Stuttgart, Varnbüler's Report, 22 January 1909; Bülow, *Reden*, III, 19 January 1909, pp. 165ff.; Landtag, 19 January 1909, 1040–1050.

210 HSA München, 2687, Lerchenfeld to Podewils, 22 January 1909.

211 Zedlitz, *Zwölf Jahre*, 20 January 1909, p. 212; HHSA Wien, 168, Szögyényi to Aehrenthal, 21 January 1909.

212 ZSA Merseburg, Rep. 53J, Lit. B. no. 16a, IV, Bülow to Wilhelm II, 9 February 1909 and 10 February 1909.

213 HHSA Wien, 168, Szögyényi to Aehrenthal, 17 February 1909.

214 ZSA Merseburg, Rep. 53J, Lit. B. no. 16a, IV, Bülow to Wilhelm II, 13 February 1909; Cole, *'Daily Telegraph* Affair', p. 263.

215 HSA München, 1081, Lerchenfeld's Report, 22 February 1909.
216 ZSA Merseburg, Kronrat, 6, 18 February 1909; Staatsministerium, 158, 13 February 1909.
217 GLA Karlsruhe, 34814, Berckheim's Report, 22 February 1909; HSA München, 1081, Lerchenfeld's Report, 22 February 1909.
218 ZSA Merseburg, Hausarchiv, Adjutants' Diaries, 12, entries for January and February 1909.
219 HSA Stuttgart, Varnbüler's Report, 1 March 1909.
220 Zedlitz, *Zwölf Jahre*, 15 February 1909, pp. 222f.
221 HSA Stuttgart, Varnbüler's Report, 1 March 1909.
222 HSA München, 1081, Lerchenfeld's Report, 17 March 1909.
223 ZSA Merseburg, Valentini Papers, 13, Loebell to Valentini, 10 March 1909; HSA Stuttgart, Weizsäcker Papers, Varnbüler to Weizsäcker, 14 July 1909.
224 ZSA Merseburg, Hausarchiv, Adjutants' Diaries, 12, 11 March 1909; Zedlitz, *Zwölf Jahre*, 12 March 1909, p. 223.
225 Bülow, *Denkwürdigkeiten*, II, pp. 446–50; cf. Witt, *Finanzpolitik*, p. 270, n. 435, who prefers Bülow's interpretation to the 'melodramatic' version of the Kaiser.
226 Zedlitz, *Zwölf Jahre*, 12 March 1909, pp. 223f.; HSA München, 1081, Lerchenfeld's Report, 17 March 1909.
227 See for example HSA München, 1081, Lerchenfeld's Report, 14 July 1909; HSA Stuttgart, Weizsäcker Papers, Varnbüler to Weizsäcker, 14 July 1909.
228 Zedlitz, *Zwölf Jahre*, 15 March 1909, p. 224.
229 HSA München, 699, Lerchenfeld's Report, 12 March 1909.
230 See for example BA Koblenz, BP, 112, Bülow to Wilhelm II, 14 December 1902.
231 Vierhaus, *Spitzemberg*, 25 March 1909, p. 501. This story gained such currency that Bülow had it officially denied in the *Norddeutsche Allgemeine Zeitung* on 20 April 1909. See PA Bonn, IA, Deutschland, 122, no. 13, Bd. XIV, Bülow to Foreign Office, 16 April 1909.
232 Zedlitz, *Zwölf Jahre*, 15 March 1909, p. 224.
233 Ibid., 12 March 1909, p. 262.
234 HHSA Wien, 167, Szögyényi's Report, 13 March 1909; ZSA Merseburg, Hausarchiv, Adjutants' Diaries, 12, entries for March 1909.
235 HSA München, 699, Lerchenfeld's Report, 12 March 1909.
236 Vierhaus, *Spitzemberg*, 4 April 1909, p. 502.
237 Ibid., 16 April 1909, p. 503.
238 HSA München, 699, Lerchenfeld to Podewils, 13 March 1909.
239 See HSA Stuttgart, Weizsäcker Papers, Varnbüler to Weizsäcker, 14 July 1909.
240 See Zedlitz, *Zwölf Jahre*, 17 April 1906, pp. 148f. and Zedlitz to his father, 15 September 1907, pp. 168f.
241 HHSA Wien, 167, Szögyényi's Report, 13 March 1909.
242 HHSA Wien, 168, Szögyényi to Aehrenthal, 1 April 1909.
243 Bülow, *Denkwürdigkeiten*, II, p. 457.
244 Rogge, *Holstein und Harden*, Holstein to Bülow, 6 April 1909, pp. 452ff.
245 PA Bonn, Eisendecher Papers, 1/7, 'Notiz betreffend Aeusserungen S.M.', 16 May 1909.
246 PA Bonn, Brockdorff–Rantzau Papers, 2/3, Wedel to Rantzau, 30 May 1909.
247 ZSA Merseburg, Hausarchiv, Adjutants' Diaries, 13, entries for April–June 1909.
248 HHSA Wien, 168, Szögyényi to Aehrenthal, 26 May 1909.
249 PA Bonn, Eisendecher Papers, 1/2, Eisendecher to Bethmann Hollweg, 14 September 1909.
250 PA Bonn, Brockdorff–Rantzau Papers, 2/3, Wedel to Rantzau, 30 May 1909.

251 ZSA Potsdam, Reichskanzlei, 798/2, memorandum of late 1908/early 1909 (Bl. 266) and Loebell to Bülow, 14 April 1909; Rogge, *Holstein und Harden*, pp. 456ff. The third Moltke–Harden trial took place on 20 April 1909.

252 FCO London, Holtein Papers, 34, Bülow to Holstein [25 November 1908].

253 Tirpitz, *Politische Dokumente*, pp. 104ff. See also Willy Becker, *Fürst Bülow und England 1897–1909* (Greifswald, 1929).

254 Jäckh, *Kiderlen-Wächter*, II, Kiderlen-Wächter to Hedwig Kypke, 24 November 1908, p. 16; HSA München, 2687, Lerchenfeld to Podewils, 1 April 1909. See also Rich, *Holstein*, II, pp. 830f.

255 Vierhaus, *Spitzemberg*, 28 March 1909, p. 502. See also HHSA Wien, 168, Szögyényi's Report, 27 April 1909.

256 HSA–KA München, D4, II, Report of Bavarian military plenipotentiary, 11 July 1909. Schön claims Bülow left him a freer hand in foreign policy than he had expected and even left to the State Secretary the discussions with the Kaiser on current affairs and personnel questions. See Schön, *Erlebtes*, p. 102.

257 See also Witt, *Finanzpolitik*, pp. 229ff.

258 HSA München, 1080, Lerchenfeld's Report, 4 December 1908; HSA Stuttgart, Varnbüler's Report, 4 December 1908.

259 HSA Stuttgart, Varnbüler's Report, 28 November 1908. See also BA Koblenz, Reichskanzlei, 1600, Reich Justice Office to Reich Chancellor, 28 November 1908.

260 Witt, *Finanzpolitik*, p. 255, See also Zedlitz, *Zwölf Jahre*, 14 January 1909, p. 210. Valentini's suspicions of the Chancellor appear to have been unfounded, but he may have heard of proposals to abolish the Civil Cabinet in its present form. See BA Koblenz, Reichskanzlei, 1600, Loebell's memorandum, 4 January 1909. For the Crown speech in which a reform of the Prussian suffrage was promised, see Landtag, 20 October 1908, 3–6.

261 HSA München, 1081, Lerchenfeld's Report, 8 January 1909.

262 HSA Stuttgart, Varnbüler's Report, 22 January 1909.

263 See especially, *Kaiserreich am Scheideweg*, pp. 203ff.

264 Reichstag, 19 November 1908, pp. 5540ff.; HHSA Wien, 166, Szögyényi's Report, 25 November 1908.

265 HSA München, 1080, Lerchenfeld's Report, 4 December 1908; HSA Stuttgart, Varnbüler's Report, 12 December 1908.

266 Born, *Staat und Sozialpolitik*, pp. 233f.; Huber, *Deutsche Verfassungsgeschichte*, pp. 315f. See also BA Koblenz, Rechberg Papers, 17, memorandum of spring 1909.

267 HSA München, 1080, Lerchenfeld's Report, 4 December 1908; Witt, *Finanzpolitik*, p. 236.

268 HSA München, 1080, Lerchenfeld's Report, 4 December 1908 and 1081, Lerchenfeld's Report, 8 January 1909.

269 Rich and Fisher, *Holstein Papers*, IV, Holstein to Bülow, 20 January 1909, pp. 615f.

270 HSA München, 1081, Lerchenfeld to Podewils, 2 February 1909.

271 Rich and Fisher, *Holstein Papers*, IV, Bülow to Holstein, 13 January 1909, pp. 614f. and 20 January 1909, p. 616.

272 Landtag, 19 January 1907, 1040–9; Rich and Fisher, *Holstein Papers*, IV, Holstein to Bülow, 20 January 1909, pp. 615f.

273 HSA München, 2687, Lerchenfeld to Podewils, 26 January 1909. Bülow misjudged the mood of the Conservatives in 1909 and believed that moderate Conservatives could be detached from the more extreme Bund der Landwirte. See especially Retallack, 'Conservatives *contra* Chancellor', 224ff. and *Notables of the Right*, pp. 142ff.

274 ZSA Potsdam, Hammann Papers, 14, Bülow to Hammann, 4 March 1909. See also Witt,

Finanzpolitik, pp. 276ff., 281.

275 Witt, *Finanzpolitik*, pp. 255f.

276 Ibid., pp. 284f. See also criticisms of Loebell in HSA–KA München, D4, II, Report of Bavarian military plenipotentiary, 11 July 1909.

277 HSA München, 1081, Lerchenfeld's Report, 2 February 1909.

278 HSA München, 2687, Lerchenfeld to Podewils, 10 February 1909; Witt, *Finanzpolitik*, pp. 267ff.

279 PA Bonn, IA, Deutschland, 103, Bd. XV, Hammann's memorandum, 4 March 1909.

280 Bülow, *Denkwürdigkeiten*, II, p. 445.

281 HSA München, 2687, Lerchenfeld to Podewils, 1 April 1909.

282 Ibid., Lerchenfeld to Podewils, 13 March 1909.

283 Reichstag, 29 March 1909, pp. 7799ff., 7831ff.; 30 March 1909, pp. 7869ff. See also Bülow, *Reden*, III, pp. 179–213; HHSA Wien, 167, Szögyényi's Report, 31 March 1909.

284 HSA München, 2687, Lerchenfeld to Podewils, 1 April 1909.

285 GLA Karlsruhe, 34814, Berckheim to Marschall, 5 April 1909.

286 See Witt, *Finanzpolitik*, p. 272.

287 BA Koblenz, Loebell Papers, 6, 'Besprechung' of 28 April 1909.

288 See Witt, *Finanzpolitik*, pp. 279f.

289 The complex relationship between the government and the Conservative Party is discussed in Retallack, *Notables of the Right*, ch. 10.

290 HHSA Wien, 167, Szögyényi's Report, 18 May 1909.

291 HSA Stuttgart, Varnbüler's Report, 22 May 1909.

292 Eschenburg, *Kaiserreich am Scheideweg*, p. 227; Bachem, *Zentrumspartei*, VII, p. 59.

293 PA Bonn, Brockdorff–Rantzau Papers 2/3, Wedel to Rantzau, 30 May 1909; HSA Stuttgart, Haussmann Papers, Q1/2, 116, Payer to Haussmann(?), 2 June 1909.

294 HHSA Wien, 168, Szögyényi to Aehrenthal, 3 June 1909.

295 HSA–KA München, D4, II, Report of Bavarian military plenipotentiary, 11 July 1909.

296 Vierhaus, *Spitzemberg*, 27 May 1909, p. 505.

297 See especially HSA Stuttgart, Varnbüler's Report, 14 May 1909.

298 Eschenburg, *Kaiserreich am Scheideweg*, p. 226. See also Witt, *Finanzpolitik*, p. 294.

299 HSA Stuttgart, Varnbüler's Report, 22 May 1909. Wilhelm II did not understand the Reich financial reform and had apparently lost interest by March 1909. See Vierhaus, *Spitzemberg*, 25 March 1909, p. 502.

300 BA Koblenz, Loebell Papers, 14, Valentini to Loebell, 6 May 1909; Retallack, 'Conservatives *contra* Chancellor', 230f.

301 Witt, *Finanzpolitik*, pp. 270f.

302 HHSA Wien, 167, Szögyényi's Report, 6 July 1909 (no. 22B).

303 HSA Stuttgart, Varnbüler's Report, 14 May 1909; PA Bonn, Eisendecher Papers, 2/3, Wedel to Eisendecher, 13 May 1909; HSA Stuttgart, Weizsäcker Papers, Weizsäcker to King of Württemberg, 22 May 1909.

304 Bülow, *Denkwürdigkeiten*, II, pp. 475f.

305 HSA Stuttgart, Weizsäcker Papers, Weizsäcker to King of Württemberg, 7 July 1909.

306 BA Koblenz, Hertling Papers, 37, Praschma to Hertling, 5 June 1909; Hertling, 'Bülow, Hertling, Zentrum', p. 150.

307 Cf. Bismarck's tactics in 1889–90. See especially Röhl, *Germany Without Bismarck*, pp. 45–55; Gall, *Bismarck*, II, pp. 201ff.

308 HHSA Wien, 167, Szögyényi's Report, 6 July 1909 (no. 22B).

309 HSA München, 1081, Lerchenfeld's Report, 27 June 1909 (no. 336). See also HSA Stuttgart, Weizsäcker Papers, Speth(?) to Weizsäcker, 24 August 1909, who was told by Bülow's niece that Bülow had realised that he would never regain the Kaiser's confidence

after November 1908 and had decided to resign regardless of the fate of the finance reform.

310 HSA Stuttgart, Weizsäcker Papers, Varnbüler to Weizsäcker, 14 July 1909.

311 Witt, *Finanzpolitik*, p. 294; Reichstag, 16 June 1909, pp. 8585ff.

312 HHSA Wien, 167, Szögyényi's Report, 6 July 1909.

313 BA Koblenz, Loebell Papers, 6, Bülow to Loebell, Whit Monday 1909.

314 HHSA Wien, 167, Szögyényi's Report, 25 June 1909; Bachem, *Zentrumspartei*, VII, p. 60. The voting was 194 to 186.

315 HSA München, 1081, Lerchenfeld's Report, 27 June 1909 (no. 336). See also HHSA Wien, 167, Szögyényi's Report, 25 June 1909; Loth, *Katholiken im Kaiserreich*, pp. 176f.

316 HSA München, 1081, Lerchenfeld's Report, 27 June 1909 (no. 336); BA Koblenz, BP, 152, Losungen, 25 June 1909.

317 HSA München, 1081, Lerchenfeld's Report, 27 June 1909 (no. 337).

318 BA Koblenz, BP, 22, Rüger to Bülow, 26 June 1909; Bülow, *Denkwürdigkeiten*, III, p. 338.

319 HSA München, 1081, Lerchenfeld's Report, 27 June 1909 (no. 336); HSA Stuttgart, Weizsäcker Papers, Weizsäcker to Varnbüler(?), 28 June 1909.

320 BA Koblenz, BP, 153, n. 291, Wilhelm II to Bülow, 25 June 1909; Hiller, *Fürst Bülows Denkwürdigkeiten*, p. 219, n. 34.

321 HSA München, 1081, Lerchenfeld's Report, 27 June 1909 (no. 336).

322 HHSA Wien, 167, Szögyényi's Report, 6 July 1909 (no. 22B).

323 HSA München, 1081, Lerchenfeld's Report, 27 June 1909 (no. 337).

324 Ibid. (no. 336). See also Bülow, *Denkwürdigkeiten*, II, p. 517.

325 HSA München, 1081, Report of Bavarian *chargé d'affaires*, 29 June 1909.

326 See Witt, *Finanzpolitik*, pp. 297ff.

327 HHSA Wien, 167, Szögyényi's Reports, 6 July 1909 (no. 22A) and 8 July 1909.

328 Sydow, 'Fürst Bülow', p. 130; Witt, *Finanzpolitik*, pp. 299f.

329 ZSA Potsdam, Rath Papers, 7, *Neue Freie Presse*, 11 July 1909.

330 HHSA Wien, 167, Szögyényi's Report, 6 July 1909 (no. 22B).

331 Monts, *Erinnerungen*, Monts to Felix von Oppenheimer, 9 July 1909, p. 463.

332 HHSA Wien, 167, Szögyényi's Report, 6 July 1909 (no. 22B).

333 HHSA Wien, 168, Szögyényi to Aehrenthal, 8 July 1909.

334 BA Koblenz, BP, 36, extract of Bethmann's speech at meeting of 13 July 1909; Bülow, *Denkwürdigkeiten*, III, pp. 18f.

335 ZSA Merseburg, Staatsministerium, 158, 13 July 1909.

336 BA Koblenz, BP, 152, Losungen, 14 and 15 July 1909. See also ZSA Merseburg, Hausarchiv, Adjutants' Diaries, 13, entries for July 1909.

337 HHSA Wien, 167, Szögyényi's Report, 20 July 1909.

338 BA Koblenz, Reichskanzlei, 1608, Wilhelm II to Reich Chancellor, 14 July 1909. Einem, Moltke and Holle also resigned in the summer of 1909, and Loebell was appointed *Oberpräsident* of Brandenburg.

339 HHSA Wien, 167, Szögyényi's Report, 8 July 1909; HSA München, 1081, Lerchenfeld's Report, 27 June 1909.

340 ZSA Merseburg, Staatsministerium, 158, 13 July 1909, at which Bülow intimated that the choice was between Bethmann, Rheinbaben and Wedel. In his memoirs Bülow omits Bethmann and suggests he recommended Schorlemer instead, *Denkwürdigkeiten*, II, p. 514. Bülow and Valentini sabotaged Monts's appointment. See Monts, *Erinnerungen*, Valentini to Monts, 13 July 1909, p. 25 and Monts to Oppenheimer, 9 July 1909, p. 463. Goltz had been considered for the post earlier in the year but was too busy in Turkey. See PA Bonn, Brockdorff–Rantzau Papers, 2/3, Wedel to Rantzau, 7 February 1909. For

Tirpitz's possible candidacy, see SA Köln, Bachem Papers, 283, Bachem to Eisele(?), 7 July 1909. In August 1909 Szögyényi reported that he had heard from a best-informed source that Wilhelm II had first thought of Botho Eulenburg as Bülow's successor and that Bülow had warmly supported his candidacy though Botho had refused. This was later confirmed by the Kaiser. See HHSA Wien, 168, Szögyényi to Aehrenthal, 19 August 1909 and 24 November 1909. See also Witt, *Finanzpolitik*, p. 300, who claims that both Botho and August Eulenburg refused the Chancellorship. For Wedel's candidacy, see HSA Stuttgart, Weizsäcker Papers, Speth(?) to Weizsäcker, 24 August 1909. Dernburg claimed the Kaiser considered him as Bülow's successor and that he, Dernburg, had felt this such an error of judgement that he withdrew increasingly from 1909 and decided to resign (in 1910). See BA Koblenz, Wolff Papers, 8, Dernburg to Zedlitz, 4 January 1927 (unsent).

341 HSA München, 1081, Lerchenfeld's Report, 27 June 1909 (no. 336). Bülow clearly claimed in his memoirs that he had not supported Bethmann so as to dissociate himself from the Chancellor who had led Germany into the war.

342 HHSA Wien, 167, Szögyényi's Report, 20 July 1909.

343 Bülow, *Denkwürdigkeiten*, III, ch. 5; BA Koblenz, Loebell Papers, 6, Bülow to Loebell, 11 August 1909.

344 HSA München, 1081, Lerchenfeld's Report, 14 July 1909; HSA Stuttgart, Weizsäcker Papers, Varnbüler to Weizsäcker, 14 July 1909. The following is based on these two reports.

345 Cf. Bülow, *Denkwürdigkeiten*, II, pp. 509f.

346 HSA Stuttgart, Weizsäcker Papers, Varnbüler to Weizsäcker, 14 July 1909.

347 HSA München, 1081, Lerchenfeld's Report, 14 July 1909.

348 HSA Stuttgart, Weizsäcker Papers, Varnbüler to Weizsäcker, 14 July 1909.

349 HHSA Wien, 168, Szögyényi to Aehrenthal, 24 November 1909.

350 Bülow, *Denkwürdigkeiten*, III, p. 29.

351 Monts, *Erinnerungen*, Monts to Oppenheimer, 9 July 1909, p. 463.

Conclusion

1 Landtag, 29 March 1901.

2 Monts, *Erinnerungen*, Monts to Tschirschky, 14 January 1901, p. 411.

3 Zedlitz, *Zwölf Jahre*, 18 January 1908, pp. 185f.

4 Ibid., 4 March 1910, p. 240.

5 BA Koblenz, Loebell Papers, 7, Bülow to Loebell, 15 November 1911.

6 Röhl, *Eulenburg*, III, Bülow to Eulenburg, 27 May 1898, p. 1897.

7 PA Bonn, Eisendecher Papers, 3/2, Tirpitz to Eisendecher, 23 August 1909.

8 See also Klügmann's Report, 21 December 1908, in Hartmann, 'Innenpolitik', 276; *Berliner Tageblatt*, 24 July 1901, 'Der Januskopf im Reichskanzlerpalais'.

9 HSA München, 1079, Lerchenfeld to Podewils, 5 November 1907; HSA Stuttgart, Varnbüler's Report, 14 December 1907.

10 BA Koblenz, BP, 105, Mirbach to Bülow, 10 July 1913.

11 See for example Monts, *Erinnerungen*, Monts to Jagow, 11 April 1907 and 4 October 1907; Hertling, 'Bülow, Hertling, Zentrum', 29 April 1907, p. 146.

12 BA Koblenz, Loebell Papers, 7, Bülow to Loebell, 3 March 1913.

13 Bülow professed great satisfaction in retirement (see ZSA Merseburg, Valentini Papers, 3, Bülow to Valentini, 6 August 1909), but he abandoned neither his political ambitions nor his concern for his reputation (see BA Koblenz, Loebell Papers, 6, Bülow to Loebell, 1 August 1909). He went on a special mission to Rome in 1915 to try to secure Italian

neutrality during the First World War (see Bülow, *Denkwürdigkeiten*, III, pp. 193ff.). Throughout much of the war he hoped to be German representative at a peace conference (see BA Koblenz, Schwertfeger Papers, 208, Wahnschaffe to Valentini, 29 June 1915; BA Koblenz, BP, 126, Tirpitz to Bülow, 4 June 1916 and 30 September 1917). During the Chancellor crisis of 1917 he pushed his own candidacy and had already promised Gustav Stresemann the *Reichswirtschaftsamt* (see BA Koblenz, Schwertfeger Papers, 210, Hatzfeldt to Valentini, 22 October 1917).

14 BA Koblenz, Loebell Papers, 6, Bülow to Loebell, 9 August 1909.
15 Ibid., Bülow to Loebell, 23 January 1910.
16 Ibid., Bülow to Loebell, 10 February 1911.
17 Bülow, *Denkwürdigkeiten*, III, pp. 328ff.
18 Monts, *Erinnerungen*, p. 155.
19 Röhl, *Eulenburg*, III, Eulenburg's essay [February 1917], p. 2231.
20 BA Koblenz, Wolff Papers, 8, Dernburg to Zedlitz, 4 January 1927.
21 BA Koblenz, Loebell Papers, 6, Bülow to Loebell, 21 August 1909.
22 BA Koblenz, Schwertfeger Papers, 207, Loebell to Valentini, 15 January 1910.
23 Röhl, *Eulenburg*, III, Eulenburg's essay [February 1917], p. 2232.
24 Ibid., Varnbüler to Moltke, 6 November 1901, p. 2078, n. 1.
25 Bülow, *Denkwürdigkeiten*, III, p. 26.

Unpublished sources

BUNDESARCHIV (BA), KOBLENZ

Files of the Reich Chancellery (Reichskanzlei), microfiche, R43F
Max Bauer Papers
Ludwig Boas Papers
Karl von Boetticher Papers
Bernhard von Bülow Papers
Hans Delbrück Papers
Bernhard Dernburg Papers
Philipp zu Eulenburg-Hertefeld Papers
Ernst Francke Papers
Johannes Haller Papers
Maximilian Harden Papers
Karl Helfferich Papers
Karl Herold Papers
Georg von Hertling Papers
Alexander zu Hohenlohe-Schillingsfürst Papers
Siegfried von Kardoff Papers
Friedrich von Loebell Papers
Arnold Rechberg Papers
Hartmann von Richthofen Papers
Oswald von Richthofen Papers
Franz von Rottenburg Papers
Bernhard Schwertfeger Papers
Wilhelm Solf Papers
Friedrich Thimme Papers
Hans Wehberg Papers
Theodor Wolff Papers
Philipp Zorn Papers
Minor Acquisitions (KE):
   310 Paul Lindau
   339 Felix von Eckardt
   341 Rudolf von Valentini
   455 Wilhelm Recke
   565 Sidney Whitman

BUNDESARCHIV-MILITÄRARCHIV (BA–MA), FREIBURG

Files of the Kaiser's Naval Cabinet (Kaiserliches Marinekabinett), RM2
Files of the Reich Navy Office (Reichsmarineamt), RM3

Files of the Admiralty Staff (Admiralstab der Marine), RM5
Wilhelm Büchsel Papers
Eduard von Capelle Papers
Otto von Diederichs Papers
Karl von Einem Papers
August von Mackensen Papers
Helmuth von Moltke Papers
Georg von Müller Papers
Alfred von Schlieffen Papers
Gustav von Senden-Bibran Papers
Alfred von Tirpitz Papers
Alfred von Waldersee Papers

POLITISCHES ARCHIV (PA) DES AUSWÄRTIGEN AMTES, BONN

Files of Foreign Office, IA
Ulrich von Brockdorff–Rantzau Papers
Hermann von Eckardstein Papers
Karl von Eisendecher Papers
Emil Mechler Papers
Friedrich von Pourtalès Papers
Paul Weitz Papers

STADTARCHIV (SA), KÖLN

Karl Bachem Papers

ZENTRALES STAATSARCHIV (ZSA), DIENSTSTELLE MERSEBURG

Files of the Royal Household (Hausarchiv), Rep. 53J (Correspondence) and Rep. 53F (Diaries of the Kaiser's Adjutants, 1898–1909).
Files of the Kaiser's Civil Cabinet (Zivilkabinett), Rep. 89H, 2.2.1
Minutes of the Prussian Ministry of State (Staatsministerium), 1900–9, Rep. 90a B III 2b no. 6, 140–58
Minutes of the Prussian Crown Council (Kronrat), 1900–9, Rep. 90a, B III 2c no. 3, 5–6
Friedrich Althoff Papers
Konrad von Studt Papers
Rudolf von Valentini Papers

ZENTRALES STAATSARCHIV (ZSA), POTSDAM

Files of the Reich Chancellery (Reichskanzlei)
Ernst Bassermann Papers
Otto Hammann Papers
Friedrich von Holstein Papers
Hermann von Rath Papers

BADISCHES GENERALLANDESARCHIV (GLA), KARLSRUHE

Reports of the Baden ambassadors to Berlin, 1899–1909, 233/34806–34814 (only drafts available for 1904, 49/2037)

HAUPSTAATSARCHIV (HSA), MÜNCHEN (GEHEIMES STAATSARCHIV)

Reports of the Bavarian ambassador to Berlin, 1900–9, MA III/2678–2687
Files of State Ministry:
  The Legation in Berlin
  Bavarian Foreign Ministry
  German Empire

HAUPTSTAATSARCHIV-KRIEGSARCHIV (HSA–KA), MÜNCHEN

Reports of the Bavarian military plenipotentiary to Berlin, 1900–9, D4

HAUPTSTAATSARCHIV (HSA), STUTTGART

Reports of the Württemberg ambassador to Berlin, 1897–1909, E73 12e
Conrad Haussmann Papers
Felix von Müller Papers
Axel von Varnbüler Papers
Karl von Weizsäcker Papers

MILITÄRARCHIV (MA), STUTTGART

Files of the War Ministry, M1/2, 24–6, 43–8
Otto von Marchtaler Papers

OESTERREICHISCHES HAUS- HOF- UND STAATSARCHIV (HHSA), WIEN

Reports of the Austrian ambassador to Berlin, 1898–1909, PA III

FOREIGN AND COMMONWEALTH OFFICE (FCO), LONDON

Friedrich von Holstein Papers (photocopies of originals in Bonn)

PUBLIC RECORDS OFFICE (PRO), LONDON

Files of Foreign Office, FO 64 (Germany).

Select bibliography

Achterberg, E. *Berliner Hochfinanz. Kaiser, Fürsten, Millionäre um 1900*. Frankfurt, 1965.

Alff, Wilhelm (ed.). *Deutschlands Sonderung von Europa 1862–1945*. Frankfurt, Bern and New York, 1984.

Allen, Ann Taylor. *Satire and Society in Wilhelmine Germany. Kladderadatsch and Simplicissimus, 1890–1914*. Kentucky, 1984.

Altrichter, Helmut. *Konstitutionalismus und Imperialismus. Der Reichstag und die deutsch-russischen Beziehungen 1890–1914*. Frankfurt, 1977.

Anderson, Eugene N. *The First Moroccan Crisis 1904–6*. Chicago, 1930.

Anderson, Margaret L. *Windthorst. A Political Biography*. Oxford, 1981.

Anderson, Pauline. *The Background of Anti-English Feeling in Germany, 1890–1902*. Washington, 1939.

Andrew, C. *Théophile Delcassé and the Making of the Entente Cordiale, 1898–1905*. London, 1968.

Bachem, Karl. *Vorgeschichte, Geschichte und Politik der deutschen Zentrumspartei*. 9 vols., Cologne, 1927–32.

Bald, Detlef. *Der deutsche Generalstab 1859–1939*. Munich, 1977.

Vom Kaiserheer zur Bundeswehr. Sozialstruktur des Militärs. Politik der Rekrutierung von Offizieren und Unteroffizieren. Frankfurt, 1981.

Balfour, Michael. *The Kaiser and his Times*. London, 1964.

Barkin, K. D. *The Controversy over German Industrialisation 1890–1902*. Chicago, 1970.

Baudis, D. and Nussbaum, H. *Wirtschaft und Staat in Deutschland vom Ende des 19 Jahrhunderts bis 1918–19*. Berlin, 1978.

Becker, Willy. *Fürst Bülow und England 1897–1909*. Greifswald, 1929.

Berghahn, V. R. 'Der Bericht der Preussischen Oberrechnungskammer. "Wehlers" Kaiserreich und seine Kritiker', *Geschichte und Gesellschaft*, 2 (1976).

'Die Fischer-Kontroverse – 15 Jahre nach', *Geschichte und Gesellschaft*, 6 (1980).

Germany and the Approach of War in 1914. London, 1973.

Modern Germany. Society, Economy and Politics in the Twentieth Century. Cambridge, 1982.

Der Tirpitz-Plan. Genesis und Verfall einer innenpolitischen Krisenstrategie unter Wilhelm II. Düsseldorf, 1971.

'Zu den Zielen des deutschen Flottenbaus unter Wilhelm II'. *Historische Zeitschrift*, 210 (1970).

Beumelburg, Werner. *Wilhelm II und Bülow*. Oldenburg, 1932.

Blackbourn, David. *Class, Religion and Local Politics in Wilhelmine Germany. The Centre Party in Württemberg before 1914*. London and New Haven. 1980.

Populists and Patricians. Essays in Modern German History. London, 1987.

Blackbourn, David and Eley, Geoff. *The Peculiarities of German History. Bourgeois Society and Politics in Nineteenth Century Germany*. Oxford, 1984.

Blaich, F. *Kartell- und Monopolpolitik im kaiserlichen Deutschland. Das Problem der Marktmacht im deutschen Reichstag zwischen 1879–1945*. Düsseldorf, 1973.

Staat und Verbände in Deutschland 1871–1945. Wiesbaden, 1979.

Bleyberg, Derek Michael. 'Government and Legislative Process in Wilhelmine Germany: the Reorganisation of the Tariff Laws under Reich Chancellor von Bülow, 1897 to 1902'. D. Phil. thesis, University of East Anglia, 1979.

Boelcke, Willi (ed.). *Krupp und die Hohenzollern. Krupp-Korrespondenz mit Kaisern, Kabinettschefs und Ministern 1850–1918*. Frankfurt, 1970.

Boldt, H. *Deutsche Verfassungsgeschichte*. Munich, 1984.

Bonham, G. 'State Autonomy or Class Domination: Approaches to Administrative Politics in Wilhelmine Germany', *World Politics*, 35 (1983).

Born, Karl Erich. *Staat und Sozialpolitik seit Bismarcks Sturz*. Wiesbaden, 1957.

Brauer, Arthur von. *Im Dienste Bismarcks*. Ed. Helmuth Rogge. Berlin, 1936.

Brocke, Bernhard von. 'Hochschul- und Wissenschaftspolitik in Preussen und im deutschen Kaiserreich 1882–1907: das "System Althoff"', *Preussen Geschichte*, 1 (1980).

Bullen, R. J., Pogge von Strandmann, H. and Polonsky, A. (eds.). *Ideas into Politics. Aspects of European History 1880–1950*. London and Sydney, 1984.

Bülow, Bernhard von. *Denkwürdigkeiten*. 4 vols., Berlin, 1930–1.

  Deutsche Politik. Berlin, 1916.

  Fürst Bülows Reden. Ed. J. Penzler and O. Hötzsch. 3 vols., Berlin, 1907–9.

  Letters of Prince Bülow. Translated by F. Whyte. London, undated.

Bussmann, Walther (ed.). *Graf Herbert von Bismarck. Aus seiner politischen Privatkorrespondenz*. Göttingen, 1964.

Cambon, Jules. 'Bülow and the War', *Foreign Affairs*, 10 (1932).

Cecil, Lamar. *Albert Ballin. Business and Politics in Imperial Germany 1888–1918*. Princeton, 1967.

  'Coal for the Fleet that Had to Die', *American Historical Review*, 69 (1964).

  The German Diplomatic Service 1871–1914. Princeton, 1976.

  'Jew and Junker in Imperial Germany', in *Leo Baeck Year Book*, 20, London, 1975.

Chickering, Roger. *Imperial Germany and a World without War. The Peace Movement and German Society 1893–1914*. Princeton, 1976.

  We Men Who Feel Most German. A Cultural Study of the Pan-German League, 1886–1914. Boston, 1984.

Clapham, J. H. *The Economic Development of France and Germany, 1815–1914*. Cambridge, 1936.

Cole, Terence F. 'The Crisis in Bülow's Chancellorship 1905–6'. M. A. thesis, University of Sussex, 1975.

  'The *Daily Telegraph* Affair and its Aftermath: the Kaiser, Bülow and the Reichstag, 1908–9', in J. C. G. Röhl and Nicolaus Sombart (eds.), *Kaiser Wilhelm II: New Interpretations*. Cambridge, 1982.

  'Kaiser Versus Chancellor: The Crisis of Bülow's Chancellorship 1905–6', in Richard J. Evans, *Society and Politics in Wilhelmine Germany*. London, 1978.

Craig, G. A. *The Politics of the Prussian Army, 1640–1945*. Oxford, 1955.

Crothers, G. D. *The German Elections of 1907*. New York, 1941.

Dahrendorf, Ralf. *Society and Democracy in Germany*. New York, 1967.

Dehmelt, Bernard Karl. 'Bülow's Moroccan Policy 1902–1905'. Ph.D. thesis, University of Pennsylvania, 1963.

Deist, Wilhelm. *Flottenpolitik und Flottenpropaganda. Das Nachrichtenbüro des Reichsmarineamts, 1897–1914*. Stuttgart, 1976.

Demeter, Karl. *Das deutsche Offizierkorps in Gesellschaft und Staat 1650–1945*. Frankfurt, 1962.

Doerry, Martin. *Übergangsmenschen. Die Mentalität der Wilhelminer und die Krise des Kaiserreichs*. Weinheim, 1986.

Domann, Peter. *Sozialdemokratie und Kaisertum unter Wilhelm II*. Wiesbaden, 1974.

Duggan, P. Robert. 'Currents of Administrative Reform in Germany 1907–1918'. Ph.D. thesis, University of Harvard, 1969.

Dukes, Jack R. and Remak, Joachim (eds.). *Another Germany. A Reconsideration of the Imperial Era*. Boulder and London, 1988.

Ebel, Gerhard (ed.). *Botschafter Paul Graf von Hatzfeldt. Nachgelassene Papiere, 1838–1901*. 2 vols. Boppard am Rhein, 1976.

Eckardstein, Hermann von. *Die Entlassung des Fürsten Bülows*. Berlin, 1931.

Lebenserinnerungen und Politische Denkwürdigkeiten. 3 vols. Leipzig, 1919–21.

Einem, Karl von. *Erinnerungen eines Soldaten 1853–1933*. Leipzig, 1933.

Eley, Geoff. 'Defining Social Imperialism: Use and Abuse of an Idea', *Social History*, 3 (1976).

From Unification to Nazism. Reinterpreting the German Past. London, 1986.

'The German Navy League in German Politics 1898–1914'. D. Phil. thesis, University of Sussex, 1974.

'Die "Kehrites" und das Kaiserreich: Bemerkungen zu einer aktuellen Kontroverse', *Geschichte und Gesellschaft*, 4 (1978).

Reshaping the German Right: Radical Nationalism and Political Change after Bismarck. London and New Haven, 1980.

'Reshaping the Right: Radical Nationalism and the German Navy League 1898–1908', *Historical Journal*, 21 (1978).

'The View from the Throne: the Personal Rule of Kaiser Wilhelm II', *Historical Journal*, 28 (1985).

Elias, Norbert. *Die höfische Gesellschaft. Untersuchungen zur Soziologie des Königtums und der höfischen Aristokratie*. Darmstadt and Neuwied, 1969. (English edn., *The Court Society*, Oxford, 1983).

Über den Prozess der Zivilisation. 2 vols. Bern, 1969.

Elm, Ludwig. *Zwischen Fortschritt und Reaktion. Geschichte der Parteien der liberalen Bourgeoisie in Deutschland 1893–1918*. Berlin, 1968.

Epstein, Klaus. *Matthias Erzberger and the Dilemma of German Democracy*. Princeton, 1959.

Eschenburg, Theodor. *Das Kaiserreich am Scheideweg. Bassermann, Bülow und der Block*. Berlin, 1929.

Eulenburg, Philipp zu. *Mit dem Kaiser als Staatsmann und Freund auf Nordlandreisen*. 2 vols. Dresden, 1931.

Eulenburg-Hertefeld, Philipp zu. *Aus 50 Jahren. Erinnerungen, Tagebücher und Briefe aus dem Nachlass des Fürsten*. Ed. Johannes Haller. Berlin, 1925.

Evans, Richard J. *The Feminist Movement in Germany 1894–1933*. London, 1976.

Rethinking German History: Nineteenth Century Germany and the Origins of the Third Reich. London, 1987.

Evans, Richard J. (ed.). *The German Working Class 1888–1933. The Politics of Everyday Life*. London, 1982.

Society and Politics in Wilhelmine Germany. London, 1978.

Evans, Richard J. and Lee, W. R. (eds.). *The German Family*. London, 1981.

The German Peasantry. London, 1986.

Eyck, Erich. *Das Persönliche Regiment Wilhelms II*. Zurich, 1948.

Farrar, L. L. *Arrogance and Anxiety. The Ambivalence of German Power 1848–1914*. Iowa City, 1981.

Fehrenbach, Elisabeth. *Wandlungen des deutschen Kaisergedankens 1871–1918*. Munich, 1969.

Finer, Hermann. *The Theory and Practice of Modern Government*. 2 vols. London, 1932.

Fink, Carole, Hull, Isabel V. and Knox, Macgregor (eds.). *German Nationalism and the European Response 1890–1945*. Norman, 1985.

Fischer, F. *Bündnis der Eliten. Zur Kontinuität der deutschen Machtstrukturen 1871–1945*. Düsseldorf, 1979.

Fischer, Fritz. 'Exzesse der Autokratie – das Hale-Interview Wilhelms II vom 19 Juli 1908', in Alff, Wilhelm (ed.), *Deutschlands Sonderung von Europa 1862–1945.* Frankfurt, Bern and New York, 1984.

Griff nach der Weltmacht. Düsseldorf, 1961.

Krieg der Illusionen. Düsseldorf, 1969.

'Der Stellenwert des ersten Weltkriegs in der Kontinuitätsproblematik der deutschen Geschichte', *Historische Zeitschrift,* 229 (1979).

Flemming, J. *Deutscher Konservatismus 1780–1980.* Frankfurt, 1985.

Fletcher, Roger. *Revisionism and Empire: Socialist Imperialism in Germany 1897–1914.* London, 1984.

Förster, Stig. *Der doppelte Militarismus. Die deutsche Heeresrüstungspolitik zwischen Status-quo-Sicherung und Aggression 1890–1913.* Stuttgart, 1985.

Fraley, J. David. 'Government by Procrastination. Chancellor Hohenlohe and Kaiser Wilhelm II, 1894–1900', *Central European History,* 7 (1974).

Frank, Walter. 'Bernhard von Bülow', *Historische Zeitschrift,* 147 (1933).

Frauendienst, Werner, ' "Fürst Bülow und England 1897–1909". Kritische Bemerkungen zu Willy Beckers Buch', *Berliner Monatshefte,* 8 (1930).

Fricke, D. (ed.). *Die bürgerlichen Parteien in Deutschland, 1830–1945.* 2 vols. Leipzig, 1968 and 1970.

Fuchs, Walther Peter (ed.). *Grossherzog Friedrich I von Baden und die Reichspolitik 1871–1907.* 4 vols. Stuttgart, 1968–80.

Gall, Lothar. *Bismarck. Der weisse Revolutionär.* Frankfurt, 1980.

Gall, Lothar (ed.). *Das Bismarck-Problem in der Geschichtsschreibung nach 1945.* Cologne and Berlin, 1971.

Geiss, Imanuel. *Das deutsche Reich und die Vorgeschichte des Ersten Weltkriegs.* Munich and Vienna, 1978.

German Foreign Policy 1871–1914. London, 1976.

Geiss, Imanuel and Wendt, Bernd Jürgen (eds.). *Deutschland in der Weltpolitik des 19 und 20 Jahrhunderts.* Düsseldorf, 1973.

Geyer, Michael. *Deutsche Rüstungspolitik 1860–1980.* Frankfurt on Main, 1984.

Goetz, Walter (ed.). *Briefe Wilhelms II an den Zaren, 1894–1914.* Berlin, 1920.

Gol, M. M. 'Der Koenigsberger Prozess von 1904 – Ein Beispiel des proletarischen Internationalismus', *Beiträge geschichtlicher Arbeiterbewegung,* 31 (1979).

Gorlitz, W. (ed.). *Der Kaiser . . . Aufzeichnungen des Chefs des Marinekabinetts Admiral Georg von Müller über die Ära Wilhelms II.* Berlin, Frankfurt and Zurich, 1965.

Gottgetreu, Erich. 'Maximilian Harden: Ways and Errors of a Publicist', in *Leo Baeck Year Book,* 7, London, 1962.

Grimm, D. *Deutsche Verfassungsgeschichte 1806–1980.* Frankfurt, 1985.

Groh, D. *Negative Integration und revolutionärer Attentismus.* Frankfurt and Berlin, 1973.

Gutsche, W. *Aufstieg und Fall eines kaiserlichen Reichskanzlers: T. von Bethmann Hollweg 1856–1921.* Berlin, 1973.

Gutsche, W. (ed.). *Studien zur Geschichte des deutschen Imperialismus von der Jahrhundertwende bis 1917.* Berlin, 1977.

Gutsche, W. and Kaulisch, B. (eds.). *Bilder aus der Kaiserzeit. Historische Streiflichter 1897–1917.* Leipzig, Jena and Berlin, 1985.

Herrschaftsmethoden des deutschen Imperialismus 1897/98 bis 1917. Berlin, 1977.

Haffner, Sebastian, 'Der letzte Bismarckianer. Zur politischen Korrespondenz Eulenburgs', *Merkur* (November 1977).

Hagen, William W. *Germans, Poles and Jews. The Nationality Conflict in the Prussian East, 1772–1914.* Chicago, 1980.

Hall, Alex. *Scandal, Sensation and Social Democracy: The SPD Press and Wilhelmine Germany.* Cambridge, 1977.

Haller, Johannes. *Die Aera Bülow. Eine historisch-politische Studie.* Stuttgart and Berlin, 1922.
Aus dem Leben des Fürsten Philipp zu Eulenburg-Hertefeld. Berlin, 1924.
Hallgarten, G. W. F. 'Fritz von Holsteins Geheimnis. Neues Licht auf die Lebensgeschichte der "Grauen Eminenz" ', *Historische Zeitschrift,* 177 (1954).
Imperialismus vor 1914. 2 vols. 2nd edn, Munich, 1963.
Hammann, Otto. *Bilder aus der letzen Kaiserzeit.* Berlin, 1922.
Der Neue Kurs. Berlin, 1918.
Um den Kaiser. Erinnerungen aus den Jahren 1906–9. Berlin, 1919.
Zur Vorgeschichte des Weltkrieges. Erinnerungen aus den Jahren 1897–1906. Berlin, 1918.
Harden, Maximilian. *Köpfe.* Berlin, 1910.
Hartmann, Hans-Georg. 'Die Innenpolitik des Fürsten Bülow, 1906–9'. Ph.D. thesis, University of Kiel, 1950.
Hartung, F. 'Das persönliche Regiment Kaiser Wilhelms II', *Sitzungsberichte der deutschen Akademie zu Berlin,* 1952.
Staatsbildende Kräfte der Neuzeit. Berlin, 1961.
Heckart, Beverly. *From Bassermann to Bebel. The Grand Bloc's Quest for Reform in the Kaiserreich, 1900–1914.* London and New Haven, 1974.
Heilbron, Friedrich. 'Nekrolog auf Otto Hammann', *Deutsches biographisches Jahrbuch,* 10 (1931).
Henning, Hansjoachim (ed.). *Die Sozialpolitik in den letzten Friedensjahren des Kaiserreichs (1905 bis 1914).* 2 vols. *1 Band. Das Jahr 1905.* Wiesbaden, 1982. *2 Band. Das Jahr 1906.* Stuttgart, 1987.
Hentschel, Volker. *Wirtschaft und Wirtschaftspolitik im Wilhelminischen Deutschland: Organisierter Kapitalismus und Interventionsstaat?* Stuttgart, 1978.
Hertling, G. von. *Erinnerungen aus meinem Leben.* 2 vols. Munich, 1919–20.
Herwig, Holger. *The German Naval Officers Corps: A Social and Political History 1890–1918.* Oxford, 1973.
Politics of Frustration: The United States in German Naval Planning 1889–1914. Boston, 1976.
Herzfeld, Hans. *Johannes von Miquel.* 2 vols. Detmold, 1938.
Hickey, S. H. F. *Workers in Imperial Germany. The Miners of the Ruhr.* Oxford, 1985.
Hiller von Gaertringen, Friedrich. *Fürst Bülows Denkwürdigkeiten. Untersuchungen zu ihrer Entstehungsgeschichte und Kritik.* Tübingen, 1956.
Hohenlohe-Schillingsfürst, Chlodwig zu. *Denkwürdigkeiten.* Ed. A. Hohenlohe and F. Curtius. Stuttgart and Berlin, 1907.
Denkwürdigkeiten der Reichskanzlerzeit. Ed. Karl Alexander von Müller. Stuttgart and Berlin, 1931.
Holl, Karl and List, Günther (eds.). *Liberalismus und imperialistischer Staat: Der Imperialismus als Problem liberaler Parteien in Deutschland 1890–1914.* Göttingen, 1975.
Horn, Hannelore. *Der Kampf um den Bau des Mittellandkanals. Eine politische Untersuchung über die Rolle eines wirtschaftlichen Interessenverbandes im Preussen Wilhelms II.* Cologne, 1964.
Huber, Ernst Rudolf. *Deutsche Verfassungsgeschichte seit 1789. Bd. 4. Struktur und Krisen des Kaiserreichs.* Stuttgart, Berlin, Cologne and Mainz, 1969.
'Das persönliche Regiment Wilhelm II', *Zeitschrift für Religion und Geistesgeschichte,* 3 (1951).
Hull, Isabel V. 'Bernhard von Bülow', in Wilhelm von Sternburg (ed.), *Die deutschen Kanzler von Bismarck bis Schmidt.* Königstein, 1985.
The Entourage of Kaiser Wilhelm II 1888–1918. Cambridge, 1982.
Hutten-Czapski, Bogdan von. *Sechzig Jahre Politik und Gesellschaft.* 2 vols. Berlin, 1936.
Iggers, Georg (ed.). *The Social History of Politics. Critical Perspectives in West German Historical Writing Since 1945.* Leamington Spa, 1985.

Jäckh, E. (ed.). *Alfred von Kiderlen-Wächter. Briefwechsel und Nachlass.* 2 vols. Berlin, Leipzig and Stuttgart, 1924.

Jagemann, E. von. *75 Jahre des Erlebens und Erfahrens.* Heidelberg, 1925.

Jarausch, Konrad. *The Enigmatic Chancellor. Bethmann Hollweg and the Hubris of Imperial Germany.* New Haven, 1973.

Jilg, G. 'Der neue Kurs in der deutschen Pressepolitik 1890–1914: Die Pressestelle des Auswärtigen Amtes unter Dr. Otto Hammann'. Ph.D. thesis, University of Vienna, 1959.

Kaehler, Siegfried A. 'Legende und Wirklichkeit im Lebensbild des Kanzlers Bernhard von Bülow', *Studien zur deutschen Geschichte des 19 und 20 Jahrhunderts.* Göttingen, 1961.

Kaelbe, Hartmut. *Industrielle Interessenpolitik in der Wilhelminischen Gesellschaft. Zentralverband deutscher Industrieller 1895–1914.* Berlin, 1967.

Kehr, Eckart. *Der Primat der Innenpolitik. Gesammelte Aufsätze zur preussisch-deutschen Sozialgeschichte im 19 und 20 Jahrhundert.* Ed. Hans-Ulrich Wehler. Berlin, 1965.

Schlachtflottenbau und Parteipolitik 1894–1901. Berlin, 1930.

Kennedy, Paul. 'German World Policy and the Alliance Negotiations with England, 1897–1900', *Journal of Modern History*, 45 (1973).

The Rise of the Anglo-German Antagonism 1860–1914. London, 1980.

The Samoan Tangle. A Study in Anglo-German Relations, 1878–1900. Dublin and New York, 1974.

'Tirpitz, England and the Second Navy Law of 1900: a Strategical Critique', *Militärgeschichtliche Mitteilungen*, 2 (1970).

Kennedy, Paul and Nicholls, Anthony J. (eds.). *Nationalist and Racialist Movements in Britain and Germany before 1914.* London, 1981.

Kissinger, Henry. *The White House Years.* London, 1979.

Kitchen, Martin. *The German Officer Corps 1890–1914.* Oxford, 1968.

Klein, E. 'Funktion und Bedeutung des Preussischen Staatsministerium', *Jahrbuch für die Geschichte Mittel- und Ostdeutschlands*, 9/10 (1961).

Klein, F. (ed.). *Studien zum deutschen Imperialismus vor 1914.* Berlin, 1976.

Klein, Walther. *Der Vertrag von Björkoe. Wilhelm II, Bülow und Holstein im Kampf gegen die Isolierung Deutschlands.* Berlin, 1931.

Koch, H. W. 'The Anglo-German Alliance Negotiations', *History*, 54 (1969).

A Constitutional History of Germany in the Nineteenth and Twentieth Centuries. London and New York, 1984.

Koch, H. W. (ed.). *The Origins of the First World War. Great Power Rivalry and German War Aims.* London, 1972.

Koch, W. *Volk und Staatsführung vor dem Ersten Weltkrieg.* Stuttgart, 1935.

Köhler, W. *Der Chefredakteur. Theodor Wolff. Ein Leben in Europa 1868–1943.* Düsseldorf, 1978.

Koszyk, Kurt. *Deutsche Presse im 19 Jahrhundert.* Berlin, 1966.

Krieger, L. and Stern, F (eds.). *The Responsibility of Power. Historical Essays in Honor of Hajo Holborn.* New York, 1967.

Kühlmann, Richard von. *Erinnerungen.* Heidelberg, 1948.

Lambi, Ivo N. *The Navy and German Power Politics 1862–1914.* London, 1984.

Langewiesche, Dieter. 'Das deutsche Kaiserreich – Bemerkungen zur Diskussion über Parlamentarisierung und Demokratisierung Deutschlands', *Archiv Sozialgeschichte*, 19 (1979).

Lepsius, J., Mendelssohn-Bartholdy, A. and Thimme, F. (eds.). *Die Grosse Politik der europäischen Kabinette, 1871–1914.* 40 vols. Berlin, 1922–7.

Lerchenfeld-Koefering, Hugo von. *Erinnerungen und Denkwürdigkeiten, 1843 bis 1925.* Berlin, 1935.

Kaiser Wilhelm II. Als Persönlichkeit und Herrscher. Kallmünz, 1985.

Lerman, Katharine A. 'Bernhard von Bülow and the Governance of Germany, 1900–1909', D. Phil. thesis, University of Sussex, 1983.

'The Decisive Relationship: Kaiser Wilhelm II and Chancellor Bernhard von Bülow, 1900–1905', in J. C. G. Röhl and Nicolaus Sombart (eds.), *Kaiser Wilhelm II: New Interpretations.* Cambridge, 1982.

Lohmeyer, Hans. *Die Politik des Zweiten Reiches 1870–1918.* Berlin, 1939.

Loth, Wilfried. *Katholiken im Kaiserreich. Der politische Katholizismus in der Krise des Wilhelminischen Deutschlands.* Düsseldorf, 1984.

Lowell, A. L. *Governments and Parties in Continental Europe.* 2 vols. Boston, New York and Chicago, 1896.

Martin, Rudolf. *Deutsche Machthaber.* Berlin and Leipzig, 1910.

Mayer, A. J. 'The Lower Middle Class as Historical Problem', *Journal of Modern History*, 47 (1975).

The Persistence of the Old Regime: Europe to the Great War. London and New York, 1981.

Menning, Ralph R. and Menning, Carol Bresnahan. ' "Baseless Allegations": Wilhelm II and the Hale Interview of 1908', *Central European History*, 16 (1983).

Meyer, Klaus. *Theodor Schiemann als politischer Publizist.* Frankfurt, 1956.

Miller, Susanne and Potthoff, Heinrich. *A History of German Social Democracy: From 1848 to the Present.* Leamington Spa, 1986.

Mittmann, Ursula. *Fraktion und Partei. Ein Vergleich von Zentrum und Sozialdemokratie im Kaiserreich.* Düsseldorf, 1976.

Mock, Wolfgang. ' "Manipulation von oben" oder Selbstorganisation an der Basis? Einige neuere Ansätze in der englischen Historiographie zur Geschichte des deutschen Kaiserreichs', *Historische Zeitschrift*, 232 (1981).

Möckl, K. *Die Prinzregentenzeit. Gesellschaft und Politik während der Ära des Prinzregenten Luitpold in Bayern.* Munich, 1972.

Moeller, Robert G. 'The Kaiserreich Recast? Continuity and Change in Modern German Historiography', *Journal of Social History*, 17 (1984).

Moeller, Robert G. (ed.). *Peasants and Lords in Modern Germany. Recent Studies in Agricultural History.* Boston, 1986.

Molt, P. *Der Reichstag vor der improvisierten Revolution.* Cologne, 1963.

Moltke, Helmuth von. *Erinnerungen, Briefe, Dokumente 1877–1916.* Stuttgart, 1922.

Mommsen, Wolfgang J. 'Der deutsche Liberalismus zwischen "klassenloser Bürgergesellschaft" und "Organisiertem Kapitalismus" ', *Geschichte und Gesellschaft.* 4 (1978).

'Domestic Factors in German Foreign Policy before 1914', *Central European History*, 6 (1973).

'Gegenwärtige Tendenzen in der Geschichtsschreibung der Bundesrepublik', *Geschichte und Gesellschaft*, 7 (1981).

'Die latente Krise des Wilhelminischen Reiches. Staat und Gesellschaft in Deutschland 1890–1914', *Militärgeschichtliche Mitteilungen*, 1 (1974).

Max Weber und die deutsche Politik 1890–1920. Tübingen, 1959.

Das Zeitalter des Imperialismus. Frankfurt, 1969.

Monts, Anton. *Erinnerungen und Gedanken des Botschafters Anton Graf Monts.* Ed. Karl Nowak and Friedrich Thimme. Berlin, 1932.

Morrow, Ian F. D. 'The Foreign Policy of Prince von Bülow', *Cambridge Historical Journal*, 4 (1932–4).

Morsey, R. 'Die deutschen Katholiken und der Nationalstaat zwischen Kulturkampf und dem ersten Weltkrieg', *Historisches Jahrbuch* (1970).

Die oberste Reichsverwaltung unter Bismarck 1867–1890. Münster, 1957.

Moses, J. A. *The Politics of Illusion*. London, 1975.
Trade Unionism in Germany from Bismarck to Hitler 1869–1933. 2 vols. London and New York, 1982.
Moy, Carl von. 'Was mir Minister Witte erzählte', *Berliner Monatshefte*, 8 (1930).
Muncy, L. W. *The Junker in the Prussian Administration under Wilhelm II, 1888–1914*. Rhode Island, 1944.
Münz, Sigmund. *Fürst Bülow. Der Staatsmann und Mensch. Aufzeichnungen, Erinnerungen und Erwägungen*. Berlin, 1930.
Muschler, Reinhold Conrad. *Philipp Eulenburg. Sein Leben und seine Zeit*. Leipzig, 1930.
Namier, Lewis. *Vanished Supremacies. Essays on European History 1812–1918*. London, 1958.
Naumann, F. *Demokratie und Kaisertum*. Berlin, 1900.
Nettl, J. P. 'The German Social-Democratic Party 1890–1914 as a Political Model', *Past and Present*, 30 (1955).
Neumann, Wolfgang. 'Die Innenpolitik des Fürsten Bülow von 1900–1906', Ph.D. thesis. University of Kiel, 1949.
Nicholls, J. Alden. *Germany After Bismarck. The Caprivi Era 1890–1894*. Cambridge, Mass., 1958.
Nipperdey, Thomas. *Die Organisation der deutschen Parteien vor 1918*. Düsseldorf, 1961.
'1933 und Kontinuität der deutschen Geschichte', *Historische Zeitschrift*, 227 (1978).
'Wehlers "Kaiserreich": Eine kritische Auseinandersetzung', *Geschichte und Gesellschaft*, 1 (1975).
Nolan, Mary. *Social Democracy and Society. Working Class Radicalism in Düsseldorf, 1890–1920*. Cambridge, 1981.
Nolte, Ernst. 'Deutscher Scheinkonstitutionalismus?', *Historische Zeitschrift*, 228 (1979).
Peck, A. *Radicals and Reactionaries. The Crisis of Conservatism in Wilhelmine Germany*. Washington, DC, 1978.
Pezold, Dirk von. 'Cäsaromanie und Byzantinismus bei Wilhelm II'. Ph.D. thesis. University of Cologne, 1971.
Pflanze, Otto. 'Bismarcks Herrschaftstechnik als Problem der gegenwärtigen Historiographie', *Historische Zeitschrift*, 234 (1982).
Pflanze, Otto (ed.). *Innenpolitische Probleme des Bismarck-Reiches*. Munich, 1983.
Philippi, Hans. *Das Königreich Württemberg im Spiegel der preussischen Gesandtschaftsberichte 1871–1914*. Stuttgart, 1972.
Pogge von Strandmann, H. (ed.). *Walther Rathenau: Tagebuch 1907–1922*. Düsseldorf, 1967.
Puhle, Hans-Jürgen. *Agrarische Interessenpolitik und preussischer Konservatismus im Wilhelminischen Reich*. Hanover, 1967.
'Deutscher Sonderweg. Kontroverse um eine vermeintliche Legende', *Journal für Geschichte*, 4 (1981).
'Zur Legende von der "Kehrschen Schule"', *Geschichte und Gesellschaft*, 4, 1978.
Rassow, Peter. 'Schlieffen und Holstein', *Historische Zeitschrift*, 173 (1952).
Rassow, Peter and Born, Karl-Erich (eds.). *Akten zur staatlichen Sozialpolitik in Deutschland 1890–1914*. Wiesbaden, 1959.
Rauh, Manfred. *Föderalismus und Parlamentarismus im Wilhelminischen Reich*. Düsseldorf, 1973.
Die Parlamentarisierung des deutschen Reiches. Düsseldorf, 1977.
Raulff, Heiner. *Zwischen Machtpolitik und Imperialismus: die deutsche Frankreichpolitik 1904–6*. Düsseldorf, 1976.
Retallack, James N. 'Conservatives *contra* Chancellor: Official Responses to the Spectre of Conservative Demagoguery, from Bismarck to Bülow', *Canadian Journal of History*, 20 (1985).
Notables of the Right. The Conservative Party and Political Mobilization in Germany 1876–1918. Boston, 1988.

Rich, Norman. *Friedrich von Holstein. Politics and Diplomacy in the Era of Bismarck and Wilhelm II.* 2 vols. Cambridge, 1965.

Rich, N. and Fisher, M. H. (eds.). *The Holstein Papers.* 4 vols. Cambridge, 1955–63.

Rieger, Isolde. *Die Wilhelminische Presse im Überblick 1888–1918.* Munich, 1957.

Ritter, G. *Der Schlieffenplan. Kritik eines Mythos.* Munich, 1956.

Staatskunst und Kriegshandwerk. Das Problem des Militarismus in Deutschland. 4 vols. Munich, 1954–68.

Ritter, G. A. *Arbeiterbewegung, Parteien und Parlamentarismus.* Göttingen, 1976.

Die Arbeiterbewegung im Wilhelminischen Reich. Berlin, 1959.

Die deutschen Parteien 1830–1914. Göttingen, 1985.

Ritter, G. A. (ed.). *Gesellschaft, Parlament und Regierung. Zur Geschichte des Parlamentarismus in Deutschland.* Düsseldorf, 1974.

Ritter, G. A. and Niehuss, M. (eds.). *Deutsche Parteien vor 1918.* Cologne, 1973.

Robson, S. T. 'Left-Wing Liberalism in Germany'. D. Phil. thesis, University of Oxford, 1966.

Rogge, Helmuth. 'Affairen im Kaiserreich. Symptome der Staatskrise unter Wilhelm II', *Die Politische Meinung,* 81 (1963).

Rogge, Helmuth (ed.). *Friedrich von Holstein. Lebensbekenntnis in Briefen an eine Frau.* Berlin, 1932.

Holstein und Harden. Politisch-publizistisches Zusammenspiel zweier Aussenseiter des Wilhelminischen Reichs. Munich, 1959.

Holstein und Hohenlohe, 1874–1894. Stuttgart, 1957.

Röhl, J. C. G. *Germany Without Bismarck. The Crisis of Government in the Second Reich, 1890–1900.* London, 1967.

Kaiser, Hof und Staat. Wilhelm II und die deutsche Politik. Munich, 1987.

Röhl, J. C. G. (ed.). *Philipp Eulenburgs politische Korrespondenz.* 3 vols. Boppard am Rhein, 1976–83.

Röhl, J. C. G. and Sombart, Nicolaus (eds.). *Kaiser Wilhelm II: New Interpretations.* Cambridge, 1982.

Rosenberg, Arthur. *Imperial Germany. The Birth of the German Republic 1871–1918.* Translated by Ian Morrow. Boston, 1964. (German edition, Berlin, 1930.)

Ross, Ronald J. *Beleaguered Tower. The Dilemma of Political Catholicism in Wilhelmine Germany.* Notre Dame, Indiana, 1976.

Roth, Guenther. *The Social Democrats in Imperial Germany: A Study in Working-Class Isolation and National Integration.* Totowa, 1963.

Saul, K. *Staat, Industrie, Arbeiterbewegung im Kaiserreich. Zur Innen- und Aussenpolitik des Wilhelminischen Deutschland 1903–1914.* Düsseldorf, 1974.

Schieder, Theodor. 'Strukturen und Persönlichkeiten in der Geschichte', *Historische Zeitschrift,* 195 (1962).

Schiefel, U. *Bernhard Dernburg 1865–1937. Kolonialpolitiker und Bankier im Wilhelminischen Deutschland.* Zurich, 1975.

Schmidt, Gustav. 'Innenpolitische Blockbildungen am Vorabend des ersten Weltkrieges', *Aus Politik und Zeitgeschichte,* 20 (1972).

Schmidt-Bückeburg, R. *Das Militärkabinett der preussischen Könige und deutschen Kaiser: Seine geschichtliche und staatsrechtliche Stellung 1787–1918.* Berlin, 1933.

Schmoller, Gustav. *Zwanzig Jahre deutscher Politik 1897–1917.* Munich and Leipzig, 1920.

Schöllgen, Gregor. 'Wer machte im Kaiserreich Politik', *Neue Politische Literatur,* 25 (1980).

Schön, Wilhelm von. *Erlebtes. Beiträge zur politischen Geschichte der neuesten Zeit.* Stuttgart and Berlin, 1921.

Schorske, Carl E. *German Social Democracy 1905–1917: The Development of the Great Schism.* Cambridge, Mass., 1955.

Schottelius, H. and Deist, W. (eds.). *Marine und Marinepolitik im Kaiserlichen Deutschland, 1871–1914*. Düsseldorf, 1972.

Schröder, E. *Zwanzig Jahre Regierungszeit. Ein Tagebuch Wilhelms II. Vom Antritt der Regierung 15 Juni 1888 bis zum 15 Juni 1908 nach Hof- und anderen Berichten*. Berlin, 1909.

Schüssler, Wilhelm. *Die Daily-Telegraph-Affaire: Fürst Bülow, Kaiser Wilhelm und die Krise des Zweiten Reiches 1908*. Göttingen, 1952.

Kaiser Wilhelm II. Schicksal und Schuld. Göttingen, 1962.

Schulte, B. F. *Die deutsche Armee 1900–1914*. Düsseldorf, 1977.

Schwabe, K. *Das diplomatische Korps 1871–1945*. Boppard am Rhein, 1985.

Schwarz, Max. *MdR. Biographisches Handbuch der Reichstage*. Hanover, 1965.

Schweinitz, H. L. von. *Briefwechsel des Botschafters General von Schweinitz*. Berlin, 1928.

Schwertfeger, Bernhard (ed.). *Kaiser und Kabinettschef, nach eigenen Aufzeichnungen und dem Briefwechsel des Wirklichen Geheimen Rats Rudolf von Valentini*. Oldenburg, 1931.

Sheehan, James J. *German Liberalism in the Nineteenth Century*. Chicago, 1978.

Sheehan, James J. 'Political Leadership in the German Reichstag, 1871–1918', *American Historical Review*, 74 (1968).

'The Primacy of Domestic Politics. Eckart Kehr's Essays on Modern German History', *Central European History*, 1 (1968).

Sheehan, James J. (ed.). *Imperial Germany*. London, 1976.

Smith, Woodruff D. *The German Colonial Empire*. Chapel Hill, 1978.

The Ideological Origins of Nazi Imperialism. Oxford, 1986.

Sösemann, Bernd. 'Die sog. Hunnenrede Wilhelms II. Textkritische und interpretatorische Bemerkungen zur Ansprache des Kaisers vom 27 Juli 1900 in Bremerhaven', *Historische Zeitschrift*, 222 (1976).

Spectator. *Prince Bülow and the Kaiser*. London, 1931.

Steenson, Gary P. *'Not One Man! Not One Penny!' German Social Democracy, 1863–1914*. Pittsburgh, 1981.

Stegmann, D. *Die Erben Bismarcks. Parteien und Verbände in der Spätphase des Wilhelminischen Deutschlands*. Cologne, 1970.

Stegmann, D., Wendt, B.-J. and Witt, P.-C. (eds.). *Deutscher Konservatismus im 19 und 20 Jahrhundert. Festschrift für Fritz Fischer*. Bonn, 1983.

Industrielle Gesellschaft und politisches System. Beiträge zur politischen Sozialgeschichte. Bonn, 1978.

Steinberg, Jonathan. 'The Copenhagen Complex', *Journal of Contemporary History*, 1 (1966).

'Germany and the Russo-Japanese War', *American Historical Review*, 75 (1970).

'The Kaiser and the British: The State Visit to Windsor, November 1907', in J. C. G. Röhl and Nicolaus Sombart (eds.), *Kaiser Wilhelm II: New Interpretations*. Cambridge, 1982.

'The Novelle of 1908: Necessities and Choices in the Anglo-German Naval Arms Race', *Transactions of the Royal Historical Society*, 21 (1971).

'The Tirpitz Plan', *Historical Journal*, 26 (1973).

Yesterday's Deterrent. Tirpitz and the Birth of the German Battle Fleet. London, 1965.

Stenographische Berichte über die Verhandlungen des Preussischen Abgeordnetenhauses. Berlin, 1897–1909.

Stenographische Berichte über die Verhandlungen des Reichstags. Berlin, 1897–1909.

Stürmer, Michael. 'Staatsstreichgedanken im Bismarckreich', *Historische Zeitschrift*, 209 (1969).

Stürmer, Michael (ed.). *Das kaiserliche Deutschland*. Düsseldorf, 1970.

Suval, Stanley. *Electoral Politics in Wilhemine Germany*. Chapel Hill, 1985.

Taylor, A. J. P. *The Struggle for Mastery in Europe 1848–1918*. Oxford, 1954.

Thimme, Friedrich (ed.). *Front Wider Bülow. Staatsmänner, Diplomaten und Forscher zu seinen Denkwürdigkeiten*. Munich, 1931.

Tirpitz, Alfred von. *Erinnerungen.* Leipzig, 1919.
Politische Dokumente. Bd. 1. Der Aufbau der deutschen Weltmacht. Berlin and Stuttgart, 1924.
Trefz, Friedrich. 'Fürst Bülows Denkwürdigkeiten', *Süddeutsche Monatshefte,* 6 (1931).
Treutler, Karl Georg von. *Die Graue Excellenz. Zwischen Staatsräson und Vasallentreue. Aus den Papieren des Kaiserlichen Gesandten Karl Georg von Treutler.* Ed. Karl-Heinz Janssen. Frankfurt and Berlin, 1971.
Uhland, Ludwig. *Gedichte.* 5th edn. Stuttgart and Tübingen, 1831.
Ullmann, H. P. *Der Bund der Industriellen.* Göttingen, 1976.
Vierhaus, Rudolf (ed.). *Das Tagebuch der Baronin Spitzemberg: Aufzeichnungen aus der Hofgesellschaft des Hohenzollernreiches.* Göttingen, 1960.
Vietsch, Eberhard von. *Bethmann Hollweg: Staatsmann zwischen Macht und Ethos.* Boppard am Rhein, 1969.
Vogel, Barbara. *Deutsche Russlandpolitik. Das Scheitern des deutschen Weltpolitik unter Bülow 1900–1906.* Düsseldorf, 1973.
Vogel, Georg. 'Die Konservativen und die Blockpolitik Bülows'. Ph.D. thesis, University of Berlin, 1925.
Waldersee, Alfred von. *Aus dem Briefwechsel.* Ed. H. O. Meisner. 3 vols. Stuttgart, 1928.
Denkwürdigkeiten. Ed. H. O. Meisner. 3 vols. Stuttgart, 1922–3.
Wehler, Hans-Ulrich. *Aus der Geschichte lernen? Essays.* Munich, 1988.
Das deutsche Kaiserreich 1871–1918. Göttingen, 1973.
'"Deutscher Sonderweg" oder allgemeine Probleme des westlichen Kapitalismus? Zur Kritik an einigen "Mythen deutscher Geschichtsschreibung"', *Merkur* (1981).
Krisenherde des Kaiserreichs 1871–1918. Studien zur deutschen Sozial- und Verfassungsgeschichte. Göttingen, 1970.
'Kritik und kritische Antikritik', *Historische Zeitschrift,* 225 (1977).
Wermuth, A. *Ein Beamtenleben.* Berlin, 1922.
Westarp, Kuno von. 'Die Konservative Partei und das Ende des Bülowblocks', *Süddeutsche Monatshefte,* 6 (1931).
Konservative Politik im letzten Jahrzehnt des Kaiserreichs. 2 vols. Berlin, 1935.
White, Dan S. *The Splintered Party. National Liberalism in Hessen and the Reich 1867–1918.* Cambridge, Mass., 1976.
Wile, Frederic William. *Men around the Kaiser. The Makers of Modern Germany.* Indianapolis, 1914.
Wilhelm II. *Ereignisse und Gestalten 1878–1918.* Leipzig and Berlin, 1922.
Wilke, Ekkehard-Feja P. W. *Political Decadence in Imperial Germany: Personnel-political Aspects of the German Government Crisis 1894–1897.* Urbana, Chicago and London, 1976.
Winzen, Peter. *Bülows Weltmachtkonzept. Untersuchungen zur Frühphase seiner Aussenpolitik 1897–1901.* Boppard am Rhein, 1977.
'Die Englandpolitik Friedrich von Holsteins 1895–1901', Ph.D. thesis (second part), University of Cologne, 1975.
'Prince Bülow's *Weltmachtpolitik'*, *Australian Journal of Politics and History,* 22 (1976).
Witt, Peter-Christian. *Die Finanzpolitik des deutschen Reiches von 1903–1913.* Lübeck, 1970.
Witte, Sergei. *The Memoirs of Count Witte.* Ed. A. Yarmolinsky. London, 1921.
Young, Harry F. *Maximilian Harden. Censor Germaniae. The Critic in Opposition from Bismarck to the Rise of Nazism.* The Hague, 1959.
Zedlitz-Trützschler, Robert. *Zwölf Jahre am deutschen Kaiserhof.* Berlin and Leipzig, 1924.
Zeender, John K. *The German Centre Party 1890–1906.* Philadelphia, 1976.
Zmarzlik, Hans Günther. *Bethmann Hollweg als Reichskanzler, 1909–1914.* Düsseldorf, 1957.
'Das Kaiserreich in neuer Sicht?', *Historische Zeitschrift,* 222 (1976).

Index

Bülow, Alfred von, 27, 35, 199

Bülow, Count (later Prince) Bernhard von; assumption of Chancellorship (1900–1), 41–73; attitude to Wilhelm II (pre-1897), 22–4; becomes *Fürst* (1905), 97–8, 127, 129; biographical details, 10; character assessment, 1, 2, 36; conception of role of Chancellor, 23–9, 48–9; consequences of Chancellorship for Germany, 258; contemporary opinion of, 4; correspondence (1880s), 13–16; decline, 189–90, 210–21; domestic policy, *see* domestic policy; early political career (1849–97), 10–18; early political ideas (1849–97), 19–29; education, 10; fall (1909), 243–7; first submission of resignation (1905), 128–33; foreign policy, *see* foreign policy; given Order of the Black Eagle, 58–9; illness (1906), 141–9, 151; inheritance, 97–8, 129; intellectual influences, 19–22; last speech in Reichstag (June 1909), 242; law training, 10; literature on, 2–8; marriage, 15–17; memoirs, 2, 31, 123–4, 255; military career, 10, 121; personal preoccupations, 121–6, 257–8; physical description, 1; political rise (1849–1900), 10–40; relationship with Wilhelm II, 18, 249–51: (1897–1900), 29–32; (1901–5), 86–102; (1906), 153–5; (1907), 190–5; (1908–9), 228–35; resignation (1909), 8, 242–7; role as Chancellor, 3, 6–8, 248–9, 251–8; role in Eulenburg scandals, 195–202; as State Secretary of the Foreign Office (1897–1900), 18, 29–40; summary of career, 248–58; watershed of Chancellorship, 148–55

Bülow, Bernhard Ernst von (father), 10, 21

Bülow, Karl-Ulrich von, 199, 213

Bülow, Countess (later Princess) Marie von (née Beccadelli di Bologna; first married Dönhoff), 15–17, 19, 29, 146

Bülow Bloc (1907–9), 3, 7–8, 127, 167–209, 213–18, 254–5; collapse, 235–42; crisis (December 1907), 202–9; victims of the, 174–83

'Bülow Cabinet', 67–73

Bülow system: (1901–5), 74–126, 130, 258; collapse of (1908–9), 210–47; political context, 74–86

Bülow–Brand trial (1907), 198–9

Bundesrat, 41–2, 59–60, 78, 79–80, 218, 224, 247, 253; Committee on Foreign Affairs, 224, 253

Byzantinism, 63, 91

camarilla, possible existence of, 160, 195–7, 210, 231, 232

Cambon, Jules, 189

Canal Bill: First (1899), 61, 77; (1901), 39, 55, 61–7, 71–3, 93, 256; (1904), 78, 80; passed (1905), 108, 120

Caprivi, General Leo von, 17, 23, 30, 43, 71, 75, 116; comparison with B., 48, 52, 53, 54, 86, 91, 99, 171

Catholicism, 16–17, 24, 59–60, 82, 167, 169–70, 175, 215

Centre Party, 32, 42, 53, 55, 63, 73, 237; and the Bloc, 167–74, 191, 201, 203–8; B.'s break with (1906), 80, 145, 154, 165, 166; B.'s relations with (1901–5), 78–86; (1908), 214–18; and inheritance tax, 245; and social policy initiatives, 78; Tolerance Motion, 59–60

Chamberlain, Joseph, 89, 96, 118

China debate (1900), 48, 58, 61, 93

China expedition, 40, 56–7

Civil Cabinet, 155: Chief of, 98, 226

class interests, 63, 249

Cole, Terence, 7–8

colonial administration, reform of, 135–7, 145–7, 150–1, 153–4

commercial treaties, *see* trade treaties

Conrad, Alfred von, 109, 110, 113

Conservatives, 32, 42, 73, 127, 237, 254; and the Bloc crisis (1907), 202, 203–4; B.'s relations with (1909), 238–42, 246; on the Canal Bill, 61–7; and the tariff issue, 75, 77; German Conservative Party, 52, 66–7, 238–9; *Reichspartei*, 237

Conservative–Centre coalition ('Blue-Black Bloc' 1909), 238–42, 245, 247

Conservatives, coalition with liberals, *see* Bülow Bloc

Constitution, Reichstag debate on the (1908), 227

Constitution (1851), 43

Constitution (1871), 4, 41, 42

constitutional reform, 149, 235, 254, 257

Court, 5, 8, 32, 63, 82, 163, 230, 232, 249

criminal procedure reform, 149, 235, 254, 257

criminal procedure reform, 186, 214

Crown Council (1898), 30; (1903), 111; (1906), 141, 144; (1909), 141, 232

Daily Telegraph crisis, 211, 221–7, 251; repercussions of, 191, 218, 228, 230–1, 233, 235–6, 239, 247, 256

Dauphin (grandson of Louis XIV), 90

Dehmelt, Bernhard, 3

Delbrück, Clemens von, 135, 140, 203, 245

Delcassé, Théophile, 127, 128, 129

democracy, growth of ideas in Europe, 150

democratic reform, myth of, 255–6

Derenthall, Eduard von, 34

Dernburg, Bernhard, 163–5, 179, 200, 256